D0344530

"T. J. English, one of the great reporters of our time, has outdone himself with this amazing panorama of strivers and thugs. The continuities over nearly two centuries are so striking that the past seems improbably close. *Paddy Whacked* is a page-turner and a revelation."

—Luc Sante, author of *Low Life*

"Finally, a book that gives us the social, political, and economic context of the Irish American mobster. *Paddy Whacked* is a riveting history of Irish thug life inextricably linked to some of America's most cherished institutions. T. J. English's page turner is the moral counterweight to all of the mythologizing and intrigue that often pervades tales of this murderous enterprise."

—Michael Patrick MacDonald, author of
All Souls: A Family Story from Southie

"*Paddy Whacked* is at once a brilliant social history, a startling examination of the dark side of the American Dream, and a great rip-roaring yarn spun by a master storyteller. Never have so many vivid characters—some famous, some mad, some lost, most larger-than-life, and all indelibly drawn—been packed into a single volume. *Paddy Whacked* gives us enough character, story, and verve to fill a dozen novels. English's feat of tying it all together is nothing short of a literary triumph."

—Thomas Kelly, author of *The Rackets* and *Empire Rising*

"In *Paddy Whacked*, T. J. English offers a rich and memorable tale of crime that has never been told before. The audacious, violent Irish American gangsters in these pages are fascinating, and the great revelation that unfolds here is their staying power—one hundred and fifty unbroken years, right into the new century, in which the FBI's most wanted mobster remains Boston's Whitey Bulger."

—Vincent Patrick, author of *The Pope of Greenwich Village*
and *Family Business*

paddy whacked

The Untold Story of the Irish American Gangster

Featuring

Whitey Bulger, Jack *"Legs"* Diamond, Dean O'Banion, George *"Bugs"* Moran, Owney Madden, Vincent *"Mad Dog"* Coll, Mike McDonald, Jimmy Walker, John Morrissey, Buddy McLean, Danny Greene, Mickey Featherstone, Tom Pendergast, Edward *"Spike"* O'Donnell, Jimmy Coonan, Mickey Spillane

T.J. English

10 ReganBooks
Celebrating Ten **Bestselling** Years
An Imprint of HarperCollinsPublishers

paddy whacked

Copyright © 2005 by 𝕿. 𝕵. 𝕰nglish.

All rights reserved. Printed in the United States of America. No part of this book may be used or reproduced in any manner whatsoever without written permission except in the case of brief quotations embodied in critical articles and reviews. For information address HarperCollins Publishers Inc., 10 East 53rd Street, New York, NY 10022.

HarperCollins books may be purchased for educational, business, or sales promotional use. For information please write: Special Markets Department, HarperCollins Publishers Inc., 10 East 53rd Street, New York, NY 10022.

FIRST EDITION

Designed by Kris Tobiassen / Richard Ljoenes

Printed on acid-free paper

Library of Congress Cataloging-in-Publication Data
English., T. J., 1957-
Paddy whacked : the untold story of the Irish-American gangster / T. J. English.— 1st ed.
  p. cm.
Includes bibliographical references and index.
ISBN 0-06-059002-5
  1. Organized crime—United States—History. 2. Irish-American criminals—United States—History. 3. Gangsters—United States—History. I. Title.

HV6446.E54 2005
364.1'092'39162073—dc22

2004065051

05 06 07 08 09 RRD 10 9 8 7 6 5 4 3 2

FOR *Kate and Patrick*

with a knick knack
paddy whack give a dog
a bone, this old man
came rolling home . . .

—Early 20th century children's rhyme

i guess we thought we
had to be crazier than
everybody else 'cause we
were the irish guys.

—MICKEY FEATHERSTONE, *Westies* hitman

may god have mercy
on my soul.

—Last words of DANNY DRISCOLL, co-leader of the *Whyo* Gang,
before his execution on January 23, 1888

contents

Part 2: A Long Way from Tipperary

introduction

ho would have guessed that in the early years of the twenty-first century—in an era of rampant jihadism and global paranoia—the highest ranking organized crime figure on the Federal Bureau of Investigation's (FBI) Ten Most Wanted List was neither a Mafia don nor a Latin American *narcotraficante* nor a Russian *mafiya*, but rather an old-style Irish American mob boss from around the way?

During the years of his reign, James "Whitey" Bulger, formerly the kingpin of South Boston, was like a character out of an old Cagney movie— tough but sentimental, kind to his mother, politically connected, and a ruthless sociopath who murdered at least nineteen people. Bulger created a criminal organization based in "Southie" that ruled the roost for over twenty years, from the early 1970s until 1995, when Bulger was tipped off that the Feds were coming to get him and went on the lam. The Age of Bulger transpired during a time when most U.S. citizens probably thought the Irish American gangster no longer existed outside of black-and-white Warner Bros. movies from the 1930s. Bulger not only existed, but he also thrived, making millions of dollars annually through racketeering, killing people at will, and getting away with it through expert manipulation of "the System." He eluded capture and prosecution in a manner that would have made a Mafia boss like John Gotti weep with envy.

As an Irish American gangster, Bulger flew mostly below the national radar. Certainly in the later decades of what was an unprecedented 150-year run for the Irish Mob, old-style mobsters like Whitey were content to operate in the shadows. Let the mafiosi walk the red carpet, their exploits made larger-than-life by the likes of Brando, DeNiro, and Pacino. Let the Italians come under the scrutiny of the FBI, which during Director J. Edgar

Hoover's administration had denied the existence of the Mafia, but would eventually go after "La Cosa Nostra" with the zeal of a jilted lover. Each headline-grabbing arrest and prosecution of "LCN" made it possible for the FBI and other law enforcement agencies to promote their own exploits, creating a self-fulfilling mythology that was great for the G-Men but not so great for the Italians. With the Mafia dominating the headlines, the Irish Mob soldiered on mostly by staying local, keeping their operations small, and working within underworld parameters that had been in place for more than a century.

Whitey Bulger may have been the last of the last, a man whose staying power was unique to South Boston, but the circumstances of his rise in the underworld were the result of a long and violent history. Like most Irish American mobsters, his power was based in part on two major elements: He had a corrupt FBI agent in his pocket and a younger brother in the State House, Massachusetts State Senator William Bulger. The degree to which Whitey was able to finagle these two factors—the lawman and the politician—was part and parcel of his inheritance as an Irish American gangster.

Like a neighborhood godfather from long ago, Bulger doled out turkeys to the needy on Thanksgiving and Christmas, lent money to school kids, did favors for his "constituents," and settled local disputes. He understood the aggrieved nature of the Irish in Boston, whose legacy was fundamentally the same as that of the Irish in New York, Chicago, Philadelphia, early New Orleans, and myriads of other U.S. municipalities large and small. The ravages of colonialism, famine, pestilence, anti-Irish and anti-Catholic bigotry had shaped the Irish American identity and created a people who were sometimes criticized for being clannish or overly parochial. The Irish themselves didn't see it that way. Arriving in America en masse under the most dire circumstances imaginable, they did what they had to do: They looked out for one another and created social systems that allowed them to advance, even though American society at large was determined to keep them in their place.

It is a common misconception among most people—even many Irish Americans—that the American Mob began as an Italian institution transplanted directly from Sicily. Indeed, criminal traditions in Sicily, known variously as vendetta societies or la Mafia, were transported to the United States with the beginnings of Italian immigration in the late 1880s and 1890s. But the Irish had been in the United States for over forty years by then, and the American underworld—which was based on criminal infiltration of the System for social advancement and economic gain—was already firmly entrenched. The earliest progenitors and organizers of this underworld were

Irish refugees whose desire to make it in the New World was informed by oppression, starvation, and the threat of total extermination.

To understand the roots of organized crime in the United States, it is necessary to make a leap of the imagination back to the Old Country. In the early nineteenth century, Ireland was a dreary place, a colony of the British Crown where the Irish people lived as virtual slaves on land that had once belonged to their ancestors. They tilled the soil at the behest of their British landlords who controlled the property through laws that made it nearly impossible for tenant farmers to achieve even a semblance of social mobility, and they could be evicted at any time. The names of all streets and towns had been changed from their original Gaelic into English, and the native language was banned by law. This oppressive colonial system was enforced at the end of the lash and the hangman's noose.

After a history of failed rebellions and squelched political uprisings, what remained of an anticolonial movement in Ireland was to be found among the "secret resistance societies," loosely structured organizations that used a strategy of sabotage and violence to disrupt the colonial government, especially in rural areas of the country. The Whiteboys, the Ribbonmen, and the Molly Maguires were comprised of members of the community who circulated openly, but whose membership in the underground resistance movement was a well-guarded secret. These groups represented the earliest inklings of American gangsterism in that they presented themselves as custodians of their communities and were just as likely to prey on their own people as they were to go after Crown forces.

In 1845, the rural resistance societies and all other forms of social interaction—underground or otherwise—were brought to a halt by a tiny agricultural virus known as *Phytophthera Infestans*. There had been blights before in the country's potato crop, which both as a product for export and a food source sustained the nation. Normally, the potato was a hardy tuber that always bounced back. This time, however, the virus struck at the root and spread like wildfire, wiping out the entire crops of 1845, 1846, 1847, and so on. Over a period of nearly a decade, the country's potato crop was decimated; one-third of the island's population perished from starvation and disease or were forced to flee into permanent exile.

The Great Potato Famine is a vague and distant memory for most Americans, even though an overwhelming majority of the forty million Americans of Irish descent in the United States can trace their ancestry back to what was the most cataclysmic human event of the nineteenth century. Many of the personality characteristics that were lampooned in U.S. newspapers of the era as "typically Irish" were a result of famine and mass starvation.

The famine wasn't just a crop failure; it was politically mismanaged genocide. For nearly a century leading up to the disaster, the economy of Ireland had been artificially engineered to produce one product and one product only. Regressive Corn Laws were passed that made it economically impossible for Irish farmers to make a profit off the export of any product other than the potato. When the crop was wiped out, it was a complete and total devastation for Irish culture. Families starved to death in their cottages or begged in the streets and were reduced to subhuman levels of subsistence. An archdeacon who toured the village of Kenmare wrote, "On one road . . . the deaths are three each day. The people are buried without coffins. I daily witness the most terrible spectacles: women, children, and old men crawling out [of their homes] on all fours, perhaps from beside a corpse, to crave a morsel of any kind."

Another witness wrote, "The cries of starving hundreds that besiege me from morning until night actually ring in my ears. . . . I attended myself a poor woman whose infant, dead two days, lay at the foot of the bed, and four others nearly dead in the same bed. . . . A famished cat got up on the corpse of the poor infant and was about to gnaw it but for my interference. I could tell you such tales of woe without end."

Bodies were piled like refuse on the side of the road. If it wasn't starvation that got you, it was famine-related disease. "The swollen limbs, emaciated countenances, and other hideous forms of disease are innumerable," wrote a medical relief worker. "A dreadful disease is breaking out amongst them. I allude to Dysentery with discharge of blood from the bowels." Another ailment, sore mouth, appeared as well, "which I think has been produced by the unwholesome food the poor were obliged to use in the early part of the season and which so injured the coat of their stomachs and bowels, that now they are not in a state to bear strong food and the consequence is the living membrane of the intestine is coming away."

These and other medical reports were delivered to Charles Trevelyan, permanent secretary of the Treasury in London and the man who single-handedly controlled most relief expenditures. The British response to reports of mass starvation in their Irish colony just a few miles across the English Channel has been most charitably characterized as a kind of "criminal negligence," best personified in the public comments of Charles Trevelyan. "Ireland's great evil," he stated, was not famine but "the selfish, perverse, and turbulent character of the people."

British relief efforts were late and insufficient to stem the tide of disease, death, and exile. And so the Irish masses took to the seas, carrying with them a deep-seated bitterness over the genocidal mismanagement of their British overlords, along with a legacy of shame, desperation, and famine-related dementia.

At sea, the Vale of Tears continued, with thousands of refugees dying on the "coffin ships," in which disease spread among the multitudes crammed together in steerage. All told, the Great Famine lasted ten years, from 1845 to 1855. In a country of eight million, one million died, and another million and a half were forced into exile hoping to find refuge in places like Liverpool, Australia, Canada, and especially the United States.

The ways in which the Irish were able to establish a foothold in the United States were inexorably linked with the growth and development of the country's most vibrant cities. What was not eradicated during the famine years was the innate sociability of a people who believed in the power of human interaction. The saloon, the parish hall, and the political clubhouse became the foundation of an immigrant dynasty where the terms of survival and social advancement were negotiated and dispensed according to a person's willingness to play the game.

In the history books, much has been made of early Irish Americans' use of Tammany Hall, the vaunted nineteenth and early twentieth century political organization, as a means of consolidating power. The implication is that "Tammany politics" and all that they represented were an Irish creation, a veritable hijacking and perversion of the democratic process. In truth, Tammany Hall existed from the beginning of the American republic. It was founded in Philadelphia in the years immediately following the American Revolution as a social, fraternal, and benevolent organization. Named after Saint Tammany, a mythical Indian chief rooted in American Indian lore, the organization was designed as a means for exerting influence over the political process. Members elected their leader, known as a grand sachem, and sought to influence legislation favorable to their own business interests.

This system was in place for nearly a century by the time of the Great Potato Famine and the huge Irish influx of the 1840s, 1850s, and 1860s. In New York, where Tammany Hall had by then consolidated most of its power, Irish immigrants worked their way into the Tammany structure like salmon swimming upstream to spawn. They became precinct captains, ward bosses, and aldermen, injecting energy and imagination into an elaborate ward system that dispensed favors and provided an edge in exchange for a vote. Tammany put forth candidates, mostly Democrats, under their banner, and the entire Machine was well-represented by the organization's official symbol—a ferocious Bengal tiger.

The Tiger became the short-hand name for an organization that was to become the model for like-minded political machines located far beyond the boundaries of New York. In cities large and small, political machines dominated by first and second generation Irish Americans became a common mode of localized government that lasted well into the next century. In many ways, Irish-style politics became the politics of America, especially within the ranks of the Democratic Party, whose benevolent stance toward immigration, the working man, and ethnic politics in general can be traced to the first great influx of Irish immigration.

Organized crime was, in many ways, a natural outgrowth of the Tammany structure. Director Martin Scorcese's movie *Gangs of New York* (2002), based on a venerable 1927 book by Herbert Asbury, is somewhat misleading when it determines that the beginnings of organized crime occurred within the universe of the early Irish gangs. In fact, the gangs operated at the behest of the political apparatus. They were the muscle that lurked behind the symbol of the Tammany Tiger, their unique skills most notably required on election day when all political parties—Democratic, Whig, Republican, and Native American—unleashed their bully boys to police the polling sites.

The vast universe of criminal rackets that flowed from the daily workings of the Machine became the basis for organized crime in the United States. Municipal corruption, graft, boodling, illegal gambling and prostitution proceeds, street-level extortion, and gangsterism were a consequence of men and women maneuvering for power, clawing and scratching to gain a foothold within the Machine structure and advance in society.

Despite wars, sporadic corruption scandals, changing political administrations, and the exigencies of the American economy, this remained the model for organized crime in the United States until the years of Prohibition, which changed everything. Prohibition provided something the underworld never had before—a single, dominating racket that was so profitable that it tipped the balance of power. With the establishment of illegal booze as an unprecedented source of profit and influence, the gangsters were now calling the shots, not the politicians.

For Irish American mobsters and their fellow travelers, Prohibition represented the "glory years," a time of social ascendancy and high profits in which the gangster became a kind of cultural archetype. New York and Chicago evolved into the central domains of a vast, interconnected underworld that included not only mobsters and bootleggers, but also politicians, judges, lawyers, ward bosses, speakeasy operators, financiers, corporate overseers, police precinct captains, cops on the beat, and corrupt federal agents who made it all possible. In many ways, the era was the culmination of a way of doing business that had begun seventy years earlier with the first wave of desperate, destitute refugees from "Paddy's green shamrock shores."

Things began to change with the end of Prohibition in 1933, and the Irish Mob took an even greater hit during the years of the New Deal. A number of prominent practitioner's of Machine politics were prosecuted or forced from office via corruption scandals. Political reforms were enacted that brought about an end to the long era of the Machine.

In the years following World War II, the Irish American gangster scattered far and wide. Many were absorbed into the labor movement, either as strikebreakers hired by corporations, or as tough guys and facilitators connected with trade unions, most notably the International Longshoremen's Association (ILA) and the International Brotherhood of Teamsters. Some Irish American gangsters became notorious hitmen for hire who carried out murder contracts either for forces in the labor movement or for the Mob, also known as the Syndicate or the Outfit, which was a consortium of multiethnic mobsters. The Italian Mafia—a faction within the Mob that gained such a grandiose level of cultural notoriety in the later decades of the twentieth century that it came to represent the Mob itself—frequently employed Irish gunmen, particularly if the intended target of a hit was an Irishman.

The image of the independent Irish American criminal, a man who went wherever the money was, became a common trope in the underworld of the 1960s, 1970s, and 1980s. Working-class hoods who usually specialized in a specific brand of criminal activity—whether it was B & Es (breaking and entering), safe cracking, the snatch racket (kidnapping), murder-for-hire, or body disposal—saw themselves as underworld tradesmen. (One Irish American hitman of this era even referred to what he did as "carpentry work.") Often, these were men who wound up on the losing end of a long, ongoing rivalry between Irish and Italian mobsters that was rooted deep in the history of the American underworld. With a far larger and more organized structure, Italian organized crime groups inevitably dominated these confrontations, leaving a trail of dead Irishmen across the land.

Far more successful for the Irish were the neighborhood-based gangs that came to represent the last of the Irish Mob. In New York and Boston, the Irish Mob remained a viable force in the underworld long after most Irish Americans had assimilated into the suburbs and became generic white people in America. Mobsters in these cities inherited certain criminal rackets that had traditionally been controlled by Irish gang factions going back more than a century. The Westies gang in New York and Whitey Bulger's Winter Hill Gang in Boston were comprised of tough-talking, street-savvy

Irish hoods who appeared to be caught in a time warp. They were tough, emotional, paranoid men who adhered to the underworld dictum that three men can keep a secret, but only if two of them are dead.

The fact that the Irish Mob in its later decades engaged in a kind of macabre, internalized violence that can only be characterized as self-destructive should not be surprising. When a vast, morally corrupt universe that has murder as its ultimate principle goes through a kind of death throes, violent thrashing and internal self-immolation are the likely result. The Irish American gangster was always known for his wild, impulsive, anti-social behavior, which certainly characterized the last bloody days of the Irish Mob in America.

The main events of this saga take place in New York, Chicago, and Boston, with side trips to New Orleans, Kansas City, and Cleveland. Although the Irish Mob did not have the kind of initiation rights or agreed-upon rules of interaction that made Cosa Nostra such a cohesive underworld force throughout the United States, there were certain social systems put in place by the Irish that were remarkably similar in all of the aforementioned municipalities. An Irish mobster in Chicago might not be bound by the same rules as an Irish mobster in Boston, but the way they went about conducting business in these different cities made it seem as if Irish underworld players had all gone to the same divinity school. Whereas the Mafia was a private club, the Irish Mob was more of a philosophy, a shared social contract characterized by a loosely-connected sphere of influence in which the underworld and upperworld intersected under the guise of the lawman, the politician, and the gangster.

The men and women who populate this long march through the under-belly of American society are not easy to characterize. At the street level, there are numerous examples of the kind of doomed, untamed desperado who would come to symbolize the Irish gangster for many Americans. Leaders and followers populate this yarn, as do sociopaths and tragic cases. Many of their lives were tawdry, some downright despicable, but they were almost never boring. The life of the gangster was harsh, dangerous, fraught with paranoia, and sometimes exciting to the point of delirium.

The history of the Irish Mob includes a fair number of criminal vision-aries, men and women who might have done well for themselves if they had applied their skills to more legally acceptable modes of commerce. The Irish Mob stretched into the legitimate world, more than most underworld fra-ternities, entangling the fortunes of untold policemen, federal agents, union men, political figures, and at least one prominent tycoon whose lifelong dal-liance with the underworld changed the course of U.S. history.

Over the decades, much hot air and ink has been expended in the media's attempt to understand why the rise and fall of the gangster has remained such an enduring myth throughout the country's history. Certainly part of the attraction is the way in which the underworld has become a metaphor for American capitalism. Anyone who has tried to get ahead and make a living in the United States, from the lowliest street vendor to the most powerful corporate CEO, recognizes the brutal, dog-eat-dog reality of the American Dream. Some fantasize about taking matters into their own hands. In defiance of the laws and mores of polite society, the gangster does just that. In fact, everything about the gangster's life is a rebuke to the mundane, everyday life of the solid citizen. He lives in the moment, pursues immediate gratification with reckless abandon, and revels in his own narcissism like a slop-house pig. The gangster lives according to his own rules, as if he were judge, jury, and executioner—as if he were God.

There must be a little something of the suppressed gangster in the imagination of many people, given the prominence of gangster lore in popular culture. This tradition far precedes the most recent cinematic incarnations. From the days of the earliest newspapers and photographs to the present, Americans have exhibited a fascination and identification with the dark recesses of American commerce.

The American mobster as we perceive him today—violent, impulsive, disreputable, often irredeemable—is tethered to the earliest days of the Irish immigrant experience, when the Mob was born out of starvation, disease, desperation, and bigotry. Over the last century and a half, men and women of innumerable ethnicities and social backgrounds have taken a bite of the apple, from the lowliest criminal to the most esteemed members of society. But for sheer audacity and reckless ambition, few plied their trade with as much staying power or as much panache as the originator: the Irish American gangster.

PART ONE

birth of the underworld

blood at the root

ohn Morrissey was a young ruffian—a teenage, Irish punk with no job, no money, and few possessions other than the clothes on his back. The year was 1849, and Morrissey had just arrived in New York City from the upstate town of Troy, where he had been raised after moving from Ireland with his parents at the age of three. In Troy, Morrissey developed a reputation as a brawler and a troublemaker. He'd been indicted for burglary, assault, and assault with intent to kill; served a sixty-day stint in the county jail; and was under constant harassment from local authorities. They said eighteen-year-old Morrissey was a gangster, but the young man knew in his heart that his ambitions were too great for that two-horse town. And so, possessing a restless energy that could not be contained in the placid, confined roads of small-town America, he set out for the great metropolis 160 miles to the south, where pilgrims, immigrants, and refugees were presently arriving in droves.

Morrissey knew exactly where he needed to go: the Empire Club, a gambling parlor and political clubhouse that was famous throughout the state. Located on Park Row in lower Manhattan, the club was the home base of Captain Isaiah Rynders, legendary sporting man, gambling impresario, and political fixer for the Democratic party. Rynders was the employer of hundreds of political operatives, gambling club workers, saloon keepers, and gangsters; his organization was at the heart of a political machine that made the great city hum. Morrissey—hungry, hard-headed, and propelled by the desires of youth—was determined to harness the power of Rynders's organization to raise himself out of the ghetto and make his mark in the world.

He arrived at the Empire Club on one June afternoon, stood overlooking the gaming tables and declared, "I'm here to say I can lick any man in this place."

Captain Rynders himself, presiding at a gaming table, looked up at the intrepid young man—five-foot-eleven inches tall, maybe 175 pounds, with a barrel chest and hands the size of meat hooks; impressive, yes, but not so imposing that he could intimidate with sheer physical presence alone.

"And who might you be?" Rynders asked the young Irishman.

"My name is John Morrissey, and I'm the toughest pugilist on the eastern seaboard. I'm here to prove it."

Rynders pursed his lips in an enigmatic Mona Lisa-smile for which he was famous and glanced around at his fellow club members. He assessed the brash youngster, looking him over from head to toe, then nodded for his underlings to advance. They descended upon the young punk with fists, bottles, chairs, slung shots, and other weapons. Morrissey more than held his own until Big Tom Burns smacked him behind the ear with a spittoon, knocking the young hooligan unconscious.

When Morrissey awoke he was laying on a cot in the back of the Empire Club with a knot the size of an acorn on the crown of his skull. Captain Rynders, dressed in finery the likes of which Morrissey had never seen before, stood over the bruiser and said, "You're a bold, young bastard."

Morrissey felt the lump on his head and said nothing.

"I want you to come work for me. You'll make a fine shoulder-hitter for the organization. You can stay at my boarding house and work the docks."

And so began the political career of young John Morrissey.

He was put to work as an immigrant runner, one of hundreds who worked Castle Garden wharf in lower Manhattan, where the immigrant ships disgorged their human cargo. Each day he watched the arrival of his countrymen, and his heart ached at what he saw.

Having been born in Templemore, County Tipperary in 1831 and raised in an Irish slum in America, Morrissey knew a thing or two about poverty. In Troy, whenever his father was able to find work, it had been at the local wallpaper factory or on the docks alongside other Irish laborers. Young John had grown up believing his family was dirt poor, but what he saw at Castle Garden made him reassess his circumstances. Gaunt, haunted Irish peasants arrived by the boatload, weak from dropsy and gout, clinging to satchels that contained all that they owned. They told shocking tales of the Great Famine that had ravaged the Old Country over the last few years and of the horrific, disease-ridden journey across the ocean in hopes of a better future.

It was Morrissey's job to greet these new arrivals and direct them to soup kitchens and boarding houses controlled by the Rynders organization. Mixed in among the many legitimate immigrant runners were dozens of con artists and "land sharks," men who preyed upon the ignorant new arrivals. Later accounts of the era often characterized the job of the immigrant runner as that of a parasite, which may have been a bit harsh. Certainly the position straddled the line between charity and exploitation. Among runners, Morrissey developed a reputation as a tough though fair man who directed hundreds of desperate immigrants to food and lodging. In exchange, they signed voter cards and pledged their support to the political organization that Morrissey represented. On election day, it was Morrissey's job to see that these people delivered on their pledge—under the threat of violence, if necessary.

Along with tens of thousands of other Irish immigrants arriving in New York City on a monthly basis, Morrissey found lodging in Five Points, the infamous slum neighborhood that dominated the Sixth Ward at the lower tip of Manhattan island. For a time, he lived in a boarding house on Cherry Street and frequented a grog shop, or speakeasy, on lower Broadway known as the Gem Saloon.

Five Points was a lively area though the physical conditions of the district were awful. Laid out on top of what had once been a sewage pond known as the Collect, Five Points had evolved from being mostly an industrial district of tanneries, glue factories, and turpentine distilleries to a residential haven for the city's growing immigrant class. Poor Germans, Irish, Jews, and African Americans were crowded into two-story wooden structures built unsteadily on landfill over Collect Pond.

The district contained what was ostensibly the nation's first tenant house, or tenement. The Old Brewery was a former beer factory that had been converted into living quarters. A five-story monstrosity that glowered over the Five Points district like a slovenly toad, the building housed an impoverished collection of newly arrived immigrants and freed African Americans. For less than two dollars a month, lodgers resided in conditions that were stifling, overcrowded, and with a sanitation system so haphazard that the building and surrounding area were sometimes buffeted by waves of cholera that reached epidemic proportions.[1]

---

1. In 1832 thousands of New Yorkers died during a cholera epidemic; the disease spread especially rapidly in tenement districts like Five Points, where outhouses and water wells were located far too close together. Cholera is a bacterial infection that spreads primarily through water contaminated by feces. Symptoms include a hellish fever and rice-like diarrhea in which the "rice" is, in fact, the interior lining of the victim's colon flaking away. The result can be a slow and hideous death. (For an incisive overview of living conditions in Five Points and of the era in general see *Five Points* by Tyler Anbinder.)

Fetid conditions in the Old Brewery almost guaranteed that the building would become the center of much violence and depravity in the district. In the sprawling basement, known locally as the Den of Thieves, gambling, organized dog fights, prostitution, and all manner of robbery and assault were not uncommon. For local authorities, be they police or officials of the Association for Improving the Conditions of the Poor (AICP), the Old Brewery was a virtual no-go zone; the belief was that if you entered uninvited you were not likely to come out alive. Within the building's many warrens and hallways, violent crimes—including rape and murder—were so commonplace that years later, when the building was finally demolished, observers claimed to see construction workers carrying out bags of bones belonging to numerous murder victims who had been buried beneath the building's floorboards and in the walls.

The abysmal conditions in the Old Brewery spilled out into the district, creating an area that became well-known for general licentiousness and depravity. There was a saloon or speakeasy on nearly every corner with drunks stumbling out into the streets to be jack-rolled by gangs of prepubescent hooligans. Organized thievery was also common, with a high concentration of pickpockets, sneak thieves, and con artists of every variety. At night, the district descended into a kind of hellish debauchery; practically every other tenement was set up as a house of assignation, and basements and backrooms were designed for even more adventurous commercial sex practices. Gaming and backroom dance parlors were also common and eventually gave rise to a vibrant new dance style that was a combination of the African American shuffle and the Irish jig. This style was called a "break down" and became the forerunner of modern tap dancing.

By the time of John Morrissey's arrival in Five Points, the dangerous and licentious nature of the area had become something of a drawing card. Numerous writers and social commentators had recently visited the area to gawk at and pass judgement upon its inhabitants. In 1841, Charles Dickens, the great social observer and illustrious English novelist, immortalized the neighborhood in *American Notes*, an account of his five-month tour of North America:

> Let us go again . . . and plunge into Five Points. Poverty, wretchedness, and vice are rife enough where we are going now. . . . This is the place, these narrow ways diverging to the right and left, and reeking everywhere with dirt and filth. . . . Debauchery has made the very houses prematurely old. See how the rotten beams are tumbling down, and how the patched and broken windows seem to scowl dimly, like

eyes that have been hurt in drunken frays. . . . Vapors issue forth that
blind and suffocate. From every corner, as you glance about you in
these dark streets, some figure crawls half-awakened, as if judgement
hour were near at hand. . . . Here, too, are lanes and alleys paved with
mud knee deep; underground chambers where they dance and game;
ruined houses open to the street, whence through wide gaps in the
walls other ruins loom upon the eye, as though the world of vice and
misery had nothing else to show; hideous tenements which take their
names from robbery and murder; all that is loathsome, drooping, and
decayed is here.

But of all the conditions that made Five Points legendary, the physical
environment was but a garland compared to its reputation as the world's preeminent stomping ground for gangs and gangsters. John Morrissey was well-
acquainted with the life of the gangster. Back in Troy by the age of sixteen,
he had become leader of the Downtowns, a small gang of mostly Irish and
German teenage hooligans who often battled with the Uptowns, an anti-
immigrant gang of American-born youths. The Uptowns frequently raided
their territory in the riverfront industrial area of town. It was as leader of the
Downtowns that Morrissey acquired his criminal record and also his reputation as a skilled street fighter who was adept with his fists.

In Five Points, fists were a throwback to a more innocent time. Even the
Irish shillelagh, the oaken cudgel that had been a part of Celtic battles since
the ancient days of clan warfare, was obsolete in Five Points, where hatchets,
knives, slung shots, spiked clubs, brass knuckles, tomahawks, and muskets
were among the more common implements of confrontation.

The gangs were ubiquitous and tended to strut their stuff in two main
areas. The primary gathering place was Paradise Square, where Canal Street,
the Bowery, Chatham, Pearl, and Centre Streets converged to form a trun-
cated triangle, giving the neighborhood its name Five Points. Paradise Square
was claimed by the earliest of the gangs, mostly Irish, including the Forty
Thieves, Kerryonions, Shirt Tails, Chichesters, Patsy Conroys, Plug Uglies,
Roach Guard, and Dead Rabbits. The other staging area for the gangs was the
Bowery, which extended north of Five Points. Here were established the
social clubs and headquarters of the native-born American gangs, most
notably the Bowery Boys, the True Blue Americans, and the American Guard.

The gangs were a highly visible presence in Five Points, particularly during daylight hours, when they traveled brazenly in packs. By 1850, when
John Morrissey was living on Cherry Street, the gangs had begun to claim
various streets and territories as their own. Some of the gangs identified

themselves with special colors or clothes. The Plug Uglies wore hi-top derbies stuffed with padding so they could use their noggins as battering rams; the Shirt Tails wore their shirts untucked; the Dead Rabbits sewed distinctive, red stripes down the outer seam of their pants to distinguish themselves from the Roach Guard, who wore blue stripes.

For the newly arrived Irish, coming from a land where colonial oppression had been the rule of law for generations, the formation of a gang carried with it the whiff of a noble gesture. These loosely organized street-corner crews were not primarily criminal organizations—not yet, anyway. Many were local versions of regional protection groups, or political resistance sects from the Old Country. Back on the Emerald Isle, these secret, loosely-structured organizations waged guerilla warfare against the British Crown's commercial and military occupation. In America, what remained were the names, which became bastardized English-language versions of the original Gaelic. Plug Uglies, for instance, was an English translation of *baill oglaigh*, which meant member of the volunteers. Patsy Conroys was an anglicization of *pairt sa conradh* (partners in league). The Whyos, a gang based in Five Points that became prominent later in the century, derived their name from the Gaelic *uathadh uais* (noble few).[2]

A gang was comprised of anywhere between ten and one hundred members. The largest of the gangs were the Dead Rabbits, who were a conglomeration of numerous Paradise Square gangs that came together under one banner. It was said that the gang's name derived from the fact that they carried a dead rabbit impaled on a stick as a calling card. More likely, the gang's name came from the Gaelic "dead *ráibéad*." In the vernacular of the times, "dead" was an intensifier that meant "very." *Ráibéad*, in Gaelic, was a galoot or big lug. Thus, a Dead Rabbit was a very big galoot. The Dead Rabbits had no leader, as such; they were broken down into subdivisions and spread throughout the Five Points district.

With so many hungry, idle young men gathered in green grocery speakeasies and on street corners, confrontations between groups were inevitable. The fights were sometimes barroom donnybrooks that spilled out into the streets, or more serious riots that grew out of organized social and political agitation. By far the most famous gang battles were those between

---

2. The author is indebted to Daniel Cassidy, head of the Irish Studies Program at the New College of California, for the Gaelic translations of gang monikers and terms in this book. As part of a study on early Irish gangs, Cassidy has undertaken the sizable task of translating *The Secret Language of Crime: The Rogue's Lexicon* by George W. Matsell, Special Justice and Chief of the New York Police, first published in 1859.

the Dead Rabbits and Bowery Boys, but there were also smaller fights between factions of the Forty Thieves, Plug Uglies, and True Blue Americans. Some of these riots were territorial in nature—Irish versus Irish—but most were racial—native-born Americans versus "the nigger Irish."

As recounted in the *New York Herald*, the *Police Gazette*, *Frank Leslie's Illustrated News*, and other periodicals of the day, the gang wars could be shockingly brutal. In rural Ireland, some of the immigrants had belonged to fighting clubs in which altercations were fought according to Shillelagh Laws, where the primary instrument of battle was the Irish stick. In America, there were no rules. Sometimes gang riots raged sporadically for two or three days, with the streets barricaded by barrels and carts while gangsters blazed away with muskets and pistols, or tussled up close with brickbats, bludgeons, fists, and teeth. Most of the combatants were men, but women also played a role, either as lookouts or as resuppliers of ammunition. A few women even achieved renown as fierce battlers, none more so than Hellcat Maggie, who fought alongside the Dead Rabbits in many of their battles with the Bowery Boys and other nativist gangs. A young woman no more than twenty-years-old, Hellcat Maggie is reported to have filed her teeth sharp as mini-daggers and wearing on her fingers long, artificial nails made of metal. She would descend on rival gang members like a screaming banshee, biting and clawing until her fingers were dripping with the blood of her enemies.[3]

With casualty totals numbering in the hundreds and a level of carnage and destruction that frequently necessitated calling in the National Guard, the gang wars were a disturbing byproduct of the times. The gangs were a potential powder keg. Sprawling and disorganized, comprised mostly of rural Irish peasants now living in a strange and terrifying new environment, they haunted the streets of Five Points like spectral figures from some pre-utopian version of the American Dream. Mostly leaderless, the gangs were replenished weekly by the waves of destitute famine refugees arriving at Castle Garden wharf and other immigrant ports-of-call. The bitterness and sense of displacement that characterized the immigrant rabble was a potent force just waiting to be organized and harnessed. Anyone who could find a

---

3. Another female gang member who rivaled Hellcat Maggie for notoriety was Sadie the Goat, so named for her head-butting proclivities. A member and eventually commander of the Charleton Street Gang, Sadie was best known for having had her ear chewed off in a fight with an Englishwoman, Gallus Mag, proprietor of the Hole-in-the-Wall bar. Sadie's ear was later returned to her, and she kept it with her in a locket she wore around her neck at all times.

way to focus the frightening energy of the gangs, to tame the wild beast and redirect its power toward some useful purpose, would be a formidable leader indeed.

Old Smoke Riseth

By mid-1851, John Morrissey had established himself as a young man on the move. Through his activities as an immigrant runner and as a political organizer for Captain Isaiah Rynders's Empire Club, he had cobbled together a small financial nest egg that made it possible for him to buy in as part-owner of the Gem Saloon. Being a saloonkeeper was an essential first step for anyone hoping to launch a career in politics. Morrissey's ambitions were somewhat hindered by the fact that he could neither read nor write, a fact he sought to rectify through long hours of tutoring and study in the back of his saloon.

The young Irishman also had aspirations as a professional boxer, which, in the rough-and-tumble world of nineteenth century America, would be instrumental to a career in politics. Men hoping to achieve elective office needed to have a following; the saloon and the boxing ring were two arenas in which a man could distinguish himself as both tough and popular. Young John Morrissey was no exception. He launched his boxing efforts in the Five Points, where he had earned the catchy sobriquet of Old Smoke.

He'd first been given the nickname at an indoor shooting gallery in the basement of the St. Charles Hotel. One evening Morrissey became engaged in an impromptu fistfight with a man named Tom McCann, an American-born hoodlum affiliated with the Bowery Boys gang. The numerous onlookers who wagered on this fight were especially amazed when McCann pinned Morrissey against a stove of burning coals. Morrissey's clothes sizzled and smoked, and the smell of burning flesh filled the room, but the Irishman never uttered a word of complaint. In fact, he eventually broke free from McCann's grasp and whipped his competitor into submission. From then on, Morrissey was respectfully referred to as Old Smoke, a fighter who was able to endure pain and even gain strength and resolve through adversity.

In early 1852 Morrissey officially began his career as a professional pugilist, even though the sport was illegal at the time. Bouts were usually held at secret locations, often on piers and barges to avoid raids by coppers. The fights themselves were bare-knuckled affairs fought according to London Prize Ring rules, which meant each round continued until one of the fighters was knocked off his feet. There was no set limit to how long a fight could last; the bout continued until one of the fighters either quit or could not answer the bell for a new round. Competitive boxing matches were brutal, bloody, and known to last as long as sixty or seventy rounds, sometimes with deadly results.

For his first major championship bout, Morrissey traveled all the way to California. At Mare Island in San Francisco Bay, Old Smoke fought and defeated the California state champion, George Thompson, in nineteen minutes for a purse of $4,000 and a side bet of $1,000. It was in San Francisco that Morrissey also made his debut as a gambling impresario, running a popular dockside faro game from which he amassed a sizable bank roll. One night, a local man named Jim Hughes claimed that he had been cheated.

"I challenge you to a duel," Hughes said to Morrissey, "so that I may restore my lost honor."

"So be it," replied Morrissey. "May I choose the weapons?"

"Of course," said Hughes.

The following night a crowd gathered in expectation of the agreed upon showdown, which never took place, for Jim Hughes fled in terror when Old Smoke Morrissey appeared on the field of honor with a pair of butcher's cleavers under his arms.

The New York Irishman returned home more popular than ever. He fought again in October 1853, this time against the man who was the recognized champion of the world, Yankee Sullivan, an Irishman by way of Australia whose real name was James Ambrose. The fight was held at Boston Corners, a remote, rural location on the border of New York and Massachusetts. An estimated three to five thousand fight fans arrived at Boston Corners that day. They came by train, stagecoach, horse, and foot, all converging on the little hamlet to witness what they hoped would be the fight of the century.

Yankee Sullivan was a skilled champion, but he was forty years old. Morrissey was twenty-two. The younger fighter was highly favored, which is why it came as a shock to onlookers when Yankee Sullivan began pounding Morrissey in the early rounds. Sullivan was a wily veteran; he would unleash a flurry of jabs and hooks on his opponent, and then, when the opponent countered, drop to the ground, taking advantage of the London Prize Ring rules in which a drop ended the round.

According to one account, as the rounds progressed, "Sullivan, cool and calculating, went at his man determinedly, pecking, slashing, hammering, connecting three times to one." Morrissey kept on coming, but soon "exhibited the most revolting appearance imaginable . . . his eye was dreadfully swollen, and the blood was flowing in a perfect stream from each nostril." In the thirty-fourth round, Morrissey took a dozen blows without return. The odds, which were posted after each round, quickly changed from the original two-to-one for Morrissey to two-to-one in favor of Sullivan.

By round thirty-seven, the old fox seemed to be in complete command. Morrissey was "fading rapidly . . . his knees shook, and his hands were down and his mind bewildered." But the youngster was amazingly game. After receiving a flurry of blows from Sullivan, he advanced with what looked like the last of his energy. He boxed Sullivan into a corner, wrapped him against the ropes, and began choking him with a forearm—which was perfectly legal according to London Prize Ring rules. A Sullivan partisan, fearing that his fighter was about to lose or be choked to death, jumped into the ring and knocked Morrissey down. This, according to any rules, was a foul. Sullivan then unloaded a roundhouse right on Morrissey, who was still on his knees. Foul number two. All hell broke loose, with various fans rushing into the ring. By the time order was restored, the referee and fight officials declared that Old Smoke Morrissey was the winner and new Champion of America.

John Morrissey returned to Five Points as the people's champion. He married Sarah Smith, the daughter of a steamboat captain, and suffered one of his few early set-backs in life when his only child died at birth. His wife, Sarah, was a well-bred Protestant; she begged her husband to forego the crude and violent world of boxing. In a letter to the *New York Tribune*, Morrissey, the self-taught writer and nearly life-long pugilist, announced that he was retiring from the ring, having reached his decision out of "an honest desire more becomingly to discharge my duties to my family and society" and that "my duties to my family and myself require me to devote my time and efforts to purposes more laudable and advantages."[4]

Morrissey may have retired from the ring, but he still carried with him the reputation of being the toughest of the tough. His stature grew accordingly. He invested his boxing proceeds in a number of gambling establishments, one of which, a faro and roulette parlor located at No. 8 Barclay Street, became especially popular among politicians and sporting men. A

---

4. As with most boxers, Old Smoke Morrissey did not stick to his pledge to retire. He fought one more time, a much-ballyhooed bout against John C. Heenan, held at Long Point, Canada in October 1858. Morrissey, true to form, was knocked down in this fight but came back to knock Heenan unconscious, winning the bout in twenty-two minutes for a side bet of $5,000. After the bout, he retired a second time and stuck to it, never fighting professionally again.

more downscale gambling den owned by Morrissey was located near Paradise Square and was frequented by members of the Dead Rabbits. Increasingly, Morrissey's circle of friends spanned two worlds: rich and poor, street hoodlums and connected politicians. Inevitably, some of Morrissey's followers began to encourage Old Smoke to challenge Captain Isaiah Rynders as the de facto mob boss of Five Points, the man who served as a nexus between the sporting men, the gangsters, and politicians who utilized the Dead Rabbits and other gang members to stuff ballot boxes and intimidate rival voters on election day.

"I owe Ike Rynders my career," Morrissey told his friends. "He put me to work when I knew not a soul in this town." Morrissey proclaimed that he would not go up against Captain Rynders unless events in the street dictated that he do so—which is exactly what came to pass.

The trajectory of Old Smoke's life changed forever on the night of July 26, 1854, when he came face to face with William Poole, a notorious nativist shoulder hitter and former Bowery Boy who presided over his own Poole Association. Poole was a butcher by trade, skilled with knives and not bad with his fists either. As a member of the Bowery Boys, he'd been in a number of gang wars with the Dead Rabbits and the Roach Guard. He was a bit of a dandy who wore a long frock coat, slicked his black hair down in an early-vintage pompadour, and tried to pass himself off as an aristocrat. Over six-feet tall and strong as a bull, he was known as Bill the Butcher to friend and foe alike. In recent months, he'd emerged as a popular representative of the Know-Nothing Party, a political organization that was the bane of Irish Catholics throughout the United States.[5]

The Know-Nothing movement began in Pennsylvania and spread to New York, Boston, and as far south as New Orleans; it started out as a secret, anti-immigrant underground that engaged in late-night burnings of Catholic churches, the murder of immigrant leaders, and all manner of organized election-day skullduggery. The criminal nature of the organization's activities necessitated its secrecy; whenever a member of the gang was asked about the private "club," he responded, "I know nothing," which is how the movement got its name.

In the wake of the Irish potato famine, which first hit the Emerald Isle in 1845 and continued over the next five to ten years, the Know-Nothing movement rode a wave of racist, jingoistic anti-Irish sentiment that had

---

5. William Poole was the basis for the character of Bill "the Butcher" Cutting, as portrayed so vividly by actor Daniel Day Lewis in the movie *Gangs of New York*.

roots early in the century. In the United States, "No Irish Need Apply" was a sentiment expressed by American-born employers as far back as the 1830s. Resistance to the Irish was partly religion-based. The United States was a Protestant country. The Roman Catholic Church was viewed not only as a pagan cult with strange customs, but as a foreign-based power with designs on subverting and maybe even overtaking the U.S. system of government. "The Catholic church is the handmaiden of the devil," was how Cotton Mather put it when American cities were first being constituted. Through the Know-Nothing movement, Mather's beliefs became a virulent sub-theme of American society.

Religious intolerance was one thing, but White Anglo-Saxon Protestant (WASP) resistance to any and all immigrants was also an economic imperative with roots in the marketplace. The Founding Fathers had never envisioned a country overrun by starving, illiterate, disease-ridden "foreigners." The Irish, in particular, were seen as ignorant, hopelessly anti-authoritarian, clannish, overly emotional, and decidedly un-WASP-like in their strong identification with the common man. The term "Mulhoolyism" became a popular synonym for what was perceived to be rowdy, primitive behavior. In newspaper editorial cartoons in Philadelphia, Boston, Baltimore, and New York, the Irish were routinely depicted as vaguely simian creatures. One famous cartoonist, Thomas Nast, even established a thriving mini-career lampooning Paddy, whose pug-nosed, slovenly representation was often placed alongside Sambo, the ignorant rural black. Paddy and Sambo became dueling caricatures that personified the "white man's burden" within America's budding Anglo-Saxon republic.

By the time Bill Poole had begun to distinguish himself as a gangster, the Know-Nothings were the shock troops of an "American purification movement." Among other things, the official Know-Nothing charter listed their principles as "anti-Romanism, anti-Bedinism, anti-Papistalism, anti-Nunneryism, anti-Winking Virginiaism, and anti-Jesuitism." Around 1850, the Know-Nothings split from the Whig Party and became bullyboys for the new American Republican Party, who believed, among other things, that the naturalization period for immigrants should be increased to twenty-one years.

For some time, Bill the Butcher Poole and John Old Smoke Morrissey had been walking opposite sides of the fence. They were, in many ways, mirror images of each other, with Poole as the hero of the Protestant ascendancy and Morrissey a living embodiment of Paddy's ability to rise above difficult circumstances. The men undoubtedly had crossed paths before, either at political rallies or in the district's many saloons (Poole's butcher shop was located in nearby Washington Market). Their bitter rivalry—based on politics, racial animosity, and bragging rights over who was "cock-o'-the-walk" in the Bloody Sixth Ward—finally came to a head on the night of July 26, 1854 when Morrissey found Poole drinking at the bar of the City Hotel at Broadway and Howard Street.

"I hear you're a wizard with a butcher's blade," said Morrissey to Poole, "but I'd wager you're a coward at the manly art of fisticuffs."

"That sounds like a challenge, Morrissey."

"It is indeed," replied Old Smoke.

The two men agreed to meet the following morning at the Amos Street dock (now Christopher Street) to have it out once and for all.

At 7 A.M. the next morning, the two bruisers and their followers arrived en masse for the confrontation. The spectators formed a circle, which served as the ring. As later described in the *Police Gazette*, the encounter was a donnybrook of legendary proportions:

> The fight began with some light sparring, Poole holding himself principally on the defensive as his opponent circled for a chance to close. For about five minutes this child's play of the giants lasted. Then Morrissey made a rush. But Poole was too quick for him. As Old Smoke made his lunge, Bill the Butcher ducked with remarkable agility and seized him by the ankles. In a flash Poole threw his opponent clean over his head and as Old Smoke went sprawling he had only time to roll over when Poole pounced on him like a tiger. Then followed terrible minutes of fighting. . . . There was a long gash in Poole's cheeks where the flesh had been torn by his opponent's teeth. The blood was streaming from Morrissey's both eyes. . . . Not a hand was raised to interfere or favor either contestant during the two or three minutes this inhuman struggle lasted.

The fight ended in what some would call a draw; others claimed that Poole got the best of it. Either way, it did not settle the ongoing rivalry between the Poole and Morrissey factions. Their war continued for months, with numerous tit for tat encounters, until the night of February 25, 1855. In this face-to-face encounter between Morrissey and Poole, two of Morrissey's henchmen gunned down the infamous Bill the Butcher at Stanwix Hall, a saloon on Broadway. Though mortally wounded, Poole lingered on for fourteen days before delivering his immortal final words: "Goodbye boys. I die a true American."

John Morrissey, along with Paudeen McLaughlin, Lew Baker, Jim Turner, and a few minor accessories, was put on trial for the murder. The case resulted in a series of hung juries before charges were dropped altogether, sealing Morrissey's legend as the man who brought about the demise of Bill the Butcher, one of the great xenophobe's of American history. Old Smoke Morrissey had been a gangster, a saloon keeper, a boxer, and gambling impresario—now he was an acquitted murderer and the most popular man in the Irish American underworld.

The First Irish Mob Boss

The term "mob boss" originated in Five Points and refers to a form of spontaneous political activity known as a mob primary. Mob primaries comprised the most basic form of political organization known to man. They were initiated by an aspiring political leader merely standing on a milk crate or soap box and orating until he had gathered a crowd, or mob, who was willing to sign a petition on the man's behalf declaring him a candidate for public office. The mob pledged its vote to the orator, who was usually a saloon keeper willing to offer free drink, a sandwich, a cellar mattress to sleep on, or all of the above in exchange for a vote. The type of voter most willing to enter into this arrangement was usually a rough character—a bum, a homeless person, a thief, or a gangster. Thus, the mob boss, or mobster, became the leader of a less than savory constituency that was, nonetheless, a powerful force capable of swinging many local elections.

The arrangement worked both ways. By aligning himself with a rising and powerful mob boss, the street hoodlum was now also a mobster. He was connected, part of a system in which he now had a vested interest. Ostensibly, he would now have the kind of protection that was necessary for him to operate an illegal business—say, a house of prostitution, gambling den, burglary ring, unlicensed speakeasy, or any manner of criminal enterprise popular throughout the underworld. A vast subterranean universe of vice, exploitation, and good times, the underworld was kept alive through a steady flow of cash from above and below. From the earliest mob primary in America, the underworld and the upperworld were intrinsically intertwined and would remain so through centuries of bloodshed, criminal prosecution, and political reform.

Since the early 1840s, the most powerful mob boss in New York City was Captain Isaiah Rynders. Rynders was the first to establish a network of saloons and gambling parlors that generated money and created an underworld constituency, which buttressed his political organization, the Empire Club. In 1844 Rynders achieved national fame for himself when he virtually delivered the presidency to James K. Polk, the Democratic candidate. He did so through a highly physical form of voter fraud. The use of gangsters on election day was a common practice of all the political parties, but Rynders was the first to perfect the art by organizing the hoodlums into cohesive voting blocks. In New York, his ability to deliver became the foundation of the powerful political organization, or machine, known as Tammany Hall. Rynders's record of success was such that he made electoral forays to Philadelphia, Baltimore, and, in 1854, the city of New Orleans, where he sought to educate local Democrats in the ways of Tammany-style machine politics.

Rynders's only problem was that he wasn't Irish, at least not Irish Catholic with roots in the Old Country. Although his mother was of Irish Protestant stock, his father was German American. Increasingly, the waves of Catholic famine immigrants who had begun to fill out the ranks of the underworld—and the lower political ranks of organizations like Tammany Hall—clamored for one of their own as titular leader of the Mob. In an era when social mechanisms for change were woefully unresponsive to the needs of the people, the Mob inevitably sought to bring about change in their own way—in the streets. It happened, oddly enough, on Independence Day, 1857.

During that time, the city's gang wars had grown considerably worse largely due to the fact that New York was patrolled by two competing police forces: The Municipals, who were loyal to the Republican Party, and the Metropolitans, stepchild of the Democrats. These two forces seemed more interested in fighting each other than actually policing the city (a situation that would be rectified two years later when the two forces were finally combined). The gangsters ran wild during what was an especially dark and turbulent year that would culminate with financial calamity for all when a run on the banks caused a massive Depression in the fall of 1857. Before it was over, scores of financial institutions and businesses would go under, with liabilities exceeding $120,000,000.

In the midst of all this, a rivalry that had been roiling between the Dead Rabbits and the Bowery Boys for more than a decade finally boiled over when, on the evening of July 4, a large contingent of Dead Rabbits and Roach Guards attacked the clubhouse of the Bowery Boys and Atlantic Guard at 42 Bowery. An all-night battle raged unencumbered by police interference, in which the nativist side appeared to prevail. The next day the gang war continued, with literally hundreds of soldiers on each side. "Brickbats, stones and clubs were flying thickly around . . ." reported the *New York Times.* "Men ran wildly about brandishing firearms. Wounded men lay on the sidewalk and were trampled upon. Now the Rabbits would make a combined rush and force their antagonist up Bayard Street to the Bowery. Then the fugitives, being reinforced, would turn on their pursuers and compel a retreat . . ."

Police finally arrived on the scene and advanced on the gangsters with unparalleled savagery, forcing scores of Dead Rabbits and Bowery Boys into the tenements and up the stairs to the roofs, clubbing them at every turn. One fleeing gangster was knocked off the roof of a house on Baxter Street; his skull was fractured when he hit the sidewalk, where his gang enemies promptly stomped him to death.

Eventually, at 7 P.M. on the second night of rioting, the police in desperation turned to Captain Isaiah Rynders, who as leader of mob forces in the Sixth Ward was believed to have influence with both sides. Rynders arrived on the scene and stood before the barricades on Baxter Street.

"I implore you to end this carnage," he declared to the rioters. "You are killing each other for what purpose? To what end?"

The gangsters, including those on the Dead Rabbits side, threw rocks and missiles at Rynders, chasing him from the scene. The riot finally ended of its own volition an hour later, but the dye had been cast. Both symbolically and in reality, the Captain's very public rebuke signaled the end of his influence in the Bloody Ould Sixth. From this point on, Rynders was out; Morrissey was in.[6]

Out of the ashes of the Great Riot of 1857 arose the first true Irish Mob boss in American history. As such, Morrissey's first order of business was to expand his gambling empire. In the nineteenth century, gambling was (as illegal booze and narcotics would be for later generations of mobsters) the secret elixir that fueled the entire underworld, as well as upperworld politicians who relied on money and muscle provided by the gambling czars. Morrissey ran two kinds of establishments: gambling dens for the poor, which consisted mostly of card games, policy, and craps, and upscale parlors for the rich, who favored faro, bagatelle, and roulette.

Morrissey achieved his greatest success when he traveled north of New York City to Saratoga Springs, a budding resort town. Having been raised in nearby Troy, Old Smoke knew the area well. Located near the foothills of the Adirondack Mountains, Saratoga Springs was a beautiful setting where the hoi polloi came to relax in the local hot springs. The Five Points mob

---

6. The official casualty totals for the Dead Rabbits/Bowery Boys riot of 1857 were 12 killed and 37 wounded, but the *Times* estimated the actual numbers to be two or three times higher. It was widely rumored that the gangs had taken away their own dead and secretly buried them in alleyways and tenement basements.

boss astutely surmised that the town needed a first class gambling parlor. He cobbled together money from a number of wealthy investors and opened the majestic Saratoga Club House, which immediately became known as "the finest gaming establishment in America."

Saratoga Springs was a conservative place, home to the first registered temperance society in the United States. Morrissey's arrival in town was not welcomed by all. There were attempts by reformists to close the Saratoga Club House. Old Smoke countered these attacks with lavish gifts, i.e. pay-offs, to the town, the churches, civic organizations, politicians, and other public officials. Remarked one local newspaper columnist in admiration, "Morrissey divides the profits of his sinning with the good people of the village with a generous hand." Thanks in part to the Irish Mob boss, Saratoga Springs would go on to build many fancy hotels, a spectacular race track, numerous fine dining establishments, and become one of the most popular destinations in the history of sporting men.

The success of the Saratoga Club House made Morrissey fabulously wealthy. The once destitute ghetto tough and immigrant runner became a leading representative of "mobster chic," the first of his generation to establish what would become a proclivity among prominent gangsters for centuries to come. He presented himself in a manner both nouveau riche and gauche. He grew a full, neatly manicured black beard in the manner of General Ulysses S. Grant and wore sparkling jewelry—a diamond studded cravat, diamond rings on his fingers, and a gold-plated pocket watch dangling from his vest. He favored striped, high-waist pants, which he combined with a swallow-tail dinner jacket and a beaver-pelt overcoat, topped off with a mink bowler hat. To go along with his ostentatious personal appearance, Morrissey was squired around town in what could only be described as the pink Cadillac of its day—a gold-embroidered carriage, custom-built in New Jersey and priced at over $2,000.

Along with his garish personal style, Morrissey exhibited another trait that would become a staple of rags-to-riches mobsters for generations to come: a desire to be accepted by aristocratic society. Born and raised in squalor, Morrissey believed that he could buy his way into high society. He was seen around town with men like Commodore Cornelius Vanderbilt and August Belmont, the wealthy WASP industrialists who patronized his Saratoga Club House. These men may have been willing to go slumming with Morrissey, the garish Irish Mob boss, but they were not his friend. Vanderbilt allegedly gave Morrissey a bogus stock tip that cost him thousands. When Morrissey tried to buy a house in the aristocratic part of town, a local syndicate led by Belmont banded together and bought the property out from under him. Morrissey was shocked to find out that beyond the gold-leaf walls of his gaming establishment, he was, to the reigning WASPs and their socialite companions, just another Paddy.

It was a hard lesson for Morrissey. Being a famous gambling impresario might make him rich, but it would not bring him acceptance among the social elite. For this, Old Smoke surmised, the real key to his aspirations was the world of politics. In 1868 Morrissey called in all his chits as Irish Mob boss and New York state gambling czar and got himself elected to Congress. Two years later he was reelected by an overwhelming majority.

Morrissey's political fortunes were aligned with none other than William Marcy Tweed, former captain of the Big Six Fire Engine Company and an alderman who had risen to become grand sachem, or boss, of Tammany Hall in 1863. Old Smoke's endorsement of Tweed, a native-born Presbyterian of Scottish descent, was an important feather in Tweed's cap. The Irish Catholic vote was huge. Morrissey's support was a decisive element in Boss Tweed's ability to deliver voters to the polls, which was the backbone of Tammany's power. As payback, Morrissey became a prominent member of Tweed's inner circle, known as the Ring. It was also Old Smoke's understanding that, as Tweed's Celtic liaison, he would be in line to assume the position of the first Irish Catholic boss of Tammany Hall.

During an eight-year stretch from 1863 to 1871, Boss Tweed and his inner circle proceeded to plunder the city of New York like no political entity ever had before—or ever would again. Tweed himself became a billionaire, amassing his fortune through a mind-boggling array of graft, kickbacks, rigged bidding on city contracts, boodling, and money from illegal enterprises such as gambling and prostitution. Tammany Hall under Tweed set the standard for what would come to be known as gangster politics. The Boss and his Ring controlled the levers of power by determining who would and who would not be elected to office. They did so largely through the use of thuggery and terror on election day. Once in office, Tweed's Ring got rich through control of the municipal government, the county government, the judicial system, the governorship, and the all-important Board of Audit, which supervised all city and county expenditures.

For a good while, the public stood idly by while Tweed and his crew siphoned off staggering amounts of money from city bonds and other pork barrel scams simply because they got things done. Under Tweed the municipal bureaucracy grew as never before, with the attendant city jobs and political opportunities for members of the tribe. The Irish, in particular, benefited greatly, and men with Hibernian names began to dominate Tammany's vast ward structure, holding down key positions as ward committeemen, ward bosses, and precinct captains.

Eventually, Tweed's own waste and arrogance brought him down. He bullied his own Board of Supervisors into building a massive, Victorian-style court house that no one wanted, then padded the construction costs to $13 million and skimmed the overage for himself. This typical act of profligacy prompted a series of damning articles in the *New York Times*. Aided by cartoonist Thomas Nast, who in *Harper's Weekly* portrayed the Boss and his Ring as corpulent hogs slopping at the trough of public beneficence, the tide finally turned against the Machine. Tweed's legitimate accomplishments—the fact that he'd presided over some of the city's most far-reaching public works projects such as improved water supplies and sewage disposal for the poor—were buried under an avalanche of vitriol and negative press.

In the early 1870s, the Boss got his comeuppance when back-to-back civil and criminal indictments laid bare the full extent of his plundering. Six million dollars in stolen funds was traced directly to Tweed. It was alleged that the Boss and his Ring together had defrauded the municipal government out of $50 million (equivalent—conservatively—to $500 million in today's currency). Facing major prison time, Tweed went on the lam, was eventually caught in Spain, and extradited to the United States, where he languished behind bars. As part of a plea arrangement, he eventually came clean, and in 1877, during an investigation of the Tweed Ring by the Board of Aldermen, the boss turned on his former protégé and Irish liaison, Old Smoke Morrissey.

In a long written statement, the disgraced Tammany boss identified Morrissey as a skillful practitioner of mass voter fraud and early bag man for the Ring. Furthermore, declared Tweed, Morrissey was "a proprietor and owner of the worst places in the city of New York, the resort of thieves and persons of the lowest character. Perhaps one of the worst faults that can be attributed to me is having been the means of keeping his gambling houses protected from the police."

Politically speaking, Old Smoke was cooked. By aligning himself with Tweed, the undisputed gambling czar of New York had backed the wrong horse. Ostracized by his rival, Honest John Kelly, who replaced Tweed to become the coveted first Irish Catholic Grand Sachem of Tammany Hall, Morrissey made one last stab at glory. He broke from Tammany and formed his own political organization called Young Democracy. His efforts were fraught with internecine struggles, and he was only partially successful. Though he was elected to the state senate in 1875 and reelected two years later, his personal life deteriorated into alcoholism and an early form of dementia brought on by his years of physical punishment in the boxing ring. With his defenses weakened, he contracted a severe case of pneumonia, and, on May 1, 1877, after being bedridden for weeks, he cried out in his sleep and then expired. At the time of his death, Old Smoke Morrissey was forty-seven years old.

In his short eventful life, this former son of the Old Sod, street tough, box-ing champ, vice lord, and skilled political operative, created a prototype for the upwardly mobile Irish American mobster. Proud, adventurous, street smart, and unencumbered by any sense of fealty to the Protestant work ethic, he became a leader among men. Although his life did not end as he would have liked, Morrissey's years were marked by many substantial though legally and morally questionable achievements. Most of all, he played a key role in helping to create a criminal framework by which the American underworld would pros-per for decades to come. He also showed that, by combining physical prowess and criminal audacity with legitimate political influence, a man could rise up out of the gutter and take on the world.

It was a lesson many of the lowly gangsters of Five Points still needed to learn.

Gangs, Gangsters, and the Women Who Love Them

In many ways, John Morrissey was the exception to the rule. Through sheer ambition and force of personality, he came to symbolize the era in which he lived. There were few coattails in the underworld, however. Morrissey's individual success did not necessarily translate into new levels of accep-tance and opportunity for the Irish American gangster. By and large, gangs continued to proliferate and were refueled from the nether regions of America's ongoing urban nightmare. By the 1880s, the squalid slum con-ditions that had given rise to an earlier generation of Dead Rabbits and Plug Uglies hadn't changed much. In Five Points, the Old Brewery had been torn down, with all traces of its sordid past eradicated, but tenement life had become more stifling and spread well beyond the bounds of the Sixth Ward.

In *How the Other Half Lives*, photojournalist Jacob A. Riis's pioneering chronicle of slum life in late nineteenth century New York City, the gangster mentality was shown to be a natural consequence of tenement life. With nearly 33,000 densely-crowded tenement houses on the Lower East Side alone, children had little choice but to lead their lives in the street. A pack mentality ruled. Riis wrote

> Every corner has its gang, not always on the best of terms with the rivals on the next block, but all with a common programme: defiance of law and order, and with a common ambition: to get "pinched," i.e., arrested, so as to pose as heroes before their fellows. A successful raid on a grocer's till is a good mark, "doing up" a policeman cause for promotion. The gang is an institution in New York.

For Riis, the roots of gang life were painfully obvious.

> The gang is the ripe fruit of tenement-house growth. It was born there, endowed with a heritage of instinctive hostility to restraint by a generation that sacrificed home to freedom, or left its country for its country's good. The tenement received and nursed the seed . . . New York's tough represents the essence of reaction against the old and the new oppression, nursed in the rank soil of the slums. Its gangs are made of the American-born sons of English, Irish, and German parents. They reflect exactly the conditions of the tenements from which they sprang.

In the years following John Morrissey's death in 1878 to the end of the century, the Whyos were by far the most notorious gang in New York. Like the Dead Rabbits before them, the Whyos were a conglomeration of numerous smaller street corner crews who, according to Riis, met in "club rooms . . . generally a tenement, sometimes under a pier or dump, to carouse, play cards, and plan their raids; their 'fences,' who dispose of the stolen property." In a city that was now fully one quarter Irish, the anti-Catholic Know-Nothing movement had been simply overwhelmed and chased out of town. The Whyos were thus less of a protection organization based on traditions founded in the Old Country and more of a criminal organization whose sole reason for existing was profit and plunder.

They were led by the two Dannys—Danny Lyons and Danny Driscoll—and presided over a sprawling domain that seemed to take in most of lower Manhattan. Their membership, almost all of whom had nicknames (a common feature of the gangs in general), included Red Rocks Farrell, Googy Corcoran, Bull Hurley, Hoggy Walsh, and Slops Connolly (not to be confused with Baboon Connolly). Piker Ryan, another Whyo who helped make the gang famous, achieved a kind of immortality when he was arrested with a "gangster price list" in his pocket that was subsequently published in the *Police Gazette.*

```
PUNCHING ............................................................$2
BOTH EYES BLACKED...................................4
NOSE AND JAW BROKE................................10
JACKED OUT (knocked out with a blackjack) ..................15
EAR CHAWED OFF......................................15
LEG OR ARM BROKE ...................................19
SHOT IN LEG ............................................25
STAB ......................................................25
DOING THE BIG JOB ..............................100 AND UP[7]
```

The Whyos were racketeers, a new breed of street-level capitalist criminal. The term itself comes from the word "racket," which was a public function—a party or a dance—held by criminals under the guise of being a fund-raiser for a worthy cause.[8] Eventually, the term was expanded to infer the use of physical intimidation or political pressure to squeeze protection money out of merchants. The Whyos collected tribute payments from saloon keepers and shop owners in the area in return for services rendered a la Piker Ryan's price list.

Racketeering was one example of how the underworld had become much more organized and stratified thanks to pioneers like John Morrissey. The organizational structure of the New York underworld was in many ways a precursor of professional baseball. The tenant neighborhood street gangs represented the minor leagues, where an enterprising hoodlum could establish a reputation and "show his stuff." If a gangster distinguished himself at the street level, he advanced to the majors and became a mobster, which was a position more connected to the levers of political and economic power. If the mobster was really good, he got to play for Tammany Hall, the New

---

7. This list appeared in Herbert Asbury's *The Gangs of New York* and has been reprinted in virtually every book ever written about nineteenth century crime in America. In recent years it has even been printed on the front of t-shirts sold at St. Mark's Place novelty shops and elsewhere around the city of New York, part of the perverse and enduring legacy of the gangs.
8. The term "racket," ironically, is today most commonly used by the ranks of the New York police and fire departments, who still refer to retirement parties and in-house fundraisers as rackets.

York Yankees of the underworld. With Tammany Hall, he could become an all-star, get filthy rich, and even—if he were truly gifted—make it to the Mobster Hall of Fame like Old Smoke Morrissey.

You could also look at street-level racketeers like the Whyos as simply mimicking the mentality, if not the tactics, of America's business elite. Early robber barons like J. P. Morgan, Jacob Astor, Andrew Carnegie, and the Rockefellers were hard-nosed men whose fortunes were built on market speculation, corporate profiteering, and organized union busting. Through burgeoning industries like coal, oil, steel, and railroad building, these men enforced a kind of labor Darwinism that created a chasm between workers and management that would become a defining characteristic of American life. Beyond the boundaries of New York's slums, the era of the Whyos unfolded at the tail end of the Gilded Age, a time of unbridled consumerism and accumulation of capital. Taking their lead from the tenor of the times, the gangsters were a gutter-snipe version of the Money Trust, as it would come to be known, a monopoly of industrial interests dedicated to the principle that a man must fight hard—by hook or by crook—for his piece of the pie and fight even harder to accumulate more and more.

Of course, the men of the Money Trust were mysterious figures rarely covered in the newspapers; it would be years before many of these men were even known by name. Gangsters, however, tended to perform their activities right out in the streets and were derided or glorified on a daily basis in the newspapers.

In fact, by the 1880s, Irish gangs in general had become so notorious that they achieved a kind of mythical status in the press. In Manhattan, most of the city's broadsheets had a daily column that covered the criminal courts and another called the police blotter that relayed arrest reports from the previous night's criminal activity in various wards around the city. The columns paid special attention to the exploits of the gangs. There were the river pirate gangs, most notably the Daybreak Boys, who were the bane of the harbor police. There were regional neighborhood gangs: the Hudson Dusters, the Gas House Gang, the Parlor Mob, and the Gophers (pronounced "goofers"). The Gophers were only beginning to take shape in the wilds of Hell's Kitchen, a burgeoning slum on Manhattan's West Side. Of all the gangs, none was mentioned anywhere near as often as the Whyos. For a time it appeared as if every jack-roller, pickpocket, sneak thief, panel house operator, and jaywalker in the state of New York was a member of the "notorious Whyo Gang."

The aggrandizement of the Whyos and other gangs in the press was great for the cops and government lawyers whose reputations were enhanced by the pursuit and prosecution of what had been identified as "a national scourge." It was not so great for the gangsters themselves, whose street-level criminal shenanigans were now part of a vast underworld conspiracy that came to be known as the Shame of the Cities.

Two well-known gangsters who certainly did not benefit from the unprecedented notoriety of the Whyos were the two Dannys, Lyons and Driscoll. Of the two, Lyons inspired more fear. He was also considered to be devilishly handsome, with a mustache that was always freshly waxed and curled up at the ends (Driscoll sported an identical mustache). Lyons was a pimp and whoremaster who strolled the streets of the Sixth Ward with his stable of girls at his side. Among his most popular girls were Lizzie the Dove, Gentle Maggie, and Bunty Kate.

Lyons was always on the lookout for fresh recruits. Sometime in early 1887, he seduced and enlisted the talents of a new girl named Pretty Kitty McGown, a virginal redhead whose skin was white as alabaster. No one knew how he did it, but Lyons had a Svengali-like ability to bring women into the fold. Some credited his good looks and natural charms; others said he used drugs and other forms of coercion. In any event, in order to become a part of Lyons' "white slave ring," Pretty Kitty McGown left her boyfriend, Joseph Quinn. Quinn became enraged and vowed to get revenge against Lyons. For several months, he and the Whyo leader were gunning for one another. They finally came face to face on the morning of July 5. In Paradise Square, the heart of the Five Points, Quinn declared, "Daniel Lyons, you're a whoremaster and a coward and a corrupter of women to boot. You will pay for your deeds."

According to an eyewitness, Lyons was attacked by Quinn. In self defense, Danny pulled out his revolver and proceeded to shoot Joe Quinn dead in the middle of Paradise Square.

Immediately after the shooting, Lyons went on the lam, hiding out in tenement basements in Brooklyn and in the sage brush hinterlands of Long Island. His brothel operation fell into disrepair. Without the pimp master's guidance, the girls quarreled. One night, Gentle Maggie and Lizzie the Dove got into a bitter shouting match at a saloon on the Bowery.

"You're nothing but a filthy whore," said Gentle Maggie.

"You bet I am," replied Lizzie the Dove, "but at least I'm not a *diseased* filthy whore like you."

Gentle Maggie ended the argument by stabbing the Dove in the throat with a cheese knife. Lizzie died. Her last words were that she would meet Gentle Maggie in hell and scratch her eyes out.

Shortly thereafter, Danny Lyons was captured and put on trial. The evidence suggested that Lyons—admittedly a disreputable criminal and all-round bad person—was merely defending himself on the day in question. As coleader of the notorious Whyo gang, however, he never stood a chance. Lyons was found guilty of murder and sentenced to the gallows.

Around the same time Lyons had been having it out with Joe Quinn; Danny Driscoll, the other leader of the Whyos, was embroiled in a situation that would have seemed fantastical were it not so strikingly similar to the predicament faced by his partner.

Late one evening in a Five Points saloon, Driscoll had been approached by Beezy Garrity, a comely, young whore who worked at a cheap panel house in Whyo territory at 183 Hester Street. Among the most notorious of prostitution enterprises, panel houses were usually located in an out-of-the-way residence. They had rooms with sliding walls that hid creepers, or sneak thieves. Once a john was preoccupied in bed with a hooker, a creeper would come out from behind the sliding wall and quietly rifle through the unsuspecting john's belongings, stealing money, jewelry, or whatever else was there for the taking.

Beezy was upset because she had been ripped off by the operator of the panel house, an Irish immigrant named John McCarthy. "He took my earnings and kicked me out in the street," said Beezy.

Despite his long criminal record that included a seven-year stint in prison for grand larceny, Danny Driscoll was considered something of a gentle soul. Nonetheless, Beezy's claims of mistreatment raised his ire.

"By God, let's go see the bastard," he suggested.

Around 3:30 in the morning, Driscoll and Beezy went to the panel house and confronted John McCarthy. A shoot-out ensued. McCarthy escaped out a back window. Driscoll, while attempting to shoot McCarthy, accidentally plugged Beezy Garrity in the stomach with his .44-caliber revolver.

Beezy lingered in the hospital for a few days, swearing with her last breath that it was McCarthy—not Danny Driscoll—who had shot her. Then she died.

Driscoll was put on trial for murder. The most damaging evidence against him came from Beezy Garrity's mother, Mrs. Margaret Sullivan. Although Beezy had, before her death, publicly maintained the lie that McCarthy pulled the trigger, her mother's testimony refuted that claim. Mrs. Margaret Sullivan had always believed that it was the Whyo gang who had lured her daughter into a life of prostitution. On the stand, dressed in black, she testified to having had the following conversation with her dying daughter at St. Vincent's Hospital:

MOTHER: Beezy, I knew something like this would happen to you for not doing as I told you.

DAUGHTER: Mother, what's the use of you talking to me that way now; I'm going to die.

MOTHER: There's many a person been shot before and are still alive.

DAUGHTER: But not with such a ball as the one I was shot with. You had to shoot the pistol like this—and Beezy placed both hands together.

MOTHER: Who did it to you?

DAUGHTER: 'Twas Danny Driscoll done the deed.

Driscoll was finished. Even though the killing was an accident (manslaughter, not murder), this was Danny Driscoll—Danny Lyons's sidekick and coleader of the Whyo gang. Driscoll was found guilty of the murder of Beezy Garrity and sentenced to hang.

When the date for his execution arrived, Driscoll spent his last hours writing letters to friends, his wife, and his mother. He also wrote a poem dedicated to Mary, a Sister of Mercy who was kind to him during his imprisonment.

At 7:15 on the morning of January 23, 1888, Driscoll was led to the gallows. His last words were "May God have mercy on my soul."

At 7:42 A.M., he was executed; three hundred pounds of iron jerked him three feet into the air and the thin rope of rare Italian hemp snapped his neck like a twig. He died in under two minutes.

Eight months later, the other Danny was led down the same hallway to the same gallows. The rope was placed around his neck, and the trap door dropped open. Lyons bucked and kicked for a few seconds, then he was gone.

A reporter for the *Brooklyn Eagle* observed "So far as a hanging can be good, it was a good hanging."

"Hurrah for Big Tim!"

The execution of a prominent gangster always made the papers. With a gang like the Whyos, you could never kill enough of them, or so the reports and editorials seemed to suggest. The irony, of course, was that the more law enforcement sought to eradicate the Whyos, the more press attention they received, until the gang was elevated from the grubby ink of the police blotter to mythical status.

For some people, the notorious reputation of the gang was a godsend. An ambitious ward boss or Tammany assemblyman, for instance, rose or fell in the political arena based on his ability to deliver, which translated into bodies, which translated into votes. Votes were a primary particle of survival in the big city. Votes fed the hungry, gave solace and power to the weak, and, more importantly, opened the door to a vast multitude of patronage jobs that the Irish were determined to use as stepping stones up and out of the slums of New York, Philadelphia, Boston, and elsewhere. Nobody enforced the will of the bosses and delivered votes better than a gang.

Old Smoke Morrissey had already laid the groundwork. An ambitious politician who was conversant with the world of the saloon, the ruffian, and the gambling den, and who could also find a way to organize and bleed the bordellos, the drug dens, and other untoward forms of vice, would be a powerful man indeed. Morrissey had started at the beginning as an immigrant runner and formulated an underworld narrative that included the Dead Rabbits as a kind of Greek chorus. The man who would do the same with the Whyos, benefiting greatly from their reputation for mayhem and their connection to the entire constellation of rackets in Five Points, was a rising young Tammany stalwart named Timothy Daniel Sullivan.

Of the Whyos' many impromptu club rooms, the most well known was Tim Sullivan's saloon on Chrystie Street, where, among others, the two Dannys appeared on a nearly daily basis in the years before their respective executions. Sullivan, Lyons, and Driscoll had many things in common: All three were born into considerable poverty in and around the Sixth Ward. All were the children of potato famine immigrants. And all understood the true nature of upward mobility for an Irish Catholic in the New World, none more so than Sullivan.[9]

Sullivan was born in Five Points on July 23, 1863 and lived with his mother, six siblings, a stepfather, and three boarders in a run-down tenement apartment at 25 Baxter Street, just south of Paradise Square. His mother and father were immigrants from Landsdowne, County Kerry who, upon their arrival, were among the very poorest of the Five Points poor. Sullivan's stepfather was a ne'er-do-well who contributed little to the survival of the family, leaving Tim, the oldest, as the man of the house.

Young Tim became quite an entrepreneur. He worked as a newspaper delivery boy and had by his early teen years developed a network of contacts

9. It was in his bar on Chrystie Street that Sullivan was given the nickname "Dry Dollar" for his habit of lifting wet dollars off the bar counter and carefully drying them before putting them in the till. He later became known as "Big Tim" or "The Big Fella." "Big" was a common Irish appellation that could either denote physical stature or a person's standing in the community. In Sullivan's case, it referred to both.

among the city's other newsboys and periodicals dealers. He formed his first business enterprise by giving orphans and runaways just starting out as newsboys their first stack of papers free, both to help the struggling street urchins and to win their loyalty. It worked. "Every new newspaper that came out, I obtained employment on, on account of my connection with the newsdealers all over the city of New York," Sullivan recalled years later. He took most of what he earned home to his mother but still had enough left over to expand his business interests. His saloon on Chrystie Street was the first of four that he opened in and around the Sixth Ward; one of them, across from the Tombs Police Court, became a center of political activity in a sprawling district that included the city's primary center of vice, the Bowery.

Sullivan was a towering, bigheaded, and gregarious Irishman with a loquacious manner. He was sentimental and generous. In 1886 he established a fund for delivering shoes to the ward's sizable homeless population. From that point on, noted the *New York Herald*, the "young element" in the district "hailed him as their chief." By the age of 23, as a result of his popularity in the ward, Sullivan was put forth as a candidate for the state assembly. Despite his youth and inexperience, he won by a landslide. On the night of his victory, a large crowd gathered at his campaign headquarters on the Bowery and chanted loudly, "Hurrah for Big Tim! Hurrah for the Big Fella!"

Within a few short years, Sullivan was the most powerful politician in lower Manhattan. Although an avowed teetotaler with not so much as an arrest for loitering on his record, his power was based largely on his mastery of the art of the shakedown. Local merchants, gambling bosses, pimps, liquor vendors, saloon keepers, and gangsters were required to buy tickets to Big Tim's clambakes, chowder suppers, and summer outings at College Point. Like John Morrissey before him, he acquired great influence within the halls of Tammany for his ability to deliver votes, which was based on the principle of the repeater, or as the Big Fella called them, "guys with whiskers." In a speech delivered on behalf of a recently elected alderman, he explained his technique of altering a hoodlum's appearance so that he could vote multiple times undetected:

> When they vote with their whiskers on, you take 'em to a barber and scrape off the chin-fringe. Then you vote 'em again with the side-lilacs and mustache. Then to the barber again, off comes the sides, and you vote 'em a third time with just a mustache. If that ain't enough, and the box can stand a few more ballots, clean off the mustache, and vote 'em plain face. That makes every one of 'em good for four votes.

By the onset of the Gay Nineties, Sullivan had replaced Morrissey in the hearts and minds of Tammany stalwarts as the new Irish vice lord. Only Big Tim was a newer, improved version with few of the flaws; he had a clean criminal record, he didn't drink, and he had no desire to be loved, coddled, or even accepted by the WASP elite. Through guile, charity, personal magnetism, and a willful manipulation of the ward's rougher elements, Sullivan was in the process of establishing a domain of power that would render the WASP elite irrelevant.

However, there was a new challenge on the horizon that was much more immediate than social ostracism or judgement by the uptown swells. And that had to do with a new generation of immigrants arriving in America's big cities. For decades, the Irish had occupied the lower rungs of the immigrant ladder virtually unencumbered. They had begun the process of institutionalizing a system by which they would climb that ladder, a process based in part on the symbiotic relationship between the gangster and the politician. By 1890, the results of this process were only beginning to be seen; through patronage, the Irish had begun to dominate civil service jobs in the fire department, police department, and elsewhere in the city. They had begun to rise.

Of the newer immigrants now arriving, the most ambitious were the Italians; they were also, by far, the greatest in number, with tens of thousands arriving in many of the same cities and locales where the Irish had already paved the way. Like the Irish before them, these immigrants came with little more than the clothes on their backs. What some of these immigrants did bring, however, was their own criminal tradition of commerce and respect rooted in the villages of Sicily. This tradition was known to some as the *onorata societa* (the honored society), to others as *la mano nera* (the Black Hand), and to others simply as *la mafia*.

Like the American gangs founded by a generation of Irish famine immigrants and their offspring, the mafia was based at least in part on intimidation, the threat of violence, and even murder. The Sicilian version in America would come to be known as *cosa nostra* (our thing) and would be comprised of *gli amici* (the friends), who had to be Italian-born and *gli amici degli amici* (the friends of friends), extended business associates who could be non-Italian. The mafiosi even had their own version of racketeering, which in Sicilian was called *pizzu*. Defined literally, *pizzu* meant the beak of a small bird, such as a canary or a lark. Back in Sicily, when the mafia don referred to *fari vagnari a pizzu* (wetting the beak), he was talking about the same system of tribute that already existed throughout the Irish American underworld.

The manner by which this arcane Sicilian tradition infiltrated, ascended, and operated alongside the world of the Irish mobster would come to define the American underworld over the next century. But first there would be inevitable power struggles. Merciless, bloody, rooted in a street-level explication of brute capitalism in its purest form, this war of the underworld would play itself out in many domains. But the saga's earliest and most defining confrontation would take place in a unique and colorful locale, way down south amidst the festering swamps of Southern Louisiana, in a port city world-renowned for its licentiousness and crime—the city of New Orleans.

a perfect hell on earth

ate on the night of October 15, 1890, Police Superintendent David C. Hennessy stepped out into the damp New Orleans night and pointed himself toward home. He was accompanied by another man, William J. "Billy" O'Connor, a retired policeman, friend, and captain of the Boylan Protective Police, a private detective agency closely aligned with the New Orleans police department. Earlier that night, Hennessy and O'Connor had adjourned a meeting of the Police Board at old City Hall. Afterward, the two men stopped by Hennessy's office in the Central Police Station, located at South Basin and Common Streets on the outer fringe of the French Quarter. By the time the two men left the station, it was near 11 P.M. O'Connor suggested to the chief that he accompany him at least part of the way home; he knew there had been threats against Hennessy's life by the city's criminal element. Hennessy, a proud man, said nothing, which was his way of saying "okay."

"We're about to get a soaking," said Bill O'Connor, looking out from under an awning at the steady drizzle. Earlier that day it had rained so hard that male pedestrians were inclined to take off their shoes and roll up their pants before crossing the muddy streets from one wood-planked sidewalk to another.

"We best go along Rampart," suggested Hennessy. "The sidewalks on Basin Street are very bad."

Holding umbrellas overhead, the two men walked through the dense mist. An uncharacteristic quiet hung over the Vieux Carré. Even in the off-season, the French Quarter normally bustled with daytime merchants and hustlers. The night brought about a different kind of activity—and not just the prostitutes and drunkards who lingered in the shadows. According to many denizens of the Quarter, the area was haunted by the ghost of Jean Lafitte, the notorious French pirate, and other spirits conjured up by Marie Laveau, the recently deceased voodoo priestess. Some people believed that if you listened closely, you could even hear the screams of those killed during the great fire of March 1788, when a lighted candle from the alter of a Catholic chapel burned down this section of the city, paving the way for the construction of the French Quarter.

On this night, there were no screams. No sound at all. Even the ghosts seemed to be in hiding, perhaps in anticipation of the trouble that this dark, misty night seemed to portend.

Hennessy and O'Connor approached the corner of Rampart and Poydras streets and came upon the gas lit exterior of Dominick Virget's Oyster House. The Chief suggested they stop for a snack.

"Why not?" agreed O'Connor.

The two men ducked out of the rain and took a seat in the back of the room. Each ordered and consumed a half dozen oysters on the half shell. Hennessy, thirty-two years of age, was a conservative, young man and a tee-totaler; he washed his oysters down with a glass of milk.

By the time they finished and headed back out into the night, the rain had let up a bit. The two men continued walking along Rampart Street until Hennessy said to his friend, "There's no need to come any further with me now, Bill. You go on your way."

They shook hands and went their separate ways—O'Connor splashing across the street in the direction of the Mississippi River, Hennessy in the opposite direction toward his home at 275 Girod Street.

The area where Hennessy lived was not the best. Rooming houses, dilapidated cottages, and shanty housing for poor blacks, Irish, and Italians lined the streets. The only reason Hennessy, a man of stature and notoriety in the community, lived in such modest surroundings was because his mother insisted. She had lived in the same house for some time and grown attached to the area.

A lesser man might have been frightened or at least concerned walking along the neighborhood's dark, deserted streets late at night, but David C. Hennessy was no ordinary citizen. In his years as a lawman in New Orleans, he had established a reputation as a fearless crime fighter. He was especially well-known as the man who had single-handedly taken on the Sicilian stiletto and vendetta societies, also known as the mafia, which had only just begun to emerge as a mysterious new criminal threat with tentacles that stretched throughout the city.

As Hennessy approached his house, a figure emerged out of the drizzle. It was a teenage boy, who looked at Hennessy, whistled loudly, and then continued on down the block: strange, but no big deal. Hennessy thought little of it. He walked up the steps to his porch and slipped a key into the front door.

Just then, a fusillade of gunfire erupted, rumbling through the night like rolling thunder. Hennessy barely had time to turn before he was hit by a full volley: three heavy slugs ripped into his abdominal area, puncturing his stomach and intestines; one entered his chest, piercing the membrane around his heart; a fifth smashed his left elbow; a sixth broke his right leg; shotgun pellets riddled his entire body—torso, arms, legs.

Chief Hennessy writhed in agony. He heard the sound of his assailants scurrying away. Barely conscious and bleeding like a sieve, he drew his pistol and stumbled after the gunmen. As they approached the corner of Basin Street, Hennessy raised his gun and fired two shots through the thick gun smoke that hung over the street like cloud cover. As the men scattered, Hennessy got a decent view of the shooters; there were many, possibly five or six. In his haste, Hennessy tripped on the steps of a secondhand goods store and fell to the ground; he forced himself to his feet and staggered twenty yards to Basin Street, where he fired another shot. He saw figures running in the smoke and fog and tried to follow, but his strength was dwindling fast. In front of a frame house at 189 Basin Street, he called out, "Billy, Billy!" and crumpled to the ground.

Bill O'Connor was walking on Girod Street when he first heard the rumbling fusillade of gunfire. He immediately turned and ran toward the noise, becoming momentarily disoriented in the darkness and fog. As he approached Basin Street, he saw gun flashes and heard more shots. While dashing toward the commotion, he came upon a patrolman.

"Which way did they run?" O'Connor shouted.

"Uptown, I think," answered the cop.

They both ran toward Basin Street, just in time to hear Hennessy call out, "Billy, Billy!"

O'Connor and the patrolman found Hennessy lying in the cobblestoned street, blood oozing from multiple wounds.

"They gave it to me good," said the chief, "and I gave it back the best I could." This statement seemed to take the last of Hennessy's strength. He gurgled with pain.

O'Connor held the chief in his arms. "Who, Dave? Who gave it to you?"

Hennessy motioned for O'Connor to lean in closer. O'Connor bent down, and the chief whispered, "Dagos."

Dagos. O'Connor knew what the word meant. Italians. Mobsters. Mafiosi. O'Connor hurried to a nearby grocery store and telephoned for an ambulance. Hennessy was rushed to Charity Hospital, but it was obvious there wasn't much hope. By noon the following day, the chief was history.

News of the assassination wafted through the streets of New Orleans like a malodorous breeze. David Hennessy had been a popular man in the Crescent City. Throughout his law enforcement career, he frequently made the newspapers and was especially lionized by the city's Irish population, who embraced him as one of their own. He was young and square-jawed, with a graceful, confident manner—attributes that would come to be known by a later generation of Americans as "Kennedyesque." And like the dashing, young president for whom that term was coined some seventy years later, David C. Hennessy was gunned down in the prime of his life by an assassin's bullet.

The shock of Chief Hennessy's murder gripped the city and indeed the nation. The fact that he had been killed by the mafia, as reported in the New Orleans *Times Picayune*, the *New York Times*, and elsewhere around the United States, was a red flag in the face of God-fearing, law-abiding citizens throughout the land. In recent years, sensationalistic tales of the mafia had enflamed the anti-immigrant sentiment that bubbled below the surface of the American republic since before the famine ships arrived from Ireland. Only now the new "scum of Europe" were a strange, olive-skinned breed from the Mediterranean believed to be shrouded in secrecy and a tradition of criminality.

Among lawmen who had made a name for themselves as experts and pursuers of this new criminal scourge, none was more vaunted than David Hennessy. His exploits had brought him national attention. He was a hero.

Of course, as with most heroes, the image put forth was only half the picture. In the months following Hennessy's death, interesting facts would begin to emerge about his career and his involvement with the city's criminal underworld. For those who cared to know the truth, a more complex reality took shape. Hennessy, it seemed, was not a plaster saint after all; his life had been marked by tragedy and violence. He was the son of a cop—a cop who had himself been murdered under mysterious circumstances. Years ago, Hennessy had even quit the New Orleans police force in near disgrace only to be politically reappointed. And most surprising of all, contrary to his reputation as a crusader against the mafia, he had recently gotten embroiled in a violent rivalry between two Italian crime factions in the city. For mercenary reasons, the chief had aligned himself with one family against the other, which may have led directly to his death.

The fact that Hennessy's true legacy was messy should have been surprising to no one. Being a policeman in the city of New Orleans meant that, unless you had your head in the sand, you developed an intrinsic understanding of—if not a working relationship with—the city's criminal class. It had been that way ever since the early population of Nouvelle-Orléans was deliberately fleshed out with thieves, vagabonds, and prostitutes released from French dungeons. (Who else would want to live in the middle of a swamp?) From the beginning, the city's institutions were founded on a kind of interpretive morality that would buttress the careers of untold pirates, slippery politicians, gamblers, madams, gangsters, shady entrepreneurs, and ambitious policemen at all levels of the force looking to consolidate power and supplement their meager incomes.

David Hennessy may have been a shining light to some, but he was still a product of his environment; his mentality and ambition were a manifestation of the city's unique moral universe. His mastery of the bureaucracy and his penchant for self-promotion were second-to-none. That he achieved national stature was no small accomplishment for someone so far from the commercial nerve centers of the Northeast. A self-made man, he had risen from the muck of a star-crossed diaspora. The circumstances of his ascension—and his demise—were rooted deep in the narrative of the city's Irish underclass.

Shamrocks, Shillelaghs, and Yellow Fever

Of all the strange and hellish locales in which the scattered Irish peasantry found themselves in the wake of famine and exile, none was more alien than the swamps of Southern Louisiana. Constructed on a spit of land between the Mississippi River and Lake Pontchartrain, the city of New Orleans was actually below sea level. The natural environment was fetid, with sweltering summers and extreme humidity; the surrounding area was prone to hurricanes, flooding, and infestations of exotic, disease-carrying insects.

The common belief that the Irish were drawn to New Orleans by the city's inherent Catholicism is only partially true. Mostly, they came because they were tricked into it. Throughout the late 1840s and early 1850s, Louisiana cotton merchants recruited Irish immigrants in Liverpool, where many had first disembarked to flee the famine. Taking advantage of the immigrants' ignorance of American geography, the brokers sold them tickets to New Orleans with the assurance that it was only a few days journey to New York, Boston, Albany, or wherever else might have been their desired destination. The Irish arrived by ship in a land of alligators, swamp rats, strange fruits and vegetation, incessant subtropical sun, and humidity. Some never recovered from the initial shock.

Also in abundant supply in New Orleans was work. Since the city was erected in swamp land, its very survival was dependant on an elaborate system of canals and levees, many of which were only in the planning stages. Somebody had to dig those ditches. Paying an average $1.25 per day, the work was of the backbreaking, pick-and-shovel variety, with a staggering mortality rate. For this reason, the immigrants were initially welcomed in the city. The *Times Picayune* summed up the feelings of many potential employers when it editorialized about the arriving ships filled with "Irish, green as shamrocks. . . . What a valuable acquisition they will prove in carrying out [the city's] internal improvement."[1]

The employer's enthusiasm was based on avarice and greed. In the antebellum South, slaves cost money. The slave owners considered their Negroes too valuable to risk at such dangerous work (especially their top-of-the-line house Negroes). Better to get an Irishman, who had no choice but to accept the rough and dirty work. If an Irishman died on the job, he could be replaced at no cost, since starving Paddies were arriving by the boatload on a near daily basis.

The biggest project of the era was the New Basin Canal, a navigational outlet conceived by merchants and promoters to link Lake Pontchartrain with the Mighty Mississippi. Irish labor from all over the country was recruited. Over a four-year period, hundreds, if not thousands, of Paddies slipped into the cypress swamp and dug on a straight line toward the lake.

---

1. The sight of Irishmen in New Orleans was not an unprecedented phenomenon. Don Alexander O'Reilly, an Irish soldier of fortune in the service of the King of Spain, was one of the city's original founding fathers. Appointed governor and captain general of the province of Louisiana after Spain first wrested the colony from France, O'Reilly arrived in August 1769 with a mandate to quell an incipient Creole and Acadian rebellion. He did so with unparalleled brutality, for which he is remembered as "Bloody O'Reilly." The Don also instituted the province's first police force, known as the *Santa Hermandad*, or Holy Brotherhood.

Many other Irishmen came later, after Louisiana passed through Spanish, British, and into American hands. Most were Protestant Irishman of the land-owning, slave-owning class drawn to New Orleans from places like Kentucky and Virginia. As card-carrying members of the Southern gentry, they went to great lengths to separate themselves from the Catholic famine Irish, who they considered to be nothing more than "bogtrotters" and "turf-diggers"—lower than "the niggers" (see *The Irish in New Orleans 1800–1860* by Earl F. Niehaus).

Given the rampant cholera, malaria, and yellow fever, everyone knew the mortality rate would be high. The precise cost in terms of human lives can never be known, for even contemporaries argued over the number of diggers who died. One account stated that 3,000 Irishmen were buried along the canal, while another quoted a figure closer to 30,000. A popular song of the era put the number somewhere in between:

> Ten thousand micks, they swung their picks,
> To dig the New Canal
> But the choleray was stronger 'n they,
> An' twice it killed them awl.

The work conditions were disease-ridden and abysmal, and the living environment for the workers wasn't much better. At the height of the post-famine "invasion," destitute immigrants moved into shacks abandoned by Negroes in an extremely poor section of what was known as the Third Municipality. The city at the time was divided into three municipalities, each with its own council (board of aldermen) and executive officer (called a recorder but, in effect, a police court judge). The First Municipality was the Latin Creole district, the Second Municipality or uptown area was regarded as the American and progressive quarter, and the Poor Third was for immigrants—mostly German and Irish.

The crowded, unsanitary living conditions were a nightmare. In the spring of 1847 the *Times Picayune* reported that "a small house in Dauphine Street contains about fifty immigrants, worn down by starvation and disease to mere skeletons . . . some of them . . . eating straw that they gathered in the street." Newly arrived passengers on the plague ships were described as "food for fever," which certainly rang true in 1853, when one of many yellow fever epidemics devastated the city. Yellow fever is a deadly virus transmitted through mosquitoes; once bitten, the victim carries a parasite in his red blood cells that causes fever, jaundice, physical debilitation, hemorrhaging, and possibly death.

The disease originated in the swamps among the working men and then spread. There was no cure. Before the sweltering summer of 1853 had come to an end, twelve thousand people died, of whom one-third were Irish. Among working men, seven out of ten fell to the sting of yellow jack.[2]

---

2. According to Herbert Asbury's book, *The French Quarter*, until the latter years of the nineteenth century, New Orleans held the distinction of being the dirtiest and

Disease led to hunger, hunger to despair. Those lucky enough to survive were left emotionally and spiritually scarred. The famine refugees acquired some of the characteristics of a hunted animal. One of the many who had been reduced to begging on Canal Street expressed his plight to a reporter: "What'll I do!? I have no place to go and no means but what I beg."

Out of this bitch's brew of slave labor, disease, and squalor arose the city's criminal underworld. New Orleans had always been a wild and licentious place, a haven for pirates, international adventurers, riverboat gamblers, professional snake oil salesmen, and the like. The great Irish rabble merely put their own spin on things.

The earliest record of gang activity in the city can be traced back as far as 1834, when a back-of-town gang called the Corkonions waged a bloody war with another Hibernian gang known as the United Irishmen. Like the early Five Points gangs in New York, the Corkonions and United Irishmen were offshoots of Ireland's rural terror societies, which in recent years had given rise to the Young Ireland Movement, a determined effort to free Ireland from the yoke of British rule. In the Old Country, these gangs were engaged in a war of resistance. In New Orleans, their activities usually revolved around labor-related issues. The war between the Corkonions and the United Irishmen had been fomented by a sugar refinery company that wanted a canal dug and encouraged underbidding between gangs of Irish diggers. In February 1834, the gangs turned on each other, resulting in four deaths and numerous arrests after the City Guard was called in to quell the riot.

By the 1850s, Irishmen had themselves become labor contractors, and the labor riots were mostly a thing of the past. Gang activity was now more commercial, and it was generally centralized in one area: the highly colorful Gallatin Street district of gambling dens, concert-saloons, dance houses, and abundant bordellos.

The district is long gone now, with little or no trace of its ribald past, but from the early 1840s to the mid-1870s, Gallatin Street thrived on vice and

---

unhealthiest city on the North American continent—and municipal authorities consistently defeated every attempt to make it otherwise. "The water supply was bad," writes Asbury, "swamps remained within the city limits, and the sanitary arrangements were unbelievably primitive. The sewage system consisted simply of open gutters between the sidewalks and the streets. Into them filth and refuse of every description were emptied, and when they overflowed, as they frequently did in the rainy seasons, the streets became well-nigh impassable." As a result, the death rate in New Orleans, even after deducting those killed during the many cholera, malaria, and yellow fever epidemics, was nearly double that of New York, Boston, or Philadelphia.

sin of every variety, with nary a legitimate business in sight. In the words of author Herbert Asbury, the district "was completely filled with barrelhouses where for five cents a man could get not a meager tumblerful of liquor, but all he could drink; dance houses which were also bordellos and gin mills; and sailors' boarding houses from which seaman were occasionally shanghaied. . . . From dawn to dusk the district slept off its debauches behind closed shutters; from dusk to dawn the dives roared full blast, and Gallatin Street was crowded with countrymen, sailors, and steamboat men seeking women and diversion. And they in their turn were sought by a horde of harlots, sneak thieves, garroters who openly carried their deadly strangling cords, and footpads with slung shots looped about their wrists. There was crime and depravity in every inch of Gallatin Street; the stranger who entered it at Ursuline Avenue with money in his pocket and came out at Barracks with his wealth intact and his skull uncracked had performed a feat which bordered on the miraculous."

The most notorious gang on Gallatin Street went by the name the Live Oak Boys, so called because they carried what the New Orleans *True Delta* described as "elaborately carved oaken cudgels." These cudgels, no doubt, were in fact shillelaghs, the weapon of choice for the rural resistance societies back in the Old Country.

The Live Oaks were formed in 1858 by Red Bill Wilson, a well-known criminal figure in the district who carried a knife concealed in his bushy, red beard. The gang was not a large, politically oriented organization like those found in New York, but rather a loose collection of rowdies with no recognized leaders. Among the gang's members were a tough bunch of fighters, including Bill Swan, Jack Lyons, Jimmy O'Brien, his brother Hugh O'Brien, and Hugh's sons, Matt and Hugh, Jr.

It was the O'Brien family who achieved the greatest infamy and brought the Live Oak Boys into the realm of legend. In 1867, Jimmy O'Brien was the first to enter the annals of New Orleans criminal lore when, after a night of drinking and thieving with fellow Live Oak Henry Thompson, he sought to rob Thompson in his sleep. Thompson awoke to find O'Brien rifling through his pockets. When he struggled, Jimmy calmly pushed a knife deep into Thompson's heart and continued his search. Jimmy O'Brien might have gotten away with this murder if he hadn't been seen by a Negro and a small boy. Their testimony at trial was enough to seal O'Brien's fate; he was convicted and sent to the penitentiary for twenty years. He died in prison.

Next up was Jimmy's brother Hugh, who stole a rowboat and set out from the Dumaine Street wharf with dreams of becoming a pirate. He was killed when he tried to rob a fisherman on the Mississippi River.

Hugh left behind his two sons, Matt and Hugh, Jr., who were then nineteen and twenty-one years old, respectively. Unlike the thousands of Irish immigrants who slaved away in the swamps every day, the O'Brien brothers and the rest of their crew were known for never having performed a stroke of honest work. Their nights were devoted to carousing and brawling in Gallatin Street dives, their days to sleeping, lounging, and planning new crimes. They were especially feared and disliked by the dance-hall proprietors; a night rarely passed when they didn't raid one or more of the district's resorts. Usually, when the Live Oaks came charging into a dance house brandishing their oaken shillelaghs and looking for a fight, the bouncers, bartenders, musicians, and customers rushed out the back door. The gangsters were left to wreck and rob the place at their leisure.

One establishment that welcomed the O'Brien brothers and the rest of the Live Oaks was Bill Swan's Fireproof Coffee House. Swan, a member of the gang, was the city's premiere promoter of dogfighting and rat-killing, an illegal though popular sport of the era. Swan advertised his events through printed handbills that were handed out in neighborhood saloons. One such flyer advertising an event to be held on March 10, 1879 read in part:

> Grand national rat-killing match for $100, to take place at Bill Swan's saloon, corner Esplanade and Peters streets, third district, Sunday afternoon, at four o'clock, precisely.
>
> Harry Jennings, of New York, has matched a certain New York dog, whose fighting weight is twenty-three pounds, to kill twelve full-grown rats per minute, for five consecutive minutes, being one of the greatest feats a dog can accomplish—sixty full-sized rats in five minutes . . .

In the backyard of Swan's property was constructed a pit twelve feet long and ten feet wide, with two-foot high side walls, and a viewing area to accommodate hundreds. On the afternoon of March 10, dozens were in attendance, though, as reported by the *Times Picayune*, they were not exactly high rollers: "The rougher element of life predominated . . . the men representing business interests and the gentlemen of the town might have been counted upon the fingers of either hand."

At four o'clock, the rat master released his rodents into the pit, where a dog named Skelper killed twenty-one rats in three minutes and forty-five seconds, but retreated yelping in pain when one rat nipped him on the nose. Another dog was brought in to take on the remaining rats. The audience cheered on the dog, or the rats, depending on the nature of their wager. The only big winner was Bill Swan, the proprietor, who gave a percentage of the take to the Live Oak Boys.

Matt and Hugh O'Brien reigned as leaders of the gang for years, though death and imprisonment thinned their ranks considerably. The wanton violence that distinguished the gang was bound to catch up with the O'Briens, which is exactly what happened on the night of October 2, 1886.

While drinking in Bill Swan's saloon, the two brothers become involved in a bitter quarrel. Their brother-in-law Johnny Hackett and Jack Lyons, a fellow Live Oak and Gallatin Street old-timer, tried to intercede—in a fashion. While Matt shouted abuse at his brother, Hackett handed Hugh a knife and said, "Here. Shut him up with this."

Matt saw the knife and clammed up. After a few more drinks, the brothers left the saloon on good terms, walking together into Gallatin Street. A few yards from the corner of Barracks Street they stopped and talked for a moment, then Matt drew a pistol and shot Hugh in the side.

"Hughy was drunk," Matt O'Brien told the police when he was arrested a few hours later, "and he was goin' to do me up, and I shot him to keep him from doin' it. I didn't give him no cause, only he was drunk and wanted blood."

Hugh was not seriously hurt and left New Orleans to avoid testifying against his brother. Even so, based on eyewitness testimony, Matt was convicted at trial of assault less than mayhem and sentenced to the penitentiary. With one O'Brien gone and the other in prison, the Live Oak Boys drifted from the scene.

Violence in New Orleans did not come to an end. In fact, robbery, muggings, and murder continued to be so common throughout New Orleans that one parish sheriff described the city to a visiting British journalist as "a perfect hell on earth."

The sheriff, presumably, was speaking metaphorically, while the city's Irish inhabitants were living in a more literal state of hell that began with hunger and exile, continued with squalor, death, and disease, and was headed God-only-knew where.

Gambling Men, Wharf Rats, and Ladies of Ill Repute

Ruffians like the Live Oak Boys were the scourge not only of the police, but of the many other underworld figures who were trying to make their living off the cornucopia of sin and vice that flourished in the French Quarter. There was no Tammany Hall to organize the district's criminal structure and link it to a larger political framework. Compared to New York City, New Orleans was small—barely one-third the size in terms of population. There was no Mob as such, no overriding set of rules that officially bound the underworld and upperworld together. Cops, politicians, and city officials were definitely still on the take, but unlike New York City where the vice rackets were spread far and wide, the French Quarter was a universe unto itself, a delicate microcosm with an ethnic polyglot of independent mid- and low-level operators seeking to establish their niche.

Gambling, of course, was a mainstay in the French Quarter and had been since the earliest days of the Mississippi River paddle boats. By the 1850s, when New Orleans became a major port for American armies operating in Mexico and a principle point of departure for the California Gold Rush, the city was thronged with soldiers, adventurers, and fortune hunters en route to and from San Francisco by way of Nicaragua and the Isthmus of Panama. The bulk of this immense transient population was composed of sharpies, bunco men, and reckless young fellows looking for quick ways to double their bank rolls—in other words, they were looking for suckers.[3]

One man who made the most of the city's hospitality toward anyone looking to turn a card or toss the dice was an Irishman of the Protestant persuasion named Price McGrath. A native of Versailles, Kentucky, a small town near Lexington, McGrath started out as an aspiring tailor, but soon abandoned that profession to devote himself to the life of sporting men. He began as a steamboat card player and later became a roper and dealer of faro at gambling houses in Lexington, Frankfort, Louisville, and Cincinnati. In 1855 he arrived in New Orleans, and, with $70,000 to his name, founded McGrath & Company, a luxurious palace of chance at 4 Carondelet Street. With croupiers that wore frock coats in the afternoon and full evening dress after dinner, it was the sort of establishment where riffraff like the Live Oak Boys were most definitely not welcome.

---

3. "Bunco" is a term originally derived from "banco," a crooked card game similar to three-card monty with origins in London. Initially in San Francisco's Barbary Coast, and then elsewhere around the United States, bunco became a word to describe con men and scam artists of infinite variety. Bunco men always dressed nicely, but never loud or showy. Usually working for a gambling boss of some type, they made it their business to know when gamblers of stature or other "players" were in town. It was their job to steer likely prospects toward the gambling bosses' roaming dice and card games, for which they received the right to operate their own low-level scams.

"Sucker" comes from the Irish *sách úr*, meaning a "fresh, well-fed fellow" or "fat cat" ready to be fleeced like a ripe Donegal sheep.

Through judicious payoffs to the necessary authorities—politicians, police, and various officials of state and city government—McGrath & Company's palatial house was in operation for six years, and during that time the annual profits ranged from $80,000 to $100,000. The success of Price McGrath's operation spawned many imitators, which was a great boon to the city's growing netherworld of commercialized vice. In many ways, gambling in New Orleans—and other American cities, for that matter—served the same function that narcotics would a century later: as the economic engine that powered the underground economy. Organizations like McGrath & Company set the standard for dozens of lesser establishments catering to men of more modest means. Through municipal kickbacks and graft, money from gambling generated an underworld cash flow that kept the upperworld fat and happy.

Price McGrath was an entrepreneur. With profits from his gambling parlor on Carondelet Street, he ventured north to New York City and introduced himself to none other than Old Smoke Morrissey, who was at the time organizing his syndicate of gambling operators. Together the two men opened a gambling house at 5 West 24th Street that was highly successful. In 1867, with Morrissey increasingly preoccupied with his Saratoga Springs operations and preparing for his initial foray into electoral politics, McGrath sold his interest in the Manhattan gambling parlor and returned to his native Kentucky, where he became a famous breeder of thoroughbred horses at a stud farm he called McGrathiana.

Back in New Orleans, the French Quarter continued to percolate. If there was a racket that rivaled the world of cards, dice, and roulette as an essential aspect of the local economy, it had to be "the word's oldest profession." In many ways, prostitution had given birth to the French Quarter. Without the lure of the harlot, it's doubtful that the many cabarets, dance houses, and concert saloons of the district could have sustained themselves. Of course, prostitution was not restricted to the world-famous Vieux Carré. By 1870, when New Orleans had a population of 190,000 inhabitants, bordellos of every variety—from the ten-dollar parlor house to the fifteen-cent Negro chippy joint—were running openly in virtually every part of town. According to Asbury, "there was scarcely a block in New Orleans which did not contain at least one brothel or assignation house."

For the young, destitute Irishwomen arriving in New Orleans in the postfamine years, the business of prostitution was both a horrible trap and a means of economic advancement. Immigrants just off the boat were met by assorted wharf rats, among them seemingly friendly women with names like Bridget Fury, Nellie McGee, and Irish Suze. These seemingly sympathetic women steered the newly arrived young girls toward lodging for the night—lodging that invariably turned out to be a house of ill repute.

As a profession, prostitution was certainly demeaning, fraught with potential violence and disease, but in many ways the harlots of nineteenth century New Orleans were better off than the escorts and streetwalkers of today. Many establishments were relatively safe and well-protected. The nearly legitimate or at least ubiquitous status of the profession allowed for mostly above board interactions between patron and prostitute. Occasionally, a young, Irish lass even rose to a level of prosperity and renown as a madam in the red light, lace curtain world of the New Orleans bordello.

One such woman went by the name of Fanny Sweet, a legendary figure in antebellum New Orleans.[4] Not only was she an important figure in local red light lore, but Fanny Sweet was also an adventuress of great renown, a practitioner of voodoo, a professional grifter who slept with a knife and pistol under her pillow, and, according to a rather florid description in the *True Delta*, "a modern Lucretia Borgia . . . a hardened murderess . . . one of the most remarkable female desperados ever known." For pure cunning and what would today be called sociopathic behavior, Fanny Sweet deserves mention among the most renowned gangsters of her generation.

By most accounts, she was not a physically attractive woman. She was tall and gangly with masculine facial features: a big nose, bushy eyebrows, and a noticeable mustache. Apparently, to compensate for her less than stellar looks, she developed many special tricks in the boudoir that endeared her to a steady stream of lovers or at least lovemaking partners.

She first came to New Orleans in 1844 and started out in a lowly whorehouse on Dauphine Street, where she met a young banker known only as "Mr. D." Once introduced to Fanny's special talents, the man became infatuated with her; she resigned her position in the bordello to become his personal mistress. Within a year after this relationship began, Mr. D stole a large sum of money from his own bank, later fleeing to Havana to escape arrest.

Fanny Sweet also fled the city. Disguised as a man, she set out for San Francisco and then Sacramento, where she ran a boardinghouse for miners.

---

4. Given the stigma of prostitution among most classes—and certainly among Irish Catholics—it was common for women involved in the trade to use a pseudonym. An exposé of Fanny Sweet in the December 8, 1861 issue of the *True Delta* revealed that her real name was Mary Robinson, and that she was an Irish American girl born in a small New York town in 1827.

She was eventually accused of poisoning to death a stage-coach driver who had slapped her in public. Rather than face trial, she fled California to the Isthmus of Panama and then returned to the Crescent City, where she resumed her life as a prostitute and con artist who fleeced older men of means.

It was during this period that Fanny came to embrace voodooism, which was outlawed in New Orleans. She attended many secret meetings, bought great quantities of charms and love potions from Marie Laveau and other voodoo masters, and was part of a group that was arrested when the police broke up what was described in the papers as a "voodoo orgy."

On Gasquet Street, Fanny ran a well-known assignation house that provided young girls for reputable elderly gents, and then blackmailed them. It was a dangerous game that finally caught up with her. She was forced to flee the city when one of her victims tried to kill her. She did not leave town alone, however; she took with her a wealthy widower whom she led on a wild overland adventure through Louisiana and Texas into Mexico, where, among Fanny's numerous elaborate moneymaking plans, they would purchase quinine and munitions for war, then sell it to the Confederate Army at huge profit.

Somewhere between Houston and Corpus Christi, the wealthy widower became ill and died. Back in New Orleans, the press and local prosecutors, wise to the ways of Fanny Sweet, were convinced that she must have killed the man. Police searched her house on Gasquet Street and found a miniature voodoo casket that held several packets of white powder, believed to be love potions if not poison, and a lock of bloodstained hair, one of the most potent of voodoo charms. The mayor of New Orleans immediately sent a squad of detectives to Brownsville, Texas to apprehend Fanny Sweet and bring her back to the city to stand trial.

Fanny proclaimed her innocence. She was held in the city jail while tests were conducted on the secret voodoo powder found in her house. When it turned out to be medicine, not poison, public sentiment turned in her favor. A prominent criminal defense attorney, certain that she was being railroaded, took on her case pro bono. Eventually, on December 12, 1861, the attorney general of Louisiana threw in the towel, announcing officially that Fanny was exonerated of all charges. She was released from jail.

The case did not destroy Fanny, but her criminal schemes and shenanigans were exposed in the press to such a degree that she was never able to operate in New Orleans again.

When the *True Delta* published its long exposé identifying Fanny's place of birth and revealing her real name as Mary Robinson, she penned a response that was published in two installments under the headline: "Autobiography of Mrs. Fanny Sweet—A Card to the Public." Although she willingly admitted to many of the most egregious accusations against her, she steadfastly held to the fiction that she was of aristocratic origin, born and reared in England in comfort and even luxury. And yet, she was somehow unable to divulge the exact location of her birth or her real name. It was a telling commentary on the social pecking order of the day that, while Fanny Sweet would admit to being a prostitute, a killer, and a gold digger of the highest calling, she persisted in trying to fob herself off as a British aristocrat. Apparently, under no circumstance was she willing to admit that she was of Irish origin.

Fanny Sweet was unusual in that she was a freelance operator—a reckless and daring enterprise. In the New Orleans bordello business, there were more secure ways to make a living. The best whorehouses in town became local institutions. If a nineteenth century madam provided a top-notch product and greased the necessary palms, she was bound to accumulate important friends and become something of a fixture in the city's political and social circles.

Such was certainly the case with Kate Townsend of Basin Street, the only other madam to rival Fanny Sweet for notoriety in the red light lore of New Orleans. No bordello operator in the history of the city was more successful than Sister Kate. Her legend was based in part on her formidable talents as a businesswoman, but also on other endowments. In the words of one newspaper, "Kate was a very portly woman and attracted general attention on the street . . . as she grew in age she became afflicted with what was properly a deformity, a voluminous bust which never failed to provoke astonishment in those who chanced to meet her."

Kate's career would have made a great rags-to-riches story were it not for the ending, which was bloody and premature. Instead, the story of Kate Townsend would live on for years as a cautionary tale to those enticed by the prospect of a reputable career in the bordello business.

She was born in Liverpool in 1831, as Katherine Cunningham, the daughter of an Irish dock worker. By the age of fifteen, she was a dance house barmaid working in a dive on Paradise Street. There she met and romanced a handsome young Irish sailor named Peter Kearnaghan. Though unmarried, Kate became pregnant and gave birth to twins. Kearnaghan was rarely around, and she was left to fend for herself. In early 1857 she left her two children with a relative and departed from Liverpool, never to return again. Kate Cunningham set out for America and eventually arrived in New Orleans, where she was reborn as Kate Townsend.

For a young woman living on her own in a big American city, no other profession came close to that of the "working girl" as a means of support. At a time when women could not vote, drink in a saloon, gamble, or even circulate unaccompanied in public without being looked down upon, working as a brothel prostitute was a statement of independence. Among other things, the whorehouse provided lodging, protection, and a steady income all in one.

Kate Townsend first went to work at Clara Fisher's place on Philippa Street, where she spent six months, then moved to a two-story, red-brick bagnio on Canal Street between Basin and Rampart, and then to Maggie Thompson's brothel on Customhouse Street—the last place she would ever be looked upon as just one of the girls.

As a young woman, Kate was attractive, with a voluptuous figure. Her early success was based, in large part, on her looks and talents in the boudoir. But by the time she left Maggie Thompson's place to open her own establishment in 1863, Kate had begun to put on weight at an alarming rate. From this point on, Kate would spend much less time in the bedroom and much more time as a greeter, bouncer, and businesswoman of considerable distinction.

Kate Townsend's business flourished like no other; she made influential friends among the politicians and police captains who came to her place. With their help she was able to expand her business, eventually opening a three-story palace of marble and brownstone at 40 Basin Street that was probably the most luxurious bordello in the entire United States. She presided over this lace-curtained house of ill repute for nearly two decades. As she acquired more wealth and influence, her waistline and other physical attributes kept pace. By most accounts, as she became more obese, she also became more irascible and short-tempered. Kate was especially mean to a mild-mannered man who served as her bookkeeper. One evening in November 1888, after she had berated and physically abused the man in front of the working girls, he could take no more. He got even with Kate Townsend by stabbing her eleven times with a pair of pruning shears and leaving her to die in a pool of blood on the floor of her bordello.

The killer was put away for life, and Kate was remembered not as a corpulent, mean-spirited boss, but as a pioneer in the bordello business who provided employment and a home for generations of immigrant girls. Her burial was lavish even by the standards of New Orleans, a city known for its colorful, outlandish funerals. The body of the famous madam—sheathed in a six-hundred-dollar, white, silk dress, trimmed with lace at fifty dollars a yard—was laid out in the drawing room of her bordello. The furniture was also covered with white silk, and a Dixieland band played "Nearer My God to Thee" as champagne was served to all. Kate's enormous body rested in a four-hundred dollar, metallic casket adorned with a silver cross, beneath which were inscribed her name and the date of her demise. The open casket was followed through the streets of the French Quarter by a procession of twenty carriages accompanied by hundreds of working girls, with nary a man in sight. The body was interned at Metarie Cemetery.

Sister Kate was gone.

Her funeral was a memorable, over-the-top tribute to an underworld figure of great renown, and as such would serve as a precursor to the extravagant mob boss funerals that would become commonplace in many U.S. cities in the decades that followed.

The Policeman as "Gangster"

It was into this broiling cauldron of street thugs, gambling impresarios, immigrant swindlers, whores, and madams that David C. Hennessy immersed himself as a young New Orleans policeman. By the time he was a young man, he was already a star detective with an intuitive understanding of the city's newest criminal peril. Ever since Sicilian immigrants had begun flooding into New Orleans in the 1880s—the first of many such waves that would redefine the ethnic makeup of many U.S. cities—sensationalistic accounts of the camorra and Mafia were commonly featured in the press. The general belief that the Sicilians' secretive nature was proof of a criminal mentality would be dramatically reaffirmed when the city's beloved Chief Hennessy was ambushed by gunfire and died in a gutter on Basin Street—an event that rocked the city of New Orleans to its core.

Given Hennessy's past, it was no great surprise that he would one day be top copper in a city where the Irish had begun to rise up from the lowest of the low. Hennessy's father, also named David, had been a citizen of some distinction. The elder Hennessy first arrived in the city as a member of the union army when David Jr. was just three years old. He was a Civil War hero, wounded three times, who had stayed in the Crescent City following the war—a mean, unstable era commonly known as Reconstruction. In October 1864, Hennessy, Sr. was appointed to the Metropolitan Police force by his Yankee commanding officer. Hennessy excelled as a policeman, navigating his way through the cities criminal underworld with skill. He also soon met his end in a violent manner that would resonate years later when his only son was also murdered.

It was in a French Quarter saloon that the elder Hennessy met his fate. While drinking one night, he was approached by an unreconstructed Confederate enthusiast who was not enamored with the Yankee carpetbaggers who now ruled his town.

"You're a cad and a carpetbagger and a stinking Irishman to boot," the man told Hennessy.

"And you, my friend," answered the policeman, "are nothing more than defeated rebel trash."

Accounts of what happened next are unclear, long lost in the haze of history. Some claimed there was a wild shoot-out; others said that the belligerent Confederate accosted the off duty policeman without provocation. Either way, the senior Hennessy wound up dead with a bullet in the back.

David Hennessy, Jr. was just nine years old when his father was violently snatched from the world. His mother had no visible means of support other than the small pension then paid to the widows of killed policemen. In 1870, the elder Hennessy's former commander, feeling an obligation to the family, appointed eleven-year-old David Hennessy to be his office messenger at police headquarters. In later years, the commander liked to say that the boy turned out to be so clever, diligent, and courageous that he had no choice but to promote him speedily through the ranks of the force.

In nineteenth century New Orleans, being a policeman was an agreeable profession for an enterprising Irishman. Especially in the years following the Civil War, citizens with Hibernian surnames flocked to the profession. And why not? For at least two decades, ditch digging, gangsterism, hustling, and whoring were the only avenues of advancement available to the average lass or laddie. That began to change as street gangs, transients, and vice peddlers multiplied like mosquitoes in a mangrove. During Reconstruction, the murder rate in New Orleans jumped to three times higher than any other city in the States. With old Civil War grudges being settled in the saloons and crime running rampant, the city's overseers came to an obvious conclusion: They needed more cops. The WASP aristocracy sure as hell didn't want the job; it paid shit, required long hours, and was also dangerous. For such an unappealing task, who better than a Paddy?

Despite efforts by an emerging Know-Nothing Party to rid the police force of all immigrants,[5] the Metropolitans became a major patronage plum

---

5. During a two-year period in the 1850s when the Know-Nothings were in power, they fired hundreds of Irish cops and spitefully auctioned off the police department's

of the Irish. By 1865, though their representation in the city's population stood at thirteen percent, Irish immigrants made up thirty-three percent of the police force, second only to native-born Americans, many of whom were also of Irish extraction. Men with Irish surnames filled out the ranks of the department at all levels, but especially at the entry level, where many famine immigrants for the first time found themselves empowered after years of starvation and humiliation. For these hardheaded coppers, the taste of vengeance was swift and indiscriminate. According to police records, Irish cops were the most likely to be brought before the Board of Police on abuse-of-authority charges. Some became known for a reckless willingness to become involved in the violent activity of riot control—a handy opportunity for head-breaking and ass-whupping of a wholesale nature. Within the department, these cops became known as "Hibernian leatherheads."

David C. Hennessy was not a Hibernian leatherhead. Unlike those of the Irish masses who had embraced police work for the simple reason that it was safer and more remunerative than joining a street gang—and less likely to get them a prison sentence—Hennessy became a cop because it was his birth right. From the beginning he seemed destined for great things in the department and beyond, which is why the Irish and many others in the city followed his career as they might the rise of a promising politician.

His legend took shape almost from the start. On one notable occasion, while still an eighteen-year-old patrolman, Dave Hennessy single-handedly caught two grown men in the act of burglary, beat them in a street fight, and delivered them to a police station for arrest. On his twenty-first birthday, he met the age requirement for the detective division and was immediately promoted by Thomas N. Boylan, the department's newly appointed chief and fellow Irishman.

The biggest coup of Hennessy's career occurred on July 5, 1881, when he and his older cousin, Mike Hennessy, also a detective, apprehended a notorious Sicilian criminal named Giuseppe Esposito, who was wanted by Italian authorities on multiple murder and kidnapping charges. Dave, Mike, and two New York detectives had staked out Esposito for months, waiting for just the right moment to make their arrest, which they did in broad daylight near Jackson Square, in the middle of the French Quarter.

The incarceration and eventual extradition of Esposito was big news both locally and internationally. Hennessy's bold capture of an infamous

---

two prized mule-drawn paddy wagons, the Red Maria and the Black Maria. By the end of the decade, the Know-Nothings were voted out, never to return again.

mafia killer living incognito in the city's Little Palermo district catapulted his name into the headlines. His career ambitions appeared limitless. The only thing that could derail him now would be a scandal of his own making, which is precisely what occurred just a few months after his spectacular arrest of Giuseppe Esposito.

The seeds of Hennessy's derailment were rooted in a bitter power struggle within the ranks of the New Orleans police force. Emboldened by the success of the Esposito caper, Hennessy, with the support of his cousin Mike, had begun campaigning to get the highly political Police Board to appoint him Chief of Detectives, what Hennessy believed would be the first of many steps in his rise to the top. Among those who supported David Hennessy was Police Chief Tom Boylan, who was set to retire soon.

Both Hennessy and Boylan were infuriated when Hennessy was inexplicably passed over for appointment as Chief of Detectives. The position went instead to a man named Thomas Devereaux, Hennessy's main political rival. A bitter contest ensued between Hennessy and Devereaux over who would take over for Boylan once he retired. The Police Board became the arena for their fight. Its meetings became increasingly heated as the two factions maneuvered for position. In the meantime, another candidate for the top job emerged, Detective Robert Harris; he, too, had support on the board and within the department.

This third detective was dramatically eliminated from the competition one day when, in broad daylight, Thomas Devereaux blew Harris' brains all over the street with his Tranier pistol, which fired an unusually large bullet. Devereaux claimed self defense. His enemies called it murder. Devereaux was tried and found not guilty; he remained Chief of Detectives.

The battle between Devereaux and the two Hennessys continued unabated. Mike Hennessy, in particular, was often seen having heated words with Devereaux in public. Tempers rose a notch when Devereaux accused Mike Hennessy of insubordination before the Police Board. When the board dismissed Devereaux's accusations, he became enraged and verbally attacked the board's members. For this, they ordered *him* to stand trial for insolence and insubordination. The first witness scheduled to testify against him was Mike Hennessy.

The entire matter finally boiled over on October 13, 1881, just four months after David Hennessy first became an international celebrity. On that day, a three-way gunfight erupted between Devereaux and the two Hennessys. In the office of a downtown stockbroker friend of Devereaux's, the Chief of Detectives shot Mike Hennessy in the jaw. In response, David

Hennessy drew his pistol and shot Devereaux in the head at close range. Devereaux died instantly. Mike Hennessy was rushed to Charity Hospital and eventually recovered from his wounds.

Over the months that followed, a desperate behind-the-scenes campaign was waged by Hennessy to get the killing of Devereaux dismissed as a justifiable homicide. However, Devereaux's stockbroker friend claimed that he saw what happened, and that David Hennessy was nothing more than a cold-blooded killer.

In April 1882, six months after the shooting, David and Michael Hennessy went on trial for murder. After a relatively short three-week proceeding, the Hennessy cousins were found not guilty. The verdict kept David Hennessy from going to prison, but it wasn't enough to repair the damage done to his career. The negative publicity forced Chief Tom Boylan, who had testified on David's behalf at the trial, to ask for the resignation of both Hennessys from the police force.

Mike Hennessy left New Orleans for good. He moved to Houston, Texas, where he became the head of a private detective agency. In 1886, while returning home from the theatre one night, he was murdered—shot five times by parties unknown.

David Hennessy stayed in New Orleans and went to work for the Farrell Protection Police, one of the city's many private detective agencies run by Irish ex-cops. Slowly but surely, he worked his way back into the public's good graces as the Devereaux shooting receded from the collective memory. When Tom Boylan finally retired as city Police Chief, he formed the powerful Boylan Protective Police, with David Hennessy as his cofounder. In 1884, the New Orleans city council commissioned the Boylan police "as patrolmen with full police powers," making them equals of the city police force. Hennessy was now, in fact, the second most powerful policeman in New Orleans, right behind the city department's chief. Four years later, when Joseph Shakespeare was elected mayor of the city, one of his first moves—by popular demand—was to appoint David C. Hennessy Chief of the New Orleans police department.

It had been a long, circuitous journey, but Hennessy had finally arrived where he felt destined to be. He picked up right where he left off, only now he was slightly less gregarious, less trusting, and more protective of his position. Emboldened by the city's newspapers, which ran banner headlines proclaiming that the city was infested by "1,100 Dago Criminals," he resumed his career as a famous enemy of the mafia—or at least that's how it appeared.

The Matranga family of New Orleans, headed by two brothers, Charles and Anthony, were one of two competing Italian factions overseeing what had once been an Irish and German domain along the city's commercial wharves. The bounty at stake was substantial. New Orleans was the busiest port in the south, with the shipping trade flowing from inland cities via the Mississippi River and arriving from international destinations by way of the Gulf of Mexico. The stevedore union was the largest active labor union in the city, and competition among crime-connected labor factions on the wharves was fierce, if not violent. On May 6, 1890, a group of Matranga longshoremen got into a shootout with their main rivals, the Provenzano family. Three Matrangas were wounded by gunfire, including Anthony, whose injuries required the amputation of a leg.

Police Chief Hennessy was at the scene of the Matranga-Provenzano shooting just a few minutes after it occurred. He was approached by one of the Provenzanos, who said, "Chief Hennessy, a little misunderstanding, that's all this was. I'm sure you will agree that you have much to gain by hearing our side of the story, yes?"

Hennessy listened and said nothing, but he liked what he heard. It was the beginning of a beautiful relationship.

In the weeks that followed, the Chief was seen often in the company of one or more of the Provenzano brothers: Joseph, George, Vincent, and Peter. He allegedly went into business with the brothers and became part-owner of a popular bordello called the Red Lantern Club, located near Hennessy's home in a part of the French Quarter known as the Swamp.

The fact that a cop, even the chief of police, would enter into a partnership with a criminal faction in the city was as endemic to life in New Orleans as jazz, jambalaya, and Mardi Gras. Since at least 1874, when the hated Metropolitan police force was ousted during an armed coup and a city-run department was instituted in its place, cops in New Orleans were the lowest paid of any big city police force in the United States. The only consolation was that they were allowed, even encouraged, to make money on the side by hiring themselves out to local business establishments as security guards, private detectives, silent partners, or guns for hire. This arrangement opened up untold opportunities for graft and corruption, as individual contractors sought out high-ranking officers to serve as their own private lawmen.

In this regard, David Hennessy was no more or less venal than many other New Orleans policemen. Hennessy's record reveals a man who was certainly ambitious, but not without virtue. Once, when an Irish cop named McCabe tried to have two African American cops removed from the force for not backing up his story of a dirty police shooting, Hennessy vouched for the black officers' good characters in their hearing before the Board of Police

Commissioners; the charges against the black officers were dropped. For a white policeman to testify on behalf of two black cops against a white cop in the Deep South at that time was an act of considerable courage. Clearly, Hennessy was a complex man. On the take? Perhaps. Entangled with mafiosi? Certainly. But he was not as blatantly corrupt as many other officers on the New Orleans police force.

To the Matranga family, however, the relative merits or deficiencies of David Hennessy's character were of no interest whatsoever. To them, Hennessy was an all-too-familiar type, an Irish cop who had gotten himself involved in the city's criminal rackets, in this case by aligning himself against them in a bitter labor war. The fact that Hennessy's reputation in the city was impeccable, that he was seen as a great enemy of the Mafia, only added fuel to the fire. By their estimation, the man was a hypocrite, plain and simple, a dirty cop who passed himself off as a pillar of society. Only now, the Chief's reputation was being used against them. It was rumored that Hennessy would be testifying on behalf of the Provenzanos in an upcoming trial for their role in the shooting of the Matranga brothers. This was an affront that could not be ignored. The Sicilians had a way of dealing with such matters.

The time had come for David C. Hennessy to pay for his sins.

"Who Killa de Chief?"

In the wake of Hennessy's assassination, Mayor Shakespeare expressed outrage and ordered the wholesale arrest of Italian males between the ages of twelve and fifty-five. There were no witnesses to the shooting, of course, and little immediate evidence other than detective William O'Connor's retelling of Hennessy's dying word: "Dagos." No one other than O'Connor heard this alleged identification of the killers, but it was enough to reconfirm the ardent belief of lawmen, public officials, and citizens throughout the city that the dreaded Mafia needed to be addressed.

Within three hours of the chief's death on October 16, 1890, five of the dozens of Italians questioned and arrested were charged "for the willful murder of David C. Hennessy." Outside the Central Police Station, an angry mob of citizens gathered.

"They killed our hero!" exclaimed one man in utter disbelief.

"We must have our revenge!" shouted another.

"Yes," someone agreed, "an eye for an eye."

When a number of wives and other female relatives of the scorned Italians attempted to enter the jail, they were cursed at, jostled, and spat upon.

Around 1:30 A.M., the five who had been booked were transported in a mule-drawn Black Maria to the New Orleans Parish Prison. The angry mob followed. When the prisoners were transported under heavy guard from the paddy wagon to the prison, the crowd began a loud, mocking chant: "Who killa de chief? Who killa de chief?" Eventually, they were dispersed by police.

In the subsequent editorials and post-mortems on Hennessy's career, there was no mention of his controversial past, which included the shooting of Devereaux, his forced resignation, and his shadowy relationship with the Provenzanos—an especially pertinent detail that would not be revealed until many months after the fact. In death, David Hennessy was offered up as a martyr. At his lavish funeral, candlelight wreathed his face in a glow that the press described as "saintly" and "otherworldly," which is exactly how the public chose to remember their fallen hero.

Among the many citizens driven to despair by the murder of Chief Hennessy was a twenty-nine-year-old newspaper peddler named Thomas Duffy. Duffy had occasionally sold a morning newspaper to Hennessy outside police headquarters and had become enamored of the man who had risen to become perhaps the single most powerful Irishman in the city. At Hennessy's funeral, Duffy was seen crying and muttering to himself. Afterward, he wandered the city streets with a gun in his pocket, came upon an exhibit of drawings of Chief Hennessy at the entrance of the Grand Opera House, and then headed for Parish Prison. What he did next would resemble the actions of another vengeful gunman seventy-three years later—Jack Ruby—following the assassination of President John F. Kennedy.

The Irish newspaper peddler was known to many at Parish Prison. Duffy presented himself at the bullpen area and announced that he heard a man named "Scafiro" had been arrested for the shooting of Hennessy and that he could identify him as one of the killers. A guard went to get Anthony Scaffidi, who had been charged as the main assassin.

While waiting, Duffy paced nervously.

"What've you got for the dago?" joked a guard. "Some kind of bomb?"

"No," Duffy answered curtly, not seeing the humor.

Scaffidi was brought into the bullpen. Duffy stiffened and asked the Italian to raise his hands. Scaffidi complied. Then Duffy whipped out his .32-caliber revolver and pointed it at the prisoner. The guards pounced, but not before Duffy got off one shot that hit Scaffidi in the throat. As Duffy was wrestled to the ground, he called out, "If there were seventy-five more men like me in New Orleans, we'd run all the dagos out of the city!"

Scaffidi was rushed to the hospital and eventually recovered from his wound.

Duffy was lionized by many as some kind of Irish avenger. Months later, he was tried and found guilty of the shooting, but was sentenced to a mere six months in Parish Prison.

In the end, nineteen men were indicted for planning and carrying out the execution of Chief Hennessy. On February 16, 1891, nine men went on trial. Apart from detective O'Connor's testimony, the prosecution still didn't have much evidence. The proceedings lasted less than a month. Despite the public's demand for vengeance, a jury found the nine defendants not guilty.

Outside of Little Palermo, where there was much celebration, the populace was outraged. A rumor started that the jury had been bought off by one Dominick O'Malley, a wily Irishman and former city detective who had been hired by the defense. A meeting of prominent citizens was called, and an angry crowd gathered in the public square. Many political leaders stood at the podium beneath a public statue and exhorted the crowd to take matters into their own hands.

"This is our city," shouted one man. "Justice must be done. We will not live in fear of the Mafia."

What followed would go down as one of the most shocking events in the city's history. Banding together into groups of ten and twenty men, the citizens stormed the Parish Prison. Armed with guns and clubs, they crashed the gates and made their way inside. Seven Italians were dragged into the prison yard and shot down execution-style. Two more were found hiding in a doghouse where the warden normally kept his bull terrier. They were shot dead on the spot. Another prisoner was dragged from the prison and hanged from a lamppost outside. Still another was found lying among the dead in the prison yard, pretending to be dead himself. To the excitement and satisfaction of the crowd, he was hanged from a tree in front of the prison, on Orleans Street. All told, eleven Italian Americans were lynched to death by a mob of over twenty thousand people that day.

While some newspapers denounced the actions of the mob, the people of New Orleans and the nation generally greeted the event with approval. Among the papers that voiced support and understanding were the *Washington Post*, the *San Francisco Chronicle*, and the *New York Times*, who editorialized that the death of the Italians made "life and property safer" in the southern metropolis. Closer to home, Mayor Shakespeare declared, "I do consider that the act was—however deplorable—a necessity and justifiable. The Italians had taken the law into their own hands, and we had to do the same."

If the citizenry of New Orleans believed that by slaughtering eleven Italians they were flushing the Mafia out of their nest, they were wrong. The city's Sicilian community retreated behind closed doors. Driven underground, they resumed their commitment to a secret society that they vowed would never be penetrated by American law enforcement, or anyone else for that matter.

It would be inaccurate to portray what happened that day in New Orleans as primarily a conflict between Irish and Italian factions in the city. After all, the mob's swift and brutal charge against the dagos was led by some of the city's most prominent citizens—WASP, southern aristocrat, German, and Irish. But to the Sicilian mafiosi in New Orleans and elsewhere, the message was clear. Hennessy represented a certain faction of the city's power structure: the police. The New Orleans police department was a bastion of the Irish, many of whom received tribute from Italian gangsters on the docks and elsewhere. To the Italians, Irish cops were part and parcel of the underworld. They were mobsters in uniform.

Somehow, by killing Chief Hennessy, the Italians had unleashed the wrath of American moralism and unmasked the hypocrisy of American life. They knew David Hennessy was no saint, but the public refused to see him that way. Never again could the Sicilian underworld trust the delicate system of financial appeasement between them and city authorities to work in their favor. Clearly, the city, the mayor, and the country at large were against them. At the heart of this treachery was the corrupt Irishman—be he a cop, a gangster, or both.

One person who carried this message deep in his heart was a young boy named Giuseppe Imburgio. His father was one of the eleven Italians murdered that day. In the wake of fear and hysteria, Giuseppe was spirited to safety by a Cajun woman. She took the boy up the Mississippi River to a relatively new and fast-growing city on the banks of Lake Michigan: Chicago. Given the anti-Sicilian climate of the times, the boy's name was changed to Joseph "Bulger," an Irish surname most common in the eastern regions of County Clare. The boy was an unusually serious-minded youngster; he applied himself to his studies with the discipline of a Trappist monk. Eventually, Joe Bulger would graduate from law school at the age of twenty and become one of the most influential behind-the-scenes legal advisers, or consiglieri, for the Windy City's growing Italian crime fraternity.

But if young Giuseppe Imburgio thought that moving to Chicago, Hibernicising his name, and acquiring a fancy law degree would protect him from the enveloping influence of the Irish American underworld, he was in for a hell of a surprise.

up from mud city

he Chicago World's Fair of 1893 was a real doozy. Among the tens of thousands of revelers who came from all over the United States to partake of what had been advertised as "the greatest Public Expo in human history" were a phenomenal number of grifters, con artists, gamblers, whores, bunco men, pickpockets, sneak thieves, and mobsters.

Officially, the fair was known as the World's Columbian Exposition, a celebration of Christopher Columbus's discovery of America. Although the theme of the Expo changed from year to year, the festivities were an annual event. The previous World's Fair had been held in Paris, the cultural center of Europe. The selection of Chicago as the site of the 1893 fair was an enormous tribute to the city. Chicago—not New York or Philadelphia—was being showcased as an example of the true American spirit. Money from all over the world was pumped into the local economy to finance the fair's exhibits and underwrite the many social events that would entertain the hoi polloi during the exhibition's long run, which began in late spring and continued well into the autumn months.

Considering that much of the city had been burned to the ground just twenty-two years earlier in the Great Chicago Fire of 1871, the Fair was trumpeted as a major coming out party for the Gem of the Prairie. Chicago was a rambunctious, wide-open American metropolis that had risen from mud flats along the banks of Lake Michigan to become the country's fourth largest city after New York, Philadelphia, and Baltimore.

To the city's WASP aristocracy, the World's Fair may have been an opportunity to showcase Chicago's many cultural attributes (such as its museums, architecture, and great universities), but for the men and women who made their living from the city's thriving underworld of vice and crime, it was a showcase of another kind. Since Mrs. O'Leary's cow allegedly kicked over the lamp that started the great conflagration that devoured the city, Chicago had reasserted itself in large part by becoming the most gleefully sinful city-for-sale in the entire United States. Many a traveling businessman had stopped in the City by the Lake and marveled at the largest, most diverse red light district in the country, a sprawling riverfront area known as the Levee. The South Side Levee had become a catchall name for Satan's Mile, Hell's Half-Acre, the Black Hole, Shinbone Alley, and a half dozen other vice districts that had existed before the fire. Gambling parlors, multiple saloons, opium dens, and cat houses of every variety thrived in the Levee, which was bounded on one side by Lake Michigan and on the other side by the south branch of the Chicago River.

In the decades leading up to the World's Fair, it was a well known fact that money generated by various illegal enterprises in the Levee was the secret elixir that fueled the city and kept it afloat. Chicago's founding fathers had long ago accepted the notion that vice was an irrefutable fact of big city life. Better to designate a specific locale for sin and avarice and to contain it in one easily identifiable and controllable neighborhood than try to suppress human nature and thereby create a subterranean economy that benefited no one except the criminals. Chicago's politicians and community leaders understood that dirty money could be washed and used to build parks, play-grounds, and schools. And so, in the heartland of America, a booming city had developed that no fire could destroy—a city in which the underworld and upperworld were virtually indistinguishable. That was the Chicago way.

It was no coincidence that the development and institutionalization of the Chicago way happened to coincide with a steady influx of new immigrants. Germans, Poles, Slovaks, and Bohemians flocked to the city, but few ethnic groups were as insistent in making their presence felt as the Irish. Though the number of citizens claiming Hibernian roots in Chicago would never be as high as in New York, Boston, and some other East Coast cities, the nineteenth century Irish would become more influential in Chicago than anywhere else.

Most of the early Chicago Irish had first touched down in other U.S. cities—in New York, the initial port-of-call for many immigrants, or New Orleans, where a generation of famine immigrants suffered tropical heat and subhuman working conditions. In Chicago, there was opportunity, and, for anyone with a touch of larceny in his or her soul, there was something more. The city's all-encompassing approach to urban development, which practi-cally embraced gangsterism and the dictates of the Mob as part of the municipal charter, insured that vice lords and politically connected mobsters were among the town's most renowned movers and shakers.

The greatest of them all was "King Mike" McDonald. In the pantheon of Chicago's great civic innovators, Mike McDonald, gambling czar, political overlord, and the man who coined the phrase "there's a sucker born every minute," is right up there with Marshall Field, Charles Pullman, and Cyrus McCormack, though you wouldn't know it by driving around modern-day Chi-Town. Today, there are no statues or monuments honoring the accomplishments of King Mike and no edifices adorned with his name. Given the morally questionable nature of his reign and, as we shall see, the tawdry nature of his demise, the oversight is understandable. Nonetheless, if there were a Mount Rushmore for the founding fathers of the Irish American underworld, Mike McDonald's mustachioed face would be right up there alongside Old Smoke Morrissey. For over forty years—from the beginnings of the Civil War to after the turn-of-the-century—no one played a more significant role in the day-to-day machinations of Chicago than Mike McDonald. He was the town's Irish American godfather, a man whose early life and glory days were synonymous with the fabulous rise of Mud City.

See Mike

Michael Cassius McDonald was born in Niagara Falls, New York in 1839. As a boy, he apprenticed to be a bootmaker, but this trade held no enduring interest for the youngster whose Irish immigrant parents had encountered virulent anti-Catholic bigotry in the Northeast and been confined to an immigrant ghetto on the city's west side. Young Mike yearned for something more; he yearned for the open road. As a teenager, he left home to take a position with the Michigan Central Railroad as a train butcher, a kid who sold magazines and confections to passengers commuting between cities. Around 1857, at the age of eighteen, McDonald's job on the railroads took him to New Orleans, where he first experienced the glamour and excitement of the city's gaming parlors and river steamboats; he saw the rich and influential sporting men in their natural habitat, and was inspired by the idea that the New Orleans model could be adapted to other cities—especially a fast growing, wide-open town like Chicago.

McDonald first visited Chicago sometime in 1855. At the time, the Gem of the Prairie was not much more than an idea waiting to take shape. The city had been built, inexplicably, in the middle of a mud flat, which necessitated raising portions of the downtown area on stilts above the sloshy earth, giving Chicago the first of many nicknames: Mud City.

The less-than-ideal geological conditions did not deter young Mike McDonald. He settled in the city around 1860, and, in less than a year, he had established himself as enough of an influential figure to cosponsor a petition calling on "all Irishmen" to join Corcoran's Illinois Irish Brigade and fight on behalf of the Union in the Civil War. McDonald, of course, had no intentions of joining the brigade himself. Instead he organized his first major criminal scam, in which he colluded with army deserters who agreed to turn themselves in, reenlist, and split the commission that McDonald received for recruiting them to join.

But McDonald's Civil War profiteering was small potatoes compared to the money he began to amass through his gambling interests. Dressed like an undertaker, always in black, with stark white shirts, a prominent sage-brush mustache, and a bowler derby hat, McDonald was a regular along a stretch of the First Ward known as Gambler's Row. Although he never gambled himself, he financed a traveling faro bank, and, in 1867, he opened his first gambling establishment at 89 Dearborn Street. It wasn't long before he got into trouble with the law. In 1869, he was accused of stealing thirty thousand dollars from an assistant cashier of the Chicago Dock Company, who had given him the money to finance his gambling operations. Unable to furnish bail, McDonald spent three months in jail before he was acquitted at trial. He returned to his gambling operation on Dearborn Street, although the expense of his criminal trial made it difficult for him to continue the necessary protection payments to the police. As a result, the place was raided two or three times a week, and McDonald was frequently arrested and fined.

The constant harassment by greedy cops with their hands outstretched engendered in Mike a resentment toward the men in blue that persisted until his dying day. Later in life, when he became politically powerful, he enjoyed nothing more than to put the squeeze on a cop. His dislike for policemen became so well-known that it even gave rise to a famous Chicago anecdote that was repeated for years in the city's saloons and by local vaudevillians. With occasional variations, the story went like this: King Mike McDonald was in his club one afternoon when a community organizer came in and said "Mike, we're raising money for a good cause, and we were looking to put your name down for two dollars."

"What's it for?" asked McDonald.

"Well," answered the man, "sadly, we're burying a policeman."

"B'jaysus," responded Mike. "In that case, here's ten dollars. Bury five of 'em."

McDonald's antipathy toward the coppers became an ancillary motivator that drove him toward higher and higher levels of accomplishment. The fact that the Chicago of his day was perhaps America's first truly wide-open big city—relatively free of the anti-Catholic, anti-immigrant bigotry so common in New York, Boston, Philadelphia, and the southern states—contributed to his success. Sure, Chicago had its share of Protestant old wealth, and there were certainly pockets of anti-immigrant bigotry in city, county, and state government, but by and large, the Know-Nothing Movement never really flourished in Chicago as it did in and around the original thirteen colonies.[1]

First generation Irish Americans like Mike McDonald were typical of Chicago's Irish population in that they weren't immigrants at all, but native-born Americans. They were the children of a pioneering immigrant generation that had suffered through starvation, exile, discrimination, and squalor. That generation had managed to survive and pass along their enterprising nature and psychological scars to their offspring. Mike McDonald and his generation—restless, daring, and relatively unfettered by the constraints of the past—were the first to venture forth with a sense of entitlement. They were determined to make their mark within the bounds of popular norms and dictates of American capitalism—which, in the case of Chicago and many other booming towns and cities, allowed for considerable moral leeway.

McDonald's first major venture came in 1873, with the opening of a gambling emporium unlike anything ever seen outside the riverboat parlors of New Orleans. A four-story building on the northwest corner of Clark and Monroe streets, King Mike's place, which he owned with a consortium of silent partners and financial backers, went by the name the Store and included a saloon, a hotel, and a fine dining establishment. The second-floor

---

1. There had been attempts to establish an antiforeigner movement in Chicago as early as 1855, when the city's mayor, Dr. Levi Boone, grandnephew of frontiersman Daniel Boone, pledged publicly to "rid the city of its rowdy Irish and low Dutch (German) elements." The mayor and other nativist political leaders banded together to pass legislation that prohibited the sale and consumption of alcohol on Sundays and increased saloon licensing fees to exorbitant levels. The legislation was aimed squarely at the city's Irish and German immigrant population. The result was Chicago's first major social disturbance, a bloody siege that broke out on April 21, 1855 between an angry German/Irish mob and the city's under-equipped, part-time police brigade. The Lager Beer Riot, remarkably, resulted in no deaths, but there were sixty arrests and scores of injuries. From then on, the immigrant vote played a major role in Chicago's political affairs.

gambling room was so extravagantly equipped with roulette wheels and faro tables that even McDonald's partners expressed concern.

"It's too much," said one partner upon seeing the dozens of gaming tables being installed. "We'll never get enough players to fill up the games."

It was then that McDonald uttered the phrase for which he became famous. "Don't worry about that," he said. "There's a sucker born every minute."

The Store was a success almost from the start. To gain entrance, a gambler first had to knock on the door and be recognized by the elegant black doorman in a waistcoat and cummerbund who was trained to recognize all sporting men of note. If the gambler was not known to the doorman, he could gain entrance by using the name of one of the many ropers or bunco men who King Mike employed to hang out at the city's train stations and finer hotels to steer newly arrived gamblers toward the Store.

Once inside, the prospective gambler was overwhelmed by the caliber of gaming establishment that presaged the grand casinos of Las Vegas by more than a hundred years. The room was furnished with the most expensive oak furniture and illuminated by gaslight chandeliers. Dealers and croupiers were formally dressed, as were the waiters. There was not a woman in sight, though McDonald's wife, Mary Noonan McDonald, did run the establishment's fourth-floor boarding house, which accommodated hard core sporting men who needed only an afternoon nap to revive themselves, replenish their bankrolls, and return to the tables.

Primary among the Store's many games of chance were faro, poker, craps, and Chuck-a-Luck, a dice game of British origin where the dice are spun in a wire-mesh cage shaped like an hour glass. By far the most popular game of the era was faro, which had spawned a New York derivative called stuss. The exact origins of faro are unknown, but the game is believed to have first been played in France and brought to America by way of Louisiana in the eighteenth century. No other card or dice game—not even poker or craps—ever achieved faro's level of influence; faro became the primary foundation for the elaborate gambling parlors throughout the United States, long before Atlantic City or Vegas centralized the country's insatiable appetite for games of chance.

Faro was played at a gaming table, with a dealer who was variously called a mechanic or an artist. The dealer drew cards from a dealing box and laid them out on a folding board adorned with a suite of thirteen cards, usually spades, pasted or painted on a large square of enameled oilcloth. To the left of the dealer was a case keeper, a scoring device with beads affixed to metal rods that resembled a billiard counter. Once the cards had been dealt, the bank, or dealer, determined the size of the bet; he announced, before bets were placed, the amount for which he would play.

The rules of the game were complicated, and the various plays and betting methods shrouded in arcane terminology made faro an especially perilous game for a neophyte. Some believed that faro, when overseen by a square dealer, was the fairest banking game ever devised. Others felt there was no such thing as a square dealer, and that the game was no more or less fair than the average card game in which the odds are always tipped in the bank's favor. In a seminal study of America's nineteenth century gambling culture, author John Phillip Quinn quotes a gambler describing the perils of faro:

> "Suppose a player wagers a dollar on the queen. If one of the three cards exposed happens to be a queen, he wins one dollar; if two are queens, he receives double the amount of his stake; if all three should prove to be queens, the dealer returns him his original stake augmented by three times the amount; if no queen is shown, the house gathers in the stake. It does not require a particularly erudite mathematician to discover that the odds at this game are enormously in favor of the bank."[2]

The success of Mike McDonald's faro game energized gambling operations in Chicago unlike anything ever seen before. The Store became the center of a sprawling empire in and around Gambler's Row that included many dinner pail gambling houses, roaming crap games, and bunco operations designed to soak the low-level degenerate gamblers who feasted on the fringes of the gambling underworld. All of the gaming lords, whether their operations were large or small, paid a percentage to King Mike. If they did not, they were put out of business through political pressure, police raids, or unannounced visits from brawny Irishmen with thick brogues just off the boat from places like Cork, Kerry, and Tipperary.

---

2. Quinn's book, *Fools of Fortune or Gambling and Gamblers*, published in 1892, is one of two important works, both written by Irish Americans, chronicling America's nineteenth century gambling underworld. The other is *Wanderings of a Vagabond: An Autobiography* by John O'Connor, a novelist of the period writing under the pseudonym John Morris. *Wanderings of a Vagabond*, published in 1873, is a fictional account of the adventures of a gambler from 1820 until after the Civil War. Unfortunately, neither book is available, though both are cited copiously by Herbert Asbury in his 1938 classic, *Sucker's Progress: An Informal History of Gambling in America*.

McDonald's connection to the city's criminal element was comprehensive in nature. He cultivated a relationship with numerous killers and political sluggers[3] through another entrepreneurial scheme that was nearly as remunerative as his gambling operation. For many decades in Chicago, if you were arrested and needed bail money to get out of jail, Mike McDonald was the man to see. Motivated perhaps by those three months he spent in jail without being able to post bail back in 1869, he devised a system that benefited everyone—especially himself.

The bail bondsman business was highly competitive, but McDonald kept an upper hand by employing numerous small-time lawyers to troll the sheriff's office and criminal courts. At Mike's behest, they offered to post bond for those charged with crimes on short notice and easy terms. Everyone was in on the scam, as police courts were little more than justice shops where the judge, the policeman, and the bondsman could receive a dollar a head for releasing an offender on a straw bail. Everyone came out ahead: The cops made money on the side while satisfying the reformers and the press that they were making arrests, the judge also got his cut, the criminal got out of jail, and bail bondsmen like Mike McDonald put every criminal in town in his debt as he amassed a small fortune through usurious loans and bounty payments—which, if an offender were to skip town, the bondsman, by law, was allowed to keep as pure profit.

By the mid-1880s, Mike McDonald was a millionaire many times over, but the true measure of his power and influence was only partially based on money. White-haired even in his youth and with a patrician manner that inspired confidence, McDonald was a friend and benefactor to Chicagoans at every level of society. He is credited with having handpicked and anointed the city's mayor Carter Harrison, a beefy, boisterous Democrat who came to symbolize the spirit of Chicago during the 1880s, when the city doubled in size from five hundred thousand to over a million people and was never again referred to as the Mud Flats of the Prairie. In 1882, McDonald bought part ownership in the *Globe* newspaper with which he sought to influence elections and the passing of favorable municipal ordinances. He fleeced the city coffers through his ownership of various contracting firms that secured sweetheart deals with the city using a bevy of aldermen popularly known as Mike McDonald's Democrats. He became copartner in a

---

3. In Chicago, young gangsters who supplied muscle for political interests were called "sluggers." In New York they were known as "shoulder hitters." Either way, their role was the same: they threatened and intimidated people and committed violent acts at the behest of the Machine.

powerful bookmaking syndicate, which dominated gambling at the Illinois and Indiana race tracks, above all the Garfield Race Track in Chicago, which in one season alone took in $800,000. At the time, this was the largest profit ever taken at a single track.

Day after day, the newspapers excoriated King Mike. In a typical editorial, the *Chicago Times* wrote "Mike McDonald is an unscrupulous, disreputable, vicious gambler, a disgrace and menace to the city. He should be driven from the city and the race tracks closed forever."

The negative press only added to the legend. Throughout the town, if you were looking for a job, a place to live, or small kernel of respect, there was only one way to get results:

See Mike.

Looking to nominate a stout lad for alderman and need the necessary backing of the ward bosses?

See Mike.

Looking to get your son, or husband, or cousin bailed out of jail and exert some influence on the judge presiding over the case?

See Mike.

Looking to pass a city ordinance that could provide jobs, money, and power for you and yours?

See Mike.

Mike McDonald's power became so ubiquitous that, in 1885, one newspaper bemoaned the fact that these two words—*See Mike*—had quite possibly become the most common phrase in the entire municipal and criminal lexicon of Chicago.

The Man Behind the Man

During the years of his reign, Mike McDonald never held elective office. For decades, he remained the proverbial "man behind the man," a stalwart and powerful figure in the long history of Irish political and criminal affairs. The Irish American underworld was based, at least in part, on a clan structure with roots going all the way back to various Celtic, Viking, and Anglo-Norman invasions in Ireland. Long before the rural resistance societies of the nineteenth century, Ireland had developed a sociopolitical system that included elements of guerrilla warfare in which clan members could associate openly with one another without appearing to be plotting against the forces of occupation. The Irish figurehead, or political leader, was in many cases a diversionary figure while the real influence lay with the man responsible for putting the recognized community leaders into positions of power. Being the man behind the man had certain advantages, not the least of which was that, when the shit hit the fan so to speak, it was "the man," not the man behind the man, who usually took the fall.

In some accounts of Mike McDonald's subterranean career as the god-father of Chicago, it is suggested that he really longed for the kind of approval that comes from being voted into power. If so, those hopes were irrevocably derailed by a series of public and personal scandals that flushed King Mike out of the woodwork and exposed his back-door role in civic affairs.

The first incident erupted on November 23, 1878. During a police shakedown at the Store, a cop was shot down in the establishment's upstairs boarding house by none other than McDonald's wife, Mary. The killing was front page news in all the papers. McDonald's influence, along with the efforts of an esteemed criminal defense attorney, was enough to bring about Mary's arraignment before a judge who determined that she had killed the invader of her home in justifiable self-defense. Having dodged that bullet, McDonald moved his wife and their two children out of the Store and into a mansion he had built on Ashland Avenue, near the home of his friend Mayor Carter Harrison.

Within months of this move, Mrs. McDonald made news again by elop-ing with a noted minstrel singer who had come to Chicago as part of a famous singing troupe; the two lovers fled the city together. Much to the entertainment of the local press, Mike McDonald set out after the pair, with daily newspaper reports informing Chicago's citizens of his progress. McDonald finally traced his wife and her lover to the Palace Hotel in San Francisco. He was waiting in front of the hotel one afternoon when Mary and the singer returned from a carriage ride in the country. He stopped the horses, but before he could do anything else, his wife jumped from the car-riage, threw her arms around her husband, and declared, "Don't shoot, Mike, for God's sake! It's all my fault! Take me back, for the love of God."

King Mike ushered his wife to the railroad station, and they took a train back to Chicago.

He reinstalled his wife in the house on Ashland Avenue, and their life seemed to return to normal. Mike had forgiven his wife, but he did not for-get. He became a remote husband and was gone from the house on business most of time. No longer employed by the Store and with little to occupy her mind, Mary turned to religion. She had a magnificent marble alter built in her home, and she recruited her own private priest to say mass and adminis-ter the sacred rights. The priest, Reverend Joseph Moysant, assistant rector of the Church of Notre Dame, provided extra-papal ministrations as well.

One day, Mike McDonald came home to find a note from his wife explaining that she and the priest had become lovers. They had run away to Europe together. In a fit of rage, McDonald smashed the alter to pieces.

In the weeks that followed, he renounced Catholicism and officially divorced his wife to whom he vowed never to speak again. Mrs. McDonald and Father Moysant lived together in Paris for a few years, but the repentant priest eventually returned to his flock; Mary returned to Chicago and opened a boarding house.

Meanwhile, McDonald became embroiled in an even bigger problem—a municipal scandal that left him with the title King of the Boodlers.

Today, the word "boodler" is an anachronism, an appellation long ago relegated to the dustbin of history. But for a time boodling seemed to be the dominant criminal activity in America—at least according to the newspapers of the day. McDonald had certainly been a practitioner of the art, which involved fleecing municipal government through judicious bribes, the creation of fraudulent shell companies that were the beneficiaries of fraudulent contracts, and the billing of government agencies for services never rendered.

The scandal of 1887 involved the sort of boodling scheme McDonald and his trust, or syndicate, had pulled off to one degree or another many times before. This time it involved a lucrative city contract to renovate the Cook County Courthouse. Through a longtime city official named William J. McGarigle, the McDonald group bribed the Board of County Commissioners to extend the renovation contract to the American Stone & Brick Preserving Company, a front for McDonald. When the job was completed in December 1886, McDonald presented a bill for $128,250. With limited money in the treasury, the Board of County Commissioners paid McDonald in warrants, sixty-seven thousand of which he had cashed into dollars when a newspaper investigation began to unravel the scam. Among other things, it was revealed that the expensive secret preserving fluid that McDonald's company had insisted on using to paint the exterior of the court house was nothing more than a mixture of chalk and water.

The scandal forced William McGarigle, a former police superintendent, to flee the country to avoid prosecution; numerous other aldermen and government co-conspirators wound up with jail sentences. McDonald was dragged through the mud in the press but was never charged with a crime. He even got to keep the $67,000 paid to him by the Board of County Commissioners.

For King Mike, it was a hollow victory. The scandal created a bad stink with the public that tainted the entire McDonald machine. The fallout was enough to prohibit Carter Harrison—known to the McDonald syndicate as Our Carter—from running for a fourth two-year term as mayor. McDonald himself went into retreat; he sold the Store and, for a time, disappeared from the scene.

All of that changed five years later when it was announced that the World's Columbian Exposition was coming to town.

The thought that the city of Chicago would be showcased on an international scale was enough to throw the city's overseers into a tizzy. They felt that preparing the city for such an event required the efforts and presence of the best the city had to offer—whether or not the participants had been tainted by scandal. In the months leading up to the opening of the World's Fair, the venerable Carter Harrison was carried along in the rush of enthusiasm and re-elected as mayor after a three–term absence. The manager of his re-election campaign was Mike McDonald.

The World's Fair was an unprecedented five-month long extravaganza in the city of Chicago. Participants from all over the world flocked to the White City, an area inside the downtown Loop district where buildings had been constructed, white tents put up, and bright lights strewn around giving the town a saintly glow. The frequent sound of French and other European dialects gave the city an international flavor that more than rivaled eastern metropolises like Philadelphia and New York. City officials became darlings of the international media and, for the first time, figures of national prominence. There was even talk that presiding over the World's Fair might be just the event to launch Our Carter as a serious presidential contender.

At the street level, the benefits of the Fair were even more immediate. The bordellos and gambling parlors went on a hiring binge to keep up with the influx of trade. Visitors from Paris, Berlin, London, and elsewhere made their way to the South Side Levee district, where the dance halls, panel houses, and honky-tonks stayed open till the crack of dawn. Grifters, bunco men, scam artists, pickpockets, sneak thieves, and gangsters from all over the country flocked to Chicago to prey on the immense gathering of suckers.

It seemed the party would never end, but then, on the night of October 28, 1894, it did. Just hours after Carter Harrison had given a speech praising his native city for its fearless, enterprising spirit, a city official who felt he had been overlooked for a plum municipal appointment entered the mayor's residence and shot him three times at close range. Within minutes, Our Carter was dead.

The shocking murder of the mayor threw the city of Chicago into an uncharacteristic funk. Although the criminal underworld had nothing to do with his death, the tawdry nature of Harrison's assassination reverberated throughout the gaming parlors, whore houses, and saloons where the city's political schemes were hatched. The revulsion at such an act brought about by perverse political ambition on the part of the killer did not reflect well on the city's political machine. Consequently, Mike McDonald once again slipped into retirement and disappeared from the scene.[4]

The rackets went into remission, but they did not disappear. Those in the know understood that the death of Harrison and retirement of King Mike created a vacuum that needed to be filled. There were many suitors from a legion of alderman, vice lords, and would-be gangsters who relished the possibility of following in the footsteps of Mike McDonald. But none were more skilled and formidable than two aldermen from the First Ward, a couple of Irish bull terriers who were so notorious that they were known almost exclusively by their colorful monikers: Hinky Dink and Bathhouse John.

Dawn of the Irish Political Boss

In the long history of American politics, few figures had more influence over the day-to-day livelihood of their constituents than the ward bosses of the late nineteenth and early twentieth centuries. Today, their legacy is largely forgotten. If they are remembered at all, it is as crude, bellicose minidictators who practiced a kind of gangster politics that existed in the decades before the New Deal and long before the political reforms of the 1960s and 1970s. Their historical image has largely been determined by the negative

---

4. King Mike's retirement kept his name out of the papers for a while, until another marital scandal once again turned his personal life into a cause celebre. In 1898, years after he had dissolved his marriage to the perennially unfaithful Mary Noonan, he met and married Flora Feldman, a woman thirty-eight years his junior. Flora was a dancer at the Chicago Opera House and Jewish. Having already renounced his Catholicism, he now converted to Judaism. Mike's new wife was notoriously high-strung; she once got into a physical altercation with one of his sons, who felt she was a gold digger. But Mike was blindly loyal to Flora. For years he would remain totally unaware of her longstanding affair with a fifteen-year-old school boy. But in February 1907, when the school boy (now a young man) tried to end the relationship, Flora became hysterical, pulled out a gun and shot him in the neck, then flung herself through a plate glass window. Flora was arrested and institutionalized. Still, Mike McDonald would not abandon her, not even after police discovered a cache of photographs in her lover's office—photos that showed Flora in many half-naked, provocative poses. Much to McDonald's embarrassment, a few of the photos were published, but he continued to visit his wife in the sanitarium on a regular basis, until the burden became too much to bear. On August 9, 1907, at the age of sixty-eight, the former most powerful man in Chicago died, some say of a broken heart.

press they received in the newspapers and magazines of their day, most of which were owned by wealthy WASP families and were pro-big business, pro-Republican Party, and solidly against labor unions.

Out in the streets of America's most bustling municipalities, however, it was a different story. Political bosses in many large and midsize cities were tolerated—if not enthusiastically supported—by working men and women, immigrants, and small business owners who viewed their boodling and other forms of political graft as nothing more than a redistribution of the country's riches.

Early on, Irish immigrants and Irish Americans were ceded an inordinate amount of political capital by the nation's burgeoning immigrant population. Generations of Germans, Swedes, Poles, Jews, and Italians supported and even promoted Irish political leaders, for a variety of reasons. In the Irish they recognized a taste for politics that came from a culture based on social gatherings at the local saloon and parish. The Irish understood the craft of giving and receiving favors as the basis of a political system. Also, they did not shy away from—and even seemed to relish—the art of confrontation, which was important in American politics, where nothing was given away free. It was apparent that immigrants would not get far in the United States without putting up a fight, and the Irish were good fighters (most of the early boxing champions were Irish) or at least wily enough to know how to manipulate a hostile political system in their favor. After all, they had been doing it for generations back in the Old Country.

Finally, and most importantly, the Irish spoke English. Other immigrant groups that did not speak the native tongue saw this as a tremendous advantage. Thus the Irish were designated as political leaders by generations of nonnaturalized citizens who not only recognized them as fellow immigrants, but also saw the qualities that transformed the best of the lot into natural leaders.

This is, of course, a broad oversimplification; not all immigrants were willing to extend political power to what some perceived to be a rowdy, fast talking, alcohol-swilling race of hooligans. But the record is impressive: Throughout the land, in big cities and small towns, Irishmen and Irish Americans filled out the ranks of local political machines in numbers that far exceeded their percentage of the overall population.

Without a doubt, the granddaddy of all political machines was the Tammany Tiger. In New York City, the Irish did exist in large numbers, and they exerted this numerical strength in a manner that shaped the direction of the city (and, by extension, the nation) for generations to come. Tammany-style politics became synonymous with political gangsterism and corruption, particularly in the years following the downfall of the Tweed Ring. In U.S. cities large and small, whenever local aldermen or other municipal figures became embroiled in any kind of financial scandal, they were inevitably satirized in the press by editorial cartoonists who sought to link local corruption with the same mentality that flourished in New York. "We don't want that kind of politics here" was the implied message, as if political corruption were some kind of big city, Irish immigrant phenomenon that was being foisted on an unsuspecting public. In fact, the political bosses were able to seize the levers of power in these cities for one simple reason: They delivered.

It all began at the entry level with the precinct caption, who was hand picked by the ward boss. Each ward was divided into numerous precincts; the local captain was almost always a saloon owner whose place of business served as a central meeting hall for disseminating information throughout the neighborhood. Next up the chain of command was the ward boss, a figure of note in the community who probably started as a precinct caption and rose above the fray by way of physical and political muscle. The ward boss was chosen by consensus from within the controlling democratic club or society, which voted semiannually on such matters. Both the precinct captain and the ward boss were commonly referred to as ward heelers, a term used to describe anyone who "worked the ward" by giving out turkeys to the poor and needy on holidays and soliciting votes and support for the organization.

If you served the party with distinction as a ward boss, you might be put forth by the Machine as a candidate for alderman. Alderman was an elected position and as such required certain skills many ward bosses might not have—such as a talent for oratory. Although many aldermen were not necessarily good public speakers, those who were tended to get the most press and became symbols of the Machine.

Almost every localized political organization throughout the United States had its unofficial bard, or public speechifier, who personified the Machine mentality as it applied to the local political arena. Perhaps no one became more famous than George Washington Plunkitt, alderman from New York City's Fifteenth Assembly District, whose long-winded, off-the-cuff political tracts were recorded by a journalist and in 1905 published under the title *Plunkitt of Tammany Hall: A Series of Very Plain Talks on Very Practical Politics*. In the book, Plunkitt distinguished between "honest graft" and "dishonest graft," famously summarizing his philosophy as "I seen my opportunities and I took 'em." According to Plunkitt, honest graft was the simple use of insider information or sweetheart contracts to enrich the organization; dishonest graft was "blackmailin' gamblers, saloon keepers, disorderly people, and the like."

At the heart of Plunkitt's treatise is the sacred belief that "all politics is local," and any political leader worth his salt must have the common touch:

> There is only one way to hold a district: you must study human nature and act accordin'. You can't study human nature in books. Books is a hindrance more than anything else. If you have been to college, so much the worse for you. You'll have to unlearn all that you learned before you can get right down to human nature, and unlearnin' takes a lot of time. Some men can never forget what they learned at college. . . . To learn real human nature you have to go among the people, see them and be seen.[5]

Plunkitt's published talks, and later his book, made the rounds in various precincts and wards throughout the United States, becoming a kind of bible for aspiring political bosses. The wit, wisdom, and methods of the Tammany bard were adapted to a staggering number of U.S. municipalities.

By the turn of the century, Irish-run political machines were flourishing or in development in a number of localities, including obvious "Irish towns" like New York, Brooklyn (which merged with New York in 1898), Albany, San Francisco, and Boston, where James Michael Curley, a young ward boss, exhorted his followers to "Vote early and often for Curley." Alderman Curley's popularity was such that when he was convicted of fraud for taking a civil service exam on behalf of a constituent, he was reelected by a huge margin from his jail cell.

Curley's electoral success was not surprising given Boston's large Irish population, but political machines also sprung up in cities with minimal Irish constituencies. For example, in Kansas City, Missouri, a young saloon keeper named James Pendergast (the son of immigrants from County Tipperary) founded a Machine that would pass leadership from one sibling to another and dominate the local political scene for half a century.

Of all the places where the Irish political bosses plied their trade, however, none was more storied and rambunctious than the city of Chicago.

---

5. *Plunkitt of Tammany Hall* (republished in 1995 by Signet Classics) is a small book—less than one hundred pages. You can open it almost anywhere and be entertained. Plunkitt's loquaciousness, malapropisms, and slippery morality are the stuff of vaudeville comedy; in the mid-1990s the book was turned into a humorous one-man stage show by the esteemed New York Irish actor and author Malachy McCourt.

Although the city's Irish population never topped more than fifteen percent, Irish political leaders in Chicago were everywhere, especially in the river wards, where vice mongers, wharf rats, dock workers, labor vampires, corrupt cops, and gangsters gathered excitedly like rats at a cheese factory.

The First Ward Levee district was the center of all vice in Chicago, and it was presided over by John "Bathhouse John" Coughlin and Michael "Hinky Dink" Kenna. Of the two, The Bath was the loudest and most ostentatious. Born in a tough Irish slum neighborhood in the First Ward known as Connelly's Patch, Coughlin was an outgoing, good-natured youth who made friends wherever he went. At the age of nineteen, he landed a job as towel boy and errand runner at a Turkish bath at 205 Clark Street in the heart of the First Ward. At this bathhouse, where prize fighters, jockeys, race-horse trainers, politicians, and prominent merchants hung out, young John Coughlin acquired his nickname as well as his seemingly magnanimous world view.

"I formed my philosophy," The Bath liked to say in later years, "while watching and studying the types of people who patronized the bathhouses. Priests, ministers, brokers, politicians, and gamblers visited there. I watched and learned never to quarrel, never to feud. I had the best schooling a young feller could have. I met 'em all, big and little, from La Salle Street to Armour Avenue. You could learn from everyone. Ain't much difference between the big man and the little man. One's lucky, that's all."

The Bath was a snazzy dresser—or at least snazzy by his own standards, which usually involved Prince Albert vests, loud plaids, the garish colors of sporting men, the bowlers and silk top hats of the aldermen and gamblers, along with lavender gloves and tan spats.

He was a stout man, six feet tall, with a belly that began to grow in his early twenties and just kept growing for the rest of his days. He sported a stylish handlebar mustache and a carefully coifed pompadour. When Bathhouse John entered a room, the whole world took notice.

He got his political start courtesy of King Mike McDonald, who gave Coughlin the okay to run for First Ward alderman after a sit-down at Billy Boyle's chophouse off Gambler's Row, where McDonald liked to conduct business while eating huge helpings of salt pork with truffles. It was there that McDonald passed along a piece of advice that would become Bathhouse John's avowed guiding principle.

"Never steal anything big," King Mike told the aspiring alderman. "Stick to the little stuff. It's safer."

With Mike McDonald's blessing and through his own innate talents as a campaigner, Bathhouse John easily won his first election in April 1892. For the next forty years, he was the First Ward's primary representative on the city council.

Almost immediately, Coughlin recognized that the surest means for an alderman to create advantageous financial opportunities for himself and his supporters was to become a committeeman. It was in committee hearings that city ordinances were considered, jobs created, and patronage schemes hatched. Well-placed committeemen were very likely to be offered bribes by shady businessmen looking for certain favorable ordinances to pass into law. Behind closed doors, these entrepreneurs might grumble that doing business in Chicago involved a kind of extortion, but they paid willingly because the alternative was likely to be just as costly. Thus, committeemen who were paid an official rate of three dollars a council meeting wound up with huge summer homes, racing stables, and prosperous side businesses, claiming they were able to acquire such amenities through "good investments."

For the aldermen, being on a prized committee was also a tremendous display of power, which is why Bathhouse John Coughlin was thrilled to have maneuvered his way onto the prestigious Reception Committee for the 1893 World's Fair after less than a year in office.

Much of Coughlin's power resided in his oratory skills, which he displayed on a regular basis in the city council meetings at which he might debate the pros and cons of a particular ordinance for hours. Once, when a new political alliance that called itself the Municipal Reform Party vowed to field candidates and drive corrupt aldermen from office, The Bath delighted his fellow council members and the press with his opinion on the matter.

"This new movement is the mist which rises skyward before one's eyes," offered Coughlin, "and while it may become thick enough to make a cloud and look scarlet and silver and gilt-edged in the sunlight, it will yet be the cloud that will blind good political vision. That means that the Municipal Party is a Jonah, an orphan, a child without parents which will cry for a little while an' die. It means I count myself too smart to associate with 'em. Honest, I'd ruther be a Republican—put that on record—than associate with such a party that stands for nothin' but a dream, a regular dewy mist. Rise above the mist an' look for the earth. You can see it, but keep on lookin'. The sun comes out an' drives the mist away, an' you see the solid bedrock of Democracy an' the sands of Republicanism still stickin' close to the ground. That's me. I want my feet on the earth."

With his flashy style and flowing verbiage, Bathhouse John was the ideal front man, but he wasn't much of an organizer. He was popular enough to

ensure himself reelection for the foreseeable future, but he had no real organization behind him. For this, he needed Hinky Dink.

Michael Kenna was the exact opposite of John Coughlin. Though they
were raised in similar hardscrabble conditions in the First Ward, and both
married local Irish girls, Kenna had none of Coughlin's flamboyance. An
absurdly tiny man, barely an inch over five feet tall, Kenna had acquired his
nickname as a youth when kids at the local swimming hole made fun of his
diminutive size. He may have been small, but Hinky Dink had oversized
ambitions. He dropped out of school at the age of ten to become a newsboy
and supplemented his income by running errands for saloon keepers and
porters along State Street, striking up valuable relationships with gamblers,
brothel madams, and their clients. By the time he was in his late-teens, he
had his own newsstand at the corner of Monroe and Dearborn Streets, just
outside the old *Chicago Tribune* building. At the age of twenty-four, he
opened a saloon, the Workingmen's Exchange, which would become the
most legendary gathering place in the history of First Ward politics.

In the months following Mayor Carter Harrison's assassination—and in
the waning days of Mike McDonald's empire—Mike Kenna approached
Bathhouse John Coughlin. Although they knew each other by reputation
and had most likely met before, they were drawn together for the first time
by a vexing problem. Both men were saloon owners (Coughlin's was called
the Silver Dollar) who ran modest gambling operations out of hotel rooms
above their saloons. In recent months the police had begun raiding both
their establishments. Hinky Dink thought it over and said to The Bath:
"Times have changed. Mike McDonald can't do nothin' for us now. We
need our own organization, one that can control the coppers and the people
at City Hall. You're the alderman, and you've got another year to run. I can
guarantee you reelection if you throw in with me. We stick together, and we
rule the roost like nobody ever done before."

Kenna's proposition made perfect sense to Bathhouse John. They threw
in together. For the next forty years, they were like a classic vaudeville team:
Coughlin the loud, back-slapping joke teller, Kenna the sad-eyed straight
man. Their stark differences in temperament only added to their unique
chemistry, which was both entertaining and highly effective.[6]

---

6. Kenna himself ran for alderman in 1894. A dour campaigner who rarely smiled,
Hinky Dink's idea of inspirational rhetoric was to declare, "If I am elected, I will try
to show the people I am not as bad as I am painted on account of the name 'Hinky
Dink.'" To the voters of the First Ward, it didn't matter what he said; he won by a

Bathhouse John may have been the showman, but Hinky Dink was the true genius. His street-level approach to political science was founded on an extensive benefit system that incorporated the lowest of the low. At a time when there was no government welfare system to speak of, Kenna became perhaps the best friend the city's indigent population ever had. The rooms of the Alaska Hotel above his Workingmen's Exchange became a veritable flophouse, more popular than the local Salvation Army. Bums and hobos were given hot water for bathing and a place to sleep. In the morning, they were offered soup and a sandwich at Hinky Dink's saloon and allowed to drink the spillover from the night before. All that was required in return was that they vote early and often on election day. The owner rarely showed his face, but the people knew who he was. To the poor, homeless, and hapless of the First Ward, Hinky Dink Kenna was like a saint.

The goodwill and loyalty engendered by Kenna's soup kitchen became the bedrock of a seemingly indestructible political organization. Kenna and Coughlin set up a defense fund in which a percentage of the protection money paid by brothel owners and gamblers was pooled for all organization followers who got into trouble. Prostitutes suffering from diseases were sent to private sanatoriums in Colorado. Gangsters from the ward who were arrested for fighting hooligans from other territories or for conducting violence on behalf of the organization would be provided legal council. The Machine exerted financial influence over the Chicago Police Department and brought about the installation of the organization's very own local chief, Captain Michael Ryan, who was a firm believer in the status quo. "This district has never been clean," declared the good captain, "and it never will be. We keep order as well as possible."

Election day sometimes got ugly. As in New York, Philadelphia, and other rapidly expanding big cities around the United States, politics in Chicago was a contact sport. The reelection of Coughlin and Kenna as aldermen usually went off without a hitch, but when it came to mayoral elections or elections that involved differences of opinion within the ward's many precincts, blood flowed. During one particularly contentious election, the Kenna-Coughlin camp acquired the services of the Quincy Street Boys, one of dozens of professional slugger squads who hired themselves out on election day. The Quincy Street Boys were assured that when the time came

---

landslide and remained an alderman until the city council reduced the district from two aldermen to one in 1923 (see *Lords of the Levee: The Story of Bathhouse John and Hinky Dink* by Lloyd Wendt and Herman Kogan).

for the application of billies, blackjacks, and brass knuckles on rival voters, the police would be looking the other way.

Sure enough, the inevitable showdown took place that afternoon. According to the *Tribune*, "Coughlin's men went after [their rivals] like hungry hyenas in a traveling circus at an evening meal of raw steak." Later in the evening, the roving street confrontations grew into a full-fledged riot. On State Street during rush hour, cable cars were halted while the rival gangsters beat, cut, and shot at one another. Three squads of police were called into action; they rushed the crowd, clubbing indiscriminately. Eventually the disturbance was quelled.

That night, while election judges and clerks busily tallied the votes for the day, newspapers made up casualty lists. They discovered that forty enemies of the Kenna-Coughlin organization had been wounded, two of them critically, while hundreds were arrested and held in the county jail. Only six Kenna-Coughlin men had been seriously injured, and of the dozens apprehended, all had been vouched for by counsel; none spent the night in jail. The Machine took care of its own.

The First Ward Ball

Elections in the First Ward were violent for one simple reason: The stakes were high. The ward's Levee district had become a cash cow, a depraved, sinful Shangri-la that spewed forth dirty money like a delirious bank teller high on dope and juju juice. The city's Vice Commission claimed that vice and crime in Chicago yielded an annual revenue of sixty million dollars, with net profits of fifteen million dollars—most of it generated in the Levee. Gross income from prostitution alone was estimated at thirty million dollars, with half of it paid out as protection to greedy aldermen and crooked coppers.

Over the years, many Protestant religious leaders and political reformers toured the district and issued reports claiming that the Levee represented the end of civilization as we know it, a veritable Sodom and Gomorrah. In 1910, a commission of concerned citizens investigated the district and determined that there were 27,300,000 paid-for couplings annually. More than five-thousand full-time prostitutes worked in and around the Levee, and ten thousand more freelanced on weekends.

Brothels scaled to accommodate every bankroll and coin purse existed in the district. The Everliegh Club was the most famous, a New Orleans-style luxury bordello catering to the city's leaders of industry. Along Bed Bug Row was a more motley and affordable collection of whorehouses such as Black May's, The Library, a cathouse called Why Not? and, most famously, the House of All Nations, which claimed to have a bevy of affordable whores from every country on earth.

In addition to prostitution, the Levee offered debauchery to satisfy every desire or fetish: faro clubs, dice joints, penny arcades, opium dens, peep shows, burlesque houses, dance halls, concert saloons, and animal sex acts. There were hundreds of saloons, most of the rot-gut variety with names like The Bucket of Blood, The Crib, Dago Frank's, and The Lone Star & Palm Club, which was described in a police report as "a low dive, a hang-out for colored and white people of the lowest type."

The Lone Star & Palm Club was owned and run by Mickey Finn, a foul-tempered pickpocket and jackroller who claimed at times to have been born in Ireland, and at other times in Peoria, Illinois. His saloon advertised a drink called the "Mickey Finn Special," which was comprised of raw alcohol, water in which snuff had been soaked, and a knockout powder he had acquired from a Haitian voodoo doctor. Suckers who were dumb enough to drink this mystery beverage (the price was a mere two cents) passed out and were then dragged into a back room, where they were robbed of everything, including clothes and shoes. Mickey Finn's technique was so notorious that his name later became a generic term applied to knockout potions of all varieties.

Finn, like everyone else, paid for the privilege of operating his scams in the district. The fact that local businesses paid protection to the politicians and police was an open secret. The *Chicago Examiner* even published a price scale:

Massage parlors and assignation houses, $25 weekly.
Larger houses of ill fame, $50 to $100 weekly, with $25 additional each week if drinks are sold.
Saloons allowed to stay open after hours, $50 a month.
Sale of liquor in apartment houses without licenses, $15 a month.
Poker and craps, $25 a week for each table.

Having to pay tribute did not keep the hustlers away. On the contrary, the gamblers, bums, thugs, pimps (called cadets), madams, harlots, and bunco artists all came in droves. Eventually, the varied collection of riffraff who operated daily in the district led Hinky Dink Kenna to an idea that would catapult the Levee into a unique position in the history of American vice.

It came to him in the winter of 1896, when Hinky Dink and The Bath were seated in his office at the Workingmen's Exchange. They were lamenting the fact that, this year, unlike the preceding fifteen, there would be no annual party for Lame Jimmy, a crippled pianist and fiddler who entertained in the ragtime style of Scott Joplin and Fats Waller. In the 1880s and early 1890s, the fund raiser for Lame Jimmy was a hugely popular event; police captains, patrolmen, and district leaders attended as honored guests, mingling with thugs and sluggers who were friends of the Machine. The annual event came to an abrupt end in 1895, when a cop at the party got drunk and shot another cop.

"Hey, I got an idea," said Hinky Dink, in a rare instance of excitement. "Why don't we take over the party? We put on an annual event just like the Lame Jimmy affair, only we control everything so nobody can shut us down."

Bathhouse John loved the idea. "Good God, m'boy, you got something there. We charge one dollar a head to every saloon keeper, madam, and slugger in the district, and we'll make a small fortune."

Thus was born the First Ward Ball, a legendary event that became the closest thing to an annual celebration that the Irish American underworld would ever have.

It was held at the Chicago Coliseum. Tickets were sold ahead of time for one dollar each, with a five dollar fee to sit in special roped-off boxes near the dance floor. From the start, the Ball was massively popular, attended by a who's who of the criminal class. Tom O'Brien, king of the bunco artists, was a regular, as was Billy Fagen, a religious man whose House of David gambling parlor always had one room reserved for "prayer meetings and gospel service." Buff Higgins was also a regular, until he was hanged in Cook County Jail on a murder charge. Big Jim O'Leary, an up-and-coming gambling czar whose mother Catherine O'Leary owned the cow that allegedly kicked over the lamp that ignited the Great Fire of 1871, was an annual guest.

Reporting on the ball one year, the *Tribune* surmised: "If a great disaster had befallen the Coliseum last night there would not have been a second-story worker, a dip or plug-ugly, porch climber, dope fiend, or scarlet woman remaining in Chicago." The paper only had it half-right; that same disaster would have wiped out most of the city's aldermen and a significant portion of the police department as well.

The First Ward Ball reached its zenith in 1907, when angry social reformers repulsed by the annual bacchanal pledged to print a list of the so-called "upstanding citizens" who attended. Bathhouse John came up with an idea for undercutting this cheap tactic. The ball that year would be a masquerade affair, offering everyone an opportunity to disguise their identities. The grand marshal was none other than Bathhouse John himself, who arrived not in a costume, but in his usual finery. His tailcoat was a crisp billiard-cloth green, his vest a delicate mauve. His trousers were lavender, as was his glowing cravat, and his kid gloves a pale pink. His shoes were canary yellow, and perched atop his fine pompadour was a silken top hat that glistened like a plate glass window at Marshall Field's department store.

The Bath also used the occasion to unveil a song he had written entitled "Dear Midnight of Love," sung by a professional opera star he had hired for the occasion. The song was corny and lachrymose, but the crowd loved every minute of the performance.

The irony was that, even though Coughlin and Kenna were (contrary to the district they presided over) straight-laced family men whose wives were active in local parish activities, the ball became to the reformers a symbol of all that was wrong with the city's laissez-faire philosophy of segregated vice. Local newspaper editorials railed against this "saturnalian orgy," this "vile, dissolute affair," this "bawdy Dionysian festival." In response, Hinky Dink smiled a rare smile and counted the proceeds, which ranged over the years from twenty-five thousand to forty thousand dollars of pure profit.

Elsewhere, the rest of the nation read about the goings-on in Chicago with astonishment and, in some cases, envy. One person who steadfastly followed the activities of the Kenna-Coughlin organization from afar was a man named Richard Croker, grand sachem of New York's Tammany Hall.

It wasn't just the First Ward Ball that caught Boss Croker's attention; it was also the manner in which Kenna and Coughlin aligned all the necessary forces to make the Ball possible. First and foremost among the Chicago Machine's benefactors was Carter Harrison, Jr., son of Our Carter. Just four years after his father's death, Carter Junior ran for mayor on the principle that under a new Carter Administration, Chicago would forever be a "wide open town," just as it had been under his father. Hinky Dink and The Bath rallied around their own version of "Our Carter," securing his election and reelection for an unprecedented twelve years in office.

In New York, Boss Croker had a mayoral election coming up and had put forth a non-Irish, non-Catholic candidate not unlike Carter Harrison. Curious to learn from his colleagues in Chicago, Croker invited Bathhouse John and Hinky Dink Kenna to visit New York as his guests. The two aldermen were delighted to take him up on the invitation.

Coughlin, Kenna, and a contingent of politicos known as the Cook County Democracy arrived by special train in Manhattan and were feted at Tammany's main wigwam, a stately building on East Fourteenth Street. Croker, a tough former gang member with bulging muscles and a full beard, towered over the two men, especially tiny Hinky Dink. But Tammany Hall's

"Mister Big" was exceedingly solicitous of his political brethren, stating to the press, "We are honored and gratified to have in our presence a group of men known to be political wizards in their own fair city, men of great accomplishment and civic virtue, masters in the science of political persuasiveness. We will show them a fine time here in New York and edify ourselves at their behest."

A special Tammany parade was arranged. Many of the New Yorkers who turned out to see the Chicagoans march down Broadway were especially eager to get a glimpse of the inimitable Bathhouse John and Hinky Dink. Dressed in their usual marching attire of long frock coats, pinstriped trousers, starched white shirts, silk top hats, white gloves, and umbrellas that served as walking sticks, the two alderman cut quite a figure.

After the parade, the contingent from Chicago retired to the Hesper Club on the Bowery, a Tammany district headquarters operated by Paddy Sullivan, brother of Assemblyman Big Tim Sullivan. Big Tim himself was on hand to welcome the Chicago crowd and give them an impromptu tour of the legendary Sixth Ward, which included what used to be known as Five Points. This storied neighborhood, once the home and incubation center for a generation of post-famine Irish street gangs such as the Dead Rabbits and the Whyos, was now divided into a series of smaller ethnic enclaves, including Chinatown, Little Italy, and the predominantly Jewish Lower East Side. All that remained to remind residents of the old days was a large gang that managed the area's still thriving vice rackets, the Five Points gang. This gang, of course, operated under the aegis of the local political boss, Big Tim Sullivan.

There is no record of what was discussed at this historic meeting of the minds between the nation's two preeminent political organizations. Given that the Chicago and New York Irish political leaders saw themselves as being engaged in a similar struggle, and had developed remarkably similar methods to achieve their goals, they might well have viewed this gathering as a meeting of the brain trust. At the turn of the new century, Chicago and New York were the Rome and Athens of the underworld, dominant practitioners of an up-from-the-gutter brand of politics that incorporated sluggers, shoulder hitters, and vice mongers of every variety. As the leaders of this movement, Boss Croker, Big Tim, Bathhouse John, and Hinky Dink were part of what the press sometimes referred to as an "Irish American cabal." The men themselves would have approved of that designation. For these municipal masters, there seemed to be no end in sight.

When all was said and done, the various political bosses exchanged hearty handshakes and went their separate ways. Coughlin, Kenna, and the others returned to the city of Chicago, energized by the deification bestowed on them by the preeminent Irish American political power, the vaunted Tammany Hall.

A few years later, the Chicagoans reciprocated by inviting Big Tim Sullivan to the First Ward Ball, where, among the whores, gamblers, political grafters, and mobsters of the Levee district, the assemblyman from Manhattan was honored as a special guest.[7]

Chicago Gambling Wars

In the first two decades of the new century, gambling remained the mother of all criminal rackets. Card games, craps, and roulette were as popular as ever, but the gambling business had truly made revolutionary strides with the Sport of Kings—horse racing—which was transformed in the early years of the twentieth century by the invention of the electronic wire service. Western Union and other corporate forces had created the telegraph wire as a means of transferring money. The modern bookmaker used it for the transference of illegal funds through off-track betting into their own pockets.

Before the wire service existed, you actually had to go to the racetrack to place a bet or at least to a betting parlor adjacent to the track. Now a gambler could place his bet with a bookie anywhere in town. Usually, this was done at a poolroom, originally a place where lottery tickets were sold. A lottery was called a pool because of the manner in which winnings were paid off. Since lottery tickets were sold all day and the drawings were not held until late in the evening, proprietors of poolrooms installed billiard tables to occupy their customers during the waiting periods. Now they installed betting boards as well, which posted odds on the races and a myriad of other sporting events.

Bookmaking operations now became an adjunct of the gambling parlors. The gambling czars employed a legion of bookies who worked the district. The bookies, many of whom were themselves degenerate gamblers, took bets from dozens of clients. The bookies might then lay off a portion of

---

7. The First Ward Ball did not go on forever. In 1908, after a twelve-year run, the ball was discontinued after intense pressure was put on the city's newly elected Republican mayor. In retrospect, the forces that brought about the end of the ball, which were galvanized by an organization called the Women's Christian Temperance Union, represented the beginning of a movement that would gain considerable steam over the next decade, culminating with the passage of the Eighteenth Amendment, otherwise known as Prohibition.

their action through sizable wagers of their own with their boss, the gambling czar. The bookies figured that, even if they lost their bets, they were covered by gambling proceeds they'd taken in through their own losing clients. It didn't always work out that way, of course. Bookies and their pigeons, or marks, became the bottom feeders of the underworld. When their financial ledgers dipped too strongly in a losing direction, sluggers were called in, and the bookmaker wound up in a world of hurt.

Given the newly dispersed, far-reaching nature of the business, a centralized gambling overlord like King Mike McDonald was no longer practical. Thus, the city's gambling empire broke down into mini-fiefdoms that were constantly encroaching on each other's turf.

One of the most powerful gambling czars to emerge in the new century was Big Jim O'Leary. O'Leary was a jowly, barrel-chested son of the South Side whose family had become social pariahs after his mother's prized cow allegedly touched off the largest single disaster in the city's history. Growing up, the O'Leary boys were taunted endlessly. The oldest of the brood, Con "Puggy" O'Leary, was so haunted by the family's stigma that he became a brawling, hard drinking ne'er-do-well who, in 1885, killed a woman and injured his own sister for refusing to give him a dollar to buy a pail of beer. Jim O'Leary was less tortured by the family's past; he merely chose a profession where having a tainted history was not necessarily bad for business.

O'Leary got his start as a bookmaker in the McDonald organization. By the late 1890s, he had become a financial participant in a highly successful casino run by Blind John Condon in Hot Springs, Arkansas, which in one season took in a nifty $250,000. O'Leary used his portion of the proceeds to open a gambling parlor on South Halstead Street near Chicago's famous Stockyard district and began to organize a series of poolrooms and handbooks. He also had an interest in numerous saloons, racetracks, and a gambling boat.

Big Jim's Halstead Street gambling parlor was the most elaborate establishment the city had seen since the days of King Mike's place, the Store. Not only did it provide facilities for all sorts of gambling, but there was also a bowling alley, a billiard room, a Turkish bath, and a restaurant. The main attraction, however, was the poolroom, with its luxurious chairs and sofas, servants to bring drinks, and chalkboards that gave the odds and results for every horse race in the United States and Canada. In this room, and in his outside handbooks as well, Big Jim took bets on everything from prize fights and baseball games to elections and even crops and the weather.

Unlike most gambling czars, O'Leary steadfastly refused to pay off the coppers. "I could have all kinds of [police protection]," he once proclaimed, "but let me tell you something. Protection that you purchase ain't worth nothing to you. A man who will sell himself ain't worth an honest man's dime. The police is for sale, but I don't want none of them."

Instead, Big Jim turned his Back o' the Yards gambling house into a veritable fortress. It had secret passageways, trap doors, a fake chimney with a ladder that could be drawn up, a steel-plated front door, and inner walls constructed of heavy oak and covered with zinc—making the place, according to Big Jim, "fire-proof, bomb-proof, and police-proof." Still, coppers did sometimes raid his establishment, gain entry, and seek to destroy the place. O'Leary was usually ready for them. On one occasion he even lined the walls of the gaming room with a toxic red pepper; when raiding police took their axes to the place, they unleashed a blinding powder.

When O'Leary wasn't battling with officers of the law, he was under assault from rival gambling organizations. Of the three main gambling combines in the city, the largest—even larger than O'Leary's—was run by Mont Tennes, the son of German immigrants and a former saloon keeper who had the backing of Kenna-Coughlin, among other friends in high places. In July 1907, a bombing war erupted among the city's gambling factions. The first to be hit was Blind John Condon, one of O'Leary's partners and a link to the McDonald syndicate of the past. Condon was relaxing in the rear of his home at 2623 Michigan Avenue when a bomb was tossed into the front yard. Lucky for Blind John, the bomb was time-fused and only caused partial damage to the façade.

Two days later, on July 25 at nine o'clock at night, Mont Tennes's home was hit with a steel-cased bomb that landed in a paved alley directly behind the house. Tennes, who was enjoying a bath at the time, was rattled to his feet by an explosion that shattered numerous windows in the house. The German gambling boss was not hurt. To the police he claimed ignorance of who might have wanted to do such a thing. "It must have been the work of some mischievous boys with a cannon cracker," Tennes said.

After this, the bombs kept flying. Jim O'Leary's Halstead Street gambling emporium was hit with what proved to be the biggest bomb of all. Buildings a block away shook from the explosion, and people ran madly down the street. O'Leary, who was not on the premises at the time, told the police that the explosion was the result of a cap on a gas pipe that blew out. The cops didn't believe him, but they had little in the way of details or evidence to determine the truth.

Over the next few years. Chicago's tit-for-tat bombing war raged unabated. There were dozens of bombings that took place in saloons, poolrooms, gambling parlors, residences, and even a South Side police precinct.

The pattern was always the same. A home-made explosive device would go off, creating a deafening blast. Helmeted police blowing calliope whistles and toting night sticks would arrive on the scene after the dynamiters had fled. There were occasional arrests, but no one was ever convicted for a single bombing. Amazingly, no one was ever killed either.

The city's gambling wars were an unnerving escalation of underworld competition, and they added to a growing weariness on the part of the general population. The days of the gentleman gambler, it seemed, were being replaced by a more menacing reality. Faced with frequent disruptions, destruction of property, and the threat of serious violence, political and social reformers stepped up their counter-efforts with almost daily rallies against the saloon keepers, gamblers, and vice mongers.

One of the first underworld figures to sense the turning of the tide was Big Jim O'Leary. O'Leary had gotten into the game as a way of possibly salvaging his family's name and reputation. He had even once hired a public relations firm to put a positive spin on his gambling operations. The bombing war and the wild nature of the city's commercialized vice in general convinced Big Jim that the time had come to move on. To the surprise of many, O'Leary sold off his operations and publicly announced his retirement from the underworld on December 1, 1911.

The gambling wars raged on, with Tennes strategically bombing Big Jim's many successors until a few years later, when Hinky Dink Kenna allegedly stepped in and mediated a peace settlement. A police informer claimed that Kenna had received forty thousand dollars for his efforts. Hinky Dink denounced the informant as a "big liar."

The cessation of the city's long bombing war did nothing to pacify the growing reform movement. When a cop was killed on July 13, 1914, during a wild shoot-out on West Twenty-second Street in the Levee district, the Board of Fifteen, a powerful citizens organization comprised of ministers and temperance leaders, announced to the public "We declare war on the Levee and all commercialized vice in the city. It's a war to the finish!"

The do-gooders and church leaders were not the only ones who had grown tired of the city's long accommodation with the underworld. The very nature of the wide open town was a commercial mandate that had created a world in which young men of violence were tolerated, if not openly encouraged. Among the Irish American lower middle class, which was the first generation of Irish Catholics to rise above the poverty level, a pervasive gang culture had spread and became institutionalized. A well-known study on gangs in Chicago by academic Frederick Thrasher claimed that there were 1,313 gangs in the city. The number was misleading in that Thrasher designated virtually every street corner gathering of young men—whether it was a politically-affiliated group or just four guys having a smoke together—as a gang. But the overall point was undeniable; the gang lifestyle was pervasive, and it fueled a culture of aimless violence that was "put to good use" by the mobster and political bosses.[8]

At the lowest end of the scale were the street corner gangs, comprised mostly of punks who spent their afternoons pitching pennies, stealing apples from Luigi's fruit stand, brawling with each other, or race-baiting, which sometimes escalated into racially tinged gang fights. A more advanced type of gang were the "social athletic" clubs, which were sponsored by a nebulous organization known as the South Side Clubs Association (SSCA). These gangs usually gathered on a regular basis in public meeting halls. In return for having their rent paid by the SSCA, the athletic clubs ran errands for the political bosses—mostly Democrats—and other members of the tribe looking to hire out their services.

By far the largest and most notorious of these groups was an Irish gang, Ragen's Colts, whose clubhouse was in a store at 5528 S. Halstead Street. The organization was named after their leader, Frank Ragen, a tough, street-smart operator who eventually rose above the gang and got himself elected to the Cook County Board of Commissioners. Long after he was gone, the gang kept his name and continued to grow, eventually adopting the slogan "Hit Me and You Hit 2,000," which was probably only a slight exaggeration. Ragen's Colts proved to be a veritable breeding ground for a generation of sluggers and underworld figures, among them Gunner McFadden, Harry Madigan, Stubby McGovern, and Ralph Sheldon, who became a notorious bootlegger in the 1920s.

Ragen's Colts first made a name for themselves during the city's rough-and-tumble newspaper circulation wars that began in 1910. The battle for

---

8. Lower middle class Irish American alienation of this period is captured with harsh realism by author James T. Farrell in his classic *Studs Lonigan Trilogy*. Born and raised on Chicago's South Side, Farrell set the first of his Lonigan novels in his old neighborhood in 1916, with young Studs on the cusp of adulthood, his life consisting of poolrooms, heavy drinking, constant fighting, and having to prove his manhood. Studs prefers life as a young punk because all other career alternatives—the priesthood, fire department, police, or other civil service rackets—seem numbingly dull by comparison. As for politics, whenever Studs and his friends notice one of their own getting a sizable beer belly, they refer to it as "an alderman," which is meant to imply that the person has become fat and complacent and has resigned himself to living off the municipal teat.

readership between the city's various broad sheets turned ugly and ushered in an era of athletic association gangs being utilized and financed by upperworld corporations. At the behest of William Randolph Hearst and other prominent publishers, gang contracts were extended to various athletic clubs who, using a method known as bootjacking, routinely intimidated, threatened, and even killed newsdealers to get their organizations to buy more of a certain paper. The *Chicago American*, owned by Hearst, had the most brutal enforcement arm—Ragen's Colts, who eventually jumped ship when a rival paper, the *Tribune*, offered them more money.

The circulation wars were serious business. Before they were over in 1913, twenty-seven street-level newsdealers were stabbed, beaten, or shot to death while the owners stayed securely in their ivory towers. Furthermore, the newspaper wars legitimized the practice of large business entities using the gangs in all manner of disputes, a practice that would become even more commonplace during the many labor union wars that flared up in Chicago on a semiregular basis.

Given the size of gangs like Ragen's Colts and the air of legitimacy that upperworld forces gave them, it is not surprising that they became entangled in other kinds of disturbances as well. Race, for instance, was a hot button issue in Chicago, as it was in many big, American cities. Since the athletic associations were based on ethnic affiliations—Irish, Polish, Italian, and African American being the most dominant—they often became the shock troops in the city's seething racial hostilities. These hostilities had grown worse since the beginnings of World War I, when thousands of impoverished southern blacks, drawn by the prospect of jobs at munitions plants and packing houses, sought the promise of a better life on Chicago's South Side. Frightened whites abandoned the area, while those who stayed saw their property values plummet. This social upheaval brought about civil tensions that would exist in the city, to varying degrees, for man decades to come.

The most cataclysmic racial event in the city's history was initiated on July 27, 1919, when a group of young African American swimmers accidentally strayed over an imaginary racial divide that separated the white beach at Twenty-ninth Street from the black beach at Twenty-fifth Street. A group of white boys stoned the blacks with rocks until a fourteen-year-old boy was hit in the head and drowned.

What followed was a violent race riot that flared sporadically over four days, complete with lynchings, looting, the wholesale destruction of property, and murder. The police lost control early on, and the battle was relegated—as race wars often are—to young people acting out the hatred and bigotry of their elders. In this case, the athletic associations became major players in a horrifying urban nightmare. Sections of the "black belt" were randomly torched to the ground by white gangs; prominent hotels were stormed by groups of rampaging whites looking for black porters and maids. Black snipers opened fire from rooftops on the gangs and policemen. By midnight on the third day of rioting, twenty-six Chicagoans were dead, and three hundred more were seriously injured.

Subsequent newspaper accounts of the riot singled out gangs like Ragen's Colts. Though it had nothing to do with commercialized vice per se the riot became the implement by which reformers like the Board of Fifteen would beat down sin and avarice once and for all. Negative sentiment toward the gangs and the crooked politicians who used their services was at an all time high. Years of rampant corruption, unbridled greed, political gangsterism, and now an inexplicable racial hostility had soured the public on the very notion of the wide open town. The entire system of graft, boodling, and gangsterism was on the verge of collapsing of its own accord.

It may well have, too, were it not for the overweening moralism of the reform movement. The Women's Christian Temperance Union and the Anti-Saloon League had declared: "It's a war to the finish!" They were not interested in election campaign reform, tougher gun laws, or a commission to investigate police corruption. All of these methods had been tried before with only temporary results. This time, the victory would be complete. Sin and vice would be stamped out at its very source—the saloon, a place where the evil influence of beer and liquor twisted the mind, inflamed the libido, and spawned a culture of degeneracy that was tearing down all that was good about the American republic.

By 1918, this temperance movement was well on its way to success. The war in Europe had aided their cause: grain-saving limits on alcohol production were imposed, and there was a heightened concern for the moral well-being of young men in uniform. The temperance leaders and hell-fire preachers crusading against liquor organized into a well-funded lobby. Nine states had already gone dry by the time the U.S. Senate passed legislation banning the use and sale of alcoholic spirits. In January of 1919, the House of Representatives was poised to do the same, which would bring about an unprecedented, nationwide prohibition of booze.

The anti-vice movement was about to succeed beyond its wildest dreams. Along with protecting the virtue and saving the souls of America's wayward sinners, the movement's success would also bring about an unintended result: an infusion of dirty money, black market commerce, and venality that would reshape American society and catapult the Irish American mobster into new realms of political influence, social ascendancy, and violence.

In the war for control of the underworld, the worst was yet to come.

delirium tremens or new clothes on an old dame

t is perhaps a minor quirk of history that Big Tim Sullivan, boss of what used to be the Five Points, benefactor of the Whyos, dispenser of shoes to the homeless, five-time assemblyman, state senator, and U.S. congressman, never made it to the glory days of Prohibition. He went crazy and died under mysterious circumstances in September 1913. The irony was that Big Tim, as much as anyone, had established the network of relationships that made it possible for the underworld to flourish during the years of "The Noble Experiment." Journalist Lincoln Steffens, in his seminal 1903 *McClure's* magazine series, "Shame of the Cities," used the word "System" for the first time with a capital "S" to describe Sullivan's creation. Today, it would be referred to as a racketeering enterprise and prosecuted under the Racketeer Influenced and Corrupt Organization (RICO) laws.

The whole enterprise was based on muscle and patronage; you used muscle to get yourself into a position of power, then used patronage to take care of those who got you there. If you were a card-carrying member of the tribe, it was a beautiful arrangement. At a time when wealthy industrialists like Commodore Cornelius Vanderbilt were quoted in the press saying "let the public be damned," street-level political bosses like Tim Sullivan were there to look out for the common man.

"I've never professed to be more than the average fella," Sullivan once told a crowd of adoring constituents at a political rally. "I was born in poverty, one of six children, four boys and two girls. The boys used to sleep in a three-quarter bed, not big enough for two, and the girls in a shakedown on the floor. Some nights there was enough to eat and some nights there wasn't. And our old mother used to sing to us at night and maybe it would be the next day that we would think she'd been singing but that she had gone to bed without anything to eat.

"That's the kind of people we come from and that's the kind of people who bore us down here. If we can help some boy or some father to another chance, we're going to give it to him. The thieves we have down here ain't thieves from choice. They are thieves from necessity and necessity don't know any law. They steal because they need a doctor for some dying one or they steal because there ain't any bread in the house for the children . . ."

Big Tim's business was politics, the mother's milk of patronage. His function was to bring solace to the hungry masses, and he was only as good as his ability to deliver. He once told a reporter from the *New York World*, "Every community has to have some man who can take the trouble to look out for the people's interests while the people are earning a living. It don't make any difference whether he's tall, short, fat, lean, or humpbacked with only half his teeth. If he's willing to work harder than anyone else, he's the fellow who will hold the job. . . . And so, after all, there isn't much to it to be a leader. It's just plenty of work, keep your temper or throw it away, be on the level and don't put on any airs, because God and the people hate a chesty man."

Feisty, fearless, a master at the fine art of accommodation, Big Tim was a born leader, but he never would have been able to build his uncontested empire were it not for Boss Richard Croker. Born in Blackrock, Ireland and raised in Manhattan's storied Gas House District, Croker followed Honest John Kelly as Grand Sachem of Tammany Hall after a youthful apprenticeship as a boxer and leader of the Fourth Avenue Tunnel Gang. At the age of thirty-three, he'd been arrested and tried for murder when a rival political operative was gunned down on election day. Croker denied his guilt, saying he never carried a gun and relied on his fists. He was acquitted of the crime.

As a political boss, Croker believed in letting his minions rule as they saw fit, as long as they delivered their district on election day. In Sullivan, Croker had a man whose reputation for getting out the vote was on a par with the legendary Hinky Dink Kenna of Chicago. The methods of Sullivan and other district bosses who followed his lead helped to make Croker a rich man. Although the position of Grand Sachem of Tammany Hall carried no salary, the former gang member from the Gas House District, through standard manipulation of city contracts and municipal largesse, became a multi-millionaire. In 1903, Croker retired to Ireland to breed race horses.

Tim Sullivan was the odds-on favorite to take over as the next boss of all bosses at Tammany, if he wanted the job. He didn't. Instead, he preferred to play the proverbial role of the man behind the man. In this case, the man was Charles F. Murphy, another product of the city's Gas House District, who took over following Croker and, as grand sachem, cast his shadow over city government for the next twenty-one years.

The Irish triumvirate of Kelly to Croker to Murphy that steered Tammany Hall from one century into another was good for Big Tim Sullivan. He got rich beyond his wildest dreams. By the time of his death, he was part-owner of the Sullivan-Considine vaudeville circuit, a lucrative national chain of more than forty theatres that included the Dewey Theatre on Fourteenth Street and the Gotham Theatre on 125th Street. He was co-owner of the Metropole Hotel on West Forty-third Street, a popular gathering place for the sporting crowd. He was also a partner in the incipient Nickelodeon business and made successful investments in entertainments at Coney Island, including Metropolitan Racetrack, and numerous saloons and athletic clubs.[1]

Although Sullivan's close relationship with Tammany's various grand sachems certainly enhanced his standing and paved the way for his business successes, his true power did not come from above. It came from below—from the streets. As the Lower East Side district that he represented evolved, Sullivan learned to speak a few words and phrases in Italian, Yiddish, and Cantonese. In perhaps the most ethnically diverse district in the entire United States, he made friends among saloon keepers, businessmen, shop-keepers, and mobsters of every nationality.

Primary among Big Tim's unofficial associates was the leader of the Five Points gang, Paul Kelly, an Italian immigrant whose real name was Paolo Antonini Vaccarelli.[2] The Five Pointers were a sprawling Italian gang that would give rise to some of the most noted mafiosi of the Prohibition era. In

---

1. In his years in public office, Big Tim Sullivan had some impressive legislative accomplishments as well. True to his reputation as a defender of common folk, he was a strong supporter of women's suffrage and organized labor, having fought successfully to limit the amount that women could work in factories in New York State to fifty-four hours a week. He also wrote into law a number of tenement reform bills and pioneered the state's first effort at gun control, the Sullivan Law of 1911, which is still on the books today.

2. Paul Kelly's use of a pseudonym was another example of what would become a common practice in the American underworld, that of Italians using Irish surnames. Among the most notable were New York mob boss Frank Costello (Francesco Castiglia), Chicago hitman Machine Gun Jack McGurn (Vincenzo DeMora), and Charles "Chuckie" English (Salvatore Inglese), right-hand man to Chicago mob boss Sam Giancana.

In *The Last Testament of Lucky Luciano*, mobster Luciano claims to have come up with the idea of giving his pal Francesco Castiglia an Irish name. He explained the benefits of such a practice this way: "When we got up to our ears in New York politics, it didn't hurt at all that we had an Italian guy with us with a name like Costello."

a testament to Big Tim's powers of accommodation, he was also on good terms with the Five Pointers' main rival, the Eastmans, a predominantly Jewish gang led by the indomitable Monk Eastman, a brawny, monosyllabic brute of a man. The gangsters helped Big Tim out on election day; in return, he used his influence with loyal magistrate judges to help them evade conviction. They were also allowed to run their various rackets free of harassment from local police. It was through his association with the Eastman gang that Sullivan established a relationship that would be his link with the city's bootlegging empire of later years.

Among Eastman's many minions was a fresh-faced, physically unimposing Jewish boy named Arnold Rothstein. Through Monk Eastman, Rothstein was introduced to Sullivan at his political headquarters on the Bowery.

"You're a fine-looking young Jew boy," said Big Tim.

"Thank you Mister Sullivan," responded Arnold.

"They'll be no 'mister' here," said the boss. "Call me Tim."

Barely sixteen years old, Rothstein worshipped the Tammany leader who seemed so magnanimous in his dispensation of favors. A talented billiards player and gambler with a good head for numbers, Rothstein became a regular at Sullivan's Hesper Club headquarters. He was particularly useful as a translator for the district's many Jewish immigrants who had just arrived from Poland and Austria. In later years, after Rothstein amassed a fortune through gambling profits, bookmaking, and loan-sharking, he would become a dominant financier of the underworld. He never hesitated to cite Big Tim Sullivan as his mentor, the man who made it all possible.

Given The Big Fella's stature for so many years, his decline and death was sad and ignominious. His decline started in 1912, when Sullivan was diagnosed with tertiary syphilis, an unfortunate disease for a man who often bragged over the years that he was clean as a whistle in his personal habits. He started to become forgetful and, at times, delusional; he was losing his mind. In the summer of 1913, he was institutionalized for a few weeks at a sanitarium, then moved to a house on Eastchester Road in the Bronx. It was necessary to assign several guards to watch over him. Occasionally Big Tim eluded his guards and frequented his old haunts along Broadway and the Bowery. Patrons would see a pajama-clad man in the corner of a saloon and say, "My God, that man looks like Tim Sullivan. Could it be? Is that Tim Sullivan?" And then, *poof*, in the bat of an eye, the man would be gone.

Finally, on a September night, Big Tim disappeared after exhausting his guards by playing cards with them all night. Later, the body of a fifty-year-old man was found on the rails near the Westchester freight yards. How it got there, nobody knew. An engineer on duty claimed that the man was already dead before he was run over by a train. The corpse lay in the morgue for a few days before it was identified as Timothy Daniel Sullivan.

Big Tim's funeral was attended by everybody who was anybody—three U.S. senators, a delegation of twenty members of the House of Representatives, justices of the New York Supreme Court, the Police Commissioner, the boss of Tammany Hall, not to mention assorted shoulder hitters, homeless people, and mobsters. They were sorry to see him go, but they might have been even sadder to learn that old Dry Dollar Sullivan would not be around to truly enjoy the fruits of his labors. In the following decade, Prohibition would transform the underworld, bringing in untold riches—and Big Tim, the man who helped lay the foundation, never even made it to Opening Day.

King of the Rum Runners

The Eighteenth Amendment, which prohibited the manufacture, sale, or consumption of alcoholic beverages, was ratified by the U.S. Congress on January 19, 1919. One year later, the laws that would regulate enforcement of the amendment went into effect. The laws became known as the Volstead Act, so named after Andrew Volstead, the Minnesota congressman who first introduced the legislation in the House of Representatives. The Volstead Act laid out the nitty-gritty details of Prohibition; it also spelled out the exceptions, requiring a government permit, which included sacramental wine, medicaments containing alcohol, hard liquor if prescribed by a physician (but not to exceed a pint per patient within any ten-day period), alcoholized patent medicines unfit for beverage, flavoring extracts, and syrups. The penalties for violations of the Act ranged from a five-hundred dollar fine for a first offense to a two-thousand dollar fine and five years of imprisonment for repeat offenders.

To the country's immigrants and their offspring—be they Irish, German, Scandinavian, Greek, Polish, Jewish, or Italian—the Volstead Act appeared to be part of a larger assault on life and liberty that began with the earliest formations of the Know-Nothing Movement and emerged, years later, as the Anti-Saloon League. If American born citizens who decried Prohibition tended to view it as a puritanical regression founded on the country's Protestant origins, the immigrants saw it as that and something more—a political movement that, behind the cloak of cultural purity and good Christian values, was determined to seize the levers of power and exterminate dissent through governmental mandate.

It took a while for the full effects of Prohibition to become known. Contrary to historical revisionism, the forces of organized crime did not immediately swoop down on an unsuspecting public. There was, initially, no system in place for importing illegal alcohol, manufacturing product, or distributing it through speakeasies and so on. That all came later, after it became abundantly clear that many Americans were determined to circumvent the law by distilling their own booze at home.

In the early months of Prohibition, U.S. cities abounded in shops that sold malt, hops, yeast, bottles, bottle-capping machines, rubber hosing, alcohol gauges, and other paraphernalia for home brewing. Economists estimated that the sums expended for brewing and distilling materials absorbed an inordinate portion of the country's household budgets. More alarming than the expense was the degree to which average Americans were willing to cross the line and engage in criminal activity. It was a new twist on family values, best exemplified in a popular rhyme of the era:

> *Mother's in the kitchen*
> *Washing out the jugs;*
> *Sister's in the pantry*
> *Bottling the suds;*
> *Father's in the cellar*
> *Mixing up the hops;*
> *Johnny's on the front porch*
> *Watching for the cops.*

The problem with home brewing was that the end product was usually horrible. If the corks didn't pop out of the bottle prematurely or the bottles didn't explode before their contents matured sufficiently to drink, the result was often a mud-brown liquid, stinking sourly of mash and tasting like drain cleaner. As for the effect, one amateur brewer was quoted as saying "After I've had a couple glasses, I'm terribly sleepy. Sometimes my eyes don't seem to focus, and my head aches. I'm not intoxicated, exactly, but merely feel as if I've been drawn through a knothole." Bathtub gin wasn't much better. Made with raw alcohol, water, glycerin, and juniper oil in a bathtub, its rancid taste was easily disguised in a fruity cocktail, but it often caused gastritis, heartburn, diarrhea, and other symptoms of acute alcohol poisoning.

Slowly but surely, the difficulties of manufacturing a palatable product at home made it clear to black market entrepreneurs that people were willing to venture forth and pay for the Real McCoy, whether it was legal or not.

Irishmen and Irish Americans were in a unique position to meet this demand. Many people of Irish descent saw the temperance movement and Prohibition as a direct assault on their very existence. The efforts of the Anti-Saloon League seemed to be aimed squarely at that aspect of Irish culture, which had for centuries revolved around the concept of the saloon as the central gathering place of the community, a place where political alliances were formed, stories passed on, friendships born, and old grudges either resolved or exacerbated. Furthermore, generations of Irish immigrants had made their living through the liquor business, which had been devastated by passage of the Volstead Act. Given this dual assault on life and liberty, many Irishman saw it as their cultural duty to violate both the spirit and the letter of Prohibition, especially when it became apparent that many citizens—from immigrants to upper crust WASPs—had no intention of abiding by what they perceived to be a silly and unenforceable law.

New York was by far the wettest city in the country, with a huge population of rich, poor, and working class who wanted to imbibe and were willing to pay for it. For those in the underworld who wanted to capitalize on the demand, the challenge was to devise a system for importing a top quality product, storing it, and delivering it to the consumer.

An early pioneer in this regard was a bespectacled, ruddy faced Irish American named William Vincent Dwyer. Born on Manhattan's Tenth Avenue at a time when the area was ruled by two prominent gangs, the Gophers and the Hudson Dusters, Dwyer first made a name for himself as a dock walloper and stevedore with the International Longshoremen's Association (ILA), a union that would prove to be a breeding ground for some of the toughest strong-arm men in the underworld. As a local bookmaker, Dwyer met and made friends with many underworld figures. He was neither a gang member nor a tough guy, but he was comfortable in the presence of violent men. More importantly, he knew how to cultivate muscle and use it to his advantage.

With his broad facial features and lumbering manner, Dwyer could have passed as a country farmer, but beneath the rather dull exterior was a true man of vision. Big Bill (as he would come to be known) saw from the beginning that the key to bootlegging was to develop a system whereby booze could be smuggled into the country free of harassment from Prohibition agents, the Coast Guard, and local police officials. Using money he had amassed as a supplier for a number of early garage-level bootlegging enterprises, Dwyer assembled a staff of businessmen and former gang members. He began to purchase what would eventually be a fleet of steel-plated speedboats equipped with machine guns, along with several seagoing rum ships. On shore, Dwyer's organization purchased and maintained warehouses, trucks, garages, cutting plants, and wholesale outlets.

From two midtown Manhattan offices, one in the Loew's State Building in Times Square, the other in the East River National Bank building on Forty-first Street, Dwyer threw his net far and wide. First, he established relationships with liquor suppliers in England, Canada, the Caribbean, and elsewhere. Then he devised a system for meeting liquor shipments at sea, off-loading the product, and running it ashore to islands and coastal cities, where it would be transferred by trucks to storage facilities in the New York area. From there, Dwyer shipped booze via Teamster convoys to many localities around the country, including Florida, New Orleans, Cincinnati, St. Louis, and Kansas City. In just a few short years, Big Bill Dwyer became the largest single distributor of illegal booze in the entire United States.

Using his uncanny ability to persuade otherwise upstanding citizens to join his operation, Dwyer established himself as overlord of Rum Row, a corridor of the outer-Atlantic where the transshipment of booze was a daily occurrence. His supremacy hinged on one major factor: He had the U.S. Coast Guard in his pocket. It was through a petty officer named Olsen that Big Bill found dozens of pliable coast guardsmen. Olsen would bring ashore fellow shipmates whom he felt might be open to a bribe. At Dwyer's expense, the guardsman would be treated to a night of revelry under the lights of Broadway; a sumptuous dinner, theatre tickets, a girl, and a hotel suite usually did the trick. By the time the bribe was tendered the following day, the guardsman was more than willing. An enlisted man, after all, only earned a grand total of $126 a month; a warrant officer at sea, $153. Dwyer might have offered ten times that much, if the guardsman was able to bring additional officers into the fold.

"Guardies" and other military men liked to drink, as did the police and even a few Prohibition agents. Big Bill understood this. His ability to bring coast guardsmen, coppers, and federal agents into the operation underscored a fact that would remain true throughout Prohibition's bloody thirteen-year run: None of it would have been possible without the acquiescence of a significant portion of America's law enforcement community.

Dwyer saw himself as a businessman, not a gangster. As the money flowed in, he diversified. He purchased hotels, race tracks, restaurants, nightclubs, and two Miami Beach gambling casinos. He established the New York and American Hockey clubs, virtually introducing professional ice hockey to the United States. He entertained regally at his suburban estate in Belle Harbor, Long Island, which he shared with his wife and five children.

No matter how wealthy Big Bill became, however, he could not resolve one vexing problem. He may have controlled Rum Row, and he had warehouses under armed guard to store his booze, but he was vulnerable when it came to the transportation of liquor via truck from one locale to another. In the early years of Prohibition, gangsters who had once been under the thumb of the political bosses started to become uppity. The profits from illegal booze were too good to pass up. Thus, America's backroads became lawless no-go zones as renegade gangs began hijacking liquor shipments, stealing the booze, and outletting it themselves.

To Dwyer, the problem was clear. Somebody had to organize the underworld. Big Bill realized he could not do this himself; he was not a tough guy or a gangster. He needed a major underworld partner that he could trust. An opportunity presented itself in early 1924 when two of Dwyer's shipments were hijacked in Upstate New York. The first incident was a warehouse robbery in which sixteen thousand dollars worth of booze was pilfered, the other a truck hijacking in White Plains in which Dwyer lost twenty-five thousand dollars worth of product. Dwyer put pressure on local cops to do something about it. As a result, a gang of five men were arrested for both robberies. Among this group of men was a name Dwyer recognized.

"Owney Madden!" he exclaimed upon seeing the name of the former Gopher gang leader, who once ruled the West Side neighborhood near where Dwyer was born and raised. "I'll be a son of gun," he said to a private detective on his payroll. "I thought Madden got sent away to Sing Sing on a murder rap."

"He did," said the shamus. "But he's out now and up to his old tricks."

Dwyer could have been angry and bayed for vengeance against this gang of hijackers who were costing him money. Instead, he waited quietly. A few weeks later, when the hijacking charges against Madden were dropped for lack of evidence, Big Bill Dwyer, King of the Rum Runners, put out the word to his minions: "Get me Owney Madden. I wanna talk to him. Tell him I got a business proposition we need to discuss."

Owney the Killer

In the many decades since Prohibition reenergized the underworld and ushered in a new era of American gangsterism, some of the trade's more notable practitioners have achieved a kind of immortality. Al Capone, Bugsy Siegel, Lucky Luciano, and Meyer Lansky are among those whose lives have been chronicled in countless books, television documentaries, and movies. Many of these men actively sought the limelight while they were alive. Capone, crude and verbose, held semiregular press conferences in which he pontificated on a variety of subjects, all for print and posterity. Siegel, sleek and paranoid, sought to immortalize himself through the white light of celluloid and wound up the most hoary of cliches: a failed Hollywood actor. At the time of his death in 1962, Luciano, a glorified pimp and dope pusher, had been at work on his autobiography in which he portrayed himself as a great American patriot. Lansky, a man with a lifelong persecution complex, achieved posthumous fame when he was reincarnated as "Hyman Roth," the character played by Lee Strasberg in the 1974 movie *Godfather, Part II*.

It is a backhanded tribute to Owen Victor Madden that he remains a shadowy figure many decades after his reign as arguably the preeminent mobster of the Prohibition era. True professional criminals who choose to traffic on the dark side of American society do not normally seek public acclaim. Being "the man behind the man" implies an inner confidence that allows for others to assert themselves in the arena of public aggrandizement while knowing all along that real power resides in the offstage hands of the marionette.

Owney Madden was a street punk and a killer who transformed himself into an underworld star. Feared and admired by those in the know, he was virtually unknown to the public at large. The American underworld was increasingly believed to be the exclusive domain of what in later years G-Men, prosecutors, and journalists tagged with a catchall moniker—La Cosa Nostra, which made the mafia famous, or infamous.

To Madden, fame was a whore to be kept at arm's length. This isn't to say he didn't have fun. He owned nightclubs, buried himself in U.S. currency, had a controlling interest in prizefighters and racehorses, bedded beautiful women, and squired himself around town as the Duke of the West Side. And yet, except for one youthful indiscretion, he never talked to the press and rarely allowed himself to be photographed, even though he had many famous friends. Among them were actor George Raft, whom he grew up with, and James Cagney, who modeled his tough-guy screen persona on Madden. Owney did occasionally court media types like gossip columnist Walter Winchell (whom he once bestowed with the gift of a Stutz Bearcat automobile) and Stanley Walker, city editor of the *Herald Tribune*, who later portrayed Owney as the Prince of Mobsters in his book *The Nightclub Era*. Generally, Madden cultivated these people so they would keep his name *out* of the media spotlight.

But what Madden did best was make money. After a youthful apprenticeship as a thug, he would eventually surpass Big Bill Dwyer as the most diversified bootlegger in the business and as such earn a place in history alongside Old Smoke Morrissey and King Mike McDonald atop the hypothetical Mount Rushmore of early Irish American racketeers.

Madden was born on Christmas Day in 1891 in Liverpool, England, to poor post-famine Irish parents, who had no property or social standing. The name Madden means hound in the original Gaelic. (Whether spelled Ó Madáin, O'Madden, O'Maddane, O'Madigane, or Madigan, it all comes from the same root: *Madach*.) Later in life, Owney would sometimes use an upper crust British accent, seeking to disguise his less-than-royal roots. To those who knew him well, it was a laughable ruse. He may have been born across the channel, but the look and inclinations of the Old Country clung to Owney like the smell of peat moss on a dewy morn in Connemara.

When Madden's father died in 1903, the boy was sent with his brother and sister to live with an aunt in New York City. The aunt lived in a cold-water tenement in a midtown Manhattan neighborhood known as Hell's Kitchen. Located on the West Side along the docks of the Hudson River between Fourteenth and Fifty-seventh streets (the neighborhood's boundaries would change somewhat in later years), Hell's Kitchen had supplanted the old Five Points district as the quintessential proving ground for young Irish ruffians—the kind of lovable punks who would one day be caricatured in Hollywood flicks like *The Dead End Kids* and *Angels with Dirty Faces*.

Hell's Kitchen was an immigrant neighborhood, mostly Irish, German, and Italian. The neighborhood's dominant physical features were the noisy Ninth Avenue elevated railway, which carried more passengers than any other line in the city, and the Hudson River Railroad, which carried freight and livestock along Eleventh Avenue, or Death Avenue as it was known to most West Siders because of the dust, congestion, and dangerous rail traffic.

In 1910, a privately funded report by a group of social workers painted a graphic picture of the area at its most wretched. Hell's Kitchen, they wrote, is characterized by "dull, square, monotonous ugliness, much dirt, and a great deal of despair." Their account included a description of what life was like for young kids, who spent most of their time on the bustling cobblestone streets hawking newspapers, fighting, picking pockets, swimming in the Hudson River, or flying pigeons from tenement rooftops.

By the time Owney Madden arrived in the Kitchen with his Liverpool Irish brogue, the area was under the sway of the Gopher Gang, so named because they often met in tenement basements. An amalgam of previous Hell's Kitchen gangs such as the Gorillas, the Parlor Mob, and the Tenth Avenue Gang, the Gophers were a predominantly Irish gang that sometimes clashed with the Hudson Dusters, who roamed below Fourteenth Street on the western fringe of Greenwich Village.[3]

The Gophers became famous not so much for their fights with other gangs, but for their head-to-head altercations with one another. In the decade following the turn of the century, the gang was known to be so turbulent and fickle that few of its leaders held the distinction for more than a few months. A few Gophers earned notoriety, such as Happy Jack Mullraney, who murdered Paddy the Priest for laughing at his facial disfigurement; Mallet Murphy, who routinely bludgeoned unruly customers in his saloon with a wooden mallet; and One Lung Curran, who started a fashion craze in Hell's Kitchen when he blackjacked a policeman, stole his overcoat, and delivered it to his girlfriend. The girlfriend wore it around town as if it were a prized mink. Soon all the other gang molls clamored for one of their own, and the coppers of Hell's Kitchen were seen walking around shorn of their overcoats.

If the Gophers became known for one particular criminal activity it was raiding and robbing the West Side railroad yards. In an era when freight trains were the preeminent mode of interstate transport for commercial goods, the railroad yards were a prime target for pilferage. It was here that young Owney Madden established a reputation as a fearless hoodlum ("courageous as a dock rat," one observer called him). He often led a brigade of Gophers on railroad boosting raids in which they broke into cargo shipments and made off with whatever they could—usually clothes, foodstuff, booze, and sometimes guns and ammo. Madden developed expert proficiency with all the tools of the trade: the revolver, blackjack, brass knuckles, and especially the lead pipe wrapped in newspaper, a favorite weapon of early twentieth century gangsters.

Through guile and daring more than brute force, Madden rose to become the recognized leader of the Gophers, which led to his constant arrests—fifty-seven times before all was said and done. On one early occa-

---

3. In the annals of Irish American gangdom, the Hudson Dusters merit special mention, though they were not exclusively an Irish gang. They got their name because most of the gang's members had a strong taste for cocaine. They were not ferocious fighters like the Gophers or early Irish gangs such as the Dead Rabbits or Ragen's Colts in Chicago. Mostly they were known as rabble-rousers and revelers in an incipient Greenwich Village bohemian lifestyle. According to author Luc Sante in his book *Low Life: Lures and Snares of Old New York*, "future Catholic Worker activist Dorothy Day, by her own admission, spent a great deal of time partying with [the Dusters] in her salad days, as did many others, including Eugene O'Neill."

sion when he was pinched, Owney bragged to a police reporter that he'd never worked an honest day in his life and never intended to. When the reporter asked him to jot down a record of his daily routine, the teenage gang boss obliged. It is the only firsthand account of his life that Madden ever gave to the press.

> *Thursday*—Went to a dance in the afternoon. Went to a dance at night and then a cabaret. Took some girls home. Went to a restaurant, and stayed there until Friday morning.
> *Friday*—Spent the day with Freda Horner [his girlfriend]. Looked at some fancy pigeons. Met some friends in a saloon early in the evening, and stayed with them until five o'clock in the morning.
> *Saturday*—Slept all day. Went to a dance in the Bronx late in the afternoon, and to a dance on Park Avenue at night.
> *Sunday*—Slept until three o'clock. Went to a dance in the afternoon and to another in the same place at night. After that I went to a cabaret, and stayed there almost all night.

Owney's account of his routine was highly selective, of course, with no mention of criminal activity or violence for which his gang was known. The cops had nicknamed him "the Killer" by the time he was eighteen, and it wasn't for his dashing good looks or talents on the dance floor.

He killed his first man at the age of fourteen. An Italian merchant near Owney's home on Tenth Avenue was bludgeoned with a pipe. Numerous witnesses saw Madden discard the murder weapon and flee the scene. Owney was arrested, but then released when the witnesses adhered to the neighborhood's code of silence and refused to testify. A year later, he was at it again. After a dispute over a girl with a store clerk named Willie Henshaw, Madden chased Henshaw onto a Ninth Avenue trolley car. In the middle of the day, before numerous onlookers, Owney shot Willie and fled.

This time, detectives were sure they had Madden. There were multiple eye-witnesses, and before expiring at the hospital Henshaw himself identified Owney Madden as his killer. The cops threw a dragnet over the West Side. Owney was eventually spotted. After leading the police on a wild chase across the rooftops of Tenth Avenue, Owney the Killer was apprehended.

But by the time the cocky hood was brought into court a few weeks later, the witnesses against him had vanished, the state's case collapsed, and the charges were dismissed.

Beating criminal cases was one thing, but when living in the underworld where encounters with rival gangsters were commonplace, events had a way of arranging their own version of justice or retribution, known on the street as payback. It was just such a confluence of events that took place on November 6, 1912, when Owney Madden's charmed existence took a dramatic turn for the worse at the Arbor Dance Hall on Fifty-second Street and Seventh Avenue. Here he was surrounded by a hit squad of eleven gunmen, some of whom were members of the Hudson Dusters.

"Come on, youse yellow-bellied Dusters," snarled Owney, reaching for his revolver. "Who'd you punks ever bump off?"

The sound of gunfire chased the patrons out of the dance hall. By the time police and an ambulance arrived, Madden was sprawled on the floor with a half-dozen bullets in him.

"Who did it?" asked a detective.

Barely conscious, Madden replied "It's nobody's business but mine who put these slugs in me. The boys'll take care of them."

Madden was rushed to New York Hospital and miraculously survived.

In less than a week, three of the eleven suspected shooters had been bludgeoned, shot, or stabbed to death in various locations around Hell's Kitchen.

Another pitfall of being a gang leader was the constant pretenders to the throne. While Owney Madden convalesced from the assassination attempt under armed guard at the hospital, Patsy Doyle, a minor member of the Gophers, declared that he was now the boss. Doyle's motives were partly based on jealousy, for Freda Horner, Madden's sometime girlfriend, had once been his lady.

When Madden heard what Patsy was saying, he decided to engage in a preemptive strike. A day after Owney was discharged from the hospital, Doyle was found in the street almost blackjacked to death. A couple of weeks later, Patsy retaliated by blackjacking, knifing, and shooting one of Madden's cherished underlings.

The Madden-Doyle Wars continued for many months, with periodic rumbles and shootings. In November 1914, when Madden's primary hangout, the Winona Social Club, was raided and trashed by Patsy and a few of his thugs, Madden had reached his limit. Together with Freda Horner and Margaret Everdeane, another gang moll Patsy was sweet on, Madden devised an elaborate scheme for luring his nemesis to a saloon on Forty-first Street and Eighth Avenue. On the night of November 28, the plot went down exactly as planned. Patsy Doyle met Margaret Everdeane and, much to his astonishment, was shot multiple times by two anonymous gunmen. He died in the gutter in front of the saloon.

Although Owney Madden was nowhere in sight when the shooting took place, the district attorney's office was finally able to build a case against the Gopher boss as planner and instigator of Patsy Doyle's demise. Their case was built around two squealers, stool pigeons, stoolies, rats, or cheese eaters—choose your epithet. In the end, it was the women who turned on Owney Madden. After considerable cajoling and threatening by the prosecution, Freda Horner and Margaret Everdeane testified against Madden at trial. He went down for the count—sentenced to ten to twenty years at Sing Sing, which was slightly less than the two shooters received. At the same time, the law went after other members of the gang. New York Police Department records show that by the end of the year, sixteen members of Owney's gang were in jail on a wide assortment of charges. The Gophers were no more.

Madden did his time quietly. He even got released early for good behavior. In January, 1923, after spending eight years behind bars, he was a free man. Now in his early twenties, Owney had no desire to return to his life as a glorified street thug; he yearned for greater things. But he still held tight to the principle that he would never work an honest day in his life and inevitably drifted back into a life of crime.

He first went to work for a taxi company. At the time, the taxi business in New York City was in the midst of a fiercely competitive war, much like the violent newspaper wars in Chicago a decade earlier. The Killer was put to work as a blackjacker and strong-arm man. Owney hated the work; he no longer had a taste for violence, but was still trapped in the old ways. He quit the taxi business and put together a small gang. With Prohibition in full swing, they began hijacking illegal booze shipments. Although they were fully armed, violence was a rarity. Usually the booze was turned over without a fight. There was so much supply flowing into New York at the time that it just wasn't worth dying over.

Hijacking, however, was small potatoes, a hand-to-mouth existence that was beneath the image Owney Madden had of himself. He wanted to oversee his own bootlegging operation. But he had missed the early years of Prohibition and was at a disadvantage in terms of capital and influence. He needed a leg up, which is exactly what he got when he heard that none other than Big Bill Dwyer, King of the Rum Runners, was looking to talk with him.

They first met at Big Bill's office at the Loew's State Building in the heart of Times Square. Madden, lean and feral, was a child of the streets; Dwyer, circumspect and well-fed, had risen from the docks and turned the country's desire for booze into his own private empire. Both had been raised on tenth Avenue on the West Side of Manhattan. They knew each other's reputation and precisely what they had to offer one another. While there is no existing account of the specifics of this meeting, the results have been borne out in the bloody annals of underworld history.

"You got a problem," Owney would have told Big Bill. "Gangsters been picking off your trucks like sitting ducks and what are you gonna do about it."

"That's why I called you here."

"You gotta organize the shooters and the cherry-pickers, not to mention the bulls and the pols."

"You're right. I need the hijackings to stop. I need a place to make my own brew right here in the big city, protected by the Tiger and the coppers. And I need outlets—speakeasies, nightclubs, you name it."

"You need a lot, my friend."

"Are you with me you Liverpool mick bastard?"

"Give me one good reason why."

"I can make you rich."

Here, a rare and knowing smile would have creased Owney's lips: "Pal, you and me, we're like two peas in a pod."

Thus was born what would be known forever after as the New York Irish Mob.

When New York Was Really Irish

Under the aegis of Big Bill Dwyer, Owney Madden went about organizing the underworld. Since money was no object, he started with the most costly proposition: the opening of a massive brewery right in the middle of the city. This way, the Combine, as the expanding Madden-Dwyer partnership would become known, would not have to worry about highway robbers; they could control the flow of booze from the source to the marketplace.

In early 1924, the Phoenix Cereal Beverage Company opened for business at Twenty-sixth Street and Tenth Avenue, not far from where Dwyer and Madden had both been raised. A huge red-brick building that took up the entire block, the Phoenix had formerly been home to Clausen & Flanagan Brewery, which had tried to sell near beer, a diluted product with minimal alcohol content that was legal under the Volstead Act. Nobody wanted near beer; they wanted the real thing, which the Phoenix brewery churned out in high volume.

Using a government patent that had been secured by the brewery's previous owners, the Phoenix operated under the guise of government authorization while producing an illegal product called Madden's No. 1. You could buy Madden's No. 1 by the barrel or by the bottle, with a label that had a sketch rendering of the brewery and surrounding area—Hell's Kitchen in all its glory. Apparently, nobody felt the need to hide anything. The bootleggers took care of Tammany. Tammany, in return, took care of the Prohibition agents and made well-placed contributions to the Policeman's Benevolent Association for protection. The Combine hummed like a well-oiled machine.

Madden, the former Gopher boss, formed a number of key alliances that made it all happen. He had a friend from his brief foray in the taxi business named Larry Fay. A scrawny, horse-faced Irish American from Long Island, Fay became a major player in the underworld after hitting a legendary hundred-to-one shot at Belmont Race Track. With the proceeds, Fay bought into the taxi business. He owned a large fleet of cabs and had hired a number of West Side hoodlums—including Owney Madden—to stamp out the competition. At Madden's behest, Fay was brought into the Combine. His primary role was to establish a number of popular nightclubs that would become the primary outlets for Madden's No. 1, along with bootleg rum, scotch, vodka, and champagne smuggled into the country via Big Bill's mastery of Rum Row.

As a club impresario and man-about-town, Larry Fay fancied himself a bon vivant. To compensate for his homely visage, he developed an abiding passion for fancy duds. When he returned from a trip to Europe in 1923, he allegedly brought with him trunks filled with Bond Street creations that were made for him by London's most fashionable tailors. His personal style tended toward loud neckties and gaudy suits, under which he almost always wore a bullet-proof vest. He took great pride in his flashy fashion sense; a newspaper reporter who once referred to him in print as the "Beau Brummel of Broadway" received a case of liquor and an invitation to eat and drink on the cuff for six months at one of his clubs.

The first of Fay's storied establishments was Fay's Follies, a nightclub he'd opened all on his own in 1921. His most celebrated club came three years later when, with Madden and Dwyer as silent partners, he opened El Fay at 107 West Fifty-fourth Street, which quickly became famous as the home of Texas Guinan, a bawdy and highly popular cabaret singer and entertainer who was the precursor to Mae West.

The success of El Fay helped turn smart-talking Larry Fay into a Broadway archetype, the sort of character immortalized in the writings of Damon Runyon, most notably in the Runyon-inspired play and movie, *Guys and Dolls*. Fay had the magic touch. As Prohibition progressed and the money rolled in, he married the Roaring Twenties version of a trophy wife, a beautiful Broadway showgirl named Evelyn Crowell. He went on to open many other clubs besides El Fay and was one of multiple partners in the Silver Slipper, the Rendezvous, Les Ambassadeurs, and, of course, the Cotton Club, where Duke Ellington and his Orchestra resided as the house band, introducing some of the most complex and enduring compositions in the history of jazz music.[4]

Nightclubs and speakeasies such as these were the most obvious by-product of the booze-fueled Roaring Twenties, but the most important element that kept the Combine running smoothly was something no one was supposed to see: the protection racket. Protection was purchased for a price—cold, hard cash usually stuffed into envelopes and surreptitiously exchanged between grubby hands under a desk or table, in a dark alleyway, or through contributions to a special police widow's fund. Protection usually started at the top and worked its way down. The Combine delivered the money directly to the ward boss or district leader, whose office dispersed the funds to the necessary judges and precinct captains, who in turn slipped the designated denomination to a lieutenant or shift commander, who then greased the palm of the appropriate patrolman. A judicious offer of an occasional bottle or case of booze to said lieutenant or captain was also recommended, since the boys in blue were known to have among the wettest wickets in town. In return, the Phoenix Cereal Beverage Company operated unmolested by law enforcement and Combine-controlled speakeasies, nightclubs, and dance halls stayed open for business. The booze flowed freely.

More than anyone else, the man who greased the wheel for Madden and Dwyer and made the Combine into a formidable operation was a white-haired, grandfatherly Irish American named James J. Hines, powerful leader of the 11th Assembly District on Manhattan's Upper West Side. A protégé of the late Big Tim Sullivan, Hines was the Big Fella's natural successor as the System's primary conduit between Tammany Hall and underworld forces. During the years of Prohibition, Hines would become the ultimate man behind the man, an iron-willed district leader and devoted family man who went to church every Sunday, then on Monday broke bread with the most notorious mobsters of his day. While serving as political fixer and bag

---

4. Larry Fay's impressive string of luck ran out shortly after midnight on New Years Day, 1933, when he was shot dead by Edward Maloney, a disgruntled employee, while standing in front of the Casa Blanca nightclub. Maloney, a doorman at the club, was angry that his pay and hours had been cut. Reportedly, it was the first time in six months that the forty-four-year-old Fay had not worn his bullet-proof vest.

man for the mob, he also played a significant role in the election of mayors, senators, and at least two presidents.

There was nothing in the appearance or demeanor of Jimmy Hines that would lead you to believe he was an acolyte of the underworld. On a good day he resembled the actor Spencer Tracy, with reddish-brown hair that had gone snowy white and a face that could be alternately kind and craggy. Although he was born on 116th Street and Eighth Avenue in a part of the city that would become known as White Harlem, he sometimes spoke with a trace of the Old Country in his voice, an affectation that was intended to underscore his historical connection to Tammany's Hibernian roots.

He began his career as a blacksmith, a trade he inherited from his father, who was also an occasional election captain in the 11th Assembly District. When his father became ill, Jimmy, just seventeen at the time, took over his father's blacksmith business and also his duties as political canvasser in the district. Hines was exposed early to a system in which ward politics relied heavily upon the services of gangsters to win elections.

In 1907 Hines threw his own hat into the ring by running for alderman. He won easily. Three years later, he challenged the popular incumbent district leader. During a campaign that was described as a reign of terror because of the violent tactics of both Hines and his opponent, Hines emerged victorious. Soon after the election, he formed the Monongahela Democratic Club, an outgrowth of the James J. Hines Association, from which he practiced the typical Irish version of Tammany politics—turkeys for the needy on Thanksgiving, donations to Catholic charities, and the dispensing of favors for votes. His Democratic club also became the basis for his patronage and boodling operations. With his brother Philip, Jimmy started a trucking company that, despite its limited work history, managed to be awarded many lucrative contracts on city and state construction projects. Hines also rented out the top floor of his political clubhouse for commercial gambling purposes to a young, up-and-coming Jewish gangster named Arnold Rothstein.

Despite Hines' power and growing popularity at the district level, which assured his reelection for the next twenty-five years, he appeared to have a scant future in citywide elective office. An unimpressive public speaker with none of the galvanizing personality characteristics of Big Tim Sullivan or Chicago's Bathhouse John Coughlin, Hines, to use a well-worn phrase, spoke softly and carried a big stick. He was the sort of man who, in a crowded room, liked to whisper behind a hand or in a person's ear, making his wishes known with a simple nod or gesture. If anything, he displayed his power by maintaining an air of mystery and inscrutability—unless you got on his bad side, in which case friends suddenly became enemies, municipal inquiries fell on deaf ears, and doors slammed in your face with merciless authority.

Madden and Dwyer met Hines often, either at Big Bill's Times Square office or at the Monongahela Club, where the district boss presided like a tribal chieftain. Constituents of all ages and denominations were free to enter Jimmy Hines' club, with complaints, suggestions, and requests. If they saw Owney "the Killer" Madden seated with their district leader, so much the better. In the World According to Tammany, having a gangster at the elbow of the ward boss was not a bad thing; it enhanced the boss's reputation and made good political sense. Politics, after all, was the raw meat that fed the beast. George Washington Plunkitt, the bard of Tammany and an early inspiration for Hines's career, said it best: "As a rule, [a district leader] has no business or occupation other than politics. He plays politics every day and night in the year, and his headquarters bears the inscription, 'Never Closed.' "

Money was funneled into the coffers of Alderman Hines by the leading lights of the Combine, and that became the source of his power. Hines was the money man who took care of the cops, judges, prosecutors, and bail bondsmen; he made the world go 'round.

With Dwyer, Madden, Fay, and Hines coalescing all the elements of what would eventually become known as organized crime in New York, it would not be inaccurate to say that, in these early years of Prohibition, the town was run by the Irish Mob. The high seas, the streets, the police department, and the city's political universe were all controlled by the Combine. But it was at every level of the underworld that one could see the shadow of the shamrock. There was Vannie Higgins, second only to Big Bill among rum runners and bootleggers. Higgins was the mob boss of Brooklyn, with speedboats and his own airplane, from which he controlled the flow of booze throughout Long Island. Irish Americans also predominated the strong-arm rackets. A young gunman from Philadelphia named Jack "Legs" Diamond was making a name for himself as a bodyguard for Arnold Rothstein and as an inveterate bootlegger. Also, an Irish-born orphan and teenager named Vincent Coll was fast becoming the era's most feared hired gunman. Along with his brother Peter, he was employed by Jewish gangsters, Italian mafiosi, and Irish alike.

Then there was the NYPD, which had been an Irish patronage racket for at least four decades. Before Prohibition, only saloons that wished to operate beyond licensed hours had been required to pay tribute to New York's Finest. Now any place that served liquor had to come up with the green.

Inspectors, captains, and vice cops were raking in money; even an ordinary patrolman who worked in a prominent bootlegging neighborhood like Hell's Kitchen, where many booze storage warehouses were located, could turn a nice dollar. Tough waterfront precincts, once seen largely as punishment precincts, were now highly desirable because that's where the smuggled booze came ashore.

Finally, there was Tammany Hall, which was even more Irish than the police department. The Celtic clan system that had been transplanted from pre-famine Ireland and reinvented in New York, Chicago, and elsewhere around the United States had finally reached its apotheosis in the Big Apple. Of the city's thirty-six wards, more than half were run by bosses of Irish descent, with numerous other district leaders, precinct captains, and election officials who were part of a tradition that stretched back to the earliest and most poverty-stricken days of Irish immigration. In terms of actual numbers, the Irish were a much smaller percentage of the overall population than they were in the 1860s, 1870s, and 1880s, but their power had grown. Years of dedication and allegiance to the democratic party system had paid off in an era of ascendancy—made all the more giddy by an infusion of Prohibition cash that dwarfed the proceeds of earlier vice rackets like organized gambling and prostitution.

Even with so many sons and daughters of Erin involved in the daily workings of the Combine, it was never meant to be exclusively an Irish operation. Madden, Dwyer, and the others had the foresight to realize that the underworld in New York could never operate as a hermetically sealed ethnic universe. Back in the days when the Dead Rabbits, Plug Uglies, or Kerryonians were first establishing a foothold in the Five Points, certain gangs had been Irish-only, but Prohibition was different. Prohibition was about capitalism, not ethnic solidarity. You could have an Irish American brain trust, but if you hoped to control the system and dominate the market, you had to create working relationships with every group. The genius of Tammany Hall had always been its ability to incorporate WASP, Jewish, Polish, and Italian representatives, giving everyone their piece of the pie. Using the Tammany approach, the Combine expanded to incorporate many non-Irish gangster pioneers: Jews like Rothstein, Meyer Lansky, Waxey Gordon, and Dutch Schultz (born Arthur Flegenheimer, a German Jew); African Americans like Bumpy Johnson and Madam Stephanie St. Clair in Harlem; Italians such as Lucky Luciano, Joe Bonnano, and Francesco Castiglia, born in Naples and raised in East Harlem.

The Combine enlisted the services of these men at the highest levels. In fact, when Big Bill Dwyer was finally arrested, charged, and convicted on bootlegging charges in 1925–1926, it was Francesco Castiglia who stepped in and took over the daily runnings of Big Bill's operation. That's when Castiglia changed his name to Frank Costello, a Hibernian name that was perhaps more acceptable to the Combine's less ethnically enlightened Irish distributors. Castiglia/Costello oversaw the operations of the Combine without a hitch until Big Bill was released early for good behavior (after serving thirteen months of a two-year sentence) and returned to the city to pick up right where he left off.

The ethnic diversity that kept the Combine running smoothly permeated the era. Police Commissioner Grover Whelan estimated there were 32,000 speakeasies in New York, and most were remarkably democratic in their clientele. As long as you could pay up and were savvy enough to know where the hot new establishments were located, you could gain entrance. All classes and many races mixed. Prohibition brought about a kind of ethnic interaction that might not have happened otherwise, with Greeks, Irish, Swedes, Italians, WASPs, and Jews socializing and doing business like never before: an antiestablishment, brotherhood of man bound together by their hatred of the Volstead Act.[5]

The Combine may have had ethnic variety in its operations and customer base, but it nonetheless gave off an aura that manifested seven tough decades of Irish upward mobility. After fighting and clawing their way through the worst kinds of poverty and discrimination, the Irish in New York—and many other big U.S. cities—had finally arrived at a place of social desirability. The Irish American bootlegger, in particular, with his tough-guy demeanor, quick patter, and devil-may-care attitude toward the law came to signify the way many American men wanted to see themselves. The street slang, clothing styles, and attitudes of the Irish hoodlum became popular in the way that rap and hip hop would many decades later; this trend was an opportunity for middle-class Americans, if there was such a thing in the 1920s, to adopt the look and style of the outlaw underclass.

It would be a few years before the phenomenon was codified and made explicit in the movies of Jimmy Cagney, but the desire for a drink and the surreptitious, exciting world of the illicit speakeasy had already defined a

---

5. Not everyone was welcome equally. The Chinese were excluded. African Americans were bullied into becoming part the Combine; in Harlem, local gangsters were forced to turn over a piece of their lucrative policy rackets or risk being murdered. Blacks had their own speakeasies, but when it came to the downtown speaks or establishments like the Cotton Club, located on 149th Street in Harlem, they were refused entry as patrons.

generation. The mixture of glamour and danger that fueled this world was immortalized forever by F. Scott Fitzgerald in *The Great Gatsby*. In the novel, as in real life, the bootlegger was viewed as a daring figure who took chances to deliver a service to the public. He may have been dangerous and may even have been a killer, but he was also devilishly attractive. The public face for this character, to most people, was an Irish one.

The city's love affair with this Irish gadfly persona reached a new pinnacle in 1926, when Jimmy Walker, a smart-talking former Tin Pan Alley songwriter, was elected mayor. Walker was not a bootlegger, but he was an Irish Catholic politician who liked to drink and hang out in Broadway nightclubs, where he shook hands and imbibed with such underworld leading lights as Owney Madden, Larry Fay, and Arnold Rothstein. Beau James, as Walker was known in some circles, was a product of the Tammany Machine, a Greenwich Village boyo who knew how the game was played and wasn't about to rock the boat. He professed his desire to see Prohibition repealed and appointed a police commissioner who wouldn't be too hard on the mobsters. By most indications, the general public approved.

With the Combine in power and Walker running the show, the city sang with an Irish lilt and walked with the cocky strut of a bantam rooster. Thanks in part to the underworld, Paddy had finally arrived. As never before in the city's history, it was swell to be a mick.

Diamond in the Rough

While there may have been—out of necessity—a semblance of diversity in its operations, the Combine was not a democracy. At night the clubs were thronged and people danced the lindy-hop and got tight, but the daily workings of the machine were brutal and dictatorial. Every speakeasy and bootlegging operation was connected. Like it or not, you sided with the Combine and succumbed to its commercial dictates or you went for the proverbial one-way ride and wound up dead in a ditch.

Independent operators were forbidden. The only exceptions were former members of the Combine who had branched off into ancillary rackets like the racing wire or local neighborhood scams that flew below the radar—the theory being that everything eventually trickled back into the organization. Bootlegging, however, was sacrosanct. From distilling to distributing to sales, anyone who ventured into any aspect of rum running, bootlegging, or the parsing of alcohol had to answer directly to the Combine. A few saloon keepers in, say, New Jersey or Upstate New York thought they could defy the mob because of their distance from Manhattan. They were sadly mistaken.

The long arm of the Combine reached from Southern New Jersey all the way to the Canadian border, and everywhere in between.[6]

Still, there was the occasional challenger.

One man who began to rock the boat as early as the mid-1920s was a former member of the organization. Jack "Legs" Diamond, born and raised in Southwest Philadelphia, took on the Combine as no one had before—and therefore blazed a trail across many a tabloid headline: "The Most Picturesque Racketeer in the Underworld," the *New York American* called him; "Most Publicized of Public Enemies," declared the *Post*; "Most Shot-At Man in America," surmised the *Mirror*. The newspapers loved Diamond because of what he represented: a true renegade who took on the establishment, but in this case the underworld establishment.

In *Legs*, first published in 1975, Pulitzer Prize-winning author William Kennedy captured Diamond's appeal by presenting his story through the eyes of a fictional criminal defense attorney. Like many journalists and average citizens, the fictional attorney viewed the bootlegger as "not merely the dude of all gangsters, the most active brain in the New York underworld, but as one of the truly new American Irishmen of his day; Horatio Alger out of Finn McCool and Jesse James, shaping the dream that you could grow up in America and shoot your way to glory and riches. . . .

"Why he was a pioneer . . . He advanced the cause of joyful corruption and vice. He put the drop of the creature on the parched tongues of millions. He filled the pipes that pacify the troubled, loaded the needles that puncture anxiety bubbles. He helped the world kick the gong around, Jack did."

Mostly, Legs Diamond dodged bullets; he shot people and was shot at. There would be five separate attempts on his life, all bloody near-misses until the last one, an intimate minimalist affair (just three bullets) that left no room for error. Thanks in part to Kennedy's masterpiece, a Broadway musi-

---

6. One of the more important regional offshoots of the Combine was based in Providence, Rhode Island and overseen by Daniel L. Walsh, a former Pawtucket hardware store clerk who became one of the most successful bootleggers of the era. Rhode Island was the most Catholic state in the country and virulently anti-Prohibition. Because of the state's craggy shoreline, it was an ideal location for offloading booze shipments from Rum Row. Danny Walsh was frequently in New York City on business, which fueled speculation that bootlegging on the East Coast was controlled by a consortium known as the Big Seven. Rumored to be among the Big Seven were at least four Irishmen: Walsh, Dwyer, Madden, and a millionaire banker and shipping magnet from Boston named Joseph P. Kennedy, of whom we will learn more in a later chapter.

cal based on his life, and other examples of posthumous hagiography, Legs lives on as perhaps the most well known of all Irish American mobsters.

His beginnings were inauspicious. In the Kensington mill district of Philadelphia, where Diamond was born and raised, the Irish had relocated from the filthy river wards in hopes of a higher-level of subsistence. The saga of the Irish in Philly was similar to that in New York, Boston, Chicago, New Orleans, and elsewhere. The anti-Catholic Know-Nothing Movement began in rural Pennsylvania and migrated to the City of Brotherly Love. Church burnings, the destruction of Irish shantytowns, and discrimination in every aspect of city life (particularly housing and employment) were commonplace. Irish Catholic protection gangs sprang up, most notably the Schuylkill Rangers and the Fenians, who clashed with Protestant gangs, predictably so on election day.

Diamond's parents had come from Ireland, where they first met at a public dance in Kilrush, County Clare and married two years later. In autumn of 1891, with the Old Country mired in its perennial post-famine cycle of food shortages and joblessness, they moved to Philadelphia, where they first settled with relatives of John Diamond. Six years later, in a cramped three-family house of their own at 2350 East Albert Street, their son Jack was born. Two years later they had another boy, Edward.

Diamond's father was not exactly a distinguished member of the community. A short, frail man who frequently coughed from an unknown lung condition, he bounced from one menial job to another, working as a short-order cook, a helper in a carriage-maker's shop, and a packer in a coffee-roasting plant. His greatest achievement was becoming a committeeman of the 25th Assembly District, which encompassed the 31st Ward. John Diamond found his calling as a Tammany-style election official, until a dark day in December 1913 when his wife died suddenly from a bacterial infection and high fever. After weeks of mourning, Diamond gathered his meager belongings together and moved his two boys to Brooklyn, where they would stay with relatives.

As motherless teenagers with little adult supervision, the Diamond brothers soon fell into the same kind of trouble they had first experienced in Philly, where they had hung out with a group of young toughs known as the Boiler Gang. Of the two brothers, Eddie was the better fighter. Jack, lean, gangly, and weighing only 145 pounds on a good day, was more concerned about his hair and clothes than about winning fights. He was, however, inventive and daring in his early criminal exploits, which set him apart as a leader.

Jack Diamond's first arrest came at the age of seventeen, when he got caught breaking into a Brooklyn jewelry store. He was sent to an upstate reformatory, where he was institutionalized for one year. Rehabilitation was not the goal; juvenile reformatories of the early twentieth century were medieval throwbacks to another time, rife with brutal forms of punishment and backward social thinking. Hidden behind red-brick walls and closed off to the public, these underfunded extensions of the penal system would play a role in producing some of the most disturbed and violent gangsters of the era.

Diamond's criminal record shows that, in the few short months following his release from reform school, he was arrested six times, mostly for burglary. He managed to stay out of jail, and even found time to get married to an attractive Broadway waitress named Florence Williams. They moved into a cheap cold-water flat on the West Side. By all accounts, the marriage was tempestuous; Jack drank while Flo got angry and threw things. She was once heard yelling "I'll pray for you, Jack. I'll pray for you, you no good tramp."

"Take me or leave me," answered Diamond. "I do what I want."

The marriage only lasted a few months, which was just as well, since in 1918 Diamond got drafted into the U.S. Army.

Not surprisingly, Diamond's time in the military was a disaster. His budding antiauthoritarian tendencies were exacerbated to the point where, after less than a year in the service, he tried to go AWOL. Armed with a .45-caliber pistol and carrying a sack of flare guns that he intended to sell, he managed to get by the main gate at Fort Dix but was caught a half-mile down the road. While struggling to get away, he smacked a sergeant with an iron bar and injured two other soldiers. Charged with desertion, along with several other crimes, he was sentenced to Fort Jay and then Governor's Island in New York Harbor. An attempt to escape landed him a sentence of three to five years of hard labor at the Federal Penitentiary in Fort Leavenworth, Kansas.

"No matter what happens, they'll never make me serve the full sentence," said Diamond as they carted him away.

He turned out to be right. In the spring of 1921, newly elected President Warren G. Harding, in a postwar gesture of goodwill, unexpectedly pardoned more than two dozen federal prisoners, including a troublesome though seemingly insignificant former buck private named Jack Diamond.

With his new lease on life, Diamond returned to New York and immediately plugged into the city's thriving Prohibition underworld. He and his brother Eddie fell in with a crew based on the Lower East Side that included a young burglar and narcotics dealer named Lucky Luciano. For a time, they worked in the organization of Vannie Higgins, the bootlegger boss of Brooklyn and Long Island. Diamond was arrested on an almost weekly basis, but was provided legal representation by the Combine and rarely spent more than a few days in jail. He began to partake of the city's vibrant nightlife, especially the dance halls. Some believe that he acquired the nickname "Legs" because of his talents on the dance floor, while others claim he had the name from adolescence, and it referred either to his running abilities or simply the fact that he had long, gangly legs. As with the origins of most underworld monikers, it is difficult to separate the fact from fiction.[7]

Sometime in early 1922, Lucky Luciano took Diamond to Lindy's, a Broadway diner and famous hangout for actors, writers, and sporting men. It was there that Luciano introduced Jack to Arnold Rothstein: "Jack, meet The Big Bankroll. Mister Rothstein—Legs Diamond."

Legs knew all about Rothstein, who had been weaned at the knee of the late, great Big Tim Sullivan. Arnold had come a long way since his days as Dry Dollar's Yiddish translator and gofer at the Hesper political clubhouse on the Lower East Side. Known variously as the Big Bankroll, Mister Big, and The Brain, Rothstein was considered a financial wizard with billions of dollars at his disposal. Among other things, he was rumored to have been the money man behind the fixing of the 1919 World Series, known as the Black Sox Scandal, though his role was never proved.

The Brain looked Legs up and down and said "You look like a mick."

Said Legs, "Could be. Or I could be a yid. Take your pick."

"Hey kid, you lookin' for work?"

"Hell yeah," said Diamond.

"Good. Go say hello to Fatty Walsh. You'll be workin' with him."

Tom "Fatty" Walsh, Rothstein's chief bodyguard, was seated at an adjoining booth. Legs nodded hello to the chubby Walsh. From that point on, he was part of Rothstein's entourage.

Legs quickly proved his value to Rothstein; he enforced the will of the underworld financier and reaped the benefit. He was on the payroll but free to

7. The legend that the nickname Legs was a reference to Diamond's dancing abilities is probably attributable to *The Rise and Fall of Legs Diamond*, a B-movie released in 1962 in which the gangster is absurdly portrayed as a professional ballroom dancer. Directed by Budd Boeticher, the movie has some entertainment value but bears little resemblance to the historical record. The misrepresentation was further compounded in the 1990s with the staging of a big budget Broadway musical supposedly based on Diamond's life, in which he was once again fictitiously portrayed as a song-and-dance man.

commit crimes with his gang, which he did frequently, most notably as a robber of minks, jewels, and cars. All that was expected in return was that he unstintingly protect Rothstein. His value in this regard was made abundantly clear when he played a major role in breaking up a plot against The Big Bankroll. A Chicago gangster named Eugene "Red" McLaughlin had come to town with the idea of kidnapping Rothstein and holding him for $100,000 ransom. The Chicago mobster approached Legs Diamond, thinking he might be willing to take part in the job. Legs played along, even going so far as traveling to Chicago to finalize the plot with McLaughlin. Then Chicago newspapers reported that McLaughlin, shot and weighted down with boulders, was found dead in a ditch in Cook County's Sanitary Canal.

Diamond's role in foiling this kidnapping scheme made him golden in Rothstein's estimation. He was promoted to a level higher than Fatty Walsh. This development, apparently, gave Jack Diamond delusions of grandeur. He began to see himself on a level with The Brain—both socially, through his manner of dress and almost nightly touring of the city's speakeasies, dance halls, and clubs, and professionally, through his dangerous idea to move in on the operations of the Combine.

A motivating factor for Legs was his jealousy of Owney Madden, who had also started as a lowly street thug, but was now codirector of the largest bootlegging enterprise in the United States. Feeling that he deserved a piece of Madden's action, Legs—taking a page from Owney's own play book—began hijacking Combine booze shipments throughout the New York-New Jersey area. He even enlisted the tacit cooperation of Brooklyn mob boss Vannie Higgins by leading him to believe they could create a Combine of their own just as powerful as the Madden-Dwyer operation. Diamond assured Higgins that he had been promised backing from none other than Arnold Rothstein, which was partly true.

At gunpoint, Legs, his brother Eddie, and their gang began picking off booze shipments on a semi-regular basis. They excelled particularly at hijacking the trucks of Big Bill Dwyer and Owney Madden. It was a dangerous game to say the least. When word got back to Dwyer and Madden, they were livid, especially since Legs was trying to pull others, namely Higgins and Rothstein, into his disloyal scheme. In his Times Square office, Dwyer, normally in control, was said to have yelled at the top of his lungs that Legs Diamond was "nothing more than a river pirate come to New York City" and promised "that no good son of a bitch will get his, if it's the last thing I do."

On a cool October afternoon in 1924, Legs was driving his newly purchased Dodge sedan up Fifth Avenue on his way to the Bronx to meet Dutch

Schultz, another Combine-affiliated gangster whom Diamond was trying to lure into his camp. Legs never made it to the Bronx that day. At 110th Street in Manhattan, a hulking black limousine pulled alongside his car. The long barrel of a shotgun poked out from a back window on the passenger side and opened fire. Two blasts aimed squarely at Legs sprayed the side of the car. Diamond ducked and floored the accelerator simultaneously, sending his Dodge careening down the street. Once he regained control of the car, he headed straight to nearby Mount Sinai Hospital, where he stumbled out of the car and through the emergency entrance. He had shotgun pellets embedded in the side of his head and in his foot. When police arrived at the hospital, they found Legs with his head and foot wrapped in gauze. Pen and notepads poised, they asked about the shooting. Diamond gave his version of the standard gangster response.

"I dunno a thing about it," he said. "Why would anyone wanna shoot me? They must of got the wrong guy."

Legs survived the attack and moved his operations to Greene County, in Upstate New York, where he would continue for years to pose a challenge— if not an outright threat—to the otherwise hegemonic operations of the Combine.

The fact that Diamond's rivals were able to run such a sprawling operation with only the occasional intra-ethnic menace from renegades like him was a testament to the organizational skills of the New York Irish Mob. Legs worked alone because the Combine had early and successfully incorporated all potential dissident factions. There was nowhere for a rival to turn for support. Lone wolf Irishmen like Legs would be an annoyance throughout the duration of the Combine's existence, but the biggest and most dangerous potential threat—the Mafia in New York—had already been co-opted.

By making Frank Costello and Lucky Luciano ranking members of the Combine, the Irish Mob had forestalled a possible inter-ethnic showdown in New York. Luciano, in particular, was brought into the fold for one specific reason: to handle the old Mustache Pete's of the Maranzano and Massaria families who formed the foundations of Cosa Nostra in the New York area. Luciano went about playing both sides against the middle until the two families went at each other in the famously bloody Castellamarese War later in the decade, but for years Lucky successfully kept the old guard Sicilians from encroaching on the Combine's rum running and bootleg territory.

This ethnic accommodation forged in New York in the early years of Prohibition proved to be an anomaly. Elsewhere around the United States, the bootlegging business was a more wide open affair; bloodshed was increasingly the most common by-product of a market regulated not by tariffs and taxes, but by intimidation, gunfire, and what few piddling arrests federal Prohibition agents were able to make. In the streets, the law of supply and demand prevailed: There was money to be made, and whoever had the muscle and the skills to seize control would rule the roost.

At the root of this fierce competition was a smoldering ethnic rivalry that had been bubbling within the country's criminal underworld for at least thirty years. Ever since the first wave of Sicilian immigrants began arriving in American cities, Italian and Irish gang forces had been headed for some kind of showdown. This rivalry had reared its head before, in labor battles, political skirmishes, and, most notably, in the interaction between corrupt Irish cops and early adherents of the Mafia, or the Sicilian Black Hand, down in New Orleans.

The idea that Irish and Italians in America would be at loggerheads was cruelly ironic. In many ways, the two immigrant groups were like cousins who trod many of the same paths. Sharing the same religion, both groups felt the sting of discrimination and bigotry in the New World. They also shared a similar peasant heritage that contained a strong tradition of social interaction through song, drink, storytelling, and the give-and-take of political negotiation. In their attempts to get ahead, Irish and Italian immigrants often worked side by side, lived in the same neighborhoods, and intermarried as much or more than any two ethnic groups in the history of the United States.

And yet, this very closeness guaranteed a level of competition that was inflamed by the wide open nature of underworld crime during the Prohibition era. In many cities large and small, war was declared between bootlegging consortiums looking to corner the market. Nearly every ethnicity in America got involved, but Irish and Italians, because they were more successfully entrenched in the fabric of big city life than more newly arrived groups, tended to be the overseers of these underworld organizations.

The history of Prohibition is rife with ethnic mob wars in cities like Cleveland, St. Louis, Kansas City, Boston, Philadelphia, and Baltimore, but nowhere was the Irish-Italian rivalry more pronounced than in the city of Chicago. In Chicago, there was no organizing Combine like the one Dwyer, Madden, and Hines created in New York—at least not one that maintained peace for any length of time. Hostility and brute force were the primary tools of negotiation in the former Mud City, where King Mike McDonald had once ruled a gambling empire, and Hinky Dink and Bathhouse John presided over the vice rackets. The days of the First Ward Ball, when all of the city's criminals came together under one tent, had given way to a more violent form of underworld interaction. Throughout the middle years of the Roaring Twenties, Gangland Chicago would come to define the rapacious, violent nature of Prohibition. And it would bring to a head, once and for all, a rivalry between Irish gangsters and Italian mafiosi that would determine the course of organized crime in America for generations to come.

the dagos vs. the micks

ean O'Banion was the boss of all bootleggers on Chicago's North Side. A combination of gumption, brutality, foresight, and likability got him there. People liked O'Banion because he was friendly, gregarious, and always on. A stout, cheery-faced Irishman with twinkling, blue eyes, he would always doff his fedora upon meeting a lady and would greet men with a slap on the back and a jovial, "Nice to meet ya, swell fellow" (he regularly called strangers "swell fellows"). A former singing waiter in various North Side saloons in his youth, he was sentimental and, at times, kindly to the point of piety. He gave away money, food, and clothing to indigent children. He was a weekly attendee and financial contributor to Holy Name Cathedral, where he had been a choirboy. Among his followers, O'Banion's generous and upright nature inspired a fierce loyalty. "He was a good man," said his wife, Viola, after he was gone. "He was fun loving, wanting his friends around him, and he never left home without telling me where he was going."

Dean O'Banion also killed people, which was another reason his friends and loyalists toed the line. Once, when a small-time gangster named John Duffy called him with a problem, Deanie, as he was sometimes called, immediately offered to help. Duffy, it seemed, had gotten into a violent, drunken quarrel with his wife of eight days; while she was in bed, he shot her twice in the head and left her for dead. After the drink wore off and Duffy realized what he'd done, he panicked and called a fellow hoodlum, who immediately put in a call to his boss, Dean O'Banion.

O'Banion knew Duffy as a none-too-swift gunman out of Philadelphia who had wandered aimlessly into Chicago and offered his services as a tough guy. By helping pull off a few incidental jobs for the North Side gang, he'd become a hanger-on to the O'Banion bunch. Now he had murdered his wife, which was going to attract the cops whether or not the lowly gangster left town. Dean immediately realized that the only way to cut off an investigation at the pass was to take John Duffy for the proverbial one-way ride.

Duffy was told to wait on a particular Chicago street corner. Around eight o'clock, O'Banion and another man drove up in a Studebaker. By this time, Duffy was nearly hysterical. "I need a car to get outta town," he pleaded. "And I need money. I need at least a grand."

"Sure," said O'Banion from behind the wheel. "I'll give you a grand. I'll give you more than that. Get in."

Witnesses saw John Duffy get in the car. The next time anyone saw the small-time hoodlum and wife killer was in a snow bank on a road out of town. His body was found with three bullet holes in the head from a .38-caliber revolver. Another witness had seen three men dumping Duffy's dead body in the snow bank and initially identified one of the men as Dean O'Banion. But when the witness learned who Dean O'Banion was, he developed a bad case of amnesia.

When O'Banion heard the cops wanted to talk to him about the murder, he told a reporter, "The police don't have to look for me, I'll go and look for them. I'll be in the state's attorney's office at 2:30 P.M. Monday afternoon. . . . I can tell the state's attorney anything he wants to know about me. . . . Whatever happened to Duffy is out of my line. I never even saw Duffy. I don't mix with that kind of riffraff."

The cops never came up with enough evidence even to charge O'Banion, though they had a good idea what happened. Later reports were that Deanie and two accomplices had driven Duffy out of town on Nottingham Road. On the dark, deserted road, they pulled over so that Duffy could urinate. While Duffy and O'Banion both stood relieving themselves, Dean pulled out a .38, put it to the back of Duffy's head, and pulled the trigger. After the victim went down, Dean shot him twice more, just to be sure. That was O'Banion—thorough, professional, and to the point.

He was also a helluva practical joker. Most of Dean's jokes were of the hotfoot, whoopee cushion variety, but occasionally he could be truly demented. His biggest whopper of all was the joke he pulled on Johnny Torrio.

Silver-haired "Papa John" Torrio was the Italian mob boss of Chicago. He was originally from Naples, by way of Brooklyn. As a youth in New York City, he'd been a member of the Five Points gang under Paul Kelly (Vaccarelli). In 1915, Torrio packed up his wife and kids and moved to Chicago. He had been summoned there by his uncle, Jim Colosimo, who was at that time the most powerful Italian criminal in the Windy City.

Torrio's uncle, known to his family and friends as Big Jim, got along with most people, including aldermen Bathhouse John and Hinky Dink. They gave Colosimo his start by making him a precinct captain in the First Ward. Through various gambling, extortion, and labor rackets, Colosimo rose to become a major power in the underworld.

The fact that Big Jim Colosimo remained loyal to Coughlin and Kenna did not sit well with some in the city's Italian underworld. The Unione Siciliane—a quasi-legitimate cultural organization that would eventually become a key player in the city's gang wars—distrusted Colosimo's affiliation with the city's two preeminent Irish American ward bosses. The Unione Siciliane's consiglieri, or legal counsel, was Joseph Bulger, formerly Guiseppe Imburgio, whose Sicilian-born father had been lynched to death in New Orleans following the Chief Hennessey murder trial. Bulger/Imburgio did not countenance appeasement with the Irish, whom he felt represented a faction of the establishment that could never be trusted. The position of the consiglieri and the rest of the Unione Siciliane was underscored dramatically on May 11, 1920 when Big Jim Colosimo was gunned down in the vestibule of his cafe. His killers were never caught, but it was generally believed that he had been taken out in an internal Italian American coup.

Johnny Torrio inherited his uncle's rackets, and he further enhanced his underworld standing by becoming an early supplier of booze on the city's South Side. A soft spoken man with a placid surface demeanor, Torrio saw himself as the great accommodator. He had spent the early years of Prohibition negotiating a division of territory throughout the city's many wards, the result of which was an unwritten non-aggression pact that had held, more or less, for four years. For Torrio, the most difficult aspect of keeping this peace treaty in place was appeasing his fellow Italians, who wanted to go after Dean O'Banion. Some of them disliked the man simply because he was "an Irish bastard." Others wanted Deanie out of the picture because they coveted his territory, for O'Banion's North Side domain included Chicago's Gold Coast, a strip of mansions and estates along Lake Shore Drive that was home to bankers, judges, politicians, real estate moguls, and other members of the financial elite. O'Banion supplied booze for some of the most highfalutin soirees in the city, which made him rich and well-connected.

The Italian bootleggers' covetous dislike for Deanie was mutual. O'Banion had grown up in a part of the city known as Kilgubbin when it was an Irish working-class neighborhood in the process of becoming Italian. Gangs of Irish and Italian youths routinely clashed, and O'Banion, in particular, was known as a young hooligan who was more than willing to stand up for his neighborhood against "the dark people."

By the time the Irishman had emerged as a major player among the city's vast bootlegging underworld, he was shrewd enough to realize that he would not last long without some form of understanding with the Italians. In the early decades of the twentieth century, Chicago had seen a phenomenal population growth among Italian groups. Some, like Johnny Torrio and his young sidekick, Alphonse "Scarface" Capone, came from the East Coast; others came up the Mississippi and Missouri rivers from New Orleans; and still others arrived directly from Sicily, as immigrants of modest means looking to plug into one of America's most thriving Italian American communities. There were probably more new Italian immigrants than Irish immigrants in Chicago, although the Italians had nowhere near the strength the Irish had in politics, the police department, the unions, and other spheres of municipal power.

While O'Banion may have accepted the idea of appeasement with the Italians because it made good business sense, he didn't necessarily like it. He was frequently heard grumbling about the dagos. He was especially aggrieved because Torrio and his organization were big in the prostitution business. "I don't peddle flesh," said the avid Catholic. "And I never will. It goes against God and the Mother Church."

One day in early May 1924, O'Banion approached Torrio with an astounding proposition. He was looking to get out of the bootlegging business, he said, and he wondered if Torrio wanted to buy out his interest in the Sieben Brewery, an extremely profitable beer manufacturing operation jointly owned by him, Torrio, and a few others. The brewery had been producing quality beer in O'Banion's North Side territory for three years, under the protection of the precinct police. For half a million dollars, said O'Banion, he would divest his share; he explained that he wanted out because the bootlegging business had become too dangerous. Torrio would be doing him a favor by buying him out. As a parting gesture of goodwill, he'd even assist in the turning over of one last shipment. Torrio jumped at the offer, even though his second in command, Capone, cautioned that he smelled a rat.

O'Banion and Torrio, along with two members of Deanie's crew and under the watchful eye of two uniformed police officers who were on the payroll, met at the Sieben Brewery on the morning of May 19. There Torrio delivered his payment of $500,000. In return, O'Banion escorted Torrio around the facility, showing him the recently concocted shipment of beer ready for delivery to speakeasies throughout the city. He showed him the financial ledgers listing the various bootlegging organizations that were scheduled to receive product. After Torrio had fully assessed the operation and the last of thirteen trucks was loaded by a crew of teamsters, he asked O'Banion, "So what will you do with yourself now that you're out?"

Deanie smiled. "I'm retirin' to Colorado to become a gentleman farmer."

Before Torrio had even finished chuckling at that remark, from all directions, blocking all exits, came a troop of blue uniforms led by none other than the chief of police himself, Morgan Collins. "You're all under arrest for violation of the Volstead Act," announced Chief Collins. He personally ripped the badges from the two uniformed officers on the premises. 130,000 gallons of beer were confiscated and thirty-one bootleggers arrested, including Torrio and O'Banion. Torrio went into a panic. He knew that a second offense for bootlegging could mean jail time. This would be his second offense, while it would only be O'Banion's first.

At the Federal Building downtown, O'Banion was chipper as hell. He paid his $7,500 bail and whistled on his way out of the courtroom, knowing that even if he were convicted of the offense, it would bring no more than a fine. Torrio, however, was sullen. He, too, was released on bail that day, but with the knowledge that if he were found guilty of a Volstead violation, he would be serving time in prison.

A few days later, Torrio learned an even more disturbing fact. A police informant told him something that his sidekick Al Capone had suspected all along. The Sieben Brewery bust had been a setup. The "Irish bastard" knew about the police raid from the beginning and had made sure Torrio would be on the premises to be arrested. "I guess I rubbed that pimp's nose in the mud all right," O'Banion reportedly said about his little joke on Papa John.

O'Banion did go to Colorado for a few months (he even bought property, paying cash for a 2,700-acre ranch), but he did not retire from the bootlegging business. He was soon back in the city demanding his share of the spoils and pissing off Italian criminals throughout the underworld. The fact that John Torrio and Al Capone did not immediately go after the capricious Irishman, leaving his corpse riddled with bullets in a roadside ditch, was a testament to O'Banion's status as the most popular hoodlum in Chicago.

₵ɧe ℳerry Ƥrankster

In Kilgubbin, the neighborhood where Charles Dean O'Banion[1] was raised from the age of nine, they had a saying: "You can lead a dago to water, but

1. In newspaper accounts from the Prohibition era, O'Banion is sometimes referred to as "Dion." It is not known where this name came from, whether it was an invention of

you can't make him drown himself." It was meant as a joke, but the racial denigration behind this nasty little aphorism was a pointed reminder of the hostility that existed between the Irish and Italians—part of an ethnic tribalism that defined street life in most East Coast and many Midwestern American cities in the early years of the century.

Despite the ethnic animosities that were part of his inheritance, Dean O'Banion was not raised to be a gangster. On the contrary, his upbringing was classic Norman Rockwell Americana. Born on July 8, 1892, in Moroa, a small town in Central Illinois surrounded by cornfields, Deanie remembered this tree-lined hamlet with fondness throughout his life. In later years, when he had acquired his wealth, he made financial donations to the town and was always ready to help out its inhabitants. He made an arrangement with Chicago hospitals that if anyone from the village of Moroa were ever admitted, he would be notified immediately so that he could send flowers. While this may have been the gesture of a proven sentimentalist, it's also likely that, as his life became increasingly dangerous, he found solace in maintaining ties to a more innocent time and place.

O'Banion's father, also named Charles, was a hard-working Irish immigrant plasterer and part-time barber who scrambled for any kind of work he could find. He and his wife, Emma Brophy, labored long and hard to support their family, which included Deanie's older brother, Floyd, and younger sister, Ruth. The children's upbringing was stable enough until a dark day in 1901, when their mother died suddenly from tuberculosis. Shortly thereafter, Deanie's heartbroken father moved him and his brother to Chicago to stay with their grandparents (sister Ruth was left with an aunt in Decatur).

Located on the city's near North Side, Kilgubbin had once been a respectable Irish enclave, but the area's tenement housing and local traditions had deteriorated; with the predictable upsurge in robbery, prostitution, and violence, the neighborhood lost its Celtic designation altogether and became known as Little Hell.

In Little Hell, Deanie O'Banion was often truant from school and eventually fell in with a gang known as the Little Hellions, the juvenile division of the Bloody Market Streeters, a gang known primarily for the marketing of stolen property. The Little Hellions were an ethnically mixed bunch.

---

the press or a pet name used by fellow gangsters. In *Guns and Roses: The Untold Story of Dean O'Banion* by Rose Keefe (by far the most complete account of O'Banion's life), a former classmate of the legendary bootlegger is quoted saying, "I don't know where this Dion name came from. We only ever knew him as Dean."

Among them were Earl Wojciechowsky, a Polish Catholic who later changed his name to Hymie Weiss; George "Bugs" Moran, who was half Polish and half Irish; and Vinnie Drucci, an Italian whom O'Banion nicknamed Schemer because he was good at devising schemes for boosting the merchandise that the gang would sell to the Market Streeters for a modest profit.

Even at a young age, O'Banion was known as a prankster whose desire to have a good time, more than anything else, singled him out as leader of the Little Hellions. One of his good-natured stunts left him crippled for life: Attempting to show off to his friends by sitting on the fender of a moving streetcar, he was thrown to the road when the vehicle suddenly lurched. Before he could get out of the way, the streetcar backed up and crushed his left leg. An operation saved his leg but left one leg shorter than the other; forever after he walked with a noticeable limp.

The accident did nothing to subdue Deanie's wild streak. He quit school altogether at the age of fourteen and shortly thereafter found work in McGovern's Saloon and Cabaret, a notorious dive at 666 N. Clark Street. Years before, Deanie had honed his voice in a short stint with the Holy Name Church choir; now he was a singing waiter, hustling around the tables with trays of beer steins and whiskey glasses while belting out traditional Irish crowd pleasers like "Danny Boy" and "Too-Ra-Loo-Ra-Loo-Ra (An Irish Lullaby)." He also served as a bouncer. Though only five-foot four, Deanie was solidly built and never afraid to mix it up with drunken and unruly customers when duty called.

One McGovern's regular who took a liking to O'Banion was Gene Geary, an older Irish American racketeer from Canaryville, a district in the city known for producing highly skilled gunmen. What Geary loved most was whiskey, Irish ballads, and the sound of a pistol being fired off. He took young Deanie under his wing and schooled him in the art of ambidextrous gunplay. From rooftops and in tenement basements, he and the much younger O'Banion conducted target practice. Geary even showed Deanie the best way to hide various weapons on his person by sewing special pockets into the interior lining of his clothing—a tactic that would later become one of mobster O'Banion's most well-known trademarks.

The disciple-mentor relationship between Deanie and the elder gangster was the sort of alliance that was at the heart of many burgeoning careers in the Irish American underworld. The two men remained close friends until 1921, when Geary was committed to a mental institution as a homicidal maniac.

Prohibition was made-to-order for Dean O'Banion. He served a gangster apprenticeship as a slugger during the city's brutal newspaper circulation wars (he first cracked heads for Hearst's *Herald-Examiner* then switched sides when the *Tribune* offered more money) and later as an expert safe cracker and second-story man. He and his North Side gang then pulled off two early coups that helped establish their bootlegging supremacy. One night in late 1923, they invaded a West Side railroad yard and transferred $100,000 worth of Canadian whiskey from a freight car to their trucks. A few nights later, they broke into the Sibley Warehouse, trucked out 1,750 barrels of bonded liquor, and, to conceal the robbery as long as possible, left in their place an equal number of barrels filled with water. Lieutenant Michael Grady of the detective bureau and four detective sergeants on O'Banion's payroll escorted the trucks to his North Side storage depot.

These two moves established a pattern for O'Banion. He was daring, certainly, but also a master at bribing cops and judges, which kept him out of jail. In his entire career, he only served two brief stints behind bars: once for getting caught with stolen postage stamps and another time for assault, for which he served three months. This was not a bad record for a man whom Police Chief Morgan Collins described in 1924 as "Chicago's arch criminal" who had allegedly "killed, or ordered killed, at least twenty-five men."

O'Banion led a charmed life partly because he seemed to inspire such strong loyalty among his followers. He was generous to a fault, especially with Bugs Moran, whom he treated like a son though they were nearly the same age. When a member of the O'Banion gang was wronged in any way, Dean was quick to stand up for them. In 1988, historian Rose Keefe interviewed a former truck driver of O'Banion's who remembered him in glowing terms. "I liked running booze for Dean," said the trucker, J. Barnett, who also drove for other bootlegger syndicates. "He paid well; he never stiffed his drivers like some of the other gangs did. . . . He really believed in treating his people well."

O'Banion was fair and friendly, but he was also tough. Barnett remembered seeing O'Banion in action one night at a Chicago restaurant:

> All that money and success in the booze business did not make Dean soft. Not at all. One night a group of us were at a chop suey joint on North Clark. . . . This drunken idiot and his girl sat at a table close to ours, and the man started going at it with the name-calling while the woman sat there and cried. You couldn't help but stare at a scene like that. Suddenly the guy looks right at Dean, who was sitting on the outside of our booth.
>
> "What the hell are you looking at?" he says.

"Not a hell of a lot," Dean says back. "What about you?" The guy gets up and comes right over. I was nervous as hell. He was big, and I felt sure that Dean or someone else would say to hell with it and just shoot him. But Dean just waited till he got close enough, then swung out his foot and kicked the guy in the kneecap. Hard. The guy fell down with his leg at a funny angle. Dean jumped out of his chair, got on top of him, and got him in a tight headlock. He pinned the guy's wrists with his other hand and kept choking him until he begged for mercy. Good thing he did beg because no one was helping him. Even the Chinese people who ran the place stood there and looked fascinated. . . . Some of the gang leaders were only big men because their guns made them big; without weapons they were nothing. Not O'Banion. Men like him were different from the Italian gangs, who had others do their fighting for them and were only as dangerous as the weapons they carried. Looking back now, I think that was one of the reasons they hated him so much.

O'Banion was the man. As such, his stature as a bootlegger and legitimate tough guy grew accordingly; the former singing waiter from Little Hell became a political force in the Windy City. He'd always been interested in politics. Given his convivial personality and ability to galvanize his followers, he might have made a highly effective ward boss in the manner of Bathhouse John or Hinky Dink. Instead, Deanie became a mobster, albeit one with a special knack for getting out the vote in his North Side wards. During the campaign of 1924, a common ditty heard throughout the city was: "Who'll carry the 42nd and 43rd wards?" Answer: "Deanie O'Banion, in his pistol pocket."

Local elections that year were hotly contested. On November 1, the Democrats, fearing that the powerful North Side bootlegger might defect to the Republicans, staged a black-tie testimonial dinner for O'Banion at the Webster Hotel at 2150 North Lincoln Park. Along with Democratic politicians from the Lake Shore wards, labor union leaders, and ranking members of O'Banion's organization, in attendance were a number of city officials, including the Commissioner of Public Works, six police lieutenants, and the Chief of Detectives. Deanie was presented with a $1,500 platinum watch amid an atmosphere of camaraderie and conviviality that evoked memories of the long-defunct First Ward Ball. The next day, when it was reported who had attended the dinner, there was public outcry, and the Public Works commissioner was forced to resign. The Chief of Detectives claimed that he had been told the dinner was for someone else, and when he recognized Dean O'Banion and his crew, "I knew I had been framed and withdrew almost at once."

For the Democrats, the dinner proved to be a bust. O'Banion may have been loyal to his gang members, but politics, like bootlegging, was a dirty business. Despite the dinner, O'Banion threw his support to the Republicans and delivered his ward by a two-to-one margin.

Politics and crime were Deanie's vocation, but when pressed, he would admit that the thing he loved most was flowers. To O'Banion, flowers represented beauty, and beauty tended to bring out his sentimental side. In order to surround himself in flora and fauna, O'Banion, with business partner William E. Schofield, opened Schofield's Florist Shop in 1923. It was located on North State Street, directly across from Holy Name Cathedral. O'Banion spent hours at the shop cutting and arranging bouquets himself. From the beginning, business was excellent, with near daily orders from the city's various underworld factions whose gang members were being killed at an alarming rate.

Even before O'Banion stiffed Johnny Torrio at the Sieben Brewery, fleecing him of half a million dollars and setting him up to be arrested, the peace treaty arranged by Papa John had been tearing at the seams. The primary culprits were a murderous family of immigrant Sicilian brothers known as the Gennas. For months, the six Genna brothers and their crew of feared gunmen had been muscling in on rival gang territory. On the North Side, they flooded O'Banion's district with cheap whiskey they cooked up themselves and sold for three dollars a gallon. (O'Banion sold his for six to nine dollars a gallon.) The Irishman was being undersold in his own backyard.

"You gotta do something about this," O'Banion told Papa John. "These Gennas are pissing all over my territory. I want 'em stopped, or I'll stop 'em myself. You understand?"

Torrio always talked Deanie down by advising caution and promising results, but after being set up and arrested courtesy of O'Banion, the Italian Mob boss was in no great mood to aid his sneaky Irish partner. It all came to a head on November 3, when O'Banion and his sidekick Hymie Weiss attended a weekly split-the-profits meeting at the Ship, a gambling emporium in the Chicago suburb of Cicero that was jointly controlled by Torrio, O'Banion, and others. Torrio was not there that night; he was in Italy with his family. Presiding over the meeting instead was Torrio's second-in-command, Scarface Al Capone, who was there with five or six other Italians. As Capone handed O'Banion his weekly cut, he noted that Angelo Genna of the Genna brothers had lost heavily at roulette that week and left an IOU for $30,000. Capone suggested to the group that, in the interest of general amity, they cancel Genna's debt.

"Are you kiddin' me?" said O'Banion. He picked up the phone, called Angelo Genna, and told him he had one week to pay up—or else.

Later, back at Schofield's Flower Shop, Hymie Weiss cautioned his boss to consider backing off a bit. The Gennas, after all, were known to be fiercely homicidal. Deanie, in response, uttered a phrase that would ring throughout the underworld. "You can tell them Sicilians to go to hell," he said.

In subsequent accounts of Gangland Chicago, much has been made of O'Banion's statement. But given the ethnic rivalries of the time, the Irishman had probably voiced the sentiment on other occasions. Certainly, Sicilian and Italian racketeers made similar comments about "crazy micks," "Irish pigs," or "donkey Irish bastards." It is more likely that O'Banion's fate was sealed not by this relatively benign ethnic jibe, but in a carefully devised plan by Capone, in place for months, to eliminate the Irishman and take over his territory. In any event, the result was not good for Deanie O'Banion.

On the morning of November 10, O'Banion was in the back of his flower shop clipping the stems off some chrysanthemums. The last few days had been particularly busy. Two days earlier the president of the Unione Siciliane, Mike Merlo, had passed away after a long illness. Mike Merlo was a popular man, and his death resulted in a tremendous volume of orders for flowers. Al Capone placed an order for $8,000 worth of roses, Johnny Torrio for $10,000 worth of assorted flowers. One of the Genna brothers had visited the shop to order a wreath. The various orders had required the shop to stay open late the night before, so on this morning only O'Banion and his African American porter were in the shop when three men entered the front door.

William Crutchfield, the porter, caught a glimpse of the visitors as they entered. The man in the middle, he said later, was "tall, well-built, well-dressed, smooth-shaven, wore a brown overcoat and a brown fedora hat. He might have been a Jew or a Greek." His companions were "Italians . . . short, stocky, and rather rough looking." Crutchfield saw his boss drop what he was doing and approach the men in a friendly manner.

"Hello boys," said O'Banion. "You want Merlo's flowers?"

"Yes," replied the tall man, extending his hand for Deanie to shake.

That was all Crutchfield saw. His boss motioned for him to close the door to the back room, which the porter did, assuming O'Banion wanted privacy. A few moments later, he heard gunshots and dashed into the front room to find Deanie O'Banion on the floor, surrounded by broken containers of carnations and lilacs. O'Banion was bleeding from multiple gunshot wounds, the red blood soiling a handful of lily-white peonies. By the time police arrived, Deanie was already dead.

It was a classic mob hit. In a reconstruction of the event days later, police authorities determined that the tall man shaking O'Banion's hand had jerked him forward and pinned down his arms. Before Deanie could break free, the others opened fire, six shots in all—two passed through his chest, a third through his right cheek, the fourth and fifth through his larynx. The sixth and final shot was fired at close range into his brain after he fell.

Three days later, the city of Chicago witnessed the largest funeral ever staged up to that time. At the Sbarbaro funeral chapel, O'Banion's body lay in an open casket, the bullet holes and powder burns expertly covered by the embalmer's art, a rosary clasped in his folded hands. On a marble slab beneath the casket was the inscription: *Suffer little children to come unto me.* "Why, oh, why?" wailed Viola O'Banion, as her late husband's remains were escorted by a massive cortege that would swell to fifteen thousand people by the time it reached Mount Carmel Cemetery.

Among the mourners was Al Capone, there to pay his respects along with Johnny Torrio and the Genna brothers. Anyone who knew anything about the Chicago underworld knew that these were the men who had arranged the murder of Deanie O'Banion. Members of the O'Banion gang mumbled angrily under their breath, but this was not the time for revenge. This was a time for sorrow.

At the cemetery grounds, O'Banion's body was interred in a section set aside for those who had been excommunicated by the church. In an official statement—in words that would have stung O'Banion, a devout Catholic, almost as much as the bullets that killed him—a spokesperson for the local archdiocese explained, "One who refuses the ministrations of the church in life need not expect them in death. O'Banion was a notorious criminal. The Church did not recognize him in his days of lawlessness and when he died unrepentant in his iniquities, he had no claims to the last rights for the dead."

One priest who defied the archdiocese's directive was Father Patrick Malloy, formerly of Holy Name Cathedral, where Deanie had sung as a choirboy. As grave diggers threw the last clods of earth onto the grave, the good father knelt and recited a litany of three Hail Marys and the Lord's Prayer. To those who knew and loved Dean O'Banion, it was a fitting tribute.

In life, he was a killer unworthy of the church he so cherished. In death, O'Banion's stature as the most notorious historical figure of his time became engrained in the legend of Chicago. If there were such a thing as a Mount Rushmore for the Founding Fathers of the Irish American underworld, his would be the fourth and final face on the mountain top—alongside Morrissey, McDonald, and Madden.

Kingɗom of tǥe ǥangs

Dean O'Banion's North Side bunch was not the only Irish American gang the Italians had to contend with—not by a long shot. In fact, as leader of the Irish Mob in Chicago, O'Banion had been an ameliorating presence; as long as Deanie was around, the other Irish gangs felt an obligation to observe John Torrio's peace treaty. Now that he was gone, the dogs of war were unleashed. The result was a period of gangland violence unprecedented in American history.

While a couple of Irish American bootlegging operations sided with Torrio-Capone, the majority did not. In the wake of O'Banion's murder, among the many prominent Irish gangs or gangsters to emerge and take their place in the annals of Chicago gangdom were:

Bugs Moran—Nobody revered Dean O'Banion more than raven-haired, pudgy Georgie Moran, who had an impish, playful demeanor similar to that of his boss. After O'Banion was brazenly murdered, Moran, Hymie Weiss, and the gang's other remaining members went after the Italians with a vengeance. Their first act was a blatant attempted hit on Capone, in January 1925. Big Al was having lunch at a State Street restaurant when the O'Banionites, thinking Capone was in his car, opened fire on the curbside Sedan with shotguns and automatics. ("They let it have everything but the kitchen stove," a policeman later reported.) Having missed their target, a few days later Moran and the gang kidnapped Big Al's most trusted bodyguard, tortured him with lit cigarettes and concertina wire, then shot him five times in the head and dumped his body in the woods. A week later, they set their sights on Papa John Torrio. In front of his home, they gunned him down on the sidewalk, hitting him in the jaw, arm, and groin. Moran then stood over Torrio, who was still squirming and put a gun to his temple to administer the coup d' grace, but the chamber was empty. Before he could reload, Moran was forced to flee the scene. Papa John recovered in the hospital, then quit the Chicago underworld for good. "It's all yours, Al," he told Capone on his way out of town. "I'm not ready to die."

Terry Druggan—Druggan got his start as a member of the Valley gang, a mostly Irish gang based in a now-defunct, notorious turn-of-the-century Chicago slum known as the Valley that was located on the other side of the Chicago River from the Levee district. The Valley gang was comprised mostly of sons of policemen and low-level politicos, as well as such renowned brawlers as "Paddy the Bear" Ryan and Walter "the Runt" Quinlan. At the onset of Prohibition, Terry Druggan, a former burglar and hijacker with the gang, formed a partnership with Frankie Lake, a former Chicago fireman. Druggan-Lake made millions peddling beer on the West Side, buying their product from Dean O'Banion until they built their own brewery. Druggan and Lake wore identical horn-rimmed spectacles and dressed like dandies. They were not known as men of violence. As the war between Capone and the Irish kicked into high gear, they drifted from the scene until, by the end of the decade, the Druggan-Lake organization was no more.

The South Side O'Donnells—The O'Donnell brothers, Edward, Steve, Walter, and Tommy, had been known criminals since boyhood. Edward, better known as "Spike," served as the gang's leader until 1917, when he was incarcerated at Joliet State Prison for his role in the daylight holdup of the Stockyards Trust and Savings Bank. An established pickpocket, burglar, labor slugger, and killer (he was twice tried for murder and accused of several others), Spike was also a religious man who rarely missed Sunday mass at St. Peter's Catholic Church. Upon release from prison in 1923, O'Donnell led his brothers in a mini-war with the Torrio-Capone syndicate that became known as the Chicago Beer Wars and resulted in at least two dozen gangland deaths.

In photographs from the era, Spike O'Donnell, a jaunty gangster who favored polka-dot ties and a felt fedora, is rarely seen without a smile on his face—which is remarkable, given that there were at least ten attempts on his life, two of which left him wounded. "Life with me is just one bullet after another," Spike once said. "I've been shot at and missed so often, I've a notion to hire myself out as a professional target."

One attempted hit on O'Donnell that was of particular historical importance occurred on September 25, 1925, when Spike and a police officer were conversing in front of a drug store at Sixty-third Street and Western Avenue. A car containing four men suddenly appeared, and one of the occupants called out, "Hey, Spike," followed by the rat-a-tat-tat of gunfire. Spike and the cop hit the pavement; the bullets passed overhead into the window of the drug store. During the Prohibition era, this shooting was the first known use of the World War I Thompson submachine gun, or tommy gun, which would become more commonly known in the press as "the Chicago typewriter."[2]

---

2. The tommy gun was invented by Brigadier General John T. Thompson, director of arsenals during World War I. At eight and a half pounds, it was light enough for a child

Frank McErlane—The man who used the tommy gun against Spike O'Donnell was Frank McErlane, possibly the most ruthlessly violent gunman in Chicago during the Roaring Twenties. He was often referred to as gat goofy because of the orgasmic joy he exhibited when firing his gat. Handsome in his youth, with wavy black hair and bedroom eyes, McErlane became bloated and pasty in later years due to severe alcoholism. He often managed to get beer smuggled into prison and sometimes appeared drunk in court. His gang (including his brother Vince and a hulking, slow-witted Pole named Joe Saltis) was based on the city's Southwest Side, which put them in direct conflict with the South Side O'Donnells. When gangland Chicago erupted in the mid-1920s, McErlane was the most significant Irish American gangster to side with Capone. (The others were Ralph Sheldon, formerly of Ragen's Colts, and the Guilfoyle gang, led by Martin Guilfoyle.) A professional hitman who seemed to relish killing, McErlane murdered at least nine people, including his common law wife whom he shot to death along with her two dogs.

One person McErlane thought he killed was William "Shorty" Egan, a truck driver for the South Side O'Donnell gang. Egan and a fellow trucker, Morrie Keane, were kidnapped and taken for a ride by McErlane and an accomplice. Shorty Egan miraculously survived and gave this harrowing account to the police:

> Pretty soon the driver asks the guy with the shotgun, "Where you gonna get rid of these guys?" The fat fellow [McErlane] laughs and says, "I'll take care of that in a minute." He was monkeying with his shotgun all the time. Pretty soon he turns around and points the gun at Keane. He didn't say a word but just let go straight at him. Keane got it square on the left side. The guy loads up his gun and gives it to Keane again. Then he turns around to me and says, "I guess you might as well get yours, too." With that he shoots me in the side. It hurt like hell so when I seen him loading up again, I twist around so it won't hit me in the same place. This time he got me in the leg. Then he gives me the other barrel right on the puss. I slide off the seat. But

---

to use and could fire a thousand .45-caliber pistol cartridges per minute. Retailing at $175, it was reasonably affordable and did not come under laws pertaining to pistols or rifles; anyone could buy as many as they liked either by mail order or from a sporting goods store. Given the noise and havoc wrought by this weapon, they were as de riguer to gangsters in their day as the Uzi and Tech-9 submachine gun would be during the cocaine and crack wars of the 1980s and 1990s.

I guess the fat guy wasn't sure we was through. He let Morrie have it twice more and then he let me have it again in the other side. The fat guy scrambled into the rear seat and grabbed Keane. He opens the door and kicks Morrie out into the road. We was doing about fifty from the sound. I figure I'm next so when he drags me over to the door I set myself to jump. He shoves and I light in the ditch by the road. I hit the ground on my shoulders and I thought I'd never stop rolling. I lost consciousness. When my senses came back, I was lying in a pool of water and ice had formed around me. The sky was red and it was breaking day. I staggered along a road until I saw a light in a farmhouse. . . .

In later years, Frank McErlane's life became a succession of court proceedings, attempts on his life, and extended periods in hiding from killers or the law. One dark, rainy night he was found drunk in the middle of the street firing his tommy gun into the sky. "They were trying to get me, but I drove 'em off," he told a cop. McErlane was sent to the drunk tank, but his problems were more serious than that. "Gangland Years Make Wreck of Frank McErlane" wrote the *Tribune* after a psychiatric evaluation suggested that the gangster was quite possibly insane. Crazy or not, McErlane was so loathed in the underworld that when he finally died from alcohol-related pneumonia on October 8, 1932, police had to guard the ambulance that held his body so that no one would try to break in and mutilate the remains.

The West Side O'Donnells (no relation to the South Side O'Donnells)—Myles, Klondike, and Bernard O'Donnell were the first bootleggers to establish a beachhead in Cicero, which would prove to be a primary battleground in the war between the dagos and the micks. In the early years of the decade, they operated under a treaty with Johnny Torrio that was beneficial to all. The O'Donnells controlled the beer concessions along Roosevelt Road, the town's main drag, while Torrio was allowed to sell beer elsewhere, as well as operate various cabarets and the Ship, a massive gambling house.

After Papa John fled the city, Al Capone commenced bullying his way into Cicero. The West Side O'Donnells violently resisted especially since they were dead set against the brothel business, which Capone intended to introduce to the town in a big way. Between 1925 and early 1929, Cicero would become ground zero in the war between the exclusively Irish O'Donnell Mob and the Capone syndicate. The battle would eventually result in nearly two hundred gang-style murders.

The Terrible Touhys—Born in the Valley (the same fetid turn-of-the-century Irish slum that produced Terry Druggan and many other aspiring gangsters), Roger, Johnny, Eddie, Tommy, and Joe Touhy underscored the fact that not all bootleggers were bad men. Sons of a Chicago cop and a mother who died when the boys were still young, a couple of the brothers became burglars and low-level criminals. The smartest of the bunch, Roger, became a union organizer, a Morse Code wireless operator, and eventually owner of a fleet of trucks based in Des Plaines, a sleepy Chicago suburb in northwestern Cook County. With the onset of Prohibition, Roger Touhy's trucking business became a bootlegging operation. Soon Touhy was making his own product, brewed with spring water, which became known as the best beer in the entire county. By 1926, Roger and his brothers were selling one thousand barrels a week at $55 a barrel, with a production cost to them of $4.50 a barrel. The profits were enormous.

Only five foot six, with curly hair and a big beak for a nose, Roger Touhy was intelligent and well-liked. Initially, he eschewed violence, preferring to win over customers with the superior nature of his product. But that changed when Al Capone got wind of Touhy's profitable Des Plaines operation. Capone moved his own product into Des Plaines and began terrorizing Touhy's customers. The result was a sporadic shooting war that took place first on the empty back roads of Cook County, then—after Roger secretly obtained the backing of Chicago Mayor Anton Cermack and the city's police department—erupted inside the city limits as well.[3]

---

3. Roger Touhy is unique among Irish American gangsters. In 1933 (the final year of Prohibition) Touhy was tried and convicted for the kidnapping of Jake "the Barber" Factor, a notorious stock swindler and half-brother of billionaire make-up manufacturer Max Factor. Touhy claimed vociferously that he had been setup to take the fall for a crime he did not commit, but no one listened. He was sentenced to 99 years in prison. On October 9, 1942, Touhy and four other inmates at Statesville prison made a daring escape. Touhy was free for two and a half months, until he was recaptured and resentenced for 199 years. In 1943, Twentieth Century Fox released a movie based on his life starring Anthony Quinn entitled *Roger Touhy, Gangster*. Touhy sued Fox and its distributors on the grounds that the film defamed him. In 1948, he won an out-of-court settlement for $10,000 and a guarantee that the movie would never again be exhibited domestically, though it could be shown overseas.

Throughout his time in prison, Touhy fought to prove that he had been falsely convicted. Over a five-year period, his lawyers filed documents claiming that Factor had faked his own kidnapping and framed Touhy for the crime. In August 1959, Touhy's case was finally heard. Miraculously, he was totally exonerated, his conviction overturned, and the additional time added after his escape declared unconstitutional. After twenty-two years in prison for a crime he did not commit, Touhy was released.

Around the time of his release, Touhy published an autobiography entitled *The Stolen Years*. He also announced his plans to sue Jake Factor, who was now running the

The Terrible Touhys and all of the Irish gangs that took on Capone did so with the knowledge that it was a battle to the death. Unlike Torrio, Capone had no interest in negotiation or appeasement. His bluntly stated goal was to take over not only the entire city, but also the county, the state, and the entire midwestern region of the United States. There would be no partners, only subsidiaries.

But the Irish were not his only competitors. The Sicilian Genna brothers hated Capone and would remain his sworn enemy until he had two of them killed (another Genna was murdered by Bugs Moran and Hymie Weiss in May 1925). The Chicago chapter of the Unione Siciliane resented Capone, who was not Sicilian and therefore never actually a member of the Mafia. When Big Al succeeded in installing his own handpicked choice as president of the Unione, it touched off a bloody, corpse-laden war within the organization dubbed by the press "The War of Sicilian Succession."

With Scarface Al turning up the heat, things were getting out of hand. During the three-year period from 1924 to 1927, there were, according to the recently formed Chicago Crime Commission, 150 Prohibition-related killings. The crisis became so bad that it brought about the formation of yet one more gang, this one in the police department.

With much fanfare, newly appointed Chief of Detectives William O'Connor announced the formation of an elite unit that became known as O'Connor's Gunners. Comprised of volunteers from the police force who had fought in the war in Europe and could therefore handle a machine gun, O'Connor's Gunners were further equipped with steel-plated police cars. O'Connor himself gave the unit their marching orders, in a blustery speech at police headquarters that was widely quoted in the city's newspapers.

"Men," he announced, "the war is on. We've got to show that society and the police department, and not a bunch of dirty rats, are running this town. It is the wish of the people of Chicago that you hunt these criminals down and kill them without mercy. Your cars are equipped with machine guns, and

---

Stardust Hotel & Casino in Las Vegas, which was secretly controlled by underworld figures in Chicago. On December 16, 1959, just twenty-eight days after his release from prison, Touhy was visiting his sister at her home on Chicago's North Side. Two gunmen approached with shotguns and opened fire, hitting him five times. It was a professional hit; the shooters were never identified. Later that night at a hospital, Touhy died from his wounds.

Roger Touhy is one of the few Irish American gangsters to have a movie based on his life, and the first one of note to publish an autobiography (though the book itself is not very revealing). He is also the only known former gangster to be taken out in a mob hit so many years after he plied his trade. Somebody had a long memory.

you will meet the enemies of society on equal terms. See to it that they don't have you pushing up daisies. Make them push up daisies. Shoot first, and shoot to kill. If you kill a notorious fuedist [a reference to the internal Sicilian feud], you will get a handsome reward and win a promotion. If you meet a car containing bandits, pursue them and fire. When I arrive on the scene, my hopes will be fulfilled if you have shot off the top of their car and killed every criminal inside."

O'Connor's red meat rhetoric was typical of the times, portraying cops and gangsters as players in a drama. When Capone was told about the Chief's new unit, he had a good laugh. "Whaddya know," he said. "Another bunch of Irish bastards with guns."[4]

Big Al's Better Half

Among the more curious aspects of Capone's contentious relationship with the Irish American underworld was the fact that he was married to the enemy. Mae Coughlin Capone, Al's wife, was born in Brooklyn, New York to Michael Coughlin, a construction laborer, and Bridget Gorman. Mae had four sisters and two brothers. The Coughlin family lived in a small two-story home at 117 Third Place and were respected in the local Irish community for their rectitude and religious devotion.

Mae was tall and slim, with a face that many thought would one day make her an actress or a model. Those aspirations were scuttled forever after she met Al Capone, in 1918, at a party in a Carroll Street cellar club. Capone, who already had the four-inch scar on his cheek that earned him his nickname, was rough around the edges, with thinning hair and a manner of speech commensurate with someone who never made it past elementary school. Somehow it worked, and the courtship was quick.

The man Capone worked for in Brooklyn, Johnny Torrio, had already married an Irish girl, Ann McCarthy. For Italians at the time, marrying Irish girls was a sign of upward mobility. There was also the fact that Italian men generally did not hesitate to marry and start a family early in life, whereas Irishmen tended to wait until they were financially stable—or until "ma" said it was okay. And so, Mae Coughlin and Al Capone were married on December 18, 1918, in a ceremony presided over by the Reverend James J.

---

4. O'Connor's Gunners came and went in a flash. They mostly arrived at crime scenes after the fact and were not directly involved in any significant gang prosecutions. After the so-called "War of Sicilian Succession" died down, the unit was quietly disbanded.

Delaney, pastor of St. Mary Star of the Sea Church, where the Coughlins worshipped. The following year, Mae bore her first and only child, Albert Francis, nicknamed Sonny. The child's godfather was Papa John Torrio.

In 1919, Torrio, having already moved to Chicago, summoned Capone. Al packed up his wife and son and moved to the Windy City, where they lived in a shack. In public, Capone went by the name "Al Brown" and passed himself off as a used furniture salesman. In truth, he was a pimp and strong-arm man who roughed up people on behalf of his boss. Then Prohibition came and changed everything.

Throughout Al Capone's reign as the overlord of Chicago, Mae Coughlin remained a mysterious figure. She rarely shared her husband's suite at the Metropole Hotel, where he conducted his affairs (business and otherwise). She did not accompany him to the theatre, nightclubs, or the racetrack. Few members of the gang and even fewer outsiders ever knew her. On those rare occasions when Mae was seen in public, usually at one of Capone's many court appearances, she was the bane of press photographers; she always partially covered her face, never spoke to the newshounds, and tried to keep her son out of the limelight. In the tradition of the old country Italian dons, Capone kept his wife confined to the home. Mae would eventually spend most of her time in Miami at the lavish Palm Island estate that Capone purchased in 1927.

A rare insight into Mae Capone's personality was revealed in *Capone*, an essential biography of the gangster written by John Kobler and published in 1971. Kobler relates the story of a woman who owned a bungalow in Miami that was rented out by a real estate agent to a man named "Al Brown." The absentee owner was appalled when she learned that Al Brown was Al Capone. For weeks, the woman worried that her bungalow would suffer damage at the hands of the notorious gangster and his underlings, who were eventually joined by Mae and Sonny Capone. The woman needn't have worried. Not only did the Capones leave the place in impeccable condition, but Mrs. Capone wrote a note asking the owner to accept as gifts the sets of fine china and silverware that they left behind, as well as numerous unopened cases of wine. The only sour note was a telephone bill for $780 in calls to Chicago. The owner needn't have worried about that either. According to Kobler:

> Soon after the [bungalow owner] received the phone bill, a Cunning-ham 16-cylinder Cadillac pulled into her drive, and out stepped a slender woman, quietly dressed, her blond hair falling below her shoulders, her pearly skin lightly tinted by the Florida sun. "I'm Mrs. Capone," she said in a soft, low voice. The telephone bill had slipped

her mind, she apologized, and she wanted to pay it without further delay. When [the owner] mentioned the charges, she handed her a $1,000 note. "Never mind the difference," she said. "We may have broken a few little things, but this should cover it."

If Mae Capone intended to bring a civilizing influence into her husband's life, she was swimming against the tide. Scarface Al was, by most accounts, a famously brutish man who killed many people with his own hands, ordered the torture and deaths of probably hundreds, and on one notorious occasion bludgeoned to death a criminal associate with a baseball bat in the middle of a fancy, black-tie dinner. His psychosis was undoubtedly complex and far-reaching (he would eventually lose his mind and die after being diagnosed with tertiary syphilis), but one persistent source of aggravation was the feelings of hatred he harbored toward the Irish thugs he'd had to confront throughout his life of crime.

Whether Al ever vented these feelings around his Irish wife would never be known. Having been born and raised near the Brooklyn waterfront, Mae would have known about the battles between Irish and Italian dock wallopers, a brutal labor war that sent ripples of fear through the borough. If her knowledge of these ethnic hostilities was lacking, she definitely got a crash course in late December 1925, seven years into her marriage, when she and her husband returned to Brooklyn to seek medical treatment for their son.

Seven-year-old Sonny had developed a severe mastoid infection, necessitating radical surgery. Al and Mae preferred that the operation take place in New York. They consulted various doctors, all of whom said the procedure would be risky but unavoidable. "I'll give you a hundred thousand dollars if you pull him through," Capone told one doctor. The surgery was performed the day before Christmas. Little Sonny came through okay, although he was left partially deaf and had to wear a hearing aid.

Of the events that followed, Capone later explained to a reporter: "It was Christmas Eve when my wife and I were sent home to get some sleep. We found her folks trimming the Christmas tree for her little nieces and nephews, and it broke her up." The following night, according to Al, "a friend of mine dropped in and asked me to go around the corner to his place to have a glass of beer. My wife told me to go: It'd do me good. And we were no sooner there than the door opens, and six fellows come in and start shooting. My friend had put me on the spot. In the excitement two of them were killed and my friend got shot in the leg. And I spent the holidays in jail."

Capone's version of the incident left out many crucial details, starting with the probability that the killings had been planned ahead of time. It all took place at the Adonis Social Club, a no-frills speakeasy located near the waterfront in Red Hook, Brooklyn. Capone himself had frequented the Adonis Social Club back in his early days as a Brooklyn dock walloper (he was known to use the club's basement for target practice). In fact, both Capone and Johnny Torrio first made their bones in the underworld during the violent labor war between Brooklyn Italians and what the papers dubbed "the White Hand," a gang of Irish racketeers led by the notorious William "Wild Bill" Lovett.

Lovett had been a machine gunner with the 11th Infantry in France during the war and was awarded the Distinguished Service Cross. After returning stateside, he became a ruthless extortionist in a section of the Brooklyn waterfront known as Irishtown, a rough-cobbled area between the Brooklyn Navy Yard and Fulton Ferry, under and around the approaches to the Brooklyn and Manhattan bridges. After assassinating Dinny Meehan to take over the Brooklyn rackets, Lovett fought to keep the Mafia off the docks. The hostilities that developed between Irish and Italian criminal interests on the Brooklyn waterfront resulted in over a hundred unsolved murders between 1915 and 1925. They were a key instigating factor in a war between the dagos and the micks that would spread throughout the country and continue to the end of the century.

Wild Bill Lovett was shot multiple times and hacked to death with a longshoreman's hook on Halloween night, 1923, by a mysterious Sicilian assassin imported from Palermo, known only as Dui Cuteddi (Two Knives). Afterward, leadership of the so-called White Hand fell to Lovett's brother-in-law, Richard "Peg Leg" Lonergan, who was believed to have authored a dozen professional murders. It was the red-haired, pugnacious Lonergan, along with five of his buddies, who stumbled into the Adonis Social Club on Christmas night, 1925, where Al Capone and a room full of his old Brooklyn *paisans* were waiting.

Peg Leg Lonergan was a well-known bigot. Although he had lost his leg in a trolley car accident as a youth, he was an accomplished brawler who first distinguished himself in Irishtown by killing a Sicilian drug dealer in a bike shop on Navy Street. Later, he and his fellow gangsters occasionally went on ginzo hunting expeditions in saloons and dives along the waterfront. According to witnesses at the Adonis Social Club, Lonergan and his people came into the club drunk and unruly, loudly referring to the patrons as "dagos" and "ginzos." When three Irish girls entered the club on the arms of some Italian boys, Lonergan chased them out of the place, yelling, "Come back with white men, fer chrissake!"

At this, someone in Capone's group gave the nod: The lights were cut off and bullets flew. In the ensuing melee, chairs and tables were overturned, glasses shattered, and customers rushed for the exit. When cops arrived on the scene, they found one of Lonergan's men lying in the street with the back of his head shot off. The cops followed a trail of blood back into the social club, where they found Lonergan and another member of his group shot execution style in the head. A fourth member of Peg Leg's crew was found a few blocks away, crawling in the street; he'd been shot in the thigh and leg and was rushed to the hospital.

Capone and six others were held without bail until the Lonergan man in the hospital had recovered enough to talk. The man refused to testify or even admit that he was in the Adonis Social Club on the night of the shooting; he was wounded in the street, he insisted, by a stray bullet from a passing car. Al and the others were released on bail bonds of $5,000 to $10,000. Without any witnesses willing to take the stand and testify, the case was soon dismissed.

Lonergan's sister, Anna, who was also Wild Bill Lovett's widow, attributed the slaughter at the Adonis Social Club to "foreigners." "You can bet it was no Irish American like ourselves who would stage a mean murder like this on Christmas day," she said.[5]

The Capone family returned to Chicago. There is no known record of how Al might have tried to explain the carnage to his Brooklyn Irish wife, but it's clear that his loathing for gangsters of the Celtic persuasion grew over the years. The extent of his loathing—not to mention his own innate narcissism—was best exemplified in a statement he made late in his life to a fellow prison inmate, Morris "Red" Rudensky. Rudensky had been gently needling him about O'Banion, O'Donnell, Moran, et al., to which Capone

---

5. Anna Lonergan was herself quite a piece of work. She often bragged that the three men in her life—her brother, Peg Leg, and her two husbands, Wild Bill Lovett and Matty Martin (who succeeded Lovett as a "dock organizer" in Irishtown) were responsible for at least twenty waterfront killings, though she always made a distinction between professional murders related to the rough-and-tumble world of the docks, and "stupid" killings attributable to such things as honor, bad temper, and misunderstanding. A tough broad from a family of fifteen, she once let her husband Wild Bill shoot off her toe to prove that she "could take it." She herself was shot once and stabbed twice in her life. Sometimes referred to as the Queen of Brooklyn's Irishtown docks, she is thought to hold the all-time record for morgue identifications. The only time anyone ever saw her cry was when she claimed Peg Leg's body. (For a deft and flavorsome profile of Anna Lonergan see *The Eight Million* by Meyer Berger.)

replied "Those silly Irish bastards. They got more guts than sense. If we ever woulda all hooked up, I coulda been President."

Who Killed McSwiggin and Why?

As long as the gangsters only killed each other, the public didn't get too upset. In some quarters, the Beer Wars were like a blood sport, with daily accounts in the newspapers serving as box scores. In 1925, the recently formed Chicago Crime Commission instituted the first ever use of a public enemies list. Printed semiannually in the papers, complete with mug shot photos and abbreviated rap sheets, it became a virtual player program, helping the public to keep names and territories straight. Of course, some people were horrified by the killings and growing lawlessness, but others among the cities many ethnic enclaves rooted for their side in a bloody game that sometimes seemed like a surreal microcosm of life in the big city.

Even those who viewed the city's crime wars with frivolity and "ethnic pride," however, were shocked by the events of April 27, 1926, a mob hit so outrageous that it would significantly reconfigure the way people looked at "those lovable bootleggers."

William H. McSwiggin was a smart, highly touted twenty-six-year-old prosecutor in the state's attorney's office. He had been handpicked by the top man himself: Robert Emmett Crowe, a stern, beetle-browed Irish American who for five years had served as state's attorney for Cook County, with an eye on higher elective office. Crowe's tenure happened to coincide with one of the most violent periods in the county's history. According to records compiled by the Better Government Association of Chicago and Cook County, of the 349 murders that occurred in Crowe's first two terms in office, 215 involved gangsters killed in the Beer Wars. Yet, despite the size of the state's attorney's office (with seventy assistant state's attorneys and fifty police, it was the largest in the history of the prosecutor's office), it obtained a mere 128 convictions for murder, none involving gangsters. Bombings during the same period totaled 369 without a single conviction.

With daily broadsides in the press suggesting that Crowe was either inept or corrupt, the prickly state's attorney placed a high level of emphasis on his rising young star, Bill McSwiggin, who in one year alone won convictions in nine straight capital cases. Little Mac, as McSwiggin was known to his friends, was the son of a decorated Chicago cop. The product of a Catholic education that included undergraduate studies and law school at DePaul University, McSwiggin was a registered Republican who had helped deliver votes for State's Attorney Crowe, which led to his appointment at a young age. Five foot nine, with the build and bearing of an athlete, McSwiggin dressed beyond his means and was known to have a sharp wit. In an office still largely comprised of WASP holdovers from a previous generation, he was a tough, street-wise Irish American who'd grown up on the West Side alongside kids who were now among some of the city's most notorious bootleggers. In fact, he was still friendly with various members of the West Side O'Donnell gang, who were presently engaged in a rambunctious shooting war with Al Capone for control of Cicero.

Despite McSwiggin's occasional fraternization with known disreputable characters, his reputation as a public servant was squeaky clean. The belief that he was incorruptible was underscored by his father's long years of service to the Chicago police department. But given the abysmal record of the state's attorney's office in recent years, the public lionization of the handsome, young prosecutor involved a fair amount of fanciful myth-making on the part of the citizenry and the press—all of which made it doubly shocking when McSwiggin wound up dead in the company of scoundrels.

At six o'clock P.M. on the evening of April 27, McSwiggin was eating supper at 4946 West Washington Boulevard, where he still lived with his parents and four sisters. He was visited by Tom "Red" Duffy, a boyhood chum and known member of the West Side O'Donnell gang. McSwiggin left his meal unfinished, saying he was going to play cards with some friends.

Outside the McSwiggin home, Bill and Red climbed into a car waiting at the curb. Behind the wheel sat Jim Doherty, another known gangster whom McSwiggin had only recently prosecuted (unsuccessfully) on a murder rap. Seated next to Doherty was his co-defendant from that case, Myles O'Donnell. In the back seat of the car sat Klondike O'Donnell, Myles' brother. These four men, crammed in the car alongside Assistant State's Attorney Bill McSwiggin, represented the entire upper echelon of the notorious West Side O'Donnell gang.

Jim Doherty had driven only a few blocks when his engine began to sputter. He pulled into a West Side garage and left the car there for repairs. The entire group got into Klondike O'Donnell's new Lincoln sedan. A sixth man joined the party: Edward Hanley, a former police officer now working for the O'Donnells. Hanley drove. They cruised around Cicero for about two hours, drinking beer in several saloons and speakeasies. Their last stop was the Pony Inn, a two-story, white-brick saloon owned by Harry Madigan, once a member of Ragen's Colts. At 5613 West Roosevelt Road, the Pony Inn was a mile north of the Hawthorne Inn, Al Capone's new headquarters in Cicero.

The rivalry between the O'Donnells and Capone for control of Cicero had been heating up. Mostly it was about beer, but it also had to do with

Capone's having opened a massive brothel (managed by his brother Ralph) on the southern edge of town near the Hawthorne Race Track. Like Deanie O'Banion before them, the O'Donnells made a distinction between illegal booze and gambling on the one hand and prostitution on the other; whoring, after all, was a corruption of the flesh, a sin that was biblical in nature. It was a quaint distinction, perhaps (the illegal beer business killed more people than prostitution ever did), but it was one that held considerable sway with Cicero's sizable Catholic population, both Irish and Italian, who viewed Capone as a degenerate vice peddler.

Even so, Capone had managed to take over Cicero through political intimidation, corruption of the local police, and brute force. The O'Donnells had resisted to the extent that they could. Mostly, they were a thorn in Capone's side, one that he viewed in the larger context of his war with the Irish who were spread far and wide throughout the area and coming at him from all directions.

A Capone scout spotted Klondike O'Donnell's Lincoln parked in front of the Pony Inn. He notified his boss, who impulsively saw the occasion as an opportunity to consolidate his business interests in one fell swoop. Capone grabbed a tommy gun and quickly assembled a team of men. Applying Machiavelli's theory of massive retaliation, they deployed five cars with a total of four gunmen. The cortege of vehicles lined up a half block away from the Pony Inn and waited for the Irishmen to appear.

Bill McSwiggin and his group of gangster buddies emerged from the saloon shortly after eight o'clock P.M. Pleasantly stewed, they ambled across the sidewalk toward the Lincoln. Capone's motorcade immediately swung into action. While cruising past the group of six men, they cut loose with a barrage of machine gun fire. An eyewitness who lived above the saloon later testified: "I saw a closed car speeding away with what looked like a telephone receiver sticking out the rear window and spitting fire. . . ."

Duffy, Doherty, and McSwiggin took the brunt of the hit, while Hanley and the O'Donnells were spared by throwing themselves to the pavement behind the sedan. Once the dust settled, the O'Donnell's surveyed the damage. Duffy was beyond help, riddled with holes and maybe already dead. Doherty's legs had been shattered and his chest ripped open, but he was still alive. McSwiggin was also alive, but hurt badly, shot multiple times in the back and neck.

A dog barked in the distance, and lights flicked on in the surrounding apartment buildings. "Fuck, oh fuck, oh fuck . . ." mumbled one of the injured men.

"Think, think, think," muttered Myles O'Donnell, trying to decide what to do.

In the tense moments that followed, the O'Donnell brothers panicked. Hoping to avoid a scandal that would surely ensue if they took the assistant state's attorney to the hospital, where they would face a battery of police and newspapermen, they decided to move the injured men to Klondike's house nearby on Parkside Avenue and call a doctor from there. They quickly loaded Doherty and McSwiggin into the back seat of their car. Duffy, they figured, was a hopeless case; they left his bleeding body propped up against a tree. But before the brothers ever reached Klondike's house, Doherty and McSwiggin both expired.

The O'Donnells now had two dead bodies on their hands, one of them a renowned public official. Leaving Doherty's corpse in the car, they decided to cart McSwiggin into the house. There they removed all identifiable belongings from his pockets and clothes, then took the body back to the car and put it in the trunk. With one brother following in a smaller car, they drove out of town to a lonely stretch of prairie and stopped. The O'Donnells removed the bodies of their two boyhood friends from the Lincoln and dumped them in a ditch. Then they continued on to Oak Park, where they abandoned the Sedan. After that, they vanished, not to be seen or heard from for more than a month. (Capone also vanished that night and hid out for the next three months.)

Duffy was the first to be found that night. He was still alive when a passing motorist discovered him seated against a tree in a pool of his own blood. The motorist drove him to a hospital.

"Pretty cold to leave me lying there," Duffy muttered in the emergency room. Those were his last words. In his pocket, the police found a list of sixty Cicero speakeasies and saloons, many of them checked off with pencil marks. Before the night was over, the list mysteriously disappeared.

A few days later, McSwiggin's and Doherty's corpses were discovered and identified. The bare details of what happened that night were established. Though it was not immediately known whether McSwiggin was the target of the hit or who had done the shooting, the circumstances surrounding the bloody triple homicide were discouraging. At the very least, Bill McSwiggin, the county's crusading prosecutor, had been killed while in the presence of known desperados, two of whom he had tried for murder just a few months before. Why was he hanging out with these men, and what had they been discussing?

The ensuing investigation did not answer these questions, but it did uncover many disturbing truths. Among other things, it was learned that once the bodies of McSwiggin and the others had been discovered, Cicero policemen visited every saloon in town and warned the owners: "There's gonna to be a big investigation. Don't tell nobody nothin'. If you open your face, you get ratted out to the Prohibition office and face federal prosecution. Understood?"

The *Tribune* asked the question in a page one editorial: "Who Killed McSwiggin and Why?" Every week, this same headline appeared on the editorial page with an update on the investigation. Despite state's attorney Crowe's guarantee that an unprecedented amount of investigatory firepower would be brought to bear, the investigation floundered. "The police have no more actual evidence as to the motives of the shooting and the identity of the killer than they did when it happened," stated the *Tribune*.

The frustrating lack of progress led to an irrefutable conclusion: Justice was ineffectual when stacked up against the forces of the underworld. If the cops were in on it and telling people to clam up, who else had a vested interest? Maybe state's attorney Crowe's laughable gangster prosecution record was not a result of ineptitude, as some felt, but of a process of collusion between the System and the gangsters. Maybe it wasn't corrupt politicians who were calling the shots, as it had been since the earliest days of the Machine. Maybe the gangsters were in control now. Maybe they—not the judges and the prosecutors—decided who would be convicted and who would go free. Maybe the whole of American justice was rotten to the core.

When Al Capone finally reemerged in Chicago after numerous grand juries had been empanelled and disbanded for lack of evidence, he quickly tossed fuel on the fire. "I didn't kill [McSwiggin]," he told reporters. "Why would I? I liked the kid. Only the day before he was up to my place, and, when he went home, I gave him a bottle of Scotch for his old man."

He told another reporter, "I paid McSwiggin. I paid him plenty and got what I paid for . . . Doherty and Duffy were my friends, too. I wasn't out to get them. Why, I used to lend Doherty money. Big-hearted Al I was, just helping out a friend. I wasn't in the beer racket and didn't care where they sold. Just a few days before that shooting, my brother Ralph and Doherty and the O'Donnells were at a party together."

Out of frustration, McSwiggin's old man took matters into his own hands. The retired sixty-year-old cop told reporters, "I thought my life's work was over, but it's only begun. I'll never rest until I've killed my boy's slayers or seen them hanged. That's all I have to live for now." After a year-long investigation, Sergeant McSwiggin publicly named the men he felt were responsible for his son's death. Al Capone and three other men manned the machine guns, he said, while two others acted as look-outs. An oath of secrecy prevented him from revealing the source of his information.

The names offered by the grieving father were nothing new. Months earlier, State's Attorney Crowe had himself publicly identified Capone as the killer, stating that Big Al had fired the tommy gun himself as an example to his underlings. So everyone knew who the killers were. The problem was that without some kind of evidence linking them to the shooting, and no witnesses or accomplices willing to testify, there was nothing anyone could do. The gangsters were above the law.

Like many notable Prohibition-era killings, the murder of Assistant State's Attorney McSwiggin remains unsolved to this day. A report compiled at the time by the Illinois Crime Survey surmised that "The very failure of the grand juries in solving the mystery of McSwiggin's death raises many puzzling and disturbing questions in the minds of intelligent citizens about the reasons for the breakdown of constituted government in Chicago and Cook County and its seeming helplessness when pitted against the forces of organized crime."

Meanwhile, the war between the dagos and micks raged on.

Gunning for Bugs

On September 20, 1926, Bugs Moran and his gang opened fire on Capone's headquarters at the Hawthorne Inn in Cicero, reducing the hotel lobby, the adjoining restaurant, and neighborhood storefronts to ruins. Capone, who was in the restaurant having lunch, narrowly escaped with his life. A few weeks later, he exacted revenge. Hymie Weiss, the former Little Hellion and boyhood chum of O'Banion and Moran, was gunned down in broad daylight along with his bodyguard, Paddy Murray, and William J. O'Brien, one of Chicago's leading criminal defense lawyers. It would have been labeled a "shocking triple homicide," with photos and banner headlines, except that murders of this vintage were now so commonplace in Chicago that they sometimes didn't even make the front page.

The tit-for-tat shootings, bombings, and killings continued until a gangland summit meeting was finally held at the downtown Sherman Hotel, located within the shadows of both Chicago City Hall and police headquarters. At this meeting, which was attended by Capone, Moran, the West Side O'Donnells, and others, a five-point peace treaty was put forth and agreed to. The treaty stood for a few weeks, until Moran and his remaining crew started hijacking Canadian booze shipments out of Detroit that belonged to Capone.

More than anyone else in the underworld, crazy Bugs Moran worried Capone. Scarface Al was enough of a student of human nature to know that Moran had harbored deep-seated revenge fantasies against him ever since the murder of his mentor, Dean O'Banion. The Polish-Irish gangster was unusually vociferous in his dislike for Capone, routinely referring to Capone in public as "the Beast" or "the Behemoth." Bugs sometimes seemed to be baiting Big Al, trying to draw him into an angry mistake or miscalculation that would cost him his life. When asked by a reporter one time to expound on the difference between himself and Capone, Bugs explained, "The Beast uses his muscle men to peddle rot-gut alcohol and green beer. I'm a legitimate salesman of good beer and pure whiskey. He trusts nobody and suspects everybody. He always has guards. I travel around with a couple of pals. The Behemoth can't sleep nights. If you ask me, he's on dope. Me, I don't even need an aspirin."

The hostilities between Moran and Capone continued for two years, with hijackings, shootings, killings, and other acts of insurgency that seemed to be building toward some kind of crescendo, which is exactly what came to pass. On the night of February 13, 1929, Bugs got a call from a hijacker offering him a truckload of whiskey from Detroit at the bargain price of fifty-seven dollars a case.

"Great," said Moran. "Bring it to the warehouse around ten thirty tomorrow morning. We'll all be there."

Bugs hung up the phone. He could hardly contain himself; the shipment was one of Capone's, snatched along the Chicago-Detroit highway, according to the hijacker. Bugs spent the rest of the evening calling around to various members of his gang, informing them to meet at the North Clark Street warehouse the following morning to help unload the shipment.

The next day, Bugs Moran rose late, as was his usual style. A gang associate who sometimes acted as his driver met Moran at his Parkway Hotel apartment. Together, the two men drove the short distance from the hotel to the gang's warehouse at 2122 North Clark Street, and arrived in the area shortly after ten thirty.

A bone-chilling wind whipped in off Lake Michigan, dropping the temperature to fifteen below zero. Rather than pull up in front of the warehouse, park, and have to walk through the freezing cold, Moran and his associate decided to enter via an alleyway in the back. As their vehicle approached the red-brick warehouse sandwiched between two taller buildings, Moran saw a car with uniformed police officers inside. Thinking it was a raid or police shakedown of some kind, he told his driver to continue on past the warehouse and head back to the hotel.

Upon his return to the Parkway Hotel, it took only minutes for Bugs Moran to begin receiving bits of information about what had gone wrong at the warehouse. In the days and weeks that followed, the rest of the city and the nation would also find out. In fact, enterprising newspapermen gave the events of that day a memorable designation: the St. Valentine's Day Massacre.

Moran's entire gang was slaughtered. The only reason Bugs survived was because he was late; a lookout for the killers had mistakenly identified one of the other bootleggers as Bugs. The gunmen, dressed as Chicago police officers, entered the warehouse and showed their identification, claiming it was a police bust. Then they lined the six North Side bootleggers (and another man who just happened to be there) against the wall and mowed them down, thinking Bugs Moran was among them.

Even to a city and nation inured to the violence that Prohibition had wrought, the headlines that day were shocking: "Seven Slaughtered on Valentine's Day" read the *Tribune*; "Gang 'Firing Squad' Kills 7," trumpeted the *Herald-Examiner*; "Massacre 7 of Moran Gang," splashed the *Daily News*. Initial reports did not name Capone; they focused instead on the four policemen seen entering the North Clark Street warehouse.

"The killers were not gangsters," the local Prohibition administrator was quoted as saying. "They were Chicago policemen. I believe the killing was the aftermath to the hijacking of five hundred cases of whiskey belonging to the Moran gang by five policemen six weeks ago on Indianapolis Boulevard. I expect to have the names of these five policemen in a short time. It is my theory that in trying to recover the liquor the Moran gang threatened to expose the policemen, and the massacre was to prevent the exposure."

The administrator's comments would go down in history as one of the most wrong-headed assessments ever recorded in print (he later claimed it was a misquote), but the fact that he was initially believed was an indication of how low the Chicago police had sunk in the estimation of many citizens.

When informed of the details of the massacre, Bugs Moran's assessment proved to be more trenchant. "Only Capone kills like that," he said.

Not surprisingly, the Behemoth had an airtight alibi; he was at his Palm Island estate in Miami at the time of the shooting, though phone records showed that he was in constant contact with key underlings back in Chicago in the days leading up to the killings.

Like most mob-hit investigations, numerous rumors and details came to the forefront, but few that could be bolstered by evidence or testimony. Within days, newly appointed Chief of Detectives John Egan and his investigators had identified one of the gunmen, a professional killer out of St. Louis who went by the name Fred "Killer" Burke. Despite the Hibernian surname, Burke was not an Irishman. His real name was Thomas Camp; he was an Okie by way of Kansas, though he was associated with Egan's Rats, a mostly Irish gang based in St. Louis that Capone sometimes drew from when contracting professional hits. Burke/Camp was known for using the policeman ruse when conducting his assassinations.

Eventually, the full details of the St. Valentine's Day Massacre would be revealed; the event stands as perhaps the most thoroughly discussed and written about gangland hit in the history of organized crime. One person who didn't need to wait around for the slow drip of history to reveal to him what had gone down that day was Bugs Moran. With virtually his entire gang wiped out in one shooting, his standing in the Chicago underworld never recovered. Although he stayed in the area a few more years, his power waned. Eventually, he fled Chicago and was never again a major player in the underworld.[6]

The St. Valentine's Day Massacre changed everything. The event was not only front page news in Chicago; it dominated the newspapers for days in every big city in the United States, including New York. People had grown accustomed to bootleggers killing bootleggers, but this was something different—a cold-blooded execution of seven people carried out by fake policemen. It seemed to capture the full flavor of an era that had become so corrupt and violent that only a shocking event like this could jar the public back to reality.

---

6. Some believe that Bugs Moran may have exacted a degree of revenge for the St. Valentine's Day Massacre in 1936. On February 13 of that year, the eve of the anniversary of the massacre, Machine Gun Jack McGurn (real name Vincenzo De Mora), long believed to be a planner and principle in the St. Valentine's Day hit, was gunned down by a five-man hit team in a Chicago-area bowling alley. When cops arrived they found a nickel in McGurn's left hand; in his right they found a note that read: "You've lost your job,/ You've lost your dough,/ Your jewels and handsome houses./ But things could be worse, you know./ You haven't lost your trousers." The jokiness of this message smacked of Moran, who was a prankster in the tradition of his mentor, Dean O'Banion.

After leaving Chicago, Moran's crimes turned petty compared to the glory days of Prohibition. In July 1946, he was arrested in Ohio for robbing a bank messenger of a paltry $10,000, an amount that would have been chump change twenty years earlier. He was convicted and sentenced to ten years. After his release, he was again arrested for an earlier bank raid and sent down for another ten-year stretch at Leavenworth, where he eventually died of cancer in 1957. Unlike O'Banion's burial, which was an event to remember in the annals of Chicago history, Bugs was given a pauper's burial in a wooden casket in a potters field just outside the prison walls.

The press and the public weren't the only ones who sensed a shift in the zeitgeist. For some time now, prominent rum runners and bootleggers following the broiling gangland wars in Chicago had sensed the changing attitudes. The violence and general air of lawlessness brought about by Prohibition had gradually turned nearly everyone against the Volstead Act. Politicians and law enforcement people routinely condemned the act, acknowledging that it was unenforceable. The St. Valentine's Day Massacre had precipitated a crisis. Nationwide, discerning underworld leaders realized that disaster was imminent; something needed to be done to stem such flagrant acts of carnage. Otherwise, the public and the press were going to turn so strongly against the gangs that they would be unable to operate, or, even worse, political pressure would lead to the repeal of Prohibition—whereupon the party would really be over.

The war between the dagos and the micks was about to enter a new phase.

requiem for a mad dog

he briny shores of Atlantic City were a fitting locale for an unprecedented meeting-of-the-minds among the country's most distinguished masters of Prohibition. Through guile and brutality, these men had redefined the American Dream and catapulted the gangster beyond the urban slum into the realm of the corporate robber baron. In times of turmoil, corporate chieftains held summit meetings in which profits were assessed, roles reassigned, projections made, and the concerns of investors discussed. Likewise, the nation's top mobsters met to discuss the widespread concern that the level of violence associated with the booze business had gotten out of hand. Something needed to be done. What that something would be was the reason the country's mobster elite arrived in the resort town of Atlantic City for a three-day conference, which would be cited in later years as the dawn of an organized crime commission in the United States.

The conference was the brain-child of Papa John Torrio, who had left Chicago four years earlier, moved to New York, and become a mobster diplomat without portfolio. Luciano, Costello, Lansky, and other leading lights of the underworld frequently consulted the older and wiser Torrio, mostly to discuss Scarface Al Capone—whom Torrio had snatched from the docks of Brooklyn, moved to Chicago, and ceded an enormous amount of power and profit (newspaper assessments of Capone's holdings in 1929 put his wealth at forty million dollars, with an annual income of six million).

Luciano, who fancied himself a leader in the Torrio mold, asked Papa John, "What the fuck are we gonna do 'bout Al? That fat bastard is gonna take us all down with his tommy gun hysterics."

Torrio agreed, but cautioned, "I know Al. If you make it seem like you're coming down on him and him alone, he'll go off in a snit. You gotta frame it just right."

The conference took place over the weekend of May 13–16, just two months after the scandalous slaughter on St. Valentine's Day. Checking into two Atlantic City Boardwalk hotels for the event was a gathering unparalleled in modern history: thirty top-ranking mobsters representing virtually every region of the United States. New York represented the largest contingent, with Luciano, Costello, Lansky, Dutch Schultz, and Owney Madden in attendance. Chicago had Capone. Nig Rosen and Boo-Boo Hoff came from Philadelphia, Moe Dalitz from Cleveland, King Soloman from Boston, and Waxey Gordon from New Jersey. From Kansas City came Johnny Lazia, who was said to represent the interests of the Pendergast Machine, an Irish American consortium that had turned Kansas City into an unlikely underworld haven during the years of Prohibition. Representatives from South Florida, New Orleans, Detroit, and other localities were also in attendance.

The conference was no great secret. Local newspapers carried pictures of Capone and some of the other mobster celebrities as they cruised the world famous boardwalk and dipped their toes in the ocean. When it came to conducting more serious business, the men convened privately in conference rooms atop the Ritz and Ambassador hotels.

Along with the untoward level of gangland violence in Chicago that had become a concern to all, there were numerous other items on the agenda, not the least of which was the recent murder of Arnold "the Brain" Rothstein. The former protégé of Big Tim Sullivan and primary financier of the mob's gambling rackets had been shot in a Manhattan hotel room six months earlier. His death left a huge vacuum; among other things, Rothstein's role in the organization necessitated the designation of a successor.[1] More long-term matters that needed to be discussed were the likely repeal of

---

1. Arnold Rothstein's murder on November 4, 1928 remains one of the great mysteries of the Prohibition era. He was shot during a card game at the Park Central Hotel. Underworld conspiracy theorists believed that the hit had likely been arranged by higher-ups. Prominent among many suspects was Legs Diamond. Rothstein had been forced to cut Diamond loose after Legs became a thorn in the side of the Combine. The betrayal angered Legs, whose ability to harbor a grudge was second-to-none; of the twenty-four murders Legs is believed to have played a role in, many were revenge killings. Diamond himself always claimed that though he might have wanted Rothstein dead, he had nothing to do with his murder. Was Legs telling the truth? Outside of pure speculation, there has never been any evidence to suggest otherwise.

Prohibition and the country's general financial uncertainty (the Wall Street crash of '29 and Great Depression were on the horizon), which would have profound consequences for the country's black market economy.

Among historians and organized crime folklorists, the Atlantic City conference is often noted as the beginning of a representative multiethnic governing body, or commission, designed to guide the Syndicate into the future. While it may be true that the conference had a major impact on the future direction of the underworld, the notion that the gathering was an ethnically representative accounting of organized crime in America is pure fiction. After all, there were only two Irishmen in attendance.

One of those Irishmen was Chicago's Frank McErlane, a glorified gunman and degenerate alcoholic whose gang never numbered more than six or seven members. The idea that McErlane was a representative leader of the Irish mob in Chicago is laughable. Frank was there for one reason only: He was "Al's boy," the only significant Irish American gang boss to side with Capone during the city's bloody Beer Wars.

The other Irishman in attendance was Owney Madden, who was a special case. Although he was a gangster with an impressive early resume—five murders and over forty arrests as leader of the Gopher Gang—Owney was no longer connected to the streets. In creating the Combine and rising to the pinnacle of underworld success, he had become Duke of the West Side, a self-made man in the Jay Gatsby mold. And like Fitzgerald's mysterious and mythical Roaring Twenties protagonist, he'd paid a price, which was an estrangement from the people and places he once knew. Owney Madden may have represented the Combine and those business interests that he helped to mold and sustain, but he no longer represented the Irish. He represented Owney Madden.

Which begs the question: Where were the South Side O'Donnells, the West Side O'Donnells, Bugs Moran, and the Terrible Touhys? Where was Danny Walsh of Providence? Brooklyn's Vannie Higgins? Legs Diamond and Vincent Coll? Where were the untold dozens of Irish American gang leaders who'd played such a formative role in the creation of the political-criminal alliance that made Prohibition a hugely lucrative racket in the first place?

The simple answer is that they were shut out. When viewed this way, the Atlantic City conference can be seen for what it really was: not the nation's first gathering of a multiethnic underworld coalition, but the beginning of a process by which Sicilian, Italian, Italian American, and Jewish gangsters would move the Irish to the fringe of the criminal underworld. The reasons for this development were more complex than mere ethnic animosity. To Italian and Jewish gangsters, the argument for marginalizing the Irish had more to do with the fair distribution of criminal spoils. The Irish, after all, already controlled the police departments and a sizable portion of the political organizations in many of the underworld's most lucrative domains. Why should they also be acceded equal share in the underworld as well? What's fair is fair, right?

The Syndicate was more than willing to deal with Irish American cops and politicians who knew how to play along. In New York, Luciano and Costello delivered cash to City Hall and police headquarters through Joe Cooney, a freckle-faced Irish American bagman they sometimes referred to as Joe the Coon.[2] Paying off Irish cops and politicians was accepted as the price of doing business; it had its benefits, most notably as a potential entrée into the upperworld, which held the promise of connecting with certain legitimate rackets that would be essential in a post-Prohibition environment. In later years, when Luciano or Meyer Lansky would ask, "What about the Irish? Who's taking care of the Irish?" They didn't mean Irish mobsters. They meant the Irish cops, politicians, and establishment figures who were "friendly." In the eyes of many Italian and Jewish gangsters, this was the fair and proper role for the Irish in the underworld; since they had "gotten here first," so to speak, and had infiltrated the upperworld, that was their function. The rest should be left to the Italians, Jews, Poles, and even the blacks.

Of course, for this New World Order to work properly, certain Irish gangsters had to be held in check. In New York, there were already a few prominent Irish American bootleggers angry about being sidelined by the Combine. One of them was the dangerous young gangster, Vincent Coll, who had started as a gunman for Dutch Schultz and lately begun muscling in on his former boss's operations. Dutch Schultz was not happy about this. The near psychotic mob boss, whose gangland murder would later be sanctioned by many of the same men he dined with at the Atlantic City conference, voiced his concerns to all.

"This crazy maniac Coll is causing me no end of grief," he told those gathered atop the Ambassador Hotel on the second night of the conference. "I want it stopped, or I want him dead. Either way."

---

2. According to Luciano in his autobiography, he and Costello were greatly amused by Joe Cooney's displeasure when they referred to him as "Joe the Coon"—in other words, "our Irish nigger."

In a strange bit of underworld symmetry, the primary Irish American bagman for Al Capone at the time was also named Cooney—Dennis "Duke" Cooney, owner of the Rex Hotel in Chicago and ostensibly the highest ranking mick in the Capone organization.

Waxey Gordon then stood and chimed in, "Yeah, and what about this bastid Legs Diamond? He's hijacking my trucks and raiding our clip joints all over north Jersey."

The men around the table mumbled their concerns over this growing threat.

Because Coll and Diamond were both Irish, the job of rectifying the problem fell on Owney Madden. He may have been a Liverpool-born Irishman who, in his current incarnation, saw himself as more of a WASP businessman than a street hoodlum, but to the others in attendance he was the only New York mick in the room.

The next day, Madden left the conference early and returned to Manhattan. The Commission seemed to be asking him to take responsibility, not only for Coll and Diamond, but for every Irish American gangster who was disgruntled about the rise of the Italian-Jewish Syndicate and the marginalization of the micks. In Owney's estimation, it was a hell of a tall order.

"Come and Get Me, Coppers!"

Few Irish American gangsters were students of organized crime. In fact, few were students of anything. Coming from the gutter, they got their information—not through books, newspapers, or even the radio—but through an underworld system known as the kite. At its worst, the kite was a rumor mill. At its best, it was a version of the news wire, except that it was entirely verbal, with nothing ever being written down for posterity or potential prosecution. Meant to be a few steps ahead of the cops and the newspapers, the kite disseminated information by way of saloons, smoke shops, political clubhouses, candy stores, and the streets. Information received through this process was notoriously suspect—prone to embellishment, misinterpretation, and outright deception—but you ignored the kite at your own risk. In the underworld, information received on the street could sometimes save your life.

No one knows the exact origins of the kite. The word itself has many meanings: A kite is flown high in the air to serve, perhaps, as a signal. A kite is also a bird, a member of the hawk family with long, narrow wings and the ability to swoop down and snatch its prey. A kite is also a bad check drawn against insufficient funds. Whatever its etymology, the kite as an information mill seems to be based on the Celtic clan system of long ago, when anticolonial Irish rebel groups passed information among themselves without ever submitting anything to public record. This philosophy also permeated the earliest Irish political machines throughout the United States, where it sometimes meant the difference between a scurrilous accusation with no actual record of wrongdoing and criminal prosecution by way of circumstantial evidence, i.e. public documents and financial records. As the legendary Boston ward boss Martin "the Mahatma" Lomasney once said "Don't write when you can talk; don't talk when you can nod your head." Lomasney was referring to the world of politics, but he could just as easily have been outlining the philosophy of the Irish American underworld.

By the dawn of the 1930's, as the nation began its descent into the harsh realities of the Great Depression, the word on the kite was that the underworld was in transition. The Irish were out; Jews and Italians were in. Irish American bootleggers looking to make a buck increasingly ran up against a brick wall. Some never even made it to the starting gate.

One such hoodlum was a young punk named Francis "Two Gun" Crowley, who probably hoped to be a bootlegger one day. In February 1931, he was little more than a bank robber and petty stick-up man, though he had shot and wounded a detective who tried to arrest him during a running gun battle in Manhattan. Crowley got away, and, a short time later, he turned up in New Rochelle, Westchester County, where he held up a bank at high noon. His crime spree continued over the next month, until May 6, 1931, when he shot and killed a Long Island cop who chanced upon him and his sweetheart necking in a car.

"Francis Crowley . . . who glories in the nickname of Two Gun Frank and is described by the police as the most dangerous criminal at large was hunted through the city last night," began a May 9 article in the *Daily News*. Authorities in New York didn't need to look far. Francis Crowley, a babyfaced kid who stood five foot three and barely weighed 145 pounds, had commandeered the apartment of a former girlfriend at 303 West Ninetieth Street, where he barricaded himself with a small arsenal (while his current girlfriend hid under a bed). There he waited, as a massive gathering of police and spectators filled the streets below.

When two detectives tried to enter the apartment via the building hallway, Crowley appeared with two guns blazing. "Come and get me, coppers!" he shouted while firing.

The detectives were forced to retreat.

Crowley then turned on the cops in the street. "I'm up here! I'm waiting for you!" he called down from a fifth-floor window, before opening fire and sending cops and onlookers scattering for cover.

The Siege of West Ninetieth Street continued for hours. At one point, police cut a hole in the roof and dropped canisters of tear gas into the apartment. Crowley fired shots through the ceiling, grabbed the canisters and tossed them into the street. Smoke clouded the area. The staccato sound of machine gun fire echoed through the streets; police hid behind their vehicles as bullets rained down from above.

Between volleys of gunfire, police and onlookers alike heard Crowley's demented laughter at the destruction. "You ain't gonna take me alive, coppers!" he called out the window.

Finally, a heavily-armed squad of police commandos stormed the apartment and wrestled Crowley to the floor. The crazed gangster had been shot four times, but he did not die. He was rushed to the hospital, where he would recover from his wounds to face criminal prosecution.

The saga of Two Gun Crowley was a media sensation. Over the radio and in the city's newspapers, Crowley was often described as a "mad Irish gunman" with "the face of an alter boy." The characterization was an example of what was becoming a common stereotype of the era—that of the genetically reckless Irish gangster who was always willing to take on the System. Never mind that Crowley was possibly not even Irish (his German immigrant mother had given him up for adoption at birth; "Crowley" was the name of his adopted family). But with his irrational brand of courage, boyish good looks, and steely blue eyes, he fit the stereotype to a T.[3]

Owney Madden must have read the newspaper accounts of Two Gun Crowley's rampage with a sense of relief. Although the crazy young hoodlum may have been identified as Irish, he was not in any way affiliated with the Combine and therefore could not be seen as Madden's responsibility. Such was not the case with another "crazed Irish gunman" making headlines on a near-daily basis, Vincent "the Mad Mick" Coll.

It was Madden who had brought Coll into the organization in the first place. Back in 1926, when the kid was just seventeen years old, Owney introduced the young gangster to Dutch Schulz, sometimes referred to as

---

3. The legend of Two Gun Crowley and the Siege at West Ninetieth Street are believed to have been the inspiration for the memorable finale to the James Cagney movie *White Heat* ("Look ma! I made it. Top of the world!") As for Crowley himself, he was dispatched within record time. On May 29, 1931, less than a month after his capture, he was found guilty for the murder of the Long Island police officer. He was held at Sing Sing Prison, where at nineteen years old, he was one of the youngest convicts ever on death row.

Capital punishment was all the rage. At Sing Sing alone, twenty men went to their deaths in the electric chair in 1932; eighteen men the following year. In his six months at Sing Sing, Crowley saw thirteen men walk "the last mile" before it was his turn. "My last wish is to send my love to my mother," he said at eleven o'clock on the night of January 21, 1932. He was then hit with two thousand volts of electricity and declared dead within minutes.

"the Dutchman." Vincent and his older brother Peter had formed a gang made up of the usual assortment of Irishmen, Italians, and Jews. Madden thought they might be useful to the Dutchman, who was then expanding his bootlegging operations into the Bronx. Coll's reputation as a fearless killer was immediately put to use by Shultz and others as well. Sometime in 1930, unbeknownst to Madden, Vincent Coll was hired by the Maranzano family to bump off Lucky Luciano. Coll was on his way to kill Luciano when the hit was called off. He got to keep the $25,000 advance payment, and the incident secured his reputation as one of the more noteworthy hitmen for hire in the New York underworld.

In Vincent Coll, Madden may have seen something of himself or at least an image of the kind of doomed gangster he might have become had he not risen above his station. Born in the tiny Gaelic-speaking village of Gweedore, in County Donegal, Coll was brought to New York as an infant in 1909 and lived in a cold-water tenement in the Bronx. His family quickly became mired in a cycle of poverty and despair that evoked the worst hardships of potato-famine immigrants. Before Vincent was twelve, five of his siblings would perish from childhood accidents or disease. His father, Tony, fled the home, never to return. His mother, Anna, died from pneumonia when Vincent was seven. He and his brother Peter were taken away by the state of New York and institutionalized in Staten Island at the Mt. Loretto orphanage, a house of refuge known for its punitive approach to reform. Vincent lived there for three years, escaping repeatedly. He was diagnosed as an adolescent deviant, and one early psychiatric report noted his deep-seeded problems with authority.

By the time he hooked up with Dutch Schultz, Vincent had already developed the brazen, self-destructive streak that was to become his most distinguishing characteristic as a gangster. At nineteen, authorities charged him with the murder of a speakeasy owner who refused to buy Schultz's booze. (At trial, Coll was acquitted, probably through Schultz's influence.) Vincent was gawky and boyish, with a full mane of unruly reddish-blond hair, a prominently dimpled chin, and a broad toothy grin. It was not brains but cold-blooded efficiency as a killer that catapulted the young hoodlum to the leadership position of his gang. Some of Coll's most devoted fellow gang members were Italian Americans who saw the Mad Mick as their ticket to the upper echelons of the Prohibition rackets. Vincent's girlfriend and true love, Lottie Kriesberger, was of German extraction—just like his boss and nemesis-to-be, Dutch Schultz.

Following the mobster conference in Atlantic City, Vincent stepped up his war with the Dutchman, who was getting filthy rich off bootlegging, nightclubs, and the policy racket, while Coll was paid a measly hundred dollars per week by the Schultz organization.

"I ain't your nigger shoeshine boy," Coll told Schultz. "I'll show you a thing or two."

After Vincent and his gang staged an outlandish daytime robbery at the Sheffield Farms dairy in the middle of the Dutchman's Bronx territory, Schultz waltzed into the 42nd Precinct station house and declared, "I'll buy a house in Westchester for anybody in here who can stiff the mick."

A squad room full of cops looked at the Dutchman in utter disbelief.

"You know you're in the Morrisania police station?" asked a detective.

"I know where I am," snapped Dutch. "I been here before. I just came in to tell ya I'll pay good money to any cop that kills the mick."

Could Schultz's offer be taken seriously? Who the hell knew, but the hunt was on.

Madden tried to intermediate a truce to save the young Irish kid's life. He and Vincent met at the Stork Club, located in a town house on West Fifty-eighth Street near Central Park. Fast becoming the most renowned speakeasy in the city, the club was partly owned by a silent partnership of Madden, Big Bill Dwyer, and a business associate of Owney's named George Jean "Big Frenchy" DeMange.

"See this place?" Madden told Coll at a private booth inside the glamorous Stork Club. "You could own a place like this one day, Vincent. This could all be yours. But you gotta learn to play along."

Coll knew when he was being used, and he knew when he wasn't wanted.

"I'm the fool who takes all the risks," he told Owney. "Me and my brother, we been shot at, chased down, and arrested. You want I should be a good little boy while you, the Dutchman, and the dagos get rich? No. We should be equal partners, plain and simple."

In the early months of 1931, at least ten gunmen associated with the Combine were stabbed, shot, and beaten to death by Coll's gang. One of those men, Carmine Borelli, was executed when he refused to take part in a scheme to set up his boss, the Dutchman. Borelli's girlfriend witnessed the murder, so Coll chased her down and shot her in the head in the middle of a Bronx street.

A few days later, the Combine retaliated by murdering Peter Coll; he was machine-gunned to death on a Harlem street corner while driving home. Vincent was overwhelmed with grief at the loss of his older brother. Instead of going into mourning, however, he responded with calculated rage. He began kidnapping business associates of the Combine, first Big Frenchy

DeMange, whom he snatched off the street and held in an apartment in Westchester County until a ransom of $35,000 was paid, and then Sherman Billingsley, the celebrity proprietor of the Stork Club. Vincent then set out after Joey Rao, one of Schultz's prime movers in East Harlem, where the lucrative uptown policy rackets were based. What happened next would shock the entire country and seal Coll's fate as the most reviled man in the underworld.

On the afternoon of July 28, 1931, Rao was lounging in front of his headquarters, the Helmar Social club on East 107th Street. Accompanied by two bodyguards, Rao had a pocketful of pennies which he was distributing to a group of neighborhood children. A touring car came around the corner and opened fire with a tommy gun on Rao, his protectors, and the children. When the fusillade was over, five children lay wounded on the sidewalk. One of those children, five-year-old Michael Vengali, died before he reached a nearby hospital. Rao and his bodyguards escaped without a scratch.

Everyone in town knew Coll was behind the shooting. The newspapers called it the "baby massacre" and clamored for immediate action. Coll, the Mad Mick, was now christened "the Baby Killer." Mayor Jimmy Walker referred to gangster Coll as a "Mad Dog" and declared that the police department would pay $10,000 to anyone with information leading to his capture and prosecution. Even the underworld was repulsed. Both Madden and Shultz put out a $25,000 bounty on Coll, the lunatic gunman who was giving all bootleggers a bad name.

Vincent and Lottie went on the run. Wearing disguises and using false identities, they drove north to the Canadian border, then zig-zagged into Western Massachusetts, then back to Upstate New York. When they felt they had been spotted, they ditched their car and traveled by train. Heavily armed at all times, they lived in roadside motels, so they could escape quickly if necessary. They bought every meal to go. Occasionally, with his hair dyed black, a fake mustache, and glasses, Coll stepped out into the early morning or chilly evening to buy a newspaper or make a phone call; danger lurked in every wayward glance, every unwelcomed stare.

In October 1931, two and a half months after "the baby massacre," authorities began to zero in on Coll. The incident that started it all was a hit on Dutch Schultz's Bronx headquarters. Schultz wasn't on the premises at the time, but the two gunmen who sprayed the storefront with gunfire killed one of the Dutchman's underlings. A couple of Edison Company repairmen working in a nearby manhole happened to spot the two gunmen and got a good look at their license plate number. The number was traced to two members of the Coll gang. One by one, the cops tracked down and arrested Coll's fellow gang members, until one of them supplied the police with a hot tip on Vincent's whereabouts.

Apparently, Coll had recently snuck back into the city, thinking he could resume his bootlegging activities. The informant told the cops that he was hiding out in a room at the Cornish Arms Hotel on West Twenty-third Street. A squad of more than two dozen cops quietly surrounded the hotel. A smaller group entered and made their way to Coll's room. They banged on the door and announced their arrival. Vincent was undoubtedly armed to the teeth. He could have fought back and tried to escape, but the Mad Mick had no desire to wind up like Two Gun Crowley, shooting it out with the entire police force. He opened the door and turned himself in to the cops.

With the money he'd made from his various kidnapping escapades, Coll hired Samuel Liebowitz, one of the best criminal defense attorney's in town. Along with another member of his gang, he was facing attempted murder and manslaughter charges for the botched hit on Joey Rao and the killing of five-year-old Michael Vengalli. The whole town probably wanted him found guilty and executed in the electric chair, just like Crowley was.

His metamorphosis was complete: Vincent was now a total outcast. His gang had betrayed him. Everyone wanted him dead. Lottie, his fiancée, was all he had left. The only other solace left to him came from the knowledge that, as bleak as his own situation had become, there was another famous Irish American gangster out there who actually had it worse.

Happy Days and Lonely Nights

On December 18, 1931, as Mad Dog Coll's murder trial got under way in Manhattan, the dark angels of the underworld finally caught up with Jack Diamond. After numerous assassination attempts over the years, Legs was no more. This time, his killers left nothing to chance. They shot him three times in the head at close range, while he lay in bed in his room at an Albany boarding house.

Coll knew Diamond well. In fact, years earlier, while he was still working for Dutch Shultz, Coll was assigned to kill Jack Diamond. He and members of his gang tracked Legs around Manhattan from one speakeasy and nightclub to another. They finally met face to face at the Hotsy Totsy Club, Diamond's own popular speakeasy located on the second floor of 1721 Broadway, between Fifty-fourth and Fifty-fifth streets. Although Diamond knew Coll by reputation, he had no idea that the gawky, young, Irish kid with the red hair was there to kill him. They hit it off so well that Vincent reneged on the murder contract and formed a casual friendship with the older, wiser Irish American racketeer.

That was the first time they met. The last was when Vincent and Lottie were on the run in Upstate New York. The two gangsters convened secretly near Diamond's home base in Acra, a small town in Greene County. There they commiserated about their mutual predicaments as gangsters in exile, shut out by the Combine, which had morphed into the Syndicate, an Italian-Jewish consortium that seemed determined to wipe all Irish mobsters off the face of the earth

"It's that bastard Owney Madden," Coll told Diamond. "He's the one I blame for this."

Legs couldn't have agreed more. Although it was Dutch Schultz who'd initiated gangland wars with both Diamond and Coll, and Lucky Luciano who'd devised the plan to shut out the Irishers, they both felt Madden should have been on their side. "If the bastard ain't gonna stand up for his own fucking people, what good is he?" asked Diamond.

The two talked about starting their own bootlegging/crime consortium based in Upstate New York. It sounded like a great idea. They could be the Beer Barons of the Catskills, hiding out in the mountains and firing shots at whoever tried to come after them. Problem was, neither of them had the finances to pull it off. Vincent had lately been cut off from his bootlegging revenues, and Diamond had costly legal problems in the form of a murder trial that was scheduled to take place within weeks. As they said their good-byes that day, they had no way of knowing it would be the last time they saw each other alive.

For Jack Diamond, in particular, the long descent from Combine insider to hunted animal had been a saga of near biblical proportions. Back when Coll was first making his bones as a young upstart with the Dutchman, Legs had already established himself as an independent racketeer in a city crawl-ing with overly ambitious gangsters. Ever since the first known attempt on his life—when his car and body were riddled with buckshot back in October 1924—he'd led a precarious existence. For a time, he tried to steer clear of bootlegging by getting involved in the heroin trade. Luciano had already made millions off dope and so had Rothstein. The potential profits were enormous: In the mid 1920s, one kilo (2.2 pounds) of heroin could be pur-chased for $2,000. By the time it was cut, diluted, and sold, that same kilo brought in $300,000.

There were plenty of users. Heroin had not yet been classified as a serious narcotic, so the penalties for use were not overly severe. Some World War I veterans had developed a narcotics habit. Among African American jazz musicians and their predominantly white followers (most blacks were banned from or unable to afford entry to the era's swankiest nightclubs), heroin had become a trendy high, as had cocaine. The most nettlesome commercial problem with both of these drugs was importation.

It was Arnold Rothstein who reestablished ties with Legs in an attempt to strike a major narcotics deal, perhaps the largest ever undertaken at the time. In late 1926, Rothstein sent Legs to Europe to make the necessary purchase and arrange for smuggling the product into the United States. Diamond's efforts paid off months later when a huge shipment of heroin, morphine, and cocaine—hidden inside bowling pins—was delivered to the Valentine's Importing Company on Walker Street in lower Manhattan. Over a period of months, drug-peddling middlemen from all over the New York area arrived at Valentine's to purchase narcotics, conducting their business in the presence of the police—who were in many instances involved in the trade. In July 1928, a special intelligence unit conducted a raid on police department lockers at the 1st Police Precinct and caught seven cops with drugs and cash. Eventually, nearly fifty detectives would be implicated in one of the largest narcotics scandals in the history of the NYPD.

Diamond himself was arrested, but then released on $15,000 bail. The bail bond was posted by the Detroit Fidelity and Surety Company and guaranteed by Rothstein. The charges against him were later dismissed.

Diamond and Rothstein had a falling out over the drug business—one of numerous disagreements in their relationship, which ran hot and cold; they were like two lovers who knew they shouldn't be together but couldn't stay apart. This time, as always, the rift was over money. Legs wanted a bigger piece of the pie, and Rothstein resisted. The stakes were enormous. They had been negotiating a massive narcotics transaction with a millionaire Belgian financier named Captain Alfred Lowenstein. It was the sort of deal that, had it gone through, would have made it possible for both men to retire in splendor. The deal disintegrated when Lowenstein, the third richest man in the world, died under mysterious circumstances: He fell—or was tossed—from his private plane while crossing the North Sea from England to Belgium. Four months later, Rothstein's time on earth also came to a sudden end, when he took a bullet in the belly at the Park Central Hotel.

Lucky for Legs, he was out of town at the time with an airtight alibi—though that didn't stop Rothstein partisans from exacting revenge. In the months following Rothstein's death, numerous gangsters associated with Diamond's crew began to disappear from the face of the earth. They even went after Legs's brother, Eddie, who was in Denver, Colorado convalescing from a serious bout of tuberculosis (TB). He managed to survive an ambush in which more than a hundred .45-caliber machine gun bullets were unloaded into a car he was driving. Eddie fled Colorado and returned to New York, where his TB worsened. In May 1929, while Capone, Luciano, Lansky, and the others were convening in Atlantic City, Eddie Diamond died in a hospital bed in Upstate New York.

Legs had now entered what would prove to be a permanent state of affairs as an underworld outsider. Other mobsters didn't seem to like Legs much. Jealousy might have had something to do with it. He was the snappiest-dressed mobster of the era, easily spotted in his custom-fit dark suits, flashy ties, and sporty black-and-white checkered cap. He had a handsome, black-Irish look that fit the public's idea of a glamorous gangster. He traveled around town by limousine, with an entourage of bodyguards that made him seem like a dignitary. And he almost always had a pretty dame on his arm.

He'd been married to his second wife, Alice Kenny, since 1926, but was seen most often on the nightclub circuit with a striking Ziegfield Follies showgirl from Boston who called herself Kiki Roberts (her real name was Marion Strasmick). Kiki was a "bombshell," according to the tabloids—a red-haired, tough-talking career girl who saw Jack Diamond as her ticket to fame and fortune. While Alice was home tending the domestic front, Legs squired Kiki to the Cotton Club, El Fay, the Stork Club, and, of course, his own Hotsy Totsy Club, where he first met the kid, Vincent Coll.

It was at the Hotsy Totsy that Diamond got himself into a heap of trouble, sending him on a course that would eventually lead to his assassination.

On the night of July 13, 1929, Diamond and a member of his gang, Charles Entratta, were in the club when three dock wallopers from the West Side became drunk and rowdy. When one of the rowdies physically accosted the club's manager, Diamond intervened.

"I'm Jack Diamond, and I run this place," he told the three men. "If you don't calm down, I'll blow your fuckin' head off."

One of the men responded, "You no good for nothin', you can't push me around."

In a matter of seconds, bullets began to fly. The three dock wallopers, all of whom had criminal records, were heavily armed, as were Diamond and Entratta. As shots were exchanged across the dance floor, club patrons rushed for the exits. The band abruptly ceased playing. By the time the dust settled, two of the intruders were dead, shot multiple times in the body and head; the third was rushed to the hospital in critical condition.

More than fifty people, including employees and patrons, saw the shooting, but none would be available to testify against Legs and Entratta. Within six weeks of the double homicide, the club's manager and three waiters mysteriously disappeared. Their bullet-riddled bodies started turning up in various locations around New Jersey. Other potential witnesses, those who were not eliminated by the dirt nap, were so terrified that they developed a collective loss of memory. The police case against Diamond and Entratta never got off the ground.

The shootout at the Hotsy Totsy Club and murderous elimination of any and all witnesses was one of those Prohibition-era horror shows that was bad for business. The authorities felt compelled to crack down on everyone, much to the annoyance of the Syndicate leaders.

"I told you that playboy Legs was trouble," the Dutchman chastised Owney Madden.

"I know, I know," was all Owney could say.

Over the next year there would be three separate attempts on Diamond's life, all of them close calls. In one of the shootings he was drinking with Kiki at the bar of the Aratoga Inn, six miles outside Acra. Three gunmen dressed as duck hunters burst in the door and filled Diamond with lead. He was rushed to nearby Albany Hospital, where he lingered at death's door for three days. A doctor who treated him said, "I had to tie off the vessels inside the lung which later collapsed, and then, as the wound started to heal, the lung was expanded by inserting into it a tube of air. The man is a medical wonder." After three hours of surgery and four weeks of convalescence, Legs was discharged.

"Well," said Legs to a gaggle of reporters waiting outside the hospital, "I made it again. Nobody can kill Legs Diamond. I am going to settle a few scores just as soon as I get my strength back, you just wait and see."

Despite the constant threat of assassination, Legs boldly attempted to expand his business operations. He made a second trip to Europe in August 1930, but "big, bad Jackie," as he was described in the *Fleet Street* tabloids, received so much negative press that he was constantly under surveillance by Scotland Yard and harassed by German police. Unable to make the major narcotics deal he had hoped for, he left Europe; upon his return via ocean liner, he was again surrounded by reporters. His arrival was even captured by *Movietone News*, who had only recently developed the technology to accompany their newsreel footage with direct sound.

"Was your trip a success, Legs?" asked an intrepid reporter. "Did you get what you were after?"

For the first time, the general public heard the voice of Legs Diamond: "You fellows know I went to Europe for my health. You aren't trying to pin something on me, are you? You can tell the public that most of what they have been reading about me is all bunk. I've got a lot of legitimate interests."

Jack returned to his compound in Acra and resumed bootlegging. Upstate, the new thing was applejack, cheap brandy made from apples. In a warehouse distillery Diamond had constructed on his own property, he made Applejack. At a large brewery in the nearby town of Kingston, he produced beer. Most of Diamond's product, according to local imbibers, was terrible, but Jack took over the booze business upstate the same way bootleggers did in the city—by eliminating the competition through intimidation and murder. Diamond counterbalanced his reputation as a thug by cultivating a reputation for generosity; he gave huge tips everywhere he went and made donations to local youth and church organizations. One local newspaper even described him as "the Robin Hood of Greene County."

Local authorities frequently raided his compound, at one time estimating his bootlegging operation to be worth $10 million. Despite the profitability of his operation and somewhat glamorous reputation, the harassment from federal agents and violent attempts on his life took their toll. In newsreel footage from the era, Legs often appears as a haunted, spectral figure, gaunt and pale. Granted, much of this footage was compiled as Diamond shuffled to and from hospitals and courtrooms, when he was presumably not in the best of moods. Even so, Diamond's temperament was becoming a concern.

Those who knew him commented that he seemed to be increasingly irritable and sadistic. The fact that he still carried buckshot embedded in one lung from the most recent attempt on his life couldn't have helped. Of course, Diamond had always been a cruel and viscous killer, but he now seemed to derive sustenance from his violent acts; it was as if the power he wielded over the lives of his victims was a substitute for the lack of power he had within the granddaddy of all bootlegging empires, the New York City underworld.

Diamond's nasty side was revealed on the night of April 18, 1931, when he, two members of his gang, and girlfriend Kiki Roberts were driving on a country road near the town of Catskill. Diamond and his gang spotted a truck carrying a load of Applejack belonging to a rival bootlegger. They stopped the truck, and, at gunpoint, forced the truck's two occupants to come with them. Kiki Roberts was told to go powder her nose. The two rival bootleggers were taken to a garage in back of Diamond's house. The truck's passenger, a terrified seventeen-year-old kid who knew nothing, was let go.

The driver, a bald-headed unassuming laborer named Grover Parks, was tied and bound.

"Give us the name of your boss," demanded Legs, "or we'll beat you to a pulp."

"I dunno nothing," said Parks. "Please, let me go."

Diamond's gang beat the man with fists and a shovel, then suspended him from the limb of a nearby tree. Parks screamed for mercy to no avail. Legs and his cohorts slugged him in the face and applied lit cigarettes to his bare feet. Every time Parks screamed for help, they beat him some more. Eventually, exasperated by the bastard's unwillingness to talk, Legs and his crew decided to take a beer break. Diamond told Parks, "When we come back, if you're not ready to tell us what we want, we're going to kill you."

While Legs and his gang were off drinking, the man managed to break free and escape. Bloodied and beaten, he made his way on foot to the Catskill Police station and begged for protection from local authorities.

The county prosecutor's office was sure they had an airtight case: Diamond and two of his gang were arrested and charged with kidnapping. Legs was released after posting twenty-five thousand dollars bail. Over the following months, publicity surrounding the case was so intensive that a judge moved the proceedings to Troy, in nearby Rensselaer County.

At the trial, prosecutors produced multiple witnesses who claimed to have seen Legs Diamond in or around the area of the kidnapping on the night in question. A terrified Grover Parks took the stand and told his story. Upon cross-examination, Diamond's attorney sought to portray Parks as a pathetic publicity hound who was hoping to enhance his social standing in the refracted glow of the defendant's legend. The trial lasted four days. The jury deliberated for three hours. Legs was found not guilty.

"Gang Law Beats State Law in Diamond Case" blared a headline in the late edition of the *Albany Evening News*. The verdict seemed to confirm everyone's worst fears: Justice was a whore.

That night, amid the inevitable cries of jury tampering, Diamond and his entourage retired to the bar of the Kenmore Hotel in nearby Albany. Jack's wife Alice was there, as was his mistress Kiki, who'd been hidden away in a separate apartment during the trial. That night Legs danced to his favorite tune, "Happy Days and Lonely Nights." Later, without wife or mistress, he went to a celebration at a popular speakeasy across from Union Station. He got drunk, then went to Kiki's apartment and got drunker. At some point, Legs stumbled back to the boarding room where he was staying under the name Kelly. He stripped to his underwear and fell into bed.

Around five-thirty in the morning, two visitors entered the boarding house and went to Diamond's room, which was apparently unlocked. The landlady would later state that she heard Jack Diamond pleading for his life. She also heard one of the visitors reject mercy and tell Legs, "Others pleaded with *you*." Shortly thereafter, the sharp retort of gunfire pierced the dawn: three shots, up close and personal. After a lifetime of close calls and near misses, Legs was finally, absolutely, positively dead.

The killers were never identified, though they were seen speeding away in a red Packard. The way the hit went down, it had to have been at least partly set up by local players. In the months that followed, there was much speculation. Could Jack Diamond have been set up by Alice, his long-suffering wife? Was he possibly betrayed by members of his own gang? Did local cops, a fair number of whom were on the payroll of one mobster or another, play a role or even provide shooters to take out the area's most notorious criminal?

Whoever pulled the trigger, it made little difference. The result was the same: Luciano, Schultz, Lansky, and the others were now one step closer to their grand scheme of establishing an underworld free of uppity Irish gangsters.[4]

With friends Like These . . .

Vincent Coll's trial for the killing of five-year-old Michael Vengalli got under way in Manhattan on December 16, 1931. If the lad from Gweedore was concerned about his fate, it was with good reason. All he had to do was look at the papers. Jack Diamond had been dramatically acquitted, then summarily executed. Under these circumstances, Coll might have viewed his own trial with considerable trepidation. Would he be better off being found guilty and sent to the electric chair a la Two Gun Crowley? Might his

---

4. In *O Albany!*, author William Kennedy's literary peon to his hometown, many local survivors from the Prohibition era, including saloon keepers, cops, newspapermen, and politicians, are quoted giving their theories on the Legs Diamond hit. Some believe that at least one participant was a tough Albany cop named William J. Fitzpatrick, whose nickname was "Doc" because his frequent comment to those who brought him problems was: "I'm the doctor. Why didn't you come to me sooner?" The accepted wisdom is that Doc Fitzpatrick and two other cops killed Legs at the behest of Syndicate bosses in New York City. Fitzpatrick later flourished in the Albany police department (becoming head of the notoriously corrupt "Night Squad" and later, chief of the department) until January 5, 1945, when he was shot dead at police headquarters by his best pal, drinking buddy, and fellow detective, John W. McElveney.

chances be worse if he were acquitted and sent back out into the streets, where he could be hunted down and murdered by the Syndicate?

These were tough times for an enterprising Irish racketeer. The press and the public had already convicted Coll of the horrendous act. Vincent the Mad Dog was a renegade Irish gangster, enemy of the establishment, which made him GUA (Guilty Upon Arrival). Compared to Jack Diamond, Coll was like a platypus wallowing in the mire. Legs had been acclaimed, while Vincent was despised—though they did represent flip sides of the same coin that had been designated for extinction.

At trial, the prosecution's star witness turned out to be a man who claimed to have been walking along 116th Street in East Harlem on the day in question. While minding his own business, lo and behold, he saw four men in a car driving by. One of those men stuck a machine gun out the back window of the car and opened fire, aiming at a man identified as Joey Rao, but striking instead a gaggle of young children. The triggerman's face was partially obscured by a fedora pulled low on his head, but the intrepid witness was able to identify the shooter as Vincent Coll because of the prominent dimple in the middle of his chin.

Coll's criminal defense attorney, Samuel Liebowitz, was on the case. During pre-trial investigations, Liebowitz had learned that the witness, along with being a convicted felon who did time as a jewel thief, was little more than a professional witness, a breed endemic to the criminal justice system. The man had only recently been paid for his testimony at a murder trial in St. Louis, where he was found to have committed perjury.

"Have you ever testified in a criminal proceeding before?" Liebowitz asked the witness on the stand.

The man denied that he had.

"Have you ever been paid, sir, to testify in a criminal proceeding?"

"Uh . . . no. I have not."

Liebowitz produced the records from the trial in St. Louis, and the government's case against Mad Dog Coll was finished. Their star witness was exposed as a cheap fraud. Before it was over, the judge would be compelled to instruct the jury that, given the mendacity of the government's case, they had no choice but to find the defendant not guilty.

Coll, dressed in his best suit, stepped into the afternoon chill outside the Criminal Courts Building with Lottie, his twenty-three-year-old fiancée, beaming at his side. To the assembled reporters, he read a rare public statement: "I have been charged with all kinds of crimes, but baby-killing was the limit. I'd like nothing better than to lay my hands on the man who did this.

I'd tear his throat out. There is nothing more despicable than a man who would harm an innocent child."

Vincent Coll was released from custody that day, but he was hardly a free man.

In the euphoria of acquittal, he and Lottie were married on January 4, 1932, in a civil ceremony. There was no honeymoon. In the weeks that followed, the two lovebirds were stopped a half dozen times and harassed by cops. They were held on minor matters, such as not having their registration for their automobile. Police authorities made it clear that they would not stop pestering Vincent Coll until he left town and never returned.

The reasons Coll and his bride stayed in the area remain something of a mystery. Vincent may have been delusional enough to believe that he could reemerge as a player in the city's underworld, though the murder of Legs Diamond should have disabused him of those notions. Nonetheless, he and a small handful of young loyalists sought to reestablish themselves. They set up an informal headquarters at a four-family frame dwelling on Commonwealth Avenue in the northern reaches of Vincent's home borough, the Bronx.

On February 1, less than one month after Vincent and Lottie's marriage, three members of Coll's crew, along with two women and two babies, were in the Bronx apartment. The men were playing cards, and the women were tending to the infants, when a team of four gunmen burst in and began shooting. There was no time for the occupants to return fire. Methodically, the gunmen shot everyone in the room, except for the two babies, who cried hysterically in their cribs. After they were finished, the killers made a hasty retreat.

When the cops arrived, there was blood splattered everywhere. Two of the men and one woman were dead. Another man and woman were badly injured. The whole scene was underscored by the sound of screaming babies. Even by Prohibition-era standards, it was a grisly incident. The tabloids, in typical hyperbolic fashion, compared the shooting to the St. Valentine's Day Massacre. Police sources speculated that the executioners were actually on the hunt for Vincent Coll and had gone on information that he was due there that night with his bride, Lottie.

Yet again, Vincent and Lottie holed up at the Cornish Arms Hotel on West Twenty-third Street. The entire city knew the underworld was out to get the man; many probably wished that the gangsters would get it over with so that the carnage might end. Star columnist Walter Winchell turned up the heat by narrating the whole thing through his radio broadcasts and his column in the

Daily Mirror. Wrote Winchell, "Five plains brought dozens of machine guns from Chicago Friday. Local banditti have made one hotel a virtual arsenal and several hot spots are ditto because Master Coll is giving them the headache."

Vincent sought to buy some time by establishing contact with the only man in the upper echelon of the Syndicate whom he could even remotely call a friend: Owney Madden. He did so in his usual hotheaded, counter-productive style—by threatening to kidnap Madden and hold him for ransom, just as he had done with Madden's sidekick, Big Frenchy DeMange.

"Just imagine how the dagos and kikes is gonna feel if they gotta shell out a hundred grand to save your sorry ass," Vincent told Owney. "Pay me now, up front, and I'll save you the trouble."

Madden told Coll he'd get back to him. Meanwhile, Madden conferred with Dutch Schultz and decided that the best way to get to the Mick was through one of his bodyguards.

Just after midnight on February 8, Vincent received a call from Madden, who was in his office at the Cotton Club. Concerned that the phone at the hotel might be tapped, the two men agreed that Coll would step out to a pay phone inside a candy store on Twenty-third Street and call Madden back from there. Vincent and his bodyguard, part of a rotating crew he kept on the premises at all times, left the hotel together.

Arriving at the New London Pharmacy and Candy Shop around twelve-thirty A.M., Coll stepped into a phone booth in the rear of the store. The bodyguard took a seat at a counter near the soda fountain. Vincent called Madden at the Cotton Club and was jabbering away when a car pulled up in front of the store. Four men, one of them wearing an ankle-length coat and gray fedora, got out of the car. Three of the men positioned themselves around the drugstore entrance. The man with the long coat and fedora entered the store and nodded to Coll's bodyguard. Coll's betrayer swiftly climbed off his stool and skedaddled out the front door.

From beneath his coat, the man in the gray fedora produced a tommy gun. While Vincent chattered on the phone heatedly and obliviously, the gunman approached, raised his machine gun, and fired a short burst into the booth, shattering glass and creating a loud racket. He paused, corrected his aim, and fired again, making sure to riddle Coll's body from head to toe. The whole thing was over in a matter of seconds.

Vincent's wife Lottie arrived on the scene around the same time as the police. She was hysterical, of course, seeing her betrothed reduced to a mass of barely recognizable blood and flesh. The police badgered her with questions, a few of which she answered until she lost control and said, "I don't want to be stubborn, but I'm not going to say anything more about Vincent and me." To a bystander she confided that she was madly in love with Coll, and the dress she was now wearing was the same dress she had worn on the day they were wed. Their current lifesavings, she said, was a hundred dollar bill she kept pinned inside her bra.

By and large, the city greeted news of Coll's gangland execution with a sense of relief. Police Commissioner Edward P. Mulrooney called the act "a positive defiance of law and order," with the accent on "positive." Mayor Walker said, as disturbingly violent as the killing had been, he hoped that it might signal the end of the open warfare that had claimed so many lives. Dutch Shultz declared, "The Mad Mick got what he deserved."

With the murder of Legs Diamond and now Vincent Coll, the Syndicate had eliminated two of their biggest headaches in New York. But they weren't done yet. The mobster conference in Atlantic City had established a new directive: The Irish mobsters must go. Even before Diamond and Coll were murdered, the bloodletting had begun. Earlier in 1931, prominent Boston bootlegger Danny Wallace, leader of the Irish Gustin Gang, was lured to the North End Italian section of Boston and assassinated, along with his number two man, Barney Walsh (a third Gustin, Timothy Coffey, was hit but managed to escape). Next on the hit parade were Diamond and Coll. Then came Vannie Higgins, the mob boss of Brooklyn; he was gunned down while strolling along a Brooklyn street with his wife and seven-year-old daughter, who was grazed by a stray bullet. The next to be murdered was Danny Walsh of Rhode Island. He was last seen on February 2, 1933, at a diner in Pawtucket, a few days before a group of Italian men were spotted digging a grave on his property and lacing it with lime.

Over the three-year period from 1931 to 1933, virtually every high-ranking Irish American bootlegger in the Northeastern United States was systematically eliminated, gangland-style. If the underworld needed a reminder that there was a New World Order in place, in which the wild, renegade behavior so famously associated with the Irish gangster would no longer be tolerated, all anyone had to do was count the bodies.

No one understood this better than Owney Madden. The Duke of the West Side had risen from the gutter to the top of the underworld hierarchy, and he had done so partly by turning against the very forces that got him there. He was a highly circumspect individual whose thoughts and feelings were intentionally never recorded for posterity (the man behind the man does not tell all). But we do know this about Madden: In 1932, a few months after the murder of Mad Dog Coll, he was arrested on a minor parole violation charge. With his connections and access to high-powered legal representation, Madden could easily have contested the charge. But he chose not to. Given the current climate in the underworld, a year off the streets was preferable—even attractive—to the man whose role as planner and facilitator in the deaths of both Diamond and Coll had left him with a reputation as an Irishman who betrayed his own.

So Owney gladly removed himself from the scene and did a year in the joint. Upon his release, he negotiated a formal exit strategy with Luciano, Costello, and the others. By agreement, Madden would leave New York altogether and retire to Hot Springs, Arkansas, where he would preside over a collection of casinos, brothels, and luxury hotels that were controlled by the Syndicate. The idea was that Hot Springs would serve as a virtual resort town for mobsters on the lam, a southern outpost for organized crime figures. And Owney Madden, the former Gopher from Hell's Kitchen, would tend to this relatively peaceful racketeer's paradise like a player coach—valued for his experience and wisdom, but also capable of taking the mound and throwing the occasional screwball or knuckler when circumstances required it.

In Hot Springs, Owney resided peacefully and—unlike so many other men he knew—lived long enough to experience the autumnal glory of his golden years. It was a sweet deal indeed.[5]

Playing at a Theater Near You

In the underworld, there was no pension plan. Long-term survivors like Owney Madden were the exception, and everyone knew it. For most, betrayal and death were daily companions, survival of a perilous game of

---

5. Hot Springs, Arkansas was a town steeped in Irish mobster history. In the 1880s the town was controlled by two rival gambling combines—one run by Major S. A. Doran, a Confederate veteran, the other by Frank Flynn, a professional card shark. The Flynn-Doran War dominated the local scene for years, until, after a bloody shootout along Bathhouse Row that killed numerous innocent bystanders, the two men were run out of town by a federal militia. Later, during the years of Prohibition and beyond, the town was run by Mayor Leo P. McLaughlin, who was a stooge of the city's criminal class, which included Owney Madden.

In Hot Springs, Madden married the postmaster's daughter, lived next door to St. John's Catholic Church, and became a local legend. He lived there until he died of natural causes in 1965. His years as the mobster patriarch of Hot Springs are touched upon in a wonderful memoir, *The Bookmaker's Daughter* by Shirley Abbott.

three-card monty—a game you played even though you knew the result was largely predetermined. The payoffs were obvious: money, dames, material comfort, the illusion of power and respect. By the early 1930s, if you weren't able to achieve some portion or combination of the above, there was one other possible perk: immortality.

In May 1931, around the same time the exploits of Two Gun Crowley, Legs Diamond, and Mad Dog Coll were being chronicled in the daily press, a movie called *The Public Enemy* opened in theatres across the country. It starred a thirty-one-year-old actor named James Cagney, who had played a secondary role in four previous Hollywood pictures but was relatively unknown beyond the New York stage. In the movie, Cagney played Tom Powers, an Irish American hoodlum who rises from the fetid Stockyard District in Chicago as a kid to become a successful bootlegger. From the day it opened, the movie was a sensation; it would outsell the two other most popular gangster pictures of the era, *Little Caesar* and *Scarface*, and go on to become perhaps the most influential gangster flick in the history of American movies.

The storyline of *The Public Enemy*, loosely drawn from an unpublished novel *Beer and Blood* by John Bright and Kubec Glasmon, incorporated many details from the life of Chicago mob boss Dean O'Banion, including his specially designed suits with the special pockets for his guns. The details may have been O'Banion's, but the character of Tom Powers, in Cagney's hands, embodied the actions and attitudes of every Irish American gangster from Spike O'Donnell to Legs Diamond and Owney Madden.

In the movie, Tom starts out as the wayward son of a recently widowed Chicago policeman. He becomes involved in a youth gang based on O'Banion's real-life Little Hellions. With the dawn of Prohibition, Tom finds work as a truck driver and strong arm man, and then, through a combination of brains, brutality, and charm, he rises to experience the good life before running afoul of rival bootleggers.

Produced by Warner Brothers Studios and directed by William Wellman, the movie had an unusual degree of authenticity for its time, though the rags-to-riches-to-death plotline certainly adhered to the proverbial moralism that crime doesn't pay. In theatres, *The Public Enemy* was accompanied by an on-screen disclaimer that read in part: "It is the ambition of the authors of [this motion picture] to honestly depict an environment that exists today in a certain strata of American life, rather than glorify the hoodlum or the criminal." There was much gunplay in the movie, the highest degree of physical violence allowable under the newly instituted

Production Code, and a shock ending, wherein a rival gang leaves Tom's dead body at his mother's doorstep wrapped in a grotesque, bloody parcel.

None of these elements were what made *The Public Enemy* a hit, however. What made the movie a box office smash was Jimmy Cagney. Lincoln Kirstein, primarily a dance critic at the time (he went on to form the New York City Ballet with George Balanchine), summarized Cagney's appeal in *Hound & Horn* magazine: "Cagney is mick-Irish . . . [he] has an inspired sense of timing, an arrogant style, a pride in the control of his body and a conviction and lack of self-consciousness that is unique. . . . No one expresses more clearly in terms of pictorial action the delights of violence, the overtones of a subconscious sadism, the tendency toward destruction, toward anarchy, which is the base of American sex appeal."

Cagney developed his physical grace and timing as a Tin Pan Alley song-and-dance man, but he picked up his swagger and his "overtones of subconscious sadism" as a youth growing up in rough-neck Manhattan and through his occasional acquaintance with known underworld figures.

Born on July 17, 1899, in the notorious Gas House District around Tompkins Square—the same neighborhood that produced Richard Croker, Honest John Kelly, and other legendary bosses of Tammany Hall—Cagney learned to speak near fluent Yiddish before his family moved north to Yorkville, an ethnic melting pot district on the Upper East Side. In his autobiography, *Cagney by Cagney*, the actor describes his childhood as being "surrounded by trouble, illness, and my dad's alcoholism . . . we just didn't have time to be impressed by all those misfortunes, though we did realize the desperation of life around us. I recall the Fitzpatrick family of Ninety-sixth Street who were put out on the sidewalk when they couldn't pay the rent, and this was not long after they had seen their little child run over by a refuse wagon. The Cagney's never had that kind of experience, thank God, and it never occurred to us, despite the poverty, to hold our heads or feel sorry for ourselves . . ."

The streets of Yorkville could be tough. "Red," as Cagney was sometimes known because of his hair, tried to stay out of trouble, but it wasn't always easy. One day he heard the sound of pounding feet behind him. When he turned to look, he saw a boy collapsing with a butcher knife sticking in his back. Another time he saw a boy sobbing, walking down the street, holding his slashed testicle. Violence and physical confrontations were common. Unless you wanted to be a victim, you learned to defend yourself.

"There was almost a kind of chivalry about fighting in our neighborhood," wrote Cagney. He fondly remembered the antics of a girl named

Maude, whose prowess as a fighter would have put her in good stead with the Dead Rabbits, Whyos, and other gangs of the previous century:

> A dope addict ("cokie" or "hophead" we called them then) named Daly was urging the little blocky girl on very loudly. Fat Bella, one of Maude's pals, said a few words to him, he replied in kind to her, and she retorted with an overhand right. Daly grabbed the wide, tightly wired ribbon in her hair and swung her off her feet, making her go round and round like a roman candle. Then we young kids jumped Daly and heaved rocks at him as he scuttled up the street. Maude's fight flowered into another between two girls about ten years old. The brother of one of the girls stepped in, slapped his sister in the face, and told her to go home. Then this little child said indignantly to her brother, "Well, she ain't gonna call *me* no whore!"

The rambunctious nature of the city streets fueled young Cagney's ambitions. A talented amateur boxer, he considered a career in the ring, but his mother was against it. He became more of a joker and dancer than a fighter, but he observed everything. He picked up mannerisms and attitudes deeply ingrained in the lower-middle-class Irish of his neighborhood and turned them into the raw material of a movie persona variously described as "hard-boiled," "smart alecky," and "street-wise." What he didn't pilfer from the characters of his youth, Cagney got from his mobster associations. The man who made the introductions was a friend and fellow actor, George Raft.

A suave tough guy born and raised in Hell's Kitchen, Raft was friendly with Owney Madden, having once served long ago as a junior member of the Gophers. Sometime in the late 1920s, at the world-famous Stork Club, Raft introduced Cagney, the budding movie star, to Madden, the Duke of the West Side. Cagney soaked up Owney's style, demeanor, and especially his manner of speech, a talking-from-the-side-of-the-mouth sarcasm endemic to Manhattan's West Side Irish. A cop once described Madden back in his Gopher days as "that little banty rooster from hell," which was also a good description of early-vintage Cagney, whose cocky strut was modeled at least partly on Madden and his Hell's Kitchen influences.

Cagney's portrayal of Tom Powers in *The Public Enemy* was so utterly convincing that there were no protests against the movie by Irish American groups. In the previous two years alone, crime movies such as *Little Caesar*, *Chinatown Nights*, and *Wheel of Chance*, which featured a Jewish racketeer named Schmulka Turkletaub (played by a WASP actor) had stirred the ire of the respective ethnic groups. A year later, the release of *Scarface* would bring about even louder denunciations from The Order of the Sons of Italy, who threatened to picket theatres showing the movie until Warner Brothers caved into pressure and retitled the picture, *Scarface, Shame of the Nation*. *The Public Enemy* met with no such public disavowals. Although the movie did not soft-peddle the vicious, sociopathic nature of Tom Powers (he kills a cop in the movie's first twenty minutes and later famously smashes a grapefruit in his girlfriend's face), Cagney, like an *Our Gang* kid gone wrong, imbues the character with a kind of rot-gut humanity.

"I doubt there is an actor extant who could have done what James Cagney does with the character of Tom Powers," wrote playwright Robert Sherwood. "He does not hesitate to represent Tom as a complete rat—with a rat's sense of honor, a rat's capacity for human love; and when cornered, a rat's fighting courage. And what is more, although his role is consistently unsympathetic, Mr. Cagney manages to earn for Tom Powers the audience's affection and esteem."

For the Irish, Cagney's performance transcended this one character in this one movie. The Cagney persona, which the actor introduced in full flower in *The Public Enemy* then honed in numerous gangster movies throughout the Thirties, was the culmination of a process that had begun decades earlier with Thomas Nast's ape-like, brutish characterizations of Paddy in magazine and newspaper editorial cartoons. The Irish, so vilified at the time as ignorant, slovenly, and baffoonish, had come from the most backward agrarian culture in Western Europe to the most heavily industrialized environment in the world. They made their way despite resistance at every turn, partly by recreating themselves in a new image. The tough, hyperalert, fast-talking, street-smart operator was an evolutionary adaptation to America's mean streets, who not only looked and acted like he belonged, but at some level embodied what urban life was all about.

Cagney's characterization was based partly on a modern urban reality: The understanding that the line between legal and illegal in the Big City was often a question of convenience rather than morality. In the nineteenth century, Paddy had viewed his new country's capitalist economy as a rigged game. That's how the political machine and the mobster came into being in the first place. Now that attitude was infused with the ethos of the Roaring Twenties, a time of moral ambiguity and playful liberation, giving birth to a new character—"Jimmy," the toughest of the tough, but also a natty dresser, a hit with the ladies, possessed of verbal agility and an ironic sensibility that set new standards in urban cool.

To say that the Irish American gangster played an essential role in this incremental transformation from Paddy to Jimmy may be anathema to some, but it's hard to deny. Society may choose to put forth more stalwart types such as soldiers, firemen, and policemen as heroes, but when it comes to setting trends, the outlaw and the gangster have always been more influential.

The irony, of course, is that just as Jimmy Cagney emerged as the avatar of a new kind of street-wise Irish American style, the mobsters who inspired that style were dropping at an expeditious rate. Deanie O'Banion, Legs Diamond, Mad Dog Coll, Vannie Higgins, Frankie Wallace, and Danny Walsh—among others—were all dead. In Chicago, Al Capone alone had virtually eradicated a whole generation of Irish mob bosses. The era of the Irish mobster that had flowered in the late nineteenth century and peaked during Prohibition was not quite over yet, but the role of Jimmy the Gangster as cock-of-the-walk and master of the underworld appeared to be heading into an ominous era of remission.

You wouldn't know it by going to the movies, though. In glorious black-and-white, Cagney reprised, refined, and expanded his creation in *Angels With Dirty Faces, The Mayor of Hell, Jimmy the Gent, The Roaring Twenties,* and other memorable 1930s crime pictures, insuring that the image of the Irish hoodlum—no matter what happened out in the streets of America—would glimmer on celluloid for time immortal.

the smoke-filled room and other tales of political malfeasance

P rohibition came to an end on April 7, 1933, when newly elected President Franklin D. Roosevelt asked Congress to modify the Volstead Act to permit the manufacture of beer with an alcohol content of more than 3.2 percent. Congress did so immediately.

Beer trucks once again rumbled through the streets, free of gangster escorts, and thousands of speakeasies flung their doors wide and became legal beer saloons once again. Later in the year, with passage of the 21st Amendment, all Prohibition-era statutes relating to the sale and manufacture of liquor were officially repealed. The long disaster could now be forgotten, except, of course, for the thousands of dead bodies, the legacy of corruption, and the criminal framework that was fine-tuned, expanded, and—in some respects—still exists to this day.

Mobsterism did not end with the repeal of Prohibition. Why would it? The underworld was larger than any one racket. Spawned amidst the squalor of famine-era immigration, it had sustained itself through civil and international wars, the Gilded Age, economic downturns, changing political regimes, the Industrial Revolution, and the folly of the Noble Experiment. The underworld survived because the underworld *was* America, an inexorable aspect of American capitalism so deeply ingrained in the fabric of big city life that no social revolution or human law could legislate it out of existence.

Still, the end of Prohibition did bring about certain alterations. The rampant gangland murders associated with the infamous bootlegger turf wars in Chicago, New York, and elsewhere died down considerably. The huge revenues from illegal booze dwindled. This was a problem mostly for low-level, working-class gangsters who—in the absence of brewing, packing, truck driving, distribution, and strong-arm jobs associated with Prohibition— would now have to find subsistence through other rackets such as union-related thuggery, the snatch racket (kidnapping for ransom), numbers-running, sports betting, bank heists, the beginnings of a burgeoning narcotics trade, murder-for-hire, and other stand-bys of the American hoodlum.

For the upper echelon mobsters, or the masters of Prohibition, the end of illegal liquor as a source of revenue required a shift in focus, certainly, but money was not the primary concern. Most of them had amassed fortunes bigger than anything they had expected to see in two or three lifetimes. The biggest problem for these scions of crime was what to do with the proceeds. Bank accounts and safe deposit boxes were no good; they left a paper trail. Money laundering was not yet the sophisticated racket it would become in later decades.

The smartest of the mobsters, men like Owney Madden, had foreseen Prohibition's end and funneled their criminal proceeds into a wide variety of "legitimate" ventures. Along with his many nightclubs and trucking and taxi rackets, Madden had money in laundries, milk delivery, and real estate. He owned racehorses and prizefighters, including Primo Carnera, an Italian-born heavyweight who toured the country like a carnival act scoring knock-outs in set up bouts before finally winning the championship on June 29, 1933. Carnera was quickly dethroned by Joe Louis; Madden owned a piece of him, too. From the late 1920s through the 1930s, Owney had a financial interest in five straight heavyweight champions.

Of all the ways for a mobster to disperse funds and utilize profits, how-ever, the best way had always been and still was politics. The manner by which dirty money from gangsters had for years infiltrated and compro-mised the inner workings of government probably had more to do with the repeal of Prohibition than any other single factor. By the early 1930s, American democracy was in a shambles, and everyone knew it. Whole police departments, federal agents, judges, prosecutors—the entire electoral pro-cess had been implicated to one degree or another. The roots of this crimi-nal alliance ran deep, starting at least with the earliest machinations of the Tweed Ring, where honest graft was not a privilege but a right. This philos-ophy, which became deeply entrenched in many municipal governments throughout the land over roughly a seventy-year period, had been turned on its head during Prohibition. Because of the ungodly amounts of money involved and the violent extremes to which bootleggers were willing to go in order to protect their interests, the gangster had superseded the politician.

The underworld, it appeared, could not be eliminated; the more law enforcement tried, the more lucrative these illegal activities became (the price of illicit whiskey rose by an average of 520 percent during the thirteen years of Prohibition). What could be stopped, however—or at least regulated—were those aspects of the upperworld that were in cahoots with the gangsters.

Implicit in Prohibition's repeal was an unwritten directive. "All right," the government said to its people, "you can have your booze. But the graft, corruption, and criminal subjugation of the System must come to an end."

Thus began an assault on the alliance between the gangster and the politician—a relationship that was at the heart of the Irish American underworld. The battle had been initiated even before Prohibition was repealed, back in 1928, following the murder of Arnold Rothstein. Most mob hits were usually professional contract jobs, conducted in such a way that there would be no serious investigation. The Rothstein murder was different. He'd been shot during a card game; many believed it had been some kind of weird accident. In any event, because no one in the underworld had authorized Rothstein's killing, no one stood in the way of a formal investigation.

Even a cursory examination of Rothstein's life was bound to lead in a number of incriminating directions. Like Big Tim Sullivan and King Mike McDonald, Rothstein's criminal authority was based on a basic principle: The man who gets criminals out of jail in a time of need is the man who controls criminals. Rothstein's role as a bail bondsman, more than anything else, was the source of his power. It was said that he owned virtually every judge in the magistrate's court. After his murder, this fact was prominently reported in practically every newspaper in town, embarrassing many judges who were named, and led to a statewide investigation.

Franklin Roosevelt, then governor of New York, was the first to establish a panel to investigate corruption in the magistrate's court. To oversee the investigation, Roosevelt approved the appointment of retired judge Samuel Seabury, an upright, patrician, septuagenarian who was no friend of Tammany Hall. An Episcopalian by birth, he was the son of a professor of canon law at the General Theological Seminary. Seabury insisted on still being referred to as Judge, even though he left the Court of Appeals in 1916. With his pince-nez spectacles, white hair parted in the middle, and aloof, superior air, Seabury epitomized the WASP crusader who carried a banner of righteousness as his main weapon.

Roosevelt knew exactly what he was doing. Though he had not yet formally announced his candidacy for president, it was common knowledge that he was running. His biggest rival for the Democratic nomination, also as yet unannounced, was Al Smith, who had run in 1928 as the first Catholic candidate for president in the nation's history and lost to Herbert Hoover. A Manhattanite of Irish descent, Smith was Tammany Hall's choice to run again in 1932. Through the Seabury Investigation, as the magistrate's probe became known, Roosevelt held Al Smith's viability as an opponent in the palm of his hands. If Tammany's criminal underpinnings were exposed, Smith would be tarnished and forced out of the race.

Roosevelt was smart enough to stay out of the picture. Safely ensconced in Albany, he merely set Seabury loose, allowing him free reign in his investigations, which soon led the judge and his panel to an inevitable target: the NYPD. Everyone knew many cops were on the take to one degree or another. Even so, ears perked up when a low-life criminal named "Chile" Acuna took the stand during public hearings and admitted that he and others worked regularly with plain-clothes officers to set up innocent women on prostitution charges—in order to shake them down for money.

"This is how it worked," the diminutive, Chilean-born stool pigeon told a packed courtroom. "I went into a whorehouse. The vice cops and I set our watches together. They would give me a five or ten dollar bill in marked money, whatever it cost. I went into the house and had a woman or girl, whoever was available. I'd go into a room so that when the officers came in I would be in a compromising position with the girl. I would also see if she had any marks on her body, so that if the officers arrived late, and we were already dressed, they could identify her in court and say that they had seen her undressed and that they had seen those marks on her body. Then they arrested her, shook down the house [for a cash payment], and brought the girl to court the next day. The magistrate asked me if I gave her any money. I said 'five dollars, your Honor, marked. I found the money under her pillow.' "

In a slightly more sophisticated operation, which the witness called "the doctor's racket," Acuna, posing as a patient, entered an office while the doctor was out and demanded immediate treatment for some fictitious ailment. Over the nurse's protests, he placed money in a conspicuous place in the office and began to undress. Just as he dropped his pants, the cops would burst in and arrest the nurse for prostitution. This was followed by the suggestion that a cash payment might make the phony case go away.

There was another scam called the "landlady racket," where innocent landladies were falsely arrested for running a house of prostitution. But when all else failed, the vice squad would simply swoop down on Harlem, break into people's apartments, and make random arrests of women. The magistrates, who in some cases were in on the scam, chose to believe the cops rather than the innocent women charged as prostitutes. If a woman refused or was unable to make a payoff, she might languish in jail for up to a hundred days. Sometimes, testified Acuna, these false arrests were made to meet a precinct house quota. If the vice squad members didn't maintain cash flow, their supervisors would reduce them in rank or have them transferred to an undesirable precinct.

Acuna named names—fifty policemen and vice detectives in all. He was ridiculed in the press as "Chili Acuna the Human Spittoona," but his testimony was a revelation. Some of the houses of prostitution who paid money were connected to saloons. Acuna collected thousands of dollars a month from speakeasy owners. He shared these payoffs with high-ranking officers from the West Sixty-eighth Street precinct station in Manhattan. It wasn't long before Seabury's investigation ensnared a number of these officers. By the fall of 1931, a parade of vice sergeants, captains, and inspectors had been called to explain how they had accumulated so much money—in some cases six-figure bank accounts on salaries ranging from $3,000 to $10,000 a year. The most enlightening of these witnesses was Thomas M. Farley, sheriff of New York County, president of the Thomas M. Farley Association, boss of the 14th Assembly District, and Tammany Hall sachem. During Farley's testimony it was revealed that, in 1929, he had deposited $83,000 in cash on a salary of $8,500.

"Where did you keep these monies that you had saved?" asked Judge Seabury.

Farley answered that he kept his cash in a tin box, which he kept in a safe in his house. He had occasionally removed the cash and deposited it in increments in three different banks.

"Now, in 1930," asked the Judge, "where did the extra cash come from, Sheriff?"

"Well, that is—my salary check is in there."

"No, Sheriff, your salary checks are exclusive of the cash deposits which during the year you deposited in those three banks."

Farley chuckled, "Well, that came from the good box I had."

"Kind of a magic box," said Seabury.

"It was a wonderful box."

"A wonderful box," agreed the Judge. "What did you have to do—rub the lock with a little gold and open it to find more money?"

"I wish I could," said Farley.

The testimony of "Tin Box" Farley was underscored by a half dozen other police officials who admitted to having similar magic boxes filled with cash at home hidden in safes, in closets, or under their beds. The momentary levity provided by the tin box brigade was abruptly shattered when, in the midst of the hearings, the body of an important witness, Vivian Gordon, was discovered in Van Cortland Park in the Bronx. The red-haired, thirty-one-year-old divorcee had been strangled with a clothesline. Only a few days before, the woman had been questioned in private by Seabury investigators; she had testified that she'd been framed by a member of the police department's vice squad. Gordon was scheduled to appear again and provide even more damaging evidence about the police who had falsely arrested her for prostitution. After her body was discovered, Vivian Gordon's distraught sixteen-year-old-daughter committed suicide.

Chief among the suspects in the Gordon murder was Andrew G. McLaughlin, the vice cop who had arrested her for soliciting and caused her to be convicted of prostitution. At first, McLaughlin could not be reached because he was all too conveniently on vacation in Bermuda. When he returned, the cocky McLaughlin smugly told reporters that "this whole Seabury mess" was a farce; he would willingly take the stand and defend the actions of the vice squad.

When called before Judge Seabury, McLaughlin came down with a sudden case of policeman's amnesia. He couldn't recall his arrest of any woman named Gordon or even whether she was black or white.

"Well," said Seabury, "can you tell me this: How is it that you managed to bank $35,800.51 in two years despite the fact your salary as a member of the vice squad is exactly $3,000 per annum?"

To this and all remaining questions, the vice cop took the Fifth.

After a departmental trial, McLaughlin was fired for making false arrests and refusing to answer questions at the Seabury hearings. But there was never any evidence linking him directly to the Vivian Gordon murder, and the crime went unsolved.

Dirty cops and dead witnesses were only the beginning. As the Seabury investigation dragged on over two years and three public sessions, bail bondsmen, judges, and assistant district attorneys were implicated. It seemed as if the proverbial rock had been lifted, and the ground below was crawling with maggots. It was only a matter of time before the trail led to the top.

During his term and a half in office, Jimmy Walker, the Night Mayor of New York, had mostly led a charmed existence. A whirling dervish of the Jazz Age, he seemed to embody the times in which he lived. He had a mistress, Betty Compton, a vivacious, uninhibited, brown-eyed dancer twenty-three years his junior. His wife, Allie, was aware of the affair; her husband and his paramour were a regular item in the gossip columns, sighted in nightclubs and restaurants all over town. Allie remained the dutiful wife, spending most of her time alone in the mayor's mansion, until events finally overwhelmed her talents for self-abnegation.

Beau James was a creation of Tammany Hall, designated for the job of mayor by Grand Sachem Charles Murphy. Boss Murphy would die before Walker was elected, but he recognized in the charming, witty, and politically undistinguished state senator from Greenwich Village a man who would preserve the status quo while waltzing above the fray. Walker himself memorialized this philosophy with one of his many critiques of the Goo Goos, or Good Government reformers who were the bane of Tammany Hall. "A reformer," said Walker, "is a guy who rides through a sewer in a glass bottom boat"—implying that, in the real world, a politician must know how to look the other way when circumstances required it.

Walker's ability to look the other way, for a time, was a big part of his charm. Prohibition necessitated having political leaders who were believed to be men of moral integrity without being moralists. Walker may have cultivated the image of a Broadway star, but, like so many other Irish American politicians, he maintained an almost mystical connection with the little guy. One of his biggest accomplishments was arguing before the U.S. Supreme Court to preserve the five-cent subway fare. Mostly, he appeared at public functions, made wisecracks to reporters, and provided a kind of gaiety that was infectious. He spent more time at prize fights and in speakeasies (his drink of choice was a Black Velvet, a mix of champagne and Guinness stout) than he did in his office. When a rival politician balked at raising Walker's mayoral salary from $25,000 to $40,000, Walker quipped, "Why, that's cheap. Imagine what it would cost if I worked full-time."

In July 1930, Walker and Compton were present during a police raid of a gambling house in Montauk, Long Island. As the gambling patrons scattered like cockroaches, the mayor explained to the federal coppers who he was. They let him go, but his mistress was taken into custody and held for two hours before being released. For most politicians, this incident would have been a career-altering scandal. For Walker, it was in keeping with his rakish nature. The public tittered and looked the other way—for a time, anyway—until the various murders, shakedowns, and overall civic corruption began to give off a foul stench that seemed all the more unseemly during a time of food lines, soup kitchens, and makeshift Hoovervilles.

In early 1932, the mayor was called to appear before the Seabury panel, whose mandate had been broadened to encompass every department and official in the city. Walker had been served with a subpoena calling for all records of his personal financial transactions from January 1, 1926 to May 25, 1932. It was an astounding request. Jimmy ridiculed the investigation in the press, went on vacation, and made himself generally unavailable until the day of reckoning could not be forestalled any longer.

On May 25, the mayor—dapper as always, with a cigarette dangling from his lips—approached the county courthouse in lower Manhattan. A throng of spectators were gathered, many of them sympathetic to Walker. Voices called out, "Atta boy, Jimmy!" "You tell 'em, Jimmy!" "Good luck, boyo!" The mayor acknowledged the crowd by clasping his hands over his head like a jubilant prizefighter.

Inside, the courtroom was filled with seven hundred people in a space designed to hold half that many. When Walker entered, Judge Seabury and his aides were already seated at the counsel table. The two sides did not acknowledge each other. Applause and cheers broke out for the mayor.

Walker's testimony, under questioning from Seabury himself, took place over two days. The mayor was feisty on the stand, and at one point said under his breath to the politically ambitious Seabury, "You and Frank Roosevelt are not going to hoist yourself to the presidency over my dead body."

The various vice squad and magistrate scandals were embarrassing enough, but they could not be directly linked to Walker. More problematic for the mayor were his finances, which involved numerous beneficences (cash payments) from business interests that later won lucrative contracts with the city. Through cancelled checks, it was shown that some of the mayor's side money made its way into the account of his mistress, Betty Compton. Another person who benefited from his relationship with Beau James was Dr. William H. Walker, the mayor's older brother. In four years, Dr. Walker had deposited close to half a million dollars as a result of being given a virtual monopoly in treating patients with Workman's Compensation matters before the city. Evidence showed that, in many cases, the bills had been padded and the government ripped off.

Although there was no "smoking gun," the hearings were humiliating for the mayor, mostly because his mistress and brother had been dragged into the mess. When Jimmy's brother passed away unexpectedly not long after Walker's appearance before the Seabury committee, the mayor fell into an uncharacteristic funk. Seabury smelled blood and went for the jugular, delivering a detailed recommendation to Governor Roosevelt that Mayor Walker be removed from office for gross improprieties and other instances of political malfeasance. While FDR brooded over Seabury's recommendation, weighing the political ramifications vis-à-vis his own ongoing campaign for the presidency (he hoped to be nominated at the Democratic Convention in Chicago, just weeks away), Mayor Walker beat everyone to the punch. On September 1, 1932, he resigned from office.

Ding dong, the mayor was dead.[1]

---

1. Initially, it was Walker's intention to resign and then run again for mayor in the next election; he hoped to shame Seabury/Roosevelt by going over their heads directly to the people. Slowly, however, it became clear to the ex-mayor that he did not have the votes. Adding insult to injury, the Catholic Church came out against his reelection.

The forces of reform—growing in number as the economic woes of the Depression deepened—saw in Walker's defeat the end of "bossism" and a blow to the dark forces of the underworld. Roosevelt, in particular, reaped tremendous political benefit heading into his party's all-important national convention. Editorial writers nationwide gave him full credit for spearheading a tough and scrupulous examination of municipal corruption in his own home state. The kudos were not lost on the Goo Goos and Tammany-haters.

The Tiger had spawned many imitators. Now, bloodied and weakened, the Tiger was looking more and more like a seriously wounded animal. Ambitious prosecutors everywhere commenced to sharpen their knives.

Revenge of the Goo Goos

For many decades, the Machine had depended on men like Jimmy Walker, a public official who projected an image of viability while the world around him seethed and sizzled with moral turpitude. Walker was the smiley face out front, a figurehead who, like the Tin Pan Alley songwriter he had once been, was supposed to create an entertaining diversion while the organization's lesser lights fleeced the city's coffers. (Because of his high profile, a man like Walker could not be seen amassing huge amounts of money; he was not going to get rich.) It was the Night Mayor's job not to get too deeply enmeshed in the dirty dealings of the ward system—enough to be compromised and forced into resignation, perhaps, but not so much that he might wind up dead or in jail.

Not all Tammany acolytes were so lucky.

Municipal corruption was an essential element of the underworld, and it was fueled by money, plain and simple. Somebody had to deliver that money from Point A to Point B. Furthermore, someone had to take the responsibility for seeing that services were rendered in exchange for these surreptitious cash payments. Whoever took the money was going to be held responsible. It was a dirty business, not to mention a dangerous one. Over the past decade, judges, corrupt cops, lawyers, and all kinds of ward officials had dis-

---

Walker was devastated; like many other machine politicians and some Irish American mobsters, he was a devout church-goer.

In 1933 Jimmy divorced his wife Allie and married Betty Compton. They lived in exile in London for three years before returning to New York. After eight years of marriage, Walker and Compton also divorced, though they remained close. Walker was at Compton's side when she died prematurely from a malignant tumor. Beau James resisted many offers to get back into electoral politics. He died from natural causes in 1946 at the age of sixty-five.

appeared, their bodies found later or not at all. It was the price of doing business in the Irish American underworld.

One man who walked this tightrope with more skill than most was Jimmy Hines. Since the earliest days of Prohibition, and even before, Hines had fulfilled his duties as the city's preeminent bag man, or emissary, between Tammany Hall and the mob. In many ways, his Monongahela Democratic Club on Manhattan's West Side was the epicenter of the Irish Mob in New York. And everyone knew it. In fact, with his Spencer Tracy-like white hair and piercing, mercurial blue eyes, the longtime alderman from the 11th Assembly District became quite possibly the most revered man in the entire Tammany universe because of his willingness to take on the riskiest responsibilities. He was considered to be the person who made it possible for everyone to get over, which placed him in a rarified position.

In mid-1933, with Prohibition finished and Mayor Walker banished into exile, Hines was approached by perhaps the only major gangster in town with whom he hadn't yet formed an alliance: Dutch Schultz. The Dutchman knew all about "the Old Man," or "Mister Fix-It," as Hines was variously known. Schultz knew that Hines had played a formative role in helping Owney Madden and Big Bill Dwyer establish the city's first major bootlegging empire. He knew that Hines had also been paid by Lucky Luciano and Meyer Lansky to promote certain aldermen who were friendly to the Syndicate. And he knew that, in 1932, Hines had attended the Democratic convention in Chicago and shared a suite of rooms at the swanky Drake Hotel with another prominent underworld figure, Frank Costello. Schultz knew this because he, too, had attended the convention.

That was twelve months ago; much had changed in the past year, with prosecutors zeroing in on some of Prohibition's most renowned former bootleggers. Most famously, Scarface Al Capone was nailed on tax evasion charges and sentenced to prison in 1933. Waxey Gordon, the Beer Baron of New Jersey, also got himself prosecuted on tax charges. During his trial, it was shown that in 1930, Gordon's income from beer alone was $1,338,000; in 1931 he brought home $1,026,000. And that was documented income. Everyone knew his real net worth was much higher. For the first time, the public at large began to get a clear picture of just how much the bootleggers had taken in during the years of the Noble Experiment.

Dutch Schultz made a lot of money, too, but his payroll was sizable, and he had legal expenses. He'd been indicted for tax code violations of his own in Upstate New York; while he would eventually beat the charges, the lawyers' fees and related costs were enormous. He'd been forced to come up with new revenue streams, which led him to muscle in on the lucrative policy rackets in Harlem.

Thanks to average working stiffs and grannies wagering untold dimes and nickels, the numbers game was enormously profitable, but it was also risky. Aggressive law enforcement could stop the racket in its tracks by disrupting or shutting down known policy banks—the warehouses, apartment rooms, and empty storefronts where betting slips were registered and proceeds tabulated. Thus the numbers racket could not function without political protection. That was where Jimmy Hines came in.[2]

The first place Hines and Schultz met was well outside the bounds of Hines's uptown barony and a long way from Harlem. The district leader waited on a street corner on Sixth Avenue in Greenwich Village, underneath the El tracks. The Dutchman drove up in a bulletproof Caddy with his right hand man, George Weinberg, and his lawyer. Hines climbed in the back seat. Schultz introduced everyone and, as they drove aimlessly around town, got right to the point. In his typically blunt manner, he made it clear to Hines that the biggest problem with his policy business was "the goddamned, no good honest cop" who wouldn't take "the ice" and kept coming around making the same pinches over and over. It was hard to keep things running smoothly when the little people, the runners and controllers, were being hauled off the streets and locked up.

Years later, on a witness stand in county court, George Weinberg recalled this conversation between Schultz and Hines in the back of the Dutchman's Caddy. It was Weinberg who explained to the district leader exactly what the Combination needed: "I told [Hines] that in order to be able to run our business and bring it up the right way, we would have to protect the controllers that are working for us. We would have to protect them from going to jail. And if we got any big arrests that would hurt our business, we would want them dismissed in Magistrate's Court so that they wouldn't have to go downtown [a reference to the sometimes tougher three-judge Court of Special Sessions]. I

---

2. The way the numbers racket worked was simple: Through "runners" associated with Schultz's operation, known as "the Combination," people put down small change on a three-digit number. Each day's winning number was determined by the last three numbers of the para-mutual betting totals, or "total mutual handle," at the local race track, which was printed daily in the newspaper. Depending on how much was bet on any given day, the return on a wager could be huge—as much as nine hundred to one. If no one hit the number that day, the entire betting totals were pure profit for the Combination. Author Paul Sann, in his book *Kill the Dutchman!* estimates that the Combination, based in Harlem, was taking in as much as $20 million a year in the mid 1930s.

explained to him that we did not mind the small arrests but if we got any large arrests we would want them dismissed in Magistrate's Court to show the people in Harlem that are working for us that we had the right kind of protection up there, and that we would want to protect them from going to jail."

Hines's reply to Weinberg and the Dutchman that day was, "Well, gentlemen, you've come to the right place."

It was agreed that Weinberg would pay the Old Man fifteen hundred dollars a week. In addition, Schultz would give the district leader a down payment of one thousand dollars right there on the spot. From this point forward, James J. Hines was on the payroll; he was a key member of the Combination.

The district leader's involvement paid dividends almost immediately. Policy arrests by the police department's Sixth Division in Harlem dropped from twenty a day down to eight and then to four thanks to the clout of Jimmy Hines. If for any reason the heat came back on and arrests started going back up, George Weinberg picked up the phone and called Hines. Mister Fix-It then picked up the phone and called his friend, John F. Curry, Grand Sachem of Tammany Hall, who had risen to the top with the backing of Hines's Monongahela political club. Boss Curry picked up his phone and called James S. Bolan, his hand-picked police commissioner. Bolan called Inspector John O'Brien, head of the Confidential Squad. By the time all the calls were completed, the arresting officers in Harlem were reassigned to a precinct or unit based far out in goatsville. That was the power of the Irish Mob in a nutshell.

Hines didn't stop with the police department. Many magistrate judges met the district leader at his spacious apartment at 444 Central Park West. The words he used with the magistrates, in general, were identical to the request he specifically made one afternoon to Judge Hulon Capshaw.

"I have a policy case, a very important one, coming up before you that I'd like you to take care of," Hines said to the judge at his apartment.

Magistrate Capshaw replied, "Haven't failed you yet, have I? Don't worry, I'll take care of it."

Having political leaders, police commissioners, and judges in your back pocket might seem comprehensive, but Hines, a man whose long career was devoted to manipulating the levers of power within the System, left nothing to chance. Through George Weinberg, he funneled thirty thousand dollars directly from the Combination into the election fund of the prospective Manhattan District Attorney, a man Hines called "stupid, respectable, and my man." Jimmy's man was elected, and he made sure that no major organized crime prosecution went forward without first consulting the white-haired commissar from the 11th Assembly District.

That might have been the whole story, with Hines getting wealthy by facilitating underworld activities with Schultz the same way he had with Madden, Dwyer, Rothstein, and others. But with the Dutchman, for some reason, the Old Man crossed the line. He socialized with Schultz to a greater degree than he would have with his other gangster associates during the halcyon days of Prohibition. Over many months, Hines and Schultz were often seen together at the swanky Embassy Club on West Fifty-seventh Street, where they dined with their wives. The two men went to boxing matches and the racetrack together. Hines was a frequent visitor to the Dutchman's riding stables in Connecticut, while Schultz and his associates were regulars at the Monongahela club, where cash payments were exchanged. All of this made it exceedingly easy for prosecutors to link Schultz with the district leader when the inevitable heat came down from above.

The man who came after Hines was Thomas E. Dewey. A professional mob buster who had been a U.S. attorney, special prosecutor, and district attorney, Dewey first set his sights on Hines's benefactor, the Dutchman. Hot off his conviction of Waxey Gordon and an indictment that would soon lead to the prosecution and conviction of Lucky Luciano, Dewey saw Schultz as his ticket to a career in electoral politics (Dewey eventually became governor of New York and, in 1948, the Republican Party nominee for president). In early 1935, he indicted Schultz on charges relating to his control of the numbers racket. The Dutchman was livid, and he began complaining loudly to high-ranking members of the Syndicate that Dewey must be taken out. The Syndicate would not sanction such a hit, fearing that the murder of someone as visible as Dewey might bring down on them the wrath of the entire U.S. government.

"Fuck you," was Schultz's response. "Maybe I'll remove the cocksucker my own damn self."

The Dutchman's temper and loud mouth got him killed; on October 23, 1935, a team of gunmen entered the Palace Steak House in Newark, New Jersey and filled him with an assortment of high-caliber bullets. Schultz lingered for two days, mumbling a series of delusional nonsequiturs ("A boy has never wept nor dashed a thousand kin. . . ." "Mother is the best bet, and don't let Satan draw you too fast. . . .") before dying in his hospital bed.

Unfortunately for Jimmy Hines, the gangland elimination of his business partner and friend did not lessen his own problems. In fact, Dewey, the crusading and ambitious district attorney, merely shifted his prosecutorial focus from Schultz to Hines, whom he identified as "a coconspirator and indispensable functionary of the Schultz organization." Dewey had the goods. In the wake of the Dutchman's murder, his sidekick, George

Weinberg, turned state's evidence. Weinberg had been the primary go-between for the Schultz organization and Hines, often meeting the district leader at his Central Park West apartment and political clubhouse.

The case against Hines was unprecedented, the first in which a prominent political leader was prosecuted for being a high-ranking member of a criminal organization. Dewey was not just saying that Jimmy Hines was a politician who had committed crimes; he was saying, clearly and unequivocally, that Jimmy Hines was every bit as much a gangster as Dutch Schultz.

After many long delays, the *People v. James J. Hines* got underway in August 1938. George Weinberg took the stand and spilled the beans on Pops, as Weinberg referred to Hines. Four days into the trial, the judge declared a mistrial on a technicality. Dewey was not deterred. He reindicted Hines on the exact same charges. In January 1939, a second trial got underway, with one major difference. On the eve of his testimony in the second trial, George Weinberg, feeling depressed and remorseful, blew his brains out with a revolver. The dramatic suicide was a potential disaster for the prosecution, but their case was saved when the judge ruled that Weinberg's testimony from the first trial could be entered into the record.

Hines was cooked. Not only was Weinberg's devastating testimony used, but a host of witnesses—including John Curry, the Grand Sachem of Tammany Hall, police commissioner Bolan, and even Hines's hand-picked district attorney—took the stand and gave details on how Hines had gone about establishing the most corrupt political/criminal network since the earliest days of the Tweed Ring.

Throughout the proceedings, Hines rarely spoke. Unlike Jimmy Walker, who was the public face of the Machine, Hines was the ultimate man behind the man. He rarely gave speeches or talked to the press. He did not sponsor legislation; that was not his function. He was a money man who remained behind the scenes. Therefore, he did not take the stand and testify on his own behalf. As noted by a news service reporter covering the trial: "[Hines] sits in the well of the court and listens closely. And he looks like a paternal father who is watching his kids cut up. His tiny mouth is drawn into a line, his button of a nose supports his spectacles. Sometimes he bites his lip. . . . When things get hot, Hines rubs his big, thick fingers across his thumb. During a lull, he looks around at gray-haired, patient, well-preserved Mrs. Hines. 'Tired?' he asks, and he comes over."

When Hines was finally found guilty on all thirteen counts of the indictment, he made a rare comment to the press. Asked by a reporter how he felt, the district leader replied, "How would you feel if you were kicked in the belly?"[3]

The dramatic fall of the two Jimmys—Walker and Hines—seemed to suggest that the world had been turned upside down (they not only got the man, they got the man behind the man). For decades, the Tammany Tiger had been a force of nature that powered the Irish American underworld—in New York and beyond. The Tammany model had been copied and adapted to cities large and small. Now, with Franklin Roosevelt in the White House looking to institute a New Deal for America, a strong wind swept across the land, gaining in intensity as it went. Political reform was no longer a pipe dream to be derided and laughed at by powerful ward bosses. The Goo Goos were in charge now, and they would make the scoundrels pay.

Kansas City Stomp

Of all the Irish American political organizations to be dismantled during the Age of Roosevelt, none had seemed more indestructible than the Pendergast Machine of Kansas City. Located far from the urban centers of the Northeast where the Irish had first settled, the political framework that helped to transform Kansas City from a nondescript cow pasture into a bustling midwestern metropolis was remarkably similar in tone and temperament to Tammany Hall. Although it had a miniscule immigrant population (less than six percent) and an overall Irish population that never exceeded two or three percent, Kansas City was controlled by an organization that looked, sounded, and acted as if it had been hatched in South Boston or in Manhattan's notorious Five Points. One writer analyzing Kansas City's government noted that the names of local politicians read like the roster of a unit of the Irish Republican Army.

For many decades, the town was run in the classic Irish American style for one reason: That was how its citizens wanted it. Kansas City had sprung up relatively late, well after the Civil War. The city's business leaders and founding fathers were anxious to establish their town as a thriving economic outpost in the Midwest. They looked to the country's most vibrant and rapidly growing metropolitan areas—New York, Chicago, and New Orleans—and copied what they saw as a political and economic system that delivered.

Vice was always part of the equation. Flat, industrial, and somewhat drab, the town and surrounding area was not known for its physical beauty.

---

3. Hines was given a sentence of four to eight years in the state penitentiary. After his appeals were exhausted, he went to Sing Sing prison in 1940, served four years, and was paroled. He died in 1957 at the age of eighty, the last of a breed.

If Kansas City was going to lure traveling salesmen and big spenders from Chicago, Denver, Galveston, and Minnesota—not to mention laborers and migrant workers from the South—it needed a draw. From at least the early 1880s, that draw consisted largely of gambling parlors, dance halls, prostitution, and other forms of vice. Much of this activity was centered in a section of the city known as West Bottom, an industrial area along the banks of the Missouri River that became Kansas City's version of the Levee District in Chicago, the French Quarter in New Orleans, or the Bowery in New York.

By the turn of the century, West Bottom was renowned as the best vice district west of Chicago, a favored stomping ground for cowboys, travelers, transients, and townspeople alike. The area was clustered with saloons, bawdy houses, and honky tonks. Bunco and floating craps tables were everywhere, especially in the blocks around Union Station, which became the center of Kansas City's red light tenderloin district. The American House, a multipurpose saloon that featured gambling tables and rooms upstairs for quick assignations, became the virtual City Hall for West Bottom. It was owned by Jim Pendergast, a former factory worker who became a Democratic party committeeman from the First Ward in 1887.

Big Jim dispensed favors in the classic style, extending loans to packinghouse workers and distributing welfare to the poor, primarily in the form of bags of coal and—that old Tammany standby—holiday turkeys. His machine was built along the same lines as those in New York, Chicago, Boston, and elsewhere; the block system, as Pendergast called it, was a constellation of block captains, precinct captains, ward heelers, and aldermen, all of them on friendly terms with the boss. "That's all there is to this 'boss' business—friends," said Jim. "You can't coerce people into doing things for you. You can't make them vote for you. I never coerced anybody in my life. . . . All there is to it is having friends, doing things for people, and then later on they'll do things for you." This statement was standard boss fare and gave little indication that the Pendergast Machine would be described in later decades as "a state within a state, a virtual invisible government."

Jim Pendergast was from a large Irish Catholic family of nine. Both of his parents hailed from County Tipperary and had come to America as potato-famine refugees. His mother first arrived in the United States through the city of New Orleans, at a time when Irish immigrants were dying in the thousands from yellow fever and hellish labor conditions. His mother's stories of starvation and death in the Louisiana swamps haunted Jim Pendergast and his siblings, instilling in their clan a drive and ambition that would dramatically reshape the environment in which they lived.

Although Jim Pendergast was a hugely popular district leader, the era he presided over was known for its fierce political rivalries. Kansas City was a Democratic town, but the Democrats were divided into two factions known as the Rabbits and the Goats. Rabbit Democrats were so named by their enemies for the way they flocked to the polls in close elections like scared rabbits. The Goats, led by Boss Jim, were so called because many of them lived in shanties clinging to the sides of the West Bluffs like mountain goats. Others claimed the name came from the large number of billy goats Pendergast registered as legitimate voters in the First Ward.

Two of Jim's brothers served important roles in his Machine. Mike, boss of the Tenth Ward, was a dedicated organizer, but his stage fright undermined his role as a leader. Thomas Joseph "T. J." Pendergast, however, was dynamic and charismatic. A stocky, former semiprofessional baseball player, he'd gotten his start as a bouncer in his brother's saloon. Whereas Jim was soft-spoken and a master of the art of political compromise, Tom (twelve years Jim's junior) was blustery and tough, a man's man who would not hesitate to use his fists if circumstances called for it. He also carried a revolver.

In 1910, not long after his wife died, Jim Pendergast retired from politics, turning his council seat over to Brother Tom, who was elected the following year by an overwhelming majority. Jim's health soon deteriorated, and in September 1911, after weeks of being bed-ridden with an unknown respiratory ailment, he woke and asked a nurse, "Where's Tom?" Tom hurried to his bedside. Jim looked at his brother and said cheerfully, "Hello Tom." Those were his last comprehensible words before he expired in his bed.

Tom Pendergast picked up the mantel bequeathed to him by his older brother and turned it into one of the most astounding municipal operations in twentieth-century America. The guiding principle of the Pendergast Machine was an epigram that Jim kept posted behind the bars in his saloons: "You can't saw wood with a hammer." Inspired by blunt practicality, Tom Pendergast improved upon his brother's model by first appeasing and then combining the Goat and Rabbit factions under one organization. This was done in the usual manner; thuggery, voter fraud, and intimidation were all part of the Pendergast arsenal. The machine that he devised was loyal and generally responsive to the needs of the people, with a monolithic system of patronage that compelled the *Kansas City Star*, an avowed enemy of the Pendergast Machine, to refer to it as "Little Tammany."

In his modest office at 1908 Main Street, the unassuming, brick-façade headquarters of the Jackson Democratic Club, T. J. (as Pendergast preferred to be called) received a daily stream of small business owners, senior citizens, aspiring aldermen, clergymen, lobbyists, and mafiosi. Fat and animated, with huge ears and a lively, salt-of-the-earth face, Pendergast was the opposite of

New York's Jimmy Walker. Where Beau James was witty and attractive, T. J. was blunt and earthy. Even his enemies were sometimes beguiled by his larger-than-life persona. He was a local chieftain who laughed, cried, and seemed to care genuinely about the lives of his constituents. He could be kindly and sentimental, especially when it came to his Irish heritage. He was also a tough-as-nails, gravelly-voiced brute who mangled the English language and wasn't afraid to get rough with anyone he felt deserved it.

In a newspaper interview, Pendergast once explained how he handled two underlings who questioned an order: "One of them hesitated, said he didn't know anything about it. Well, I slapped him with my open hand. The other tried to protest. I hit him with my fist and knocked him through the glass door."

T. J. didn't have to get rough very often. As his power grew, so did his reputation. Locally, City Hall became known as "the House of Pendergast." The state capital in Jefferson City was referred to as "Uncle Tom's Cabin." Harry S. Truman, who was hand-picked by Boss Tom to run for the senate and eventually became the thirty-third president of the United States, was sarcastically known as "the Senator from Pendergast." The boss was unapologetic about his power: "I'm not bragging when I say I run the show in Kansas City. I am the boss. If I were a Republican, they would call me a leader."

Prohibition had much to do with T. J.'s ability to establish a prosperous and powerful dictatorship. Borrowing from Chicago's pioneering example of the wide open town, Kansas City promoted itself as a city where anything went. Not a single felony conviction for violation of the Volstead Act was ever imposed in Kansas City. Saloons and speakeasies doubled as gambling dens and assignation houses. The Blue Goose, the Winnie Winkle, the Oriental, and the Jubilesta were known Pendergast sin places.

The most notorious was the Chesterfield Club, located only one block from the federal courthouse downtown. The establishment pretended to operate as a swank supper club, offering a menu of soup and striptease. The waitresses wore only shoes and a change belt. On Friday afternoons, members of the Machine held regularly scheduled ribald parties featuring nude dancing and backroom sex as a reward for male precinct workers and local lobbyists. Given the mix of booze and nudity, the club could get unruly. A gang of bouncers routinely rolled drunks and beat up overly randy customers. One night, a Texas cattleman who became amorous with a waitress was beaten to death inside the Chesterfield, then taken over the state border to Kansas City, Kansas, dumped in the street, and reported as a hit-and-run accident.

Even more important than booze and sex to the financial well-being of the Machine was gambling. Wrote one visitor from New York, "If you want excitement with roulette, cards, dice, the races, or a dozen other forms of chance ask a patrolman on the Kansas City streets. He'll guide you. It's perfectly open. You just walk in." It was reported in the press that the annual take for the Pendergast Machine from gambling alone was $20 million.

The Kansas City underworld also gave birth to a unique brand of jazz that thrived in the black-and-tans, a cluster of clubs that sprung up in the vicinity of Eighteenth and Vine, east of downtown in a large African American district. For a musician to secure a booking, the man to see was Bennie Moten, a dapper African American pianist and bandleader who controlled many of the music jobs in town. Moten was an adjunct of the Pendergast Machine, a regular visitor to the boss's Jefferson Democratic Club headquarters at 1908 Main.

The Kansas City sound was characterized as "dirty jazz," a hard-driving Southwestern variation on the Delta blues, much different from the sophisticated European-influenced orchestrations of Duke Ellington and others in New York City. The Panama Club, the Elk's Rest, the Boulevard Lounge, the Hi Hat, the Hey-Hay (where customers sat on hay bales), and Dante's Inferno (where the waitresses wore devil costumes) were just a few of the clubs that became home to jazz musicians who flocked from all over the United States to take part in the most vibrant musical epoch since the glory days of Storyville in New Orleans. Countless luminaries like Lester Young, Jay McShann, Coleman Hawkins, Count Basie, and Charlie Parker developed and honed their styles in the Eighteenth and Vine district.

While Kansas City may have represented a kind of hell for the Goo Goos and other reform-minded citizens, for musicians it was, according to pianist Mary Lou Williams, "a heavenly city." Amidst the myriad forms of vice, including booze, drugs, and prostitution, a musical culture and classic American style was born. Perhaps none of it would have been possible were it not for the wide open, laissez-faire morality of the Pendergast Machine. In fact, if the Volstead Act had been enforced, few of the clubs in Kansas City, Harlem, Storyville, or anywhere else in the United States where jazz was born would ever have been able to exist.

Of course, the gangsters and cops on the take who fed off the flourishing jazz scene in Kansas City did not restrict their extortion to the downtown nightclubs. The cost of doing business in town often involved exorbitant fees paid to men like Johnny Lazia, a local mafiosi closely aligned with the Capone syndicate. Starting in the years of Prohibition, the Kansas City family would become an integral aspect of the Mob, later referred to as the Outfit. Many years later, the Outfit would pull off its biggest power play with the systematic skimming of casino gambling money in Las Vegas, which was funneled back into the underworld through the Kansas City family.

The Mob—and Al Capone—had no problems with T. J. Pendergast. Kansas City, like Chicago, was a pioneer of the attitude that money generated by organized vice worked its way back into the system, not only through graft and payoffs, but through licensing fees and taxation that funded untold civic projects; the city grew fat on the concept of dirty money. The man who benefited most, not surprisingly, was Boss Tom. Neither an elected official nor a political appointee, Pendergast was that classic avatar of American capitalism, the businessman. As owner and president of the Ready-Mixed Concrete Company, he held an exclusive contract on every cubic inch of concrete that was poured in the city and surrounding county. The man who gave final approval on all public works projects in Kansas City was the city manager, Henry McElroy, a partisan member of the Pendergast machine (as was Water Commissioner O'Malley and Director of Police Higgins). Every time a highway, city park, parking lot, or building foundation was initiated and put in place, Pendergast got the contract. In so doing, he violated no laws. Simply through political maneuverings and the force of his personality, the man seemed to control everything. No wonder they called the place "Tom's Town."

Fall of the House of Pendergast

During the years of his reign, Pendergast made many enemies. Most of them were local Republican businessmen who had a hard time getting projects off the ground in a city and county where the Machine had a lock on everything. The disgruntled and the bitter formed a loosely structured coalition, a vocal opposition that expressed itself often in the pages of the *Kansas City Star*, a newspaper founded and owned by one of the areas wealthiest WASP families, the Nelsons. The *Star* had positioned itself as a harsh critic of the Democratic Machine since the early days of Jim Pendergast's tenure as alderman, though they reserved their harshest attacks for Brother Tom. In editorial cartoons inspired by Thomas Nast's anti-Tammany depictions from an earlier era, Pendergast was portrayed as a gangster-politician in the Boss Tweed mold, complete with a monstrously oversized stomach, Irish derby hat, and piggish inclinations. Knowingly or unknowingly, this portrayal evoked the most virulent anti-Irish stereotypes of the postfamine era.

For a time, the *Star*'s anti-Pendergast crusade played right into the boss's hands. Irish American machine politics had always been based on an element of populism, if not outright demagoguery, the perception that the powers that be—namely the WASPs and the blue bloods—deemed themselves morally and socially superior to the average Joe. The bosses rarely missed an opportunity to twist this latent American snobbery in their favor by attacking the institutions of the well-to-do. The unparalleled master at this was James Michael Curley of Boston. Once, in response to an anti-Irish editorial in the *Boston Globe* (a newspaper that served basically the same function in Boston as the *Star* did in Kansas City), Curley declared to a gathering of the faithful, "A strange and stupid race, the Anglo-Saxon. Beaten in a fair, stand-up fight, he seeks by political chicanery and hypocrisy to gain the ends he lost in battle, and this temperamental peculiarity he calls fair play. . . . No country is ever ruined by a virile, intelligent, God-fearing, patriotic people like the Irish."

Pendergast did not possess Curley's verbal dexterity, nor were there enough Irish in Kansas City to make playing the shamrock card a big winner. Nonetheless, Pendergast benefited by positioning himself as a self-made man who'd risen from the gutter and understood the needs of common folk—as opposed to the desires of bankers, corporations, and newspaper editorialists. This philosophy played well in the Heartland of America, among the cowboys and the cattle ranchers, until the excesses of "bossism" began to appear ever more venal and corrupt during the hard, lean years of the 1930s.

The roots of Boss Tom's downfall, like that of many larger-than-life public figures, were to be found in the man's character. Generally a proud family man, content to while away evenings in his mansion with his wife and three kids, Pendergast was a teetotaler who rarely partook of the criminal rackets that his regime helped to create. But he did have one uncontrollable vice: gambling. Although he was known occasionally to go to the track to bet on the ponies (he owned several thoroughbreds and an interest in two local tracks), Boss Tom was mainly a gambler in the way some people are masturbators; he gambled behind closed doors, by himself. He had a wire service teletype installed in the basement of his mansion, enabling him to communicate directly with bookmakers. He used an elaborate system of fictitious names to cover his transactions, betting as much as $20,000 on a single horse race. At the behest of his family, he sometimes promised to stop, only to resume his addiction. His son, Tom Pendergast, Jr., said of his father, "He was like a man on dope. He needed a fix. A fix for him was each race."

Boss Tom's lawyer described his client's habit this way: "He told me that when the afternoon was here, two-thirty, three o'clock, he would go into a little room, and there he would take the form sheet, and with the advice of a friend of his would handicap horses, and then he would sit with the telephone at his ear and he would hear the call, 'They're at the post.' Later, 'They're off,' and so over that telephone, by ear and not by eye, he watched those horses run to the finish line—all the thrill that can come to any man, for which possesses him and which he cannot down." The lawyer quoted a remorseful Pendergast as saying, "I don't know what it is, but [this addiction] has been with me all my life."

Informants claimed that Boss Tom lost as much as $100,000 per week to big New Jersey and New York bookmakers, who code named him "Sucker." Pendergast once told an associate he needed to "slow down" because "bookies from the Atlantic to the Pacific have me pegged as their biggest sucker." He did not slow down.

To avoid leaving a paper trail, Boss Tom rarely used money from his personal accounts to finance his habit. Given his stature and reputation, he was extended credit by bookmakers, or he borrowed directly from Capone's man in Kansas City, Johnny Lazia. In return, Lazia was given the run of the town. This arrangement was especially beneficial to Lazia during the years of the Noble Experiment. After Prohibition, however, the federal government came after him the same way they had Capone, Waxey Gordon, Dutch Schultz, and all the others. In February 1934, Lazia was found guilty of tax evasion.

T. J. Pendergast wrote a letter to the U.S. Postmaster General, pleading for leniency for Lazia, claiming he was "being jobbed because of his Democratic activities." At the same time, rumors circulated in the street that Lazia was going to turn canary and detail the many loans Pendergast had been extended by local racketeers.

In the early morning hours of July 10, 1934, Lazia, free on parole, arrived with his wife and driver at his fashionable midtown apartment. A gang of four hitmen pulled up alongside his car, aimed a tommy gun and shot gun, and opened fire. They hit Lazia eight times without hurting his wife or driver. An ambulance rushed the bleeding mafioso to St. Joseph's Hospital. Boss Pendergast arrived and exhorted his personal physicians to save Lazia, but all their efforts failed. "Kansas City's Al Capone," as the newspapers called the local mafia boss, was dead by dawn. As the end neared, he reportedly said to a doctor, "If anything happens, notify Tom Pendergast, my best friend, and tell him I love him."

Front and center at Lazia's funeral was Boss Pendergast, but that did not stop the rumors from swirling like buzzards at a garbage dump. Many believed that T. J. himself must have ordered the hit to silence Lazia before he had a chance to sing. It was an outlandish notion; Pendergast could be a bully, and he often engaged in threats and verbal intimidation, but he was basically a white collar criminal—not a killer. Furthermore, there was never any real evidence that Lazia was about to turn informant. More than likely, Lazia was taken out in a professional mob hit. While there were many theories about why it might have happened, there was no evidence, and the murder went unsolved.

Boss Tom, who was nothing if not loyal, found the accusations that he killed Johnny Lazia insulting, but he only had himself to blame. He could hardly deny that his relationship with the city's preeminent mobster was far-reaching and complicated. For decades, Pendergast had flourished in that gray zone between right and wrong, good and evil. He had made it possible for the underworld to hold sway in Tom's Town, to kill or be killed depending on which way the dice rolled. Now he was being portrayed not as the political facilitator and benign manipulator he saw himself to be, but as a common gangster.

The seamy nature of the Lazia-Pendergast alliance, as it was splashed across newspaper headlines in the weeks and months following the mafioso's murder, emboldened the anti-Pendergast forces, who had been gaining steam since the inception of the New Deal. It is a testament to Pendergast's arrogance that, even as public sentiment turned against him, he refused or was unable to change his ways. He continued to run up huge gambling debts. Since Lazia was no longer available as a source of money, he had to look for other ways to feed the beast.

In January 1935, Pendergast began a series of meetings with a St. Louis insurance broker who was looking to influence legislation in the state of Missouri. Pendergast had considerable pull with Robert Emmett O'Malley, the superintendent of insurance for the state. For a price, Pendergast told the St. Louis broker, he could make his troubles go away. The man readily agreed, promising a series of payments to Pendergast and O'Malley totaling $750,000. The first of these payments was made at Pendergast's political headquarters. Another payment, totaling an astounding $330,000 in cash, was made at a Chicago hotel and later delivered directly to Pendergast at his home, where he counted out the bills on his dining room table.

In all, Boss Tom received a grand total of $440,000, keeping $315,000 and giving $125,000 to O'Malley. Technically, the money did not constitute a bribe. Pendergast and the insurance broker had merely engaged in a classic form of American-style influence peddling. If the boss had paid federal income taxes on the money, there would never have been any problem. But he apparently used the entire amount to settle pressing outstanding debts owed to bookmakers.

Pendergast's shady insurance kickback lit a fire under the Goo Goos and antimachine crusaders. For the first time, Pendergast candidates for office began routinely losing at the polls, leading the governor of Missouri, Lloyd C. Stark, to declare, "The political boss can be licked. He and the corrupt machine are in the main responsible for organized crime in our cities. I propose to lead the fight against Boss Tom Pendergast and keep at it until

Kansas City is cleaned up." Keeping his pledge, the governor put pressure on President Franklin Roosevelt who, in May 1938, answered Governor Stark by unleashing investigators from the Bureau of Internal Revenue Services on Tom Pendergast and his Machine.[4]

In April 1939, after months of investigation, the IRS went public with their findings: In a period from 1927 to 1937, the Boss failed to report as income the staggering figure of $1,240,746.55, defrauding the government of $501,078.75 in taxes. Tracing all of the money that Pendergast had received proved difficult, said the investigators, since he kept "negligible records, rarely used a bank account, almost always accepted only cash payments, made virtually all expenditures in cash, and sent large amounts by wire under assumed names." They were able to determine, however, that, in 1936 alone, Pendergast wagered $2 million on horse races and lost $600,000. In 1938, he lost $75,000 in November and won back $43,000 the following month.

On April 7, 1939—Good Friday—a federal grand jury indicted Pendergast on two counts of tax evasion. The boss, more corpulent than ever, his hair now thinning and gray, appeared in court to be fingerprinted and to give bond. He was unrepentant. In an uncharacteristic display of self-pity, he snarled at reporters and compared himself to the Man from Nazareth: "There's nothing the matter with me. They persecuted Christ on Good Friday and nailed him to the cross too." Later, in a more reflective mood, he said, "Every human being, including myself, has to live with his own conscience. There comes a day when he has to account for himself. There's no one there but himself. It's a fearsome time when a man faces his own conscience. But I'm willing to live with mine. I haven't an elastic one either. I'm living with my conscience today in peace and contentment."

A month after the indictment, to the surprise of many, Boss Tom entered into plea negotiations with the prosecution. Suffering from a chronic heart condition, he did not look forward to a contentious, embarrassing trial that he could not win. There was also the threat of other indictments directly related to the insurance kickbacks. Consequently, Pendergast pleaded guilty

---

4. On April 24, 1939, *Life* magazine ran an article speculating that by agreeing with Stark to go after Pendergast, President Roosevelt intended to elevate the Missouri governor as a Democratic version of the crusading New York "Mob Buster" Thomas E. Dewey. "It was clearly a New Deal effort to dim some of Tom Dewey's crusading glory by destroying a political boss even more powerful than New York's Jimmy Hines." Though *Life*'s reasoning was specious—the magazine was notoriously pro-Republican—the point was well-taken: Going after the political bosses had become a kind of buffalo hunting. They were easy prey and made wonderful trophies.

in exchange for a sentence of fifteen months in federal prison. In addition the judge announced, "The defendant will not be permitted to bet on the races or gamble in any form. He will not be permitted, directly or indirectly, to take part in any sort of political activity unless his full civil rights shall be restored by presidential pardon. He will not be permitted to visit 1908 Main Street during his probation."

Tom Pendergast served his time in prison and lived out his remaining years in ill health. In keeping with the terms of his probation, he steered clear of politics (although his nephew James Michael Pendergast kept the family name alive in Missouri politics well into the 1950s). On January 15, 1945, at the age of seventy-two, T. J. suffered a heart attack in his office at Ready-Mixed Concrete. He was rushed to the hospital and passed away the following day.

In death, as in life, Pendergast inspired extreme points of view. His family had played a major role in the political and economic fortunes of Kansas City for more than half a century; Boss Tom presided over this dynasty like a portly potentate. To some, he was the devil incarnate. Wrote one local judge who'd butted heads with Boss Tom:

> He thoroughly understood the psychology of the underworld, and the habitues of the shadowy kingdom followed him blindly as well as devotedly. He protected them from prosecution for their misdeeds and granted them commissions to sin against the laws of God and man. His past experience had qualified him to lead and rule the refuse in society. He understood the life of the brothel and houses of ill fame. . . . He derived immense revenues from graft in public office and from his levies on crime. To support his invisible government, he deemed it prudent to increase his power over elections and to take away every element of chance. . . . All citizens, to be secure, were forced to acknowledge the uncontrolled and despotic power of one man with his invisible empire.

Pendergast loyalists, of course, saw things differently. At his funeral, attended by an enormous crowd that included Vice President Harry Truman (whose career Boss Tom had initiated and sponsored), a Catholic priest eulogized the deceased. "He had a noble heart," said Monsignor Thomas B. McDonald. "His word was his bond. If he was your friend, he was a true friend. In regarding his life, it would be best to recall the injunction, 'Let he who is without sin cast the first stone.'"

T. J. himself, in an interview published in the *St. Louis Star-Times* just a few months before his death, gave the best defense of his regime. With his usual mix of arrogance and Christian piety, he proclaimed, "I've done a lot for Kansas City—for the poor of Kansas City. I've done more for them than all the big shots and bankers, all of them put together. We used to take care of our poor, with coal and wood and food and rent, and we helped them in their trouble. We never asked the poor about their politics. . . ." Finally, in what could be his epitaph, the boss declared, "And I've never broken my word. Put this down: I've never broken my word to any living human being I gave it to. That is the key to success in politics or anything else."

Reform

The prosecution and banishment of the political bosses—Walker, Hines, Pendergast, and others—was only one factor in the decline and fall of the Irish political machines. From the beginning, the New Deal had been designed as a federal system to dispense the same sort of services that had once been provided by political organizations like Tammany Hall at the ward level. Federal work projects, food stamps, and low-income housing were functions of the New Deal that had once been monopolized by Irish-run machines for close to a hundred years, when no other organization within government seemed to give a damn. Over time, the general public grew weary of seeing bosses like Sullivan, Croker, and Pendergast get rich off backdoor deals in smoke-filled rooms, which sometimes involved mobsters and a primitive form of muscle. In the brotherly glow of the New Deal, such operations seemed perversely out-of-date.

Even the Irish had seen enough. One hundred years after the Great Potato Famine, which had facilitated the birth of the American underworld, the Irish no longer needed the fierce upperhand that had been provided by the political machines. As a group, the Irish had made inroads into virtually every profession in American life. Moreover, they had a controlling interest in many of them, especially municipal professions such as police forces, fire departments, and public works. Quite simply, by the mid-twentieth century, the political bosses were no longer needed. As they dropped off one by one, the attitude among many second and third generation Irish Americans was "good-bye and good riddance."

For the Irish American gangster, however, the end of the Machine as a powerful political entity was bad news indeed. The Machine had helped to keep the underworld organized and stratified. Street-level Irish hoodlums, those who had survived the bloody purges of the Prohibition years, rose up the social ladder thanks in part to their association with various Machine-affiliated political organizations. Now that they were in decline, the Irish gangster had nowhere to turn. The only organization out there now was some version of the mafia, variously known as the Syndicate, the Outfit, or Cosa Nostra. From here on out, Irish American gangsters looking to do business in the underworld would be doing so over some variation of pasta and meat sauce.

The culture that had spawned and sustained the concept of the Irish American gang for so long appeared to be dying out. This gradual social metamorphosis was institutionalized on June 22, 1944, when President Roosevelt signed into law a piece of legislation that, inadvertently, probably had more to do with the death of Irish American gang culture than any other single factor. It was called the Servicemen's Readjustment Act, otherwise known as the G.I. Bill.

Since the days of the Civil War, military service had been a possible alternative to the gang life, an arena in which physical aggression and other violent tendencies were given an acceptable outlet. Wars ended, however, leaving the veteran with sometimes troubling memories and few adaptable job skills, which put him right back where he started. What the G.I. Bill did was make military service attractive by offering money for education and housing to veterans. For many young Irish American males raised in a culture where violence, early alcoholism, and machismo comprised the true Holy Trinity, the G.I. Bill offered a clear path out of the ghetto. Irish Americans, perhaps more than any other ethnic group, took advantage of the benefits provided by the bill, leaving behind in droves the street-level gang mentality that would now be adopted by Puerto Ricans, African Americans, Asians, and other ethnic groups.

Given the powerful social forces that conspired to stamp out the Irish American underworld, the Irish mobster appeared to be on the verge of extinction. Like the Paleolithic creatures of a previous age, however, Irish mobsters would prove to be a pesky, irascible organism whose carnivorous ways would continue to sustain them long after the ecosystem at large had passed them by. While the political framework that had given rise to the Irish mobster may have been rendered obsolete through prosecution and political reform, independent Irish mobsters lived on—feasting, as before, on rackets associated with organized labor, police graft, gambling, narcotics, murder-for-hire, and, of course, politics.

The extinction of the Machine was not the final blow; it was merely the shedding of a layer of skin. The foundation of the Irish American underworld, dictated by a flexible morality that involved manipulation, coercion, subterranean alliances—in a word clout—was alive and well. With the machine structure now cast off, the Irish American way of doing business, heretofore restricted to the ward, the city, and the state, was now free to range far and wide and advance to new heights. And so it would—all the way to the White House and beyond.

2

PART two

a long way
from
tipperary

❧ ❧

hard hats & hard men

F rom the earliest inception of the Irish American underworld, the waterfront was where it all went down. In any port city the pattern was the same: Immigrant ships arrived at the docks and unloaded their human cargo. Native-born Americans and wily immigrants who had arrived years earlier were there to meet the new arrivals. Like jackals gathering for a feed, hustlers, con artists, sneak thieves, and wharf rats descended on their prey. Even the official greeters who represented legitimate social organizations like Tammany Hall had ulterior motives. Sure, an immigrant runner from the river wards might lead a new arrival past the riffraff; he or she might suggest lodging or a place to find a bowl of soup and a piece of bread. But it all came at a price. By partaking of the immigrant runner's largesse, the greenhorn had virtually sold his or her soul to the Machine, knowingly or not.

The waterfront was not only a port of entry, but also a vast commercial bounty. Especially in the decades before commercial trucking, seafaring ports were the primary source of national and international trade in the United States. Valuable cargo of every variety—including illegal contraband—arrived and departed by way of the docks. Organized pilferage, a huge racket for the gangsters, was considered the price of doing business; the losses were part of an inflated bottom line that was passed along from the stevedoring companies to the consumer. Luxury cruise ships of the Cunard and Grace Steamship lines were another wonderful source of exploitation; they paid huge tariffs and disgorged an unending supply of well-to-do passengers who, in the eyes of the gangsters and their facilitators, were ripe for the taking.

Most of all, the docks represented jobs. A steady supply of manual labor was needed to service the vast commercial machinery along the waterfront.

A young, brawny lad with little or no education could, by cultivating relationships with the right people, find work loading and unloading freight. Eventually, through organized labor agitation, waterfront jobs became a highly prized, well-paying form of employment, especially for unskilled laborers with few other opportunities.

On wharves and docks throughout America, tough men gathered on a daily basis. Among them were the poor, immigrants, ex-cons, and those simply looking for a solid day's work, a bimonthly pay packet, money for rent, shoes, a warm winter coat, a beer-and-a-shot, or food and sustenance for their families at home. There were never enough jobs to go around. To procure a day's wages, a strong back and conscientious work habits were *not* the primary consideration. More valuable was a man who knew the routine, who showed a willingness to submit to the System as it was—a system based mostly on greed, exploitation, and the threat of violence.

The shape-up was a ubiquitous method of employment on the piers. Men arrived twice a day and gathered in a huge mob outside a designated loading dock. A stevedore, or hiring boss, surveyed the crowd and decided who would work and who would not. If you were a lone, unaffiliated individual looking for a day's labor, *fuggettaboutit*. The only way to procure work was to form into a crew or gang and pay tribute to the hiring boss, who in turn paid tribute to the stevedore companies, who in turn paid tribute to union officials, who in turn paid tribute to politicians and cops, and so on up the ladder. The result was an elaborate kickback system with tentacles that reached into virtually every aspect of modern industrial society—in other words, organized crime in a nutshell.

In the early decades of the twentieth century, Irish and Italian laborers waged a bloody battle for control of the commercial piers in many big cities. The Brooklyn dock wars, led by Wild Bill Lovett and Peg Leg Lonergan, may have produced the highest body count, but similar battles sprang up all over the United States. In New Orleans, huge shipping companies deliberately manipulated Irish and Italian longshoremen, pitting one against the other, eventually adding a new element—African Americans, who were brought in at low wages to undercut both groups. In New England, some of the cities' most renowned gangsters got their start in the region's dock wars, shuttling from Boston to Providence to Portland, Maine during strikes or when competing work crews clashed. In the Great Lakes region, particularly in Chicago and Cleveland, Irish American longshoremen fought to hold onto jobs that had passed from one generation to another since at least the 1870s, when Irish laborers first arrived in sizable numbers to help build the Ohio and Erie Canals.

Of all the locales where gangsters fought and eventually seized control of commercial mechanisms along the waterfront, none compared with the Port of New York. By the 1940s, especially during the years of World War II and immediately after, the Port of New York emerged as the most lucrative commercial port in the world. The shipping business in New York and elsewhere had survived the lean years of the Depression, which saw a dwindling workforce and a number of crippling strikes. Labor subterfuge and political turmoil may have kept workers from organizing, but it also hindered commercial trade on the waterfront. From an international standpoint, strikes and violent confrontations between workers and police made shipping freight more trouble than it was worth.

All of that changed on December 7, 1941, when the Japanese air attack on Pearl Harbor initiated U.S. involvement in World War II. Among other things, the war years turned out to be an unprecedented boon to the maritime industry, with New York harbor at the epicenter of an economic revival that would continue for at least the next fifteen years.

At the time, the Port of New York included all seaborne commercial activity in Manhattan, Brooklyn, and New Jersey, a gigantic waterfront trade covering 750 miles of shoreline with 1,800 piers. By the middle of the decade, nearly 10,000 ocean-going ships cleared New York harbor a year, or one ship every fifty minutes. These ships were owned and operated by steamship lines that sailed to 155 ports in every corner of the world. With more than a million passengers a year, they carried thirty-five million tons of cargo in foreign trade alone.

Within the harbor itself, cargo handling was serviced by approximately 2,500 tugs, barges, lighters, derricks, car floats, and scows. The adjacent railroad fleets moved more than 750 carloads of export freight daily to 200 steamship piers. Domestic freight was believed to be four or five times higher than foreign trade, with a total cargo somewhere around 150 million tons annually. New York harbor handled between 32 and 38 percent of the nation's overall cargo, or money cargo in longshore terms, with an annual value that ranged from fourteen to sixteen billion dollars.

This huge flow of commercial activity was bound to attract its share of criminal parasites and bottom feeders. In fact, many sluggers, shoulder hitters, and bootleggers who had survived the Prohibition years drifted into rackets associated with the waterfront trade. The hiring boss, in particular, was frequently a gangster from the booze running days who was adept at attracting and also controlling "dock wallopers." The docks were a rough-and-tumble universe; shylocks, or loan sharks, fronted money to workers so they could pay tribute to the hiring boss. Workers who were tardy in repaying the loans could be roughed up or even killed. Longshoremen who were on the wrong side of labor disputes also became victims of violent intimidation. And everyone kept their mouths shut; killings on the waterfront almost always went unsolved. Violence became the underpinning of a vast racketeering underworld that included gambling concessions (bookmaking and policy), payroll padding, no-show jobs, organized thievery, murder-for-hire, and all manner of labor corruption.

By the mid-1940s, the International Longshoreman's Association in the Port of New York boasted a membership of 40,000 workers. Most were part-time employees, and many were beholden to a particular hiring boss or waterfront gang—all of which guaranteed a desperate and compliant workforce. The ILA may have advocated for workers during labor disputes, but it also ruthlessly enforced the shape-up system, which was the foundation for the entire constellation of waterfront rackets. With thirty-two locals from the Gulf Coast to the Great Lakes and a national membership over 100,000, the ILA had become the glue that held together the vast, interconnecting array of criminal elements, making the waterfront the most lucrative underworld universe since Prohibition.

The ILA, in other words, was more powerful than any Mafia family. It was a legitimate organization with hegemony over a massive commercial and criminal marketplace. Anyone who ruled this universe was destined to be a man of great power, widely revered and feared. Such was the case for the man who ruled as the international president of the ILA for twenty-six years: a tough, proletarian individual known to his workforce simply as Boss Joe.

King of the Dock Wallopers

In all the years that Joseph P. Ryan reigned as supreme commander of the International Longshoreman's Association, he was never once voted into office by the union's general membership. In 1927, the year Joe Ryan first ascended to the presidency of the ILA, he was simply handpicked by a cadre of New York–based delegates representing locals from around the country. For the next two and a half decades, Ryan maintained his power, even though rank-and-file longshoremen on the West Coast completely rejected his leadership and eventually bolted from the ILA to form their own union—the International Longshoremen and Warehousemen's Union (ILWU), which Ryan denounced as a "communist conspiracy." In 1943, after years of strikes and labor agitation in many ILA ports from the Gulf Coast to the Northeast, the Boss was given an unusual vote of confidence:

He was named "president for life"—again, not by the union's general membership but by a proclamation of union business agents.

For a long time, Joe and his union cronies all got fat together, with Boss Joe somehow netting millions on a modest annual salary of $20,000 plus $7,200 for expenses. At the same time, he became perhaps the most powerful labor leader in the country, a benefactor to mayors, senators, presidents, and assorted killers and hoodlums. He was a kingmaker, of sorts, until his own greed and arrogance finally led the rank-and-file to rise up against him. Eventually, the public turned against him. On May 5, 1953, not long after being compelled to testify before a public tribunal known as the New York State Waterfront Commission, Boss Joe was convicted of stealing union funds and carted off to prison.

Joe Ryan's long march to the penitentiary was rooted in his childhood. He was born on May 11, 1884 to Irish immigrant parents in Babylon, Long Island. At the age of nine, Ryan became orphaned when both his mother and father died of natural causes within a few months of one another. After languishing in an orphanage for a time, young Joe was eventually adopted and went to live with his stepmother in a cold-water flat in Chelsea, a neighborhood on the West Side of Manhattan, just south of Hell's Kitchen.

Ryan began his working life as a floor sweeper, stock clerk, and trolley car conductor before landing a job on the Chelsea Piers in 1912. Four years later, at the age of thirty-two, Ryan joined the ILA by purchasing his union book for the going rate of two dollars and fifty cents. Within months, while working in the hold of a freighter, Ryan suffered a minor injury when a heavy sling load snapped and dropped onto his foot. Following a brief recovery in the hospital, he was assigned to the post of financial secretary for ILA Local 791 in Chelsea. Ryan would never again have to callus his hands or stain his shirt collar with sweat while working in a dock or hold gang on the waterfront.[1]

By most accounts, young Joe Ryan had natural talents as an administrator and organizer. Although he had dropped out of school and terminated his formal education at the age of twelve, he possessed a facility with the English language; his red-meat rhetoric was frequently humorous and sentimental.

---

1. A member of Local 791 at the time was William "Big Bill" Dwyer, who would go on to become King of the Rum Runners, founding father of the Combine, and business partner of Owney Madden. During Prohibition, the headquarters for Local 791 was located in a building on Tenth Avenue, just a few blocks from Dwyer and Madden's massive Phoenix Brewery.

Unlike many union leaders, however, Ryan preferred to exert power mostly as a behind-the-scenes figure. In the book *Dock Walloper*, a lively memoir of New York's longshoreman culture, written by Richard "Big Dick" Butler, the author describes how he tried to use then Vice President Joe Ryan as a Trojan Horse in his battles with a rival union leader.[2] Butler knew Ryan well, both as head of the ILA's district council and later as a Tammany-sponsored alderman. Knowing that young Joe Ryan had designs for obtaining the union presidency, Butler suggested to Ryan that, with the backing of Butler and others, he run against the union's current president, T. V. O'Connor.

Ryan may have been ambitious, but not so ambitious that he would allow himself to be used in what was essentially an internal power struggle, even though it may well have propelled him to the presidency. He respectfully declined Butler's offer, keeping both Butler and T. V. O'Connor as friends. A few years later, Joe Ryan became president anyway—on his own terms, with all of the necessary relationships and alliances intact.

With his thick torso, barrel chest, huge hands, and a face that only a mother could love, Ryan had the grizzled look and demeanor of a tough guy, but his greatest skills were as a classic Tammany-style fixer. In the mid-1920s, he formed the Joseph P. Ryan Association, a political club devoted to one thing: promoting the career of Joe Ryan. The ILA leader held fundraisers, solicited campaign contributions, and helped get out the vote for numerous Tammany candidates, including Mayor Jimmy Walker. As president of the Central Trades and Labor Council, Ryan was able to garner huge crowds for Walker at political rallies. When Beau James was forced to resign from office following the Seabury Investigation, Ryan issued a statement that read: "The labor movement in the city of New York regrets that political expediency has deprived them of a mayor whose every official act has been in conformity with the Americanistic policies of organized labor."

---

2. Butler, the son of Irish parents from Tipperary, was born in London's East End, immigrated to New York, and joined the Longshoreman's Association in 1898. *Dock Walloper* was written during his retirement years and is especially good at detailing the rambunctious early twentieth century connection between labor sluggers, politicians, and gangsters—especially on election day. Writes Big Dick: "Elections nowadays are sissy affairs. Nobody gets killed anymore, and the ambulances and patrol wagons stay in their garages. There's cheating, of course, but it's done in a polite, refined manner compared to the olden days. In those times murder and mayhem played a more important part in politics. To be a challenger at the polls, you had to be a nifty boxer or an expert marksman. A candidate, especially if he ran against the Machine, was lucky to escape with his life. I was lucky—I only had my skull bashed, and my front teeth knocked out, and my nose broken."

From the beginning, Ryan envisioned an ILA so powerful that he would literally be able to control the fate of presidents and dictate the ebb and flow of international commerce. His plans were altered considerably, however, when longshoremen in Boston dramatically repudiated his leadership in October 1931 by going on strike against his wishes. In 1934, an even bigger labor dispute involving a dozen commercial ports from San Francisco to Seattle reached a boiling point in the ILA's Pacific Coast District. Not wanting to be shut out like he had been in Boston, Ryan traveled to the West Coast to take part in labor negotiations with local employers. Ryan spent more than a month in San Francisco, finally emerging with a settlement that he declared was "fair and in the best interests of our members."

The grizzled New Yorker made the rounds of various strike committees in San Francisco, Portland, Tacoma, and Seattle, urging them to ratify his settlement agreement. In every location, Ryan was voted down, and the president of the Tacoma local declared in the press, "No body of men can be expected to agree to their own self-destruction."

The primary issue was the way in which workers were hired. Ryan urged his members to accept the shape-up system, which had been the sole manner of employment in ILA ports since the turn of the century. West Coast longshoremen astutely viewed the shape-up system not only as pernicious and humiliating for the workers, but also as the central way in which organized crime became institutionalized on the waterfront. The West Coast longshoremen preferred a hiring-hall system in which time in the hold and other seniority factors determined who was first in line for employment.

The West Coast longshoremen's strike of 1934 went down without the support of the ILA president; it was a memorably violent and contentious affair that culminated in San Francisco with the Battle of Rincon Hill—a street confrontation between strikers, professional strikebreakers, and cops that resulted in two deaths and scores of injuries. The National Guard was called in to quell the disturbance.[3]

---

3. The West Coast longshoremen's strike of 1934 ended in victory for the workers; a hiring-hall system was instituted and would be overseen not by a hiring boss, but by a dispatcher chosen by a labor board comprised of employers and workers.

The longshoremen's repudiation of Joe Ryan and business as usual in West Coast ports had much to do with minimizing the development of organized crime in cities like San Francisco and Seattle. Criminal rackets like loan-sharking, organized gambling, policy, and systematic labor corruption were never institutionalized in the same way they were in the Northeast. These factors help to explain why the Irish American mobster and labor racketeer appear rarely on the West Coast, although they remained a viable factor in cities like New York and Boston until the end of the twentieth century.

Joe Ryan left town denouncing West Coast labor leaders as malcontents and communists, but his rhetoric could not mask what had been a crushing defeat for his leadership. Back in New York, Boss Joe sought to mitigate his West Coast failure by enforcing his will even more resolutely than before. One way the ILA president regulated who obtained power and who did not was through his ability to dispense union charters, which made it possible for groups of workers to form their own locals. Joe Ryan alone dictated who would be given this power. He allowed for the establishment of union locals only by workers who pledged absolute loyalty to Joe Ryan. They also kicked back a percentage of all monthly membership dues directly to the president for his own personal use and consumption (of course, there would never be any records to prove that this was the case).

Although waterfront mobsters tended to come in all shapes, sizes, and ethnic denominations, over a fifteen-year period, from the late 1930s to the early 1950s, the ranks of the ILA in the Port of New York became a haven for the some of the toughest characters in the Irish American underworld. Thanks to Boss Joe, many unreconstructed bootleggers found new life as dock wallopers and union enforcers through the institution of a system that was beneficial mostly to stevedore companies, union business agents, and waterfront employers, not to the workers. Individual locals broke down along ethnic lines; Italian American locals controlled business on the waterfront in Brooklyn, Staten Island, Bayonne, and Hoboken, while the Irish controlled the docks in Jersey City and on Manhattan's West Side.

Among the many notorious members of the waterfront mob who owed their power to President Ryan were:

Edward J. "Eddie" McGrath—A former truck driver for Owney Madden and Big Bill Dwyer during the glory days of Prohibition, red-haired Eddie McGrath first became an ILA organizer in 1937, just six months after being released from Sing Sing prison. He'd been arrested thirteen times over the years on charges ranging from burglary to murder. An elite member of the New York underworld, McGrath controlled the lucrative numbers racket in the Port of New York and was believed to be on close terms with many high-ranking mafiosi. In 1943, Joe Ryan appointed Eddie McGrath an ILA adviser for life, later sending him south to shore up ILA operations in South Florida.

John M. "Cockeye" Dunn—As Eddie McGrath's brother-in-law and designated muscle, Cockeye Dunn was perhaps the most feared gunman on the waterfront. Born in Queens, New York, he was four years old when his father, a merchant marine, was lost at sea. Dunn bounced in and out of various Catholic reform schools and was often in trouble with the law, garnering early arrests for assault and robbery. In 1932, he was convicted of robbing a card game at gunpoint and sent to Sing Sing for two years.

Once out of prison, Dunn teamed up with McGrath, who was part owner of Varick Enterprises, a front company whose main function was to make collections for waterfront boss loaders to whom every truck man on Manhattan's West Side was paying tribute, usually in cash. The collections were enforced by goon squads armed with guns and blackjacks. In 1937, when a reluctant truck man was found dead, Dunn and McGrath were arrested on a charge of homicide but were eventually discharged for lack of evidence.

Dunn went on to form his own powerful local with the American Federation of Labor (AFL) and became the overseer of all waterfront rackets on Manhattan's Lower West Side, which included some sixty piers. In 1947, Dunn was arrested along with two other men for the murder of a hiring stevedore in Greenwich Village; his trial was one of the more memorable events of the whole waterfront era. Cockeye was found guilty and given the death penalty. He died in the electric chair.

Andrew "Squint" Sheridan—On the waterfront, any rising underworld figure worth his salt had to have a more violent junior partner to do the dirty work. Joe Ryan had Eddie McGrath. Cockeye Dunn had Squint Sheridan, a psychopath who found his calling as a notorious ILA enforcer. Once, when a longshoreman on the West Side piers threatened to start a dissident movement and take on the union leadership, Sheridan stopped by the pier and asked the man to step into a portable toilet for a conference. There Sheridan shot the man in the head and left him to die. When another dockworker had some negative things to say about a prominent ILA business agent, Sheridan drove up in a car, walked to the platform, and asked, "Who's Moran?" When Moran stood up, Sheridan pulled a gun, fired two shots, and killed the man in front of numerous witnesses—none of whom were willing to testify against him.

Squint Sheridan eventually became a victim of his own bad karma. In 1947, he was arrested along with Cockeye Dunn in the famous Greenwich Village murder of hiring stevedore Andy Hintz. They went on trial together and met the same fate: Sheridan was put to death in the chair just a few minutes after Cockeye, his friend and mentor.

Pistol Local 824—With Hell's Kitchen as its base, it was no surprise that Local 824 became one of the ILA's most powerful crews, presiding as it did over the luxury piers where the *Queen Elizabeth* and *Queen Mary* were docked. Harold Bowers was a neighborhood delegate appointed by Joe Ryan to Local 824, commonly known as the Pistol Local because its mostly Irish American membership was comprised of so many convicted felons. Bowers himself had been arrested for grand larceny, robbery, and gun possession, done time in prison, and was suspected of being an accessory in numerous waterfront murders.

The real power behind Local 824 was Harold Bowers' cousin, Mickey, whose criminal record showed thirteen arrests between 1920 and 1940. Mickey Bowers was believed to be behind the death of (among others) Tommy Gleason, a rival for control of the Pistol Local who was gunned down in a Tenth Avenue funeral parlor—a convenient spot for a mob hit if ever there was one. Local 824 was legendary for its nepotism, with brothers, cousins, and barely qualified ex-con-in-laws first in line for lucrative administrative positions within the union.[4]

George "the Rape Artist" Donahue—Donahue got his start as a loading boss on the Jersey City piers and served as an ILA liaison with the political administration of Mayor Frank Hague, the least charming of all the big city Irish American political bosses. Hague's influence reached beyond Jersey City to include Hoboken and much of Hudson County; his reign lasted from 1915 to 1949 and was militantly enforced by a famously brutal police department. Boss Hague was known to use the New Jersey waterfront as a major patronage plum, doling out jobs and favorable contracts as payback to loyal operatives. He was also tight with Joe Ryan, frequently serving as cochairman alongside New York Mayor Jimmy Walker at the annual testimonial dinner of the Joseph P. Ryan Association.

George "the Rape Artist" Donahue, Hague's waterfront overseer, first became president of Local 247 after he and two bodyguards stormed into the Local's headquarters and demanded the resignation of the president and vice president. When the two men refused, Donahue pulled out a gun, stuck it in the president's mouth, and told him either his signature or brains would be on the resignation papers. The president signed away his leadership. When the vice president hesitated to sign, his front teeth were knocked out with a gun butt. He also signed.

Donahue's leadership of Local 247 was marked by violence. When Boss Hague left office in 1949, after a thirty-four-year run, Donahue lost much

---

4. John Bowers, son of Harold and nephew of Mickey, became a member of Local 824 in the 1940s, a union officer in 1956, and, in 1987, president of the ILA and head of the union's Atlantic Coast Division, for which he currently pulls in an annual salary of half a million dollars. Accusations of corruption in the ILA have continued, with the most recent racketeering indictment against the union coming in 1990.

of his clout. In January 1951, a bomb went off under the hood of his automobile when he started the ignition. Miraculously, Donahue survived unhurt, but his days as president were numbered. He was lucky to live to see retirement.

Many of the hoodlums, union men, and politicians who operated within the Port of New York were rulers in their own right, but none could hold a candle to Boss Joe. On a daily basis, Joe Ryan's ILA created the illusion of democracy; there were local meetings, district councils to hear complaints, an ILA executive board, and a national convention held every year. But none of that mattered to Ryan. If ever he harbored aspirations for a unified workforce, for whom he would be a magnanimous advocate, those dreams were crushed in Boston and on the West Coast, when his attempts to negotiate a strike settlement had been so dramatically repudiated.

Boss Ryan was determined to show that such humiliation could never occur on his home turf. In the Port of New York, thanks to his unprecedented gathering of ex-cons, killers, and various political sycophants, his authority would remain absolute.

You Push, We Shove

In the long history of the American labor movement, the ILA was not alone in its use of hard men and questionable tactics. The reasons for this are buried deep in the history of America's industrial beginnings and inexorably intertwined with the Irish American experience.

Before Joe Ryan ever rose to the top of the longshoreman's association, labor politics in the United States were steeped in bloodshed. Among the first laborers in the country to become advocates for basic principles of employment such as a minimum wage, safe working conditions, and some version of Workman's Compensation were Irish immigrants and Irish Americans. Paddy dug the canals, built the bridges, and, along with Chinese, African American, and Italian laborers, laid down the tracks of the transcontinental railroad. The work was brutal and often lethal. In the anthracite coal mining region of Pennsylvania, black lung disease and mining accidents took the lives of thousands of workers, including more than a few under the age of ten.

Secret labor organizations like the Molly Maguires sprang up in direct response to an owner's unwillingness to address abysmal working conditions. In rural Pennsylvania's Schulykill County, where nine out of ten Irish immigrant males worked in the mines, the Molly Maguires took matters into their own hands, embarking on a campaign of sabotage and

violent acts aimed at specific mining companies, with the intention of forcing management to the bargaining table. The coal mining companies
responded by hiring the Pinkerton Detective Agency, who planted an Irish
American spy deep inside the organization. Thus, the tactic of labor espionage on the part of management was established, injecting an aura of
paranoia and fear into America's industrial workplace that would persist
for at least the next century.

The Industrial Revolution only intensified the deep-rooted animosities
between workers, management, and the corporate manufacturers who pioneered the staple of American industry: the factory assembly line. There
were few significant labor laws at the time and only the beginnings of a
union movement. Whereas in the mid-nineteenth century the proletarian
rabble was mostly forced to engage in full-scale rioting to bring about social
change, the new century saw the emergence of labor agitation, or the strike,
as a viable strategy of mobilization.

Due to their spectacular success at infiltrating the Molly Maguires, the
Pinkerton Agency became the leader in a brutal and systematic campaign to
undermine union agitation wherever it occurred. Strikebreaking became a
hugely profitable enterprise for Pinkerton and other private detective agencies that specialized in recruiting and transporting antiunion goon squads
and armed guards. Finding men willing to partake in violent strikebreaking
activities for pay was not difficult. From 1870 until at least the 1920s,
employment among the working class was chronically unsteady, and each
year there were several hundred thousand people who were unable to find
work for at least a few months. In industries such as slaughtering and meat-
packing, iron and steel, brick and tile, garment manufacturing, and the
building trades, work was seasonal, with no unemployment insurance or
social welfare system of any kind to help get a worker over the hump. Men
desperately in need of work were willing to do almost anything to make a
buck, including spying for the company store or strikebreaking, in which
men armed with lead pipes, rocks, and guns set upon picket lines and union
halls looking for heads to smash.

The same sort of person who might once have hired himself out as a
bootlegger, political slugger, dock walloper, or gangster also had the right
stuff to be a strikebreaker. Given that such a high percentage of the workforce was of the Celtic persuasion, Irishmen, in the eyes of management,
made ideal spies and strikebreakers. Some even found their calling in the
fink markets.

One such man was James Farley. Born into a lower-middle-class Irish

American family in the Upstate village of Malone, New York, Farley began his career in organized labor as a street car motorman who, in the midst of a general strike, turned against his fellow workers and joined forces with the corporation. Not only did Jim Farley go on to become a notorious commander of professional strikebreakers with a standing army of twenty-five hundred men, but he also achieved the highest level of cultural notoriety a man could receive in pre-Hollywood America when Jack London, the top commercial novelist of his day, mentioned Farley by name in his novel *The Iron Heel*. Farley was singled out by the famous writer as an example of a pernicious trend, men who were "private soldiers of the capitalists . . . thoroughly organized and well-armed . . . held in readiness to be hurled in special trains to any part of the country where labor went on strike or was locked out by employers." In London's apocalyptic vision of the class struggle between labor and "the Oligarchy," strikebreakers were an ominous sign of bad times ahead.[5]

As a young man, Farley was adventurous and reckless. At the age of fourteen he ran away from home to join the circus. When the circus went to the wall in the town of Monticello, he obtained employment in a hotel there, first as a poolroom attendant, then as a bartender and clerk. One day he became uncontrollably violent when he accidentally swallowed an overdose of cocaine during a visit to the dentist and ended up being chased into the woods, where he was hunted for weeks as a wild man. Unemployed and penniless, he drifted to Brooklyn and found work there as a detective.

Detective work led Farley to a career in strikebreaking, which began in the 1895 Brooklyn streetcar strike, when the company put him in charge of a squad of fifteen special officers. After taking part in other antiunion cam-

---

5. *The Iron Heel* was first published in 1908 and is still in print. Set in the near future, the novel describes a class war in which corporate America has coalesced into a ruling oligarchy and taken over control of the country. The nascent labor movement is crushed by a fascist plutocracy. Although London's vision is certainly paranoid and anticapitalist, it proved to be prophetic in many details. Among other things, the novel captured the tone of fear, subterfuge, and distrust between workers and corporations that led certain unions, out of self-defense, to utilize their own gangster squads.

The fact that corporate management in America was out to divide and conquer trade unionism—by force, if necessary—became the self-justification for union bosses like Joe Ryan and Jimmy Hoffa to resort to strong-arm tactics and gangsterism. Over time, wily racketeers within the movement found ways to exploit the labor/management paradigm and plunder their own unions for personal profit.

paigns in Philadelphia and Richmond, Virginia, Farley realized that what was needed was a more organized approach: Successful strikebreaking required that a single boss assume complete command from the company and supply all the men. Over the next eight years, Boss Farley put together an underground strikebreaking network that was tops in the country. Farley was always at the forefront, overseeing an organization that broke strikes from the Atlantic to the Pacific. In newspaper advertisements, he claimed to have at his command an "army of forty thousand men ready to do his bidding." No one doubted him. The Farley organization broke over fifty strikes without suffering a single defeat.

Much of Farley's reputation as a champion strikebreaker was based on what one newspaper described as his "imperturbable demeanor." He was a physically imposing man who wore his Colt .38 in a holster, like a gunslinger from the Old West. He was covered from head to toe with bullet wounds and scars from knives, clubs, pistol butts, bricks, and baseball bats. Reputedly, he smoked fifty to sixty Havana maduro cigars a day, preferring big, fat Carona Specials. According to an article in the *United Mine Workers Journal*, he stood before his mercenaries, mostly tough lumpenproletarians from big city slums, "with the air of a potentate," wearing "a long Cassock overcoat," and the men "looked up at him with gaping mouths." Farley's power was legendary. During the 1905 New York IRT subway strike, a reporter mentioned IRT President August Belmont, one of the nation's wealthiest men, to a strikebreaker. The strikebreaker responded, "Who the hell is Belmont? Farley's runnin' this road."

Farley's near mythical strikebreaking career culminated in San Francisco in 1907. Summoned by the city's largest private transit company to stop a rumored strike before it began, he arrived in San Francisco Bay on a steamer with four hundred of his mercenaries, recruited from all over the country. In the weeks that followed, there were numerous skirmishes; Farley's men descended on union members whenever they attempted to gather. The streetcarman's union accused Farley of deliberately placing explosives on the tracks to turn public opinion against the strikers, an old detective agency trick designed to connect labor with terrorism. He had used similar tactics before, in Cleveland, where a bomb blew up a trolley car injuring ten people, and in Bay City, Michigan, where Farley had been convicted of placing obstructions on the tracks designed to cause wrecks that would be blamed on the union.

In San Francisco, the bloodiest night of strikebreaking occurred on May 7, when Farley's gang finally faced off against union activists near the Turk and Fillmore street car barn. The workers were armed with clubs and pipes, the strikebreakers with revolvers. Farley's men opened fire on a crowd, killing four union sympathizers. According to an eyewitness account, the union people were "shot down like dogs." When all was said and done, the San Francisco transit strike never took place. The union, intimidated by the strikebreakers, voted against the strike. Farley had succeeded once again.

During his strikebreaking career, Boss Jim Farley was paid millions by American corporations to intimidate, brutalize, browbeat, and kill labor activists. He was a mercenary who undertook his violent antiunion campaigns purely for personal profit. Was Jim Farley a gangster? The press of his day did not characterize him as such. The *San Francisco Chronicle* meant it as a compliment when they described the world's most famous strikebreaker as "a man who prefers hot blood to water as a beverage." Other newspapers around the country lionized Farley, characterizing his penchant for violence and mayhem on behalf of employers as a noble calling. He was sometimes taken to task for his use of extreme tactics, but this too was often portrayed as a kind of daring in which criminal deception and thuggery were regrettable although justified in the face of flagrant social agitation (big city newspapers, most of them notoriously antiunion, frequently editorialized that the labor movement was socialist- or communist-inspired).

Whereas Jim Farley was portrayed as a hero and a necessary response to a social ill, violent activists on the other side were not. During the massive West Coast·longshoreman's strike of 1934, for example, violence occurred on all sides. A small group of ILA members known as the Tacoma Flying Squad frequently roamed from port to port defending strikers, chasing away scab workers, and clashing with overzealous police. Overseen by Paddy Morris, leader of a Tacoma longshoreman's local, the Flying Squad was revered within the union, but not by the press. The *Tacoma Daily Ledger* and other West Cost newspapers characterized the Flying Squad as "a union mob of thugs and gangsters." Yet most of these men had no criminal record and had adopted their defender strategy on behalf of their union, not for personal gain.

The fact that union activists were characterized as gangsters while strikebreakers were viewed as defenders of society goes a long way toward explaining why certain trade unions became paranoid and defensive. The dichotomy was forceful and blunt: One man's gangster was another man's labor activist. The union could not trust that the press or even the general public would understand or sympathize with their position. Thus, labor leaders like Joe Ryan were able to brazenly accumulate a standing army of hard men, ex-cons, and gangsters within his union without anyone batting an eye. Ryan could count on a general atmosphere of fear and paranoia brought on by a long tradition of industrial exploitation, subterfuge, and violence, so that if a discerning member of the union were to ask himself, "Are there gangsters in the ILA?" he would have to conclude, "Sure. But at least they're *our* gangsters."

Cockeye and Squint Get the Chair

Early on the morning of January 8, 1947, stevedore Andy Hintz left his apartment on Grove Street in Greenwich Village, just a stone's throw from Pier 51, where he had worked as a waterfront hiring boss for the last seven months. Hintz never made it to work that day. In front of his building, three men appeared. One of them said, "Hey, Andy." Then they all opened fire and pumped him with six bullets. Hintz was a tough bastard. He lingered for three weeks in a hospital, drifting in and out of consciousness. Before he expired on January 29, he told his wife, "Johnny Dunn shot me."

Three longshoremen, Cockeye Dunn, his sidekick Squint Sheridan, and a third man, former prizefighter Danny Gentile, were immediately arrested for the murder of Andy Hintz. The shooting and arrest were major stories in the local newspapers. Murders on the waterfront were part of the city's lore, and this one appeared to be a humdinger as it involved a couple of notorious gunmen for the ILA.

Dunn, Sheridan, and Gentile were all held without bail, but that didn't stop Andy Hintz's wife from fearing for her life. The word was out that Mae Hintz would be the district attorney's primary witness in the upcoming murder trial of the three men. As a forty-one-year-old former nightclub owner, Mae knew all about how things operated on the waterfront. She knew that Cockeye Dunn and his thugs had been trying to oust her husband and replace him with someone more friendly to the waterfront mob. Before his death, when Hintz had been harassed by a gang of rival longshoremen, he said to the gangsters, "You can tell Cockeye Dunn to go to hell." Mae Hintz had been living in fear ever since.

As the date of her husband's killers' trial approached, Mrs. Hintz disappeared. For a while, foul play was suspected. It looked like the government's main witness was no more, in which case the evidence against the three gunmen was weak. Lawyers for Dunn and Sheridan gloated, alleging that their clients would soon be set free. But they were wrong: Mae Hintz turned up in Miami, where, out of stark, raving fear, she had gone on the run. Under heavy guard, she was brought back to Manhattan and kept under lock and key.

Where it all began: Five Points, New York City. This famous photo by Jacob Riis was taken in 1881, during the reign of the Whyo Gang, who were led by "the two Dannys," Lyons and Driscoll.

(MUSEUM OF THE CITY OF NEW YORK)

John "Old Smoke" Morrissey was the first Irish mob boss in America.
This editorial cartoon from the 1870s depicts his epic career in the most unflattering light possible.
(LIBRARY OF CONGRESS)

From the 1860s to the turn-of-the-century, Michael "King Mike" McDonald (right) was the man to see in Chicago. Bail bondsman, gambling impresario, political kingmaker, and infamous cuckold, McDonald was the Irish American Godfather of Mud City. (CHICAGO HISTORICAL SOCIETY)

New Orleans Police Chief David C. Hennessy, an early casualty in the war between the dagos and the micks (TULANE UNIVERSITY, LOUISIANA COLLECTION)

Two vice lords of early Chicago: Michael "Hinky Dink" Kenna and John "Bathhouse John" Coughlin.
For nearly forty years, the two aldermen ruled over the Levee District, the city's primary area for prostitution,
gambling, drugs, and more.

Owney Madden, Duke of the West Side
(NEW YORK *DAILY NEWS*)

Legs Diamond, nemesis of the Combine,
lived his life like a hunted animal.
(NEW YORK *DAILY NEWS*)

A rogues gallery—Eddie Diamond, Jack "Legs" Diamond, Fatty Walsh, and Lucky Luciano
(LIBRARY OF CONGRESS)

Chicago bootlegger Dean O'Banion and his wife Viola on their wedding day, February 5, 1921.
(ROSE KEEFE COLLECTION)

Alphonse Capone, primary nemesis of the Irish Mob during Prohibition
(LIBRARY OF CONGRESS)

Edward "Spike" O'Donnell (center), leader of the South Side O'Donnell Gang, with friends.
There were so many attempts on his life that Spike once joked, "Life for me is just one bullet after another."
(CHICAGO HISTORICAL SOCIETY)

George "Bugs" Moran,
Capone's least favorite Irishman, circa 1932
(AP PHOTO)

Bodies being removed from the killing grounds following the most notorious hit in gangland history, the St. Valentine's Day Massacre.
(CHICAGO HISTORICAL SOCIETY)

THE COLD-BLOODED HOT-HEAD WHOSE GUNS ROARED ACROSS THE 'DECADE OF DEATH'!

"PUBLIC ENEMY"

JAMES CAGNEY

JEAN HARLOW · JOAN BLONDELL · WILLIAM A. WELLMAN

On screen, actor James Cagney created the archetype of the Irish American gangster.

The lad from Gweedore, Vincent "Mad Dog" Coll (left), shakes hands with "the mobster's best friend," a highly skilled criminal defense attorney. (NEW YORK *DAILY NEWS*)

New York City Mayor Jimmy Walker (center) struts into court to give testimony before the Seabury Hearings. It would prove to be his undoing. (BETTMANN/CORBIS PHOTO)

Thomas "T. J." Pendergast (center) presided over the Pendergast Machine in Kansas City, the most steadfast Irish American political organization in the country—until Pendergast was convicted of financial improprieties and sent

An editorial cartoon lampooning the Pendergast Machine, one of many that appeared in the *Kansas City Star*

(AUTHOR'S COLLECTION)

At the McClellan Hearings, Bobby Kennedy and J.F.K. went after some of the very people Joe Kennedy leaned on to get his son elected president—with disastrous consequences.
(JOHN FITZGERALD KENNEDY LIBRARY: DOUGLAS JONES/LOOK)

Mafia boss Sam Giancana, who smirked at Bobby Kennedy during the McClellan Hearings, received this retort from the chief counsel: "I thought only little girls giggled, Mister Giancana." (LIBRARY OF CONGRESS)

Joseph P. Kennedy—whiskey baron, financial genius, the ultimate Man Behind the Man, seen here with a young J.F.K.
(BETTMANN/CORBIS PHOTO)

Buddy McLean, originator of Boston's Winter Hill Gang, of whom it was said: "He looks like a choir boy but fights like the devil." (**BOSTON POLICE DEPARTMENT**)

James "Whitey" Bulger, age 23
(BOSTON POLICE DEPARTMENT)

Danny "the Irishman" Greene, age 26
(CLEVELAND POLICE DEPARTMENT)

Francis "Mickey" Featherstone, feared hitman for the Westies, is arrested in 1978 for a murder he did not commit.
(NEW YORK *DAILY NEWS*)

Jimmy Coonan would eventually become boss of the Westies. This arrest photo was taken in 1966 at the height of the Coonan-Spillane Wars in Hell's Kitchen.
(NEW YORK *DAILY NEWS*)

Last of the Irish American mobsters, Whitey Bulger (right), on his home turf in South Boston
(FBI SURVEILLANCE PHOTO)

FBI Agent John Connolly strikes a defiant pose following his conviction for racketeering and obstruction of justice. Said Connolly: "The government put me in business with murderers." (*BOSTON GLOBE*)

RIGHT: The most wanted mobster on the planet, James "Whitey" Bulger (FBI POSTER)

FBI TEN MOST WANTED FUGITIVE

RACKETEERING INFLUENCED AND CORRUPT ORGANIZATIONS (RICO) - MURDER (18 COUNTS), CONSPIRACY TO COMMIT MURDER, CONSPIRACY TO COMMIT EXTORTION, NARCOTICS DISTRIBUTION, CONSPIRACY TO COMMIT MONEY LAUNDERING; EXTORTION; MONEY LAUNDERING

JAMES J. BULGER

Photograph taken in 1994 — Photograph taken in 1994 — Photograph retouched in 2000

Aliases: Thomas F. Baxter, Mark Shapeton, Jimmy Bulger, James Joseph Bulger, James J. Bulger, Jr., James Joseph Bulger, Jr., Tom Harris, Tom Marshall, "Whitey"

DESCRIPTION

Date of Birth:	September 3, 1929	Hair:	White/Silver
Place of Birth:	Boston, Massachusetts	Eyes:	Blue
Height:	5' 7" to 5' 9"	Complexion:	Light
Weight:	150 to 160 pounds	Sex:	Male
Build:	Medium	Race:	White
Occupation:	Unknown	Nationality:	American
Scars and Marks:	None known		

Remarks: Bulger is an avid reader with an interest in history. He is known to frequent libraries and historic sites. Bulger is currently on the heart medication Atenolol (50 mg) and maintains his physical fitness by walking on beaches and in parks with his female companion Catherine Elizabeth Greig. Bulger and Greig love animals and may frequent animal shelters. Bulger has been known to alter his appearance through the use of disguises. has traveled extensively throughout the United States, Europe, Canada, and Mexico.

CAUTION

JAMES J. BULGER IS BEING SOUGHT FOR HIS ROLE IN NUMEROUS MURDERS COMMITTED FROM THE EARLY 1970s THROUGH THE MID-1980s IN CONNECTION WITH HIS LEADERSHIP OF AN ORGANIZED CRIME GROUP THAT ALLEGEDLY CONTROLLED EXTORTION, DRUG DEALS, AND OTHER ILLEGAL ACTIVITIES IN THE BOSTON, MASSACHUSETTS, AREA. HE HAS A VIOLENT TEMPER AND IS KNOWN TO CARRY A KNIFE AT ALL TIMES.

CONSIDERED ARMED AND EXTREMELY DANGEROUS

IF YOU HAVE ANY INFORMATION CONCERNING THIS PERSON, PLEASE CONTACT YOUR LOCAL FBI OFFICE OR THE NEAREST U.S. EMBASSY OR CONSULATE.

REWARD

The FBI is offering a $1,000,000 reward for information leading directly to the arrest of James J. Bulger

www.fbi.gov

August 1999
Poster Revised November 2000

Mrs. Hintz had good reason to be afraid. Cockeye Dunn was no ordinary criminal. As Eddie McGrath's brother-in-law and business partner at Varick Enterprises, Dunn was tied into the ILA's underworld network at the highest levels. Short and slight, with a wisecracking manner ("the midget gunman," the *Daily News* called him), Dunn had spent the previous summer at a hotel suite in Hollywood, Florida, as Meyer Lansky's guest. At the time, Lansky was shuttling back and forth between Florida and Cuba, where he was establishing a working relationship with the corrupt government of General Fulgencio Batista. One of Lansky's grandiose schemes was to use Cuba as a transshipment point for the importation of heroin and cocaine into the United States. The longshoreman's association was a key element in this plan, as the product would have to be shipped via freighter and offloaded at U.S. ports. Dunn would be the one to coordinate the importation of Lansky's drugs, and hotel phone records from his stay in Florida would show that, over a one-week period, he put in calls to some of the biggest names in organized crime, including Frank Costello and Eddie McGrath in New York, Bugsy Siegel in Los Angeles, and Lucky Luciano at the Hotel Nacional in Havana.

Cockeye, of course, was also tight with Boss Joe Ryan. It was Ryan, through his underling Eddie McGrath, who first sponsored Dunn's membership in the union. Not only had Dunn become the overlord of all the piers on the Lower West Side, but he was also on the Arrangements Committee for the annual dinner/dance put on by the Joseph P. Ryan Association. Tickets for the event, which was held at either the Hotel Commodore or the Waldorf-Astoria, were highly coveted. Police commissioners, district attorneys, judges, and ranking bureaucrats in the city's many governmental departments were regularly in attendance, as were various notorious figures from the waterfront mob. The guests were there for one reason: to kiss the ring of Joe Ryan, which could bring a political endorsement and/or campaign contribution from his powerful union. Those who couldn't make it always sent a note, as was the case in 1950 when the reputedly incorruptible, racket-busting governor of New York was unable to attend.

Dear Joe:

I would surely be delighted to come to the annual affair of the Joseph P. Ryan Association on Saturday, May 20 if possible. As it happens, Mrs. Dewey and I have accepted an invitation to the marriage of Lowell Thomas's only son that weekend, and we just can't possibly make it.

It is mighty nice of you to ask me, and I wish you would give my regards to all the fine people at the dinner.

On behalf of the people of the entire state, I congratulate you for what you have done to keep the Communists from getting control of the New York waterfront. Be assured that the entire machinery of the governor of New York State is behind you and your organization in this determination.

With warm regards,

Sincerely yours,
Thomas E. Dewey

Ryan's annual dinner was the capstone on a social profile that placed the ILA president among the city's reigning elite. He was a regular at Toots Shor's, the famous sportsman's watering hole, and a member of the Elks, the New York Athletic Club, and the Winged Foot Golf Club in Westchester County. Apart from Eddie McGrath, Cockeye Dunn, and a small cadre of ILA operatives who comprised his inner circle, Boss Joe, once a man of the people, rarely mingled with the rank-and-file. His flagrant social climbing even caught the attention of activist Dorothy Day. After spending a typical Thanksgiving Day serving dinner to the homeless (a dinner paid for and coserved by delegates from the hospital and prison unions), Day wrote in the *Catholic Worker*

> That day I could not help but think how different was the position of Joseph P. Ryan, head of the longshoremen, who has had a position of trust and power for many years. Where are the hiring halls, the recreation rooms, the library, the communal repasts, the works of mercy performed by the prison and hospital delegates, in the longshoreman's union? Are Ryan's offices open to the rank-and-file? Ryan is more often to be found at the tables of the rich than with his men.

Ryan may have been immune to criticism from "radicals" and "communists" like Dorothy Day, but he was not immune to criminal prosecution. The murder trial of two of his underlings hit close to home—too close as far as Ryan was concerned. In the months leading up to the trial, he was nowhere to be seen, not even at Toots Shor's.

The trial got off to a bang when Danny Gentile, Dunn and Sheridan's accomplice in the shooting of Andy Hintz, flipped and turned state's evidence against the defense. The two waterfront gangsters could do nothing but sit and watch as Gentile described, on the witness stand, how the three of them had shot the hiring stevedore. In the end, it was as if Andy Hintz had spoken from his grave through his wife and identified the killers. The verdict was swift and sure: guilty as charged.

The real fun began after the trial. The verdict and sentence—death by execution—weighed heavily on Cockeye Dunn's mind. As the date for his electrocution approached, the man who had for years served as a waterfront enforcer, doling out beatings and even death to those who violated the mob's code of silence, put out the word to the Manhattan district attorney's office that he might be ready to talk. Dunn suggested that, if his sentence were commuted to life imprisonment, he could supply information that would solve over thirty murders along the waterfront. Beyond that, said Cockeye, he could name the higher-ups in the field of politics who had protected all the rackets along the docks, including the very top boss of all. One man, Dunn claimed, was Mister Big for all the waterfront rackets, and he was a very powerful man, indeed, with high political connections.

While Dunn and the Manhattan D.A.'s office began negotiating the terms of a potential deal, the town was abuzz with speculation. Who was this behind-the-scenes kingpin on the waterfront? So far, Dunn's only clue was that it was a reputable businessman known for his charitable works, church affiliations, and political activities. Did this mean others would be dragged into the mess as well? Would this kingpin's political connections be implicated and exposed?

Contributing to the swirl of speculation was the fact that Mayor William O'Dwyer abruptly announced that he would not be running for a second term. His decision was a shocker. An Irish-born ex-policeman and former magistrate judge who rose to prominence as the district attorney in Brooklyn, O'Dwyer had, in his day, prosecuted many mob cases, most notably those relating to the murderous Brooklyn Jewish gang known as Murder Incorporated. Despite his reputation as a racket-buster, O'Dwyer had been dogged throughout his political career by allegations that he received campaign contributions from underworld sources. He was linked most often with the waterfront mob, partly because he had started his career as a waterfront cop and received strong support from the ILA when he first ran for mayor.

Whether or not his decision to forego reelection was influenced by the anticipated revelations from Cockeye Dunn, O'Dwyer would not say. The point became moot when, a few weeks after O'Dwyer first went public with his decision not to run, the D.A.'s office announced that they were unable to make a deal with Cockeye Dunn. While much of what Dunn had told them during confidential negotiations was tantalizing, little of it could be backed up with provable facts. Dunn had named one city official as his contact in getting a fat city contract; this official was also allegedly a participant in some of the waterfront rackets. But Dunn failed to back up his charges with any substantial details. The prosecutors concluded that Dunn was merely yanking their chain, insisting on commutation first, testimony later. No go, said the district attorney.

On July 7, 1949, the day scheduled for Dunn's execution, the waterfront gangster was given one last chance to tell all. He declined, saying only that he was prepared to meet his maker. With his friend and partner in crime, Squint Sheridan, he walked the last mile. The gallows were no more, of course. The hangman's noose had been replaced by the slightly more anti-septic electric chair. Cockeye and Squint took turns in the hot seat—a rare double execution.

In the wake of Dunn's death, many people in and around the waterfront must have breathed a collective sigh of relief, including the man Cockeye described as kingpin of the rackets, who wore a mask of respectability.

Two days after the execution, a committee of labor leaders, including Joe Ryan, called on Mayor Bill O'Dwyer at City Hall and asked him to change his mind and run for reelection. He would have their endorsement, they assured him. O'Dwyer said that he was flattered and would think about it. A few days later, he announced that he had reversed his decision and would indeed be campaigning for reelection.

O'Dwyer won his second term as mayor, beating Fiorello Laguardia by ten thousand votes. Thirteen months later, he was forced to resign under a cloud of accusations that he had ties to organized crime—accusations unrelated to the life and death of Johnny "Cockeye" Dunn.[6]

---

6. Mayor Bill O'Dwyer's resignation from office was fraught with irony. His downfall originated with a meeting he'd had with mobster Frank Costello at a Manhattan townhouse apartment in 1942, before he was mayor. At the time, O'Dwyer was on leave of absence as Brooklyn district attorney, serving during the early months of World War II as a major in the procurement division of the army air force. O'Dwyer claimed that he had arranged to speak with Costello, known in the press as the Prime Minister of the Underworld, because he was investigating contract fraud at an airbase in Ohio that Costello might know something about. It was never shown that anything criminal took place or was even discussed at this meeting, but, in the post-Machine era, get-togethers between a notorious mafioso and a district attorney/future mayor were no longer accepted by the public.

O'Dwyer was not a Tammany-sponsored politician. In fact, he'd run for mayor on an anti-Tammany ticket, claiming that his racket-busting past as district attorney showed that he was above reproach. This claim was damaged when his meeting with

Ʈḫe Waterfront Commission

The circumstances surrounding the sensational trial and execution of Cockeye and Squint proved to be the beginning of the end for Boss Joe Ryan. The rank-and-file had never been more dissatisfied with Ryan's leadership, and, in 1951, longshoremen in New York did something they had never attempted before: They staged an unauthorized wild cat strike by walking off the job in defiance of Boss Joe. The strike was costly. It lasted twenty-five days and shut down 118 piers. Thirty thousand men went without pay for almost a month. But in the larger scheme of things, calling attention to corrupt practices within the longshoreman's union was worth every penny.

The man behind the strike was not a longshoreman at all. He was a stubborn, courageous man of the cloth who had made the waterfront his personal parish. Father John Corridan was the child of Irish immigrants. Born in Harlem, he was the eldest son of a New York policeman who died when John was just ten years old. After fifteen years of theological study, he was ordained a Jesuit priest in 1944. One year later, at the age of thirty-four, he was assigned to the Xavier Labor School on West Sixteenth Street, just a few blocks from the Chelsea and Greenwich Village piers. The labor school was an adjunct of the Catholic university system. With courses taught by both priests and lay instructors, the curriculum was designed to teach the use of Christian principles in dealing with labor management problems.

Costello became public knowledge and was further destroyed by a sensational investigation into police corruption in Brooklyn. In that investigation, it was shown that the NYPD command structure in Brooklyn, from beat cops all the way up to lieutenants and captains, had for years been receiving illegal cash payments from bookmakers and gambling houses throughout the borough. The "bag man" for this operation was James J. Moran, a former assistant district attorney and close political confidant of O'Dwyer's. The suspicion was that Moran had been delivering some of this dirty money directly into the campaign coffer of his former boss and friend. Moran was eventually convicted and sentenced to prison on charges of perjury, conspiracy, extortion, and tax evasion, although he steadfastly refused to implicate O'Dwyer in any criminal wrongdoing.

With accusations from newspaper editorialists and Goo Goos ringing in his ears, O'Dwyer resigned from office in August 1950, he claimed, so that he could accept the position of ambassador to Mexico that had been kindly offered to him by President Harry Truman. Ambassador O'Dwyer served in Mexico for two years and then retired from public life, dying of coronary thrombosis in November 1964.

Corridan was a chain-smoking, no-nonsense man, comfortable in the profane and muscular world of the waterfront. He became friendly with the many longshoremen who attended Xavier Church, adjacent to the school. These men saw in Father John a kindred spirit, and they told him things about how the waterfront really operated—things they would never have told any other outsider. Corridan began to compile index files on the waterfront's key players and went on walking tours of many piers to inspect working conditions. He attended union meetings, listened to complaints and accusations on all sides. It didn't take long for the priest to see that the waterfront was a violent universe, fueled by intimidation and exploitation. Clearly, at the heart of the problem was a collusive arrangement between the New York Shipping Association and the mob-dominated ILA, with the common laborer getting the shaft.

Corridan set out to call attention to corrupt labor conditions in the Port of New York. In his quest to expose injustice, he was not afraid to utilize the press. One of his more notable contacts was reporter Malcolm Johnson, who in 1950 published a series of articles in the *New York Sun* entitled "Crime on the Waterfront." The series, which eventually won Johnson a Pulitzer Prize, was a revelation; it named names and spelled out operating procedures within the ILA that had been hidden for years.

The explosive series in the *Sun* happened to appear in print around the same time that the celebrated Kefauver Committee arrived in town. The Kefauver Hearings, led by Senator Estes Kefauver, Democrat from Tennessee, had been authorized by governmental mandate to undertake a nationwide investigation of organized crime. In a series of hearings held in fourteen cities that included New Orleans, Chicago, Cleveland, and New York, a parade of hoodlums were subpoenaed to testify in front of a five-man panel known as the Senate Select Committee to Investigate Organized Crime in Interstate Commerce. Over a twelve-month period, from mid-1950 to mid-1951, the Kefauver Hearings made headlines around the United States. The most sensational of the hearings, by far, were those held in February 1951 in New York City. These were the first to be broadcasted across the country through the relatively new phenomenon of television. An estimated twenty- to thirty-million citizens viewed the hearings, the highlight of which turned out to be Frank Costello's hands.

Trusting his innate intelligence and lawyerly ability to bamboozle the committee, the man formerly known as Francesco Castiglia had agreed to testify, but only if his face was not shown. The committee accommodated Costello's wishes by agreeing to televise only his hands. A rapt national audience watched Costello's beefy hands close-up, accompanied by his disembodied voice. The hands twitched nervously, reached for a glass of water, and kneaded a ball of paper between thumb and forefinger. Costello was lured into revealing far more than he wanted to about his shady business relationships. The hands became a symbol of the underworld's grip on American commerce.

Also testifying at the Kefauver Hearings was former Mayor Bill O'Dwyer, who arrived in town from his current posting as ambassador to Mexico. Silver-haired and tanned, O'Dwyer defiantly defended his record as mayor, although he did not enhance his historical standing when he said of Frank Costello, "It doesn't matter whether a man is a banker, a business-man, or a gangster. His pocketbook is always attractive."

The Kefauver Committee concluded its barnstorming tour in September 1952. In a highly anticipated report, the senatorial panel, for the first time in American history, officially surmised that there was a vast National Crime Syndicate operating in the United States. "These criminal gangs have such power," stated the Committee, "that they constitute a government within a government in this country and that second government was the govern-ment by the underworld. . . .

"This phantom government nevertheless enforces its own law, carries out its own executions, and not only ignores but [also] abhors the democratic pro-cesses of justice which are held to be the safeguards of the American citizen.

"This secret government of crimesters is a serious menace which could, if not curbed, become the basis for a subversive movement which could wreck the very foundations of this country."

Although the hearings had not focused specifically on the activities of the ILA, the Committee did conclude that "racketeers were firmly entrenched along New York City's waterfront" and recommended further investigation. Given the popularity of the hearings, it didn't take long for an enterprising and ambitious public official to answer the call. Days after the Kefauver Committee delivered its explosive concluding report, New York Governor Tom Dewey, shamed into action by Father John Corridan's labor activism and Malcolm Johnson's scathing investigation in the *Sun*, announced that the state crime commission would begin public hearings on criminal activity in the Port of New York.

The Waterfront Hearings, as Dewey's investigation became known, were not televised and therefore did not garner the same amount of national attention as Kefauver's traveling road show. But over the course of the next seven months, hundreds of waterfront figures would be dragged out of the dark and exposed to the glare of public inquisition. Although the over-whelming majority took the Fifth and declined to answer questions on the grounds they might be incriminated, the parade of union officials with extensive and violent criminal records left the impression that the East Coast ILA might more accurately have been named the Ex-con Benevolent Association.

Among the most revealing witnesses—not for what he said but for what he represented—was a man named William J. "Big Bill" McCormack. McCormack was a multimillionaire industrialist who had risen from hardscrabble roots in Jersey City to become a powerful behind-the-scenes figure in New York area politics. Although nearly seventy years old at the time of the hearings, with a long career in business and public affairs, he was something of a mysterious waterfront figure; McCormack was a man whose name was well-known but whose face was rarely seen—except, of course, for his annual appearance as a guest of honor at the Joseph P. Ryan Association's prestigious dinner/dance.

Born to Irish potato-famine immigrants from County Monaghan, Bill McCormack and his brother, Harry, first became known in the Port of New York as owners of a small trucking business. They were also stout pillars in the New Jersey political organization of Frank "I Am the Law" Hague, for whom they got out the vote. The McCormack brothers, like so many children of famine immigrants who started out with less than nothing, were esteemed as fearless street brawlers. Bill McCormack was also shrewd. In 1920, he banded together with several others truckers and formed the U.S. Trucking Corporation, installing himself as executive vice president in charge of labor relations. It wasn't long before McCormack branched off into other waterfront-related businesses—everything including delivering produce, dredging sand from the bottom of Long Island Sound, a concrete company, a waterfront hiring agency, and the largest independent chain of filling stations in the state of New York.

The key to McCormack's success was his ability to cultivate powerful political connections, a classic first-generation Irish trait. Along with Boss Hague, McCormack was close to Alfred E. Smith, who would eventually become the first Irish Catholic to receive the Democratic nomination for President of the United States. In 1920, Governor Al Smith was defeated in his campaign for reelection. McCormack and his business associates shrewdly made Smith the president, or front man, of their U.S. Trucking Corporation. When Smith was reelected governor, he paid Bill McCormack back by appointing him chairman of the New York State Boxing Commission.

Over the years, the former street kid from Jersey City became a rich man, with an annual income from his various businesses estimated at $20 million a year. Somewhere along the line, McCormack became a close friend and business partner of Joe Ryan. They came from similar humble beginnings and shared a tough, hard-bitten view of the world. They helped each other out whenever possible.

In 1950, when the controversy surrounding labor conditions on the waterfront were at a peak and Mayor Bill O'Dwyer was forced to do something about it, Joe Ryan suggested to the mayor that McCormack be named to lead a prestigious blue-ribbon panel to investigate allegations of racketeering. After months of investigation at the taxpayer's expense, and contrary to everything that was known about the inner workings of organized crime, this panel concluded, "We have found that the labor situation on the waterfront of the Port of New York is generally satisfactory from the standpoint of the worker, the employer, the industry, and the government."

McCormack's name came up often during the Waterfront Hearings. Perhaps the most damning testimony came from a supervisor of employment for the division of parole. The witness stated that he had never met Mr. McCormack personally but had dealt many times with his brother, Harry. Many an application for parole had crossed his desk with a note that read, "Mr. H. F. McCormack will make immediate arrangements for this inmate's union membership upon his release." The witness estimated that McCormack enterprises had sponsored the parole of some two hundred men from prison, promising that they had jobs waiting for them with McCormack's Penn Stevedoring Company.

When called to testify before the Waterfront Commission, Bill McCormack explained his reasons for springing so many convicted felons in humanitarian terms: "It's because I take a human view of employee problems. I'm human, and they're human."

McCormack's explanation was in keeping with his recent anointing by the Archdiocese of New York as their "Catholic Layman of the Year," but it didn't go over well when stacked up against the reputations of men like Cockeye Dunn, Squint Sheridan, members of the Pistol Local, and others who'd been grandfathered out of prison to become the muscle behind Joe Ryan's leadership of the ILA.

The press had a field day, believing that Cockeye Dunn's Mister Big had finally been revealed. The *Herald Tribune* editorialized, "Mr. McCormack's activities on behalf of the longshoreman's union suggest that he has been pulling the strings for Joseph P. Ryan for years and may, in fact, be a more powerful figure on the waterfront than the Boss himself."

The 209th and final witness in the Crime Commission's public hearings was none other than Joe Ryan. After the sensational testimony and headlines concerning McCormack, his friend and patron, Ryan's long day on the stand seemed like an anticlimax, but it directly resulted in his complete downfall, both as a union leader and politician, and to his trial in a criminal court on charges of theft of union funds.

Ryan was forced to concede that he had knowingly appointed convicted thieves and violent felons like Eddie McGrath and Harold Bowers to important positions within the union. Ryan claimed not to know that as many as 30 percent of ILA officials had police records, that more than half of forty-five locals in the Port of New York could produce no financial records or minutes, and that many of his union officials had increased their own salaries from time to time without ever consulting their members. It also came out that, in 1948, Ryan had sent a stern warning to Manhattan District Attorney Frank S. Hogan—a "threat," Hogan called it—that if he continued his investigation of a string of waterfront murders, it might precipitate a strike on the piers.

None of these revelations hurt Ryan among his own members; in fact, the argument could be made that he was merely standing up for the rights of his men, whether or not they had criminal records. What even Ryan's biggest supporters could not countenance, however, was his personal plundering of union funds, especially when it was revealed that the Boss had used $50,000 from the ILA's Anti-Communist Fund for things like luncheons at the Stork Club, repairs to his Cadillac, expensive clothes, and a cruise to Guatemala.

Ryan sought to portray these expenses as mere bookkeeping mistakes or even venality on the part of his underlings. Commenting at the end of his long day of testimony, he laughingly asked, "When the teller of a bank is guilty of something, they don't hold the bank president, do they?" It was vintage Joe Ryan—dismissive, evasive, and imperial—but the damage had been done. Ryan's reputation as a great anti-Communist was in tatters. Within weeks of the conclusion of the crime commission's hearings, the Boss was indicted by a New York County grand jury for stealing money from his union and was under investigation by the FBI, the IRS, and two other grand juries in connection with his tax returns and additional matters.

At the same time that Ryan's lawyers were dealing with his mounting legal problems, the American Federation of Labor (AF of L), in an unprecedented move, announced its intention to expel the ILA from its membership. In September 1953, as top labor leaders from around the country gathered for the AF of L's annual convention in St. Louis, Missouri, President George Meaney announced: "We've given up all hope that the officers or members of that union will reform it. We've given up hope that the ILA will ever live up to the rules, standards, and ethics of a decent trade union."

Upon hearing of Meaney's announcement, Joe Ryan growled and uttered the last words he was ever quoted saying in public: "We'll hold on to what we got."

In St. Louis, Ryan waged a losing battle to maintain control of the union he had ruled for twenty-six years. As part of a deal for the ILA to remain a member of the AF of L, Ryan was forced to resign. One year later, in a New York courtroom, he was found guilty of having accepted gratuities from employers in violation of the Taft-Hartly Act. He was sentenced to six months in prison and fined $2,500.

Ryan did his time quietly and retired in obscurity. In the years that followed, on those rare occasions when his name was mentioned at all, it was usually by some old-time stevedore, longshoreman, or dock walloper who asked, "Hey, whatever happened to Joe Ryan?"

The answer, invariably, was, "Beats me."

The man whose name had once been synonymous with fear, power, and racketeering on the waterfront was relegated to the dustbin of history.

Corridan's Legacy

The person who was most responsible for the purging of flagrant mobsterism on the docks did not testify at the Waterfront Hearings. Father John Corridan had been invited to appear, but he declined the invitation. He later explained his reasoning: "Any testimony that I might have given would weaken the belief of people around the waterfront in my trustworthiness as a priest to keep confidences. Some of the information had come to me in the confessional. Much of the rest of what I knew had been given to me in confidence."

Members of the commission conceded the validity of Corridan's position. They asked if he would be interested in submitting a proposal for waterfront reform, which he did. The proposal became known as "Corridan's Law" and served as a blueprint for leading the ILA out of the stone age and into the bright light of twentieth century labor reform.

Corridan's contribution did not end there. In 1952, just as the crime commission hearings were getting under way, Corridan had been approached by an eager young screenwriter named Bud Schulberg. Schulberg had been enlisted to write a screenplay loosely based on Malcolm Johnson's Pulitzer Prize–winning series in the *New York Sun*. Although

Father Corridan had never heard of Schulberg, he was familiar with the screenwriter's creative partner, Elia Kazan, the famous director who'd already directed *A Streetcar Named Desire*, *Viva Zapata*, and other well-known Hollywood movies.

Corridan viewed Schulberg and Kazan's interest as a golden opportunity to call attention to conditions on the waterfront. He spoke at length with Schulberg and introduced him to numerous contacts on the docks. The savvy, street-smart screenwriter took it from there.

Schulberg was fascinated by Father Corridan, whom he later described as "the antidote to the stereotyped Barry Fitzgerald-Bing Crosby 'Fah-ther' so dear to Hollywood hearts. In West Side saloons I listened intently to Father John, whose speech was a unique blend of Hell's Kitchen baseball slang, an encyclopedic grasp of waterfront economics, and an attack on man's inhumanity to man based on the teachings of Jesus Christ."

Having gotten his start as a boxing writer, Schulberg was comfortable in the brawny, profane world of the waterfront. His personal politics were on the side of the working man. He immersed himself in the world of the piers, guided mostly by a devoted disciple of Father Corridan's named Arthur Browne—an Irish American longshoreman who was proud to be one of the stand-up "insoigents" in the Chelsea local run by "fat cats and their pistoleros."

Following months of research, Schulberg fashioned a script that contained a character named Father Pete Barry, based on Corridan. The screenplay's other main character was a working palooka named Terry Malloy, a former boxer and sometime strong-arm man for waterfront racketeers who, inspired by the crusader priest, develops a conscience and becomes disillusioned with business as usual on the docks. Terry eventually turns against the union's corrupt overseer, a petty dictator named Johnny Friendly, and testifies against him in front of a commission looking into mobster activity on the waterfront.

In their quest to get Schulberg's screenplay financed as a movie, the writer and Kazan were turned down by every major studio in the business. Kazan's cache as an Academy Award–nominated director made no difference. Hollywood had little interest in making a film about common laborers. "Who's going to care about a lot of sweaty longshoremen?" asked Warner Bros. Studio head Daryl Zanuck after reading the script.

Eventually, once Marlon Brando agreed to play the character of Terry Malloy, Schulberg and Kazan were able to find financing at Columbia Studios. The budget was modest, with much of it going to Brando. Veteran stage actor Karl Malden was chosen to play the Corridan stand-in, Father Barry.

The movie was filmed primarily in Hoboken, New Jersey, utilizing numerous nonprofessional bit actors culled from various ILA locals. The emphasis was on authenticity, with actual waterfront locations, believable dialogue, and a general level of realism that was unheard of for a big-studio Hollywood movie in the 1950s.

On the Waterfront contains many classic scenes, but the moral center of the movie is a scene in which Father Barry, after a longshoreman has been killed in a work-related "accident," climbs down into the hold of a freighter to deliver last rights. There he makes a fighting speech about "Christ in the shape-up," comparing the longshoreman's death to the Crucifixion. His dialogue is taken almost verbatim from a famous speech Father Corridan once gave to a group of longshoreman that became known as "the Sermon on the Docks."

When *On the Waterfront* opened in theaters in September 1954, it was an immediate sensation, garnering rave reviews, impressive box office totals, and, eventually, Academy Awards for Schulberg, Kazan, and Brando. Today, the movie is rightfully considered a classic, but, at the time of its original release, its main power was as a "straight from the headlines" exposé. Appearing in theaters on the heels of the New York Waterfront Hearings, the movie was that rare item: an explosive, socially relevant presentation of a contemporary labor condition, told unabashedly from a proletarian point of view. Among other things, the movie played a major role in the turning-of-the-tide against corrupt forces within the ILA, most notably Joe Ryan, whose legal comeuppance in the courts was taking place at the same time that *On the Waterfront* played to large audiences around the country.

To the extent that movies are able to reach the masses and enlighten minds, *On the Waterfront* was a landmark. The movie helped to expose a culture of gangsterism in the ILA that had existed for decades. While the awards for this went to Schulberg, Kazan, and Brando, the moral imperative that made it all possible came from the Waterfront Priest. According to Bud Schulberg, "Without the life, activism, and example of Father John Corridan, there's no way *On the Waterfront* ever would have happened. It was Father John who took on the mobsters—and the rest is history."[7]

---

7. Bud Schulberg, age ninety-two, was interviewed by the author in March 2004.

the patriarch

n the decade of the 1950s, America was in the throes of committee fever. Secret agendas, subterranean alliances, and subversive activities were a national obsession, and it appeared that the only way to root out the enemy within was through official governmental investigation. Hot on the heels of the Kefauver Hearings on organized crime and the Waterfront Commission's public tribunal in New York came the anti-Communist witch hunts of the Senate Permanent Subcommittee on Investigations led by Senator Joseph McCarthy of Wisconsin. The McCarthy Hearings were televised and, like the Kefauver Hearings, captured the public imagination. McCarthy was allowed to run rampant, making wild accusations and destroying careers, until he eventually overstepped his boundaries by taking on the U.S. Army.

Before Joe McCarthy's vile and divisive subcommittee crashed and burned in December 1954, he appointed an eager young attorney named Robert F. "Bobby" Kennedy as his assistant counsel. Kennedy was the seventh of nine children born to Joseph P. Kennedy, the well-known billionaire banker, tycoon, ex-movie mogul, and former U.S. ambassador to the Court of St. James during the Franklin Roosevelt Administration. The elder Kennedy was a friend and financial benefactor of Joe McCarthy's. Over the years, the alcoholic senator from Wisconsin had occasionally been a guest at the Kennedy family compound in Hyannis Port, where he once almost drowned after falling from a sailboat into the bay. He was saved by another son of Joe Kennedy's—John—at the time a congressman from Massachusetts, who dove into the water and helped pull McCarthy back into the boat.

On McCarthy's Senate Subcommittee, Bobby Kennedy served under Roy Cohn, the senator's vicious and unscrupulous lead counsel. As the subcommittee became more wantonly unethical in its pursuit of phantom

communists and subversives, Kennedy bolted, astutely surmising that Mc-
Carthy's crusade was headed for disaster.

Bobby Kennedy may have recognized the flaws and public relations limitations inherent in McCarthy's scorched-earth approach, but that did not
mean he was against the notion of high-profile governmental committees. In
late 1956, when Kennedy was approached by Senator John J. McClellan of
Arkansas to take part in yet another major senate investigation—this one
looked into the role of mobsters and labor racketeers in the Teamsters
Union—the young lawyer jumped at the chance.

Officially, the investigation was to be called the Senate Select Committee
on Improper Activities in the Labor or Management Field. The committee
and their investigators would be given the power to subpoena whoever they
wanted. For Kennedy, thirty-two years old and looking to put his career on
a par with that of his older brother John, the offer was irresistible. As chief
counsel, he would be given the opportunity to square off with major mafiosi
and corrupt union officials similar to ILA boss Joe Ryan and others of his
ilk. Kennedy, notoriously competitive, relished the prospect.

When Bobby told his father that he had accepted the offer to become
chief counsel for what would come to be known as "the McClellan
Committee," the patriarch of the Kennedy family was livid. According to
Bobby's sister Jean Kennedy Smith, the argument that ensued at the family's
annual Christmas gathering at Hyannis Port was bitter, "the worst one we
ever witnessed." Bobby argued that by taking on organized crime in the
labor movement, the Kennedy family would be establishing a reputation for
independence. Recalled longtime Kennedy confidant Lem Billings, "The old
man saw this as dangerous. . . . He thought Bobby was naïve."

Joe Kennedy's main argument against Bobby's involvement was that it
was going to cause an upheaval that would turn organized labor against
Senator John Kennedy, thus damaging his quest for the presidency. Ever
since the tragic death of his first son, Joe Jr.—a fighter pilot whose plane was
shot down in World War II—Papa Joe's desire to see J.F.K. elected as the
first Irish Catholic president of the United States had become his overriding
ambition in life. His own personal designs on higher office had been perma-
nently derailed long ago, during his disastrous tenure as ambassador to England, so Kennedy had transferred his hopes to his children, becoming for
them the ultimate man behind the man, cajoling and manipulating with the
skill of a master puppeteer.

The emotional force Papa Joe exhibited when arguing against Bobby's
potentially damaging decision to oversee the McClellan investigation was no
surprise to those who knew him—nor was the rigidity of his son's counter-

argument. To even his best friends, Bobby was known at times to be a "stubborn bastard." In the weeks that followed Bobby's Christmas announcement, Joe enlisted some of his son's closest mentors and advisers to try to talk him out of it to no avail. Bobby held his ground.

R.F.K.'s decision to proceed as planned caused a rift between father and son that continued over the next two years. The rift was regrettable but expected, given Joe Kennedy's proprietary interest in seeing J.F.K. ascend to the presidency. Most everyone who knew Papa Joe accepted his argument at face value: He was against Bobby's involvement in a crusade against organized crime because it would "stir up a hornet's nest" that might hurt John's chances. But there was more to this argument than the elder Kennedy was able to fully vocalize at the time.

Papa Joe knew that chasing after mobsters was not like chasing communists, as both Bobby and John had done during the McCarthy hearings. Chasing "Reds" had been like shooting fish in a barrel; communists were social pariahs, with no one to advocate on their behalf. Mobsters, however, tended to strike back. They created corrupt, subterranean alliances that could destroy careers, resorted to violent intimidation, or sought revenge through sensational acts of murder and mayhem.

At the very least, taking on the mob was messy business. Joe Kennedy knew this intuitively and from firsthand experience, not because he read it in a book or heard it through the grapevine. Although very few people, not even members of his own family, were cognizant of it at the time, Joe Kennedy's rise to power was riddled with potentially compromising underworld alliances. Kennedy had been dealing with mobsters nearly his entire adult life. By and large, they had served him well. He had amassed millions of dollars, in part, by cultivating certain nefarious relationships. Were these relationships to become known, they would destroy the hopes and dreams he had for his family. This was, in effect, Papa Joe's dirty little secret. For decades, he had been not only the patriarch of an attractive and politically ambitious Irish clan, but also, in a number of interesting ways, the patriarch of the entire Irish American underworld.

Portrait of tfje Artist as a Young Wfjiskey Baron

In the nearly forty years since Joseph P. Kennedy's death in 1969, a more complete portrait of the man's life has slowly emerged. It has taken this long partly because Kennedy shrouded his personal and professional activities behind a veil of secrecy. Even today, the official record is carefully sanitized. Voluminous FBI records released under the Freedom of Information Act (FOIA) are comprised mostly of innocuous security reviews and fawning letters between Kennedy and FBI Director J. Edgar Hoover. There is no mention of Kennedy's associations with organized crime figures. FBI communiqués about Kennedy's links to mobsters have come to light in recent years, leaked to various biographers and investigative reporters, but they are not part of the official file. For a more well-rounded profile of the man, we have a library full of memoirs and remembrances from nonofficial sources, people who knew Kennedy or were directly affected by his actions throughout history.

According to those who knew or did business with the man, Kennedy's involvement with gangsters began, not surprisingly, with Prohibition. The Kennedy family fortune, which Joe inherited as the oldest son of five-time Massachusetts representative and state senator Patrick Joseph "P. J." Kennedy, made it possible for the young businessman to dabble in banking and shipbuilding before the onset of Prohibition in 1919. As the full dimensions of the Volstead Act became apparent, enterprising entrepreneurs like Kennedy were in the right place at the right time. With his family fortune and money he made from the stock market, Joe had the capital. He also had the contacts. His father's political career had been largely financed by the Boston liquor lobby, and his father-in-law, John F. Fitzgerald, was a Boston saloon keeper who rose to become the city's highly popular mayor and served proudly in local politics from 1892 to 1919.

In accounts of his life, Joe Kennedy is sometimes called a bootlegger, which is not exactly accurate. The term itself comes from old-time moonshiners hiding flask bottles of whiskey in their boots and refers to the process of distribution. Kennedy was more precisely a rum runner or whiskey baron—an importer and wholesaler. He purchased large quantities of alcohol, mostly Scotch, from England or Canada and facilitated its shipment along Rum Row. The booze was usually transferred from Nova Scotia to the Eastern Seaboard, where it was off-loaded under cover of darkness along the Massachusetts or Rhode Island coastline or somewhere in Long Island, New York. The bootleggers and crime syndicates took over from there. There were literally thousands of bootleggers in operation during Prohibition, but there were very few overseers like Joe Kennedy, who supplied the suppliers and kept up the steady flow of product that made the entire booze racket possible.

The relationships Kennedy forged through whiskey smuggling were the same types of alliances he depended on at various stages throughout his career. In the fledgling movie business, in real estate, and in politics, the scion of the Kennedy clan did not hesitate to utilize the influence of the underworld as an edge in his professional life. He understood how spheres of power interacted in big-city America. Kennedy gained this knowledge at the knee of his father and later from his father-in-law, "Honey Fitz" Fitzgerald, a quintessential Irish pol who sang "Sweet Adeline" at campaign stops and seemed politically invincible until he was forced to relinquish his hold on the mayoralty because of a sex scandal.

In biographies and other accounts of the Kennedy clan, Papa Joe is often described as having been tough and ruthless in his business dealings. In fact, he was probably no more ruthless than the Cabots, the Lodges, and other Brahmin family dynasties of his Boston youth. He was certainly no more ruthless than American industrialists like J. P. Morgan and Henry Ford who used violent strikebreaker squads and labor espionage to keep workers in their places. In the early years of the twentieth century, for a man to rise to a level of corporate esteem, the ability to play hardball was highly valued. What Kennedy also possessed in abundance was an inherent sociability and charm, the byproduct of a vibrant cultural heritage.

Joseph Patrick Kennedy was born on September 6, 1888, at a time when Boston was fiercely divided between New England's entrenched Yankee aristocracy, the Brahmins, and the growing mass of Irish immigrants who had been flooding into the city since at least the 1840s. Boston, more than any other city, became a center of hostility between native-born Protestants and Irish Catholics. The Know-Nothing Movement achieved its highest level of electoral success in Boston, where church burnings and other acts of intimidation against Catholics were part of the city's heritage.

The most famous attack was the torching of the Ursuline Convent in 1834. A small group of nuns operated the convent as a boarding school for children of local families. The nuns and children were chased from the building by a Protestant mob, and the convent was burned to the ground. Eight people were eventually brought to trial for the capital offense of arson, but they were all acquitted, a verdict that was greeted with cheers of delight by their supporters. For Irish immigrants throughout the United States and especially in Boston, the burning of the Ursuline Convent and its aftermath was a watershed event in the history of anti-Catholic bigotry.

By the end of the century, the Irish had grown in significant enough numbers to overwhelm the Know-Nothings and ensure that there would be no more church burnings. By 1900, Irish immigrants and Irish Americans represented more than a third of the city's population and acquired clout in all of the typical areas of employment—police, firefighting, saloons, and politics—but were still relegated mostly to ghetto neighborhoods in the North End, Charlestown, and South Boston.

Joe Kennedy's father was the son of famine immigrants from County Wexford. Thick and square-shouldered, with neatly-parted brown hair and a luxurious handlebar mustache, P. J. Kennedy had made his way in the New World in the traditional Irish fashion—first as a stevedore on the East Boston waterfront and then as a saloon keeper, from which he launched his political career. After nearly two decades in state politics, he became the city wire commissioner, responsible for electrifying Boston. From there, P. J. went on to infiltrate the most sacrosanct territory of the Brahmins, the banks.

Kennedy's success as a banker made him rich. With all that wealth, he diversified. Although a lifelong teetotaler, he became the owner of three Boston-area saloons as well as a prosperous liquor importing business that handled shipments from Europe and South America. By the time his oldest son Joe was a teenager, P. J. Kennedy was perhaps the most powerful Irish American in Boston. Even so, young Joe came of age in a city where class divisions were pronounced, not only between the Brahmins and the Irish, but also between the lower-class, shanty Irish and the "two toilet" Irish such as the Kennedys.

The fact that the Kennedy family was more prosperous than most other Irish in Boston but still looked down upon by the WASP establishment engendered a fierce ethnic inferiority complex in Joe that became a guiding principle throughout his life. Kennedy was raised to be an Irish Brahmin; his mother indoctrinated him in the ways of the WASP upper class, insisting that he forego the Catholic school system and attend Boston Latin, a monument to Protestantism with an alumni that included Cotton Mather, Benjamin Franklin, and John Hancock. Kennedy continued his higher education at Harvard University. After graduation, he immediately established himself as young man to watch in the world of high finance. By the age of twenty-five, he was the youngest bank president in the country. In public, he excelled amidst the most entrenched WASP aristocracy in America. In private, with his receding hairline, steely blue eyes, and pronounced Kennedy teeth, he was a Boston Irishman.

Despite his breathtaking upward mobility, Kennedy maintained links with his Irish American roots, mostly through his father-in-law, Honey Fitz. Joe had married Rose Fitzgerald in October 1914, when her father was in the midst of his remarkable political career. Papa Fitzgerald's reputation as something of a stage Irishman, sentimental and comically verbose, was contrary to Joe Kennedy's upbringing, but it appealed to his ethnic pride and sense of fun. He also admired his father-in-law's embodiment of hardball politics, a classic Irish American means to an end involving the use of friendships, political chicanery, and the skillful manipulation of power, of which Joe Kennedy would become an unparalleled master.

In 1918, Joe Kennedy became involved in Papa Fitzgerald's last winning foray into elective politics. As a key campaign organizer in Honey Fitz's drive to unseat incumbent Massachusetts congressman Peter F. Tague, Joe acquainted himself with the city's growing Italian immigrant population. In the Fifth Ward, where the Italians had supplanted an earlier generation of Irish immigrants, Kennedy recruited and paid local paisano to intimidate potential Tague voters. Kennedy achieved his goal; his father-in-law defeated the incumbent by a mere 238 votes. But one year later, after a congressional inquiry into circumstances surrounding the campaign, Fitzgerald was formally accused of voter fraud and his election was overturned.

The repudiation of Honey Fitz was a stinging last blow to the once-vaunted politician, but for young Joe Kennedy the party had only just begun. The Volstead Act made Kennedy a popular man. The earliest recorded example of his ability to slake the thirst of those in need occurred in 1922, two years into Prohibition, when he arranged for the overseas delivery of bootleg Scotch to a Cape Cod beach party, celebrating the ten-year reunion of his Harvard class of 1912. Within the following months, Kennedy organized the importation of another major shipment to Carson Beach in South Boston, believed to be the biggest single shipment of whiskey in Boston Prohibition history.

The profits for Kennedy were staggering. The best Scotch cost $45 a case on Saint-Pierre and Miqueloon, a group of eight, small craggy islands in the North Atlantic Ocean, situated about sixteen miles south of Newfoundland. The cost of shipping along Rum Row added another $10 per case, labor and payoffs perhaps another $10, for an adjusted total of $65 a case—or $325,000 for a typical five-thousand-case shipment. Before it ever reached the marketplace, the Scotch was usually "cut" with other liquids, diluting it by half. It was then rebottled and sold to bootleggers for $85 a case. Thus the net profit for Kennedy on a $325,000 investment could be $525,000: a markup of roughly two-thirds.

How did Kennedy distribute his booze? Over the years, some of the most legendary gangsters from the Prohibition era have given first-hand testimony of their relationship with Joe Kennedy. Frank Costello, in interviews for an autobiography he intended to have ghost-written by author Peter Maas, told the writer shortly before his death that he and Kennedy were "in the liquor business together during Prohibition." Q. Byrum Hurst, a former

Arkansas state senator and a longtime attorney for Owney Madden during his retirement years in Hot Springs, told investigative journalist Seymour M. Hersh, "Owney and Joe Kennedy were partners in the bootleg business for a number of years. I discussed the Kennedy partnership with him many times. . . . Owney controlled all the nightclubs in New York then. He ran New York more than anyone in the 1920s, and Joe wanted the outlets for his liquor." The lawyer added that Madden "told me he valued Kennedy's business judgment. He recognized Kennedy's brains."

Kennedy appears to have reached out to Owney and the New York Combine sometime in the mid-1920s, when Big Bill Dwyer was away in jail. That's why Kennedy found himself dealing with Paul Costello, who was shepherding the operation while Dwyer served his sentence. In numerous Manhattan meetings with Madden, Costello, and Danny Walsh of Providence, the whiskey baron and the bootleggers finalized distribution arrangements. These surreptitious meetings led to speculation that the entire bootlegging racket in the Northeast was led by a group known as the Big Seven—including Kennedy, Madden, Dwyer, Costello, and Walsh.

The most far-reaching member of this group, purely from a business standpoint, had to be the Man from Boston. Having come from the most intensely parochial Irish city in the United States, Joe Kennedy was not content to settle for local success, either in his home state of Massachusetts or even the entire Northeast. Kennedy's vision, which he applied to his life, his career, and later to the lives of his children, was breathtakingly audacious for a man from Irish Catholic immigrant stock. As a corporate entrepreneur, he was always looking for ways to expand and increase profits, which, in the bootlegging business, inevitably led him to Al Capone.

In 1926, Capone was firmly entrenched as the bootlegger boss of Chicago and much of the Midwest. He'd rubbed out Dean O'Banion and taken over his lucrative North Side territory, expanding into the Illinois suburbs and even adjoining states like Indiana, Missouri, and Wisconsin. Kennedy wanted Big Al's business. Allegedly, the two men met over dinner at Capone's home in Cicero. The meeting was seen and overheard by a young piano tuner named John Kohlert. Capone was a jazz lover who sometimes invited musicians to his place for jam sessions after the clubs closed. He had Kohlert keep his piano tuned on a monthly basis. On this particular night, the young man was invited to stay for a spaghetti dinner, which was attended by Kennedy. The young piano tuner listened while Kennedy and Capone struck a deal wherein Capone traded his whiskey for a shipment of Kennedy's Seagram's brand. The exchanges were to be made in Lake Michigan, off Mackinac Island.

Kennedy's role as a supplier for Capone's syndicate is further documented in *The Outfit*, author Gus Russo's thorough delineation of the Chicago underworld from Prohibition to the present. Russo unearthed records of a 1926 Canadian government investigation into Canadian alcohol being exported to the United States, primarily by way of Detroit and Chicago. At the time, Canadian authorities were trying to discern how much export tax they were owed by the American bootleggers. The commission's paperwork showed that the one purchaser whose name appeared time and again was Joe Kennedy; he had been buying up liquor from Canada's Hiram Walker facility, which had upped its production 400 percent to meet Kennedy's demand. In the same Hiram Walker record book was the name of Al Capone and other U.S. "partners" of Kennedy's.

The extent to which Kennedy profited from this arrangement was made clear in mid-1925, when *Fortune* magazine estimated Joe Kennedy's wealth at $2 million, equal to roughly $20 million today. Yet Kennedy had left his most recent job as a stock broker at the firm of Hayden, Stone, and Company in 1922. While he undoubtedly made hundreds of thousands of dollars via stock market investments, only his role as the country's preeminent whiskey baron could account for such sudden and fabulous wealth.

Through it all, Kennedy maintained his upperworld reputation as a stock tycoon and rising star in the world of high finance and public service—a term Kennedy virtually invented to disassociate himself and his family from the more small-minded, unsavory aspects of Boston-style politics as usual. Publicly, Kennedy's reputation remained unbesmirched; his meetings with people like Madden, Costello, and Capone were handled in the most discreet manner possible, taking place in hotel rooms or some other highly guarded setting. Although he was known to present expensive bottles of Scotch as gifts or gratuities in his business dealings, Kennedy, like his father, was a teetotaler; he rarely patronized speakeasies or swanky nightclubs. His public life rarely intersected with the mobsters with whom he did business, with one notable exception.

In 1933, shortly after Prohibition had been repealed, Kennedy began an affair with Evelyn Crowell, a Broadway showgirl and the widow of Larry Fay. Fay was the business partner of Owney Madden and fashionable club owner who was gunned down by a disgruntled employee in front of his Casa Blanca nightclub. Before Fay's corpse was even cold in its grave, Kennedy and Crowell were romantically involved. The affair was well-known enough that, three years later, it appeared as a blind item in Walter Winchell's widely read *New York Daily Mirror* gossip column: "A top New Dealer's mistress is a mobster's widow."

After publication of the item, Kennedy arranged to meet with Winchell. The two men became confidants, with Kennedy, legendary for his ability to co-opt journalists, thereafter becoming one of Winchell's most valuable unnamed sources. In return, there were no more Kennedy references, veiled or otherwise, in any of Winchell's columns.

The Friends of Joe Kennedy

There is no record of Joe Kennedy's involvement in whiskey smuggling after 1926. Perhaps, as Prohibition became increasingly homicidal in the latter years of the Roaring Twenties, Kennedy was put off by the untowardly violent nature of the business. Essentially a corporate predator and white-collar criminal, Joe Kennedy was not a mobster in the sense that Owney Madden, Frank Costello, and Al Capone were mobsters; he did not kill men with his own hands. Like most legitimate businessmen who traffic on the dark side of American commerce and profit at some level from organized crime, Kennedy's role was predicated on the assurance that he would be able to sleep nights without the metaphorical sight of blood on his hands. It may have become increasingly difficult for Kennedy to justify his role as primary supplier in a business that yielded a higher weekly body count than some U.S. wars.

In 1927, Joe Kennedy took his fortune and his penchant for underworld alliances and headed to Hollywood. Kennedy's years as a Hollywood producer spanned the Silent Era and the dawn of the talkies. Although his cinematic output as a producer at RKO Studios and Film Booking Office (FBO) was decidedly unimpressive, Kennedy manipulated the situation to his advantage and made millions.

In Hollywood, Joe immediately established contact with Johnny Roselli, the underworld's main representative in the movie business. Years later, at the Church Committee hearings before the U.S. Senate in 1975, the dapper Roselli testified that Joe Kennedy had begun courting him almost as soon as he arrived in town. At the time, Roselli was very familiar with the Kennedy name. Born in Italy and raised in East Boston, the same area where Kennedy's Irish immigrant grandfather had first settled, Roselli was still living in Boston in 1918 when young Joe Kennedy showered the city's Italian neighborhoods with money, looking for sluggers to serve as campaign operatives on behalf of his father-in-law, Honey Fitz.

As a youngster, Roselli was a lean and scrappy thug. By the age of seventeen, he'd been arrested twice for narcotics trafficking, once due to a sting operation involving an informant. After spending six months in jail,

Roselli was released, and the informant was soon found murdered. When local authorities came looking for Roselli, the young gangster fled to Chicago, where he soon took on an envied role as Al Capone's personal driver. A handsome man and slick dresser, he became known in the underworld as Mr. Smooth. He was also known to have mastered the art of malocchio, or the evil eye. In later years, he once counseled a friend: "The secret is not to look in [a person's] eyes. You pick a spot on their forehead and zero in. That way you don't blink, you don't move. It intimidates the hell out of them."

Joe Kennedy was himself known to have this skill, which his family and friends referred to as "Hickey eyes" because he had inherited the trait from his mother, whose maiden name was Hickey.

The Kennedy-Roselli relationship was not exactly a secret. Far removed from the bootlegging centers of the East and Midwest, Joe was more sanguine about mixing with known underworld figures than he had been in the past. The two men occasionally played golf and cards together, and Roselli was an occasional guest at Kennedy's Beverly Hills mansion. Among other things, the budding movie mogul used Roselli's influence with various Hollywood trade unions to stave off potentially costly strikes.

Kennedy didn't need Johnny Roselli to get rich in the movie business. Using techniques he had developed in his years as a Wall Street broker, where he became a master at driving up the price of stocks and then dumping them at enormous profits, Kennedy was an expert at recognizing undervalued corporations. Hollywood had become the fourth largest business in the United States, although few major investors took the industry seriously. "It looks like another telephone industry," Kennedy told several friends, meaning that it was brand new and ripe for the taking. People in the underworld referred to Hollywood as the new booze.

At the same time that Joe presided as chairman of FBO, he moved around town from company to company, making money wherever he went. He was chairman of RKO Studios for five months, special adviser to First National Pictures for six weeks, special adviser to Radio Corporation of America for two and a half months, and adviser to Paramount Pictures for seventy-four days. He made his biggest killing at Pathé, the venerable newsreel company that had been around since the beginning of motion pictures. Kennedy was brought in as a special adviser and proceeded to plunder the company's stock. He arranged to pay himself eighty dollars a share, while the average stockholder received a dollar-fifty a share.

Favoring insiders to such a degree was a form of corporate robbery that would be punishable by a prison sentence today. Since Kennedy had acquired his Pathé stock at thirty dollars a share, he more than doubled his investment in little over a year. Stockholders filed suit, but nothing came of it. In Joe's private papers, Kennedy family biographer Doris Kearns Goodwin found anguished letters from stockholders at Pathé. Wrote Ann Lawler of Boston, who lost her life savings to Kennedy: "This seems hardly Christian-like, fair, or just for a man of your character. I wish you would think of the poor working women who had so much faith in you as to give their money to your Pathé."

Kennedy's avarice appeared to know no bounds. He realized that, to truly make a killing in the movie business, he needed to own his own theater chain to distribute his pictures. In late 1929, he sought to purchase the Pantages Theatre chain, whose primary showcase was a resplendent Art Deco movie palace at the corner of Hollywood and Vine. Kennedy made an offer to buy out the entire Pantages chain, the second largest on the West Coast. The company's owner, Alexander Pantages, an illiterate Greek immigrant, did not want to sell. After several bullying maneuvers against Pantages failed, Kennedy resorted to other means.

On the evening of August 9, a seventeen-year-old woman named Eunice Pringle, wearing a low-cut red dress, went to Pantages' office inside his theater on South Hill Street in downtown Los Angeles. Several minutes later, the woman ran screaming into the lobby, where she collapsed into the arms of a theater employee, crying, "There he is—the beast. Don't let him get at me." She pointed at Alexander Pantages.

A cop arrived on the scene. Pringle, barely coherent, her clothes torn, told the police that Pantages had tried to rape her.

"It's a lie," protested Pantages, whose command of the English language was barely adequate. "She raped herself," he told the cop, meaning that it was some kind of setup. Pantages was arrested and booked on a charge of assault with intent to rape.

The trial was a Hollywood sensation. The main witness, Pringle, was described in the *Herald-Examiner* as "the sweetest seventeen since Clara Bow." On the stand, she told a lurid tale of Pantages ripping at her clothes and biting her breast. Pantages, in denying her story, broke into tears and repeated over and over in broken English, "I did not; I did not." Compared to the seemingly angelic Pringle, Pantages came off as a crude, paranoid foreigner. The jury found him guilty, and he was sentenced to fifty years in prison.

But Pantages appealed the verdict. A team of private investigators unearthed evidence showing that Eunice Pringle was a girl with a past; she was at the very least a professional con artist, if not an outright prostitute. At a second trial, Pantages was acquitted of the attempted rape charge, but the notoriety caused his business to go down the tubes. In November 1931, a few months after Joe Kennedy had made a final offer of $8 million to buy him out, the theater chain owner was forced to cut his losses and sell out to Kennedy's RKO for less than half that price.

Two years after the Pantages acquittal, Eunice Pringle told her lawyer she wanted to come clean. Rumors began circulating that she was about to blow the lid off the rape case and name names. Suddenly, she died of unknown causes. The night she expired, she was violently ill and red in coloring, the tell-tale signs of cyanide poisoning. On her deathbed, Pringle confessed to her mother and a friend that men representing Joe Kennedy had paid her to set up Pantages. For her perjured testimony, said Pringle, she and her agent/boyfriend were paid $10,000, with the additional promise that studio boss Joseph P. Kennedy would make her a star. Whether or not Kennedy had Pringle killed to silence her, no one would ever know. For one thing, no autopsy was conducted. All that remained was Pringle's accusation.[1]

The idea that Kennedy might resort to such tactics may have seemed far-fetched to some. Certainly, it was not in keeping with his public image as a reputable business tycoon. However, Joe Kennedy had been living a dual existence ever since he entered public life. At the same time that he was routinely promoted in the press as a business genius and charitable benefactor of the Roman Catholic Church, he was on a first name basis with some of the most ruthless gangsters alive—men who had personally killed or ordered the deaths of literally hundreds of people over the last decade.

Joe Kennedy's own success was based on a kind of bullying and ruthlessness commensurate with a man in his position (other studio moguls such as Jack Warner, Sam Cohn, and Daryl Zanuck are not generally remembered as wonderful human beings). In this regard, blackmailing Alexander Pantages, a stubborn business competitor who refused to submit to his will, was not inconsistent with tactics Kennedy used throughout his life. The silencing of Eunice Pringle was, perhaps, a regrettable but unavoidable consequence.

---

1. Joe Kennedy's role in "the Pantages Affair" and the death of Eunice Pringle were not publicly revealed until years after the fact, after he had moved on to other endeavors. The incident became part of Hollywood lore, chronicled in Kenneth Anger's book *Hollywood Babylon,* as was Kennedy's highly public affair with starlet Gloria Swanson and his relationship with mobster Johnny Roselli. Joe Kennedy's exploits in Hollywood were later eclipsed by those of his son, J.F.K., who befriended mobster acolyte Frank Sinatra and bedded the greatest "trophy" of them all—Marilyn Monroe.

If Kennedy did play a role in the woman's mysterious death, or in the frame-up of Pantages, as Pringle alleged on her deathbed, it's likely he would have handled the matter in such a way that he'd never be directly implicated. The former whiskey baron and aspiring studio boss cultivated the kinds of relationships he did for precisely this reason: to maintain a reliable buffer zone between the man who gives the order and those who carry it out.

Kennedy's less-than-distinguished although profitable stint as a movie mogul and producer ended in late 1931, when New York Governor Franklin Roosevelt summoned him to the East Coast to become a key operative in his bid for the presidency of the United States. Coming from a political family as he did, Joe jumped at the chance to establish a direct line to the White House. He personally contributed or helped to raise $200,000 for the campaign—equal to $2.5 million today. According to Timothy A. McInerny, a former *Boston Post* editor who later worked for Kennedy, Joe also served as Roosevelt's money collector or bag man, arranging for cash contributions from underworld figures and others who wanted to hide their identities. After F.D.R.'s election as president, Kennedy was rewarded with appointments as chairman of the Securities and Exchange Commission, later as chairman of the Maritime Commission, and finally as ambassador to England.

At the same time that Kennedy served in the Roosevelt Administration, he pursued his own business interests. In 1933, through inside contacts in the government, Joe learned that Prohibition would soon be repealed. He immediately began buying up huge quantities of Scotch—fraudulently—by claiming that it was for "medicinal purposes." The Scotch, mostly Haig & Haig and Dewars, was stockpiled in warehouses near the Canadian border. When Prohibition was finally repealed, Kennedy became overnight the largest single distributor of Scotch in the United States and remained so until 1946, when he sold his interest in Somerset Importers, Inc. for a huge profit.

Following his resignation from the Roosevelt Administration in 1941, Kennedy resumed his relationship with underworld figures in various U.S. locales. In 1943, Joe purchased 17 percent, a controlling interest, of the Hialeah Race Track in Miami, which was frequented by South Florida mob boss Santo Trafficante, Meyer Lansky, and other notable mobsters. Rose Kennedy, in her memoir, wrote of visiting the track with her husband "a couple times a week." Kennedy was also a regular at roulette tables in Miami Beach carpet joints owned and operated by Lansky during and immediately after World War II. It was also alleged that, through a silent partner, Kennedy purchased a 10 percent interest in the Tropicana Hotel & Casino in Las Vegas, which was co-owned by a consortium of gangsters, including Johnny Roselli, Frank Costello, and New Orleans mob boss Carlos Marcello. And in 1945, with $12.5 million of his own money, Kennedy bought the Merchandise Mart in Chicago, then the world's largest building and a center of organized crime and corruption in the Windy City.[2]

The Merchandise Mart, a massive commercial/office building, brought Kennedy directly into the realm of the Outfit, the Chicago-based syndicate that would play such a crucial role in the creation of Las Vegas, the plundering of the Teamsters Union pension fund, and other major post-World War II criminal rackets. Once home to the most renowned speakeasy in the city, Kennedy's latest purchase was located just north of the Chicago River in the East Chicago Avenue police district, famed for having what senior police officials called a solid setup of corruption. Organized crime controlled the bars, gambling, and prostitution that dominated the area's economy, as it had back in the days of the old Levee District. It was understood that any illicit business could operate without disruption, as long as two payoffs were made at the beginning of each month—one to the East Chicago Avenue police and one to the local ward committeeman.

Joe Kennedy was nothing if not astute. He knew exactly what he was inheriting when he purchased the Merchandise Mart. He rarely showed his face in the area and didn't need to. He was now, economically speaking, at the center of a nexus of corruption from which the city of Chicago had derived its very personality. It was a nexus he would come to rely on in later years, especially during the frantic runup to his son John's landmark election as president.

All the Way With J.F.K.

By late 1944, with too many skeletons in his own closet to attain higher political office for himself, Papa Joe was free to turn his attentions to his oldest living son, John Fitzgerald Kennedy. Known as "Jack" to his friends and family, J.F.K., like his father, had a reputation as a flagrant womanizer. He'd come back from World War II with at least one notorious affair under his

---

2. Even at such a high price, the Merchandise Mart was believed to be a steal for Kennedy. At the time of his death in 1969, it was valued at $75 million. Observed his wife Rose, "Joe had a genius for seeing something and knowing it would be worth something more later on. And with the Mart, he was absolutely right . . . it skyrocketed in value and became the basis for a whole new Kennedy fortune."

belt (with a married Scandinavian journalist and alleged Nazi spy), along with medals for bravery that would eventually become the basis for his best-selling book, *Profiles in Courage*. Upon Jack's return from oversees, Joe sent him to a well-known Massachusetts political sage to assess his prospects for elective office. "He has poise, a fine Celtic map. A most engaging smile," reported the sage. Kennedy should "buy him in."

Joe immediately began plotting the details of John Kennedy's introduction into the local political landscape. The problem was that Massachusetts, the home base of the Kennedy dynasty, was a highly competitive political universe crowded with veteran incumbents and eager wannabes. Joe quickly determined that the most likely prospect for Jack was to run as the congressman from the 8th Assembly District, which included a couple of Irish working-class neighborhoods as well as Cambridge, home to Joe and Jack's Harvard alma mater. The district's current representative, James Michael Curley, was soon up for reelection. A legendary figure in Massachusetts politics for the last four decades, Curley was unbeatable in a one-on-one contest, but Joe Kennedy had other ideas.

The relationship between Kennedy's family and the most renowned Irish pol in all of Boston history went back at least to the days of Honey Fitz and his tenure as mayor. Curley had blackmailed Fitzgerald into not seeking reelection as mayor in 1914, by threatening to go public with information on his extramarital affair with a woman named Elizabeth "Toodles" Ryan. Curley, who'd once been reelected as ward boss from jail, was as shrewd a hardball politician as ever lived. He merely hinted to the Fitzgerald camp that he was about to deliver a public address entitled, "Great Lovers: From Cleopatra to Toodles." Fearing public scandal, Honey Fitz stepped aside. Curley went on to serve multiple terms as mayor, governor, and congressman.[3]

---

3. James Michael Curley, beloved by the electorate, was throughout his career under constant attack from the press, especially the *Boston Globe*. Frequently under investigation for political and financial improprieties, he was sentenced to jail a second time in 1946, for influence peddling. Five months later he was granted executive clemency by President Truman. Curley lost his final election bid in 1950, at the age of seventy-six, but soon found himself to be more renowned than ever when writer Edwin O'Connor's novel, *The Last Hurrah*—based loosely on Curley's life and career—became a national bestseller. Two years after its release, the book became a classic Academy Award–nominated movie starring Spencer Tracy and directed by John Ford, securing Curley's place in history as perhaps the most glorified of all the old Irish political bosses.

Joe Kennedy knew that Curley's dream was to be elected mayor of Boston once again. He also knew that Curley, who'd recently had to defend himself in court on various charges of political malfeasance, was deeply in debt. By Curley's own estimations, he needed somewhere in the neighborhood of $100,000 to run in the city election, which was to be held in November 1945. Curley did not have access to that kind of money. That's where Joe Kennedy came in.

In November 1944, on the eve of Curley's reelection as congressman from the 8th District, Kennedy approached Curley with a classic Irish American proposition: *You scratch my back; I scratch yours.* Specifically, Kennedy told Curley that if he agreed to step down from his congressional seat and run for mayor, Joe would pay off his debts, finance his campaign, and even subsidize the salary of Curley's campaign manager. It was, quite simply, an offer too good to refuse. Curley stepped aside, and Jack Kennedy got himself elected to congress in 1946, serving with a minimum of distinction. In 1954, activating phase two of Joe Kennedy's master plan, J.F.K. was elected U.S. Senator from the state of Massachusetts.

By the time Joe's other son, Bobby, became chief counsel for the McClellan Committee, J.F.K. had emerged as an attractive, well-spoken senator with serious potential as a national candidate. Joe the Patriarch, meanwhile, had virtually disappeared from public life. A millionaire many times over (Kennedy's worth at the time of his death was estimated at $500 million), he was content to stay in the background and manipulate the levers of power on behalf of his offspring. Jack was now the golden boy. In 1956, as a trial balloon, he'd entered his name into nomination as a Democratic party candidate for president and quickly stepped aside when it became clear that Adlai Stevenson would be the party's nominee. The gesture served the purpose of elevating J.F.K.'s name and face into the national scene, making him appear to be a viable and even likely future candidate. This is why Papa Joe was so concerned about Bobby's involvement in a potentially embarrassing and dangerous investigation into the activities of organized crime.

The McClellan Committee turned out to be one of the longest and most expensive senatorial investigations in history, lasting over two years, with fifteen hundred witnesses whose recollections (or, at least, recitations of their Fifth Amendment privilege not to testify on the grounds of self-incrimination) filled dozens of volumes totaling over twenty thousand pages of testimony. Most of the dominant mafiosi in America were dragged before the committee, including Johnny Roselli, Carlos Marcello of New Orleans, and, of course, Sam Giancana of Chicago, who smirked at Bobby Kennedy from the witness stand and famously received this retort from the pugnacious chief counsel: "I thought only little girls giggled, Mr. Giancana."

Bobby's strongest vitriol was reserved for Teamsters Vice President Jimmy Hoffa, who was short, fiery, and equally as stubborn as Kennedy. The rivalry between the two men was intensely personal, at least on Bobby's part, which Hoffa could never fully comprehend. Years later, in his own defense, Hoffa commented, "You take any industry and look at the problems they ran into while they were building it up—how they did it, who they associated with, how they cut corners. The best example is Kennedy's old man. . . . To hear Kennedy grandstanding when he was in front of the McClellan Committee, you might have thought I was making as much out of the Teamsters pension fund as the Kennedys made out of selling whiskey."

Throughout the hearings, Bobby Kennedy seemed hell-bent on establishing "the Mafia" as *the* source and instigator of organized crime in America. Mobsters with Italian immigrant roots, in particular, were linked together in a "conspiracy of evil," as Kennedy called it. One of the more riveting encounters was between the chief counsel and forty-nine-year-old Carlos Marcello, who oozed contempt as he sat in the spacious, high-ceilinged senate hearing room and invoked his Fifth Amendment privilege no less than sixty-six times. Marcello even refused to tell the committee where he was born. Kennedy moved on from Marcello to Giancana and others—badgering, ridiculing, and excoriating them all in his sometimes shrill, Hyannis Port-by-way-of-Harvard manner of speech.

Most Kennedy biographers agree that it is unlikely the aggressive young chief counsel, at this point in his life, knew the full extent of his father's history with underworld figures. Even so, Bobby's sometimes obsessive fascination with the Mafia seemed to contain an undercurrent of expiation—as if, by underscoring the fraternal Italian and Sicilian nature of organized crime in America, he was shifting the focus away from others (like his own father) who may have occasionally benefited from or played a role in the underworld's conspiracy of evil. Bobby's zeal was undoubtedly inspired by events outside the hearing room as well.

In November 1957, roughly midway through the hearings, an extraordinary event shifted the focus of the committee. In Apalachin, a small town in Upstate New York, local police stumbled onto a large gathering of mobsters at the home of a local resident. The mobsters fled into the woods, where many were caught, rounded up, and held for questioning. The large-scale mobster meeting dominated newspaper headlines throughout the country.

Of the fifty-eight men who were detained, fifty had arrest records, thirty-five had convictions, and twenty-three had served prison terms. Eighteen had been involved in murder investigations, fifteen netted for narcotics violations, thirty for gambling, and twenty-three for illegal use of firearms. Clearly, this was not a gathering of the Rotary Club. The conference seemed to suggest something that FBI director J. Edgar Hoover had been discounting for years; there was, in fact, a commission or syndicate of gangsters in the country who met and operated together. The round-up at Apalachin would go down as a landmark in organized crime history and give the McClellan hearings added impetus as part of a vital, straight-from-the-headlines crusade against organized hoodlums.[4]

As the McClellan Committee finally began to wind down in early 1959, Joe Kennedy was not in the mood to wait around for the dust to settle. His son Jack had already announced his candidacy for the presidency, and there was much to be done. Joe knew that Bobby had ruffled feathers in the underworld, but this was not the time to placate bruised egos or simmering grudges. Joe had been dealing with underworld personalities for decades; he had helped many criminal figures make money through bootlegging, stock scams, and political influence. Now was the time to call in his chits.

In February 1960, Papa Kennedy reached out to his old friend, Johnny Roselli. Through the underworld's Mr. Smooth, he arranged for a sit-down with a number of high-ranking mobsters to discuss J.F.K.'s candidacy. The gathering took place at Felix Young's Restaurant in Manhattan. One of the people in attendance was Manhattan attorney Mario Brod, a mysterious figure who had served as a liaison between various mobsters and the U.S. government since the days of Lucky Luciano. Many years after the fact, Brod revealed the details of the Kennedy-mobster powwow to historian Richard Mahoney; he said that many of the New York and Chicago crime bosses whom Kennedy had asked Roselli to invite failed to show up. There were,

---

4. The Apalachin conference was an interesting indicator of just how successful the old Italian-Jewish consortium had been at eradicating the Irish mobster from the equation. Of the fifty-eight men rounded up and held for questioning, the overwhelming majority were Italian or Italian American, with only a few Jews. There was not a single Irish mobster in attendance. In the years since Prohibition, when they dominated operations in New York, Chicago, and elsewhere, Irish American mobsters had been completely shut out of the operations of the Syndicate. The result, as we shall see, was an increased hostility between Irish and Italian racketeers, with decades of bloodshed to come.

however, a fair number who did.[5] Once the attendees were settled in, Kennedy got right to the point; he asked for a large campaign contribution and, more importantly, for the mob's help in ensuring that organized labor support his son's campaign. A number of people at the table objected, reminding the elder Kennedy of son Bobby's recent high-profile, anti-Mafia crusade. Wrote Mahoney in his book *Sons & Brothers:* "The elder Kennedy replied that it was Jack who was running for president, not Bobby, and that this was business, not politics."

After making his case, Kennedy left the restaurant. The mobsters discussed Kennedy's overture amongst themselves. Most were lukewarm in their response, but Roselli reminded the men that Kennedy had come to them, which was significant. He asked his associates at least to consider the Kennedy alliance. Meanwhile, the patriarch did not wait around to see if this meeting in Manhattan bore fruit. He was not deterred by the fact that there was resistance due to Bobby's activities with the McClellan committee. Joe had other names in his mobster rolodex—other fish to fry.

Having studied Jack's prospects carefully, Joe determined that there were two main areas of concern: the West Virginia primary in May, which J.F.K. desperately needed to win, and the state of Illinois, which would be crucial in the general election. Both were heavy labor states that could be turned around with the right kind of mob support.

In April 1960, Papa Joe invited entertainer Frank Sinatra to the Kennedy compound at Hyannis Port. Kennedy knew Sinatra through his son-in-law, actor Peter Lawford. He also knew that Sinatra had a special relationship with Sam "Momo" Giancana, boss of the Outfit. The Chicago Outfit, through Johnny Roselli, their man in Hollywood, had helped boost Sinatra's career on numerous occasions. The singer was eternally grateful and even closed his live shows by singing "My Kind of Town (Chicago Is)" as a tribute to Sam Giancana.[6] For decades, Sinatra remained mum about his initial

<hr />

5. According to Edna Daulyton, who was a hostess at Felix Young's Restaurant at the time of this meeting, "It was as though every gangster chief in the United States was there." In 1988, Daulyton told Irish journalist Anthony Summers: "I took the reservations. . . . I don't remember all the names now, but Johnny Roselli was there . . . they were all top people. I was amazed Joe Kennedy would take the risk."
6. Singer Eddie Fisher, a friend of Sinatra's, once remarked, "Frank wanted to be a hood. He once said, 'I'd rather be a don of the Mafia than president of the United States.' I don't think he was fooling." Born and raised in Hoboken, New Jersey, Sinatra was the product of a typical Italian-Jewish-Irish neighborhood familiality common in so many American cities at the time. His father, Marty Sinatra, an aspiring boxer early in his life, fought under the alias "Marty O'Brien."

meeting with Joe Kennedy, until 1997, when he authorized his daughter Tina Sinatra to give the following account:

> A meeting was called [between Joe and Frank]. Dad was more than willing to go. It was a private meeting. I remember it was over lunch. . . . Dad was ushered in. He hadn't been to the house before. Over lunch Joe said, "I believe you can help me in Virginia and Illinois with our friends. I can't approach them, but you can."
>
> It gave Dad pause. . . . But it still wasn't anything that he felt he shouldn't do. So off to Sam Giancana he went. Dad calls Sam to make a golf game and told Sam of his belief and support of Jack Kennedy. And I believe that Sam felt the same way.

Once Frank Sinatra broke the ice with Giancana, Kennedy took matters into his own hands. Again, it would be many decades before the full extent of his meetings with the mob on JFK's behalf were fully documented. Gus Russo's *The Outfit* offers the most detailed account. Russo quotes numerous first-hand sources who were party to a highly secretive meeting between Kennedy and Giancana, which was arranged by a First Ward alderman and circuit court judge William J. Tuohy, one of Kennedy's oldest friends in Chicago. The meeting took place inside the judge's private chambers. Behind closed doors, Kennedy made certain assurances that, Bobby Kennedy's recent history notwithstanding, the election of J.F.K. would benefit Giancana and his friends. Certain known mob figures currently facing legal and/or deportation problems would see those problems disappear. "Any administration led by the Kennedy family will be good for your people," Joe assured Sam.

Given the way Giancana had been ridiculed by Bobby Kennedy during the McClellan hearings, the mobster had every right to be skeptical. But he was apparently dazzled by the Irish patriarch; in later months, he was often heard bragging that he was "trying to get that Joe Kennedy's kid elected president."

There were other meetings that summer, most of them held covertly at the Cal-Neva Lodge, a luxury resort that straddled the California-Nevada state line on the north shore of Lake Tahoe, a region known as Crystal Bay. In this bucolic setting, described in brochures as "Heaven in the High Sierras," Kennedy maintained a series of bungalows that became headquarters for the unofficial Kennedy campaign braintrust. It was a short hop by plane from Cal-Neva to Las Vegas and on to Chicago, which became a well-worn path for Joe, Sinatra, Giancana, and others involved in a subterranean effort to ensure J.F.K.'s election as the country's first Irish Catholic president.

In hindsight, Giancana's willingness to trust Joe Kennedy and go to bat for his offspring may seem inexplicable. Many people in Giancana's own organization told him he was crazy. Murray Humphreys, a high-ranking member of the Outfit who remembered Joe Kennedy from his bootlegging days, bad-mouthed Kennedy as an untrustworthy "four-flusher" and a "potato eater." Others told Giancana he was putting his neck on the line by working for the Kennedys after Bobby's excoriation of "our friends." Some mobsters flatly refused to help with Kennedy's election in any way, most notably Carlos Marcello in New Orleans, who later made a personal cash contribution of $500,000 to the campaign of Kennedy's rival, Richard Nixon. The money was picked up in New Orleans and delivered to the Nixon campaign by another avowed Kennedy hater, Teamster boss Jimmy Hoffa.

But Momo Giancana had his reasons. An underworld traditionalist, his motives for cooperating with Joe Kennedy were rooted in a tacit agreement between certain Italian underworld figures and Irish Americans that had been in effect since at least the big Atlantic City conference of 1929. That conference had established new ground rules by redefining the role of the Irish in the eyes of Italian and Jewish racketeers. Irish mobsters were shut out or killed, nowhere more so than in Chicago, where young Sam Giancana had established a reputation as a fierce gangster described in one police report as "a snarling, sarcastic, ill-tempered, sadistic psychopath." Giancana started out as member of the 42 Gang, a notorious Italian street gang, and eventually caught the attention of Al Capone, who enlisted the young gangster's services as a wheel man. Giancana became a key player in the mob's hostile takeover of Irish American bootlegging operations, forcing many would-be Irish crimesters to seek refuge in ward politics and police work, which is exactly where the Syndicate wanted them.

By forcibly assigning the Irish this role, the Italians accepted as a quid pro quo that they at least listen when approached by an Irish American politician, lawman, or businessman looking to play along with the mob. After all, the Irish had arrived before everybody else and infiltrated mainstream society in a way the Italians and Jews had not. Their function was to hatch schemes from the inside, which is exactly what Joe Kennedy was offering Sam Giancana. Kennedy was dangling the prospect of an inside track on American political and business affairs unlike anything the Syndicate had ever experienced before. How could Sam Giancana say no to such an offer?

The truth of this hypothesis is to be found in the way Giancana dutifully carried out Kennedy's wishes, as if he were fulfilling an obligation that was at the very heart of the mob's multiethnic agenda. Giancana didn't just agree to go along with Kennedy's plan; he leaned on others in the underworld to do so also, mortgaging his own reputation on the alliance with Papa Joe.

The first order of business was to guarantee Jack Kennedy's victory in the upcoming West Virginia primary, thus proving the candidate's electability even in rural, non-Catholic regions of the country. Overnight, mob-controlled juke bosses throughout West Virginia began featuring J.F.K.'s campaign theme song, a reworded version of Sammy Cahn's current hit "High Hopes," sung by Sinatra. A Kennedy aide traversed the state (one of the poorest in the United States), paying tavern owners twenty dollars each to play the song repeatedly.

Money began to fall out of the sky. Suitcases full of cash were delivered by silk-suited men named Vinnie, Tony, and Rocco. As FBI wiretaps would later disclose, Sinatra and Giancana's close friend Paul "Skinny" D'Amato spent two weeks in the state dispensing $50,000 worth of contributions, most of it in the form of desks, chairs, and supplies for politicians around the state. According to D'Amato, Joe Kennedy even paid him a personal visit and, in exchange for his help in the campaign, promised that, if elected, his son Jack would allow deported New Jersey mobster Joe Adonis to return to the United States. This was just one of many Joe Kennedy promises to the mob that would go unfulfilled.

J.F.K. won in West Virginia and went on to secure the nomination by August. By all indications, the general election that fall was going to be close, with Nixon and Kennedy neck-and-neck in most polls. Every vote would count. Just as Joe Kennedy had predicted, it looked like the race was going to come down to the state of Illinois. The Kennedy patriarch would pull out all the stops.

There were continued meetings with Giancana, at least one of them arranged by Mayor Richard Daley of Chicago. In the long history of Irish American political bosses, Daley was truly the last of his breed—a quick-tempered, salt-of-the-earth product of the Chicago Machine who was fiercely proud of his working-class Irish roots. "Da Mare" had known Joe Kennedy for years. Having come from opposite ends of the Irish American spectrum—Kennedy, the Irish WASP by way of Harvard, Daley, the aggrieved proletarian from blue-collar Bridgeport—their relationship was based more on political expediency than friendship. Kennedy cultivated the mayor to be his Irish lackey, and Daley soaked Kennedy for campaign cash. They met occasionally for lunch at the patriarch's Merchandise Mart, no press allowed.

At the Ambassador East Hotel in downtown Chicago, over the course of three meetings, Kennedy, Daley, and Giancana discussed strategy. It was agreed that certain key districts, including the First Ward, would be delivered on election day by large pluralities. Mayor Daley, through the Chicago police department, would make sure there was no outside interference.[7]

On election day, November 11, 1960, everything fell into place. J.F.K. won by the slimmest margin in history, with the key districts in Chicago proving to be the margin of victory. The election was a classic Machine-style effort. Subterranean Irish and Italian criminal forces coalesced as they had in many old-style city, county, and state elections since the birth of the American underworld. In many ways, it was a replay of the election Joe Kennedy had engineered for his father-in-law, Honey Fitz, way back in 1918. Only this time, Papa Joe had outdone himself by making grandiose promises to the powerful underworld figures who had dutifully followed his every command. These were not men to be taken lightly. Now that they had done what was asked of them, they expected to see results.

The Kennedy Double Cross

The first shocker came with J.F.K.'s naming of his attorney general. The appointment of brother Bobby as the nation's top cop had come at the insistence of Papa Joe, who saw the choice as a fait accompli. Joe must have

---

7. The meetings between Joe Kennedy, Mayor Daley, and Giancana are detailed in *Double Cross*, written in 1992 by Sam and Chuck Giancana, the brother and nephew of Momo, who was murdered in his home in 1975. As described in the book, the details of these meetings are somewhat specious, slanted in such a way as to make Giancana look strong-willed and Kennedy look like a fool. Although the "you are there" nature of these scenes—complete with bad Hollywood dialogue—are to be taken with a grain of salt, their having taken place is not entirely surprising given Mayor Daley's benign relationship with the Outfit. In 1955, Daley won the Chicago mayoral election with a 13,275 to 1,961 plurality in the Outfit-controlled First Ward. At Ward Headquarters on election night, the mayor boasted of his record of giving city jobs and civil contracts to Outfit associates. "I've been criticized for doing this," he said, "but I'll make no apologies. I'll always stand alongside the man with a criminal record if I think he deserves a second chance."

In fairness to Daley, his feelings about mobsters was based on more than self-interest. His views on the subject were rooted in the belief that the American social structure was slanted in favor of the WASP, and that ethnic mobsters were a regrettable although legitimate aspect of immigrant upward mobility (for an insightful presentation of Daley's philosophy, see *Don't Make No Wave Don't Back No Losers* by Milton Rakove). Either way, his approach was good for the Outfit. A high-ranking member of the Chicago mob was once captured on wiretaps saying of Daley, "This mayor has been good to us. And we've been good to him. One hand washes the other."

known that Bobby's appointment would not sit well with Giancana, Roselli, and the rest of the boys, but he was faced with an even more pressing concern. J. Edgar Hoover had come to Joe immediately after J.F.K.'s election with the startling information that Jack had been carrying on an affair with a woman named Judith Campbell (later Judith Campbell Exner), who was at the same time having an affair with Sam Giancana. Hoover claimed to be concerned that the president, at the very least, was opening himself up to potential blackmail. Joe Kennedy was concerned that Hoover would hold this information over the president's head. The elder Kennedy believed Bobby's appointment as attorney general would provide an essential buffer that would protect J.F.K. from internal government attack from the likes of J. Edgar Hoover.

Bobby Kennedy undertook his role as attorney general with the same kind of zeal he had exhibited during his stint with the McClellan Committee. In fact, at his first press conference under his new title, Kennedy announced that dismantling organized crime would be the Justice Department's highest priority, and added that he had his brother's full support in the effort.

Kennedy's actions were swift and unprecedented. The number of attorneys in the Department's Organized Crime and Racketeering Section ballooned from seventeen to sixty-three; the number of illegal bugs and wiretaps grew from only a few to more than eight hundred nationwide; Bobby drew up a hit list of top mob targets—a list that included Johnny Roselli and Sam Giancana, the very men whom Papa Joe had leaned on to get J.F.K. elected. To the gangsters, Bobby's antimob initiative was inexplicable and seemed highly personal in nature. Among the many acts undertaken by the Kennedy Administration that rocked the underworld were

1. The "kidnapping" of Carlos Marcello: Tops on Bobby's mafiosi hit list was New Orleans crime boss Carlos Marcello, who had defied Bobby during the McClellan hearings and, as Kennedy later learned, made a secret $500,000 contribution to the Nixon campaign through arch-enemy Jimmy Hoffa. On April 4, 1961, under pressure from the Justice Department, Marcello was literally snatched off the streets of New Orleans by federal agents, put in an airplane, and flown to Guatemala, where he was summarily deported under the pretext of traveling under a false passport.

Outraged to the point of hysteria, Marcello snuck back into the United States two months later and filed suit against Attorney General Robert Kennedy. At the same time, he apparently tried to broker a truce. According to author John H. Davis in *Mafia Kingfish*, an FBI wiretap picked up a conversation between two well-known northeastern mob bosses about how Marcello had tried to use Frank Sinatra to help get Bobby Kennedy off his back. Sinatra was successful in getting Bobby's ear, but the overture only made matters worse. Instead of getting Kennedy to take it easy on the Louisiana mob boss, the stubborn attorney general, suspecting perhaps that his father had put Sinatra up to it, stepped up his efforts against Marcello. The U.S. government reinitiated criminal proceedings against the mafioso on charges of conspiracy in falsifying a Guatemalan birth certificate and committing perjury. Marcello's brother also was indicted.

Down in New Orleans, the volatile Marcello seethed and cursed the Kennedy name, telling anyone who would listen, "You just wait; you wait an' see if that son of a bitch Bobby Kennedy is gonna take me away from my wife an' kids."

2. The hit on Fidel Castro: Unbeknownst to the Kennedy Administration, a few months before J.F.K.'s election as president, certain members of the underworld had linked up with the CIA in a misguided plot to assassinate Cuban president Fidel Castro. The CIA, knowing that the Syndicate was angry at Castro for shutting down their lucrative Cuban casinos, initiated the plot. Joe Kennedy's old Hollywood friend, Johnny Roselli, served as the point man in this operation, but Sam Giancana was assigned the role of actually recruiting the hitmen to carry out the various harebrained assassination schemes then under consideration.

As a quid pro quo for getting involved in the CIA's "Get Castro" operations, Roselli, Giancana, et al. understood that there would be a moratorium on federal mob prosecutions or at least a lessening of pressure on the Chicago Outfit. Apparently, no one in the CIA had informed Bobby Kennedy about this arrangement. In light of the joint CIA-Mafia operation, the attorney general's fervid legal onslaught against the mob felt, to the mobsters themselves, like yet another betrayal engineered by those "Irish bastards" in the White House.

3. The Valachi hearings: In mid-1963, the Department of Justice announced "an extraordinary intelligence breakthrough" in their battle with organized crime. Bobby Kennedy asserted that disclosures by Joseph M. Valachi, a federal prison inmate, had revealed for the first time the whole picture of organized crime, its organizational structure and initiation rites, which included sacred oaths and bloodletting. Overnight, this small-time underworld hood from the streets of New York became an international celebrity.

A few months later, to the further shock and dismay of underworld figures everywhere, the McClellan Committee was reconstituted to provide a forum for Joe Valachi to be paraded in front of television cameras. As pure theater, Valachi's testimony before the senate committee in September and

October outdid the Kefauver Hearings, the Waterfront Commission Hearings, and the previous McClellan Hearings put together. With his gravelly, straight-from-central-casting New York accent, the sixty-year-old Valachi introduced words like don, caporegime, and consiglieri into the American lexicon, and insisted that what was known to the public as the Black Hand, the Unione Sicilione, or the Mafia was most commonly known to the mobsters themselves as cosa nostra.

Italian gangsters from coast to coast were stupefied by Valachi's testimony, mainly because they believed he was a fraud. Valachi wasn't even Sicilian; he was a New York Neapolitan who had never been anything more than a low-level thug. Yet he sat before the McClellan Committee and all of America on television making observations on how Sicilian gangs were organized and operated, including supposedly inside accounts of top-level decision making. As mob boss Joseph Bonnano later observed, it was like a "New Guinea native who had converted to Catholicism describing the inner workings of the Vatican."

The breadth and scope of Bobby Kennedy's assault on organized crime was unparalleled in modern history. To high-ranking members of the underworld, his actions were like a knife in the back, strategically plunged for maximum damage and then twisted around for the pure sadistic fun of it. The Outfit had helped put the Kennedys in the White House. Joe Kennedy, the Irish Godfather, in the eyes of Giancana, Roselli, and other Italian mobsters, had brokered an arrangement that was supposed to work in everyone's favor. Now here was Bobby Kennedy on a holy crusade, casting aspersions on Italian organized crime as if his family's lily-white Irish hands had never been sullied by dirty money. FBI bugs and wiretaps around the country began to pick up a steady stream of anti-Kennedy commentary about those "Irish bastards" and "those filthy, Irish cocksuckers."

In Upstate New York, Peter Maggadino: "He should drop dead. They should kill the whole family, the mother and father, too."

In Pennsylvania, Mario Maggio: "[Bobby Kennedy] is too much; he is starting to hurt too many people, like unions. He is not only hurting the racket guys, but others."

In New York City, Michelino Clements: "Bob Kennedy won't stop until he puts us all in jail all over the country."

In Chicago, Sam Giancana: "I never thought it would get this fucking rough. When they put the brother in there, we were going to see some fireworks, but I never knew it was going to be like this. This is murder."

The angriest words of all came from New Orleans, where Carlos Marcello was embroiled in his titanic battle with the Justice Department.

Marcello had run up close to $1 million in legal fees and frothed at the mouth every time the Kennedy family name was mentioned in his presence.

One afternoon, Marcello and a group of friends and acquaintances were gathered at Churchill Farms, the mobster's weekend resort located outside New Orleans in Louisiana bayou country. Among those present was Edward Becker, a former director of public relations of the Riviera Casino in Las Vegas who was now a private investigator. Becker made the mistake of bringing up Kennedy's name: "Man, isn't it a shame the bad deal you're getting from Bobby Kennedy? I've been reading about it in the papers. All that deportation stuff. What are you going to do about it, Carlos?"

Marcello's face flushed red. *Livarsi 'na pietra di la scarpa*, he said in Sicilian (*Take the stone out of my shoe*). "Don't worry about that little Bobby son of a bitch. He's goin' to be taken care of. I got—"

"But you can't go after Bobby Kennedy," Becker interrupted. "If you do, you're going to get into a hell of a lot of trouble."

"No, I'm not talkin' about that." Marcello stood up, gesticulating as he spoke. "You know what they say in Sicily: If you want to kill a dog, you don't cut off the tail, you cut off the head." The Kennedys, explained Carlos, were like a mad dog; the president was the head and the attorney general was the tail. "That dog will keep biting you if you only cut off its tail. But if the dog's head is cut off, the dog will die—tail and all."

Marcello continued yapping, seized by a deep personal animosity toward the Kennedys. He explained that the death of the attorney general would not solve anything, since his brother, the president, would surely go after Bobby's enemies with a vengeance. The president himself would have to go, and it would have do be done in such a way that it could not be directly linked to the organization. He had already given some thought to setting up a nut to take the blame, "the way they do it in Sicily."

To Becker, Marcello's tirade, which lasted no more than five minutes, seemed fantastical, if chilling. But Marcello's feelings went even deeper than his own personal animosities. The New Orleans branch of the Mafia was the oldest and most Sicilian of all the regional factions of Cosa Nostra. They often carried out operations on their own, without ever having to consult the governing commission in New York or the Outfit in Chicago. They had a deep and abiding sense of history—a bloody history that harked back to the assassination of Police Chief David Hennessy and the subsequent lynching of fourteen Italians, a landmark event in the history of the Mafia in the United States. In fact, Marcello's leadership of the New Orleans family, which began in the early 1940s, could be traced directly to the Matrangas, the same family that Chief Hennessy had betrayed in his dealings with the Mafia seventy years earlier.

The New Orleans mob's problems with the Kennedys was a case of history repeating itself. Like Chief Hennessy, Joe Kennedy was another "Irish bastard" who represented the legitimate world but was as duplicitous as any underworld hoodlum. To Carlos Marcello and other mafiosi with a deep connection to the region's Sicilian bloodline, the insult struck at the core of the underworld's twisted code of honor. They had been betrayed by people who were passing themselves off as incorruptible and above reproach, when they were as dirty as the lowliest mobster. The mob had been used, manipulated, and played for a fool, and now they were being persecuted. There was no worse insult. It was a transgression punishable by death.

Death to Giovanni

Joe Kennedy was unable to react much to the heartbreaking events that occurred in Dallas on November 22, 1963. Twenty-three months earlier, the patriarch had suffered a massive stroke that rendered him speechless and practically immobile. Confined to a wheelchair, the once powerful leader of the Kennedy clan retreated into his own private universe. The alliances he had formed and promises he'd made to help get his son elected president were now a blur. Whether or not he had any cognizance that the murder of his son might have been a kind of blowback effect from his own dealings with the mob, the world would never know. When told of President Kennedy's assassination, he did not cry, although a family assistant claimed later to have seen the remnants of tears on his cheeks.

For Carlos Marcello, November 22 was a good day. Almost simultaneous with the announcement that his nemesis had been shot down in Dallas, he and his brother were found not guilty in a New Orleans courtroom on conspiracy and perjury charges. Marcello embraced his attorney and hurried home to watch reports of the assassination on television.

In the years that followed, theories on the Kennedy hit were hatched and expounded upon, with the official explanation put forth by the Warren Commission—that it was a single gunman acting alone—turning out the be the least likely scenario of all. Much credible evidence led back to New Orleans; respected criminal defense attorney Frank Ragano related a chilling snippet of conversation he had with his client, mobster Santos Trafficante, Carlos Marcello's closest associate in the underworld. "Carlos fucked up," Trafficante told his lawyer. "We shouldn't have gotten rid of Giovanni. We should have killed Bobby." Ragano, adhering to lawyer-client constraints, kept this and other details he learned from Trafficante under wraps until after the mobster passed away in 1987.

One person who was convinced that the Mafia killed the president was Bobby Kennedy. The attorney general went into a deep depression in the months immediately following his brother's murder. Those who knew him best said he seemed to be racked not only with sorrow, but also with guilt. His personal vendetta against the Mafia had quite possibly boomeranged with horrible consequences. Bobby admitted as much in the summer of 1967, when he told close family friend Richard Goodwin that he believed his brother was killed by "the guy from New Orleans," meaning Carlos Marcello.

History shows that the volatile melding of forces that brought about the assassination of J.F.K. was not without precedent. Police Chief Hennessy had straddled the same fault line with similar results. The Mafia had been dealing with characters like Joe Kennedy all along. To them, Papa Joe was merely a grandiose variation of all the other micks—Jimmy Walker, Jimmy Hines, T. J. Pendergast, Richard Daley—legitimate citizens whose careers were enhanced by their willingness to stoke the flames and play along. Bobby Kennedy was from the new generation; either he didn't know the rules, or he knew the rules and was deliberately setting out to undo what his father had done. Either way, it was a lethal game, and Bobby's posturing as a knight in shining armor was, to the aggrieved mafiosi, the height of hypocrisy and an insult that demanded retribution.

"The flower may look different, but the roots are the same," was how Sam Giancana once put it to his brother, describing how he and the Kennedys, despite outward appearances, were operating within the same universe. Giancana, no doubt, was referring to the roots of the underworld, which had sprouted up to entangle people like Joseph P. Kennedy. Irish and Italian immigrants had been among the progenitors of the underworld, and so their offspring found themselves inheriting the old grudges. The Kennedys and the Mafia were engaged in a high-stakes game of social ascendancy that could be traced back to the earliest maneuverings for power in neighborhoods like Five Points, Little Hell, the Valley, and Hell's Kitchen. In the wards and on the waterfront, Irish and Italian racketeers, gangsters, and quasi-legitimate operators had been engaged in this dance for nearly a century. Players like Joe Kennedy, Sinatra, and Momo Giancana raised the stakes to new levels, but the game was the same.

Key details surrounding the J.F.K. assassination would take decades to surface. When they finally did, the most compelling explanation, that the killing was a mob-generated conspiracy enacted as payback for Joe Kennedy's double-crossing, had roots that could be traced back nearly to the beginning of organized crime in America. The Kennedy hit was merely the latest and loudest salvo in the ongoing war between the dagos and the micks. The war wasn't over yet.

irish vs. irish

The assassination of JFK altered the course of U.S. history, but for most Irish Americans the significance of the Kennedy presidency had been carved in granite three years earlier, on Inauguration Day, 1960. The moment Jack Kennedy was swept into office, the issue of his Catholicism was effectively taken out to sea, given a ten-gun salute, and dumped overboard. Three years later, after the shots were fired on a November day in Dallas, the transformation was complete. How could anyone, WASP or otherwise, question the fidelity of Irish Catholics when they had just offered up one of their most fortunate sons, an Irish prince whose youth and idealism, among other things, made terrific television. The shackles of anti-Catholic bigotry were shattered once and for all. Paddy was home free.

And so began the second great Irish exodus; this time from the city to the suburbs. It wasn't as dramatic as the Great Potato Famine, but the numbers were, over the course of the next two decades, almost as startling. This process of white flight, later chronicled by untold social historians and academic ethnographers, would eventually lead to the reconfiguration of many U.S. cities, among them New York, Chicago, and Philadelphia. In urban areas that had once served as incubation centers for the Irish American gangster, shifting ethnic trends in formerly white neighborhoods would lead to a slow dissolution of the Irish Mob over the next forty years.

Some cities were slower to change than others. In Boston, where Joe Kennedy's family dynasty had been founded and forged, a stubborn Irish American working class was deeply entrenched. Having encountered an unparalleled level of WASP resistance, the city's embattled Irish Catholics were not inclined to relinquish what they had fought so hard to obtain. By the early 1960s, neighborhoods like Charlestown and South Boston had become staunch working-class districts, predominantly Irish American, with a localized system of politics, civil service, law enforcement, and crime that had been in place for generations.

Gangs and gangsters were part of the equation in these neighborhoods and had been for decades. The Gustin Gang, named after a street in South Boston, had been a force in the city during the years of Prohibition and was one of the first bootlegging operations to do business with Joe Kennedy. More recently, the Mullin Gang, a gaggle of wharf rats based along the South Boston waterfront, had spawned a whole new generation of gangsters. In Charlestown, gang factions tended to be broken down into small groups of five or six members (many were family affairs comprised of brothers) and sometimes operated in conjunction with larger racketeering organizations, including the Mafia.

The city's Irish American underworld was mostly a collection of working stiffs: men with wives, children, mortgages, and debt. In appearance and in terms of their family aspirations, the city's racketeers were indistinguishable from other working men—except that they committed crimes and sometimes killed people for a living. This chasm between perception and reality created a psychological disconnect for the gangsters themselves, one that hit home especially hard in the early 1960s. If televised images of Camelot were inspiring Irish Catholics nationwide to revel in their new-found upward mobility, in Boston, the rise of the Kennedys was the cornerstone of something different—an eruption of gangster violence that was without precedent in the long history of the Irish Mob.

For those who cared to notice, the irony was cruel: As J.F.K.'s election opened doors to most middle- and upper-class Irish Catholics, the world of the Irish gangster in Boston entered an era of almost total self-annihilation, which had little to do with the long-standing rivalry between the dagos and the micks, and everything to do with the concept of revenge—Irish revenge.

Gangland murders rarely take place in isolation. The laws of physics dictate that for every action there is a reaction. This would have been an appropriate motto for the Boston underworld or even the city in general. Unlike, say, New York or Kansas City, where a tradition of mobsterism sprang from would-be benevolent associations like Tammany Hall and the Pendergast Machine, Boston never had a centralized base of power, either criminal or legitimate. James Michael Curley, the most exalted of all Boston political chieftains, was not, technically speaking, a boss. Curley had been mayor, congressman, and governor—an elected official. He certainly had clout, but not so much that he could override local ward bosses, some of whom, within their own small domains of power, were at least as important as the mayor or the governor. Thus the city (much like ancient Ireland during the time of the clans) was broken down into a series of tribal villages: Dorchester, Roxbury, South Boston, and so on, each with local commercial interests and governing bodies.

The city's underworld operated as a parallel universe, the main difference being that local hoods frequently formed partnerships based on expediency with crooks from other territories. Aside from the up-and-coming Mullin Gang in South Boston, the city's underworld of the 1950s and early 1960s was comprised mostly of freelance operators—thieves, hijackers, bank robbers, bookmakers, policy runners, and hitmen-for-hire—old-style professional crooks who sold their services to the highest bidder. Irish, Italian, Portuguese, Polish, and even crooks of Arab descent mixed freely in Boston, sometimes hatching schemes together and negotiating the division of spoils amongst themselves.[1]

Partly, this unusual level of interethnic fraternization came about because the dominant mafia faction in Boston was not even based in the city. The New England Mafia, as it had been identified by Joe Valachi during his incendiary senate testimony in October 1963, was led by the Patriarca family, who was based in Providence, Rhode Island. There was a Patriarca subgroup entrenched in Boston's Italian North End, but they were small and toothless compared to Cosa Nostra families in other cities of comparable size. Therefore, Italian and Irish crooks were free to engage in joint ventures without having to kick back a percentage of their take to higher-ups—unless, of course, those higher-ups were directly involved in the planning and financing of a particular scam.

The decentralized nature of the Boston underworld made for some strange bedfellows. One of the most famous criminal capers in the city's history was the Brinks Job, a skillfully planned and executed robbery by a small-time collection of local Irish and Italian hoods. Led by James "Specs" O'Keefe, a professional criminal best known for his brazen shakedowns of gamblers and bookies in the Boston area, the seven-man robbery crew—wearing identical Navy peacoats and Halloween masks—entered a Brinks storage facility in the city's North End; they made off with $2.7 million in cash, checks, money orders, and other securities. The robbery took place on January 17, 1950, and was the largest single haul in U.S. history at the time.

---

1. For a naturalistic delineation of Boston's raffish underworld, see the fictional works of George V. Higgins, especially his first and arguably best novel, *The Friends of Eddie Coyle*, published in 1970.

The crew agreed to keep the proceeds hidden for six years, until the statute of limitations ran out.

It was a good plan, but susceptible to the same sort of mistrust and paranoia that eats away at even the strongest of underworld alliances. In the months and years following the heist, while the FBI hunted for clues and sniffed around for cracks in the plan, the Brinks robbers retreated into mutually suspicious cliques. Specs O'Keefe sided with Carleton O'Brien, an old-time bookmaker and policy boss out of Rhode Island who had helped with the planning of the heist. When, in 1952, O'Brien was mysteriously gunned down in a professional hit on a street in Pawtucket, O'Keefe got nervous. He was also concerned about his mounting legal bills from an assortment of criminal charges.

Eventually, O'Keefe approached the Italian faction of the robbery crew and demanded that they fork over sixty grand from the Brinks loot. His request was flatly denied. As crooks often do when they don't get their way, O'Keefe reacted badly: He kidnapped Vincent Costa, a member of the original break-in crew, and held him for ransom in a Boston hotel room. The Italian members of the Brinks gang arranged for Specs to be paid a portion of the ransom in exchange for Costa's release. Specs should have known that the crew's willingness to cough up the dough designated him as a marked man.

One night, while sitting behind the wheel of his car in his home neighborhood of Dorchester, a vehicle pulled alongside Specs, and someone inside opened fire. Specs ducked to the floor and survived the attack. For some reason, O'Keefe didn't flee the city, even though he must have known there would be follow-up attempts on his life. He had a mistress in the Victory Road housing complex in Dorchester, and that's where he hunkered down. Eight days later, sure enough, O'Keefe was walking on Victory Road late at night when a gunman appeared out of the darkness. Machine gun in hand, the gunman chased Specs through the courtyard of his mistress's housing complex, firing rounds as they ran. O'Keefe returned fire with a handgun. The shootout between the two men lasted for nearly a half hour, with Specs getting the worst of it. By the time cops arrived, O'Keefe was lying in a pool of blood, hit in the chest and arm, but still alive. The hitman had fled the scene.[2]

---

2. The man who'd been hired to take out Specs O'Keefe was a notorious Irish American hitman from New York City named Elmer Francis "Trigger" Burke. Best known back in New York City for having killed his boyhood pal, Poochie Walsh, Burke was born and raised on the West Side of Manhattan. A professional contract killer, he was often employed by Cosa Nostra and other underworld factions and was

Specs O'Keefe convalesced in a hospital under heavy guard. Realizing that he would forever be dodging bullets or hiding from the law, he did the unthinkable: He turned canary and testified against his fellow Brinks robbers in court.

The details of the Brinks Job became a permanent part of the local crime lore. There were many cautionary aspects to the yarn, particularly in the way that the robbery eventually unraveled, but few crooks paid any attention to that. The heist itself had been a thing of beauty—well-planned, professionally carried out, with a score that placed it high up in the Bank Robber Hall of Fame. So what if the participants all wound up in the joint. In the places where criminal schemes are hatched and discussed (saloons, social clubs, in the street) the prospect of a good score trumps a bad ending every time.

One young Boston kid who absorbed the local crime lore better than most was a brazen Irish-born thief named Patrick Nee. By the time Pat Nee had reached his mid-teens, he had become infatuated with the mostly Irish hoods and professional crooks who formed a subgroup within his home neighborhood of South Boston. Elsewhere in the city, kids may have worshipped the likes of Ted Williams, Carl Yastremski, and other local sports legends, but not young Pat. Had there been Topps bubble gum cards depicting the look and careers of men like Specs O'Keefe and Trigger Burke, Nee would have collected every one.

Since migrating with his family from County Galway in 1952 at the age of eight, the aspiring hoodlum set about to transform himself from a rural Irish *culchie* into a true-blue American. Nee's father, the middle son of fourteen brothers and sisters, had been chronically unemployed back in the Old Country. In Southie, he found work through the Laborer's Union. Gaelic speakers from Galway like Nee's dad were first in line at the laborer's local. Gaelic speakers from elsewhere in Ireland came next, followed by Irish-born who did not speak Gaelic. Irish Americans looking for work in the ancestral neighborhood of Southie came in a distant fourth.

---

believed to have committed at least a dozen murders in Boston, New York, South Carolina, and elsewhere. In 1955, after years on the lam, he was apprehended by federal agents at Folly Beach on the Carolina coast and extradited to New York State, where he was tried and convicted on multiple murder charges. Trigger Burke was handsome, with an angular face, chiseled features, and a lithe athletic frame; he was also a cold-blooded killer with ice in his veins. On January 8, 1958, Burke got what many people on both sides of the law felt was his due: He was executed in the electric chair at Sing Sing Prison.

Young Pat Nee was not interested in the pecking order of various trade unions in his new neighborhood. In fact, Nee rarely thought about gainful employment at all. By his early teen years, his main source of fascination was a bar located across the street from the Nee family home on East Third Street. Young Pat was not yet old enough to enter the Lighthouse Tavern, but he had a good view of the establishment's back patio from the creaky wooden porch in back of his house. From there, with the eyes and ears of an adolescent, he heard the music and laughter, saw men playing cards and rolling dice, witnessed the occasional barroom brawl spill out into the street, and noted the fancy clothes and sleek automobiles pulling up in front of the place at all hours of the night. In later years, Nee would say there was never any hope for him; he was hooked on the glamour of the underworld before he was even old enough to vote. The Lighthouse Tavern became an obsession that would catapult the young Irish immigrant through the highs and lows of a long and winding career as a professional gangster.

Running with the Mullin Gang

No one knows for sure the precise origins of the Mullin Gang. What is known is that the gang got its name from an intersection in South Boston at the corner of East Second and O streets that commemorated a war veteran by the name of John Joseph Mullin. In Southie, there was a long-standing tradition of naming various intersections, parks, and town squares after war heroes, complete with small plaques that bore the names under a military star. Mullin may have been a veteran of World War I or World War II, no one knew for sure. The gang that first adopted his name in the late 1940s had no connection to Mullin himself; the intersection was simply in the middle of their territory, and the name Mullin had a nice Irish ring to it. And so the Mullin Gang was born.

The original rulers of the gang were mostly World War II veterans who worked as longshoremen, men like Roger Kineavy, Pete Mansfield, and Wally Mansfield. A later generation took control over of the gang in the late 1950s—most notably Mickey McDonough and Mikey Ward, who were both veterans of the Korean War. These men often gathered at a Teamsters hiring hall located on the South Boston waterfront or at the Lighthouse Tavern, which was *the* gathering place for Boston hoodlums of every variety.

Pat Nee, late of Rossmuc, County Galway, made his first foray to the Lighthouse pub at the age of fifteen. An average-sized youth with a slight stutter, Nee began shining shoes in front of the bar and later ran errands for some of the area's better-known criminals. The criminals liked Pat; he was respectful but not the least bit timid. Eventually, Mickey McDonough and Mikey Ward put Nee to work, allowing him to serve as stick man for the neighborhood's card and dice games. The stick man's job was to hold the money during a game and call out "no dice" if a player's toss of the dice did not make contact with the wall—in which case the player crapped out and lost his wager, often blaming the stick man.

"You fuckin' little prick," they usually grumbled, smacking Nee on the head with an open hand.

Invariably, someone would come to Pat's defense. "Hey, leave the kid alone. He's only doin' his job."

Nee enjoyed every part of it, even the smacks to the head, because he knew it was all part of his apprenticeship as an aspiring hoodlum. "I knew about the Mullin Gang and wanted to be a part of it—desperately wanted to be a part of it," he would say years later. "At some level I guess I wanted to be a criminal, but I wasn't really thinking of it that way, you know, *criminal* in the legalistic sense of the word. I just wanted to be like those guys I saw at the Lighthouse. I wanted to do what they did. The money looked easy. At least they spent it like it was easy. I never saw the dark side, of course, the loans that went unpaid, the violence, the time in jail. That all came later."[3]

Eventually, Nee started hanging out with a group of young kids his own age who thought of themselves as junior Mullins. They often loitered in front of McGillicudy's, a pharmacy at O and Broadway, where they drank ice cream sodas and lime rickeys. Sometimes they gathered at Castle Island, an old fort located at the end of a peninsula that jutted out into Boston harbor. Castle Island was especially popular in the summer; it was in Mullin territory, a cherished spot along a stretch of the beach that was expected to be protected against outside forces—which sometimes resulted in gang confrontations.

One legendary battle took place in the summer of 1960, when a gang known as the Saints from the lower end of South Boston strutted onto the beach at Castle Island. Pat Nee, Mikey Ward, and a small group of fellow Mullin Gang members were drinking beer and lounging in the sun with their shirts off. The number of Saints who arrived at Castle Island outnumbered the Mullin Gang nearly two-to-one, and there was no time to call for reinforcements. "We only got one chance here," said Mikey Ward, the oldest

---

3. Pat Nee was interviewed by the author in Boston over a series of days in late March and early April 2004.

of the group. "Let's charge and break 'em up. They won't expect it." Pat Nee recalls

> So we all grabbed bottles and charged. Some of them scattered, and we started picking them off one by one. They fought back pretty good. I got sliced down to the bone on my left hand. They had knives, we didn't. But we were tougher that day. We gave them a brutal, brutal beating. I remember one kid's face; it looked like we fuckin' skinned him he got kicked so often. Others had jumped or got thrown in the water to get away from us. They dog paddled over to a big wooden raft, but we had a guy on the raft with a two-by-four. He was hitting them in the head and kicking them, trying to beat them back into the water. That was one of the roughest gang battles I ever saw. We all had cuts, concussions, broken noses. But they got the worst of it.

By the early 1960s, the Mullins were the dominant gang in the neighborhood, having supplanted the Saints, the Red Wings, the Shamrocks, and other gangs, some with roots going all the way back to the 1920s. The Mullin Gang was sprawling and haphazard, with no real hierarchy. And their activities weren't related to any organized form of racketeering—not yet, anyway. The various gang wars that took place revolved mostly around issues of friendship and loyalty. When your friends were in trouble, you could help in any number of ways. You could be an observer, a gatherer of information, or you could be a fighter, which was a primary way of distinguishing yourself within the gang.

Gang battles and acts of loyalty were one thing, but the primary reason Pat Nee had become a Mullin was to become a professional crook. By the age of seventeen, he was ready for the big time. For his first significant act of pilferage, he chose a location he knew would not only net a decent score but also attract maximum attention from the neighborhood's criminal elite: the Lighthouse Tavern.

Nee and two accomplices broke into the venerable gangster hangout through a bathroom window. They fleeced the cigarette machines, stole cases of booze, and cleaned out the money drawer beneath the bar. Afterward, when it became known around Southie that Pat Nee and a crew of young Mullins had the balls to rob the Lighthouse, they became famous in the neighborhood. Spurred on by the notoriety, the Mullins grew in stature; they were well on their way to becoming one of the most impressive collection of thieves, stick-up artists, B & E men, bank robbers, safe-crackers, and hijackers the city of Boston would ever know. According to Pat Nee

> We got to be very good at what we did. One of our better thieves was Paulie McGonigle; he was great at tailgaiting and hitting the docks. Jimmy Lydon was good, especially with B & Es. Paulie and them had their own crew. They were doing drug stores all over Boston. Pharmaceuticals. They would hit those places and sell the drugs. Plus there were safes with money in there. Back then the safes were fairly simple. You could crack them open with a pinch bar, a good hammer and chisel. We had crow bars we stole from the fire department that gave you the leverage you needed to pry open the safe. Paulie and his crew got caught one night in Newton. That was big. Paulie got away, I believe, but the others went to jail. A guy in that crew turned informer, which was highly unusual back then. We knew who it was, but we didn't bother the guy. He was young, and he'd been beaten very badly by the Newton cops. They broke his jaw, his nose, and kept on beating. Back then the cops were allowed to beat you—and they would. None of us ever thought of pressing brutality charges. You were just happy to get out of there alive.

Getting caught or bloodied by cops did not slow down the Mullin Gang. They became especially notorious along the Boston waterfront, where they raided the commercial piers on almost a weekly basis. "We stole any place we could steal and sold it to whoever could afford it," said Nee. Shipments of TVs, stereos, and clothing were good, but foodstuff like hams, crabmeat, and tuna were even better. The Mullin gang shipped their stolen merchandise to a professional fence either in Boston, Providence, or New York City. "The people we dealt with were solid, honorable professionals," remembers Nee. "We rarely had problems—unless we screwed up ourselves." One time the Mullin Gang did mess up when they set out to boost a coveted shipment of crabmeat and tuna and wound up instead with a truckload of women's cosmetics. Not having any concept of the resale value of women's cosmetics, the gang drove the shipment to a housing project in Southie and told the women to help themselves. Nee called his contact in New York and told him, "We grabbed the wrong truck. We got nothing but broad's cosmetics."

"What did you do with them?" asked the guy.

"We gave them away."

"Are you nuts!? Do you have any idea how much that stuff is worth? Its worth more than the stuff you were going to take. Get that truck back. Get that stuff over here."

It was too late. The women of South Boston had cleaned out the truck, and the Mullin Gang had lost a valuable shipment.

Mostly, the gang got the job done, even if individual gang members did get pinched on a regular basis, in which case they reached out to Dudda Flaherty, the neighborhood bail bondsman. Flaherty had them back on the street in no time, and they were soon planning their next act of professional pilferage. They moved on from the piers in Southie to the docks downtown, which were bigger, with more valuable cargo and better security. But no waterfront operation was safe from the thieving ways of the Mullin Gang.

A business owner whose warehouse was located on a prominent downtown pier once told Pat Nee and his fellow gangsters, "I know you water rats been robbing these piers blind, but you'll never get my place. The security is too good." The Mullin Gang took this as a challenge. They began to case the man's place of business, Federal Liquor Distilleries, a huge brick warehouse sandwiched between a fish company and another warehouse. They determined that the doors and windows were all wired with alarms. The building's ceiling was not wired, but the roof was exposed to a roadway overpass, so that anyone trying to break in from there would be spotted by cars driving by. The only possibility was to go in through the loading dock of the fish company next door. You could back a truck up all the way to the wall and break through the brick without being seen or tripping any alarms.

And so they did. A six-man crew, led by Pat Nee, hit Federal Liquor Distilleries at three o'clock in the morning. Dressed in black with black ski masks, they backed a large produce truck flat against the building's wall. They rolled up the truck's back gate and—from inside, undetected by night watchmen or other passersby—hammered away at the building's brick wall with crow bars and sledge hammers. A sheet of plywood was laid down to catch falling rubble. If debris did fall to the pavement, someone hopped down and swept it up, so there would be no visible remnants of the wall being taken apart.

A member of the robbery crew was stationed high on a nearby billboard, with a commanding view of all roadways. Using binoculars, he surveyed the surrounding area. If cops or detectives approached, he notified the break-in crew over a walkie-talkie. "Little Red" was the code for a patrol car, "Big Red" for a detective unit. If the message "Big Red is coming" came over the walkie-talkie, the break-in crew pulled in the plywood, closed up the truck, and everyone froze in their positions. A patrol unit might pull right into the parking lot and see the truck alongside other trucks and vehicles that were parked overnight; unless they examined the truck closely, looking through the tight six-inch space between the back of the truck and the wall, there was no way they could see the gaping hole in the side of the building. "All clear," the lookout whispered into the walkie-talkie once the unsuspecting cops drove off. The crew resumed banging away at the wall.

It took forty minutes to break through the wall and into the warehouse. From there, it was a piece of cake; working from a list, the thieves began carting crates of booze through the wall into the back of the truck. Canadian Mist, Seagram's Seven, Old Thompson's. Common bar booze was more popular than top-shelf liquor because it was easier to unload on the Black Market. It took less than an hour to grab nearly every case of booze in the warehouse. Before they left, the crew broke into the office of the owner—the very man who had challenged the Mullin Gang by saying that they would never be able to penetrate his security system. One of the crew opened the owner's desk drawer and defecated inside, leaving behind a card that read: "Having a great time, wish you were here. Yours truly, the Mullin Gang."

Explained Pat Nee, "He'd shown his contempt for us, so we had to show our contempt for him."

The robbery at Federal Liquor Distilleries was a good clean score. Afterward, the owner never said a peep to the Mullin Gang.

There were other robberies, well-thought out, professionally executed, with financial returns that usually made them well-worth the risk. Various Mullin crews distinguished themselves at different aspects of the craft: some were good with safes, some talented second-story men, some cat burglars par excellence. The gang conducted robberies far from their original Southie territory without any problems, until one day in early 1961, when they hit a prominent trucking company based on a dock in the heart of downtown Boston. Following that robbery, Nee and a few leading members of the gang were summoned to appear in Somerville, a district just north of the Boston city line that was the home base of a well-known racketeer named Howard Winter.

"We knew who Howie Winter was," said Nee. "We knew him by reputation. He was a more established criminal than we were, more connected. So we went out there to see what he had to say." Nee and the Mullins met Winter at a garage in a section of Somerville known as Winter Hill.

Howie Winter was in his mid-thirties, slight of build, with curly, brown hair and beady eyes. Despite the fact that his birthday was on March 17, St. Patrick's Day, Winter was not Irish; he was Italian and German. Although he was known primarily as a racketeer and businessman and not a man of violence, Winter was affiliated with some of the toughest criminals in the Boston area, including the city's main Mafia organization based in the North End, adjacent to Somerville.

"That trucking company you hit downtown?" Winter said to the assembled Mullin gangsters at his garage headquarters.

"Yeah?" said Pat Nee.

"They're with me."

A moment of tension passed between the men before Nee finally spoke. "Okay, Howie, no problem. From now on, we'll stay away from your interests."

"Good," said Winter, adding quickly, "Now those other companies down there, that's a horse of a different color . . ." Howie suggested that whenever the Mullin Gang hit other trucking companies and warehouses anywhere in town, they should "come over to Winter Hill, and we'll help you move product. How's that sound?"

Pat Nee saw the possibilities immediately. Howie Winter was an underworld mover and shaker, tied in with a much higher level of criminal activity than the Mullin Gang. Specifically, Winter had a major interest in gambling rackets all over the Boston area. The dogs, the ponies, and policy were the big moneymakers in the underworld, low risk and high gain. Howie had a piece of it all, and he was offering to cut the Mullin Gang in on his action if they dealt exclusively with him and his people.

"You got a deal," Nee told Howie Winter.

The alliance between the Mullin Gang and the Winter Hill operation represented a seismic shift in the Boston underworld, one that would not be fully understood for years to come. The immediate result was that Pat Nee and his crew found themselves spending a lot less time thieving and more time involved in high-end rackets and union-related activities. Many of the Mullin gang were already card-carrying members of the Teamsters and longshoremen's unions, so they were naturally put to work as labor agitators. During one especially violent Teamster strike in early 1962, Nee and a handful of Mullins were used as head bangers. They mixed in with union picket lines; when a truck operated by a scab driver approached, they hopped up on the truck and cracked the driver over the head with a blackjack, then faded back into the crowd or down an alleyway.

"We got a good day's pay for that," remembers Nee.

The relationship with Winter Hill paid financial dividends for the Mullins and vice versa, but that was not the reason Howie Winter had been so eager to bring the notorious Southie gang into the fold. While Winter and Pat Nee were making kissy-face, the Boston underworld was in the beginning stages of a major war. Much of this conflict would take place in the city's northern provinces—Somerville, Charlestown, East Boston, and the North End. Already there had been a number of gangland killings. Pat Nee and the Southie crowd were only vaguely aware of what was going on at the time. Before it was over, they would be major players in the most sustained period of underworld violence the city of Boston had ever known.

Boston Gang Wars, Part I

It all started back in 1961, on Labor Day, when two gangsters affiliated with the Winter Hill Gang rented a cottage on Salisbury Beach with their two girlfriends and an old pal named George McLaughlin. McLaughlin was a member of a notorious crew of crooks and contract killers who were friendly with Winter Hill and based in the neighborhood of Charlestown.

Located at the northern edge of Boston on a peninsula between the Mystic and Charles rivers, Charlestown was, like Southie, separated from the rest of the city by bridges and water. The origins of Charlestown are steeped in revolutionary history; the area was the site of the Battle of Bunker Hill, one of the earliest and most significant battles in the Revolutionary War. Nearly a century after the United States gained its independence, the peninsula of Charlestown was annexed to Boston and became a center of the city's maritime industry. The neighborhood became a classic longshoreman's enclave, with successive generations of Irish immigrant families working the docks. Georgie McLaughlin came from a dock worker family and had himself apprenticed as a longshoreman until he fell in with a tough crowd from nearby Winter Hill and became more of a hoodlum than a laborer.

At the cottage on Salisbury Beach, McLaughlin and his friends drank all day and into the evening. At some point, Georgie—who, at the age of twenty-two, was known to be an ardent imbiber—grabbed the breast of a girlfriend of a Winter Hill gangster. This act led to a heated discussion, which escalated into an argument and resulted in the two Winter Hill gang members giving Georgie McLaughlin the beating of a lifetime.

"Is he dead?" asked one of the guys looking down at Georgie, who was unconscious and covered with blood.

"I don't know," said the other guy. "Let's get him out of here."

The two men loaded McLaughlin into the back seat of their car, left their girlfriends, and drove to a nearby hospital. They dumped Georgie's body on the front lawn of the hospital, having no idea whether he was dead or alive.

After driving away, the two gangsters stopped at a bar in Somerville and had a few more drinks, the better to absorb the nights events. Eventually, it dawned on them that they might be in a world of trouble. Georgie McLaughlin, after all, was the younger brother of Bernie McLaughlin, leader of the Charlestown gang who occasionally did hits for some of the biggest mobsters in town. Comprised of three McLaughlin brothers, Georgie, Bernie, and Edward (whom everyone knew as "Punchy"), and the Hughes brothers, Stevie and Connie, the Charlestown boys were serious players in the underworld who, again, were friendly with the Winter Hill gang. In light of all this, the two men who had just beaten Georgie McLaughlin to a bloody pulp surmised that, unless they explained their actions to their superiors, pronto, they might wind up on somebody's hit list.

"Hey," said one Winter Hill guy to the other, "we better get over to Somerville and tell Buddy about this."

"Yeah," agreed his partner. "Before the McLaughlins or Hughes brothers get over there first and tell Buddy a pack of lies."

The "Buddy" to which the two men referred was James J. "Buddy" McLean, the unofficial Irish godfather of northern Boston. There was no more revered figure in the local underworld than Buddy McLean, originator of the Winter Hill Gang in Somerville. McLean was a longshoreman and racketeer who had built an impressive following based on his legendary toughness. But he was also believed to be a fair man, and so the two Winter Hill gangsters rushed to his home on Snow Terrace in Somerville and explained to Buddy how the McLaughlin beating had come about.

"It's a good thing you told me," McLean said to his Winter Hill associates when they finished their version of the story, "because I already heard all about it. Georgie's in intensive care right now, but he's going to make it. When he gets out, I'll see if we can't get you boys to bury the hatchet."

The two Winter Hill gangsters went home. Buddy McLean had absolved them of all responsibility, and in doing so moved himself to the front and center of a dispute that, before it was over, would claim the lives of around sixty men and become one of the most violent gang wars in American history.

In the vernacular of the underworld, Buddy McLean was a tough motherfucker. His upbringing was a classic rage-to-riches waterfront saga. Born in 1930, he'd been orphaned at a young age and later adopted by immigrant Portuguese parents. By the age of eighteen, he was working the docks in Charlestown and East Boston as a card-carrying member of the ILA. He was also a close boyhood friend of William J. McCarthy, who would go on to become president of the International Brotherhood of Teamsters.

In 1955, Buddy married a local Portuguese nurse, quickly had two children, and moved into his modest home on Snow Terrace in the Winter Hill section of Somerville. The neighborhood was mostly blue-collar Irish and Italian at the time, with many bars, lounges, and clubs along the main thoroughfare of Broadway.

McLean was medium-sized with blond hair, boyish good looks, and piercing blue eyes. He was tough and had distinguished himself in numerous labor battles and barroom disputes, one of which had left him with scars on his neck and permanent damage to his left eye. Despite his fearsome reputation, McLean was well-liked by most who knew him and his crew spanned ethnic lines, Irish, Italian, Portuguese, black, you name it. The Winter Hill Gang, as established by Buddy, dabbled in everything from numbers and loan-sharking to truck hijackings and waterfront pilferage. The gang was comprised of some of the most hardened old-school hoods in the city, including a young Howie Winter, a former cop turned gangster named Russell Nicholson, a veteran thief from Charlestown named Tommy Ballou, and Joseph "Joe Mac" McDonald, a legendary strong-arm man whom Mullin gangster Pat Nee knew as "probably the toughest guy that ever was. Joe Mac was one of those rare people who was fearless without being a psychopath. He was utterly without fear of anybody or anything or any situation, but he was also a very likable guy."

The Winter Hill Gang under Buddy McLean often gathered at a bar known as the Tap Royal, at the Winter Hill Athletic Club, or at the 318 Club (later known as Pal Joey's), all located on Broadway. In the tradition of Irish gangs going back to the days of the Dead Rabbits and the Whyos, Buddy presided more as an equal than as a boss. His approach inspired loyalty and fear among his followers. Said one old-time Winter Hill associate of McLean

> I remember his hangout, the Tap Royal on Broadway. Buddy used to have a stool in the back against the wall facing the door that was his. Even if the bar was packed and Buddy wasn't there nobody sat on his stool. I made the mistake one time of sitting on it. Right when I did, about five guys yelled, "That's Buddy's stool!!" Well let me tell you, I was up and out of that stool faster than lightening. 'Cause Buddy was a real tough, tough guy. He used to fight everywhere. The bars, the streets, the nightclubs, the docks. . . . The thing that threw you off was his baby face. One guy summed it up perfectly when he said about Buddy, "He looks like a choir boy but fights like the devil."

Even Raymond Patriarca, boss of the Patriarca crime family in Providence, revered Buddy McLean. One day Patriarca was caught on an FBI wiretap calling McLean "a real sweet guy" and "a facilitator." With his most trusted associate, Howie Winter, Buddy made biweekly trips to the Federal Hill section of Providence to meet with Patriarca and discuss various deals. McLean's ability to reconcile mobster factions of every class and ethnicity must have made him confident that he could resolve whatever hard feelings might arise from the vicious beating of Georgie McLaughlin.

On the day McLaughlin was released from the hospital—exactly one month after being admitted—his brother Bernie paid a visit to Buddy McLean at his home in Somerville. Bernie had known McLean for years; it was Buddy who usually acted as a go-between for the Charlestown boys and the Patriarca crime family, who often employed the McLaughlin and Hughes brothers for professional hits and other acts of mayhem.

With regard to the beating of Georgie McLaughlin, Buddy was disturbed to hear that the Charlestown boys were not about to let sleeping dogs lie.

"I want 'em dead," Bernie McLaughlin said of the two men who nearly killed his brother.

"For that I can't give you permission," responded McLean.

"Permission?" said Bernie. "Who said anything about permission? I want you to help me set 'em up."

McLean flatly refused. Bernie McLaughlin cursed his former friend, spat on the floor, and stormed out of the house.

Later that night, McLean awoke to the sound of dogs barking outside his home. When he looked out his window, he saw two men standing near his car, parked at the curb. He grabbed a .38 revolver, opened his front door, and fired shots at the men; they scampered away. McLean walked over to his car and examined it carefully. Underneath the hood he found a bomb made of plastique wired to the ignition.

Buddy McLean had gotten as far as he had in the underworld because he was a man of action. Instinctively, he knew who put the bomb under the hood of his car—the McLaughlin brothers. He also knew that the McLaughlins were relentless. Like many in Charlestown, the McLaughlins traced their Irish ancestry to County Donegal, bandit country in the far north of Ireland. No one held a grudge quite like the Donegal Irish; they were tough, fearless, and did not know how to back down. Knowing this, McLean did not spend much time deliberating about what needed to be done. The very next day, he began stalking Bernie McLaughlin. Then on Halloween, at twelve noon in City Square, Charlestown, in the shadow the Bunker Hill Monument, McLean shot his prey dead in front of nearly one hundred people. Not one witness would offer evidence against Buddy McLean, but he was arrested on a gun possession charge and sent away to prison for two years.

The very week McLean was released from the penitentiary, Georgie McLaughlin shot and killed a man he heard saying nice things about Buddy at a party in Roxbury. Only, Georgie shot the wrong man. When he overheard the comment, he went to get a gun, returned, and wrongfully shot Billy Sheridan, an innocent victim. Sheridan's death was typical of the kind of killings that were to dominate the Boston underworld now that Buddy McLean was back on the street.

The murders came fast and furious. On May 3, 1964, an ex-con named Frank Benjamin was heard bragging about how he was going to take out the whole Winter Hill crew, starting with McLean. A gunman loyal to Winter Hill shot Benjamin in the head. Because it happened in a bar in front of twenty witnesses, the gunman felt he needed to burn the establishment to the ground. He also talked about taking Frank Benjamin's severed head and placing it on Punchy McLaughlin's doorstep, but he decided against it. The day after the shooting, Benjamin's body was found in the trunk of a stolen car in South Boston, minus its head, which had been buried in the woods.

A week later, the Charlestown boys struck back, killing Russell Nicholson, the six-foot-seven ex-cop who had been serving as Buddy McLean's bodyguard. One month later, the Winter Hill Gang got revenge. Two Charlestown hoods were lured to an apartment by a woman friend of theirs. When they arrived at the apartment, Buddy McLean and a few of his men were there waiting. Before killing them, McLean held a blowtorch to their genitals to get information. After finding out what he needed to know, he strangled them both and dumped the bodies in Boston Harbor.

On September 4, the bullet-riddled body of Ronald Dermody was found in his car at a red light in Watertown. The case of Ronnie Dermody was a strange one. According to underworld folklore, Dermody was in love with a woman known simply as Dottie from Dorchester. Dottie, however, was in love with another guy. So Dermody approached Georgie McLaughlin with a stellar proposition. If McLaughlin would kill Dottie's boyfriend, paving the way for Dermody to marry his truly beloved, Dermody would kill Buddy McLean. To show how sincere he was, Dermody would take the initiative and kill McLean first. On September 2, Dermody stormed into the Capitol Café on Broadway in Winter Hill and gunned down a man he thought was big bad Buddy McLean. Unfortunately for Dermody, it wasn't; he had shot a petty thief by the name of Charlie Robinson. When McLean heard what happened and put two and two together, he ordered Dermody's execution.

Throughout 1964 and into 1965, the war continued: gunshots, knifings, and strangulations occurred in the dead of night, as the body count grew. Some of the killings were brazen, out in the open, while others were sneaky and surreptitious. Men disappeared and were never heard from again. In Charlestown and Winter Hill, people kept their mouths shut. Many of the murders never even made the newspapers, and most of the killings were never solved or even seriously investigated. In Boston, the underworld existed far below the radar. Sports and politics were the dominant topics of the day. The country was still grieving the assassination of their beloved president, while in the city of J.F.K.'s earliest professional accomplishments, the bloodletting was unprecedented with so many dead bodies that, had they been laid out, head to toe, they might well have spanned the entire Freedom Trail.

By 1965, the Winter Hill Gang was determined to nail Punchy McLaughlin. The feeling was that, if they could eliminate Punchy and his unquenchable Irish thirst for revenge, maybe the killings would stop. To do the job, Buddy McLean turned to a Mafia hit team led by Frank "Cadillac Frank" Salemme and Joe Barboza, an Italian-Portuguese killer who would later become famous as one of the first criminals to enter the Witness Protection Program. Twice in early 1965 the Salemme-Barboza hit team ambushed Punchy McLaughlin. The first time, the killers came dressed as rabbis and shot their target in the parking lot of Beth Israel hospital. Punchy lived but lost half his jaw. The second attempt was even sloppier; they ambushed McLaughlin in a suburban neighborhood, shooting off his right hand and spraying a number of surrounding homes with gunfire.

The attempts on Punchy's life were well-known events in the city's underworld, and in October 1965 hitman Frank Salemme was approached by a local FBI team of Agent H. Paul Rico and Agent Dennis Condon, a veteran G-man duo who had been circulating in the Boston underworld for years. Rico, in particular, was a star in the local FBI office, well-known for his ability to turn informants. With his black hair and olive complexion, Rico looked Italian, but he was actually of Spanish and Irish descent. A scheming, Machiavellian figure, Agent Rico had a well-known animosity toward the McLaughlin-Hughes faction of the Irish Mob. Among other things, he believed that they had incriminating information on the fact that he was a closet homosexual who occasionally had dalliances with underage boys.[4]

---

4. A good source on the underworld manipulations of FBI agents Paul Rico and Dennis Condon (and on the Boston gang wars in general) is the 154-page April 2003 congressional testimony of Frank "Cadillac Frank" Salemme, who became a govern-

After the second bungled attempt on Punchy McLaughlin, Agent Rico approached Cadillac Frank Salemme and said, "Boy, that was some sloppy work on your part. What are you guys—amateurs?"

"The problem," said Salemme, "is that we don't know where he's been hiding out; we don't know his address. If we had that we could track him from the moment he leaves his house."

Agent Rico nodded and said nothing. Two days later, he approached Salemme at a Boston diner and handed him a slip of paper.

"What's this?" asked Salemme, looking at the paper.

"That's the address of Punchy's girlfriend. He's been living with her."

Using the address provided by the FBI agent, Mafia hitman Salemme picked up McLaughlin coming out of his girlfriend's house on October 20, 1965. At a nearby bus stop, Punchy was shot nine times, twice in the genitals and once in the face.[5]

The killing of Punchy McLaughlin did not stop the bloodletting. On the contrary, eleven days after the bus stop murder, the Charlestown crew struck back and netted the biggest trophy of all—Buddy McLean. They got him coming out of the Tap Royal, his favorite bar. The killers were the fearsome Hughes brothers.

Howie Winter was now the undisputed leader of the Winter Hill Gang. A conciliatory person by nature, it was hoped in many quarters that Howie would try to negotiate some kind of settlement. Winter had himself survived one attempt on his life—a bomb planted under his car that detonated

---

ment witness in the late 1990s after admitting to having carried out more than a dozen contract murders for the mob.

5. The role played by agents Paul Rico and Dennis Condon in the Boston gang wars of the 1960s represents one of the most sinister violations of the public trust in FBI history. Rico, in particular, was a diabolical figure; he fed information to selected gangsters that resulted in countless underworld deaths. He once heard, through an FBI wiretap, of a planned hit against a small-time Irish gangster named Edward "Teddy" Deegan. Rico said nothing and allowed the hit to go off as planned, then sat back and did nothing as the wrong men were prosecuted and convicted for the murder.

In 1975, Rico retired from the FBI and lived in splendor in Miami Shores, Florida, where he became director of security for World Jai Alai, a sports betting enterprise. In October 2003, Rico was arrested for murder. Back in 1981, he had helped James "Whitey" Bulger, the mob boss of South Boston, to set up and kill the millionaire owner of World Jai Alai (see Chapter Fourteen).

At his arraignment, Rico was asked if he had any remorse for his long life of treachery and crime. "Remorse?" said the former FBI agent. "For what? Do you want tears or something?" In early 2004, before he could be prosecuted for murder and other charges, Paul Rico died of natural causes at the age of seventy-nine.

while he was still inside his house. The problem was that negotiating a settlement was not so easy. The Charlestown boys took pride in the fact that they had no "boss," per se; all of them were equal members of the clan. They resisted appeasement as if it were a sign of unmanliness. Although they had been reduced to just two primary members (two out of three McLaughlin brothers had been murdered, while the third, Georgie, had been convicted of homicide and sent away to prison), these were the most lethal members of the lot: Stevie and Connie Hughes.

Cadillac Frank respected and feared the Irish Hughes brothers, calling them "very capable, very dangerous guys." He and Barboza stalked the brothers for ten months. They never appeared publicly together and would have to be taken out on separate occasions. And so they were: On May 25, 1966, Connie Hughes was shot multiple times while driving on Route 1 in the suburb of Revere. Four months later, his brother Stevie met an almost identical fate; he was gunned down by Salemme and Barboza while stopped at a red light in Middleton. The legendary Charlestown crew was now completely wiped out.

From the day Georgie McLaughlin grabbed the wrong breast back in 1961 to the death of Connie and Stevie Hughes in the spring of 1966, the killings had rarely let up. It had been a strange and terrifying gangland jitterbug, an Irish version of the Hatfields and McCoys, a backwoods-style vendetta war that had nothing to do with commerce or territory or ethnic rivalry. Perhaps the war represented a kind of internal purging of the Boston underworld, an acknowledgment of a New World Order in the wake of the first Irish Catholic president and all that it represented. But that would suggest a degree of forethought, an awareness of the outside world, when in fact there was none. Rash and impulsive, the killings were based on nothing more than a deeply personal sense of grievance rooted in the dark, inbred nature of the city's Irish underworld.

Now, with most of the initial instigators of the gangland slaughter either dead or in prison, some believed the city's long period of violence was finally over. They were wrong.

Boston Gang Wars, Part II

Pat Nee of the Mullin Gang missed the most violent, early years of the Boston gang war. In 1962, not long after forming his alliance with Howie Winter, Nee saw the writing on the wall and opted for a stint in the Marine Corp. The Charlestown-Winter Hill feud was just getting underway at the time, and Nee, fully aware of the relentless nature of the Donegal Irish, sensed there was going to be a high body count. The Mullin leader had formed his partnership with Howie Winter for business reasons, not to become engulfed in a senseless slaughter that would pit Irishman against Irishman; perhaps the only real winner in such a battle would be the Patriarca crime family in Providence, who could sit back, enjoy the show, then feed off the dead carcass of the city's Irish American underworld. And so, instead of dodging bullets at the bar of the Bunker Hill Athletic Club, Pat Nee found himself with the 3rd Marine Division on a beach in South Vietnam, among the earliest of U.S. troops to set foot in the Land of the Ascending Dragon. Over the years, he took incoming fire at Phu Bai, saw American troop levels quadruple, and then returned stateside in October 1966, trading one impending quagmire for another that was already awash in blood.

For a number of months, Nee tried to live the straight life. Back in his home neighborhood of Southie, the decorated war veteran found work as a laborer. Then his cousin pulled some strings and got him into the printers union. He worked three months as a printer for the *Globe*, but the former street hoodlum found civilian life to be absurdly boring. "I tried, I really did," he said. "But the straight life just wasn't for me."

Still a young man, Nee began looking into reforming his old robbery crew. His hope was to steer clear of the kind of violent underworld carnage that had engulfed Howie Winter's Somerville operation—Strictly B & E's, waterfront pilferage, maybe a bank job if the opportunity presented itself. But Boston was an internecine universe; it was almost impossible to be a functioning criminal in the city without stepping on somebody's toes. New fault lines had been established while Nee was away in Vietnam. He was about to find out that the war that began in Somerville and Charlestown with Buddy McLean and the McLaughlins had metastasized like a cancer. It had engulfed Southie, forcing nearly everyone in the underworld to choose sides whether they wanted to or not.

Paulie McGonigle had been a Mullin Gang member almost as long as Pat Nee. The two men were close enough that they would have died for each other. Fortunately for them, that never happened, but death did become a deciding factor in their relationship when Donnie McGonigle, Paulie's brother, was gunned down in the street in early 1968. Donnie McGonigle had no connection to the Mullin Gang. He was harmless, a drinker and a lover, not a fighter. A crew of Southie gangsters led by Billy O'Sullivan trailed McGonigle home one night and took him out in a drive-by shooting. O'Sullivan, one of the most feared professional killers in Southie, mistook Donnie for his brother Paulie, who had been marked for death by an old-time group of neighborhood racketeers and mobsters known as the Killeen Gang.

The Killeen Gang was led by three brothers: Donald, Kenneth, and Edward. Donald Killeen was the boss, serving basically the same function in Southie as Buddy McLean had in Charlestown. Donald's huge head and beetle brows gave him the appearance of a brute, but he had a good head for numbers. Born in 1924, he was a bookmaker and gambling impresario from the old school, with roots going all the way back to the Gustin Gang. There had been at least five Killeen brothers; Donald's oldest brother, George, had been murdered in 1950 after being questioned by police, following the legendary Brinks Job heist in the North End. Virtually every old-time Irish crook in South Boston was affiliated with the Killeens, as were a couple of younger gunmen—including Billy O'Sullivan, better known as Billy-O.

The mistaken identity murder of Donnie McGonigle touched off the same kind of tit-for-tat pattern of revenge killings in Southie that had characterized Charlestown over the previous five or six years. In an act of vengeance for the McGonigle murder, a crew of Mullin Gang members shot and killed Billy-O in the street. Predictably, the Killeen Gang struck back, shooting and crippling a Mullin gangster named Buddy Roach. In late 1968, Eddie Killeen, the most well-liked of the Killeen brothers, committed suicide under mysterious circumstances that some considered murder . . . and on and on it went.

To outsiders, the violence in Southie was inexplicable, but to those involved it was the natural consequence of a kind of primitive street-corner code. The Mullin Gang in particular, who had a tradition of military veterans in their ranks, prized loyalty as something worth dying for. The gang was like a platoon; assaults against one gang member were effectively assaults against the entire group. This code, when fused with ethnic identity and a general sense of Southie loyalty, would be manipulated by gangsters, politicians, and community leaders. Southie would eventually become engulfed in race wars, and gentrification wars, and a fair amount of internal self-flagellation. But in the Age of Aquarius, it was mostly Southie boys killing Southie boys, with nary a word of outrage from the police, the press, or the public at large.

In early 1969, Pat Nee stopped into a bar near downtown Boston called the Mad Hatter. Far from Southie, Charlestown, or any of the other gangland hot spots in town, the Mad Hatter was a sort of demilitarized zone where members of various crews could drink and hang out, supposedly without having to worry about taking a bullet in the back of the head. It was on this particular night that Nee first met a well-known member of the Killeen Gang named James "Whitey" Bulger.

Nee knew Bulger by reputation. He was just Jim Bulger back then, before his hair receded and turned prematurely silver, earning him the nickname Whitey. Raised in Southie, Bulger was a stick-up man and bank robber who had gone off to prison at a young age and missed the early years of the Boston gang wars. Nee was intrigued by the veteran bank robber who had done time at Alcatraz prison in California. Nee suspected that Bulger, as a hitman for the Killeen Gang, had taken part in the shooting of a number of Mullin Gang members. The two gangsters from opposing camps eyed each other warily and assessed each other over drinks at the bar, while chatting about growing up in Southie and other neutral subjects.

While they were talking, a member of the Mullin Gang named Mickey Dwyer rushed into the bar. Dwyer, an ex-boxer with a harelip that made him hard to understand, was excitable in the best of times. Pat Nee looked up and did a double take at the sight of Dwyer: His nose had been completely torn off, with blood rushing down his face and all over the front of his shirt. He'd also been shot in the arm and beat up pretty badly. Dwyer was excitedly trying to explain what happened, but with the lisp, the missing nose, the bullet in the arm, and the general beating he had received, nobody could understand a word he was saying.

"Mickey," said Nee, "slow down, for Chrissake. Tell us what happened."

Turned out Mickey Dwyer had gotten into a brutal fight with Kenny Killeen at the Transit bar in Southie. Killeen shot Mickey in the arm and then bit his nose off.

"He what!?" exclaimed Nee.

"That's right, Paddy. The bastid bit my fuckin' nose off."

A couple of Mullin gangsters rushed Mickey off to the hospital, while the others said, "Fuck them Killeens. Let's go get 'em."

Whitey Bulger had been quietly watching and listening to all of this. As the only member of the Killeen Gang on the premises, he was surrounded by the enemy, although no one seemed to notice.

"You got a car?" Nee asked Bulger.

"Sure," said Whitey.

"Let's get over to the Transit."

Various Mullin gangsters piled into cars and raced toward the Transit bar, which was owned by Donald Killeen. It was only as they were driving there that Pat Nee realized he was with Jim Bulger, a member of the enemy camp. By the time all of them pulled up in front of the bar in Southie, the

Killeen brothers were long gone. "Fuck," mumbled the Mullin gangsters. Revenge would have to wait until another day.

On the street outside the bar, Nee and Bulger said their good-byes. It was an odd moment: The two men from opposing sides of Southie's underworld divide sensed that the next time they saw each other it might be from the opposite sides of a gun. But they simply shook hands and headed off in different directions.

True to form, the Southie gang war heated up, and Nee and Bulger became enemies. Their next encounter was outside the same bar, the Mad Hatter, where they'd met and conversed on the night that Mickey Dwyer rushed in with blood all over him. This time, Pat Nee was driving by the bar when a fellow Mullin said, "Hey, there's that prick Bulger." There had been a number of fresh killings in recent weeks, with the requisite increase in tension.

"Stop the car," Nee commanded.

It was after midnight, and the street outside the Mad Hatter was poorly lit. Nee was carrying a .38-caliber pistol. "Hey Bulger," he cried out, then fired off a couple shots in Whitey's direction. Bulger hit the pavement, grabbed a revolver from an ankle holster and returned fire. After exchanging a volley back and forth, Nee hopped back in his car and sped away, tires squealing.

On other occasions, Nee hid in the shrubbery across from Bulger's residence at the Old Harbor Housing Project, where Bulger shared an apartment with his mother. Every time Whitey stepped out the door, the Mullin leader cut loose with sniper fire in his direction, chasing the Killeen gangster back into his house. Sometimes Bulger would go weeks without ever leaving his mother's home, for fear that he would be cut down like a dog in the street.

The tit-for-tat Mullin-Killeen war went on for months. Meanwhile, Pat Nee sought to make a living through the usual assortment of robberies and hijackings. It was a hustle, to say the least, one that was occasionally interrupted by the vicissitudes of the gangster life—a person had be ready to avenge all slights, real or perceived.

One act that required Pat Nee's immediate attention was the murder of his younger brother Peter. On a night in April 1969, Peter Nee and a friend got into an altercation at the Coachman Bar with three neighborhood guys, two of whom were vets just back from Vietnam. Peter Nee was not a gangster or even much of a tough guy. He wasn't the one who initiated the drunken argument at the Coachman. Rather, his friend had gotten into a shoving match with Kevin Daly and Daly's two companions. From there, the fight continued throughout the night; it moved from the Coachman to

Cassidy's Bar, and finally ended up at the Iron Fort, a bar located across the street from Gates of Heaven Church. It was at the Iron Fort that Peter Nee was shot twice in the face with a .22-caliber pistol.

Within hours of the killing, Pat Nee knew who did it. There were numerous witnesses, though none who were willing to violate the neighborhood code by fingering the assailant for the cops. The word came back to Nee: Kevin Daly had pulled the trigger, aided and abetted by two others. All three men were well-known in the neighborhood and came from established Southie families. Nee set out to avenge his brother's murder.

Throughout the summer and fall of 1969, a set of circumstances considerably shortened Nee's three-man hit list. One of his brother's killers went crazy and checked himself into a mental institution, where he would stay for at least the next two decades. Another killer, a neighborhood bully who had become a Boston police officer weeks after the death of Peter Nee, was murdered in a totally unrelated barroom altercation. That left Kevin Daly, whom Pat Nee held most responsible for Peter's death.

On a rainy night in November, Nee got a call from a friend who had sponsored a Marine Corp ball in Southie that night. Kevin Daly, like Pat Nee, had served in the Marines.

"He's here," Nee's friend told him over the phone.

Nee could hear the music and revelry in the background. He knew Daly was a drinker and would be there until closing time. "Okay," said Pat. "Call me back at midnight, and let me know how he's doing."

At midnight, Nee's contact called again. "He's still here, getting drunker by the minute. We'll be closing down here at two."

"Good," said Nee. "Thanks for the info." He hung up the phone.

Nee knew where Kevin Daly lived. Immediately, he called two friends who were to act as his back-up. The three men drove over to Daly's house, parked a few blocks away, and waited. Nee remembers

The heavy rain made it difficult to see, which worked to our advantage. Me and my back-up guy waited in an alleyway, lying down behind barrels and garbage cans. We had a third guy across the street with a shotgun loaded with buck shot. Daly's two brothers were Boston cops, living in that same house; we knew that they might come running out once they heard gunfire. When they came out our guy was supposed to spray them with buckshot, chase them back into the house.

I heard Kevin Daly coming; he drove a Volkswagen with a bad muffler, so we heard him before we saw him. As luck would have it, there was a parking spot right there in the alleyway. I heard the engine turn off. With the rain pissing down, I crept up the alleyway. I had a .38 automatic, which turned out to be a mistake. I was more comfortable with a rifle, but that would have been too big for such tight quarters. He was locking his car with the key. When he turned and saw me, I was no more than two feet away. I simply told him, "Now it's your turn." And I started shooting. Hit him five times. After he went down I kicked his teeth in and spit on him in the street.

Pat Nee went home that night thinking he had avenged his brother's murder by killing Kevin Daly. A few days later, much to his surprise, Nee was arrested for assault with intent to kill and taken to Charles Street Jail. Daly, it seemed, had not died. "My brother got hit twice and died. I shot this guy five times—once above the heart, once below—and he lived. Go figure." Daly had not only survived; just when he thought he was about to expire, he had identified Pat Nee as the assailant.

Two months after the shooting, Nee was escorted into municipal court. Kevin Daly was brought in, in a wheelchair. Having miraculously and unexpectedly survived the brutal attack, Daly was now confronted with his deathbed statement, in which he had fingered Pat Nee.

"Does your client stand by his statement?" the judge asked Kevin Daly's attorney.

"Your honor," said the lawyer. "My client now believes that that statement was made under duress, in a delusionary state, and he would like to rescind that statement. The truth is he did not get a good look at whoever shot and assaulted him on the night in question."

The judge was dumbfounded, and the court was thrown into disarray. Not wanting to let Pat Nee go free, the judge threatened to prosecute Daly for perjury, but that was only a ruse. There was nothing anyone could do. Kevin Daly, a child of Southie, was reneging on his identification of Pat Nee, whose brother he had killed months earlier. Against the court's wishes, Patrick Nee was set free.

Having dodged a bullet, Nee laid low for awhile. He began to grow weary of the neighborhood's relentless cycle of violence and revenge. He wasn't a kid anymore. Through the news media, he began to follow the explosive political situation in the country of his birth—Ireland. There was a rebel war going on in the country's northern counties, with British troops storming the streets and shooting Catholic citizens dead in their homes. Nee was deeply affected by what he saw and began to wonder whether there was some way to use his daring and underworld acumen for a purpose other than personal gain. More and more, these ideas began to dominate Nee's thinking. Eventually, he would see himself less as a gangster and more as a revolutionary—a man with a higher calling.[6]

Meanwhile, the Boston gang wars continued to be the biggest boon to the local funeral business since the Battle of Bunker Hill.

Wɧitey Makes ɧis Move

Early on the evening of May 13, 1972, Donald Killeen, the Irish mob boss of Southie, celebrated his daughter's birthday at his home in Framingham, a Boston suburb. At some point during the celebration, Donald got a call. After hanging up the phone, he told his wife and father-in-law that he needed to run a quick errand and would be right back. He left the birthday party and headed outside to his car, which was parked in front of his pleasant $70,000 brick house (it had once been featured in a national magazine as a model suburban home). A few minutes later, Killeen's five-year-old daughter asked her mother, "Why is daddy shooting off fireworks out by his car?"

Donna Mae Killeen and her father rushed outside and found Donald slumped in the front seat of his car, riddled with bullets and bleeding like a sieve. By the time cops arrived, Donald Killeen, age forty-eight, was dead—the victim of a professional hit. Apparently, as soon as the Irish mob boss had settled into the front seat of his car, somebody had come up behind him with a Thompson submachine gun and opened fire. Killeen had reached for a .38 revolver that was either in the car or on his person; the revolver was found unfired on the car floorboard.

The gangland murder of the Killeen Gang boss was a monumental event in the history of Boston's underworld. The killing was swift and brutal, but not unexpected. The Southie gang wars had seemed to be heading in this direction. Like many famous, carefully planned hits, the murder would go unsolved, although everyone had a theory. Most neighborhood people sus-

---

6. In the late 1970s, Pat Nee was one of the key organizers of a major gun smuggling operation in which guns from the United States were shipped to Ireland aboard the *Valhalla*, a fishing trawler that set out from East Boston. The Valhalla was intercepted at sea, courtesy of an informant inside the Irish Republican Army (IRA), which was to receive the shipment of weapons. Nee was arrested and prosecuted on federal weapons smuggling charges; he served eighteen months in prison for the crime.

In 1989, Nee was caught in the act of robbing an armored bank vehicle; he was sentenced to thirty-seven years in prison but released early due to a legal technicality after serving eight years. Today, Nee is a retired gangster and ex-IRA gun-runner working as a laborer in South Boston. He is currently working with a writer on a memoir of his criminal years.

pected that the Mullin Gang, probably acting in consort with Howie Winter and the Winter Hill Gang, had done it

On the surface, the man who stood to lose the most by the murder of Donald Killeen was Whitey Bulger, primary muscle for the Killeen brothers. With Donald out of the picture, it was assumed that other racketeers—most notably the Winter Hill Gang—would be moving in to pick up the pieces of Killeen's operation. This put Bulger in a vulnerable position. Whitey did not have the manpower to stand his ground against a combination of Winter Hill and Mullin gangsters coming at him from all sides. For Bulger, the situation appeared bleak. But, as he would time and again over the following decades, Whitey Bulger demonstrated an uncanny ability to, in the vernacular of the streets, "turn chicken shit into chicken salad." He treated the execution of his boss not as a disaster, but as an opportunity. A few weeks after the murder, he reached out to the very men who were believed to be responsible for Killeen's death and demanded a meeting.

It was a bold move. Aside from Kenny Killeen, Donald's thuggish younger brother who once bit off Mickey Dwyer's nose in a barroom brawl, the Killeen organization had been rendered moribund. Most of the city's gunmen were of a younger generation and had aligned themselves with the Winter Hill Gang or the Italians. Bulger, therefore, was not exactly dealing from a position of strength when he walked into Chandler's, a legendary wiseguy hangout in the South End, where a meeting of the city's reigning criminal elite was about to commence. (In the Italian American underworld, such gatherings were commonly known as sit downs, whereas the Boston Irish referred to them simply as meetings—as in, "It's time we had a meetin'.")

Present at this particular get-together was Pat Nee, representing the Mullin Gang, Howie Winter of the Winter Hill Gang, numerous mafiosi including an old-time mobster from the North End named Joe Russo, and Whitey Bulger. Over the course of eight hours at Chandler's bar and restaurant, the city's multiethnic underworld leadership negotiated a settlement. Priority number one was that the city's gang wars come to an end and that everyone start conducting themselves like businessmen instead of thugs. In this regard, Whitey Bulger had a card to play. It was believed that Kenny Killeen, Donald's brother, would resist any and all encroachments on his family's considerable rackets, which included bookmaking and gambling in the city's southern wards. If Whitey Bulger could force Kenny Killeen to step aside without further bloodshed, he would have himself a seat at the underworld banquet table.

A few days later, Kenny Killeen, clad in bathrobe and slippers, stepped out onto the patio of his South Boston apartment on Marine Avenue overlooking Dorchester Bay. From somewhere in the distance, a sniper fixed Killeen in his sights. At the moment the sniper fired, Killeen bent down to pick up his morning newspaper. The bullet hit the balcony's wrought-iron railing and splintered into pieces that hit Killeen in the wrist and torso. Killeen went down, but as it turned out, the balcony's wrought-iron railing saved his life.

One week later, Kenny Killeen was limping past a car at City Point when a voice called out, "Hey Kenny." Killeen turned to see the familiar face of Whitey Bulger thrust out the passenger side window; he was holding a gun. "It's over," said Whitey. "You're out of business. No future warnings." The car drove off.

Bulger's role in the Boston gang wars became the stuff of legend. It was the beginning of a period in which the Southie gangster would be given credit or blamed for just about everything that took place in the city's criminal underworld. By the time the full story of Whitey Bulger's life and times had been recorded and mulled over by a national audience, he would hold a special place in the U.S. gangland saga as the most revered and most vilified Irish American mobster of all time.

Like many professional criminals, Bulger started out as the bad seed in his family. Born on September 3, 1929, and named after his father, James Bulger was the oldest boy in a clan of what would eventually consist of six brothers and sisters. He was nine years old when his family moved from Everett, a Boston suburb, into the Old Harbor housing project in Southie. Bulger's dad worked as a clerk at the Charlestown Navy Yard across town, while his mother assumed the traditional role of housewife with stoic devotion. From the beginning, there was something different about Jim. The other Bulger children took after their parents—conservative, disciplined, devoted Catholics, solidly middle-class. Jim's younger brother, William "Billy" Bulger, was an especially diligent student. While Billy was showing early signs of academic achievement and what would eventually be a distinguished career in politics, Jim was already in trouble with the law.

At the age of nineteen, he was arrested for assault, the result of his activities with a Southie street corner gang known as the Shamrocks. By the early 1950s, Bulger had moved on to more serious crimes, including hijackings and bank hold-ups. Whitey never graduated from high school. Instead, he joined the air force, went AWOL in Oklahoma City, and wound up in county jail in Great Falls, Montana on a sexual assault charge. When he returned to Boston, Bulger immediately fell in with a local crew of bank robbers. He was acquitted of several minor larceny charges before setting out on a robbery spree that took him from Massachusetts to Rhode Island and Indiana. After going on the lam for awhile, dying his blond hair black, he was eventually apprehended in Revere, Massachusetts, prosecuted for bank robberies in various jurisdictions, and sentenced to twenty years in federal prison.

Bulger's first stop was a federal penitentiary in Atlanta, where he was involved in a number of scuffles and spent a total of ninety days in the hole. After two years in prison, he took part in an experimental drug program in exchange for a minor reduction in his sentence. Whitey's small volunteer unit at Atlanta was part of a CIA project to find out how people reacted to LSD, a program documented in a 1977 book entitled *The Search for the Manchurian Candidate*, which exposed medical abuses by the intelligence agency. In exchange for dropping acid and submitting himself to testing, Bulger had three days a month taken off his sentence.

In late 1959, Whitey was transferred to Alcatraz. While incarcerated at the infamous "Rock" in San Francisco Bay, Whitey adopted a lifelong habit of studying World War II and military strategy, reading biographies of Rommel and Patton and dissecting battles from all sides. He also became a physical fitness buff. In July 1962, around the time Alcatraz was closed down, Bulger was transferred to a federal prison in Lewisberg, Pennsylvania before being paroled in March 1965, after serving nine years.

Upon his return to Southie, the thirty-five-year-old Bulger moved back in with his mother in the Old Harbor housing complex where he grew up. His brother Billy, by then a three–term state representative, got him a job as a courthouse janitor that paid seventy-six dollars a week. It was the classic old-style Irish arrangement—one brother pulling strings for another, trying to exert whatever influence he could to help out a loved one in need. Whitey didn't last long as a courthouse custodian, although it did serve the purpose of keeping his parole officer happy. Within the first year of his release from prison, Bulger was collecting vig and doing hits for the Killeen brothers.

Despite the fact that he was right back where he started as an inveterate Southie hood, by most accounts Whitey Bulger was not the same person he had been before he went to prison. The young Bulger had been a freewheeling, smart-mouthed punk prone to impulsive behavior. The new Bulger was disciplined and taciturn. He had spent his time in Alcatraz reading books on military history, everything from the ancient Greeks to World War II. He was a student of Machiavelli, which was de rigueur for any upwardly mobile mobster. And he had a penchant for cleanliness and overall physical health that bordered on fetishism. Exuding what would later be identified as "the Bulger mystique," he was exceedingly polite in public, and projected a courtly image even as he pistol-whipped loan shark debtors and executed selected members of the Mullin Gang.

By the time of Donald Killeen's gangland execution in 1972, Whitey was well positioned to ascend as the new Irish mob boss of South Boston. His brother Billy was a significant player in Massachusetts state politics. Although there was no indication that Billy Bulger played a role in (or even knew the full extent of) his older brother's criminal shenanigans, the relationship gave Whitey a potent symbolic edge in the local underworld. The symbiotic connection between the gangster and the politician, which had long been at the very root of the Irish Mob, was even more powerful in this case because it was contained within one family, brother to brother. The fact that Whitey and Billy never appeared together in public only added to their mystique. Just being brothers enhanced both of their careers, without either of them having to lift a finger.

The Bulger Mystique was important to Whitey. As he faced an era of uncertainty following the death of his boss, he needed every edge available to him. By the early 1970s, the underworld in Boston and other U.S. cities was entering into a new epoch whose genesis had less to do with what was happening on the streets or in the courtrooms, and everything to do with what was playing at the local bijou.

At the same time that Whitey was emerging as a major player in Boston's criminal underworld, the movies *The Godfather* (1972) and *Godfather, Part II* (1974) were filling movie houses around the country, dazzling audiences, and winning awards. Together, the two movies presented a fanciful and appealing theology of Italian American organized crime, tracing the roots of Cosa Nostra to Sicily and illustrating its emergence in New York through the fictional Corleone family. The terms "Cosa Nostra," "Mafia," or "Syndicate" are never used in *The Godfather*; instead, the film's writer and director— Mario Puzo and Francis Coppola—have their characters speak only of "the family." In the movie, the family turns out to be less of a criminal organization and more of a defender of noble values like honor, loyalty, tradition, and respect for one's elders in the midst of a sordid and corrupt world.

Since at least the days of Jimmy Cagney and *The Public Enemy*, movies had played a major role in defining the image of the gangster in American society. *The Godfather* was a new and even more powerful example of this phenomenon. Puzo and Coppola's presentation of a violent criminal tradition as an extension of old-world family values not only changed the way society viewed the Mafia; it changed the way many mafiosi viewed themselves, allowing even the most brutish of Italian American criminals to take refuge in the belief that they weren't really thugs or parasites, but part of a noble tradition that was currently enjoying new levels of deification in popular American culture.[7]

When *The Godfather* was first released, the real-life Mafia had hit an all-time low. The Valachi hearings had shattered the myth of omerta; new laws and criminal prosecutions in the late 1960s had seriously depleted families in New York, Philadelphia, Cleveland, and elsewhere. The Mafia was on the way out, but it was revived partly by Mario Puzo's book and then by a duo of cinematic masterpieces that presented Italian American criminal traditions in a manner that met with great approval from the mobsters themselves. As a result, *la famiglia* was infused with a new generation of recruits, many who fancied themselves the real-life equivalent of Sonny and Michael Corleone.

For non-Italian mobsters plying their trade in the American underworld, "the Godfather Syndrome" (as it was called in a 1977 *Time* cover story) was bound to have a deleterious effect. The Mafia had always been a part of the underworld, but now they were the star attraction. Everyone wanted to do business with "the Don." Increasingly, Italian American criminal organizations viewed themselves as part of an exclusive club. "We're in charge; you work for us," became the unofficial motto of Cosa Nostra. Emboldened by

---

7. Part of the persuasive power of the *Godfather* movies is that the story is told *solely* through the eyes of the Corleone family, with hardly a single outsider's perspective (Michael Corleone's wife, played by Diane Keaton, may be the only exception). In this regard, the movies present a striking example of how the insular Italian American mobster viewed, among other things, the role of the Irish in society. Aside from Tom Hagen, the German-Irish consigliari played by Robert Duvall, there are exactly two Irish American characters in *Godfather I* and *II*. In Part I, it's Captain McCluskey, the venal, corrupt police captain who is shot in the face by Michael Corleone. In Part II, it's Senator Pat Geary, the venal, corrupt politician who is compromised by the Corleone family, but only after he is revealed to be a soulless, hypocritical degenerate. This trend is continued in *Godfather III,* in which the primary Irish character is Archbishop Gilday (played by Irish actor Donal Donnelly), the venal, corrupt Vatican clergyman who willfully solicits a "donation" from the Mafia and is later murdered.

Taken together, the *Godfather* movies offer a blunt, undistilled interpretation of how the Irish were viewed within the Italian American underworld, with the cop, the politician, and the clergyman—all of them corrupt—fulfilling the roles that had been designated for the Irish, in real life, by Johnny Torrio, Lucky Luciano, Al Capone, and other mafiosi at the 1929 mob conference in Atlantic City. (For an insightful analysis of *The Godfather* and the role of gangster movies in American society in general, see *Crime Movies* by Carlos Clarens.)

new levels of notoriety and prestige, Mafia crews throughout the United States began to see themselves as the rightful heirs to any and all underworld rackets, regardless of historical precedent or territorial imperative.

For the Irish, this new cockiness on the part of the Mafia was less of an issue in Boston, the "greenest" of all American cities, than in other jurisdictions. In cities like New Orleans and Chicago, the Irish American mobster was virtually eradicated. In New York City, it was a whole different story.

By the mid-1970s, in the wake of "the Godfather years," the Mafia in New York had regrouped and was bigger and stronger than ever with a ruling Commission that met like the bosses of old. The Five Families—Gambino, Bonanno, Genovese, Luchesse, and Colombo—had determined that they should have a controlling interest in every racket in town. For the most part, they seized control of these rackets through a series of internal coups, in which mafiosi killed other mafiosi in an effort to stratify the business of illegal narcotics, gambling and policy, union and municipal extortion, large-scale cargo heists, the distribution of stolen goods, and so on. Since the mafia had within its operating framework a vast hierarchy of capos, consigliaris, and soldatos designed to facilitate the ebb and flow of illegal commerce, the entire American underworld willingly deferred to "the Italians," with one notable exception.

On the West Side of Manhattan, where the twentieth century version of the Irish Mob had been conceived and exalted during the glory days of Prohibition, old habits died hard. Criminal rackets that had been passed from one generation to the next still existed in this congested accumulation of tenements and saloons along the Hudson River, and the natural successors to Owney Madden, Big Bill Dwyer, and Boss Joe Ryan of the ILA were not quite ready to relinquish their piece of the pie. If the guineas wanted to move in and take over this neighborhood, it was not going to happen without the kind of gangland jockeying for position that usually resulted in dead bodies and shattered lives. And so the Irish and Italian mobsters resumed their longstanding battle with newfound ferocity, this time in the legendary cradle of the Irish Mob: Hell's Kitchen.

i left my heart in hell's kitchen

ickey Spillane was a fortunate man; he inherited the long-standing criminal rackets on the West Side of Manhattan mostly by default. As a kid, Spillane had been a numbers runner for a sweaty, 300-pound bookmaker and policy boss named Hughie Mulligan. Mulligan was soft, both figuratively and literally; he wore thick-rimmed glasses and moved with the grace of a water buffalo. His considerable stature as a bookmaker had more to do with his brains and likeability than his muscle, for Mulligan was not a violent man. He was known to be a facilitator, or bag man, a person whose sway in the underworld was based on his array of friends in city government, the police department, and among crooked contractors and shady businessmen. Mulligan had been smart enough to snatch up Mickey Spillane and turn him into a neighborhood organizer when Spillane was in his early twenties. Spillane was a handsome kid and respectful of his elders; everyone knew Mickey would one day supplant Hughie, who was from Queens and probably never should have been in charge of the neighborhood rackets in the first place.

The fact that Mulligan was running things in Hell's Kitchen was due to atrophy more than anything else. The neighborhood's rightful heir, Eddie McGrath, had fled New York City around the time of the infamous Cockeye Dunn-Squint Sheridan murder trial in the early 1950s. Ever since that trial and the Waterfront Commission hearings, the neighborhood in general had gone into a precipitous decline. This was due in part to the waterfront's dwindling appeal as an object of pilferage and plunder. Starting in the late 1950s, air freight and overland shipping via truck sent the seagoing cargo industry into a tailspin from which it never recovered. The membership of the ILA in the Port of New York dropped from a high of 40,000 in 1945 to just 18,000 by 1970. With the disappearance of all those workers, many of whom had taken part in an extortionate system that started with the shape-up, labor racketeering and peripheral moneymaking scams like policy, gambling, and loan-sharking weren't what they used to be.

Not all was gloom and doom, however. By the 1960s, when Mickey Spillane was taking over as boss of the West Side, there was a renewed sense of excitement in the air. While an Irish Catholic sat in the White House in Washington, D.C., Spillane worked out of the White House in the heart of Hell's Kitchen. The White House bar was a modest gin mill at Forty-fifth Street and Tenth Avenue from which he played the role of neighborhood benefactor, doling out favors and settling disputes like an ancient clan chieftain from the fields of Athenry. When Spillane learned a neighbor had landed in the hospital, he usually sent flowers. On Thanksgiving, turkeys went out to families in need. The man from the White House bar was especially popular with the nuns at Mount Carmel convent on West Fifty-fourth Street, to whom he made occasional donations.

What made Spillane popular—especially among neighborhood old-timers—was his sense of history. In 1960, the year of JFK's inauguration, he married into the McManus family. The McMani, as they were known to nearly everyone on the West Side, had ruled the Midtown Democratic Club since 1905. In the beginning, there was Thomas J. McManus, who first wrested control of the district leadership from the illustrious George Washington Plunkitt. After vanquishing Plunkitt, McManus became one of the most powerful district leaders in the city. When he dropped dead from a heart attack unexpectedly, the incident was treated like the passing of a monarch. Some five hundred floral pieces filled the back room of the Midtown Democratic Club, where the wake was held. Days later, New York Governor Al Smith led the funeral march of one hundred policemen and three hundred carloads of mourners.

In 1945, McManus's nephew, Eugene, proprietor of a funeral parlor on West Fifty-first Street, became district leader. Eugene McManus ruled the local Democratic club for nearly two decades until—around the same time Mickey Spillane married Eugene's daughter Maureen—his health declined, and he turned over the reigns to his son James, Maureen's brother.

The marriage of Mickey and Maureen was a big deal in Hell's Kitchen; the melding of two such archetypal neighborhood families—one criminal, the other political—carried huge symbolic weight. If Hell's Kitchen had been a wedding cake, Mickey and Maureen were the bride and groom on top, the living embodiment of the link between legitimate and illegitimate forces that had always been at the heart of the Irish Mob.

As a mobster, Mickey Spillane was more of a pseudopolitician than a tough guy; after all, he had come from the halfway respectable side of the business: bookmaking, numbers, a little loan-sharking. But like other Irish American gangsters, Spillane had grown up the hard way. His first brush with the law was in 1950 at the age of seventeen, when he was shot and then arrested by a patrolman while robbing a Manhattan movie theater. He was sent to St. Clare's Hospital, then to jail. Over the years, he would rack up twenty-four more arrests on an assortment of charges including burglary, assault, gun possession, criminal contempt, and the crime he was most often associated with, gambling. But Mickey only did short stretches in the joint, and his solicitous demeanor and neighborhood affiliations made him seem more like a gentleman gangster than a hood.

And then, of course, there was the name: Mickey Spillane. It didn't hurt at all that the most popular pulp fiction writer in America had the same name. The fact came up all the time. Once, Spillane's youngest son Bobby rushed home with a Mickey Spillane paperback he'd picked up at a Times Square candy store. "Hey pop," he said. "Did you see this?"

"Yeah," said Mickey. "I know."

"Well," asked the son, "have you read his stuff?"

"I tried," replied the father, a churchgoing Catholic. "Too much sex."

In the early 1970s, the coincidence of the two Mickeys became part of a formal inquiry when a crusading assistant D.A. dragged Spillane, Hughie Mulligan, and other West Side mobsters before a grand jury that was investigating corruption in the NYPD. Spillane, under oath, was asked a number of incriminating questions, such as: "Were you present on certain occasions when Hughie Mulligan paid bribes to police officers?" and "Have you ever assaulted anyone in an attempt to collect a usurious loan for anyone?" Other questions concerned a conversation between Mulligan and Spillane, recorded by the police, in which Mickey allegedly sanctioned the murder of a government witness.

Throughout his afternoon on the stand, Spillane refused to answer questions. Finally, the exasperated assistant D.A. asked, "Well, can you tell me this: Are you related to the other Mickey Spillane? The famous writer?" After a momentary pause, Mickey leaned over to the microphone and said, "No. But I'd be happy to change places with him at the moment." Everybody laughed, but Spillane's refusal to talk cost him a contempt charge and sixty days at the Rikers Island House of Detention.

While Spillane lost time on the street, he gained stature in his community; refusing to talk was a revered neighborhood trait. The culture of the underworld was probably as deeply ingrained in the blood and sinew of

Hell's Kitchen as in any neighborhood in the country. Unlike South Boston, which was predominantly Irish, Hell's Kitchen had always been mixed—a classic New York–style melting pot. Through criminal gangs like the Gophers and through political control of the neighborhood (courtesy of the McMani), the Irish had established an early foothold. It was Spillane's job to see to it that certain neighborhood traditions were protected from outside encroachment. In the Irish American criminal arena, that usually meant standing up to the Italians.

The Mafia had been involved in various West Side rackets at least since Prohibition, when the Combine was an ethnically diversified operation. There had been an uneasy working relationship between Irish and Italian racketeers in the neighborhood ever since. The Italians conceded the West Side docks to the Irish largely because they had their own waterfront fiefdoms in Brooklyn and New Jersey. Other areas of potential underworld commerce were more commonly in dispute; among them were two huge sources of gangland patronage, both located on the outer fringe of Hell's Kitchen territory. One was Madison Square Garden, the city's premiere sports arena, then located at Fiftieth Street and Eighth Avenue. The other was the New York Coliseum, a massive convention center at Fifty-ninth Street and Eighth Avenue.

Both of these venues employed hundreds of people. The Garden, in particular, had been a source of employment for local Hell's Kitchen residents since the day it opened in 1925, and Mickey Spillane's influence over ticket-takers, ushers, and Teamster jobs at the Garden was one of his most important symbols of power. The Coliseum, built in 1956, was another gangster's paradise, with as many as fourteen different unions involved in the daily running of the place—contractors, union management, and the mob all looking for a piece of the action.

For years, patronage jobs and rackets like gambling, policy, and loan-sharking at both the Garden and the Coliseum had been equally divided among Spillane's Hell's Kitchen Irish Mob and the Genovese crime family based in upper Manhattan. Spillane had inherited this arrangement when he succeeded Hughie Mulligan as the West Side boss. To Spillane, who was basically a neighborhood racketeer with no interest in exploring a more expansive business relationship with the Mafia, the arrangement seemed like a one-way street—a shakedown. As he once said to an underling, "Those buildings are in our territory. The Italians got no right demanding their pound of flesh."

By the 1960s, Spillane had nowhere near the muscle to even think of taking on the Italians mano a mano. Instead, he waged a guerilla war, flagrantly

violating certain ground rules that had been established by an earlier generation of mobsters. Spillane's antics elicited a degree of mutual distrust, which
no doubt took a turn for the worse when he snatched Eli Zicardi, who ran the
policy games for Anthony "Fat Tony" Salerno, boss of the Genovese family.

The snatch racket had been a common gangster activity since the earliest
days of the gangs. Spillane had been a practitioner early in his criminal
career, often snatching legitimate neighborhood businesspeople and holding them for ransom; he gave up this menacing activity once he started to
envision himself as a semilegitimate figure in the community. Kidnapping
mafiosi, however, was fair game. It was a curious aspect of Spillane's relationship with the Italians; he occasionally kidnapped wiseguys right off the
street, held them for ransom, then let them go once he was paid. The Italians
often knew that Spillane was the culprit, but they were willing to tolerate the
activity as long as nobody got hurt, and the ransom never exceeded the
$10,000 to $15,000 range.

But something went wrong with the Zicardi kidnapping. The ransom
was delivered. Zicardi, however, disappeared from the face of the earth.
There were no immediate repercussions, but Spillane must have known the
Italians would come looking for their pound of flesh.

If the relationship between the Irish Mob and Cosa Nostra had been
tense before, it was now entering a whole new era of paranoia, especially for
the neighborhood boss. Over one shoulder, Spillane had to watch out for the
guineas, who had crews and soldiers spread throughout the five boroughs of
New York. Over the other, he had to watch out for a new generation of
hoodlums coming of age in Hell's Kitchen, any one of whom might challenge his authority the minute he showed signs of weakness. It was a
predicament, to say the least, one that would pass through numerous permutations and close calls over the following months until one cold fact
became clear: As formidable an enemy as *la famiglia* might have seemed to
Mickey Spillane, the far more dangerous threat was the enemy within.

Death and Taxes

The Irish American underworld was and always had been a Darwinian universe. Those who survived did so through a combination of guile and ruthlessness. Some, like Spillane, were lucky. They ascended to the top through
attrition and being in the right place at the right time. Others had to kill to
get what they wanted.

James Michael "Jimmy" Coonan was thirteen years younger than
Spillane. Born on December 21, 1946, he grew up in Hell's Kitchen when

the neighborhood was in a transitional phase, passing through the prosperous waterfront era into the "white flight" years of the 1960s. Although there were pockets of real poverty in Hell's Kitchen, Coonan, unlike many Irish kids who got drawn into the neighborhood's glorious gangster tradition, came from a respectable middle-class background. His parents, John and Anna Coonan, were certified public accountants and the proprietors of Coonan's Tax Service located just a block away from the Coonan family home at 434 West Forty-ninth Street.

As a teenager, Jimmy was only five foot seven inches tall, but stocky, with a thick neck, broad shoulders, and a full head of striking reddish-blond hair. He showed some promise as a boxer and would later hone his skills at various penal institutions. Although he was a reasonably affable youngster, he was also known to have an explosive temper. Once, at the age of sixteen, he got in a fight with a neighborhood kid. The kid wound up in a local hospital with nearly sixty lacerations on his face and body; Coonan wound up doing a short stint at the Elmira Reformatory for juvenile delinquents.

One of young Coonan's more notable characteristics was his overriding ambition. His plans did not include school; he dropped out at seventeen and began running with the neighborhood's established criminal element. Because of his boxer's physique, it was assumed he would be one of a dozen strong-arm types, the kind of kid a more established racketeer might enlist to do the dirty work. Coonan willingly took on this role, but only as part of a larger design that involved the most renowned of underworld motivations: revenge.

Neuroscientists contend that the concept of payback is deeply rooted in human physiology; when people are wronged or insulted, a part of the brain is stimulated, the same part that triggers feelings of hunger and desire. The Irish may not have an exclusive monopoly on the notion of vengeance, but some Irishmen have been known to make it their own. The entire Irish American underworld in Boston nearly eradicated itself as the result of an overstimulated adrenal gland. The world of the gangster has always been inordinately susceptible to cycles of revenge, predicated as it is on a more direct kind of justice—street justice. This is why officers of the law sometimes refer to hot, gangster-prone neighborhoods as self-cleaning ovens.

In Hell's Kitchen, legends were based on a person's ability to do the right thing, which could mean taking matters into one's own hands. Owney Madden was able to build an underworld empire on the strength of his early reputation for revenge, which led to his ascension as boss of the Gopher Gang. Exhibiting a talent for payback was one way an Irish American hoodlum distinguished himself.

Jimmy Coonan had been weaned in Hell's Kitchen and spent time in the reformatory, which was a precursor to prison. He knew an opportunity when he saw one. Coonan had a bone to pick with Mickey Spillane, and, like an aspiring Wall Street broker fresh out of college, he seized on that fact as a way to make a name for himself in a highly competitive workplace. Back in Spillane's kidnapping days, Spillane and his crew allegedly snatched Coonan's father and held him for ransom. As Coonan would tell it over the years, Spillane pistol-whipped his father for no good reason. After a small ransom was paid, the neighborhood accountant was let go.

This act of humiliation did not sit well with young Jimmy Coonan or with his older brother Jackie. The Coonan brothers vowed to get even, first through a campaign of harassment. They routinely called the Spillane home at all hours of the day and night and said to Spillane's wife, children, or whoever else answered, "Nobody's safe in this house, you hear me? We're gonna kill every one of youse."

Mickey Spillane got wind of these calls and stormed over to Coonan's Tax Office. On the street outside the office, he slapped Jimmy Coonan's father and told him, "Leave the families out of this. Understand?"

Undoubtedly, Spillane believed that, with his reputation and standing in the community, he could force the Coonan brothers to back down. But he underestimated the extent of young Jimmy Coonan's rage. What followed was a legendary period of violence in the neighborhood that came to be known as the Coonan-Spillane Wars.

Like most underworld contretemps—at least the Irish American version—the Coonan-Spillane Wars started in the bars and spilled out into the streets. In March 1966, a neighborhood gangster affiliated with the Spillane organization was taken from a saloon on Tenth Avenue, driven to a deserted back alley in Queens, and filled with lead. It was Coonan's first known kill, undertaken with his brother Jackie and a couple of older gangsters whom Jimmy had methodically rallied to his cause. Spillane's response was to snatch one of those older gangsters, Eddie Sullivan, who had aligned himself with Coonan, and give him a beating in the back of the White House bar.

A few days later, Spillane and a group of associates were headed to a late-night card game on West Forty-sixth Street between Eleventh and Twelfth avenues. On any given night, there were half a dozen casinos operating in various Hell's Kitchen apartments, where games like blackjack, craps, and roulette were played. It made good business sense for Boss Spillane to make an occasional appearance at these casinos, as he got a sizable piece of the action. But he also happened to be a notorious addict, generally known on the street as a degenerate gambler. On this particular night, Mickey and a crew of seven or eight pals were walking along the dark street when, suddenly, someone opened fire from a rooftop. Spillane and the others all ducked for cover as bullets sprayed down like rain.

"Holy shit!" one of the crew exclaimed. "Who the fuck is that?"

Spillane leaned forward and peered up toward the roof. "It's that bug Jimmy Coonan. He's got a machine gun!"

They had to stay down for a while until Coonan ran out of ammunition. Then they scampered off to their card game.

On another occasion, in the middle of the afternoon, Coonan and Spillane were seen exchanging words on Tenth Avenue. They both pulled guns and traded fire, just like in an old-fashioned Western shootout.

For the people of Hell's Kitchen, the onset of the Coonan-Spillane Wars had ominous overtones. By the late 1960s, the era of the gangster as lovable rogue and provider of harmless vice had been buried under decades of gangland killings, exploitation of labor unions, political corruption, extortion of local businesses, and general thuggery and intimidation in the bars and on the street. For some members of the community, Spillane represented the last vestiges of decency in a tradition that had gone to seed. The fact that he was under siege seemed to be part of a larger social maelstrom that included shocking political assassinations, ongoing violence in the Vietnam War, tumultuous antiwar protests throughout the country, and a general disrespect for authority that appeared to be undermining the very foundation of American life.

In Hell's Kitchen, the fear and paranoia trickled down into the social fabric of the neighborhood and found its focus in the Coonan-Spillane Wars. Nearly everyone was forced to take sides. Rumors swirled that Spillane had flown in professional hitmen from Texas and Boston to take out Jimmy Coonan. The Coonan brothers began to circulate in the neighborhood, establishing alliances and demanding loyalty oaths from bar owners and tough guys. In a tight, cloistered community like Hell's Kitchen, where the Coonans and Spillanes were both well-known, residents found themselves in a dangerous position.

One night in March 1966, an old-time bartender at Pearlie's Bar on Ninth Avenue was accosted by the Coonan brothers and Eddie Sullivan. They looked demented, as if they'd been up for several nights without sleep. Sullivan, a large brute of a man, carried a black chrome submachine gun partially concealed by his trench coat.

"Where's Spillane?" eighteen-year-old Jimmy Coonan demanded of the bartender.

"He was in here this morning," said the man, "but I ain't seen him since."

The older Coonan, Jackie, glared at the bartender. "Whose side you on anyway?"

"What?"

"Don't play dumb. You heard me."

The bartender hemmed and hawed. He knew the Coonans well—in fact, John Coonan, Jimmy and Jackie's father, had been the best man at his wedding. But he was also friendly with Spillane, with whom he played cards on a weekly basis and thought of as the neighborhood godfather. "Come on Jackie," he said. "I'm on nobody's side, you know that. I walk right down the middle."

There was mumbling among the three gangsters. The bartender thought he heard Jackie say, "He's a fuckin' liar, and we oughta get rid of him." To which Jimmy said, "No, he's okay. Let him live." The Coonans moved on that night; the incident was just one example of the perilous nature of friendship in Hell's Kitchen during the time of the Coonan-Spillane Wars.

On April Fool's Day, 1966, Jackie Coonan got spooked at a bar in Queens and shot the bartender dead. He was arrested on the spot and hauled off to jail.

Shaken by his brother's incarceration, Jimmy Coonan only became more desperate and paranoid. Three nights after Jackie Coonan's arrest, Jimmy, Eddie Sullivan, and two others from their crew were getting drunk at an East Side bar called the Pussycat Lounge. Eddie Sullivan got into a heated discussion with two male patrons and became convinced that they were hired hitmen flown into New York by Spillane. Sullivan and Coonan produced police badges and pretended to be cops. They rounded up the two patrons and drove them across the Fifty-ninth Street bridge into the borough of Queens. In a vacant lot across from Calvary Cemetery, they stopped, took the men from the car at gunpoint, and stood them up against a stone wall. Then they shot them both, hitting one directly in the face and the other multiple times in the body, and left them for dead. Miraculously, one of the victims survived; from a gurney in a hospital emergency room, he was able to give the police a detailed account of what went down.

A week later, detectives from the 108th Precinct in Queens tracked down Coonan, Sullivan, and the others at a flophouse apartment where they had been hiding out. All four gangsters were arrested and held on various charges, including murder in the first degree. Thirty-seven days later, they were brought shackled into Queens County Courthouse. The man who had survived the shooting was wheeled into the courtroom on a gurney. Before a grand jury, he identified Eddie Sullivan as the shooter and Jimmy Coonan and the others as his accomplices. What the witness remembered most vividly was the noise that his assailants made after he was filled with lead and left to die in the lot across from Calvary Cemetery.

"I heard footsteps going back to the car," he said. "I heard the doors shut, and I heard a hysterical kind of laughter. It wasn't like somebody told a joke; it was almost an animalistic kind of laughter coming from the car."

All four men were indicted. Eddie Sullivan, a three-time loser, was convicted and given a life sentence. Jimmy Coonan plea-bargained and wound up getting five to ten for felonious assault. He served his time quietly at an assortment of prisons, including Sing Sing, where he was reunited with his brother Jackie.

Four years later, having finagled an early release, Coonan was back on the street, older but not necessarily wiser. He worked for a time as a carpet installer, which was nothing more than a ruse to satisfy his parole officer. Within months, he was up to his old tricks—hijacking warehouses, sticking up liquor stores, and (taking a page from Mickey Spillane) kidnapping local merchants.

In early 1971, just five months after his release from prison, Coonan and two accomplices kidnapped a taxi broker from Staten Island who was supposed to be mobbed up. The snatch job took a sudden turn for the worse when the kidnapee escaped from the trunk of the car he was being transported in, and, with his hands still in cuffs, fled on foot through Times Square until he found a cop. Jimmy had to go into hiding for a few months. He was eventually arrested on a kidnapping charge, but the case was dropped when the victim refused to testify in court.

Coonan dodged a bullet on that one, and he knew it. He also knew his luck wasn't going to last forever. At the age of twenty-five, he began to sense that he needed a right-hand man, someone who was at least as violent as he was, but maybe not as ambitious or conniving. In the underworld, it was a sign of stature to have underlings, people willing to do the dirty work and, more importantly, take the fall when criminal schemes went haywire. In Hell's Kitchen, there was no shortage of wayward youths willing to fill the role. In time, Coonan would find his young hooligan, a troubled soul who would prove to be a more-than-worthy bodyguard, but also, ultimately, Jimmy's undoing. The kid's name was Francis "Mickey" Featherstone.

Back from Vietnam

To many Americans, it may come as an unpleasant fact that a sizable number of gangsters throughout history were either created or seasoned in the cauldron of war. The GI Bill may have offered a path out for many young men from tough neighborhoods, but it could also be a road to nowhere, an emotional and psychological cul-de-sac that left some men staring into a world of darkness. In the military, men are taught how to kill, and some even get to practice the craft. Some come home scarred by the experience. In the post–Civil War years, gangs like the Whyos drew many of its members from the ranks of the Union Army—veterans who had taken part in battles of incomparable brutality. World War I produced Wild Bill Lovett, one of the most decorated soldiers in the war, who came home to establish a new identity as a homicidal enforcer along the Brooklyn waterfront. The Mullin Gang in Boston was created by World War II veterans, named after a prominent war veteran, and recharged every few years by the ranks of soldiers coming home from other conflicts such as the Korean and Vietnam wars.

For at least 150 years, service in the military has been an especially proud tradition among Irish Americans, many of whom first overcame discrimination in the United States by proving their loyalty on the battlefield. The Fighting 69th Regiment, an Irish unit originally comprised of men mostly from Hell's Kitchen, was established during the Civil War and reconstituted in World War I. The unit's exploits were turned into a popular Hollywood movie, *The Fighting 69th*, starring none other than Jimmy Cagney. The neighborhood's proud tradition of service continued in World War II with the 165th Infantry, another regiment made up mostly of Hell's Kitchen natives.

Throughout the early years of the Vietnam War, young men in the neighborhood continued the tradition and volunteered in large numbers. All they had to do was walk a few blocks east to the Times Square army recruitment center and sign on the dotted line. One of the many young men to make this walk was Mickey Featherstone, a scrawny, tousled-haired kid from West Forty-third Street. Featherstone would spend twelve months in Indochina and return with a penchant for violence that outstripped even Jimmy Coonan's. Mickey's damaged psyche and hair-trigger reactions to all slights perceived or otherwise would come to define a new generation of Irish American gangsters in the post-Vietnam era.

Long before he was a troubled war vet, Featherstone was a street urchin, the last of nine kids from a Hell's Kitchen family that had been in the neighborhood for a couple generations. His mother, Dorothy "Dottie" Boyle, first married a man named Charlie Featherstone in the late 1930s and started having babies right away. By most accounts, the elder Featherstone, who sometimes worked as a longshoreman on the West Side docks, was a drunk and a louse who beat his wife regularly. Eventually, he deserted Dottie, leaving her with little or no money and six kids to raise. Dottie then struck up a relationship with Charlie Boyle, a military man. They were unable to find Featherstone, who was still her legal husband, so proper divorce papers were never filed. Dottie and Charlie Boyle entered into a common-law marriage and had three children of their own, the youngest being Francis Thomas, whom everyone referred to as "Mickey."

Young Featherstone had some minor disciplinary problems in school, but mostly he was a shy boy who steered clear of physical confrontations. It wasn't until his teen years that Mickey started to manifest a need to prove his manhood. His father had been a proud soldier in Korea; two of his brothers had already enlisted and been shipped off to Nam. Mickey had every reason to believe he would establish his own identity as a warrior through military service. In April 1966, he lied about his age so that he could enlist in the army at the age of seventeen. After going through basic training, he was assigned to the Natrang headquarters of Special Forces, the elite commando unit commonly known as the Green Berets.

For the most part, Featherstone's time in the service was a bust. Although he took some pride in being assigned to a Special Forces unit, he was an ordnance supply clerk who rarely saw combat and was generally regarded by his fellow soldiers as "ash and trash." With his diminutive size and New York accent, he was a frequent target of ridicule. The kid from Hell's Kitchen suffered from a severe sense of displacement in the jungles of Southeast Asia and took to spending much of his time drinking at the local Playboy Club in town. One night, while boozing with a couple army medics, he got so drunk that he passed out. When he woke up, he found that his penis was wrapped in gauze. Apparently, while he lay comatose, the medics had performed an impromptu circumcision on Private Featherstone, leaving him scarred for life.

The botched circumcision was a good metaphor for Mickey's entire tour of duty. He returned stateside in 1968 with some pathologically unresolved manhood issues and a severe alcohol problem. He began hanging out in neighborhood bars and engaging in almost daily physical confrontations, many of which ended in bloodshed.

His first stateside kill took place in September 1968, when he shot a kid from New Jersey during a rumble outside the Market Diner on Eleventh Avenue. Mickey was held on manslaughter charges but released on bail, pending trial. Against the wishes of his mother and everyone else who knew him, he then requested another tour of duty in Vietnam. His request was denied after a psychological evaluation by an army doctor concluded that he was suffering from a nervous condition—including severe nightmares, heavy drinking, insomnia, and withdrawal from the outside world. The doctor wrote in his report: "The assigning of EM [emergency medical] back to a combat area will probably bring back the difficulties that it previously created and probably with much more intensification. . . . The experiences the young man went through while serving his one year appear to be too traumatic for even a mature, well-adjusted individual to cope with." Featherstone fulfilled the remaining fifteen months of his military commitment as a driver and mail clerk at Fort Hamilton in Brooklyn.

The fact that he had been declared "unfit for combat" left Featherstone with much to prove. He continued his routine of drinking, smoking dope, and seeing "enemies" around every corner. Inexplicably, in the midst of this downward spiral, he married a Puerto Rican girl from the neighborhood. A few months into the marriage, Mickey awoke from a nightmare and attempted to strangle his wife in bed. When he snapped out of his rage, he apologized, but it was too late. His wife fled their home and never returned.

To Mickey, the failed marriage was one more example of a life out of synch; whenever he caught his reflection in a mirror, young Featherstone hated what he saw. He withdrew deeper into himself. Whatever money he had came from his father, Charlie Boyle, and most of that was spent on whiskey and beer. Mostly, he hung out where he could drink free, places like the American Legion Post on West Forty-third Street, which was run by his father and his older brother. Mickey could be found there most nights getting stewed and watching old horror movies on TV. On those rare occasions when he roused himself and tried to mix with other people, it often ended in disaster.

On one such occasion, Featherstone was having a drink at the Sunbrite Saloon, a popular neighborhood bar on Tenth Avenue. Being a Saturday night, the Sunbrite was crowded, and the juke box was loud. Mickey had been drinking for a couple hours and was feeling no pain when a commotion broke out in the bar. A gun was being passed around, over everybody's head. The next thing Featherstone knew, the gun was in his hand. Was it his hand? It looked like his hand. A menacing figure came toward him, a guy he recognized named Mio.

"Gimme the gun," barked Mio.

Mickey heard a swirl of voices in his head: "Watch out!" "Pull the trigger!" "He's gonna kill you!"

Before he even knew what was happening, Mickey shot the guy dead.

Everyone stampeded from the bar. Featherstone was rushed out a back door and driven to an apartment, where he was told to hide out. After he'd been there a while, Mickey began to think it might be a setup. He fled the apartment and laid low at a friend's place in the Bronx for a few days. When he called an acquaintance in Hell's Kitchen, he was told, "Mickey, the fuckin' neighborhood's crawlin' with cops. They know you was the shooter."

Featherstone saw the writing on the wall. He took the subway back to Hell's Kitchen and turned himself in at the local precinct. Everything after that was a blur. He remembered being sent to the Manhattan Correctional Center, the downtown prison also known as the Tombs. Then he was dragged in front of a grand jury. Although the Sunbrite saloon had been packed on the night of the shooting, everyone adhered to the neighborhood code: *Whatever you say, say nothin'*. The grand jury wound up calling it a "justifiable homicide." They wouldn't indict for murder, only for possession of an unregistered weapon.

Given Featherstone's barely coherent state, both during the shooting and in the weeks that followed, it was determined that the kid was in serious need of psychiatric evaluation. He was shipped to a VA hospital in the Bronx, where he was officially diagnosed for the first time. "Traumatic War Neurosis," read the report. "A paranoid schizophrenic with suicidal and homicidal ideations." In layman's terms, Featherstone was a ticking time bomb waiting to go off.

They pumped the patient full of various antipsychotic medication—mostly thorazine, known in the trade as a liquid straight jacket. It didn't seem to help much. Mickey was more paranoid and unruly than ever. There was some concern that he might try to escape, so he was transferred to another veterans' hospital in Montrose, New York, that was known for its tight security.

Four days later, Mickey was considered well enough to receive visitors. His soon-to-be ex-wife came by with a psychiatrist. She was filing for divorce, she said, citing "extreme cruelty," and she'd brought the doctor along to offer his diagnosis. Mickey paid little attention. The only time he spoke was to ask if he could borrow some money. When his wife and the doctor had left, he escaped by walking past the guards and out the front door. Still dressed in his lime-green hospital garb, he hitchhiked to a local train station and used the money he'd borrowed to buy a one-way ticket to New York City. A week later, he was ready to kill again.

This time, it all started at the Leprechaun Bar, where he got into another drunken altercation. Featherstone was unarmed, so he dashed from the bar and headed out into the night in search of a gun. The Hell's Kitchen Irish were a tight-knit community; the locals usually defended one another, especially when under siege from outsiders. Mickey had good reason to hope someone would help him out in his hour of need, which is exactly what happened when he rushed into Sonny's Café on Ninth Avenue and came face to face with Jimmy Coonan.

Coonan didn't usually spend his nights drinking late in neighborhood saloons, so Mickey was surprised to spot him sitting in a booth near the back. He was with a few people Featherstone didn't recognize, so Mickey nodded for Jimmy to come into the men's room. Coonan and Featherstone had known each other on a casual basis almost all their lives. Mickey knew about the Coonan-Spillane Wars, which had landed Jimmy a four-year stretch in the pen. Coonan, of course, was more of an aspiring racketeer than Featherstone, a lost soul whose craziness and gun-blazing ways were becoming part of the neighborhood lore. Featherstone had always sort of admired Coonan and figured, one day, if things worked out, they might even be able to make some money together.

But all that meant nothing at the moment; what Mickey needed right now was a gun, no questions asked, and that's how he put it to Coonan.

With no hesitation at all, Jimmy produced a handgun, a .25-caliber semiautomatic, which he kept in his belt in the small of his back, covered by his jacket.

"Mickey, you need any help?" asked Jimmy.

"No," replied Featherstone. "This is somethin' I gotta take care of myself."

With that, Featherstone headed back out into the night. At the Leprechaun Bar, he confronted his nemesis, a loud bully with a Southern accent who was nearly twice Mickey's size. He lured the guy outside, and, on the sidewalk in front of the bar, shot the man twice—once in the chest and once between the eyes.

Mickey Featherstone was arrested and taken to the Mental Observation Unit at Rikers Island. It was his third kill in the less than two years since he'd returned from Vietnam. None of the shootings had anything to do with business or organized crime; it was merely Featherstone's damaged psyche acting out on the streets of Hell's Kitchen. His troubled history fit the legal definition of "mitigating circumstances." Mickey was put on trial for this most recent shooting and found not guilty by reason of insanity.

He wound up serving three years at the Mattaewan State Prison for the Criminally Insane on gun possession and assault charges stemming from the previous killings. Through it all, Mickey clung to one positive note, one noble gesture of friendship: Jimmy Coonan providing him with a weapon, no questions asked. This single act would develop into an alliance that would drag the Irish Mob into a whole new era of barbarism.

Mad Dog Redux

While Coonan and Featherstone were charting divergent criminal paths that seemed destined to intersect, the boss of Hell's Kitchen, Mickey Spillane, was still dealing with his Italian problem. In fact, Spillane's rivalry with Cosa Nostra was about to take a decidedly homicidal turn, due in part to a major new construction project on the West Side of Manhattan that was being discussed.

Ground had net yet been broken for what would eventually be called the Jacob Javitz Convention Center. The New York State Urban Development Corporation was still battling with various governmental licensing committees over whether or not such a major project was viable, but it looked like it was going to happen. In typical New York fashion, the project would take years to work its way through the city bureaucracy, but the mobsters and their various construction and union affiliates were already licking their chops at the prospect.

What was being proposed was the largest single convention center in U.S. history, a building that would cost $375 million to construct, with 1.8 million square feet of floor space, to be erected on a plot of land bounded by Thirty-eighth Street, Eleventh Avenue, Thirty-fourth Street, and Twelfth Avenue—the outskirts of Mickey Spillane's Hell's Kitchen territory.

At a time when the city of New York was famously headed toward bankruptcy, construction projects of this scope were few and far between. The Genovese crime family, which had for years battled with Spillane's Hell's Kitchen Irish Mob over control of the Coliseum and Madison Square Garden, had no intention of going through a similar struggle over this new convention center. The stakes were too high. The cement contract alone might net $30 million, not to mention carpentry, wiring, food concessions to feed a workforce of 12,000 workers, and the attendant loan-sharking, gambling, and policy proceeds that went along with any major construction project.

Fat Tony Salerno, boss of the Genovese family, was a crude, rotund, cigar-chomping mafioso from the old school. The man had ordered dozens, if not hundreds, of mob hits over the years. From his headquarters on Pleasant Avenue in East Harlem, he opined about the best way to neutralize the Irish Mob. It was determined that rather than kill Spillane outright, leading, perhaps, to an unruly shooting war with the West Side Irish, it would be better to take Spillane down piecemeal by first eliminating his closest associates. That way, Spillane would be forced to step aside, leaving the convention center to its rightful overlord, the Genovese crime family.

Taking out Spillane's people was not as easy as it sounded. The idea was not only to "whack" the Hell's Kitchen mob boss's three top associates systematically, but also to do it in such a way that it would be unclear who was behind the killings, creating an atmosphere of uncertainty and paranoia. For this, the Mafia would need to use a non-Italian outsider, a professional assassin who could move in and out of the insular Hell's Kitchen neighborhood without being identified as a Mafia hitman. Fat Tony found his man through an Irish American union official who served as the Genovese family's point man at the New York Coliseum. The union official was well-connected in the underworld and had no trouble identifying the right man for the job.

Joseph Sullivan was a hardened contract killer who, in May 1976, had only recently been released from prison after serving ten years on a second-degree manslaughter charge. Sullivan was a well-known figure in the New York underworld. Born in the neighborhood of Woodside, Queens, he was a virtual product of the state who had spent twenty-five of his thirty-six years on Earth incarcerated in various penal institutions. He became famous in April 1971 when he escaped from Attica Correctional Facility in Upstate New York. At the time, no one had ever escaped from the maximum-security prison in its forty-year history. Sullivan did so by hiding himself beneath some grain and feed sacks piled aboard a truck that left the prison in broad daylight. He was captured five weeks later strolling down a street in Greenwich Village.

Even Sullivan was surprised when he was paroled by the state of New York just four years later. He was aided greatly by the fact that he had a powerful lawyer, Ramsey Clark, the former attorney general of the United States during the Johnson administration and a family friend. Upon his release, Sullivan resettled back in the borough of his birth. Before long, he was circulating in the underworld looking for work.

On a warm, mid-May afternoon, Sullivan walked into the Coliseum Restaurant, located on Fifty-nineth Street and Columbus Circle, across from the Coliseum. There he met up with a man he knew only as J. J., whom he had first met in prison. J. J. was now a corrupt union official affiliated with Fat Tony Salerno. The two men sat at a booth, sipped bottles of beer, and talked about old times. Eventually, Joe Sullivan said, "Okay, enough small talk. What I wanna know is, can you use me or not?"

"Yeah, I can use you," said J. J. "In fact . . . ," he pointed toward a man sitting at a table near the door, "see that guy, the guy sitting over there?"

Sullivan looked. "Yeah. What about him?"

"Ever seen him before?"

"No. Never."

"Well, would it bother you terribly if I passed you a piece beneath the table and asked you to blow his brains out before we walked out the door?"

Sullivan laughed. "Just like that, huh?"

"Yeah, pal, just like that."

"Damn. Is he the butcher, baker, candlestick maker, or somebody like us?"

"Does it matter to you who or what he is, Joe?"

"No, J. J., it doesn't really matter. It doesn't matter at all."

J. J. explained that the man's name was Devaney, Tom Devaney, right-hand man of Mickey Spillane. He told Sullivan that Spillane and the West Side Irish Mob were on the outs with Fat Tony, who was looking to position himself as the Godfather of the Javitz Convention Center. Sullivan asked few questions. He left the diner that day without killing Devaney, but the contract was now his; over the following months, he would do the bidding of the Italians and send a ripple of fear through the Irish American underworld.

The concept of Cosa Nostra turning to an Irish hitman to do the dirty work was not new. As far back as Vincent Coll, who'd been hired by the Maranzano family to bump off Lucky Luciano in the late 1920s, the tactic had been firmly established. In the 1940s and 1950s, Elmer "Trigger" Burke was another well-known Irish subcontractor frequently used by the Italians. Throughout history, men like Coll and Burke were used to bump off an array of underworld victims—including other mafiosi—but the arrangement undoubtedly had added appeal to *la famiglia* when it involved one Paddy being whacked by another.

By the 1970s, many Irish American gangsters looking to hire themselves out as freelance gunmen had little choice but to turn to the Mafia for work. After decades of incarceration, prosecution, political reform, and assimilation, the Irish Mob barely existed outside of Hell's Kitchen and a few neighborhoods in Boston, and they already had their own supply of hitmen. A guy like Joe Sullivan, a cold-blooded mercenary who seemed to enjoy killing, was constantly on the lookout for gainful employment; in true capitalist fashion, he sold his services to the highest bidder, or, in most cases, the only bidder. His willingness to take on murder contracts involving fellow Irishmen earned him the nickname "Mad Dog," a tip of the cap to Vincent

Coll, perhaps, but also a catchall moniker for a certain type of gangster with no scruples whatsoever.

Eight weeks after agreeing to murder Tom Devaney, Mad Dog Sullivan walked into a bar-and-grill in Midtown Manhattan, where Mickey Spillane's right-hand man was having a drink with a few friends. Sullivan was in disguise, with an afro wig and darkened skin that made him appear vaguely Hispanic or Middle Eastern. He ordered a beer and observed Tom Devaney for a while until he was ready to make his move. After draining the last of his drink, he walked over to the man, pulled out a gun, and calmly did the deed.

From inside a prison cell, years later Sullivan wrote an autobiography that was never published. In it, he described the Devaney shooting.

> [Devaney] had just lifted the beer to his lips when I brought my arm straight up, stopping inches from his ear as I pulled the trigger. The dull roar of the weapon echoed in one part of my mind while the other concentrated on the three men that had been facing him—all now wearing the rictus of fear as the shattered bits of bone and blood sprayed their horrified faces. I hadn't broken stride on my way to the door, and never took my eyes off them as I stepped outside onto the deserted street, breaking into a slow jog that wouldn't attract any attention . . ."[1]

Over the following months, hitman Sullivan eliminated two more of Spillane's closest associates in similar fashion. The most significant of these

---

1. A copy of Sullivan's manuscript, entitled *Tears and Tiers* (penned by him and his wife) was obtained by the author as research for this book. The would-be autobiography focuses mostly on Mad Dog's prison years, although there are many detailed descriptions of professional killings. Throughout the manuscript, Sullivan attributes his criminal psychosis to a kind of deeply ingrained Catholic guilt (he claims to have been sexually abused at the age of ten by a nun).

Sullivan's long life of crime continued into the early 1980s, when he was eventually arrested after a bank robbery spree in Upstate New York, but not until after he engaged in a wild shootout with state troopers and FBI agents in which he was shot and wounded. During his tumultuous criminal career, Sullivan managed to marry and have three kids. At the end of *Tears and Tiers*, he offers this small chestnut of hope: "The only saving grace for the maintenance of my often elusive sanity is that, barring the ever-possible freak cruelty of nature, my sons will never have the sins of their father visited upon them. I have told them of my own less-than-noble brand of domestic terrorism, and have never glorified it like I'd care for them to emulate it."

hits was the killing of Eddie "the Butcher" Cummiskey. Cummiskey was a tough West Side gangster who, like Sullivan himself, had done a stretch at Attica prison, where he trained to be a butcher. When he returned to Hell's Kitchen, Cummiskey plied his new skills by cutting up the bodies of people he murdered, bagging the body parts, and disposing of them in the river. It was believed that Cummiskey had brought about the disappearance of Eli Zicardi, the Genovese family bookie whom Mickey Spillane kidnapped back in the late 1960s. Zicardi's kidnapping and disappearance had been a catalyst for the current hostilities between the West Side Irish Mob and the Italians.

Eddie the Butcher's introduction of vivisection into the underworld discourse of Hell's Kitchen would prove to be a landmark development. For one thing, it ushered in a new era of debauchery. The neighborhood had always been a violent place, but cutting up bodies in the basement of Tenth Avenue tenements was something new. Cummiskey's grisly proclivities were a harbinger of things to come; before he was shot and killed by Mad Dog Sullivan, the Butcher passed his skills along to Jimmy Coonan, who eventually utilized what he learned in his reign of terror as boss of the Westies.

Eddie the Butcher was taken out by Mad Dog Sullivan at the bar of the Sunbrite Saloon on August 20, 1976. When another of Spillane's men was gunned down a few months later, people began to get the picture: There was a professional assassin loose in the neighborhood who was systematically eliminating the old-guard leadership of the Hell's Kitchen Irish Mob. It was probably being engineered by the Italians, but who the hell knew?

One man who had a vested interest in finding out was Spillane himself. He'd spent much of his time in 1976 and 1977 attending funerals and wakes, where he consoled the families of men he'd known since he was a kid. Clearly, there was some sort of major power play taking place; Spillane sensed that these professional hits were leading toward his doorstep. To get to the bottom of things, he traveled to Florida to meet with Eddie McGrath.

The one-time bootlegger for Owney Madden and leg-breaker for Boss Joe Ryan and the ILA was still, at the age of seventy-five, an underworld liaison of sorts who commanded respect from the upper echelons of Cosa Nostra. Spillane met with McGrath in Miami Beach, at the bar of the Thunderbird Hotel on 178th Street. Surrounded by potted palm trees and other tropical vegetation, the beleaguered boss of the Hell's Kitchen Irish Mob asked McGrath directly if he knew anything about this recent pattern of killings back in New York City. McGrath claimed ignorance.

"Sorry pal," he said. "I'm retired and out of touch."

A troubled Mickey Spillane returned home and saw the writing on the wall. He packed up his family and moved from Hell's Kitchen, where he had lived all his life, to Woodside, Queens, home of his former boss, Hughie Mulligan.

Jimmy Coonan had every reason to be pleased by Spillane's move out of the neighborhood, except that he, too, was concerned about the Mafia's violence against the West Side Irish. Coonan was fairly certain it had nothing to do with him, but he wasn't going to sit around and wait for someone to shove a hot poker up his ass. The time had come for Jimmy to make his move—both to protect himself from outside forces and to seize control of everything that Spillane had left behind, once and for all.

The Wild, Wild Westies

Mickey Featherstone had been out of prison and back in the neighborhood less than a year when he began to hear stories about bodies being cut up and made to "do the Houdini." These wild rumors on the kite were spreading from bar to bar like a bad case of the clap. In July 1975, a boyhood friend of Mickey's named Paddy Dugan had disappeared after shooting and killing another neighborhood kid, Denis Curley. Mickey heard a rumor that Paddy Dugan's severed head had been rolled down the bar at the Sunbrite Saloon. He confronted another neighborhood hoodlum, Billy Beattie, who had supposedly taken part in the killing and dismemberment of Dugan. Beattie admitted his role but said he had been forced into it by Eddie Cummiskey and Jimmy Coonan. Said Beattie, "You shoulda seen it, Mickey. They made me put Paddy's dick and balls in a milk carton and store it in the refrigerator."

To Mickey, it all sounded rather twisted. He chalked it up to the machinations of the neighborhood's gangsters, of which he had only a passing knowledge. Featherstone had killed people and done time for his own personal reasons, not because he had designs on any of the neighborhood's traditional rackets. If the mobsters in Hell's Kitchen wanted to kill people and cut up bodies, it was none of his business. But it became his business in late 1976, when Jimmy Coonan asked to meet with Mickey at the bar of the Skyline Hotel on Tenth Avenue, where Coonan had been holding court and doing business ever since Spillane moved out of the neighborhood.

Jimmy had done well for himself over the last year or two. He had taken over the numbers racket and all loan-sharking in Hell's Kitchen, which provided a steady weekly income. He'd bought a bar at 596 Tenth Avenue called, appropriately enough, the 596 Club, which had become a primary hangout for a new generation of gangsters loyal to Coonan. He was also working as a bodyguard for a major underworld figure in New York named Charles "Ruby" Stein. Known as "the loan shark to the stars," Ruby Stein was an old-time racketeer and owner of an exclusive gambling club on the Upper West Side. A dapper Jewish hood in his sixties, Stein was tied-in with Fat Tony Salerno and just about every other big-time mafiosi in town.

Despite everything he had working in his favor, Jimmy Coonan was not a happy man. He was concerned about the recent spate of gangland killings, especially the murder of Eddie Cummiskey, who had been in the process of switching his allegiance from Spillane to Coonan. "It's probably got nothing to do with me," Jimmy told Mickey Featherstone, "but you can never be sure. The bottom line is this: I need somebody to watch my back. I want you to come in with me."

Mickey thought about it. His sense of allegiance to Coonan had run deep ever since Jimmy passed him a gun no questions asked back in 1970. He owed it to Jimmy. There was also the lure of being paid $150 a week to accompany Coonan on his weekly rounds, with the promise of much more down the road.

"Jimmy," Featherstone told his new boss, "you can count on me."

News of the alliance between Jimmy and Mickey spread through Hell's Kitchen like wildfire. Coonan, the ambitious young mobster, and Featherstone, the crazy Vietnam vet who had killed numerous people and gotten off easy with an insanity plea, were now the dynamic duo who were taking over the neighborhood rackets. Hell's Kitchen would never be the same.

Meanwhile, the city was in the throes of its worst financial crisis of the century, the Vietnam War had ended in disgrace, and drugs and random violence were rampant all over town. On the West Side, the days of the friendly neighborhood racketeer were a thing of the past. Coonan and Featherstone made their rounds with guns tucked in their belts. If a loan shark customer was late with a payment, he took a beating from Featherstone. The neighborhood ILA office, Local 1909, which had once been loyal to Spillane, was told that weekly extortion payments and no-show jobs were now under the purview of Jimmy Coonan. When the president of the local balked, he was told to meet Coonan and Featherstone at the Landmark Tavern, one of the neighborhood's more upscale saloons, at Forty-sixth Street and Eleventh Avenue. There Jimmy Coonan informed the local's president and business agent that if the bogus payroll checks didn't arrive in one week, he would blow their brains out. The checks arrived.

A group of young neighborhood toughs and older guys formerly loyal to Spillane began to coalesce around the Coonan-Featherstone duo. Jimmy McElroy, Billy Beattie, Richie Ryan, Mugsy Ritter, Tommy Collins, and others became regulars at the 596 Club. Booze and cocaine flowed freely, although Coonan, who took his role as leader seriously, rarely indulged. Featherstone did, but his relationship with Jimmy also motivated him to clean up his act. In his post-Vietnam years, he rarely wore anything other than jeans and a T-shirt, but now he dressed in a sports coat and slacks, his hair longish but neat, with a neatly trimmed beard.

The alliance also had a maturing effect on Featherstone's personality. Now that he was a professional racketeer, he was less prone to volatile mood swings and counterproductive acts of mayhem. His violent tendencies were reigned in and directed toward a purpose—the purpose of brute capitalism and a modus operandi of fear and retribution that would come to characterize this new generation of Hell's Kitchen gangsters.

By early 1977, Coonan controlled all the neighborhood rackets, but he was still worried about Spillane's old enemies in the Genovese crime family. His strategy for dealing with the problem was at once diabolical and brilliant: He simply reached out to another branch of Cosa Nostra—the Gambino crime family, based in Brooklyn.

Through the late Eddie Cummiskey, who'd once worked at a sewage treatment plant on Ward's Island, Coonan had gotten to know Danny Grillo, a coworker of Cummiskey's and a *soldato* (or soldier) in the powerful Gambino family. Grillo was connected with a notoriously violent crew based in the Canarsie section of Brooklyn that was headed by a squat, bullnecked capo named Roy DeMeo.

In the early months of 1977, Coonan began to trudge his West Side underlings over to Ward's Island, a sizable island in the East River that served as a foundation for the massive steel stanchions of the Triborough Bridge. In a small industrial trailer on the island's eastern flank, Coonan, Featherstone, McElroy, Beattie, and Ryan met a guy named Tony, who was the foreman at the sewage treatment plant. On most occasions, Danny Grillo and Roy DeMeo were there as well. Initially, the meetings had little to do with serious criminal business. Coonan seemed to be testing the waters. More than anything, he wanted to show off his virile young crew in front of the powerful Roy DeMeo and Danny Grillo.

"We can do business," Jimmy told DeMeo on numerous occasions.

DeMeo nodded. "I got no prejudice against nobody," he replied, assuring Coonan that the fact he was Irish would not get in the way.

The sewage treatment plant at "Tony's island" became a nexus point for Coonan's crew and the Italians. Coonan purchased silencers and weapons there and also used the location as a place to dump the body parts of his murder victims.

Now that he was friendly with a crew that was part of the largest Mafia family in the United States, Coonan was ready to make an audacious move that would alter the balance of power in the New York underworld. Few of Jimmy's own underlings knew what he had in mind when he told them all to meet the next afternoon, May 5, 1977, at the 596 Club on Tenth Avenue. On his drive in from Keansberg, New Jersey, where he now lived with his wife of three years, Edna, and their two kids, he stopped at a Food Town supermarket where he purchased an assortment of kitchen knives and some jumbo-size plastic garbage bags, then continued on into the city.

At the 596 Club, Coonan met by Danny Grillo, his Italian buddy from Ward's Island, as well as three members of his own crew: Billy Beattie, Richie Ryan, and Tommy Hess. Coonan and Grillo explained to the others what was about to go down. Coonan was going to pick up Ruby Stein (the legendary loan shark for whom he worked as a driver and bodyguard) and bring him here to the 596 Club. Then they were going to shoot Stein dead, cut up his body, stick the body parts in plastic garbage bags, and dump them in the East River.

The members of Coonan's crew were all small-time criminals. They looked at one another, startled by the idea that they were about to whack out a major player in the underworld who was connected at the highest levels.

Coonan had his reasons: Both he and Danny Grillo owed Ruby Stein money, $70,000 in Coonan's case. By killing Stein, they would absolve themselves of that debt, and, even more importantly, they would take over Stein's business. The ultimate plan was to inherit Ruby's many debtors as their own.

While the others waited, Coonan picked Stein up at his private gambling parlor on the Upper West Side and drove him down to the 596 Club. When the two men entered the club, all the guys in the bar greeted the dapper, white-haired loan shark, who was dressed in a customary tie and silk suit, with a hankie in the breast pocket.

"Ruby, have a seat," said Coonan. "Make yourself comfortable."

When one of Coonan's crew pulled down the shades and locked to the door behind him, Stein's life must have flashed before his eyes.

Suddenly Danny Grillo burst out of the kitchen with a .32-caliber automatic aimed straight at him. "Oh my God!" gasped Ruby, just as Grillo fired six shots, hitting him in the chest, arms, and leg. The jolt lifted Ruby an inch or two off the ground and spun him completely around. He collapsed on the floor in the middle of the bar.

It was over just that fast. One of Coonan's men stepped outside to stand guard. Coonan handed a gun to Billy Beattie and told him to fire a shot into Stein's body, which he did. Then Jimmy told Richie Ryan to do the same: *boom!* They were all accomplices now in the murder of a man who was a friend of the Mafia. If word got out that they had murdered one of the Mafia's most renowned loan sharks, there would be hell to pay. All the more reason, deduced Jimmy Coonan, to make the body "do the Houdini."

Mickey Featherstone was not present for the killing of Ruby Stein, but he arrived at the 596 Club shortly thereafter, as Stein's body was being prepared for dismemberment. Ruby's body had been stripped naked and dragged into the men's room.

"This here," said Coonan, holding up Stein's black ledger book, "this is gonna make us all rich." He put the book away in his own coat pocket and then began slicing away at Ruby's neck. "Come here," he said to Featherstone. "I want you to feel how fuckin' heavy this head is. Feel that."

Mickey took one look at the severed head and began to wretch. "Fuck that," he said, stepping behind the bar to pour himself a drink. While Featherstone and Beattie sat at the counter, they heard Coonan in the bathroom offering words of advice to Richie Ryan, the youngest of the group. "This here," said Coonan, "the elbow, this is the toughest part."

Finally, after about an hour, they were finished. The various severed body parts had been stuffed into six or seven bags. Whatever was left over in the way of excess flesh or gristle was flushed down the toilet. The walls were wiped clean, the floors mopped. They locked up the 596 Club and loaded the bags into a battered red van that Coonan liked to refer to as "the meat wagon." Then they drove across town to Ward's Island, where Tony buzzed them through the security gate.

It was dark now, and a cool breeze was rustling the trees on the grounds of the Manhattan Hospital for the Insane, which was also located on the island. They backed the van up to the river, pulled the garbage bags out of the back, and tossed them into the water's swirling currents. Ruby Stein was no more.

The legendary loan shark's disappearance was reported in the newspapers a few days later. In the *New York Post*, it was hinted that Stein had been the victim of a group of Hell's Kitchen gangsters, dubbed the Westies by one local detective because of their base on the West Side of Manhattan. The name stuck. Although no one knew it at the time, over the next decade the Westies would join the Dead Rabbits, Whyos, and Hudson Dusters as a permanent fixture in the city's underworld lore.

Last of the Gentleman Gangsters

"Hey Pop, there's somebody at the door for you," called Bobby Spillane, youngest son of Mickey, the semiretired West Side mob boss who'd moved his family to the middle-class neighborhood of Woodside, Queens.

Mickey Spillane entered the front hall, leaned toward the intercom, and said he would be right down.

"I'll be right back," he said to his son. "I gotta talk to somebody."

"I'm going to bed," said twelve-year-old Bobby.

"Okay," said Mickey. "Good night, son."

It was May 13, 1977, a somewhat chilly evening. Mickey Spillane threw on a brown leather coat and headed outside. There was a car idling on Fifty-ninth Street in front of his apartment building. Spillane walked over to the car and bent down to talk to somebody he recognized. A shot rang out. Then another and another and another and another. Five shots in all hit Spillane in the face, neck, chest, abdomen, and left arm. His body fell to the street, and the car sped away. Spillane was pretty much DOA by the time cops arrived on the scene.

News of his death cast a pall that stretched from Fifty-ninth Street in Woodside all the way over to Hell's Kitchen, where Mickey Spillane had been revered by many. To the older residents, the saddest fact of all was that the murder seemed totally unnecessary. Spillane was no longer a mover in West Side criminal circles and hadn't been for months.[2]

---

2. Spillane's murder was never officially solved, although most of the participants were identified years later, after the perpetrators were themselves killed in various gangland slayings. One key mystery remains: Whose voice was it on the intercom that lured Spillane down to the street? Obviously, it was someone Spillane knew and trusted, given the former mob boss's concern about the recent spate of killings of his West Side underlings. Spillane knew these killings had been engineered by the Genovese crime family, and he'd been trying to barter a truce at the time of his death.

Spillane had been trying to use Eddie McGrath as a go-between in his negotiations with Cosa Nostra. His meeting with McGrath at the Thunderbird Hotel in Miami Beach bore little fruit, but Spillane stayed in touch with the old-time labor racketeer who was still on a first-name basis with many of New York's most powerful mafiosi. The record shows that Eddie McGrath was in New York City attending a funeral and dealing with a legal matter around the time of Spillane's murder. McGrath, who had been a legendary figure in Hell's Kitchen during Spillane's teen

Three days after the killing, on the afternoon of May 16, mourners gathered on West Forty-seventh Street at the McManus and Ahern Funeral Parlor, which was owned and run by the McMani. Mickey's widow, Maureen, was there, as was her brother, James McManus, leader of the Midtown Democratic Association. Spillane's stature in the community had been based largely on his embodiment of the oldest tenet of the Irish American underworld: the cosy relationship between the gangster and the politician. In deference to the McMani, many power brokers from around the city stopped by to pay their respects to a man who would be remembered as the Last of the Gentleman Gangsters.

While the Spillanes, the McMani, and other Hell's Kitchen friends were mourning the passing of a neighborhood legend, Jimmy Coonan, Mickey Featherstone, and a few others were meeting four blocks away at the Skyline Motor Inn. Roy DeMeo, Coonan's contact in the Gambino family, had requested a sit-down with Coonan and his people.

"Bet you're wondering what happened with Spillane," DeMeo said to Coonan after they'd all settled in at the bar area of the motel.

"I was, kinda," replied Jimmy.

"Well," said Roy with a smile. "You got an early birthday present."

Without mentioning names, DeMeo explained how they lured Spillane from his apartment and shot him in the street. Coonan was thrilled. He embraced DeMeo and told him that, from now on, anything he needed from the West Side crew was his for the asking.

For Coonan, the removal of Spillane was like a coronation; he was now the official mob boss of Hell's Kitchen. He could have been satisfied and reigned as Spillane had, as a local chieftain with his own small piece of the pie, but that wasn't Coonan's style. Jimmy realized that, apart from the proposed convention center, the Hell's Kitchen rackets were mostly a nickel-and-dime operation. The Westies weren't going to get rich off loan-sharking, policy, and penny-ante extortion alone. There was a bigger world out there, a constellation of big ticket rackets, most of which were controlled by the Italians. Coonan already had his sights on the big prize.

Since the days of Old Smoke Morrissey, moving forward, forging alliances, and thinking big had been the essential traits of a successful mobster. But you also had to know how to cover your ass. In this regard, the most

---

years, is one of the few men he would have trusted enough to come outside, unarmed, if he was called. McGrath was never questioned about the murder. Instead, police arrested and charged Mickey Featherstone, who was nowhere near the murder scene that night. Featherstone was later acquitted at trial.

important relationship in a mobster's life, more important than his marriage, was his relationship with his right-hand man. Coonan trusted Featherstone and felt that he could depend on him for most things, but Mickey had not yet taken part in the cutting up of a body. Coonan and his new buddy DeMeo had talked about this fact. DeMeo himself had been a practitioner of vivisection ever since he, just like Eddie "the Butcher" Cummiskey, had learned the butcher trade in prison.

"Say a guy's in your crew, and you think he's a stand-up guy," said DeMeo. "You can never really know for sure unless he's willing to go all the way. You gotta break that guy, bring him into your world. Only then can he be trusted."

Coonan took DeMeo's advice to heart. A few months later, he knew the time had come to "break Mickey's cherry" and initiate him into the macabre world of human dismemberment. All Coonan needed was a victim.

Rickey Tassiello was a small-time Hell's Kitchen hoodlum with a bad gambling habit. To satiate his habit, he frequently borrowed money from Jimmy Coonan's loan shark operation. Jimmy was constantly having to chase the kid down and extend him credit. Rickey was a classic deadbeat. At one point, Coonan even went to the kid's brother, a bartender in the neighborhood, who paid Jimmy the $7,000 he was owed and begged him not to lend Rickey any more money because he was "a sick person, a degenerate gambler."

A few months later, Coonan showed up at the brother's place of business again. This time Rickey Tassiello owed him $6,000. They worked out a payment schedule whereby the brother would try to get Rickey to pay $100 a week.

Months passed. Coonan showed up again. Rickey Tassiello had stopped making his payments. He still owed $1,250. Exasperated, the brother said there was nothing more he could do.

They snatched Tassiello out of a booth at the Market Diner and drove him to an apartment on Tenth Avenue. In the kitchen of the apartment, Coonan shot Rickey once in the back of the head, then twice more as he lay on the floor. Coonan then dragged the body into the bathroom, stripped it naked, and dumped it in the tub.

"Thank God he was a small guy," said Coonan. Using simple kitchen knives, he began cutting up the body.

Featherstone watched for a while and tried to help, but he couldn't take it; he vomited in the toilet.

Coonan was sympathetic. He put a hand on Mickey's shoulder and explained why it was important to make the body disappear. It made good business sense, he said. "No corpus dilecti; no investigation," were his exact words. Then Jimmy handed Mickey a knife. "I want you to take this knife and stick it in his heart."

"But he's already dead," said Mickey.

Jimmy was insistent. "Take the knife, and stick it in his chest."

To Mickey, it seemed weird, perverse. He had killed before, out of rage or fear, but this was different—a crude blood ritual that Jimmy seemed determined to have him perform.

Mickey looked at Coonan. He took the knife and plunged it into the corpse.

Jimmy smiled and said, "Good. Good."

After that, they cut up Rickey Tassiello's body, put the pieces in jumbo-size plastic bags, and threw the bags in the trunk of the car. Then they drove out to Ward's Island and dumped the bags in the river.

In the larger scheme of things, the killing of the small-time hood was a minor murder, nowhere near as significant as, say, the killing of Ruby Stein. But in terms of the emotional sinew and intestinal fortitude of Coonan's operation, it was monumental. Jimmy had fully initiated his right-hand man into the macabre ways of the Westies. And Mickey had come through with flying colors, showing complete and total allegiance to the boss. There was no stopping them now.

As it turned out, Jimmy's gory test of Featherstone's loyalty proved to be providential, for within weeks of disposing their latest murder victim, the Italians came knocking.

"Big Paulie wants to see you," said Roy DeMeo to Coonan and Featherstone at the bar of the Skyline Motor Inn. "He wants to talk business."

Coonan smiled. Everyone knew who Big Paulie was—Paul Castellano, *capo di tutti capi*, the boss of all bosses.

Apparently, Castellano had been hearing a lot about the Westies lately. Too much. There had been so many West Side–related homicides and suspicious disappearances over the last year that Cosa Nostra was becoming concerned. Most recently, the murders of Stein, Spillane, and Tassiello even made the nightly TV news when a prominent NYPD detective squad staged an archaeological-style dig along the deserted railroad tracks of the West Side. The cops had received numerous tips that body parts had been buried there, specifically the head of Rickey Tassiello. The diggings produced nothing in the way of evidence, but they garnered plenty of media attention. Castellano was concerned that the Westies were bringing too much heat down on the entire underworld, including *la famiglia*. Something needed to done.

There was also the matter of Ruby Stein and his black book.

"Don't worry about that," DeMeo said to Coonan. "If the boss asks, just tell him you don't know nothin' about it. You don't know nothin' about Ruby getting whacked or his black book. That's it. Everything's gonna be fine. In fact, this could be the best thing that ever happened to you guys."

After DeMeo went back to Brooklyn, Featherstone told Coonan he was worried that this was some kind of setup. "Maybe we're gonna get whacked," he surmised.

"Nah," said Jimmy. He had his concerns, too, but they were eclipsed by the prospect of forming a business alliance with the Italians. It was the sort of arrangement Coonan had been scheming toward his entire adult life.

The sit-down took place one night in late February 1978, at a private dining room in the back of Tomasso's Restaurant in Bay Ridge, Brooklyn. Seated at a U-shaped table were more than a dozen of the most powerful Cosa Nostra figures in America at the time—Castellano, Funzi Tieri, Anniello Dellacroce, Carmine Lombardozzi, and others, most of them in their sixties or seventies. The two Irish kids were seated near Castellano and treated like kings. All of them ate a huge pasta feast, and it was only after the food was digested and the espresso served that Castellano asked about Ruby Stein and his black book.

"We don't know nothin' about that," said Coonan, sticking to the script.

With his wire-rimmed spectacles and conciliatory demeanor, the sixty-five-year-old Castellano was known to be a judicious man who read the *Wall Street Journal* on a regular basis and fancied himself the CEO of a legitimate corporation. Others might have pressed Coonan more strongly on the matter of Ruby Stein's murder, but Big Paulie let it go. He moved on to the main reason he had called for the sit-down, which was to tame the Westies and bring them into the fold.

"From now on, you're with us," said the *capo di tutti capi*. "You're gonna be our crew. We get 10 percent of whatever you drum up, but you also get 10 percent of our operation in Manhattan. I think you're gonna find it could be a most profitable business arrangement for you and your people. Only one thing: You gotta stop acting like cowboys. From now on, every time somebody gets whacked, it's gotta be cleared with us first. It's time for a little order over there on the West Side. Capisch?"

On the drive home to Hell's Kitchen that night, Coonan was ecstatic, telling Featherstone that things were going to be different now. They were going to be major players in the underworld. They were going to get rich. They were going to go down in history.

In at least one sense, Coonan was right. Ever since the Atlantic City conference in 1929, when it was first determined that Irish American mobsters would be marginalized, if not flat-out eliminated via gangland assassination, the Irish Mob had been forced to fight for every scrap they could get. In some ways, the Irish American gangster had been pushed to the sidelines and forced to become a fringe player who had to kick up a big ruckus just to get noticed. By inheriting the rackets on the West Side and exploiting the reputation of the Irish gangster as a wild, unpredictable factor in the underworld, Coonan and the Westies had done something no Irish gang had done since the end of Prohibition: They had stabbed, shot, and dismembered their way to the main banquet table.

At the time, it must have looked peachy. Immediately following the sitdown in Brooklyn, the money rolled in. Mickey Featherstone, for one, saw his weekly pay as Coonan's muscle increase from $150 a week to $4,000 a week. Other opportunities to make money proliferated, especially in the construction rackets where the Westies were hiring themselves out as Mafia subcontractors. And for things like murder and extortion, acts they might have committed anyway just for the hell of it, various members of the gang were now being well compensated.

Money, however, can be a whore, an illusion, or a beautiful diversion. In time, the Italians' largesse would seem less like a bounty and more like a paltry trade-off in comparison to the down side. It was bad enough that, by the late 1970s, the Mafia was an insatiable, multi-tentacled octopus who believed the entire underworld was their oyster; now they were the *official* overlords of the Irish. It was an arrangement many Irish gangsters had been trying to avoid since the earliest days of the battle between the dagos and the micks.

This new arrangement made things especially difficult for the independent operator. The Westies, after all, had been called to the table not because they were Irish, but because they had something to offer: a neighborhood bounty that, however diminished, had historical antecedents going back to the beginnings of organized crime in America. Most Irish American gangsters weren't so lucky; they operated outside Hell's Kitchen or even outside the protection of the Irish Mob, as freelance operators looking for work wherever they could find it. Shorn of any overriding ethnic structure that might guarantee them a piece of the pie or back them in underworld disputes, they were, in many cases, underworld pariahs—lone meteors in a universe that was no longer of their making.

It would take a while for the Westies to realize that their pact with the Mafia had been a gangland version of the Trojan Horse. For non–West Side gangsters, however, the consequences were as clear as a slap in the face. The era of the Irish American hoodlum as independent operator was pushed further along the road to extinction. But given the breed's reputation for irascible, hard-headed acts of mayhem, there was a better-than-even chance they would not go down without a fight.

last call at the celtic club

immy McBratney was a typical Irish American mook working the fringes of the underworld in the early 1970s. He did his criminal business mostly in the outer boroughs of New York—Staten Island, Brooklyn, and across the river in New Jersey. At a formidable six foot three inches tall and 250 pounds, McBratney was a tough hombre known more for his brawn than his brains. People who knew Jimmy best thought of him as something of a gentle giant, a slow-witted man who rarely initiated a fight unless he was riled. Eddie Maloney, a fellow small-time hood who did prison time with McBratney, wrote about him in his 1995 book, *Tough Guy: The True Story of "Crazy" Eddie Maloney.*

> Jimmy McBratney was locked up for armed robbery. He was quiet, a listener and a learner, and soon we were discussing heists we might do together. He knew about guns and wanted to become a collector, but closest to his heart was his wife and two small children and their house on Staten Island, and his goal of saving enough to own a nightclub. I learned Jimmy was very loyal to his wife, and that all the talk in the yard about "broads" upset him. His wife visited regularly and wrote every day.

McBratney and Maloney eventually did go into business together. In the early 1970s, they became part of a small multiethnic crime crew that kidnapped wiseguys from the Gambino crime family and held them for ransom. It was a dangerous way to make a living, but the remuneration could be fabulous—as much as $150,000 for a couple nights of work.

The key to a successful snatch-and-pay was to make sure the kidnapee never knew who his kidnappers were. This was done with the aid of a hood and a blindfold. McBratney and Maloney's crew also used a two-team approach. The first team, pretending to be police officers and using a stolen badge, would snatch the wiseguy, usually from his home, and hold him at a secure location. The second team would pick up the ransom money.

The first guy they kidnapped was a Gambino family capo known as Frankie the Wop. This escapade went off without a hitch, and the gang got away with a cool one hundred grand. Over the next two months, the gang completed three more successful body snatches. Their luck changed, however, on December 28, 1972, when they clubbed a Gambino loan shark named "Junior" on a street in Staten Island, threw him in the back of their car, and skedaddled out of the neighborhood. A couple of local kids, who just happened to witness the snatch and getaway, passed along the license plate number to some neighborhood wiseguys.

To keep Junior alive, the Gambinos paid the relatively small amount of $21,000 for his release. Then they set their sights on Jimmy McBratney, who had been identified as a member of the kidnapping crew.

Snatching mafiosi or Mafia-connected criminals and holding them for ransom had become a cottage-industry for a certain type of Irish gangster who liked to live dangerously. The Gambino family, in particular, had been plagued by a recent rash of kidnappings, many of which ended badly. Carlo Gambino, scion of the largest crime family in America, became distraught when his own nephew was kidnapped early in 1972. A ransom of $100,000 was paid for his release, but the young Gambino kid never materialized. In January 1973, the police acted on a tip and dug up the body of Gambino's nephew at a garbage dump in New Jersey. Although there was nothing linking McBratney to this particular kidnapping and murder, the Irish mug made a wonderful fall guy. The word went out: "Get Jimmy McBratney. He killed Don Carlo's nephew."

On the night of May 22, 1973, McBratney was drinking at a Staten Island bar and restaurant called Snoope's when three Italian-looking hoods strolled in and announced that they were detectives who wanted to take him in for questioning. McBratney smiled because he recognized the ruse as the same sort of approach he used in his own kidnappings.

The three Italians were vintage *gavones*, and one of them even wore his hair slicked back in a ducktail like it was still 1959. It would later come out that this particular *gavone* was an up-and-coming Gambino soldier by the name of John Gotti.

Gotti and the others jumped McBratney right there in the bar. The big Irishman put up a furious struggle. In front of several startled witnesses, he dragged Gotti and the other two Italians the full length of the bar, getting in a few licks of his own, before they immobilized him against a wall. Then one of the men put a gun to McBratney's head and, in full view of the barmaid, fired three shots at close range, killing him instantly. The three killers then escaped into the night.[1]

McBratney's partner in crime, Eddie Maloney, read about his pal's murder in a Staten Island newspaper. Years later, in *Tough Guy*, he wrote:

> McBratney's death saddened me as nothing else in my life had. He'd been a good friend, and he wasn't a hardened criminal like some of us. He intended to get out of the life—and I believe he would have— soon as he accumulated that nestegg. I felt bad for Jimmy's wife, also. She had been as loyal to him as he was to her. On a personal level, Jimmy would have risked his life for me—and I for him—and a person doesn't make friends like that very often.

If Jimmy McBratney had been a connected criminal, a member of the Westies or some other organization with at least a semblance of a standing army, he might have been able to barter his way out of being murdered. As it was, McBratney was a freelance criminal with no affiliation and an Irishman to boot. He was expendable.

In an underworld universe where one misstep could lead to certain death and the almighty dollar was an intermittent commodity, some Irish American gangsters did better than others. The mob was first and foremost a capitalist venture; gangsters with a talent for making money, who knew how to play by the rules and spread the wealth, tended to be treated like royalty.

Take James "Jimmy" Burke, another independent mick hoodlum plying his trade in the underworld of the 1970s. Burke had one advantage that Jimmy McBratney did not: He operated within a specific commercial territory—Queens, New York—where, for years, he was a smuggler of untaxed liquor and cigarettes, as well as a hijacker of trucks leaving JFK Airport. Burke was well-liked by wiseguys and victims alike. When hijacking a truck,

---

1. It became part of underworld lore that John Gotti "made his bones" with the killing of Jimmy McBratney. If so, he was not the first mafiosi to do so by whacking an Irishman. Al Capone's first kill was also of the Celtic persuasion, a Brooklyn dock walloper named William Finnegan.

Gotti did six years for his role in the McBratney murder. After he got out of prison, the future boss of the Gambino family was often heard on government wiretaps bragging about the killing of McBratney, whom he alternately pumped up as a major gangster with big-time connections or denigrated as "a no good Irish lowlife."

he always slipped a few hundred dollars to the driver, which earned him the nickname Jimmy the Gent. More importantly, Burke adhered to underworld protocol. He kicked back a percentage of his take to Paul Vario, an underboss with the Luchesse family. Vario's people referred to Burke as the Irish guinea and spoke his name with awe, since he was a dependable cash cow for the mob.

Not much was known about Burke's roots. He was born in 1931 to a woman named Conway and orphaned in a Manhattan foundling home. At the age of two, he was designated a neglected child and entered into the Catholic Church's foster care program. For the next eleven years, he bounced from one foster home to another. It was later revealed by psychiatric social workers that, during these years, he had been alternately beaten, sexually abused, pampered, lied to, ignored, screamed at, locked in closets, and treated kindly by so many different surrogate parents that he had trouble remembering their names or faces.

At the age of thirteen, Burke escaped from the Mount Loretto Reformatory and began his life of crime. He burglarized homes, passed counterfeit checks, and began to carry a gun. At the age of eighteen, he was arrested for bank forgery. The detectives who brought him in knew that he was passing fraudulent checks on behalf of a neighborhood mafiosi. With Burke's hands cuffed behind his back, the cops beat him silly trying to get him to implicate his partner. Burke kept his mouth shut, and when he arrived at Auburn Prison in Upstate New York to serve his five-year sentence, he was treated like a paisan by the Italian inmates who respected his adherence to the code of omerta.

In *Wiseguy*, Nicholas Pileggi's classic account of life in the mob, low-level gangster Henry Hill remembers Jimmy Burke as a kind of underworld Sir Galahad whose criminal instincts ran deep.

> The thing you've got to understand about Jimmy is that he loved to steal. He ate and breathed it. I think if you ever offered Jimmy a billion dollars not to steal, he'd turn you down and then try to figure out how to steal it from you. It was the only thing he enjoyed. It kept him alive.

Burke was exceedingly generous with his criminal partners, although his love of the life often made him violent and unpredictable. According to Hill,

> Jimmy was the kind of guy who cheered for the crooks in movies. He named his two sons Frank James Burke and Jesse James Burke. He was

a big guy, and he knew how to handle himself. He looked like a fighter. He had a broken nose and he had a lot of hands. If there was just the littlest amount of trouble, he'd be all over you in a second. He'd grab a guy's tie and slam his chin into the table before the guy knew he was in a war. . . . Jimmy had a reputation for being wild. He'd whack you.

Henry Hill, who was half Irish himself, became a part of Burke's multi-ethnic crew based out of a bar in Ozone Park, Queens, called Robert's Lounge. By the mid-1970s, Burke had become a bookmaker, loan shark, and fence for cargo stolen from JFK Airport. The Luchesse crime family not only tolerated Burke, they also revered the man. His ability to make money for local mafiosi rendered irrelevant the Old World tradition of inducting only men with pure Sicilian blood into Cosa Nostra. Jimmy Burke's reputation as an earner made him quite possibly the most well-connected Irish American racketeer in America outside of the traditional Irish mobster enclaves of Hell's Kitchen and South Boston.

In 1975, Burke got himself convicted, along with Henry Hill, on loan-sharking and assault charges. While serving time at Atlanta Federal Prison, Jimmy the Gent began to plan a major robbery that would be the crowning achievement of his criminal career—or anybody's, for that matter. The Lufthansa Heist, as it became known, would go down in the annals of crime as the largest robbery in U.S. history, even bigger than the Brinks job.

The heist was initiated by a Lufthansa Airlines security guard who worked at the airline's cargo terminal at JFK Airport. News of the terminal's vulnerability to an inside job was passed along to Burke, who masterminded the break-in plan and put together the robbery team—a mixed crew of mostly low-level cons not unlike the team that robbed Brinks. The robbery was in the planning stages for nearly two years; by the time Burke was paroled from prison, the plan was set and ready to go.

On December 11, 1978, less than a week after Burke was released to a halfway house in Times Square, he and a group of masked men, armed with rifles and pistols, hit Building 261 at the Lufthansa terminal at JFK Airport. The heist went off without a shot being fired. The robbery crew loaded bags containing $5 million in cash and another $875,000 in jewelry into a van.

After the heist, the crew stashed away the booty, designating Burke as the disperser of funds. The idea was to wait until the publicity surrounding the robbery died down before absconding with the loot, but, like any under-world plan subject to the vicissitudes of human nature, the whole thing turned bad. Wrote author Pileggi in *Wiseguy*

Lufthansa should have been the crew's crowning achievement. A dream come true. The ultimate score for anyone who ever hi-jacked a truck or moved swag out of the airport. It was the heist of a lifetime. The one robbery where there would have been enough for everyone. Six million dollars in cash and jewels. And yet, within days of the robbery the dream score turned into a nightmare. What should have been the crew's happiest moment turned out to be the beginning of the end.

The killings started in early 1979 and continued throughout the year. Before it was over, more than fifteen murders would be attributed to fallout from the Lufthansa Heist. The entire robbery crew—except for Burke—was murdered gangland style. Wives and girlfriends who knew details about the heist were also rubbed out, their bodies cut up and dumped in rivers and vacant lots.

Two million dollars from the Lufthansa take had been dispersed directly to Mafia underboss Paul Vario, making the crime traceable to the Luchesse crime family. Burke didn't have to wait around to be told that the unraveling of the post-heist plans and potential investigation were his responsibility. Most of the murders that took place following the robbery were attributed to Burke, whose role as a Mafia subcontractor put him in a highly vulnerable position. Burke himself might have been a victim of the hit parade were he not arrested on a parole violation in April 1979.

It was Henry Hill, Burke's half-Irish pal from the Robert's Lounge crew, who put Jimmy the Gent behind bars for life. Hill was facing life imprisonment on various narcotics violations at the time, and, as part of a deal with the feds, he testified against Burke—not about the Lufthansa Heist, in which Hill had no direct involvement, but about one of the subsequent murders. The Irish guinea was given a life sentence, and Hill disappeared into the Witness Protection Program, became the subject of Pileggi's bestselling book, and saw himself portrayed by actor Ray Liotta in *Goodfellas*, director Martin Scorcese's 1990 adaptation of *Wiseguy*.[2]

Jimmy Burke survived as long as he did as an Irish American hood operating in an increasingly Italian American universe for one simple reason: He lined everybody's pockets with dough. His talents as an earner put him in a unique position in the New York underworld. Elsewhere around the United States, Irish American mobsters of the 1970s tended to be rebels and under-

---

2. In the movie, Burke is memorably portrayed by Robert DeNiro. The real Jimmy Burke died in an Upstate New York prison from stomach cancer on April 13, 1996.

appreciated throwbacks to a long gone era. Whereas Burke had endeared himself to the Mafia by playing the game according to their rules, most Irish hoods did not go so quietly into the night. A primary example of this was an audacious Irish American gangster who—at the same time Jimmy the Gent was making money for the Mafia in Queens—was waging a one-man war with Cosa Nostra that would go down in history as quite literally the most explosive battle in the ongoing rivalry between the dagos and the micks. The setting was Cleveland, Ohio. The mick's name was Danny "the Irishman" Greene.

The Legend of Danny Greene

Cleveland was never really an Irish town. Unlike New York, Chicago, or even Kansas City, where the Irish were able to exert influence well beyond their numbers through political organization, Cleveland's dominant political leaders were immigrants of Eastern European extraction, due to the city's large population of Slovenians, Yugoslavians, Hungarians, and Czechoslovakians. Cleveland's Irish population peaked around the year of 1870, when Irish laborers were drawn to the city by the many new steel mills and stevedoring firms that opened for business along the Cuyahoga River. There were approximately 10,000 Irish or Irish Americans in the city at the time—10 percent of the overall population. That number dwindled in the following decades, although there remained a good number of Irish among the city's laboring class, in the police department, and within the local hierarchy of the Catholic Church.

The Irish settled mostly around the east and west banks of the Cuyahoga River's mouth, especially in the bend of the river known as the Angle, the city's first Irish neighborhood. By the turn of the century, many Irish had also begun to settle in Collinwood Village, a gritty industrial neighborhood whose central commercial hub was called Five Points (in tribute, perhaps, to the infamous New York neighborhood where so many Paddies settled in the years following the Great Potato Famine). By World War II, Collinwood had become one of the most heavily industrialized areas in the nation. Children in the neighborhood played near the railroad yards and tracks of the New York Central Railroad, or around the various factories that spewed forth toxins and industrial pollutants on a daily basis. It was here that young Danny Greene passed from adolescence into manhood.

He was born on November 14, 1933, in St. Ann's Hospital to John and Irene (Fallon) Greene, both Irish immigrants. He was the first child of the young newlyweds, who'd been married in a civil ceremony just five days earlier. The shame and embarrassment that Irene had shouldered while carrying her baby out of wedlock were dispelled by the birth of their healthy baby boy. The joy of that birth did not last long, however. Within hours, Irene's vital signs dipped to alarming levels. She was immediately moved to the intensive care ward. In the hours that followed, her blood pressure skyrocketed, and she developed a hellish fever. Nothing the doctors did seemed to help. Three days after the birth of her child, Irene Greene died from what was officially diagnosed as an enlarged heart.

"Baby Greene" hadn't even been named yet. It wasn't until after the funeral and burial of his wife that John Greene decided to name his son Daniel, after the boy's paternal grandfather.

In the wake of his wife's sudden and shocking death, John Greene sought solace in the bottle. His heavy drinking cost him his job as a traveling salesman for the Fuller Brush Company. With no source of income and the landlord banging at his door, Greene had no choice but to place his son Danny in the Palmdale Catholic Orphanage in suburban Cleveland.

In 1939, at the age of six, Danny left the nuns and priests at the orphanage and moved back in with his father, who had recently wed for the second time. The boy didn't settle in well. He was troubled by the death of a mother he never knew and uncomfortable around his new stepmother. Several times he ran away from home and was once found hiding under a neighbor's porch. John Greene lost patience with the young boy and turned him over to his grandfather, a widower who lived in a modest wood-shingle house on East 147th Street in the heart of Collinwood.

Danny Greene's grandfather worked nights as a pressman at the printing factory of the *Cleveland Plain Dealer* and slept during the day. Young Danny was left unsupervised most of the time. He attended Catholic grade school, where he was well-liked by the teachers but was an indifferent student and frequently got into trouble. He was in the Boy Scouts for three weeks but was kicked out for giving the scout master a hot foot during a troupe meeting.

Danny fared better on the streets than he did in school or other mainstream pursuits. Although average in height and weight, he was not afraid to defend himself. In Collinwood, the Irish kids were frequently targeted by corner crews comprised of Italian and Slovenian boys. Danny's lack of fear and his refusal to knuckle under to the dominant Italian ruffians would prove to be a foreshadowing of his life in the Cleveland underworld. "He was a tough kid, likeable but reckless," remembered a Collinwood native who knew Danny as a youngster and was quoted years later in *Cleveland Magazine*. "You could have guessed his life was not going to follow the straight and narrow."

In 1951, at the age of eighteen, Greene dropped out of high school and joined the Marine Corp. He served his three years with the Fleet Marine Force Division at Camp Lejune, North Carolina. He gained respect there more for his abilities in the boxing ring than as a soldier. As in school, discipline was a problem for the blue-eyed, blond-haired Irish kid whose penchant for pranks often crossed the line between humor and cruelty. He was frequently transferred from one camp to another for disciplinary reasons.

In 1953, Greene was honorably discharged from the marines and returned to Cleveland. He soon found work in a typically Irish area of employment as a longshoreman. At this time, the city's waterfront was booming. The opening of the St. Lawrence Seaway in 1959 added nearly 9,000 miles of sea coast to the United States and Canada, making the Great Lakes region a relatively new and bustling port. The number of shipping vessels carting iron ore, grain, automobiles, and general merchandise tripled over a ten year period, with the number of longshoremen in the local ILA office doubling during that same period.

Although Danny Greene was apparently a lazy worker who once got fired for sleeping on duty in the hold of a ship, he was a popular figure among his fellow dock wallopers. He had a charismatic personality and exhibited leadership traits, mostly through his fearless nature. As a result, in 1961, he was easily elected president of ILA Local 1317, which covered the Cleveland waterfront. A year later, he was also elected district vice president of the Great Lakes Office of the ILA.

As a union organizer, Danny achieved a level of maturity and discipline that had been lacking throughout his youth. He took great pride in his job. The first order of business was turning the local office into a presentable front for various union-related ventures. He started by totally refurbishing the ILA headquarters, painting the interior walls of the office kelly green in honor of his Irish heritage (he also used green ink pens, had the union bylaws reprinted in green ink, and drove a green Cadillac). He began hosting popular parties at union headquarters before and after Cleveland Browns games—parties that were attended by a Who's Who of local movers and shakers, including judges, cops, mobsters, and councilmen.

"Before I got here, union headquarters was a packing crate and a lightbulb on a cord," Greene jokingly told a reporter.

As a labor leader, Greene was a fierce advocate for his men. He was constantly at war with the stevedoring companies, who wanted to choose their own anchor men during the loading and unloading of vessels. To enforce his will, Greene formed an inner circle of ex-boxers and gangsters who threatened, muscled, beat, or bombed the opposition into submission. His victims could be stevedoring companies, or business agents, or even fellow dock workers who were not sufficiently acquiescent.

Years later, while being questioned by detectives, a member of Greene's inner circle explained the arrangement: "If someone complained, they'd get a beating. If someone went to the police, they'd get a beating. Even if one of them just said something bad about Danny, we'd rough him up."

"Was there a name for this group?" asked the police interrogator.

"Yeah. The grievance committee."

Danny Greene's stature as a union official elevated him to new levels of a power within Cleveland's tough-as-nails intersecting worlds of politics, labor, and crime. He began to hang out at some of the city's most well-known underworld night spots on Short Vincent Avenue, the city's entertainment district during the 1960s. One of his favorite spots was the Theatrical Bar & Grille; it was here that he first met Alex "Shonder" Birns, a Jew of Austrian-Hungarian extraction who was a local mobster legend. Birns had been around since the days of Prohibition, when he ran corn sugar into Cleveland from across the Canadian border. He still presided over a thriving loan-sharking and numbers operation and was believed to have numerous lawyers, judges, and policeman on his payroll.

While frequenting the nightclubs, restaurants, and strip joints along Short Vincent Avenue, Greene developed a taste for the nightlife that would eventually sully his reputation as a union official. Although his annual ILA salary came to a grand total of $6,000, Danny lived a life of conspicuous consumption; he spread money around the clubs, arrived for work in his green Cadillac, and seemed to have plenty left over for his wife and two young kids, not to mention the occasional mistress. His lifestyle—lavish by Cleveland standards—caught the attention of an enterprising reporter for the *Plain Dealer*. The paper began an investigation of the district office of the ILA that uncovered a secret building fund, which was controlled by Greene. As it turned out, the union president was fleecing his own local, forcing workers to put in overtime hours for which they were never paid. Instead, the money went into Greene's pocket.

The exposé in the *Plain Dealer* touched off an FBI investigation that led to Greene being indicted for embezzlement and falsifying union records. In 1966, he was convicted and given a five-year sentence, but he avoided jail time by resigning from his post as ILA president and being barred from further union-related activities.

The scandal may have ended Greene's career as a union official, but it did little to damage his standing in local criminal circles. In the late 1960s and early 1970s he became a behind-the-scenes figure in the city's garbage carting wars, which involved rival Mafia factions. Greene was put to work as strong-arm man for the Cleveland Solid Waste Trade Guild. He explained his duties thus: "If others don't join [the guild], we will follow their trucks and take away their stops. We'll offer to pick up for less and take away their business at the cheapest price—and knock them out of the box. . . . There are a lot of ways we can do this, and then we'll split up the stops and give them to guild members . . ."

The carting wars resulted in death and destruction. When Michael Frato, a garbage hauler, pulled out of Greene's guild, he was marked for death. An underling of Greene's was sent to attach a remote-control explosive to Frato's car. While carrying the bomb to Frato's car, the underling was prematurely blown to pieces. On the surface, it looked like a freak accident, but local cops would come to believe that Greene himself had detonated the bomb, deliberately blowing up his underling, who he believed was leaking information to Frato. It was the opening salvo in a war that would continue for years and claim many lives.

While Greene pursued a career in waste management, he also began an association with the granddaddy of organized crime in Cleveland, sixty-nine-year-old Shonder Birns.

The long tradition in the American underworld of Jewish bookmakers and loan sharks employing Irish "muscle" went back to the days of Arnold Rothstein, whose bodyguards included Fatty Walsh and Jack "Legs" Diamond. Since Irishmen had a reputation for being physically capable and could never be a member of the Mafia, they were available to the older, more experienced bookies, who were not generally men of violence. It was often a paternalistic relationship; the older, smarter man schooled the young tough in matters of points and percentages, in exchange for protection. Sometimes, the student turned out to be an ingrate or worse. In New York, Ruby Stein had employed the tough Hell's Kitchen hood Jimmy Coonan, taught him the ways of the world, and then wound up getting killed, cut up, and dumped in the river.

The Stein-Coonan relationship was similar to Danny Greene's budding partnership with Shonder Birns. Birns introduced Greene to the longstanding underworld rackets of loan-sharking and numbers. Birns was Cleveland's kingpin of the numbers racket, which had become especially popular in the city's growing African American neighborhoods. Birns lack of familiarity with his newfound "colored" clientele may have made him feel he needed a big Irish bodyguard like Danny Greene.

One of Greene's first assignments as Shonder's enforcer was to deliver a bomb to the home of a dissident numbers runner who was holding out on paying the appropriate protection money. Greene drove to the man's house with a home-made explosive device; he parked a block down the street and pulled the igniter. But Greene was unfamiliar with the military-style detonator. The fuse burned faster than he had anticipated. Danny fumbled with the bomb and tried to toss it out the passenger window, but it hit the door frame and fell back into the car. He was able to get the door open and escape just as the bomb exploded and blew the roof off the car.

"The luck of the Irish," Danny would later remark. The only consequence was a slight injury to his right eardrum that left him hard of hearing for life.

It was around the time of Greene's budding partnership with Shonder Birns that he began to embrace his Irish heritage even more strongly. He'd always been a proud Irishman, which had manifested itself in his obsession with the color green—green pens, green car, green office, and a green plaid sport's coat that he wore everywhere he went. More recently, however, Danny had begun to devour books on Celtic and Irish history. He took a special interest in the legend and mystique of the ancient Celtic warrior. The Celts were among the great nomadic tribes of Europe five hundred years before the birth of Christ. Celtic males were tall and fair-skinned, with blond or red hair—impressive physical specimens who were known to have mastered two arts with great success: the art of clever speech and the art of war. Among other things, the Celtics had stood up to and repelled the marauding Roman Empire.

A psychotherapist might have had a field day with Greene's obsessive fascination with his Celtic roots. Perhaps he was attempting to reunite with his Irish mother, whom he lost at birth. Or maybe his years as an orphan had thrown him into an identity crisis that was compelling him to connect to something larger than himself. Or maybe he was merely overcompensating for the fact that he was virtually all alone in the Cleveland underworld, an Irishman surrounded by Jews, Italians, and African Americans. Whatever the reason, Greene's strong identification with his Irish roots—and particularly his obsession with the legend and persona of the Celtic warrior—was about to turn the Cleveland underworld on its head. His actions would provoke many mafiosi in town to curse the Irishman, and one in particular to ruminate on an FBI wiretap, "That cocksucker, that fucking Irishman. How the hell did this guy ever come into the picture, anyway?"

Live by the Bomb, Die by the Bomb

The use of explosives in the Cleveland underworld was a tradition going back at least to the city's labor wars at the turn of the twentieth century. In the city's infamous streetcar strike of 1899, called by *Motorman and Conductor* "the hardest contested battle ever fought by our people in America," strikebreaking crews faced the prospect of their cars being dynamited on the tracks. On what came to be known as "Bloody Sunday," a nitroglycerin bomb that had been placed on the tracks exploded beneath a Euclid Avenue streetcar, badly wounding ten passengers and ripping an ear off a motorman's head. Nitroglycerin bombs blew up several more streetcars over the next few weeks.

Bombs continued to be used in the city's labor disputes for decades to come. Danny Greene had himself employed the use of explosives as an ILA organizer and as the president of a new business he called Emerald Industrial Relations, a labor consulting firm. Emerald Industrial Relations provided protection and helped settle labor disputes, sometimes with a bang.

The big bang theory of underworld negotiation was a risky tactic. After all, both sides could play that game, and frequently did; bombing wars were notorious tit-for-tat affairs, with the warring parties trying to out-do one another with bigger and more devastating explosions. After the bombing death of his underling, Greene found a C-4 explosive device affixed underneath his own car. He was able to diffuse the device before it detonated, but he had reason to believe there would be other bombs to follow.

This most recent exchange of homemade explosive devices in Cleveland had its roots in an earlier attempt on Danny Greene's life. On the morning of November 26, 1971, Greene was jogging along White City Beach when Mike Frato, his carting business rival, drove up in a car and opened fire. Greene pulled out a gun and returned fire. Frato's car was later found a block away with the fleshy, 250-pound wiseguy slumped over the steering wheel, a bullet hole in his head. A few hours later, Greene turned himself into the police and gave the following statement:

> About 10:30 in the morning I drove my three dogs to White City Beach like I do almost every day. I was there jogging and exercising my dogs when a car started driving slowly at me. The passenger shouted, "I've got you now you sonavabitch" and pointed a revolver at me. I recognized him as Mike Frato. He was about fifteen feet away and shot at me two times. I pulled out my gun and fired once then the car sped away. I didn't think I killed him. I thought that I hit him in the shoulder . . .

Although a number of witnesses corroborated Greene's account, the police charged him with homicide and held him in jail for a few days. The charges were soon thrown out of court. "The evidence indicates that Frato was attempting to assassinate Danny Greene . . . in a struggle for control of the rubbish hauling business," determined a judge. The incident was ruled a "justifiable homicide," and Greene was released from custody.

A few months later, there was another attempt on Danny's life, at the same location. Greene was jogging along the beach when a sniper, concealed in some bushes, fired several shots at the Irishman. The shooter probably believed that Greene would be an easy target, out in the open with no cover. But instead of ducking to the ground, Greene pulled out his revolver and started shooting while running straight at the would-be assassin. The tactic worked; the gunman turned, ran for his life, and was never positively identified.

Clearly, somebody wanted Danny Greene dead, and that person wasn't likely to stop until he got it done right. Greene had acquired many enemies in his years as a labor organizer, gangster, and resident underworld wild card, but he had a pretty good idea who was behind these latest attempts on his life: the old Jew, Shonder Birns.

Greene's relationship with his former mentor had soured one year earlier when the former ILA boss borrowed $75,000 from the aging mobster to open a cheat spot—an after-hours drinking and gambling spot on the East Side. Unbeknownst to Greene, Birns had gotten the investment money from friends of his in the Mafia, specifically the Genovese crime family in New York. Problems ensued when Birns insisted that Greene hire a local African American hood to handle some of the business at the club. The man turned out to be a drug dealer who skimmed some of the $75,000 investment money to finance his own drug deals on the side. Police had the man under investigation, and the club was raided a few days before it had even opened.

Birns and Greene blamed each other for the loss.

"You owe me that seventy grand," the aged bookmaker told Greene.

"Sorry, old man. You're the one made me hire that bastard," said Danny.

When Birns told Greene that the money had come from a source in Cosa Nostra, Danny laughed.

"Fuck 'em," he said. "Tell 'em it was a gift."

While Shonder Birns was likely at the stage in life where he placed his teeth in a glass before going to bed at night, he was not about to take such an insult lying down. He immediately put out a $25,000 murder contract on Greene, which resulted in the attempted bombing of Danny's car and various bungled assassinations.

The old Jew may not have known it, but by trying to have Greene whacked, he was playing right into the Irishman's newfound identity as a Celtic warrior. The more Danny was under siege, the more he drew on his ethnic heritage, particularly aspects of that heritage relating to Celtic mythology. The noble warrior of the ancient clans took pride in his impetuous nature, and, more importantly, he wasn't afraid to die. Weaned on the legend of Cuchulain and other gods of the north, the Celtic warrior believed that, through death, he could achieve immortality. The more you tried to kill him, the more audacious he became.

On a typically cold night in March 1975, Shonder Birns walked out of Christie's Lounge, a go-go club down the block from St. Malachi's Catholic Church. Although past his prime, Birns always looked sporty, like a high-roller just back from Vegas. Dressed in maroon pants, a white turtleneck sweater, and a sports coat, he complained to a doorman at the club of a cold he'd been unable to shake. "Maybe the warm weather in Miami will help," said Birns. "Yeah, I think this will be my last month in the rackets."

Birns strolled to the curb and reached out to unlock the driver's side door of his aqua-blue El Dorado. The explosion was so loud that it rocked the city blocks away. Birns was blown in half, his legs separated from his upper torso by more than fifty feet. The rest of his body was sprayed against a nearby chain-link fence.

The amount of C-4 explosive used in the car bomb suggested that Greene did not just want to kill Shonder Birns; he wanted to deliver a message to the old-time mobster's Mafia benefactors: *You play with me, and you're playing with fire.* The war was on.

Two months later, in May, Danny's entire apartment went up in a ball of smoke. Greene was in bed at the time, with his girlfriend. The explosion hurled Greene into a refrigerator and cracked a few of his ribs. His girlfriend was unhurt. The entire second floor of the building caved in. Danny and his girlfriend made their way through the rubble to his car and left the area.

When the police bomb squad arrived, they found a second more powerful bomb—a block of tetrytol, a military-style explosive, strapped to a three-gallon can of gasoline—affixed to Greene's back door. The bomb had been wired to go off along with the first bomb, but its fuse had been improperly placed. Had the two bombs gone off together, said the police, the blast might have turned Greene's entire Collinwood neighborhood into flaming rubble.

If the Mafia believed that by devising such a devastating attack—one with the potential to kill far beyond Greene's place of residence—they could turn the neighborhood against the Irishman, they were sadly mistaken.

Collinwood was a tough, hard-scrabble environment, and the area's residents rallied around Danny Greene as one of their own.

Greene, of course, had foreseen a time when his inevitable showdown with the city's mafia would involve the neighborhood, and so he cultivated the image of a Robin Hood figure, doling out cash from his criminal scams in the form of extravagant tips and picking up the tab at local restaurants and diners for long-time neighborhood residents. Like an old-style Irish ward boss, he purchased turkeys during the holidays for families in need and once paid the entire four-year tuition at Villa Angela Academy, a Catholic girls' school in Collinwood, for a local waitress he favored. In return, the neighborhood became Danny's eyes and ears, tipping him off when suspicious characters or FBI agents were snooping around the area.

The day after Greene's apartment building was bombed, he was back in the neighborhood. In a vacant lot not far from where the explosion occurred, Greene set up two trailers, one as a living quarters, the other an office. In front of the office he posted a sign: "Future Home of the Celtic Club." A green harp adorned the sign and an Irish tri-color flag fluttered nearby. As a gaggle of journalists and TV news reporters gathered around, Danny looked straight into the camera and fired a shot over the bow.

"I have a message for those yellow maggots," he said into a microphone. "And that includes the payers and the doers. The doers are the people who carried out the bombing. They have to be eliminated because the people who paid them can't afford to have them remain alive. And the payers are going to feel great heat from the FBI and the local authorities. . . . And let me clear something else up. I didn't run away from the explosion. Someone said they saw me running away. I walked away."

When a reporter suggested to Danny that he had nine lives, he responded, "I'm an Irish Catholic. I believe that the Guy upstairs pulls the strings, and you're not going to go until He says so. It just wasn't my time yet."

A few days later, Greene was approached by John Nardi, a local union official and Mafia associate he'd known for years. Nardi was on the outs with the Mafia's current leadership in Cleveland and Cuyahoga County. There had been a few near-miss attempts on his life, which Nardi viewed as part of a Sicilian-style vendetta that could not go unanswered. He told Danny Greene, "You got a good thing going here, pal, but your flank is wide open. Why don't we form a partnership? Your enemies are my enemies. Let's fight them together."

The arrangement made sense to Greene, especially since Nardi had access to traditional crime rackets well beyond anything Danny could cobble together on his own. In a city where there was no such thing as an Irish

Mob, Greene had little choice but to form alliances whenever it was in his best interest. "You got a deal," he told Nardi.

What followed was the sort of volatile underworld eruption that harked back to the worst days of Chicago during the gangland wars of the 1920s, with mobsters killing mobsters on a weekly basis, and innocent bystanders running for cover. In 1977 alone there were thirty-seven bombings in Cuyahoga County, twenty-one of those in Cleveland, which was dubbed "the bombing capital of America." Mobsters were bombed in their cars, in restaurants, and in their homes. Widows cried, priests and rabbis prayed, and children wondered why. The Cleveland Mafia Wars touched off such concern within the ranks of the ruling Commission in New York that Fat Tony Salerno, boss of the Genovese family, authorized the immediate induction of ten new *soldatos* just to deal with the bastard Irishman and his renegade Italian partner who were believed to be at the heart of the blood-letting. With dozens of Mafia hit teams arriving in Cleveland that spring, the town began to look like a Sicilian resort.

In May 1977, the Mafia got John Nardi with a car bomb. Nardi and Greene had a sweet deal in the works at the time, a union-related meat distribution scam based in Texas that they estimated could net $6 million over a five year period. To facilitate the deal, Greene was actually thinking of closing down his Cleveland operation and moving to Texas—all of which went up in a blaze of shrapnel and body parts in the parking lot outside the Teamsters headquarters, where Nardi had an office.

Although his only major partner was now dead, the Irishman remained typically defiant. Outside his Celtic Club headquarters, Danny stood shirt-less with a Celtic cross pendant around his neck. With his golden locks (he'd recently undergone a hair transplant procedure), full mustache, and well-toned physique, he looked more like a Celtic warrior than ever before. Flanked by several of his club underlings, he answered questions from an on camera TV news reporter.

> REPORTER BILL MCKAY: Rumor has it, Danny, that the word was out on the street back in March that John Nardi was a target. Did you talk to John Nardi at all about this?
>
> GREENE: I haven't seen John in about three and a half months, Bill, but I did send him a message very recently. "John," I said, "be careful. It's out here very, very strong on the streets that somebody's out to get you."

REPORTER: Word has it, Danny, that you are also a target in this so-called gangland war for control. What's your answer to that?

GREENE: In the world of the streets, I happen to have a very enviable position to many people because I'm in between both worlds, the square world and the street world. And I think I have trust in both sides. I have no ax to grind, but if these maggots in the so-called Mafia want to come after me, I'm over here at the Celtic Club. I'm not hard to find.

With his reckless bravado and growing cadre of adoring followers, Greene was becoming a legend in his own time. But there was an undeniable air of doom surrounding Danny Greene and his people. Everyone knew the Irishman's day was near, which only added to his warrior-like mystique. One of his young followers even wrote a poem entitled "The Ballad of Danny Greene."

> Among the Crow, the story says
> A man was judged by fiercest foe,
> Many scalps a brave Chief took
> Who fought his way to fame,
> Often he outwitted death
> Ere history prized his name.
>
> A modern warrior known as Greene
> Was very quick and smart and mean,
> He scrambled hard and fought like hell
> And led a charmed existence,
> They shot him down and blew him up
> With most regular persistence.
>
> Through guile and luck and skill
> Danny Greene is with us still,
> He does his job as he must do
> With zeal, finesse and pride,
> It's hard to keep a good man down
> With Saint Patrick at his side.
>
> Some day he'll die, as all we must
> Some will laugh but most will cry,

His legend will live on for years
To bring his friends mixed pleasure,
For he has done both bad and good
And lived his life full measure.[3]

Danny loved the poem and had it posted on the wall of the Celtic Club—in green ink.

By September, after another Greene bomb killed another high-ranking capo, the Mafia were beside themselves. They sent a note to Danny practically begging for a truce. A meeting was arranged.

At the time, Danny was stretched thin. His inner circle may have included many adoring followers, but all of the big-ticket rackets were controlled by the Italians. It was worth Greene's while to meet with Cosa Nostra if he could finagle his way into the game, which was exactly what he did. At a meeting attended by local mob leaders and a Genovese family representative from New York, Greene was told that, if he would agree to a cease-fire, he would be ceded a significant portion of Cleveland's West Side gambling operations once run by John Nardi. Danny agreed to the deal.

The truce was reported in the *Plain Dealer* and brought about a noticeable lessening of tension throughout the city, which was precisely what the Mafia wanted. They never had any intention of letting the Irishman get away. All along, the plan had been to create a scenario in which he might let his guard down. A professional out-of-town hit team had been stalking Greene for months, sleeping in cars and eating Chinese takeout, noting his every move. By and large, Danny was a cautious, elusive target. The Mafia's big break came when they were able to plant a wiretap on the phone of Greene's girlfriend. While listening to a cassette recording from the wiretap, they heard the following exchange:

GREENE'S GIRLFRIEND: Hi. I'm calling for Danny Greene.

RECEPTIONIST: Okay.

GIRLFRIEND: He has a loose filling and, um, would like to see Doctor Candoli as soon as you can get him in.

RECEPTIONIST: All right, let's see what we have available. . . . [pause]. We can squeeze him in on this Thursday—that's the sixth at three o'clock. Will that work?

---

3. "The Ballad of Danny Greene" was first published in 1998 in *To Kill the Irishman* by Rick Porrello, a book-length account of Greene's life and death.

GIRLFRIEND: That'll be fine.

RECEPTIONIST: Good. Then we'll see Mr. Greene on the sixth at three o'clock.

GIRLFRIEND: Thank you.

RECEPTIONIST: You're welcome. Have a nice day.

The Mafia hitmen listened to the tape three or four times and then laughed their asses off. Danny Greene was going to have a loose filling replaced, and then they were going to blow him to smithereens.

On the afternoon of October 6, 1977, Greene arrived for his dental appointment and parked in the lot. Danny paged an underling who was supposed to watch his car while he was inside, but the underling never got the message because the batteries in his pager were dead. From the front seat of the car, Danny grabbed his green leather gym bag that served as his survival kit. Inside was a Browning nine millimeter semiautomatic pistol capable of firing multiple rounds without reloading, an extra clip of bullets, a list of car license plate numbers of his various Mafia enemies, a box of green ink pens, and a Mother of Perpetual Help holy card.

Once Greene had disappeared inside the dentist's office, the hit men pulled up alongside Greene's car and parked. Inside their own car, on the side flanking Greene's, was planted a steel-encased remote control bomb covered with a blanket. The two hitmen vacated the rigged car and moved to a different vehicle. They sat and waited for Greene to appear. An hour later, when he did, the hitmen bristled with excitement. As Danny put his key in the car door to unlock it, they detonated their bomb by remote control.

The explosion blew out windows in a nearby store. The bomb car and part of Danny's car were completely demolished. The Irishman was killed instantly. Although much of the flesh was seared from his body, his body remained largely intact—except for his left arm, which was blown almost one hundred feet away. His prized emerald ring was still attached to a finger, and his Celtic cross pendant was embedded in the asphalt a few feet away from his body.

Greene's death was the story of the day, resonating beyond Cleveland and throughout the American underworld. He was not the most powerful Irish American mobster ever, nor the wealthiest or the smartest, but the saga of Danny Greene seemed to unfold in a place where crime and folklore were indistinguishable. To some, he was a homicidal maniac, to others, a hero. Either way, as foretold in "The Ballad of Danny Greene," his legend lives on as a testament to the bold and audacious side of the Irish American gangster.

The Informer

It was not commonly known about Danny Greene until many years after his death that he was a C.I., or confidential informant, for the FBI. Had it been known, the revelation might have been difficult for some of his followers to swallow. Irish mobsters did not have a tradition of blood oaths and initiation rituals in which they pledged undying loyalty to the family, but they were arguably more virulent than the Italians in their hatred of informers. Much of this had to do with the history of Ireland itself, where being a tout had dire political connotations. In Liam O'Flaherty's classic Irish novel, *The Informer* (1925), the main character, Gypo Nolan, becomes an outcast in his own community when he informs on a revolutionary comrade who is wanted by the authorities. The novel captures aspects of the Irish psyche that run deep. A quasi-religious ideology rooted in the struggle against colonial oppression in Ireland was transmitted to America via the early gangs and became a badge of distinction for the Irish American mobster.

Danny Greene, no doubt, would justify his actions by saying he was seeking an edge against his enemies. Acting as a dry snitch, he leaked information about his underworld rivals to his FBI handlers, and they in turn leaked information to him. It would later be revealed that Greene's FBI contacts alerted the Irishman about Mafia assassination plots against him that they overheard on government wiretaps. What information Greene gave up in return is not known, nor is it documented in his FBI file, obtained through the Freedom of Information Act.

The phenomenon of FBI agents enlisting still-active mobsters as government informants was a relatively new law enforcement technique in the 1970s. The Omnibus Crime Control Act—a massive piece of legislation enacted in 1968—had established within the U.S. Justice Department a number of new far-reaching directives. Among them was the Witness Protection Program, which was designed to induce criminals to turn against their coconspirators by offering them a new name, identity, and place to live after they testified in court. As a subtenant to the witness program, the FBI initiated an ambitious new system for cultivating informants. Individual agents were now encouraged to recruit and register C.I.s who were still active criminals.

This dramatic new approach by the FBI was open to all sorts of messy misinterpretations. Agents and mobsters would now be operating on the same playing field, entering into complex relationships built around the concept of mutual manipulation, leading to the obvious question: Who was using whom?

Nowhere was this subterranean interaction between crooks and coppers more multilayered than in the city of Boston, where local law enforcement, whether FBI, Massachusetts State Patrol, or Boston police, tended to be heavily Irish American. In Boston, cops and crooks had sometimes grown up in the same neighborhoods, gone to the same schools, or even come from the same families. A wily Irish American mobster with the right connections was in a position to play this system to his advantage, which was certainly the case for the man who emerged in the 1970s as the rising star of the Boston underworld: Whitey Bulger.

Whitey was the proverbial Irish leprechaun, a little green man with magical powers, all pluck and brass balls. He had survived CIA-sponsored LSD experiments, a stint at Alcatraz, the gangland elimination of Donnie Killeen (his boss), and come through it all smarter and stronger than ever. From 1972 to 1975, he had lived in constant fear for his life. The FBI team of Paul Rico and Dennis Condon approached Bulger on numerous occasions to tell him they had picked up underworld chatter suggesting that he was going to be killed by the Winter Hill Gang, of which he was a member. It was Agent Condon, a native of Charlestown, who took the initiative and opened a file on Bulger with the intention of signing him on as a C.I. Condon and Bulger had conversations, much of which Condon paraphrased in a series of FBI reports filed as far back as the early 1970s. In one report, dated August 7, 1971, Condon writes, "The [potential informant] is still reluctant to furnish info and is spending most of his time working for a group that has him marked for elimination."

After a couple more conversations with Bulger, Condon gave up. In 1975, he was approaching retirement and turned over the Bulger file to an ambitious young agent in the Boston office of the FBI named John Connolly.

The relationship that developed between Bulger and Connolly rightly stands as a landmark in the history of the Irish Mob in the U.S. In some ways, it was a relationship rooted in history, linked to an era when Irish American gangsters and Irish American cops were not infrequently cut from the same cloth. A century ago, the Irish gangster was sometimes viewed within the community as a necessary evil; he may have been a criminal, but at least he advocated for his people. In the long march from the ghetto to the gravy train, the gangster played his role. Consequently, the local Hibernian leatherhead might cut him some slack, especially if he knew the lad or knew his family, or if the crook had shown the foresight to factor the lawman into the financial give-and-take of his activities.

John Connolly was not some grubby cop looking to bring home a paper bag filled with cash to the missus. He was a G-man, schooled at the FBI training facility at Quantico, Virginia, exalted by Hoover, praised by presidents, and lionized by Hollywood. Connolly was at the forefront of the Bureau's new emphasis on street smarts, daring, and initiative, especially when it came to cultivating what were known as Top Echelon informants. Connolly was a brash native Bostonian who walked the walk, talked the talk, and could have been a gangster. Instead, he was a lawman whose primary goal from early in his career was to build his reputation on the scattered bones of the Mafia.

He was also from Southie, born and raised on the same block as the Bulger family. In later years, when Connolly's methods and ethics were called into question, he would go out of his way to underscore Whitey Bulger's reputation as a near-mythical figure in the neighborhood. According to *Black Mass*, Dick Lehr and Gerard O'Neill's devastating account of the Bulger-Connolly relationship, the two men first met when Connolly was eight years old. At a baseball field in Southie, Connolly was attacked by an older and much bigger kid. The future FBI agent was taking a beating when a nineteen-year-old neighborhood guy, whom he recognized, stepped in and chased the bullies away. Young Connolly's savior that day was none other than Whitey Bulger.

Connolly's family eventually moved out of the Old Harbor housing project to City Point, Southie's best address because it was on a promontory jutting out into the sea, with splendid views of the harbor and city. Like many Southie residents, Connolly's parents hailed from Galway, one of Ireland's western-most counties. The family was devoutly Catholic and imbued with the neighborhood's traditional instinct toward patriotic duty and government employment.

Connolly joined the FBI in 1969 and quickly distinguished himself. While assigned to the New York City office, he made a daring street corner arrest of one of his hometown's most notorious criminals who was hiding out in New York at the time. Cadillac Frank Salemme was wanted for the car bombing of John Fitzgerald, a well-known Boston mob lawyer. On Third Avenue in Manhattan, Connolly happened upon Salemme walking out of a jewelry store; he chased the Beantown gangster through the snow and arrested him. It was a major feather in the young agent's cap. He was rewarded with his dream assignment as a special agent with Boston's Organized Crime Squad.

In late 1975, after having been in the local office less than a year, Connolly approached Whitey Bulger. Connolly was friendly with Whitey's younger brother, state senator Billy Bulger, whose political career was on the rise. As natives of the same Southie turf, Connolly and Whitey had much in common, including a sense of pride in the accomplishments of others from their old neighborhood. As Irishmen, they also had a heightened sense of tribal loyalty stoked by years of schoolyard competition and street corner rivalries between the city's ethnic factions, especially the Irish and the Italians.

They met in a parking lot at Wollaston Beach in the shipbuilding city of Quincy, on Boston's southern border. On a pleasant moonlit night, they sat in the front seat of Connolly's Plymouth talking about old times and mutual concerns. Whitey, who'd recently turned forty-six, was no spring chicken. Although he was a physical fitness buff and as tough as a man could be at his age, the Boston underworld was crawling with younger, hungrier predators. Whitey's emergence as the boss of Southie made him a marked man; if he hoped to stay alive, maintain his position, and get ahead, he would need to massage the system.

The Mafia in New England was expanding in 1975, with the Godfather Syndrome then in full flower. Connolly told Bulger that they had a mutual enemy—what the feds referred to as LCN, La Cosa Nostra. If Whitey were willing to feed him information on the Italians and help him make cases, then Connolly would help protect Bulger from his enemies; in this mutually beneficial relationship, the Irish mobster would become an official, registered informant for the FBI and in return be virtually inoculated from criminal prosecution.

"The only thing you can't do is kill people," Connolly told Bulger.

Whitey jumped at the deal. That very month, he signed on as a C.I. and proceeded to continue his murderous ways. In fact, Bulger's newfound status as a protected informant likely gave him delusions of grandeur, leading him to surmise that the U.S. government, in the person of John Connolly, now had a vested interest in maintaining the fiction that he was some kind of honorable racketeer willing to help the FBI in their efforts to take down the dreaded Mafia.

Just one month after signing on as an official FBI informant, Whitey Bulger murdered Tom King. King was a former member of the Mullin Gang, now affiliated with Winter Hill, whose primary fault was that he had once whipped Bulger in a bar fight. In the back seat of a car near Carson Beach in Southie, Whitey shot King in the head. Then he and a couple of accomplices buried King's body in a marshy area near the Neponsit River in Quincy.

Whitey's main accomplice that day was Steve Flemmi, a savage contract killer who went by the nickname the Rifleman because he had become an expert marksman while serving as a paratrooper during the Korean War. Unbeknownst to almost everyone, Flemmi had himself been an FBI informant since 1965. Now that he and Bulger were both secretly affiliated with federal lawmen, they formed a partnership that crossed ethnic lines (Flemmi was Italian American). Over the next two decades, the duo of Bulger and Flemmi would become known as one of the most homicidal gangster partnerships in the history of the American underworld.[4]

The benefits of Bulger's newfound status as a Top Echelon informant were immediately apparent. In 1977, John Connolly got wind of the fact that Bulger was one of numerous local criminals under investigation by a federal prosecutor in connection with an elaborate race-fixing scheme. A group of mobsters led by Howie Winter, boss of the Winter Hill gang, had been fixing races for years along the East Coast by paying bribes to track officials, jockeys, and horse owners. Combined with various extravagant bets placed with designated bookmakers—some of whom were in on the scam and some not—it had been a highly profitable racket. Prosecutors estimated that the Winter Hill Gang's race-fixing scam had amassed more than $8 million in profits while operating in eight states.

A key operative in the scheme had turned canary, and more than a dozen indictments were about to come down. Connolly and his boss, John Morris, the new Chief of the FBI's Organized Crime Squad in Boston, approached the prosecutor who was overseeing the case. They informed prosecutor Jeremiah T. O'Sullivan that two of the men about to be named in his indictment—Bulger and Flemmi—were valuable Top Echelon informants for the Bureau. Furthermore, these two informants were crucial to an impending FBI investigation that would, if all went according to plan, bring about the demise of the Mafia in Boston. Bulger and Flemmi, argued Connolly, were

---

4. Before all was said and done, Bulger and Flemmi were identified as having perpetrated at least nineteen murders. Among their many victims were two women; one was a girlfriend of Flemmi's who was trying to break up with him at the time, and the other was Deborah Hussey, the daughter of another girlfriend of Flemmi's, with whom he was having an affair. Hussey, at the age of twenty-six, was strangled to death by Whitey Bulger and buried in the basement of a Southie home along with two other murder victims. A series of hidden graves throughout the Boston area were filled with the bones of mobsters, ex-girlfriends, former friends, and other unfortunate saps who happened to get on the bad side of Bulger-Flemmi.

too valuable to sacrifice on the race-fixing case. Wasn't there some way they could be dropped from the indictment? O'Sullivan was amenable to the idea, especially if Bulger and Flemmi were to provide information that would help bolster the charges against Howie Winter, et al.

About a month later, a racketeering indictment was returned against thirteen defendants. Bulger and Flemmi were not among them.

By the time the various trials and plea-bargaining arrangements were over, the race-fixing case resulted in the incarceration of nearly the entire upper echelon of the Winter Hill Gang. The venerable Howie Winter, the man who had helped negotiate an end to the Boston Gang Wars and saved Bulger's life back in 1972, was sentenced to ten years. This sentence would be superseded by other indictments that would keep him behind bars for the better part of the next two decades.

Whitey Bulger was now the de facto boss of the Winter Hill Gang. For the first time in the gang's history, their headquarters was moved out of Somerville into a garage on Lancaster Street in downtown Boston. The Lancaster Foreign Car Service became a front for Bulger's operation. On a daily basis he, Flemmi, and others met at an office inside the garage, received payments from various bookies and loan shark customers, and planned new crimes. The garage office was strategically placed midway between the headquarters of the Boston Mafia, with whom Bulger did business, and the downtown field office of the FBI.

Up until now, the relationship between Whitey and the feds had mostly been a one-way street. Bulger had been secretly spared from criminal indictment and kept abreast of underworld developments by Connolly. Bulger had even been tipped off about a bug that was planted in his Lancaster Street headquarters by the Massachusetts State Police, who had concluded in an internal memo that "virtually every organized crime figure in the metropolitan area of Boston, including both LCN and non-LCN organized crime figures, frequent the premises and it is apparent that a considerable amount of illegal business is being conducted at the garage." By leaking information about the bug to Bulger, Connolly effectively sabotaged the state police investigation.

Throughout history, there had rarely been a sweeter arrangement between a mobster and the law. Connolly was acting as Whitey's Big Brother and getting little in return. But that was all about to change.

In 1981, in a daring late-night operation, the FBI planted a bug in the North End headquarters of Gennaro "Jerry" Anguilo, the Mafia boss in Boston. Anguilo was a white-haired, cantankerous mafiosi with a Napoleon complex who didn't care much for Irishmen, especially Irish cops, whom he'd been paying off for years. "It takes a special guy to be a cop to begin with," Angiulo once said. "Disturbed upstairs . . . that's why all Irishmen are cops. They love it. Alone they're a piece of shit. When they put on the uniform and get a little power, they start destroying everything."

Angiulo's big mouth eventually brought about his demise—and the demise of the entire Cosa Nostra in Boston. The bug planted inside Angiulo's North End headquarters proved to be the centerpiece of a massive RICO case that ended with the prosecution of Jerry Angiulo, four of his brothers, and nearly a dozen others.

There has always been a difference of opinion about the extent of Whitey Bulger's contributions in the Angiulo case. FBI agents Connolly and Morris may have puffed up Whitey's role in an effort to enhance his stature within the Bureau. By most accounts, it worked. Although Bulger never had to testify in court and his role as an informant was never publicly acknowledged, in the upper echelons of the U.S. Justice Department, his contributions did not go unnoticed. With the Angiulo prosecutions of the mid-1980s, the FBI's Boston office was the toast of the law enforcement community, and Bulger's cooperation was considered by insiders to be a major coup.

For the man himself, the results were almost beyond belief. In seven short years—since climbing into bed with John Connolly and the FBI—the middle-aged mobster from South Boston had eradicated his rivals in the Winter Hill Gang, effectively taking over that organization, and presided over the fall of the Mafia in Boston. Whitey was now much more than just a wily neighborhood boss from Southie or even a major player in the Irish Mob; he was the lone man on top, king of the Beantown rackets, overseer of the city's gambling and loan-sharking operations who could rightfully claim a piece of every act of organized crime that took place in the entire metropolitan area.

It must have looked dandy, as life on top frequently does. But already planted within the story of Bulger's impressive rise to power were the seeds of destruction, not only for Whitey, but also for the entire Irish Mob.

Bulger may have outsmarted the Italians and scored a major victory in the ongoing battle between the dagos and the micks, but at what cost? His role as a government dry snitch and the use of informers in general was an insidious development with ominous implications for the mob. Apparently, the rules of the underworld had changed. The forces of the law were looking to infiltrate the mob and bring it down from within. If that meant garnering the cooperation of men who might previously have been viewed as beyond the pale, then so be it.

It was the 1980s, and the American underworld was heading into a new phase of paranoia and self-destruction. In places like New York and Boston, where the Irish American mobster was still a viable factor, old-time racketeers from the 1940s and 1950s hardly even recognized the menu. The daily special was a gastronomical disaster: a large helping of deceit and betrayal, with a topping of savage violence, and a side platter of dismemberment. The era of the informer had arrived, and the Irish Mob would never be the same.

mickey's monkey

f the Irish American underworld of the early 1980s were a celestial constellation, the latest incarnation of the Hell's Kitchen Irish Mob would be the dark star, an angry planet spinning out of control. Led by Coonan and Featherstone, the Westies had shot and Houdinied their way to the Mafia banquet table, but they didn't really know what to do when they got there. They were more accustomed to being the fly in the ointment than equal partners in a corporate-style racketeering enterprise. Coke, whiskey, greed, and the ability to kill people at will and get away with it had led them to the demonic side of American gangsterism.

Although never comprised of more of than twelve to twenty members—depending on who was in or out of jail at any given time—the Westies became synonymous with the last generation of Irish in the birthplace of the Irish Mob, a mongrel community that started with the gang and spread out from there. Brothers, sisters, nieces, and nephews claimed association with the Westies even when they were not criminals themselves because the gang represented muscle, historical continuity, and a revered brand of neighborhood loyalty that supposedly ran deeper than blood.

By claiming affiliation with the Westies, some residents of Hell's Kitchen were literally putting their lives on the line. Many of the gang's most outlandish acts had nothing to do with racketeering or profit motive. Friends killed friends over stupid barroom arguments. People got beaten up for talking to the wrong people. Old grudges were rekindled and violently resolved in the amount of time it took to snort a half gram of Colombia's finest. Innocent bystanders fled in horror or became part of the collateral damage. In January 1981, a well-known neighborhood gambler who interceded in a brawl between two brothers got himself tossed from one of the upper floors of a sparkling new forty-three-story apartment building. He splattered on top of a parked car on Tenth Avenue. In early 1982, Richie Ryan and longtime Westies compatriot Tommy Hess got into a beef at the 596 Club. Before it was over, Ryan pulled Hess's pants down around his ankles, stuck a revolver up his rectum, and pulled the trigger. Patrons stampeded toward the door. By the time cops arrived, Hess was dead, and there wasn't a witness in sight.

The fact that the gang was wild and unpredictable was terrifying, but not necessarily bad for business. "The more bodies the better," Jimmy Coonan once said. Coonan knew that dead bodies and spontaneous acts of mayhem were calling cards for a neighborhood gang; they only enhanced its reputation. As tenement gangsters from the Old School, the Westies were merely putting their own unique spin on a tradition that had been around since the days of the original Five Points gangs, when bodies were often buried in basements and tenement walls.

Mickey Featherstone was both an instigator and a victim of the Westies' mystique. He was the original loose cannon, a troubled Vietnam vet who had become Coonan's enforcer and then a major player in the New York underworld who dined with the Mafia elite. He had become a legend in his own time and was sympathetically profiled by the newspaper columnist Jimmy Breslin (himself a bona fide New York character) in the *Daily News*: "Mickey Featherstone, discharged from the army after serving as a Green Beret in Vietnam, stared at his sister. His face was the wall of a funeral parlor and his eyes were looking at a log fire that was something else."

At the age of thirty-one, with a wife and son, Featherstone had become an underworld celebrity, but he was not a happy man. By the early 1980s, he'd begun to have doubts about his role in the gang. Those doubts took root and festered while he was in the penitentiary. The circumstances that had led Mickey Featherstone to a stint in the big house were part and parcel of the Westies legend. The road to disaster started back in November 1978, a few months after Mickey and Jimmy Coonan had their sit down in Brooklyn with Paul Castellano and other high-ranking members of Cosa Nostra. Almost immediately, behind Coonan's back, members of the gang began to complain about their new status as errand boys for the Italians. Jimmy was aware of these complaints, and he had no sympathy whatsoever.

"You'll do what I tell you," Coonan said to the gang. "Or you can go out there and start your own fuckin' crew."

Coonan wasn't interested in preserving the Westies as an exclusively West Side Irish operation. In fact, Jimmy didn't even live in the neighborhood anymore. The economic realities of the modern-day underworld were such that, if the gang hoped to survive and prosper, they had to recognize that the Italians were the only game in town, plain and simple. In this regard, Coonan was determined to make the partnership work. He introduced other members of the gang to Castellano and began planning crimes with Roy DeMeo and his murderous Mafia crew in Canarsie. In Hell's Kitchen bars like Amy's Pub, the Madison Cocktail Lounge, and the bar of the Skyline Hotel, Coonan met with his own gang and pitched assignments, many of them murder-for-hire schemes that DeMeo's Brooklyn crew either didn't want or weren't able to pull off.

It was just such a job that led Coonan, Featherstone, Jimmy McElroy, and a few other Westies to find themselves drinking at the Plaka Bar on the Upper West Side late one chilly night in November. All that afternoon and into the evening, the Westies had been hunting for a union official. In fact, they'd been trying to kill this union official for days, with no luck. Tensions were running high. Many members of the gang, including Featherstone, never wanted to take on the assignment in the first place, but now that they had, they were having a hard time finding the guy. Just that afternoon, in their frustration, they'd come perilously close to gunning down the wrong man on a crowded midtown street in broad daylight.

At the Plaka Bar, Coonan was in a dark mood. By chance, the gang had just bumped into a low-level criminal they knew named Harold "Whitey" Whitehead at the bar. Coonan hated Whitehead, who had supposedly once called his brother Jackie a "fag." To lighten the mood, everyone, including Whitehead, went downstairs to the men's room to smoke a joint. Coonan stood at the urinal of the cramped restroom while the others formed a circle, handing the joint around and laughing. Coonan never took his eyes off Whitehead. Then, with no warning whatsoever, he pulled out a .25-caliber Beretta, put the gun to the base of Whitehead's skull behind his right ear and—BAM! The shot reverberated throughout the men's room, and Whitehead went down. Coonan stood over the body, eyes ablaze. He fired two more shots into Whitehead and said, "There, you bastard. Now you can burn in hell."

It was an incredibly stupid murder, uncharacteristic of Jimmy Coonan. The Plaka Bar was connected to a hotel, with people coming and going on a regular basis. The gang quickly dumped the body in a back stairwell (there was no time to make it do the Houdini) and, in their haste, left behind shell casings and other evidence.

Months later, Coonan and Featherstone were arrested and put on trial for the murder. It was a hectic time for the Westies. While being held for the Whitehead murder, Featherstone was charged with the homicide of Mickey Spillane, which had taken place almost two years earlier. And gang member Jimmy McElroy was on trial for another unrelated murder around the same time.

The Whitehead trial was a big media event that even appeared on the front page of the *New York Times*. The proceedings turned out to be something of a circus, with one witness withdrawing his sworn confession and another committing suicide instead of taking the stand. In the end, Coonan and Featherstone were found not guilty. When McElroy also beat his case in court and Featherstone was acquitted of the Spillane murder, the Manhattan district attorney's office was stunned. Thanks to their highly skilled lawyers, the Westies had apparently beaten the rap.

All was not lost for the forces of justice, however. In an all-out effort to bring down the Westies, government prosecutors cast a broad net. They got Coonan on a gun possession charge, for which he was sentenced to four and a half years. Featherstone's counterfeit currency charge was a federal rap; he could have gotten fifteen years, but he pled guilty to a reduced charge and got a nice deal, thanks again to his attorneys.

Even before he'd been shipped out of state to begin serving his sentence at a federal pen in Wisconsin, Featherstone had begun to have misgivings about his partnership with Coonan. The reason he'd gotten involved in manufacturing and selling counterfeit money in the first place was to create a revenue stream separate from Coonan and the Italians. Many of the gang's younger members had begun to coalesce around Mickey, who, unlike Coonan, still lived in the neighborhood. They felt that Mickey was more devoted to the concept of the Westies as a neighborhood gang, whereas Coonan seemed content to subcontract for the guineas.

Featherstone wasn't interested in taking over the Westies, but he was interested in making a buck and staying alive. The various trials and legal entanglements had led him to consider the fact that maybe life in the gang wasn't worth it. He had enough neighborhood contacts that, when he got out, he could find gainful employment some other way—either with the Teamsters or in the construction trades. In federal prison, far from the old neighborhood, he began to ponder the possibility of a life beyond the Westies.

The problem was that the old neighborhood ties were still strong. Mickey's wife of six years was back in New York with their two kids. In Hell's Kitchen, it had always been understood that if one of the neighborhood people wound up in prison, the other gang members would look out for his family. This tradition had existed since the earliest days of the Irish

Mob, but it was not honored in Mickey's case. The disappointment and anger that Mickey felt when he and Sissy were not given their due touched off a smoldering disenchantment that would eventually infect the entire gang and bring it crashing down.

That would all come later. In the meantime, even in Coonan and Featherstone's absence, the Westies thrived. Various no-show union jobs were controlled by the gang and doled out according to seniority. There was still loan shark and gambling money coming in on a weekly basis. In many ways, life on the West Side went on as if nothing had changed. Edna Coonan, Jimmy's wife, was making extortion collections from the unions and other local businesses for her husband, and Sissy, Mickey's wife, sometimes tagged along in an attempt to get her piece of the action. The Westies had certainly taken a major hit with the incarceration of their two top men, but the organization continued to function. While Jimmy and Mickey monitored their own personal interests from afar, the daily operations of the Hell's Kitchen Irish Mob were now mostly in the hands of the women.

Sissy and Edna

In the beginning, when the early Irish gangs were still based on political-resistance sects from the Old Country, women played a vital role in the Irish American underworld. In the era of the Dead Rabbits, females like Hellcat Maggie and Sadie the Goat were notorious gang war combatants, either as warriors or as crucial suppliers of arms, medical aid, and logistical support. Women also played a significant role in the early bordello business, especially in New Orleans, where prostitution served as a lamentable though viable source of refuge for destitute immigrants during the immediate post-famine years.

For the most part, however, women were marginalized in the underworld in the same ways they were in the upperworld. Since they were unable to vote until nearly two decades into the twentieth century, they were not a factor in forging ties between the mobster and the politician, a key aspect of the Irish Mob. They did not own saloons or work on the docks, and there were no women in the ILA or Teamsters union. During the years of Prohibition, when the American underworld-at-large first began its transformation from a series of neighborhood fiefdoms into a corporate structure modeled after Wall Street, women played about as significant a role as they did on the real Wall Street.

Above and beyond these factors was the harsh reality of violence. The American underworld was based on the law of the jungle. In most instances of gangland confrontation, brute force won out over diplomacy, at least in the short term. Gangland murders peaked during Prohibition, tapered off in the early 1930s, then continued to climb throughout the century. Increased public exposure of mob activities and prosecutions did not lessen the violence. In fact, it could be argued that, from the late 1950s (starting with Robert Kennedy's assault on organized crime) through the 1960s, 1970s, and 1980s, the forces of organized crime in America were never more violent. In cities like New York and Boston, where the Irish Mob was most active, the underworld was, to coin an old-fashioned phrase, no place for a lady.

Nonetheless, Hell's Kitchen was a tough, working-class neighborhood that produced its share of tough, working-class women. They weren't necessarily gang molls in the Hollywood sense—pistol-packing mamas like Ma Barker or Bonnie Parker—but they knew what the underworld was all about. As mothers, they sometimes saw their sons get drawn into the dangerous world of the gang. As wives, they either knew or chose not to know what their husbands were up to. They hid guns, drugs, money, or other contraband when the occasion called for it, or they played dumb when the cops came sniffing around. They may have played a subsidiary role in terms of actual criminal activity, but the life of a mobster's wife could be an existence fraught with as much fear and paranoia as that of any hoodlum on the street.

Sissy Featherstone knew what she was getting into when she hitched her wagon to the legendary kid from West Forty-third Street who'd already fought in a violent war halfway across the world, killed numerous people in the neighborhood, done time in prisons and mental hospitals, and formed a partnership with the most ambitious young gangster in Hell's Kitchen. Many women would have run for the hills upon meeting Mickey Featherstone, but Sissy was attracted to his choir boy good looks and his troubled reputation, which brought out her maternal instincts. Having grown up in the neighborhood herself, she knew what it took to survive. She was petite, just five foot three inches tall, with long sandy-blond hair, a tight, curvaceous figure, and a face that could be either glamorous or tough. People who knew her sometimes compared her to the actress Ellen Barkin, who exhibited a similar combination of toughness and vulnerability.

Her birth name was Knell, and she was German-Irish. When she was still an infant, her mother married a neighborhood laborer named Houlihan. Marcelle "Sissy" Houlihan became part of a large star-crossed Hell's Kitchen family that experienced more than its share of tough times. Over the years, six out of Sissy's eleven brothers and sister would die tragically from overdoses, murder, or suicide. The familial trauma and hardship she experienced growing up made Sissy all the more determined to create a safe haven for her own family, which had expanded with the birth of a son, Mickey, Jr., in 1977. Five years later, while Mickey was away in prison, tragedy once again struck the Houlihan family: Sissy's oldest sister became the latest family suicide. Sissy took in her daughter, and she and Mickey agreed to raise the child as their own.

Shaken by her sister's sudden death, Sissy and the two kids moved out of the neighborhood and into a small apartment in New Milford, New Jersey. Sissy had steady income from a job as a ticket taker at the *U.S.S. Intrepid*, a battleship/museum docked on a West Side pier that had been a steady source of plundering by the Westies since the day it opened for business. In addition to her job at the Intrepid, Sissy received other gang-related drips and drabs: $100 a week from Tommy Collins, who owed Mickey $5,000 from a shylock loan; $1,000 every now and then from Mugsy Ritter's coke business; and $150 a week from the neighborhood bookmaking operation, which she received from Edna Coonan.

The pittance from Edna was a source of bitterness that had eaten away at Sissy since the day Mickey and Jimmy were arrested for the Whitehead murder. While Sissy cobbled together money from various sources to make ends meet, Edna was raking in thousands every week just by making Jimmy's old rounds in the neighborhood. Initially, Sissy had accompanied Edna on her shylock runs. In the months during and after the Whitehead murder trial, she and Edna would come back from Rikers Island after visiting their husbands and spend the afternoon trying to hunt down people who owed the Westies money.

"It's funny," Edna would say. "When your husband goes away, nobody wants to pay. They always seem to disappear on you. Well, when Jimmy gets back, he'll take care of 'em."

Eventually, Sissy got fed up with the whole thing. She grew tired of listening to Edna brag about all the possessions she had in her New Jersey mansion while Sissy was living in a crowded one-bedroom apartment in New Milford. Sissy felt that Mickey was getting screwed out of money that was rightfully his, but she also knew that she wasn't going to get anywhere with stout, foul-mouthed Edna, who was at least as tough as the man she had married.

In some ways, Edna and Sissy were opposites. Where Sissy was blond, lean, and sexy, Edna was raven-haired, overweight, and manly. Sissy wore tight jeans and tiny tops that accentuated her feminine side, while Edna tended to shroud herself in one-size-fits-all dresses. On the surface they were night and day, Beauty and the Beast, but in the ways that really mattered, Edna and Sissy could have been members of the same tribe. Both were tough women who had come up the hard way.

Edna was fifteen years older than Sissy and had graduated from the school of hard knocks when Mickey's wife was still in diapers. Orphaned at the age of fourteen, she bounced from one inattentive relative to another until, at the age of twenty, she married a cop named Frank Fitzgerald. Frank and Edna had been married for a number of years and had two children when, sometime in the late 1960s, Fitzgerald died suddenly of an overdose. Now a widow in her mid-twenties with two young mouths to feed, Edna began dating a series of men who were not great husband material. Billy Beattie, a Hell's Kitchen burglar and longtime criminal partner of Jimmy Coonan's, dated Edna briefly in the early 1970s. It was through Beattie that Jimmy and Edna first met.

Coonan had never been much of a womanizer and wasn't really one for elaborate courtships. A Hell's Kitchen survivalist who spent his early years (what might otherwise have been years of sexual maturation) behind bars, he was straight-laced and even somewhat prudish. He liked and admired Edna, who was four years his senior, but he first wanted to make sure the coast was clear. One afternoon at Sonny's Café on Ninth Avenue, Coonan asked Billy Beattie, the former flame, about his intentions vis-à-vis Edna Fitzgerald.

Beattie said, "I ain't seen her in about a month. Far as I'm concerned, it's over and done with."

"Good," replied Jimmy. "That's what I was hopin' to hear. I been hangin' out with her myself."

"Hey, knock yourself out. She's all yours."

Jimmy and Edna became an item, and within four months of Jimmy's conversation with Beattie, he and Edna made plans to get married.

What Coonan liked about Edna was that she was tough, a classic defender of the throne. She was a good mother. She knew when to keep her mouth shut or when to circle the wagons. Her years as an orphan and as a struggling young widow with two kids had imbued her with a fierce sense of entitlement.

"We're gonna get what we got coming to us," she often told Sissy as they drove around Hell's Kitchen collecting money for Jimmy.

"That woman is a bitch on wheels," Sissy told Mickey on the phone while he was in prison. "She has the heart of a gangster. And she's cheap. She's cheating us outta money."

Sometimes Mickey would laugh, but he also knew his wife was right.

"Stay the fuck away from her," he told Sissy. "I'll take care of things when I get back."

In the Realm of the Westies

After serving just over four years of his six-year sentence, Featherstone was paroled and released from prison in July 1983. He spent a few weeks at a halfway house in Newark, New Jersey before being reunited with his wife and family. Still basking in the glow of his new positive attitude, which he had acquired through group therapy sessions in prison, Mickey and Sissy talked about the future. It annoyed Mickey that Coonan and the gang had not taken care of his wife while he was away, but he was determined not to let it drag him down. He and Sissy both agreed that Mickey should try to steer clear of the Westies. They should try to make it on their own.

Mickey's first big test came in September, two months after his return to civilian life, when he came into Manhattan one afternoon to pick Sissy up from work at the Intrepid Air-Sea-Space Museum. He bumped into Vinnie Leone, a union official from ILA Local 1909. Vinnie Leone was half a wiseguy who'd been instituted into Local 1909 as part of the Westies arrangement with Paul Castellano and the Gambino family.

"Hey, Mickey. I heard you was back," said Leone. The burly, silver-haired union boss gave Featherstone a hug. "You gotta come by the office; say hello to the fellas."

There were three or four men playing cards at a table in the front room when Leone and Featherstone entered the red-brick ILA offices on Twelfth Avenue. Leone introduced Mickey to everybody and then said, "Hey, I was out of state visiting Jimmy last week."

"Yeah?" said Mickey. "How's he doing?"

"Tough as can be. You know Jimmy."

"Yeah."

"Hey, Mick, everybody's happy to have you back here. No shit. Things've been goin' good, real good."

To illustrate his point, Leone pulled a wad of bills out of his pocket and peeled off a few twenties. "Here," he said, handing some money to Featherstone. "Here's a hundred. But that's chickenshit. Just some chump change to get you started. They'll be more from now on. Way more."

"Nah," said Mickey. "That's all right."

Leone laughed; he thought Mickey was joking. He tried to stick the bills in Mickey's shirt pocket. When Mickey insisted that he didn't want the money and would rather "go my own way," Leone turned serious. "All right, Mick, if you say so. But I gotta tell ya, Jimmy C. ain't gonna like this one bit."

Mickey shrugged and left the office.

For a while, Featherstone did his best to maintain the pact he'd made with himself and his wife. Through his brother-in-law, he got a job as a bartender at a catering hall in Garfield, New Jersey, where he made a modest living wage. Mickey and Sissy's most immediate problem was their apartment. It was far too small to accommodate a family of four. They went house-hunting and found a place they liked in Teaneck, a pleasant middle-class town just a thirty-minute drive from the West Side of Manhattan.

"I love the house," said Sissy. "But we can't afford it right now."

Mickey thought about it and said, "Let me try Jimmy. Just this one time. He owes me."

Sissy was against the idea. As bad as she wanted the house, she knew that if they borrowed the money from Coonan, it would come with strings attached—strings that would inevitably entangle Mickey and draw him back into the realm of the Westies.

From the inception of the mob, going straight, or staying clean, was one of the most threatening things a gangster could try to do. Becoming involved in the criminal life was usually something that happened incrementally and without much thought, but getting out often required that a person go cold turkey and sever ties in a manner that was bound to create misunderstandings and deep suspicion on the part of those left behind. Few things are more dangerous to the mob than an ex-mobster, who knows where the bodies are buried and has no compelling financial stake in keeping his mouth shut.

Featherstone, whose very identity had been established as a prominent enforcer for the Westies, had the additional problem of trying to walk away from the gang while still psychologically and financially wedded to the neighborhood. Perhaps he was living in a dreamworld, thinking he could simply move to the suburbs and leave the Westies behind. Or maybe he was thinking he could still keep one toe in the water, as Jimmy Coonan had done, living in suburban New Jersey while controlling the neighborhood as a commuter criminal. In any event, Mickey wasn't making it any easier for himself by going to his longtime buddy with his hand outstretched, especially when he had to ask for the loan through Jimmy's battleaxe of a wife.

"Gee, Mickey, I don't know," said Edna, after Featherstone asked for a loan of $40,000, which he pledged to pay back in installments. "I gotta talk to Jimmy about that, see what he says."

Two weeks later Mickey got his answer, and it didn't even come from Edna. It came from a neighborhood contact of Mickey's, who heard it from Edna's brother, who heard it from Edna, who got the word from Jimmy. The answer was "No."

At first Mickey was shocked. "After all the shit I been through with Jimmy Coonan?" he asked himself. "Murders, hacking up bodies, being willing to die for the guy? And this ungrateful motherfucker tells me no?"

Sissy said she wasn't surprised at all; she had expected it. But Mickey found it hard to believe that Coonan, for whom he had literally put himself through hell, would treat him this way.

Four weeks later, Mickey and Sissy received an invitation to an engagement party for the Coonans' oldest son, Bobby. The party was to be held in a large room at the Hazlet, New Jersey, firehouse, and everyone from the old neighborhood was expected to attend. Edna had even rented a bus to pick up a group of people in front of the Skyline Motor Inn on Tenth Avenue and transport them to and from Hazlet.

"I can't believe this bitch," said Sissy when they got the invitation. "She treats us like dogs, then expects us to come to an engagement party?"

Mickey, however, wanted to go. "We can't let her think she controls our lives. Why give her the satisfaction? We'll go there and hold our heads high just like everybody else."

It was a snowy night in November when over one hundred residents from Hell's Kitchen arrived at the firehouse in Hazlet. Edna had hired a band, so there was dancing, and tables were set up around the room where people could eat and talk. It was a festive atmosphere, with everyone drinking and getting reacquainted.

At some point in the evening, Edna sidled up to Mickey and said, "I need to talk to you."

"Okay," said Mickey.

"Jimmy feels bad about the loan. He knows you need money and all, so he's got a proposition. He's willin' to turn over the West Side piers to you, the whole thing. But you gotta do something for him."

"I'm listening."

Edna explained that there were three people Jimmy wanted whacked. One was Vinnie Leone, the ILA official the Italians had ensconced on the West Side. According to Coonan, Leone was ripping off the Westies, and Jimmy had received authorization from the Gambino family to take him out.

The other guy Jimmy wanted whacked was Billy Beattie, Edna's ex-boyfriend. Beattie had welched on a loan shark debt that was long overdue. "Jimmy wants him dead," said Edna, "and so do I."

The third person was another neighborhood guy who had run afoul of Jimmy.

Mickey listened to all of this and said, "Edna, I don't want it. Don't want no part of this shit."

"Mickey, this is serious. This is business."

"I know what it is. I don't want it."

Edna looked hard at Featherstone. "Okay, Mickey, I'll tell Jimmy. I know he's gonna be very disappointed."

Mickey shrugged.

" 'Cause you know this is gonna get done anyway, right? Whether you do it or somebody else does it, it's gonna get done."

"That ain't my problem. That's your problem."

After Mickey and Edna separated, Sissy Featherstone approached her husband. She'd overheard bits and pieces of his conversation with Coonan's wife, and she could hardly contain her anger. "Are you gettin' involved with these fucking people? Are you gettin' involved again?"

Mickey and Sissy argued loudly, attracting the attention of those around them. Mickey tried to explain that he had said no to Edna's proposition, but Sissy was so upset she was hardly listening. "That treacherous bitch!" she kept saying over and over.

Things got even more heated later on that night, when a smaller group of neighborhood people reconvened over at the Coonan house. After watching Edna gleefully show off each and every new gadget in her house and catching her once again trying to lure Mickey back into Jimmy's schemes, Sissy could no longer contain herself. She laid into Edna, calling her a "fat cunt," a "treacherous bitch," and every other insult she could think of. Edna just sat there like she was above it all.

"You just remember," snapped Sissy, grabbing Mickey to leave. "You keep that husband of yours outta our lives, or I'll come back here and burn this goddamn house to the ground."

After that, Mickey tried to stay on the straight and narrow. He got a job at Erie Transfer, a Teamster garage based in Hell's Kitchen that supplied rented trucks and trailers to the entertainment industry. He didn't have a union book yet, but he was getting work almost every day just by showing up. There was plenty of idle time on the job—and lots of cocaine. Coke was prevalent at every level of the entertainment business at the time, and it was commonly sold in working-class bars throughout Hell's Kitchen. Mickey had tried to avoid it at first, preferring marijuana and alcohol. But the boredom and routine nature of daily employment, plus his estrangement from his fellow Westies, ate away at Featherstone's resolve until he was snorting coke on the job almost every day.

Working on the West Side, he was never far away from his old haunts and old ways. As much as he may have wanted to, Featherstone could not entirely separate himself from the gang. He'd heard through the grapevine that certain people in the neighborhood were using his name, as in "You better pay up, or Mickey Featherstone is gonna be pissed." Or, "We're with Mickey Featherstone, so you better not try an' cross us." The idea that certain members of the Westies were making money off his reputation without his authorization was enough to push him over the edge.

Edna had been right about one thing: Underworld crime on the West Side was going to continue, and Jimmy Coonan's wishes would be carried out, whether Mickey was in on it or not. Featherstone found this to be true a couple months after Edna's party in New Jersey, when he heard that one of the people on Coonan's hit list had been whacked. Jimmy McElroy told Mickey how he and a fellow gang member, Kevin Kelly, killed Vinnie Leone, the ILA official who was ripping them off.

The conversation took place at McElroy's West Side apartment, which had a panoramic view overlooking the Hudson River. Kevin Kelly was also there. Nine years younger than Featherstone and McElroy, Kelly represented the next generation of gangsters on the West Side. He'd grown up hearing stories about Coonan and Featherstone and the neighborhood's glorious gangland associations. Short and black-haired (with a passing resemblance to the actor Matt Dillon), Kelly was a godson of James McManus, the neighborhood political leader, and married to Jimmy McElroy's niece. His entire life seemed to be devoted to positioning himself to take over the Hell's Kitchen rackets.

The three men—Featherstone, McElroy, and Kelly—were sitting in McElroy's front room, deep into an afternoon session of whiskey and cocaine, when McElroy and Kelly explained how, a week earlier, they met Leone at the Local 1909 offices on Twelfth Avenue. Leone lived out in Jersey near one of McElroy's girlfriends, and they asked him if he'd be willing to drop them off on his way home. "Sure," Leone said.

In the car, McElroy told Vinnie they had some good coke they wanted to try out. Vinnie was game. He exited the expressway and pulled over on an idyllic tree-lined suburban street. Kelly was in the back seat, McElroy in the front passenger seat, and Leone behind the wheel.

After Leone had just taken in a snout full of white powder, Kelly, from behind, put a small caliber automatic to the base of Vinnie's skull and began firing. He emptied the chamber, firing six shots when one would have easily done the job. Leone's head and brains splattered like watermelon over the inside of the windshield. Particles of flesh and brain matter sprayed Jimmy McElroy, who had his fingers pressed to his ears, trying to block out the deafening sound of gunfire. Kelly, an amateur, hadn't even used a silencer.

At the time, McElroy almost panicked, but he laughed about it now as he related the story to Featherstone. All the car windows had been rolled up, he said, and the shots were so loud that they rang in his ears for hours afterward.

"Two days later," said McElroy, "we drove over to the prison and visited Jimmy C. We told him we took care of that Italian fuck, Leone, and now we wanted the piers, just like he said."

"And?" asked Featherstone.

"He said, 'You got it, you know. Long as Mickey's in it with youse.'"

Okay, thought Mickey. All right. So they finally got to the point. Mickey was ready for this, so ready he even had a little speech prepared.

In a coke-induced torrent, Featherstone let it all out, expressing anger about his wife and family not being taken care of while he was gone. If he were to come back, he said, things would not be the same. "'Cause I ain't in it for friendship no more," said Mickey. "And I ain't in it for loyalty. I'm in it for one thing: money."

McElroy and Kelly both assured Mickey that things would be better this time and that the piers were theirs to do with as they pleased. From now on, anytime Mickey's name was used by any member of the crew in any transaction, he would get his cut.

"We'll make sure of that," promised Kelly.

In the days and weeks that followed, the word spread like a hot tip at the race track: Mickey Featherstone was back. He stopped showing up for work at Erie Transfer and instead began making the rounds, tying up loose ends on behalf of the Westies. He met with ILA officials from Local 1909 and told them that if they didn't resume making full weekly payments to the gang, they were going to wind up like Vinnie Leone, with their brains splattered all over the inside of a car. The president of Teamster Local 817 was told that if he didn't provide the requisite number of union books for certain West Side workers, the gang would kill one member of his local a week until there were enough openings for their people. All freelance operators on the West Side—loan sharks, drug dealers, sports betting operations—were told that they had better fork over a percentage to the Westies, or they would be put out of business.

Within months, Featherstone was pulling in $4,000 a week, twice what he'd been making while working a legitimate job. He finally had enough money to make a down payment on the house in Teaneck. The timing was perfect. Sissy had recently given birth to their third child, and she was already pregnant with a fourth.

Mickey was happy about the kids and the house, but other than that he didn't seem to give a fuck. He was zonked out on coke and booze much of the time. Those who knew him noticed that he seemed to be reverting back to the old Mickey Featherstone—angry, unfocused, violent—all of it geared toward one thing: an inevitable showdown with his former friend and mentor, Jimmy Coonan.

The Return of Jimmy C.

From the beginning of the Irish American underworld, loyalty was the glue that held everything together. In the famine years, when the Irish arrived en masse—starving, disease-ridden, and despised by the Anglo-Saxon elite—banding together was not a choice but a survival mechanism. The Irish became known as clannish for this very reason. Seen as human cockroaches by society at large, they relied on one another and devised social systems by which they were able to crawl out of the woodwork and advance, whether others liked it or not. For these social systems to operate successfully, loyalty was considered essential, whether it was to the church, the police department, the union, or the gang.

Loyalty is a positive value, but also a trait highly susceptible to manipulation. The very nature of loyalty implies a willing dispensation of power; a person pledges loyalty to something other than him or herself, knowing that he or she is giving up an element of personal choice. Given the magnitude of this proposition, a pledge of loyalty is often accompanied by a ritual or ceremony of some kind.

For Jimmy Coonan, the ritual involved the bloodletting, dismemberment, and disposal of a human body, which was always done in consort with other gang members. An outsider might surmise that Coonan was exposing himself to potential prosecution by creating witnesses to his grisly acts, but Jimmy figured that he was doing just the opposite. Men who cut up a body together entered into a pact so horrible that they were not likely to talk about it with others; it was like a pledge of loyalty: Coonan's version of the West Side Code.

Jimmy was counting on the West Side Code when he returned to the neighborhood in December 1984, after an absence of over four years. At first, everyone tried to act as if nothing had changed. There were a series of meetings on the West Side with Featherstone, McElroy, Kelly, and others in which Coonan sought to lay out his agenda for the 1980s. There were a number of people who Jimmy felt needed to be killed. One of them was a former West Side resident named Michael Holly. Coonan and other Westies wanted Holly dead because they believed he had played a role in the death of another gang member many years before. There had been a contract out on Holly's life for at least eight years, and Coonan felt it was an embarrassment to the gang that it had never been resolved.

"It makes us look disorganized, weak," said Jimmy one afternoon at the Skyline. "Who's gonna take care of this?" He looked directly at Mickey, but Mickey just glared right back and said nothing.

"Billy Bokun needs to do this job," interrupted McElroy. "It was his brother who got killed."

Coonan let it slide. After the meeting on Tenth Avenue, he and Featherstone exchanged small talk. It was awkward—like a husband and wife coming together after a long separation and realizing the magic is no longer there.

Coonan was seen in the neighborhood only sporadically after that. He was spending nearly all of his time with the Italians. His old buddy, Roy DeMeo, had been murdered by his own people; Coonan's new point man was Danny Marino, a Gambino family capo based in Brooklyn.

To people on the West Side, Jimmy looked and acted different. When he was with Danny Marino and other mafiosi, he was deferential, almost like a lackey. "I never seen the guy act the way he does with those people," said McElroy.

Featherstone particularly disliked Danny Marino, who dressed like a parody of a mafiosi, all silk, gold chains, and diamond-studded pinky rings. He made fun of Marino and the other Italians, referring to them as Al Calognes, which made Coonan angry.

"Whether you like it or not," said Coonan, "we got business to do with these people. Besides, you could learn a thing or two from them."

Among Jimmy's assorted ventures with the Italians was a construction contracting firm he was in the process of starting with his brother-in-law. Marine Construction, based in Tarrytown, just north of Manhattan, was going to serve as a front for the Gambino Crime family; Coonan would use his West Side connections to obtain lucrative no-bid contracts, with the spillover going to the Gambinos. New York was experiencing a construction boom in the mid-1980s, so the arrangement had the potential to make millions for Coonan and the Italians. Jimmy had said nothing about this arrangement to his fellow Westies and apparently had no intention of sharing Marine Construction with them.

In addition, there was the Jacob Javits Convention Center, which had finally begun construction after nearly seven years of planning. Many lives had been lost in the power struggles over who was going to control construction contracts and other racketeering-related ventures associated with the largest convention center in the United States. The building was on the West Side and belonged to the Irish Mob. Coonan, not wanting to jeopardize his relationship with the Gambinos, had not advocated very strongly for his people. It looked like the convention center was going to be up for grabs, and the Irish would have to fight for their rightful piece of the pie.

Some members of the Westies were livid. In Hell's Kitchen bars, Featherstone, McElroy, Kelly, and other longtime gang members began to voice the unthinkable: *Jimmy don't want to be one of us no more. He wants to be an Italian. He needs to be taken out.* Featherstone was considered the number two man in the gang, so everyone turned to him. Mickey was equally pissed off that Coonan was turning over everything to the Italians, but he wasn't sure whom he could trust. From deep within his own paranoia, Mickey half-believed the gang was out to get him, not Coonan. He certainly didn't trust young Kevin Kelly, who seemed to be scheming to take over the West Side rackets. McElroy, he believed, was more loyal to Coonan than to him. The others would follow whoever wound up on top.

One person Featherstone did trust was Billy Beattie, the longtime Westie who had been marked for death by Jimmy and Edna Coonan. When Beattie heard that he was on Coonan's hit list, he fled the neighborhood and never returned, hiding out in the Catskill Mountains in Upstate New York. Through Beattie's brother, Featherstone got word to Billy that he wanted to talk to him.

A frightened Billy Beattie met with Mickey one afternoon near Central Park, far from Hell's Kitchen.

"I just wanna tell you one thing," Billy told Mickey, getting right to the subject that was on both their minds. "If Coonan's gonna kill me, I want you to know why—the real story."

Mickey smiled. He'd always liked Beattie, who was the designated comic relief of the Westies, a guy who could be counted on to puncture a tense situation with a joke or a funny comment. "Hey," said Mickey. "You don't have to tell me. I'll tell you."

Beattie looked startled.

"I'll bet Edna tried to hit on you."

"How the fuck did you know?"

"I don't know, man, I just figured."

Beattie explained how Edna, whom he'd dated years ago before she married Coonan, had found out where he was staying. While Jimmy was away in prison, she'd started calling up and making sexual advances. Beattie would hang up on her, but she'd call again the next night.

"That's the whole reason she wants me dead. And that bitch probably told Jimmy I'm the one that was coming on to *her*!"

"Billy," said Mickey, "I don't wanna kill you, okay? I don't intend to kill you. Neither do any of the other guys, 'cept maybe Jimmy. I believe he wants to kill me, too. So, you know, what else can we do? It's like, kill or be killed, know what I'm sayin'?"

It had finally come to this. Featherstone, Beattie, McElroy, and the others agreed that Coonan needed to be whacked. They came up with various half-baked plans, then passed along a gun to Billy Beattie, who was given the assignment. But Billy got cold feet and refused to carry out the hit alone. At one point, the gang considered hiring a black guy to dress up as a Rastafarian, go out to Hazlet, and gun Jimmy down in his suburban Jersey neighborhood. If the shooter were black, the cops would never think to trace the hit to the Westies. Everybody liked that idea until they realized there probably wasn't a single black person in all of Hazlet; any Rasta seen in that neighborhood would probably be arrested on general principle.

The whole thing reached a low point one afternoon around St. Patrick's Day, 1985, when the gang put on bulletproof vests, piled into a car, and drove out to Hazlet, hoping to catch Coonan at home. "The house that Ruby built," they called Coonan's home at 15 Vanmater Terrace because Jimmy had purchased the place with money he saved by murdering Ruby Stein. They drove around the neighborhood for an hour or so bitching about Jimmy and Edna, passing a joint around and getting high. They never saw Jimmy that day.

Although everyone was trying to act tough, the thought of killing Jimmy Coonan was fraught with bad connotations. If the Westies had been mafiosi, the hit would have probably been cleared with higher-ups, all uncertainty assuaged and potential consequences agreed upon beforehand. But when it came to the Irish, a hit was a hit, let the consequences be damned. The gang's subterranean concerns about what lay ahead made it hard for them to pull the trigger. After Coonan was gone, who would control the West Side rackets? Who would give the orders? The possibilities were paralyzing.

Although the hit had not happened by mid-April, everyone felt it was imminent. Maybe it would take place right on Tenth Avenue when Coonan drove by in his brand new black Mercedes. Maybe it would happen in a restaurant when he was eating pasta with one of his goomba friends. Or maybe it would be quiet, and Jimmy Coonan would just disappear one day, his body made to "do the Houdini" just as he had made so many other bodies disappear over the years.

The underworld had a way of creating its own bad karma. Even though everyone believed the Coonan hit was bound to happen, it never did. Instead, the tables were turned: An old Westie nemesis named Michael Holly got gunned down in broad daylight, and Mickey Featherstone, whose life with the gang had been an emotional roller-coaster ever since he returned from prison, was going to take the fall.

The murder took place outside the Jacob Javitz Convention Center, where forty-year-old Michael Holly worked as a laborer. On the afternoon of April 25, 1985, Holly was on his lunch break, walking along West Thirty-fifth Street toward Clarke's Bar on Tenth Avenue. It was a few minutes before noon, with plenty of people on the street to witness a beige station wagon with New Jersey license plates come careening down the block. The car screeched to a halt near Holly, who had no idea what was happening. From the passenger side of the car, a man with sandy-blond hair bolted to the street and opened fire on Holly, hitting him five times. Holly's final words were, "Aaaargh . . . You dirty motherfucker." Then he fell to the pavement and died.

The morning after the Michael Holly murder, Mickey Featherstone, his wife Sissy (then six months pregnant), and their stepdaughter arrived at Erie Transfer on West Fifty-second Street. Mickey was there to pick up a paycheck. The second he stepped out of his car, he was surrounded by a swarm of NYPD cops and detectives, all with their guns drawn. He was quickly separated from his wife and stepdaughter, handcuffed, and placed under arrest.

"Mind tellin' me what for?" asked Featherstone.

"Wouldn't you like to know," said a detective.

Featherstone found out soon enough. In the days that followed, he was placed in two separate police line-ups and identified by witnesses as the person who shot and killed Michael Holly.

Mickey was dumfounded. While being held in jail for the murder, he heard from various neighborhood sources what had taken place. The Holly murder had been devised by Kevin Kelly, a criminal partner of his named Kenny Shannon, and Billy Bokun, the brother of the guy Michael Holly had supposedly setup almost a decade earlier. Kenny Shannon had been the driver and Bokun the triggerman. Billy Bokun was a young wannabe gangster in the neighborhood who admired the likes of Coonan and Featherstone. At five foot seven, with brown hair and a large, red birthmark that covered one side of his face, he looked nothing like Mickey Featherstone. From his cell, Mickey tried to figure how Boken could have been mistaken for Mickey as the shooter. Then he heard that Bokun had worn a disguise—a sandy-blond wig and fake mustache the same color as Mickey's. They had also used a rented car from Erie Transfer to commit the murder. The car was identical to one Featherstone had rented and been driving around in the days leading up to the murder.

There were dozens of other inexplicable little details that ate away at Mickey while he was being held at Rikers Island, charged with Murder One (which carried a mandatory sentence of twenty-five years to life). He began to suspect that maybe he'd been setup to take the fall, that Kelly, Shannon, and Jimmy Coonan had constructed an elaborate scheme leading to his arrest, knowing full well that the cops and prosecutors would jump at the chance to convict the legendary Mickey Featherstone, who had beaten so many murder raps in the past.

In the months leading up to his trial, Mickey descended deeper into his own paranoia and began to deteriorate. He got high whenever he could, thanks to his wife, who smuggled cocaine and marijuana to Mickey at the Rikers Island visiting room. She would wrap the illegal substance in a tiny rubber balloon, put it in her mouth, then pass the balloon from her mouth to his when they kissed. Mickey would swallow it, retrieve it later when he defecated, and snort and smoke whatever Sissy had been able to get her hands on.

On the verge of his trial in March 1986, Mickey became even more convinced that something was amiss when he heard that Billy Bokun had confessed to the legal team of Hochheiser and Aronson that he, not Mickey, had shot Michael Holly. Bokun had even told the lawyers and Mickey that he felt terrible about Featherstone facing a life sentence for the hit; he wanted to "walk into the courtroom and confess." But Hochheiser and Aronson, who were the attorneys of record for both Featherstone and Bokun, told Bokun to keep his confession to himself.

In fairness to the attorneys, their position was a complicated one. Just because Bokun wanted to confess didn't mean that he was telling the truth. Bokun worshipped Mickey Featherstone: What if Mickey had put him up to this confession? If so, Bokun would likely crumble on the witness stand and the lawyers would be left with a defendant who, in the eyes of the jury, looked even more guilty than he had before. All things considered, they felt it was best to go to trial without Bokun's confession and beat the charge against Featherstone by attacking the recollection of the government's eye-witnesses—a tactic they had successfully employed many times in the past.

To Mickey, the logic of his lawyers' position made no sense and became even more inexplicable as the trial began. For three straight weeks, Featherstone watched in a semistupor as his life went up in flames. He was identified by three eyewitnesses, none of whom were effectively cross-examined by defense counsel. Even more distressing to Mickey was when his lawyers called Kevin Kelly to testify on his behalf. Mickey told his lawyers, "Don't do it; he'll come off as a gangster," but they felt it was important to establish that Mickey was left-handed, whereas the gunman had been iden-tified as being right-handed. On the stand, Kelly was rude and menacing, reaffirming Mickey's suspicion that there was some kind of setup afoot. His conspiracy theory expanded to include his attorneys when he heard that Billy Bokun had arrived outside the courtroom one day, still wanting to confess, but the lawyers turned him away.

It was obvious to Mickey: Coonan must have heard that he and the other Westies were conspiring to take him out. Rather than kill his popular num-ber two man, Jimmy had devised a plan to make Mickey take the fall for the Holly murder. It was an ingenious plot that Featherstone might have admired were he not on the receiving end.

When the guilty verdict was delivered, Mickey was devastated but not surprised. He'd seen it coming. For weeks he'd watched his own trial like a cornered animal, frustrated and helpless, his options dwindling day by day until there was only one choice left. It was not an alternative that he relished, but he was willing to take the step. As the entire New York Irish Mob was about to find out, Mickey Featherstone felt he had nothing left to lose.

Settling Old Scores

Jimmy Coonan was mostly an offstage presence during the months of Featherstone's demise. He was a full-time Italian now, and his relationship with the Gambino family had taken some unexpected twists and turns. On December 18, 1985, while Featherstone was still awaiting trial for the Holly murder, Paul Castellano got whacked. The capo di tutti capi and his body-guard were filled with lead on a busy Midtown Manhattan street during rush hour. It was an outlandish mob hit in the old style, and it brought about the ascension of a new boss of the Gambino family, a thuggish, sartorially inclined former button man named John Gotti—the same John Gotti who first made his bones by whacking the small-time Irish gangster Jimmy McBratney.

Within weeks of the Castellano hit, Coonan was introduced to the new boss. Coonan and the Dapper Don immediately hit it off. They met numerous times in early 1986 at the Ravenite Social Club in Little Italy and also at Gotti's club in Howard Beach, Queens. With his penchant for violence and fervent belief in street justice over boardroom diplomacy, Gotti was more Coonan's style than Castellano had been. Like Jimmy, he was a brute, a man inclined to strike first and ask questions later (Gotti was once recorded on government wiretaps saying of an underling, "I'll sever his fuckin' head off."). The new boss was bound to find common ground with Jimmy Coonan, who was anxious to expand his relationship with the Italians by way of Marine Construction, his mob-affiliated contracting company.

Constantly on the lookout for ways to endear himself to the Gambinos, in May 1986, Jimmy heard about a dispute *la famiglia* was having with an Irish-born union official. At the Brooklyn funeral of a recently murdered Gambino family capo, Jimmy was told how John O'Connor, business agent for Carpenter's Union Local 608, had run afoul of Gotti and his people by ordering the trashing of a downtown Manhattan restaurant that was using nonunion labor. Unbeknownst to O'Connor, the restaurant was under the protection of the Gambino crime family.

Gotti wanted to deliver a message to O'Connor. Coonan jumped at the chance and volunteered the services of the Westies. The Dapper Don took him up on his offer. How could he resist? Using an Irishman to punish an Irishman was a proud Mafia tradition going back to the earliest days of Cosa Nostra in America.

Coonan assigned the job to Jimmy McElroy, who pawned it off on the new Westie hit team of Kevin Kelly and Kenny Shannon. They were not supposed to kill O'Connor, only deliver a pointed message. As the silver-haired union official arrived at his Midtown Manhattan office building for work one morning, he was shot multiple times below the waist by an unidentified assailant.

Meanwhile, Mickey Featherstone was supposedly awaiting sentencing on his murder conviction at Rikers Island. On the afternoon of May 16, Kevin Kelly visited Featherstone at Rikers and told him all about the O'Connor shooting in loving detail.

"We gave the guy a new asshole for being an asshole," Kevin told Mickey.

What Kelly did not know was that Featherstone was cooperating with the government at the time, and that a bug had been planted behind a picture on the wall near where he and Mickey were seated.

The recording of Kelly's description of the O'Connor shooting was just one of numerous tapes that Mickey and his wife Sissy would compile throughout the spring and summer of 1986. They had turned to the government in an attempt to prove Mickey's innocence in the Holly murder, but the government played hardball. They were not interested in whether or not Featherstone had been wrongly convicted for the murder—*unless* Mickey first signed an agreement specifying his full cooperation with the government in a broad, far-reaching RICO case against the Westies. Rather than spend the rest of his life in prison for a murder he didn't commit, Featherstone agreed.

Sissy wound up shouldering most of the burden. She was the one who was still out on the street, so she had to gather much of the evidence that would exonerate her husband. In a series of conversations with Kelly, Shannon, Bokun, and others who were involved in the Holly murder, she tried to solicit information without asking questions that were too obvious. If the men discovered what Sissy was up to, she'd almost certainly be murdered on the spot.

Of the many incriminating confessions and crucial pieces of information that Sissy was able to get, the most poignant confession came from Billy Bokun, whom Sissy had known since he was a little boy. Bokun had been conflicted ever since Mickey Featherstone was arrested for the Holly murder, and he became even more distraught after Sissy's husband was convicted. In a meeting between Sissy and Bokun that took place at the Ninth Avenue International Food Festival, an annual street fair in Hell's Kitchen, Bokun poured his heart out. Standing on the corner of Fifty-first Street and Nineth Avenue, as thousands of people flooded around them, Bokun tearfully told Sissy, "They told me, they told me to wear a wig and mustache."

"See, now, to this day, Kevin says you didn't wear a mustache."

"I wore a mustache. But it was so light and so thin I had to pencil it in. It was an eyeliner mustache."

"That's what's messin' Mickey up. Mickey's goin', 'Why the fuck?' ''Cause,' I said to Mickey, 'I don't doubt Billy. Billy says to this day they told him to wear a mustache. I don't doubt that.' Were you high, though, that day?"

"No, I was straight."

"Yeah? Did Michael Holly ever see you comin' toward him?"

"Uh, I was in the car. He didn't see nothin'. I jumped out—boom! I just shot him. One-two-three-four-five. Back in the car. Ten seconds, no more. . . . I'm not ashamed of what I did. I think what I did is absolutely right."

"Why you did it is, you feel—"

"I feel 'cause he whacked my brother. He was responsible for John. Otherwise I wouldn't have done it."

"But remember when you said, 'Kevin fuckin' set me up. And he didn't only set me up, he set Mickey up along with me.' Remember?"

"Right. I said that after the fact. After I spoke to your husband, after me and Mickey decided that it was true . . ."

Bokun sputtered; he was so upset there were tears in his eyes. "Alls I was supposed to do was go over to that corner, you know, and go and shoot the guy. And I didn't know nothin' else about the plan, see. The reason I'm by myself is, I don't know, I'm not the type of guy who can walk around and shoot everybody. I can shoot anyone for my brother, but I can't just go out and whack everybody. It's my personality. I mean, that's my big fault. I guess it's my loyalty to everybody, you know. I'm so loyal, 'cause I can't help it."

Sissy let Billy ramble on and hang himself. She got it all on tape. She felt sick about it because she liked Billy and had known him forever, but her survival and her family's survival were at stake. The way she saw it, there was no choice.

On September 5, Mickey Featherstone was brought before Judge Alvin Schlessinger, the same judge who had presided over his murder trial. The same prosecutor who had secured Featherstone's conviction now stood before the judge and read a statement: "On too many occasions to cite, the New York County D.A.'s office has gone to extraordinary lengths to investigate claims of innocence by people either charged or convicted of crimes which they claim they did not do. Usually those claims do not hold water. However, on those rare occasions when they do, our obligation to see that justice is carried out is clear: That conviction must be set aside . . .

"When all the evidence in this particular case is taken together, the People are now convinced beyond a reasonable doubt that it was William Bokun and not Francis Featherstone who shot and killed Michael Holly."

"In the interest of justice," declared Judge Schlessinger, "I am compelled to overturn this conviction."

The next morning, those citizens with even a passing knowledge of the Westies looked at the morning papers and gagged on their coffee. Not only had Mickey Featherstone's murder conviction been overturned, but it was also announced that the Westies' most notorious hitman was now cooperating with the government against the gang. "Westies Con Sings Irish Lullaby," was the headline in the *New York Post*. The long reign of the Hell's Kitchen Irish Mob had just taken a dramatic turn for the worse.

The gang scattered. Coonan went into hiding but was eventually cornered in New Jersey and placed under arrest. Edna was arrested in front of the family Christmas tree in their home in Hazlet. Others, including Billy

Bokun, Mugsy Ritter, and a woman named Florence Collins were arrested in and around Hell's Kitchen. Flo Collins, fifty-two years old, was a neighborhood coke dealer along with her husband Tommy Collins, who was also arrested.

Jimmy McElroy pulled a lambrooskie. But McElroy was a creature of habit. The NYPD knew of a place in Mesa, Arizona, where he'd gone on the lam once before, and he was arrested there by federal authorities. Kevin Kelly and Kenny Shannon also went into hiding. More successful than McElroy, they eluded capture for nearly two years until they were forced to turn themselves in after being profiled on the TV show *America's Most Wanted.*

A number of gang members, upon hearing of Featherstone's cooperation, struck their own deals with the government. Billy Beattie became a government informant, agreeing to testify in court against the Westies after pleading guilty to RICO charges. Throughout 1986 and into 1987, state murder indictments were returned against various members of the gang. Then in March, Rudolph Giuliani, the U.S. Attorney for the Southern District of New York, stepped in and announced a massive federal indictment that would supersede all others. Ten members of the Westies, including those already hit with the state indictments, were charged on fourteen counts of having taken part in a racketeering conspiracy. The RICO charges dated back some twenty years and included extortion, loan-sharking, counterfeiting, gambling, and sixteen counts of murder, attempted murder, and conspiracy to commit murder. These charges, assured Giuliani, would finally bring about an end to what he termed "the most savage organization in the long history of New York gangs."

The trial began in September, exactly one year after Mickey Featherstone's cooperation with the government was first announced. On a daily basis, family members of the defendants, residents of Hell's Kitchen, and other interested citizens filed into Room 506 in Manhattan federal court. They were there, for the most part, to see Featherstone—the once shy, neighborhood kid who became a troubled Vietnam vet, then a feared enforcer for the Westies, and now the unthinkable: a rat, a stool pigeon, an informer.

In the years of the Westies, no single person had personified the West Side Code more than Featherstone. For nearly a decade, he was the one who beat up or warned any neighborhood person who was even rumored to have spoken to the bulls. He enforced the neighborhood's revered code of silence with an iron fist. His years as a soldier in Vietnam and as a gang member had placed his loyalty beyond question. Even people who were not gangsters or associated with the criminal rackets accepted and admired Mickey. Like most of the Westies, he was not big or physically imposing, but he was always ready to fight, shoot, and kill on behalf of certain longstanding neighborhood traditions. The thought that Featherstone—*Mickey fucking Featherstone!*—was the one who was going to divulge the neighborhood's darkest criminal secrets to the public at large was too much for some West Siders to bear. They could not believe that it was true, and so they made the trek downtown to the criminal courthouse to see for themselves.

On the stand, Mickey was dressed in a suit and tie. His hair was neatly trimmed, and he had the same sandy-blond mustache that had contributed to his conviction for the Holly murder. In a soft voice that sounded like that of one of the Dead End Kids, he revealed a litany of crimes and events that spanned a lifetime. Throughout four long weeks of direct testimony and cross-examination, he was an unflappable witness. The neighborhood people listened, mostly in hushed silence.

There were many others who took the stand, seventy witnesses in all—gangsters, crime victims, collaborators, coconspirators, cops, federal agents, and organized crime experts—with a mountain of evidence that was presented throughout late 1987 and into 1988. The neighborhood people mostly disappeared during the middle months of the trial, but they returned again for the verdict. When they did, the courtroom was packed to the rafters, with many tough, grizzled Irish faces right out of a 1930s Cagney flick. Sisters, brothers, nephews, mothers, fathers, and neighbors were there to see not only the final adjudication of the core members of the Westies, but also the passing of a way of life.

The Irish hardly existed in Hell's Kitchen anymore. They had long since moved onward, upward, and assimilated into the suburbs. The Westies represented those who did not have the resources or the inclination to leave the neighborhood; they were a throwback to a different era, when the Irish had been forced to fight, claw, and scheme to survive. The criminal rackets, which they had spawned and fostered for nearly a century, were the last lethal strain of an ecosystem that should have died out long ago.

The verdict was guilty on all counts.

Facing certain extinction, the Irish Mob was now hanging by a thread, down to its final frontier, Boston, and its last boss, a man named Whitey—who would prove to be the most wily and diabolical survivor of them all.

southie serenade: whitey on the run

ccording to Pat Nee, an early leader of the Mullin gang who was also an occasional crime partner of Whitey Bulger until the late 1980s, the Irish mob boss of Boston once received a call from Jimmy Coonan, leader of the Westies. The overture was made sometime in the mid-1980s, when Bulger was sitting pretty in Southie, and Coonan, recently released from prison, was looking to expand his operation beyond the confines of Hell's Kitchen. Whitey received word of the overture through an underling, who reported that Coonan had a "business proposition he wanted to discuss."

Bulger knew who Coonan was, of course. The American underworld was a loosely interconnected private fraternity, like the Moose Lodge or the Shriners, whose regional criminals frequently crossed paths while in federal prison or on the lam. Bulger gave some consideration as to whether or not he should return Coonan's call and see what he had to say. Apparently, Whitey decided against it. As a regional criminal who had a good thing going in his own backyard, Bulger saw no benefit in forming an alliance with the Irish guys from New York. They might make their own demands, or even worse, jeopardize his secret, unprecedented partnership with the number one law enforcement agency in the United States, the Federal Bureau of Investigation.

Nothing ever came of Coonan's overture, and the anecdote can now be filed under the heading: What Might Have Been. If Bulger's Boston operation and the Westies had hooked up, they would have been a major force to contend with in the underworld, particularly in the lucrative northeastern part of the United States. Given the Irish Mob's penchant for violence, they would have posed a formidable threat to the Mafia and perhaps brought about a bloody crescendo to the war between the dagos and the micks—the longest running rivalry in the underworld. For a variety of reasons, that war never did materialize into the kind of face-to-face showdown that many had expected. One reason was that the Irish Mob had no interest in taking on the mafia's role as corporate overseers of organized crime in America. Loosely based on a pre-famine clan system in which power was dispersed through regional fiefdoms, the Irish Mob tended to be antiauthoritarian in nature, with little talent for intergang coordination, even when the other gangs were Irish.

In this respect, Lucky Luciano, Meyer Lansky, and other high-ranking originators of the Syndicate or the Outfit were probably right to exclude the Irish. Experience had taught these men that the corporate structure they had in mind—a Wall Street–style version of centralized power, augmented by a board of directors and a hierarchical system of accountability—would never fly with their Celtic brethren. The Irish Mob had little interest in centralized power (they didn't trust the concept) and were therefore averse to the kind of organizational approach that might have posed a genuine threat to the Italians. Otherwise, regional Irish gangsters like Whitey Bulger might have seen the value in returning the phone call of a fellow Irish mobster like Jimmy Coonan.

As the leading underworld chieftain in the most Irish city in America, Bulger was doing just fine with things the way they were. Through his ongoing role as a dry snitch and his cozy relationship with FBI Agent John Connolly, Bulger had vanquished all comers. He ruled with a combination of murder and treachery, but also with a total mastery of a neighborhood that was viewed by many as the last bastion of working-class Irish culture in America.

Southie was a tight-knit, proud, insular community, comprised of firemen, cops, priests, school teachers, tradesman, large families, and the occasional gangster. Unlike Hell's Kitchen, which was a melting pot neighborhood made up of every ethnicity under the sun, Southie was Irish through and through. It was the kind of neighborhood that U.S. politicians always proselytize about: self-sufficient, with a seemingly low crime rate, hegemonic voting patterns on election day, and a fierce sense of internal loyalty that held everything together.

For better or for worse, Southie's defining moment had come in the mid-1970s when a federal district judge sought to integrate the city's segregated school system through forced busing, touching off what came to be known as "the busing crisis." Residents in Southie resented being ordered to take part in a highly disruptive social experiment while more affluent communities in other parts of the city were free to send their kids to all-white schools without recrimination. The racial conflagration that erupted in Southie during the busing crisis received national and even international press. Outsiders saw it as an example of American racism at its worst; Southie residents saw it as a kind of governmental assault on their liberty. They reacted defensively, battened down the hatches, and became even more insular and circumspect in their dealings with the outside world.

Whitey Bulger played a significant behind-the-scenes role in Southie's resistance to the dictates of the federal government. He harbored teenage kids who were chased by cops for throwing rocks at buses carrying African American school kids into Southie. In addition to his reputation as the neighborhood's protector, Whitey was believed to be the muscle behind the South Boston Marshals, an armed vigilante group whose slogan "Hell No, We Won't Go!" became the rallying cry of the antibusing resistance. According to author Michael Patrick MacDonald, whose beautiful, heart-breaking memoir *All Souls* chronicles his upbringing in Southie during and after the busing years, Bulger's reputation attained near-mythical status in the wake of the crisis.

> Whitey stepped up as our protector. They said he protected us from being overrun with the drugs and gangs we'd heard about in the black neighborhoods. . . . He was our king, and everybody made like they were connected to him in some way. . . . Everyone bragged about how his uncle was tight with him, or his brother had been bailed out of jail by him, or how he'd gotten them a new pair of sneakers, or his mother a modern kitchen set. All the neighbors said they went to see Whitey when they were in trouble, whether they'd been sent eviction notices from the Boston Housing Authority or the cops were harassing their kid. Whitey was more accessible than the welfare office, the BHA, the courts, or the cops. If your life had been threatened, your mother could always visit Whitey and get him to squash a beef.

On the one hand, the neighborhood's residents believed in Whitey's power because they wanted to; on the other hand, anyone who ever dared to speak out against Whitey and "the boys" were intimidated into silence. "I knew there were drugs and even gangs in my neighborhood," writes MacDonald, "but like everyone else I kept my mouth shut about that one. Whitey and the boys didn't like 'rats.'"

It was no small feat: After a long criminal career, a secret role as a Top Echelon informant for the FBI, and, through skillful manipulation of a major civic crisis, Bulger had come to embody the entire history of the Irish

American mobster. He was a neighborhood godfather from the Old School, yet his power was not based on nostalgia; he was not relying on the reputation of past gangsters. Whitey was the real deal. He made human beings disappear. And when the bodies washed up on Carson Beach, or were found stuffed in a ten-gallon drum or appeared unceremoniously at O'Brien's Funeral Parlor, nobody said nothin'. Whitey must have had his reasons. Because Whitey was an honorable gangster. He kept the neighborhood free from street criminals and dope peddlers and made everybody proud.

Of course it was all a lie. Bulger presided from a back office at the South Boston Liquor Mart off Old Colony Avenue. A huge green shamrock was painted on the side of the building, but it was mostly just for show. Like most gangsters, he lived life according to an inverted value system. At the same time that he claimed to be protecting the neighborhood against the ravages of drugs and random crime, Bulger oversaw an infusion of cocaine into Southie, profiting from its sale to poor people living in housing projects and to the teenage sons of single mothers. He recruited underlings from the neighborhood's play fields and at McDonough's Boxing Gym, where young men without fathers were especially susceptible to the appeal of the legendary neighborhood boss. Bulger promoted the underworld as if it were all about "manliness" and "togetherness," while for him it was really about one thing: survival. Whitey's survival.

Eventually, the mob boss of South Boston's charade would be exposed for what it was. The public would be the last to know. The first to know was anyone who did business with the man, especially those whose last vision— before being stabbed, shot, or strangled to death—was of the cold, piercing blue eyes of Whitey Bulger.

Shadow of The Shamrock

Brian Halloran was typical of the kind of low-level, working-class schnook who circulated in the Boston underworld of the 1970s and 1980s. A hijacker, bank robber, and leg-breaker from the heyday of the Winter Hill gang, he had been a witness to the phenomenon that was Whitey Bulger. He watched with awe as the man from Southie rose from the ashes of the Boston gang wars by masterfully working the city's levers of power. Halloran, a high school dropout with a reading disorder, had none of Whitey's brains and finesse. Tall and hefty, with an unruly mop of jet-black hair, thick black eyebrows, and the beginnings of a double chin, he was sometimes told that he resembled Gerry Cooney—the erstwhile heavyweight contender from the 1980s known more for the sprawling manner in which he hit the canvas after a knockout than for his boxing technique. Halloran was an Irish American palooka with an easygoing manner who tread lightly in the Boston underworld, always trying to stay on Whitey's good side. The manner in which he crossed over the line from gangster-in-good-standing to hunted animal demonstrated the perils of "doin' business" in Boston during the Age of Bulger.

Halloran's descent into underworld purgatory began on a night in early 1981, when he innocently headed over to the North End apartment of a guy he was looking to do business with. The guy was a certified public accountant and consultant to a number of Boston banks named John Callahan. Halloran and Callahan had met years earlier at Chandler's, the well-known wiseguy hangout in the South End where Howie Winter, Pat Nee, Whitey Bulger, and the Italians had negotiated an end to the Boston gang wars back in the early 1970s. Callahan was a legitimate businessman from the world of high finance, but he liked to hang out with criminals—a proclivity among men of a certain type that almost always ended badly for the so-called legitimate citizen.

Halloran knew that Callahan fancied himself a "player." Years earlier, the portly CPA had once asked the Boston gangster if he would be willing to take part in a staged robbery. Each week, said Callahan, he hauled a bag of money to the bank from his place of business, a company called World Jai Alai (WJA), which was basically a front for a hugely profitable sports betting enterprise. Callahan's plan was that Halloran would rob him at gunpoint as he transported the money pouch to a Brink's truck, and then afterward they would split the bread. The bogus robbery never took place, but it was enough for Halloran to realize that John Callahan was not the upstanding citizen his bank employers, family, and friends believed him to be.

Callahan's latest proposition also involved WJA. A sport of Basque and Spanish origin that somewhat resembles racquetball, jai alai is played with a long banana-shaped scoop used to hurl a rubber ball within an enclosed court known as a "fronton." The game is hugely popular among both Latin and American fans and, thanks to WJA, became a major source of underworld betting in the 1980s. WJA owned frontons and sponsored leagues in Connecticut and Florida, where the company's director of security was none other than H. Paul Rico, the former Boston FBI agent who played a nefarious role in the early Boston gang wars before he retired and moved to South Florida.

Brian Halloran knew all about WJA, and so he was not surprised when Callahan called and asked him to come by to discuss an important criminal matter relating to the company. Halloran was surprised, however, when he walked into Callahan's North End loft and came face to face with Whitey Bulger and his partner Steve "the Rifleman" Flemmi. Halloran knew that Bulger and Flemmi were partners in WJA, which had proven to be a lucrative racket for all parties concerned, but he had not been told they would be in attendance tonight.

For reasons that weren't entirely clear to Halloran, the Southie mob boss never seemed to like him much. As far as Halloran could tell, it had something to do with a certain Southie bookie for whom Halloran had worked as a bodyguard and chauffeur. Sometime in 1980, this bookie had fallen out of favor with Bulger, and it was made clear to Halloran that, on a specified night and at a specified time, he was to drive his boss over to the Triple O bar, a notorious bucket of blood located on West Broadway, Southie's main thoroughfare.

On the night in question, Halloran did as he was told. He dropped his boss off, then parked his Lincoln behind the Triple O bar and waited. It wasn't long before Halloran saw Whitey and another man dragging a heavy green trash bag down the back stairs of the bar. They dumped the bag in the Lincoln's trunk. Halloran drove the car to the South End and left it there. Later the bookie was discovered in the trunk—dead—with a bullet hole in his head.

At Callahan's apartment, Halloran was greeted effusively by his friend. Steve Flemmi said hello. Whitey Bulger gave Halloran his usual sideways glare. Callahan explained why they were all there. There was big trouble brewing at WJA, he said. The company had a new owner, a hard-driving CEO based in Tulsa, Oklahoma, named Roger Wheeler. Within weeks of taking over the company, Wheeler had discovered that someone was skimming one million dollars a year from the company coffers. Wheeler had announced that he planned to fire the company's top financial officers and conduct an extensive internal audit, which was going to be disastrous for Callahan and the Boston boys.

There was only one way to deal with the problem, surmised Callahan. Brian Halloran should "take [Wheeler] out of the box." A clean, professional hit was the only way to stop the paper trail from leading directly to Callahan's office and to derail a likely embezzlement charge against him. The four men discussed the possible ramifications of an out-of-state murder contract, which would likely lead to a federal investigation. Bulger, who had the final say on such matters, told the others that he needed to think about it. The meeting ended, and they all went home.

Halloran, the bit player who had operated on the fringe of the underworld most of his adult life, had mixed feelings about the proposition. On the one hand, if he did the hit, he would be engaging in a high-level job with the man himself—Jimmy Blue Eyes—and that was good. On the other hand, throughout the entire one-hour meeting at Callahan's apartment, Bulger had been giving him nasty looks, leaving Halloran feeling less than loved. As a professional hood, he knew that the closer you got to a man like Whitey, the greater the chance that you too might one day wind up in the trunk of a car with a bullet in your brain.

A week later, Halloran ran into Callahan at one of their watering holes and asked him where things stood on the Wheeler job. Callahan was a little evasive and said they were still "working out the details." A couple weeks after that, Halloran got a call from Callahan asking him to stop by his North End apartment. With some trepidation, Halloran headed over to his buddy's place. When he got there, Callahan told him that his services would not be needed on the "Tulsa job." As a professional courtesy, Halloran was presented with a bag filled with $20,000 in cash. "Take the money," said Callahan. "I never should have got you involved in the first place. My apologies."

Halloran didn't need to be told twice. Perennially strapped for cash, he took the money and headed out the door. In a matter of days, he blew nearly the entire twenty grand on furniture for his Quincy apartment, a long weekend in Fort Lauderdale, and the down payment on a new car for his wife.

Through the underworld grapevine, Halloran learned that the Oklahoma hit went off without him. A hit team had been dispatched from Boston. Fifty-five-year-old Roger Wheeler, the CEO of World Jai Alai, was shot in the head at close range after having just finished a round of golf at the Southern Hills Country Club in Tulsa. The man who supplied the hit team with information on Wheeler's routine and whereabouts was H. Paul Rico, the former Boston G-man and now director of security for World Jai Alai.

Halloran would like to have been able to forget all about the Tulsa hit, but he was acutely aware that, as the only person with knowledge of the murder who wasn't directly involved in its implementation, he was a marked man. If he needed a reminder, it came in the form of a fusillade of bullets fired in his direction from a passing car one morning, while he was dumping the trash in front of his Quincy apartment.

The small-time hood became frazzled and paranoid. With a wife and a young child, he didn't feel he could just pack up and run. He tried to create an independent revenue stream for himself by getting involved in the drug trade. He was not only selling coke, but also was using it a fearsome rate and drinking heavily. Brian Halloran was a disaster waiting to happen.

On a rainy night in October 1981, it happened: Halloran shot and killed a Mafia-connected coke dealer at a restaurant in Chinatown. After hiding out for a month, Halloran turned himself in to the authorities. He was charged with first-degree murder and released on $50,000 bail, with the proviso that he could not leave the Boston area. Under the circumstances, he probably would have been better off hijacking a NASA spacecraft and leaving the earth's atmosphere. The word on the street was that the Italians wanted the Irish gangster dead for having whacked one of their coke dealers. Meanwhile, Whitey Bulger and his crowd harbored the knowledge that Halloran was the only living nonparticipant capable of ratting them out for the Tulsa murder.

Given his predicament, the low-level Irish hood took what must have seemed like the only logical step—he reached out to the FBI. Desperate, facing a possible sentence of 25 years to life, he introduced himself to a veteran agent in the Boston office named Robert Fitzpatrick. Halloran told the agent that if the FBI could help him get a reduced sentence in the Chinatown murder, he had information that could help them solve a certain homicide in Oklahoma.

"Maybe," said Fitzpatrick upon hearing Halloran's proposition. "But first I need to know what you know."

That night Halloran signed a statement that read, in part: "I was offered $20,000 by John Callahan to kill Roger Wheeler. Bulger and Flemmi were present at Callahan's apartment when the offer was made. Callahan said the owner, Wheeler, discovered someone was ripping off one million dollars a year from the Jai Alai operations and was planning to fire the executives, conduct an audit, and bring in state officials to investigate."

Agent Fitzpatrick and his partner worked Halloran like a mule. For six straight weeks, from January 3 to February 19, 1982, they pumped him for information, moving him from safe house to safe house so that his whereabouts would not be detected. They had Halloran wear a wire and circulate in the underworld, but that proved unproductive. Everywhere he went, the big Irish lug gave off the stink of desperation—the telltale aroma of a stool pigeon. When Halloran walked into the Triple O, the Mullen Club, Kelly's Cork & Bull, or other well-known Southie watering holes, even the priests headed for the exits.

The likelihood that Brian Halloran was yakking to the Man was more than just idle chatter. Southie was the kind of neighborhood that had a mainline into many things related to city government, and it didn't hurt at all that two prominent FBI agents were—for all intents and purposes— members of Bulger's organization.

As Chief of the FBI's Organized Crime Squad in Boston, John Morris was apprised of the fact that Halloran was telling tales about Bulger and

Flemmi. By this time, Morris had completely fallen under the thrall of John Connolly, the brash Southie-born agent who first brought Whitey into the fold, and Bulger himself, with whom Morris and Connolly met socially on numerous occasions. The two agents were in deep with Bulger, having tipped him off about investigations and informants and, in Morris's case, taken bribe money in the form of gratuities and cash. Morris knew full well that if other investigators in his office began to delve too deeply into Bulger's activities, his own unethical—if not criminal—relationship with Bulger would be exposed.

In a late-night bull session at the downtown FBI office, Morris told Connolly, "John, we got a problem. Brian Halloran has implicated Jim Bulger and Flemmi on the Tulsa murder. We've got to head this off at the pass."

"Don't worry," said Connolly. "I'll take care of it."

Connolly immediately set up an "interview" with his two informants, Bulger and Flemmi, supposedly to explore what they knew about the Tulsa matter. After talking to the two men, Connolly filed a report stating that Halloran's claims "could not be substantiated by the facts," after which Morris officially closed the investigation.

Bulger and Flemmi were in the clear, and they celebrated with a wine and dinner party at Steve Flemmi's mother's house in Southie. The honored guests at the dinner party were agents Morris and Connolly. The two gangsters had reason to celebrate. Not only had they once again gotten away with murder, but they also now knew for sure—thanks to the FBI agents—that Brian Halloran was a rat.

Halloran's predicament just kept getting worse. No matter which way he turned, the shadow of Whitey Bulger was upon him. He had tried to come in from the cold and deliver the top mobster in Boston to the FBI on a silver platter, and now he was in even more danger than before.

Robert Fitzpatrick, the agent with whom Halloran first established contact, was understandably concerned for his C.I.'s life. Although he did not yet know that his own agents had tipped off Bulger about Halloran, word on the street was that his informant was not long for this world. The agent approached Assistant U.S. Attorney Jeremiah O'Sullivan, whose approval Fitzpatrick needed to offer Halloran a plea-bargain deal for his cooperation and get him off the street and into protective custody.

O'Sullivan, of course, knew all about Whitey Bulger's role as an informant; he was the one who had severed Bulger from the 1978 race-fixing case, which had resulted in convictions for every high-ranking member of the Winter Hill Gang except Bulger and Flemmi. O'Sullivan also knew that, in accordance with government policy, the FBI was not allowed to keep Bulger on as a C.I. if he was under criminal investigation. In a sense, the prosecutor was being asked to choose between Brian Halloran and Whitey Bulger—a no brainer. Instead of listening to Fitzpatrick, who was telling him that Halloran's life was in imminent danger, O'Sullivan went with Morris and Connolly, who were telling him that Halloran was a wannabe and a drunk who knew nothing about the activities of a man like Whitey Bulger. Halloran was denied protective custody.

In May 1982, the low-level Irish hood's official role as an informant was terminated, and he was cut loose. The FBI had chewed him up, set him up to be killed, and spit him back out on the street. He couldn't live at home with his wife, who was pregnant with their second child, for fear that someone might bust through the door and shoot them all to death. Moving from safe house to safe house, he trusted no one and slept with a gun under his pillow.

On the night of May 11, less than a week after being dumped by the FBI, Halloran got a call from his sister, who was living near the South Boston waterfront. She wanted to see him. A friend drove him into Southie, a place he'd been avoiding for months. Around six o'clock in the evening, he and his friend were sitting in a Datsun outside a restaurant on Northern Avenue. A blue Chevy pulled alongside them. Before Halloran had time to react, a fusillade of machine-gun fire rang out. Halloran was hit; he staggered out of his car and fell in the street. One of the assassins ran up to him and shot him several more times with a pistol. Halloran died with twelve bullets in him from two different guns. His friend—an innocent bystander—was also killed.

A Boston detective at the murder scene claimed that the dying Halloran was able to identify his assailant. "Jimmy Flynn," he supposedly said with his last breath. Jimmy Flynn was an established Charlestown gangster who was angry with Halloran for having allegedly ratted him out on a bank robbery. The Boston cops thought they had an iron-clad suspect, but it was all a carefully planned diversion. Bulger himself was the triggerman that night. He'd worn a disguise—a sandy-blond wig and prominent mustache—that made him look like Jimmy Flynn.

The day after the murder, FBI agent John Connolly met with Bulger and Flemmi, who told him that, as far as they knew, Charlestown gangsters acting on behalf of the Italians had taken out Brian Halloran. Connolly quickly filed an internal report to that effect, which was later used by local authorities to build a case against Flynn.[1]

---

1. Jimmy Flynn was a rare rank-and-file survivor of the Boston Gang Wars, a Renaissance criminal weaned at the knee of the originator of the Winter Hill Gang, Buddy

In Boston's police squad rooms and prosecutorial chambers, few tears were shed for Brian Halloran. He was a gangster who trafficked on the dark side and apparently got what was coming to him. But in the city's underworld of the 1980s, looks could be deceiving. In truth, Whitey Bulger had spun a web of treachery and deception unlike anything ever seen in the annals of the Irish Mob. FBI agents Connolly and Morris were literally on the payroll, supplying information to the Bulger organization that made it possible for them to engage in pre-emptive strikes. The hits just kept on coming.

The next to go down was John Callahan, the accountant from World Jai Alai who first brought Halloran into the Tulsa murder plot. In July 1982, his body was found in the trunk of a car near Miami International Airport, having been murdered by the same Boston hit team who gunned down Roger Wheeler in Oklahoma.

Then came Arthur "Bucky" Barrett, an expert Boston safecracker who had pulled off a daring bank heist, netting $1.5 million in cash. Whitey Bulger ratted out Barrett to Connolly and Morris. They, in turn, approached Barrett with a "friendly warning" that Bulger, as the mob boss of Boston, wanted his cut of the heist. The agents then offered Barrett a "safe haven" as an FBI informant, but Barrett rejected it. In 1983, he was kidnapped, tortured, and dragged to a South Boston home, where he was murdered and then buried in the basement.

Less than a year later, John McIntyre met the same fate. He was a young boatman who ran afoul of Bulger after taking part in an IRA gun smuggling operation led by occasional Bulger associate, Pat Nee. When McIntyre started singing to federal authorities, Agent John Connolly tipped off Whitey. McIntyre disappeared, to be exhumed years later alongside Barrett and the corpse of Deborah Hussey, the ex-girlfriend of Bulger's psychotic partner, Steve Flemmi.

In the wake of all these murders, the Irish American underworld became even more oppressive than usual. In Southie, where many of the victims lived or operated, the worst thing you could be accused of was having an "Irish whisper," talking too loudly about the neighborhood's business. Residents mumbled about the latest disappearance, became defensive, or tried not to think about the reality: Bulger and Flemmi were not just mobsters, they were serial killers, racking up an ungodly body count with virtual

---

McLean. After Brian Halloran's murder, Flynn went on the run. He was caught two years later and put on trial. His lawyer was able to show that Flynn was nowhere near the murder scene on the night in question. Flynn was acquitted. Investigators later determined that he'd been set up to take the fall by Whitey Bulger.

impunity. No one was safe. Enemies, ex-girlfriends, fellow gangsters, and especially business associates who engaged in moneymaking criminal rackets with the Bulger organization all vanished, never to be seen again.

Wrote Eddie MacKenzie (yet another small-time Southie hood who worked for Bulger) in his autobiography, *Street Soldier*: "Whitey Bulger was an institution unto himself . . . Lucifer personified. If the word on the street was to be believed—and what other word could I rely on?—Whitey Bulger could kill you and your dog, fuck your wife, burn down your house, and walk away clean."

Bulger's power was mind-boggling and ubiquitous. It was based on a combination of his own innate skills and psychosis, his sinister relationship with the FBI, and his demonic partnership with Flemmi. And when all else failed, Whitey had another "ace in the hole" that seemed to hark back to the earliest days of the Irish Mob—when the underworld was a hushed intermingling of politics and gangsterism, and the American Dream a circumscribed commodity most obtainable to those with an edge. The days of Tammany Hall were a distant memory, but nobody ever told that to Whitey's brother, the Senator from Southie, Mr. William Bulger.

The Bulger Mystique

In September 1988, the *Boston Globe* published a voluminous four-part series on the Brothers Bulger, who were by now a source of endless fascination in the city. After ten years in the state House of Representatives and nearly twice that time in the state Senate, where he rose steadily to be elected senate president in 1978, Billy Bulger was a force to be reckoned with in his own right. A proficient public speaker and skilled legislator, Billy, like his brother, had ridden the angry wave of resistance that swept over South Boston during the busing crisis. Bulger's lacerating public critiques of the city's WASP and Anglo-Irish elite, whom he characterized as "drowning in a sea of hypocrisy," was a clear-eyed expression of working-class politics in the tradition of James Michael Curley, one of Bulger's political heroes.

Like Curley, Bulger had a talent for piercing rhetoric that skirted the edges of class and race-baiting, which turned out to be a much more volatile proclivity in the Boston of the 1970s than it had been in Curley's time. It was de rigueur for Southie political leaders of the busing era to have a gangster at their side, either literally or metaphorically. Louise Day Hicks, the most vitriolic of the antibusing crusaders in Southie, had as her bodyguard Jimmy Kelly, a former member of the Mullin Gang, who would himself eventually became an elected state representative. Whitey Bulger's reputation was such that he and brother Billy didn't even need to be seen together; the relationship was simply understood.

The *Globe* series on the brothers was comprehensive and revealing, and it quoted Senator Bulger at length. He waxed eloquent about growing up in Southie and expressed distaste at the way he and his neighborhood had been wrongly characterized as narrow-minded, unduly tribal, and racist. When the subject turned to his brother, Bulger was tight-lipped, as he had been since the time he entered public life. "He was always a very good brother and cared very much for his mother. . . . I worry for him," was all the Senator would say. Bulger's loyalty to his brother was reiterated when the *Globe* series appeared in print and implied—for the first time ever in a public forum—that Whitey Bulger and the FBI had a "special relationship." Billy Bulger felt that the *Globe* had accused his brother of being an informer, which was anathema to any card-carrying Irishman. In response, Bulger disowned the *Globe* and never again gave the paper an interview until his retirement from the Senate in 1996.

Loyalty among brothers is an admirable trait and should not be construed to suggest, in Billy Bulger's case, a direct criminal allegiance. In his long political career, Bulger was never overtly linked with his brother's mobster activities in any way. In fact, Billy presented himself to the public as nearly puritanical. He was a devout churchgoer, scholar, teetotaler, devoted husband, and father of nine children. With his fastidiously groomed blond hair, cherubic face, quick wit, and alert, penetrating blue eyes (not unlike his older brother's), the Senator from Southie was the kind of "good boy" who would make a mother proud. Some people even believed that Bill Bulger's drive to achieve great things in legitimate society in spite of his brother's dubious reputation was a gift to his aged mother, who lived as a veritable recluse in her own neighborhood.

In personal presentation and public achievement, Whitey and Billy may have looked like the Cain and Abel of South Boston, but it wasn't really that simple. Senator Bulger made no apologies for his brother and at times even seemed to bask in the dirty glory of Whitey's untoward reputation. Their mutual careers had risen on a parallel track, with Bill ascending to the senate presidency at the same time that Whitey (with the help of FBI Agent John Connolly) was eliminating his former associates in the Winter Hill Gang and taking over as the city's undisputed underworld boss. In the rough-and-tumble world of South Boston, where gangsterism was still perceived as a semilegitimate consequence of the city's anti-Irish, anti-Catholic roots, Whitey Bulger's mobster pedigree did not hurt Billy Bulger one bit. Some argued that it was the secret of his success.

The Senator from Southie could be a dictator and a bully, and he was known to possess a well-honed Boston Irish taste for revenge. His political opponents often noted his tendency to personalize all battles, large or small. One junior member of the legislature, trying to enlist Bulger's support for a bill on rules reform, said to the senate president, "You could be a hero, Mr. President." Bulger shook his head and replied, "You guys from Cambridge can be heroes, but guys like me can't. I'll always be a redneck mick from South Boston."

Where Billy sometimes got even was on St. Patrick's Day, at the annual breakfast that was a required stop for politicians and community leaders lucky enough to score an invitation. With Bulger presiding, the breakfast was like a Friar's Roast. Political leaders such as Boston's popular Mayor Ray Flynn (a rival of Bulger's who was another up-from-the-bootstraps Southie success story), Senator Ted Kennedy (who was sure to be lampooned about his weight and for his liberal leanings) and campaigning national politicians like Ronald Reagan and George Bush stopped by to sing songs and prostrate themselves before the man commonly referred to as "the most powerful local politician in the state of Massachusetts." The media was not allowed inside, except on rare occasions. Although never in attendance, Whitey Bulger was often referred to with jocularity at these Paddy's Day breakfasts; on one occasion, Billy good-naturedly designated his brother "the Reverend"—a comment that would come back to haunt him years later, when the truth about Whitey came out and he was no longer viewed in the neighborhood as a subject of such ribald good humor.

Senator Bulger's talent for political payback went well beyond a few pointed jibes on March 17. A political operative who identified himself in the *Globe* as "a friend" of Bulger's, put it this way: "[He] at times personifies the iron hand in the velvet glove. . . . And the stiletto in that hand is so slim, slender and sharp that it's only after it's been withdrawn that you feel that you know what happened." Some of Bulger's more notorious acts of legislative revenge could be chalked up to political hardball, an example of the kind of politics that had been practiced in the state of Massachusetts since the days of the Boston Tea Party. But other acts were more pointed in their defense of brother Whitey, giving the impression—intended or not—that the Bulgers were "in it together."

For example, when a court clerk finally eliminated James "Whitey" Bulger from the state payroll, years after he'd stopped showing up for his post-prison job as a courthouse janitor, Senator Billy—in an act of brotherly payback—froze the clerk's pay.

When Massachusetts State Police officers undertook an investigation of Whitey Bulger's criminal operation in 1981 (going so far as to plant a bug in his garage headquarters on Lancaster Street, to which Whitey was tipped off by FBI Agent Connolly), they found a strange addendum tagged onto the following year's state budget that would require state police officers age fifty or older to take a reduction in pay and rank, or retire. The amendment affected only five officers in the Boston office, three of whom had worked the Whitey Bulger case. Senator Billy's response to this mysterious budget amendment was "no comment," but many in local law enforcement saw it for what it was: another instance of one Bulger running interference for the other.

An even more ominous incident occurred in September 1987, when Whitey Bulger and his girlfriend were passing through Logan Airport and were stopped with a bag filled with $50,000 in cash. According to an incident report filed by a state trooper, Whitey lost his cool and became verbally abusive to a number of airport security workers and to the trooper. Bulger was detained but eventually let go. In the weeks that followed, the state trooper came under intense scrutiny from his supervisors, who claimed that State Senator Bulger was demanding a copy of the incident report. The trooper was an exemplary employee—a Green Beret in Vietnam who was twice awarded a Medal of Merit and the Trooper of the Year Award—but he became the target of a campaign of political harassment and payback, which turned out to be the beginning of the end of his distinguished career. The trooper's relationship with his superiors soured, and he retired early, a broken man. A few years later, in the woods of southern New Hampshire, penniless and despondent, he blew out his own brains.

According to the legend, Billy Bulger punished those who went after his brother and rewarded those who didn't. The senator, by his own admission, was good friends with FBI Agent John Connolly. Like Whitey, he'd known Connolly since they were kids growing up on the same block in Southie. Connolly had worked on many of Billy's early political campaigns, and when Southie protégé Ray Flynn got himself elected mayor, Bulger lobbied hard for Connolly to be appointed the city's new chief of police. Connolly didn't get the job, but he was still grateful and maintained a close, affectionate relationship with the senator.

Years later, Bulger claimed—none too convincingly—that he had no idea about Connolly and Whitey's "special relationship," but he did admit to telling the agent, "I expect you to take care of my brother." The implied understanding was that Connolly would be Whitey's protector inside law enforcement. In return, Bulger would write reference letters and exert his considerable influence for a steady stream of FBI agents whom Connolly brought by his senate office (many wound up with cushy retirement jobs on the state payroll). It was the classic patronage arrangement; Connolly looked out for Whitey and his friends, and Billy took care of Connolly and his people. It all seemed benign until you stopped to consider the fact that Whitey Bulger had whacked at least nineteen people—eight of them while he was a registered informant with the FBI.

There was nothing subterranean about the alliance. On at least one occasion, Whitey, his partner Flemmi, and their FBI handlers were having a celebratory dinner at the Southie home of Flemmi's mother when Billy Bulger walked in. Bulger lived next door, merely twenty feet away. A junior FBI agent who was there that night (having been invited for the first time) would later testify that he was shocked; here were the two most notorious mobsters in the city together with two leaders of the FBI's organized crime squad, later joined by the president of the state senate, all interacting as if they were longtime friends and members of the same club—which, in fact, they were. It was later revealed that at least two murders had taken place at this same home, just next door to Senator Bulger's place. One of those murders involved a twenty-six-year-old woman whose sole crime was that she wanted to break up with Flemmi, and therefore posed a threat to the Bulger-Flemmi partnership. Whitey Bulger strangled her to death with his bare hands.

There was no indication that Billy Bulger had direct information about these killings or the fact that Whitey and Flemmi had used a shed behind the house—which abutted Billy's own backyard—as an arsenal for other killings. Years later, under oath, Billy would hide behind a stream of lawyerly nondenials in the manner of "I do not remember" or "not to my recollection," even claiming before a congressional hearing that he did not know Whitey and Connolly knew each other at all, much less had a working partnership.[2]

In some ways, Senator Billy Bulger was a man operating within the vortex of history. Maybe he knew Whitey was a killing machine and dispenser

---

2. Billy Bulger's testimony on June 19, 2003 before a House Committee on Government Reform in Washington D.C. proved to be his undoing. The committee was interested in finding out if Bulger had in any way aided his brother, who at that time had been on the run for eight years. Bulger was out of state government, having retired from the senate in 1996 and taken on his prestigious new job as President of the University of Massachusetts. His testimony before the committee was widely covered by the Boston media, to whom Bulger had rarely given the time of day. Stoic, defensive, and evasive to the end, Bulger's long years of walking a tightrope between being a strong advocate for his neighborhood of South Boston and being a mobster's brother finally caught up with him. In the wake of the hearings, he was forced to

of cocaine (nearly everyone else in the neighborhood did), and maybe he didn't. By advocating so brazenly on his brother's behalf, he was taking part in an arrangement with deep roots in the Irish American underworld. In an earlier era, the intermingling of politicians, lawmen, and gangsters had been a way for the disenfranchised minority group to make some headway in the New World. But by the Age of Bulger, the overwhelming majority of Irish Americans no longer took part in or even made excuses for mobsterism, flagrant patronage, and political corruption. Put simply, Irish Americans no longer needed the extra edge that came at the end of blackjack or a gun. They had arrived long ago.

And yet, in Boston, where the fear, anger and bitterness of the Irish immigrant experience had hardened into a kind of crucible—"Hell no, we won't go!"—the Irish American underworld was hanging on. The entire 150-year run of the Irish Mob had come down to its essential distinguishing characteristic: the alliance between the gangster, the lawman, and the politician. In this light, it was not surprising that Connolly and the Bulger brothers forged their relationship as if it were well within their rights. They were like ancient legends walking among the ruins of the Irish American underworld.[3]

The Last Hurrah

John Connolly retired from the FBI in December 1990. Whitey Bulger did not attend his retirement party, but Senator Billy did. In fact, Billy Bulger

---

resign as president of University of Massachusetts and has since remained retired from public life.

3. To say that Special Agent Connolly's actions were solely a product of Irish American underworld history or the internecine culture of South Boston would not be telling the full story. Connolly was also an FBI agent, the product of a law enforcement culture that was not averse to violating internal rules or national laws. Starting with J. Edgar Hoover's COINTELPRO program, which involved the illegal wiretapping and surveillance of civil rights leaders throughout the 1960s, the Bureau established a mindset in which subverting the law was well within the bounds of standard operating procedure. The Boston office was perhaps the Bureau's most corrupt, with a pattern of using informants for conniving purposes going back at least to the murderous H. Paul Rico. Connolly was following in this tradition. The nature of his relationship with Whitey Bulger was well-known within the Boston office, and it went mostly unchallenged even as Bulger cut a huge criminal swath through the city's underworld. Connolly was aided and abetted by his FBI supervisors. The fact that Bulger was able to play Connolly to the extent that he did is just one example of how the underworld and upperworld occasionally intersect to sustain that long-running American vaudeville act known as organized crime.

was the Master of Ceremonies, as he had been at so many FBI retirement rackets in the 1980s and early 1990s that he was later unable to remember them all. Connolly's fete was termed a "raucous occasion" by those in attendance. A few months later, the former FBI agent landed a high-paying position as head of corporate security at Boston Edison, a company closely aligned with Senate President Bulger. Five other former agents from the Boston office also landed jobs with the public utility company, thanks in part to references from Bulger.

Not long after his retirement, Connolly moved into a condominium in Southie that had an adjoining unit belonging to Whitey Bulger. They were now next-door neighbors and had every reason to believe they would grow old together sitting on the porch, telling stories about how they snookered the Mafia in Beantown and lived like kings during the Age of Bulger.

With Connolly gone from the Bureau's Organized Crime Squad, Whitey was officially closed out as a confidential informant. He would now have to find other ways to establish an edge within the city's criminal underworld. Apparently, he still had enough juice to pull off a classic gangster's retirement scam: He "won" the Massachusetts State Lottery. Residents of the state were understandably suspicious when it was announced that one of numerous winning tickets was sold at Bulger's Rotary Variety Store, next door to his Liquor Mart with the huge green shamrock painted on the exterior. Whitey's portion of the $14.3 million jackpot—which came out to $89,000 a year for the next twenty years—was put on hold pending further investigation.

Also around this time, Bulger began a series of international forays, usually undertaken with one of his two girlfriends, which might have seemed suspicious if anyone in law enforcement were paying attention—they weren't. Bulger opened bank accounts and safe deposit boxes in numerous locales, including the Caribbean, Ireland, and London. He acquired driver's licenses under assumed names from multiple states, including New York.

In retrospect, Bulger's activities made perfect sense. With his FBI benefactor in retirement, Whitey would have known or at least suspected that his long run as a protected mobster was over. There was a better-than-even chance that, without Connolly to hold down the lid, the dirty little details of their long alliance would one day bubble over. Bulger had already dodged one close call: In 1991, just a few months after Connolly's retirement, a major narcotics investigation involving the DEA and Massachusetts State Police netted fifty-one Southie-based cocaine dealers, most of them associated with the Bulger organization. Bulger held no sway over the DEA, and the State Police hated him for what they felt had been years of political meddling and flagrant acts of payback on the part of his brother, the senate president. The indictments rocked the neighborhood of Southie, where Whitey's upperworld supporters had always maintained the lie that he would never sell drugs in his own backyard. But even with all the indictments, not one high-ranking member of Bulger's organization "flipped," demonstrating the kind of esteem and fear that Whitey Bulger still inspired in his home neighborhood of Southie.

The DEA case against the Irish Mob may not have netted the Big Fish, but it left Whitey vulnerable, which he would have recognized. Bulger had always been, first and foremost, a survivor. After returning to Boston in 1965, following a nine-year stint in jail, he survived and even rose above the Boston Gang Wars through a Machiavellian ability to divide and conquer. He established his role as the neighborhood godfather with a keen understanding of the historical parameters of the Irish American underworld, doling out turkeys on the holidays and doing favors for his people as if he were a turn-of-the-century ward boss. Some in the community genuinely loved Whitey Bulger or at least loved the *idea* of Whitey Bulger. The man himself was somewhat taciturn and cold and rarely intermingled directly with neighborhood residents—the better to establish his standing as a near mythical figure, always talked about but rarely seen.

Whitey had also covered his bases through an unparalleled manipulation of upperworld forces. Whereas New York Mafia boss John Gotti, who was lionized by the national media as the "Teflon Don," was constantly being brought to trial, Whitey Bulger never even stepped foot in a courtroom and was never even charged with a crime in the thirty years since he returned to his home neighborhood. His criminal life embodied the Irish mobster credo, borrowed from the Irish American ward boss, who was known to say: "All politics is local." Bulger resisted overtures from other Irish American mob bosses like Jimmy Coonan of the Westies because he knew it would take him outside his sphere of influence. Bulger's philosophy was the philosophy of the Irish Mob: Keep it small, local, even parochial, and you can make it last forever.

Granted, the forever part was a stretch, even for Whitey. As the long saga of the Irish American mobster has shown, few of them ever made it past their forties. Leaders like McLean, Killeen, and Spillane were all killed by younger, hungrier gangsters on the rise. By the 1990s, Whitey was in his early sixties, still pounding the pavement, still making money, still willing to whack people himself if the situation called for it. But as his operation grew with Whitey demanding a piece of everything that was going on in the Boston area (narcotics, gambling, loan-sharking, extortion), it was just a matter of time before Bulger got caught. Nobody knew that better than Whitey himself.

And so, in 1992, the chickens came home to roost. An aggressive federal prosecutor, working mostly with Massachusetts State Police, began rounding up a series of middle-aged bookies—Jewish, Italian, Portuguese, African American—who plied their trade in and around the city. Most of these bookies had been arrested numerous times before, pled guilty, and paid small fines. But this time, prosecutors were threatening to charge them as a group on multiple money laundering and RICO counts. One bookie in particular began to sing like a canary, and it soon became apparent that all of the bookies had one thing in common: In order to operate, they paid tribute to Whitey Bulger and the Irish Mob.

As the case grew, the FBI got involved. The local FBI office was now under a totally new regime. With John Connolly retired, John Morris long since transferred elsewhere, and other individuals out of the picture, the Bureau was finally ready to move on Bulger. His years as a C.I. were, of course, well-known throughout the FBI command structure. There was some concern that by indicting the notorious South Boston Mob boss, the special relationship between Whitey and the feds would be revealed and maybe even become an issue. But there was nothing anyone could do. The Organized Crime Strike Force was going after Bulger anyway, and the FBI figured they might as well be on board.

John Connolly was retired, but he was not disconnected. "Once a lawman, always a lawman," is a phrase commonly used throughout law enforcement. Connolly, more than most, maintained ties with friends and former colleagues throughout the law enforcement community. He monitored the grand jury investigation of Bulger and his partner Flemmi. Shortly after New Year's Day, 1995, Connolly was tipped off that the indictment would be handed down on January 9 or 10. The retired agent's next move was not surprising. He had once told his former boss, John Morris, that he had secured Bulger's cooperation as an informant partly by agreeing to the condition that Bulger be given a "head start" in the event of an indictment. And so, keeping his word, Connolly called Bulger immediately and told him everything he knew.

Whitey was already out of town when he got the call. He and his longtime girlfriend, Theresa Stanley, had been on the road since August. They visited Graceland, Elvis Presley's home in Memphis. They traveled to Dublin, London, Rome, and around the United States to New Orleans, California, and the Grand Canyon. Whitey squirreled away money in all of these locations, and he was ready for the call when it came from Connolly.

The only problem was that Theresa Stanley, the girlfriend, did not want to go on the lam. She did not want to leave her family forever.

"I want to go home," she told Whitey.

He was driving her back toward Boston when it was announced over the car radio that Steve "the Rifleman" Flemmi had been arrested. Apparently, the feds, fearing that Bulger and Flemmi would be tipped off, did not wait around for the racketeering indictment. They quickly arrested Flemmi on a criminal complaint charging him with conspiracy to extort a bookmaker, knowing they could hold him until the superseding indictment was announced.

Whitey turned his car around and headed toward a safehouse in New York state, where he dropped off his girlfriend. He then disappeared into the great unknown and has been on the run ever since.

The inability of the Organized Crime Strike Force to catch Bulger was big news, but even bigger news came months later. It had slowly dawned on Steve Flemmi that he was quite possibly going to take the fall for the entire Irish Mob—and he wasn't even Irish. The federal prosecutors had put together a big case against the South Boston Mob, and it included a number of rats, most notably Timothy Connolly (no relation to John), who was the proprietor of a South Boston tavern that had been the hub of Bulger's cocaine operation. Connolly also had information that linked Bulger and Flemmi to at least two murders, which was enough to put the two mobsters away for their natural born lives.

The myth of the stand up guy has always been one of the central precepts of the American underworld, dating back to the earliest immigrant gangs. In New York's Five Points, where the American underworld got its start, ballads were written about gangsters who refused to talk to the authorities and were willing, if necessary, to do time in prison. Being a stand up guy was akin to being a prince of the underworld, and it was a revered attribute that crossed all ethnic lines—Italian, Jewish, Latino, Irish, or whatever.

The stand up guy, however, was borne of a time before RICO, government-sponsored C.I.s, and the Witness Protection Program, which offered the illusion of a fresh start under an assumed name far from the old neighborhood. Back in the day, a gang member or racketeer with a strong constitution was willing to take the fall because it rarely involved more than a three-, five-, or seven-year bit in the joint. For many hard-core criminals, this was seen as a right of passage, one that taught them toughness and did wonders for their reputation once they returned to the underworld.

Steve Flemmi had a reputation as a stand up guy. In *Street Soldier*, Eddie MacKenzie, who was part of the South Boston coke ring, writes about the time he wound up at Danbury Federal Prison and was confronted by a big-time mafiosi who told him, "You're here because you got ratted out by your boy Whitey. We've known for years he was a canary. . . . Not Stevie, though. Stevie's good."

The Mafia clung to the myth that Flemmi was a stand up guy when, in fact, he'd been an informant even longer than Whitey Bulger. You might rightfully ask how a government informant—a rat—can be a stand up guy at the same time. Only in the underworld would such an ethical perambulation be accepted because in the underworld the myth of the stand up guy is more powerful than Santa Claus, the Easter Bunny, and the Tooth Fairy combined.

As with most gangsters, however, Steve Flemmi's instinct for survival outweighed all other criminal codes of behavior. In early 1997, after sitting in prison for two years waiting for Whitey to make things better, as he had always done in the past, Flemmi dropped a bomb that would reverberate throughout the underworld and the Halls of Justice for at least the next five years. Through his attorney, Flemmi put forth the defense that he could not be prosecuted for the crimes he and Whitey had committed together because they had been authorized by the FBI to commit those crimes in a trade for underworld intelligence. To support his claim, he began filing sworn affidavits describing his life with the Bureau and the promises he said FBI agents had made never to prosecute him and Whitey Bulger. These claims included details about a multitude of criminal acts, including many murders, that implicated just about every underworld figure in Massachusetts going back to the waning days of the Boston Gang Wars.

Even to those who had always suspected Whitey's special relationship with the FBI, Flemmi's revelations were astounding. Had the government actually underwritten one of the most murderous duos in gangland history, making it possible for the Irish Mob to survive in Boston long after it had disappeared elsewhere, so that the government could build cases against the Mafia? It was an extraordinary proposition, the truth of which was about to be dragged into the public domain. U.S. District Court Judge Mark L. Wolf, after months of closed door hearings and legal briefs filed by Flemmi's attorney, granted a defense request for an open evidentiary hearing to determine if Bulger and Flemmi had indeed been "secretly providing information to the government in exchange for criminal immunity."

What became known as "the Wolf Hearings" were held throughout 1998. In many ways, the hearings were similar to the Westies trial in New York a decade earlier—a final denouement for the Irish Mob in which numerous faces from the past were called forth to bear witness against aspects of the underworld that had been in place for over a hundred years. In this case, most of the people who were subpoenaed to testify were from the government—FBI agents, federal prosecutors, city officials, and various other representatives of the U.S. Justice Department who were compelled for the first time to come clean about what they knew of the FBI's pact with Bulger and Flemmi. For many who had observed Whitey Bulger's miraculous criminal career from afar, it was like the Nuremberg Trials; the unearthing of many long-hidden details verified everyone's worst suspicions about how Whitey had managed to get away with multiple murders and escape prosecution all these years.

Outside the room where the hearings were held, John Connolly held court. The retired FBI agent knew that his reputation, and perhaps his liberty, was at stake. In keeping with his temperament and personality, he waged an energetic counteroffensive, regaling reporters with comments like, "Handling informants is kind of like a circus . . . if the circus is going to work, you need to have a guy in there with the lions and tigers. My job was to get in there with the lions and tigers." And later: "All of them, top echelon informants, are murderers. The government put me in business with murderers."

As to whether or not the deal with Bulger and Flemmi had been worth it, Connolly said, "We destroyed the Angiulos in exchange for a gang of two, Whitey Bulger and Stevie Flemmi. Who wouldn't make that deal?" And later: "The proof is in the pudding. Look at the decimated New England Mafia."

Connolly's defense to aiding and abetting the murderous reign of Bulger's Irish Mob in exchange for taking out Cosa Nostra was a fitting parting shot in the long-running rivalry between the dagos and the micks. Engineered by the last Irish Mob boss in America, the manipulation of Connolly had been a delirious act of counterespionage, based on the knowledge that the FBI would do almost anything to nail the Mafia. The Mafia had become a victim of its own success, which included a public relations bonanza fueled by Hollywood and embraced by the mafiosi themselves, who no doubt thrilled at the sight of being portrayed by the most dynamic actors in the business. The Mafia had become so big, such a ubiquitous part of American pop culture, that the prosecution of even a small localized Mafia crew was sure to garner national headlines. Some prosecutors, like New York's Thomas Dewey and Rudolph Guiliani, had even launched political careers through their perceived prowess as mob busters. The FBI was determined to make up for all those years lost to J. Edgar Hoover's steadfast denial of the Mafia's existence. The game now was to rehabilitate the reputation of the Bureau on the backs of LCN. If that meant making a backdoor deal with the Irish Mob, who were mostly below the radar and whose prosecution was less likely to bring about major kudos, then so be it.

Paddy must have been laughing all the way to the bank.

Outside the courtroom, John Connolly talked a good game, but when called to testify before the Wolf Hearings, he invoked his Fifth Amendment privilege against self-incrimination a total of thirty-two times. At his trial in May 2002, he declined to take the stand in his own defense. He was found guilty of racketeering and obstruction of justice and given a ten-year sentence in federal prison.

Afterward, U.S. Attorney Michael J. Sullivan said of Connolly, "He abused his authority and crossed the line from crime fighter to criminal. . . . Today's verdict reveals John Connolly for what he became: a Winter Hill Gang operative masquerading as a law enforcement agent."

Old Bones and Shallow Graves

In the wake of the Wolf Hearings, the rats abandoned the last sinking ship of the Irish Mob. Longtime associates of Bulger's crew—Steve Flemmi (twenty-one murders), Cadillac Frank Salemme (twelve murders), and John Martorano (nineteen murders)—all cut deals with the government in exchange for testimony, as did numerous members of the Irish Mob, including Kevin Weeks, one of Bulger's most visible lieutenants in Southie, who admitted to taking part in four murders and gave testimony concerning four others.

Early in the year 2000, the bulky, curly-haired Weeks began to talk, leading investigators to a series of impromptu graves spread throughout the Boston area. The first was a gully alongside the Southeast Expressway in Dorchester, which contained three decomposed corpses. These three murder victims, killed between 1983 and 1985, had originally been buried in the basement of a home on East Third Street in Southie, but they had to be transferred when the house was sold in late 1985. One of the skeletons exhumed belonged to the twenty-six-year-old woman strangled to death by Whitey Bulger. Another skeleton had had its teeth ripped out before being killed, the result of a torture session, also courtesy of the South Boston mob boss.

A few months later, another killing field was unearthed, this one just a mile or two from Bulger's condo at 144 Quincy Shore Drive. The remains of Tommy King, the Southie hood who bested Whitey in a barroom brawl back in 1975 and got himself killed as a result, were unearthed, as were the remains of Debra Davis, another ex-girlfriend of Flemmi's.

Another grave was uncovered in September 2000. At Tenean Beach in Dorchester, investigators dug up a pile of bones that, through DNA testing, turned out to belong to Paulie McGonigle, an early member of the Mullin Gang who'd disappeared back in November 1975. Four days after he'd vanished, McGonigle's station wagon was found in the waters off the docks of Charlestown. With Paulie's wallet floating nearby, the cops always suspected that Bulger whacked the former Mullin gang member back during the final days of the Boston Gang Wars. Now they had the proof.

It was as if, just below the surface of the city and surrounding area, lay generations of the dead—gangsters, dirty cops, business partners, girl-friends, and others who simply got in the way. Similar diggings in New Orleans, New York, Chicago, Kansas City, and elsewhere no doubt would have unearthed similar victims of the Irish Mob, buried beneath layers of landfill, blacktop, new buildings, train stations, streets, parks, and other examples of civic progress and urban gentrification. The building of these cities often involved aspects of the criminal underworld—construction rackets, corrupt city officials, dirty ward bosses, cops-on-the-take, and, of course, the Irish American gangster who occasionally graduated to the mob-ster level and became a hidden though immutable aspect of American capi-talism in all its many permutations.

By the end of the twentieth century, the Irish American mobsters were mostly all gone, victims of law enforcement, each other, assimilation, and the long inexorable flow of history. The ranks were thinned down to just a few organizations in New York and Boston—the Westies and Whitey Bulger—until even they went through their final stages of self-immolation.

Whitey, of course, remains at large. Through the early years of the twenty-first century, sightings of the wily Irish mobster were numerous. He was known to have lived for a period with his longtime mistress, Catherine Greig, on a small island off the coast of Louisiana in the Gulf of Mexico. Other sightings were reported in Fountain Valley, California; Galway, Ireland; the island of St. Vincent's; and in London, where, it was reported, a man who had met Bulger years earlier at a gym and known him well bumped into Whitey on the street and said, "Hey, Jim, how you been?"

Bulger looked startled. "You must have the wrong person," he replied and disappeared into a crowd of pedestrians.

After the tragedy of September 11, 2001 and the subsequent passage in the United States of the Patriot Act, which placed new and more stringent restrictions on the use of passports and other kinds of identification—as well as the beefed-up security at airports and train stations—it's hard to imagination how a seventy-year-old man whose face has been plastered on every law enforcement Web site in America can make it on the run. But then again, Whitey Bulger spent nearly his entire adult life defying the odds.

He was the last of the last, inheritor of a tradition that had once pretended to represent the rising of a people and inevitably degenerated over the generations into a bloody netherworld of treachery, deception, betrayal, wholesale murder, and dismemberment. To some, the story of the Irish American gangster is the stuff of legend, a tribute to the rebellious, defiant, tough-as-nails side of the Irish temperament. To others, the saga is shameful, a best-forgotten example of antisocial behavior at its most homicidal and a desperate survival mentality personified in the diabolical, sociopathic tendencies of Whitey Bulger and his ilk.

Either way, the lives were lived, the bodies buried, and the history remains the same. Out there somewhere, Whitey exists as a living relic, or a ghostly reminder, that no criminal underworld in the history of the United States started as early or lasted as long as the Irish Mob.

epilogue

n July 2004, a book was released entitled "*I Heard You Paint Houses,*" an account of an Irish American gangster by the name of Francis "the Irishman" Sheeran. Sheeran had always been suspected by the FBI of being one of the last people to see ex-Teamster boss Jimmy Hoffa alive before he vanished way back on July 30, 1975. Sheeran was a close personal friend of Hoffa's, which meant, in the inverted moral universe of organized crime, that he was a likely suspect in the union official's demise. As even an amateur disciple of the underworld would know, or should know, when they come to get you, the person enlisted to do the deed will most likely be your closest friend or most trusted associate.

In the late 1990s, Sheeran was ready to come clean about his role in one of the great unsolved mysteries of the twentieth century. The motivating factor had been a meeting arranged by Sheeran's two daughters between him and a Catholic monsignor. In ailing health and physically disabled, Sheeran listened as the monsignor granted absolution for his sins so that he could be buried in a Catholic cemetery, but the clergyman also hinted that the Irishman would never be at peace with God until he "did the right thing." Sheeran told his family, "I believe there is something after we die. If I got a shot at it, I don't want to lose that shot. I don't want to close the door." Following his audience with the monsignor, Sheeran contacted a writer and began to tell his story. A few months before the publication of his book, he passed away at the age of eighty-three.

His deathbed confession was a doozy. Sheeran admitted to carrying out numerous acts of violence for Hoffa during his years as Teamster president and also doing contract hits for Russell Bufalino, a legendary Mafia boss. Equally close to both men, Sheeran was a professional bruiser who made his living enforcing the will of his bosses until they turned against one another, and he was forced to make a choice. It really wasn't much of a decision. The Irishman agreed to carry out a murder contract against Hoffa, his longtime friend and mentor, because he knew that if he didn't, he too would be whacked. Such was the nature of survival in the American underworld.

The first time Frank Sheeran ever met Jimmy Hoffa, the legendary Teamster boss looked Sheeran over from head to toe, all six foot three inches of brawn and toughness, and said, "I heard you paint houses." In the mid-twentieth-century vernacular of the underworld, to paint a house meant to whack somebody—the "paint," in this case, representing the blood of the victim. Sheeran had already done a fair number of paint jobs for the Italians, including the famous gangland murder of Joseph "Crazy Joey" Gallo, which went unsolved for decades. That hit took place at Umberto's Clam House in New York's Little Italy in April 1972. According to Sheeran, he carried it out with John "the Redhead" Francis, an Irish-born, New York–based "house painter" with whom he had done other contract jobs in the past.

Although he was not directly affiliated with the Irish Mob, Sheeran represented a classic type of Irish American gangster: the freelance enforcer who went wherever the money was. Vincent Coll, Jack Diamond, Mad Dog Sullivan, Trigger Burke, and others had established a long and dubious tradition as Irish gunmen from hardscrabble and often impoverished backgrounds who circulated throughout the underworld. These were tough, cold-blooded men willing to undertake the impossible and dangerous jobs that others were either ill-equipped or too scared to take on. Coll, Diamond, and Burke all died prematurely via the dirt nap or the electric chair. Sheeran survived because he did most of his jobs under cover of either the Mafia or the International Brotherhood of Teamsters.

His upbringing was typical depression-era Irish American. In Darby, Pennsylvania, the small town outside of Philadelphia where Sheeran was born and raised, unemployment was near eighty percent. Sheeran's father occasionally found work as a janitor at the Blessed Virgin Mary Church & School in Darby, but mostly he drank. Sometimes he'd drag his strapping son Frank into local saloons, where he staged impromptu smokers in which Frank fought local kids or even adults, with dad wagering on his son and keeping the winnings to pay the rent or buy beer.

For guys like Frank Sheeran, minimally educated, relatively unskilled, born into a pre–Civil Rights America that was mean and pitiless, World War II was like a gift from the gods. Sheeran lied in order to enroll in the service underage. At seventeen, he was stationed for a while at Lowry Field in Colorado, where, because of his imposing physical stature, he served as an MP with the Army Air Corp. He then went off to Europe, where he spent the war as a rifleman in the 45th Infantry Division, otherwise known as the Thunderbird Division.

The average number of combat days for a soldier in World War II was around 80. Before the war was over, the Irishman would log four hundred and eleven days in combat. Sheeran's status as a war veteran reiterates the harsh truth that the Irish American underworld drew many of its toughest adherents from the ranks of the ex-military. In Sheeran's case, the sheer number of his combat days were instrumental in establishing his ruthless proficiency as a killer. General George S. Patton himself gave the Thunderbird Division their marching orders. According to an officer of the division who was present during Patton's June 1942 speech to the division, "[He told us] to kill and to continue to kill and that the more we killed the less we'd have to kill later. . . . He did say the more prisoners we took, the more men we would have to feed and not to fool around with prisoners. He said there was only one good German and that was a dead one." The General's position on civilian casualties was equally severe: "He said . . . if the people living in the cities persisted in staying in the vicinity of the battle and were enemy, we were to ruthlessly kill them and get them out of the way."

Among the many theaters of battle where Sheeran saw combat was Anzio, a bloody killing field in which U.S. soldiers were routinely ordered to exterminate prisoners and civilians. Wrote Sheeran, "When an officer would tell you to take a couple of German prisoners back behind the line and for you to 'hurry back,' you did what you had to do." Following orders and killing people became the young soldier's stock-in-trade.

When he returned stateside, Sheeran became a bouncer, loan shark, hustler, and a ballroom dance instructor at Wagner's Dance Hall in Philly. He fell in with a notoriously tough Teamster local, which eventually brought him into the realm of Russell Bufalino, a man described by Bobby Kennedy during the McClellan Hearings as "one of the most ruthless and powerful leaders of the Mafia in the United States." According to Sheeran, Bufalino was tough enough to have once told Mafia acolyte Frank Sinatra at the 500 Club in Atlantic City, "Sit down Frank, or I'll rip your tongue out and stick it up your ass."

The Mafia boss took a liking to Sheeran and was the first to call him "the Irishman." Bufalino admired the way Sheeran carried himself, like a man who had killed before and would do it again if circumstances called for it and the price was right. When the mafiosi first introduced Sheeran to Jimmy Hoffa, he told the Teamster boss, "I've never seen a man walk straight through a crowd of people like the Irishman does and never touch a single person. Everybody automatically parts out of the way. It's like Moses parting the Red Sea."

Hoffa put the Irishman to work right away, flying him to Chicago to paint a house. Wrote Sheeran

I was used to getting put on a landing craft and now I was moving up in the world, invading Chicago on a plane. I was in Chicago maybe an hour. They supplied me the piece and they had one guy right there to take it from me after the thing and get in one car with it and drive away. His only job was to break the piece down and destroy it. They had other guys sitting in crash cars to pull out in front of cops who might go after the car I got in. The car I got in was supposed to take me back to the airport.

Sheeran did many other hits in the same manner, surreptitious killings in which he knew almost nothing about the intended target or whoever else was involved in the job. Clean. Professional. The way hits were meant to be carried out in the underworld.

Although Sheeran was loyal to Hoffa on the friendship level ("I'll be a Hoffa man 'til the day they pat my face with a shovel and steal my cufflinks," he told his Teamster brothers on Frank Sheeran Appreciation Night in 1973), he was an equal opportunity hit man. He was the only person to win a Man of the Year award from an Upstate Pennsylvania chapter of the Italian American Civil Rights League as well as a Teamsters Man of the Year award in 1973, two years before he whacked Hoffa.

By the time the order came down to take Jimmy out, Sheeran had to admit it was no big surprise. After serving fifty-eight months in prison for misappropriating $1.7 million in union pension funds and getting released early courtesy of a commutation from President Richard M. Nixon, Hoffa wanted his old job back. The mob had other ideas. Hoffa began to mouth off, threatening to tell where the bodies were buried. The legendary Teamster boss knew he was playing with fire, telling his friend the Irishman on numerous occasions, "Watch your ass . . . you could end up being fair game. . . . You're too close to me—in some people's eyes."

Sheeran got the order to take Hoffa out from his other best friend, Bufalino.

"Your friend made one too many threats in his life," said the mafioso.

Responded Sheeran, "The nuclear fallout's going to hit the fan when they find the body."

"There won't be a body," said Bufalino. "Dust to dust. That's what it is."

Wrote Sheeran: "I moved around in my seat. I couldn't show anything in my face. I couldn't say a word. . . . The wrong look in my eyes and my house gets painted."

On Hoffa's famous last day in 1975, the last thing he wrote on a notepad next to the phone in his home was "Russ and Frank." Bufalino and Sheeran. Hoffa was off to meet with them and a handful of key mafiosi to square things away with the mob. Sheeran was there to make Hoffa feel safe and at ease.

The Irishman and a couple others guys were supposed to pick Jimmy up in the parking lot of the Machus Red Fox Restaurant on Telegraph Road in Hoffa's hometown of Detroit. They arrived late, which angered the Teamster boss. When they told Jimmy there had been a change in plans, that they were now going to convene their meeting at a nearby house in a placid Detroit neighborhood, Hoffa was his usual profane self—"What the fuck. . . . Who the fuck. . . . How the fuck . . ."—but he went along with it partly because Sheeran was there.

In two cars, they drove to the house on a quiet street. Sheeran escorted Hoffa up the front stairs to the house. He opened the door and led Hoffa inside. It was only when the Teamster boss got into the front hallway and saw that there were no Mafia men on the premises to greet him that he knew he'd been setup, although he still believed the Irishman was on his side. Sheeran recalls:

> He turned fast, still thinking we were together on the thing, that I was his backup. Jimmy bumped into me hard. If he saw the piece in my hand he had to think I had it out to protect him. He took a quick step to go around me and get to the door. He reached for the knob and Jimmy Hoffa got shot twice at a decent range—not too close or the paint splatters back at you—in the back of the head behind his right ear. My friend didn't suffer.

Frank Sheeran did some other hits in later years and was lucky to live to retirement. Like most Irish American gangsters, he was a man who had pursued his version of the American Dream with a wife, kids, and an extended family. He was a working-class hood who lived a working-class life, suppressing whatever misgivings or guilt he may have had about his violent deeds behind a mask of toughness. It was only in his golden years that the ghosts of the Irishman's past began to haunt him. The year before his death, Sheeran told his coauthor that he'd started having nightmares that mixed incidents from the war with incidents from his life in the mob. He began to "see" these people when he was awake, haunting apparitions he sometimes called "chemical people," because he believed they were partly a result of the chemical imbalance that was caused whenever he neglected to take his medicine. Once, when he was driving in a car with the author, he said, "There are two chemical people in the backseat. I know they're not real, but what are they doing in the car?"

In December 2003, Francis Sheeran died and was buried underground.

In these early years of the twenty-first century, the Irish American gangster is mostly a thing of the past.

All that remains are the demons.

—Thomas Joseph English
January 2005

Sources

Interviews

The early chapters of this book chronicling events that took place in the nineteenth and early twentieth century derive mostly from archive research in libraries, museums, and city crime commissions, as well as from the books, articles, essays, manuscripts and reports listed below. The latter chapters, where participants of some events are still alive, I relied, when possible, on interviews. Given the nature of the subject matter, many contemporary sources insisted on anonymity. The following is a partial list of names that I am able to identify: Patrick Nee, James Martorano, Eddie MacKenzie, Kevin Cullen, Raymond Flynn, Ciaran Staunton, Michael Patrick MacDonald, Joe Coffey, Frank McDarby, Richie Egan, James Tedaldi, Tom McCabe, Greg Derkash, Jeffrey Schlanger, Lawrence Hochheiser, Kenneth Aronson, Gerald Shargel, Jim Nauwens, Mickey Featherstone, Marcelle Featherstone, Bud Schulberg, Edward McDonald, and Peter Quinn.

Books

Abbott, Shirley. *The Bookmaker's Daughter: A Memory Unbound.* New York: Houghton Mifflin, 1991.

Allen, Oliver E. *The Tiger: The Rise and Fall of Tammany Hall.* Reading, MA: Addison Wesley, 1993.

Anbinder, Tyler. *Five Points: The 19th Century New York City Neighborhood That Invented Tap Dance, Stole Elections, and Became the World's Most Notorious Slum.* New York: Free Press, 2001.

Arnesen, Richard. *Waterfront Workers in New Orleans, 1860–1920.* New York: Oxford University Press, 1991.

Asbury, Herbert. *The Gangs of New York: An Informal History of the Underworld.* New York: Alfred A. Knopf, 1928.

———*The French Quarter: An Informal History of the New Orleans Underworld.* New York: Alfred A. Knopf, 1936.

———*Sucker's Progress: An Informal History of Gambling in America.* New York: Dodd, Mead, 1938.

———*Gem of the Prairie: An Informal History of the Chicago Underworld.* New York: Alfred A. Knopf, 1940.

——— *The Great Illusion: An Informal History of Prohibition.* Garden City, NY: Doubleday, 1950.

Beatty, Jack. *The Rascal King: The Life and Times of James Michael Curley.* Reading, MA: Addison Wesley, 1992.

Berger, Meyer. *The Eight Million: Journal of a New York Correspondent.* New York: Simon & Schuster, 1942.

Bergreen, Laurence. *Capone: The Man and the Era.* New York: Simon & Schuster, 1994

Blumenthal, Ralph. *The Stork Club: America's Most Famous Nightspot and the Lost World of Café Society.* Boston: Little, Brown, 2000.

Brandt, Charles. *"I Heard You Paint Houses": Frank "the Irishman" Sheeran & the Inside Story of the Mafia, the Teamsters, & the Last Ride of Jimmy Hoffa.* Hanover, NH: Steerforth Press, 2004.

Brill, Steven. *The Teamsters.* New York: Simon & Schuster, 1978.

Bulger, William M. *While the Music Lasts: My Life in Politics.* Boston: Houghton Mifflin, 1996.

Butler, Richard J. & Driscoll, Joseph. *Dock Walloper: The Story of "Big Dick" Butler.* NY: G.P. Putnam & Sons, 1933.

Cagney, James. *Cagney by Cagney.* Garden City, NY: Doubleday, 1976.

Callahan, Bob. (ed.). *The Big Book of American Irish Culture.* New York: Viking, 1987.

——— *Who Shot JFK? A Guide to the Major Conspiracy Theories.* New York: Fireside Books, 1993.

Carroll, James. *The City Below.* Houghton Mifflin, 1994.

Clarens, Carlos. *Crime Movies: From Griffith to the Godfather and Beyond.* New York: W.W. Norton, 1980.

Coffey, Michael & Golway, Terry (eds.). *The Irish in America.* New York: Hyperion, 1997.

Cohen, Rich. *Tough Jews: Fathers, Sons and Gangster Dreams.* New York: Simon & Schuster, 1998.

Collins, Max Allen. *The Road to Perdition.* New York: Pocket Books, 2002.

Curley, James Michael. *I'd Do It Again: A Record of My Uproarious Years.* Englewood Cliff, NJ: Prentice-Hall, 1957.

Davis, John H. *Mafia Kingfish: Carlos Marcello and the Assassination of John F. Kennedy.* New York: McGraw Hill, 1989.

Delap, Breandán. *Mad Dog Coll: An Irish Gangster.* Dublin: Mercier Press, 1999.

Dewey, Thomas E. *Twenty Against the Underworld.* Garden City, NY: Doubleday, 1974.

Doctorow, E.L. *Billy Bathgate.* New York: Harper & Row, 1989.

Downey, Patrick. *Gangster City: A History of the New York Underworld, 1900–1935.* Fort Lee, NJ: Barricade, 2004.

English, T.J. *The Westies: Inside the Hell's Kitchen Irish Mob.* New York: Putnam, 1990.

Farrell, James T. *Studs Lonigan: A Trilogy.* New York: Random House, 1935.

Fitzgerald, F. Scott. *The Great Gatsby.* New York: Scribner's, 1925.

Fowler, Gene. *Beau James: The Life and Times of Jimmy Walker.* New York: Viking, 1949.

Fried, Albert. *The Rise and Fall of the Jewish Gangster in America.* New York: Holt, Rinehart and Winston, 1980.

Gambino, Richard. *Vendetta: The True Story of the Largest Lynching in U.S. History.* Garden City, NY: Doubleday, 1977.

Giancana, Sam & Chuck. *Double Cross: The Explosive Inside Story of the Mobster Who Controlled America.* New York: Warner Books, 1992.

Goddard, Donald. *All Fall Down: One Man Against the Waterfront Mob.* New York: Times Books, 1980.

Goodwin, Doris Kearns. *The Fitzgeralds and the Kennedys: An American Saga.* New York: St. Martin's, 1987.

Gosch, Martin & Hammer, Richard. *The Last Testament of Lucky Luciano.* Boston: Little Brown, 1974.

Hersh, Seymour M. *The Dark Side of Camelot.* Little, Brown, 1997.

Higgins, George V. *The Friends of Eddie Coyle.* New York: Alfred A. Knopf, 1970.

Hurley, John W. *Irish Gangs and Stick Fighting: In the Works of William Carleton.* Philadelphia: Xlibris, 2000.

Ignatiev, Noel. *How the Irish Became White.* New York: Routledge, 1995.

Jackson, Kenneth T. (ed.) *The Encyclopedia of New York City.* New Haven, CT: Yale University Press, 1995.

Johnson, Curt with R. Craig Sautter. *Wicked City Chicago: From Kenna to Capone.* Highland Park, IL: December Press, 1974.

Josephson, Matthew. *The Robber Barons: The Classic Account of the Influential Capitalists who Transformed America's Future.* Harvest/HBJ, 1962. Originally published in 1934.

Katcher, Leo. *The Big Bankroll: The Life and Times of Arnold Rothstein.* New Rochelle, NY: Arlington House, 1958.

Keefe, Rose. *Guns and Roses: The Untold Story of Dean O'Banion, Chicago's Big Shot Before Al Capone.* Nashville: Cumberland House, 2003.

Kelly, Thomas. *Payback.* New York: Alfred A. Knopf, 1997.

——— *The Rackets.* New York: Farrar, Straus & Giroux, 2001.

——— *Empire Rising.* New York: Farrar, Straus & Giroux, 2005.

Kennedy, Robert F. *The Enemy Within: The McClellan Committee's Crusade Against Jimmy Hoffa and Corrupt Labor Unions.* New York: Harper & Row, 1960.

Kennedy, William. *Legs.* New York: Coward, McCann & Geoghegan, 1975.

———*O Albany!: Improbable City of Political Wizards, Fearless Ethnics, Spectacular Aristocrats, Splendid Nobodies, and Underrated Scoundrels.* New York: Viking, 1983.

———*Roscoe.* New York: Viking, 2002.

Kessler, Ronald. *The Sins of the Father: Joseph P. Kennedy and the Dynasty He Founded.* New York: Warner Books, 1996.

Kobler, John. *Capone: The Life and World of Al Capone.* New York: Putnam, 1971.

———*Ardent Spirits: The Rise and Fall of Prohibition.* New York: Putnam, 1972.

Kogan, Herman & Wendt, Lloyd. *Lords of the Levee: The Story of Bathhouse John and Hinky Dink.* Indianapolis: Bobbs Merrill, 1943.

Lardner, James & Reppetto, Thomas. *NYPD: A City and Its Police.* New York: Henry Holt, 2000.

Larsen, Lawrence H. & Huston, Janice J. *Pendergast!* Columbia: University of Missouri Press, 1997.

Lehr, Dick & O'Neill, Gerald. *Black Mass: The Irish Mob, the FBI, and a Devil's Deal.* New York: Public Affairs, 2000.

———*The Underboss: The Rise and Fall of a Mafia Family.* New York: St. Martin's Press, 1989.

Levine, Gary. *Jack "Legs" Diamond: Anatomy of a Gangster.* Fleischmanns, NY: Purple Mountain Press, 1995.

Lewis, Norman. *The Honored Society.* New York: Putnam, 1964.

Lindberg, Richard. *To Serve and Collect: Chicago Politics and Police Corruption from the Lager Beer Riot to the Summerdale Scandal.* New York: Praeger Press, 1991.

———*Chicago Ragtime: Another Look at Chicago 1880–1920.* South Bend, IN: Icarus Press, 1985.

Loftus, John & McIntyre, Emily. *Valhalla's Wake: The IRA, MI6, and the Assassination of a Young American.* New York: Atlantic Monthly Press, 1989.

London, Jack. *The Iron Heel.* New York: Macmillan, 2000. Originally published in 1908.

MacDonald, Michael Patrick. *All Souls: A Family Story from Southie*. Boston: Beacon Press, 1999.

MacKenzie Jr., Edward J. et al. *Street Soldier: My Life as an Enforcer for Whitey Bulger & the Boston Irish Mob*. NH: Steerforth Press, 2003.

Maloney, Eddie & Hoffman, William. *Tough Guy: The True Story of "Crazy" Eddie Maloney*. New York: Pinnacle, 1997.

McCabe, John. *Cagney*. New York: Knopf, 1997.

Miller, Kerby. *Emigrants and Exiles: Ireland and the Irish Exodus to North America*. New York: Oxford University Press, 1985.

Mitgang, Herbert. *Once Upon a Time in New York: Jimmy Walker, Franklin Roosevelt, and the Last Great Battle of the Jazz Age*. New York: Free Press, 2000.

Moldea, Dan. *The Hoffa Wars: Teamsters, Rebels, Politicians, and the Mob*. New York: Paddington, 1978.

Morris, Ronald L. *Wait Until Dark: Jazz and the Underworld, 1880–1940*. Green, Ohio: Bowling Green Press, 1980.

Niehaus, Earl F. *The Irish in New Orleans 1800–1860*. Baton Rouge: Louisiana State University Press, 1965.

Norwood, Stephen H. *Strikebreaking and Intimidation: Mercenaries and Masculinity in Twentieth-Century America*. Chapel Hill: University of North Carolina Press, 2002.

O'Connor, Edwin. *The Last Hurrah*. Boston: Little Brown, 1956.

O'Connor, Richard. *Hell's Kitchen: The Roaring Days of New York's Wild West Side*. Philadelphia: J.P. Lippincott, 1958.

O'Connor, Thomas H. *The Boston Irish: A Political History*. Boston: Northeastern University Press, 1995.

O'Dwyer, William. *Beyond the Golden Door*. Jamaica, NY: St. John's University Press, 1987.

O'Flaherty, Liam. *The Informer*. New York: Harcourt Brace Jovanovich, 1980. Originally published in 1925.

Patrick, Vincent. *The Pope of Greenwich Village*. New York: Simon & Schuster, 1978.

Peterson, Virgil. *Barbarians in Our Midst: A History of Chicago Crime and Politics*. Little Brown, 1952.

———*The Mob: 200 Years of Organized Crime in New York*. Ottawa, IL: Green Hill, 1983.

Pileggi, Nicholas. *Wiseguy: Life in a Mafia Family*. New York: Simon & Schuster, 1985.

Porrello, Rick. *To Kill the Irishman: The War That Crippled the Mafia*. Cleveland: Next Hat Press, 1998.

Quinn, Peter. *Banished Children of Eve*. New York: Viking, 1994.

Rakove, Milton. *Don't Make No Waves Don't Back No Losers: An Insider's Analysis of the Daley Machine*. Bloomington: Indiana University Press, 1975.

Raymond, Allen. *Waterfront Priest*. New York: Henry Holt, 1955.

Reddig, William M. *Tom's Town: Kansas City and the Pendergast Legend*. Philadelphia: J.P. Lippincott, 1947.

Reedy, George. *From the Ward to the White House: The Irish in American Politics*. New York: Scribners, 1991.

Reppetto, Thomas. *American Mafia: A History of Its Rise to Power*. New York: Henry Holt, 2004.

Riis, Jacob A. *How the Other Half Lives: Studies Among the Tenements of New York*. New York: Hill & Wang, 1957. Originally published in 1890.

Riordon, William L. *Plunkitt of Tammany Hall: A Series of Very Plain Talks on Very Practical Politics*. New York: Signet Classic, 1995. Originally published in 1905.

Rousey, Dennis C. *Policing the Southern City: New Orleans, 1805–1889*. Baton Rouge: Louisiana State University Press, 1997.

Royko, Mike. *Boss: Richard J. Daley of Chicago*. New York: Dutton, 1971.

Russo, Gus. *The Outfit: The Role of Chicago's Underworld in the Shaping of Modern America*. New York: Bloomsbury USA, 2002.

Sann, Paul. *Kill the Dutchman!: The Story of Dutch Shultz*. New Rochelle, NY: Arlington House, 1971.

Sante, Luc. *Low Life: Lures and Snares of Old New York*. New York: Farrar, Straus & Giroux, 1991.

Schwarz, Ted. *Joseph P. Kennedy: The Mogul, the Mob, the Statesman, and the Making of an American Myth*. New York: Wiley & Sons, 2003.

Stoddard, Lothrop. *Master of Manhattan: The Life of Richard Croker*. New York: Longmans, Green and Co., 1931.

Thrasher, Frederick. *The Gang: A Study of 1,313 Gangs in Chicago*. Chicago: University of Chicago Press, 1926.

Touhy, Roger with Brennan, Ray. *The Stolen Years*. Cleveland: Pennington, 1959.

Tuohy, John W. *When Capone's Mob Killed Roger Touhy*. Fort Lee, NJ: Barricade Books, 2001.

Van Tassel, David D. & Grabowski, John J. (eds.). *The Encyclopedia of Cleveland History*. Bloomington: Indiana University Press, 1987.

Walker, Stanley. *The Night Club Era*. New York: Frederick A. Stokes Company, 1933.

Walsh, George. *Public Enemies: The Mayor, the Mob and the Crime that Was*. New York: W.W. Norton, 1980.

Walsh, Michael. *And All the Saints*. New York: Warner Books, 2003.

Whyte, William F. *Street Corner Society*. Chicago: University of Chicago Press, 1955.

Zinn, Howard. *A People's History of the United States*. New York: Perennial Classics, 2003. Revised Edition.

ᴀrticſes, Reports, Essays, anд Manuscripts

Beatty, Jerome. "A Political Boss Talks about His Job." *American Magazine*. February, 1933.

Becker, Ed & Tuohy, John William. "The Valley Gang." *Gambling Magazine*. Internet (undated). www.gamblingmagazine.com.

"The Bulger Mystique." *The Boston Globe*. (Spotlight Team: Gerald O'Neill, Christine Chinlund, Dick Lehr, Kevin Cullen, Mary Elizabeth Knox.) September 18–21, 1988.

Bulger, William. "The Bulger Hearings." U.S. House of Representatives, Committee on Government Reform. June 19, 2003.

Cassidy, Daniel. "Breaking the Codes of New York's Gangs." *New York Observer*. January 6, 2003.

Cohen, Henry. "An Ordinary Thug." Introduction to *The Public Enemy* (published screenplay). Madison: University of Wisconsin Press, 1981.

Czitrom, Daniel. "Underworlds and Underdogs: Big Tim Sullivan and Metropolitan Politics in New York, 1889–1913." *Journal of American History 79*. 1991.

Daly, Michael. "The Ghosts of Hell's Kitchen." *New York* Magazine. October 11, 1986.

———— "Tammany's Last Stand." *New York* Magazine. July 13, 1992

English, T. J. "The Original Irish Gangsters." *The Irish in America*. New York: Hyperion, 1997.

———— "Featherstone's Lament." *The Village Voice*. September 12, 1988.

———— "On Trial—The Wild, Wild Westies." *Irish Voice*, December 13, 1987.

Fenton, Patrick. "Still the Same." *Ways to Writing* (2nd Edition). New York: McGraw-Hill, 1988.

Firestone, David. "Stretching Legs." *New York Newsday*. January 3, 1989.

Flynn, Sean. "Good Guys, Bad Guys." *Boston Magazine*. September 2000.

Hamill, Pete. "Trampling City's History: 'Gangs' Misses Point of Five Points." NY *Daily News*. December 8, 2002.

Geringer, Joseph. "George 'Bugs' Moran: His War With Al Capone." *The Crime Library*. Internet (undated). www.crimelibrary.com

Goldstock, Ronald. "Corruption and Racketeering in the New York Construction Industry: An Interim Report." New York State Organized Crime Task Force, 1988.

Kendall, Jon S. "Who Killa de Chief?" *Louisiana Historical Quarterly*, Vol. 22, 1939.

Landesco, John. "Organized Crime in Chicago." Part III of the Illinois Crime Survey. 1929.

May, Allan. "Vannie Higgins: Brooklyn's Last Irish Boss." *Crime Magazine.* Internet (undated). www.crimemagazine.com

——— "Frank McErlane and the Chicago Beer Wars." *Crime Magazine.* Internet (undated). www.crimemagazine.com

——— "Three Thin Dimes: The Demise of Larry Fay." *Crime Magazine.* Internet (undated). www.crimemagazine.com

——— "Jimmy McBratney: A Footnote to Mob History." *Crime Magazine.* Internet (undated). www.crimemagazine.com

"The Mystery of Joe Kennedy." *Newsweek*, September 12, 1960.

O'Donnell, Ed. "United Front: The Irish and Organized Labor." *The Irish in America.* New York: Hyperion, 1997.

Quinn, Peter. "Looking for Jimmy." *The World of Hibernia.* Spring 1999.

——— "Farmers No More: From Rural Ireland to the Teeming City." *The Irish in America.* New York: Hyperion, 1997.

——— Introduction to *Plunkitt of Tammany Hall*: A Series of Very Plain Talks on Very Practical Politics. NY: Signet Classic, 1995.

Rodann, Curtis. "Big Bill Dwyer—King of the Rum Runners." *True Detective.* February 1961.

Rousey, Dennis C. "Hibernian Leatherheads: Irish Cops in New Orleans, 1830–1880." *Journal of Urban History*, Vol X. November 1983.

Salemme, Frank. "Statement of Frank Salemme." U.S. House of Representatives, Committee on Government Reform. April 10, 2003.

Schulberg, Bud. "Writing *On the Waterfront.*" Introduction to *On the Waterfront* (published screenplay). London: Faber and Faber, 1980.

Spillane, Bobby "The Real 'Road to Perdition.'" NY *Daily News.* July 21, 2002.

Sullivan, Joseph J. & Gail W. *Tears and Tiers (A Product of the State): The Life Story of the Only Man to Ever Escape from Attica Prison.* Unpublished manuscript/autobiography (undated).

Sutherland, Sidney. "The Machine-Gunning of McSwiggin and What Led Up to It." *Liberty.* July 3–August 7, 1926.

Tuohy, John William. "Joe Kennedy and the Pantages Affair." *Gambling Magazine.* Internet (undated). www.gamblingmagazine.com

"Waterfront Commission Hearings, Vol. 1–5" New York State Crime Commission. December 1952–March 1953.

Whelen, Edward P. "The Life and Hard Times of the Cleveland Mafia—How the Danny Greene Murder Exploded the Godfather Myth." *Cleveland Magazine.* August 1978.

"The Wolf Hearings." (Memorandum and Order) U.S. District Court, District of Massachusetts. Judge Mark L. Wolf. September 15, 1999.

Institutions

Essential research material in the form of newspaper archives, historical quarterlies, photos, and, in some cases, police documents were culled from some of the collections of the following institutions: American Irish Historical Society; Museum of the City of New York; New York Public Library (Newspaper Division); New York Municipal Archive; Metropolitan Crime Commission of New Orleans; Louisiana Historical Society; New Orleans Public Library (Louisiana Division); Howard-Tilton Memorial Library (Louisiana Collection), Tulane University; Chicago Crime Commission; Chicago Historical Society; Kansas City Museum; Boston Public Library (Micro-text Room); and John F. Kennedy Library and Museum.

Government Files and Trial Transcripts

Through the Freedom of Information Act (FOIA), U.S. Justice Department FBI files were obtained on the following individuals: Joseph P. Kennedy, Daniel J. Greene, and James J. "Whitey" Bulger.

Transcripts and other evidence from numerous criminal and civil trials were used in the research for this book, especially where it involved wiretap conversations that became the basis for reconstructing dialogue. The primary cases are:

The People of the State of New York v. Francis T. Featherstone aka "Mickey," Supreme Court of the State of New York, Manhattan. 1986.

United States v. James J. Coonan et al., U.S. District Court, Southern District of New York. 1987–88.

Unites States v. Kevin Kelly and Kenny Shannon, U.S. District Court, Southern District of New York. 1989.

United States v. John J. Connolly, Jr., U.S. District Court, District of Massachusetts. 2002.

acknowledgments

This book could not have come together were it not for the assistance of various friends, authors, archivists, cops, historians, college professors, newspaper people, ex-girlfriends, priests, taxi drivers, gangsters, and wizards of publishing that I have had the good fortune to know. On various research expeditions to the primary cities mentioned in this book, I was aided by archivists and librarians. In an attempt to find documents and interview living participants from the world of the Irish American gangster, I was aided by law enforcement personnel and people in the underworld—or people who knew people in the underworld. To make sense of it all, I often relied on friends and fellow professionals, especially those with expertise on the subject of Irish Americana.

For providing or leading me to key pieces of information, photos, or helping to facilitate interviews, I would like to thank the following people: Patrick Nee, Jimmy Martorano, Eddie MacKenzie, Mickey Featherstone, Sissy Featherstone, Ciaran Staunton, Tommy Lyons, Chip Fleischer, Rich Farrell, Ray Flynn, Tyler Anbinder, Edward McDonald, Rose Keefe, Kevin Cullen of the *Boston Globe*, Bill Boyle of the New York *Daily News*, Bill Gallo of the *Daily News*, and Rick Porrello of *americanmafia.com*.

Having gotten my start as a journalist writing mostly for Irish American publications, I have accumulated friends and professional contacts who were indispensable as a sounding board on the subjects of Irish American history, culture, and/or American gangsterism in general. In this regard I would like to thank: Bob Callahan, Peter Quinn, Alderman Tom Kelly, Michael Patrick MacDonald, Vince Patrick, Patrick Farrelly, Kate O'Callaghan, Danny Cassidy, Ed Moloney, Pat Fenton, Sean O'Murchu, Niall O'Dowd, Trish Harty, and Brian Rohan.

Various research institutions were essential sources of information. I was aided in my archival expeditions by the following professionals: In New York, Scott Kelly of the American Irish Historical Society. In New Orleans, Wayne Everard, head archivist at the New Orleans Public Library, Louisiana Division; Sally Reeves, archivist for the Louisiana Historical Society; and Anthony Radosti of the Metropolitan Crime Commission of New Orleans. In Chicago, Lee Lyons, research director for the Chicago Crime Commission. In Kansas City, archivist Denise Morrison of the Kansas City Museum. In Boston, archivist James Hill of the John F. Kennedy Library and Museum. In Cleveland, Lt. Wayne Drummond and Commander Edward Tomba of the Cleveland Police Department.

In many ways researching and writing this book was for me the continuation of a lifelong journey as a writer, an exploration that has been supported and sustained by friends and family. Just for being there, I would like to thank: Tom Caldarola, Barbara Henderson, Dino Malcolm, Gha'il Rhodes-Benjamin, Joan Barker, Joel Millman, Joel Popson, Frankie "the Tailor" Shattuck, Ryan Schafer, Nora Wertz, Rocky Sullivan's Bar, and, most especially, the one and only Sandra Maria Rocha English. I would also like to thank my immediate family: Joan, Terry, Ed, Maureen, Marian, Suzanne, John, Margi, Mike, and mother Suzanne.

Finally there are the people who helped launch this project into the marketplace and shape its final form. I am indebted to master agent Nat Sobel, who compelled me to expand and go deeper, to publisher Judith Regan, who knows an Irish gangster when she sees one, to editor Cal Morgan for championing the cause, and to editor Anna Bliss, who helped get the project rolling when she was under the employ of Sobel Weber Associates and ushered it across the finish line after she switched to ReganBooks.